Shakespeare and
the Middle Ages

ALSO BY MARTHA W. DRIVER AND SID RAY

*The Medieval Hero on Screen: Representations
from Beowulf to Buffy* (McFarland, 2004)

Shakespeare and the Middle Ages

Essays on the Performance and Adaptation of the Plays with Medieval Sources or Settings

Edited by
MARTHA W. DRIVER *and* SID RAY

Foreword by Michael Almereyda *and* Dakin Matthews

McFarland & Company, Inc., Publishers
Jefferson, North Carolina, and London

LIBRARY OF CONGRESS CATALOGUING-IN-PUBLICATION DATA

Shakespeare and the middle ages : essays on the performance and adaptation of the plays with medieval sources or settings / edited by Martha W. Driver and Sid Ray ; foreword by Michael Almereyda and Dakin Matthews.
p.   cm.

Includes bibliographical references and index.

ISBN 978-0-7864-3405-3
softcover : 50# alkaline paper ∞

1. Shakespeare, William, 1564–1616 — Knowledge — Middle Ages.
2. Shakespeare, William, 1564–1616 — Sources.
3. English literature — Medieval influences.
4. Civilization, Medieval, in literature.
I. Driver, Martha W.   II. Ray, Sid, 1966–
PR3069.M47S54   2009   822.3'3 — dc22   2009010123

British Library cataloguing data are available

©2009 Martha W. Driver and Sid Ray. All rights reserved

No part of this book may be reproduced or transmitted in any form or by any means, electronic or mechanical, including photocopying or recording, or by any information storage and retrieval system, without permission in writing from the publisher.

Cover photograph: Glenn Close as Gertrude in Zeffirelli's *Hamlet*, 1990

Manufactured in the United States of America

McFarland & Company, Inc., Publishers
Box 611, Jefferson, North Carolina 28640
www.mcfarlandpub.com

For our parents

and

in memoriam:
Julia Ruth Briggs
(1943–2007)

Acknowledgments

The editors wish to acknowledge first the patience and love of their spouses (Tom Rhodes and Philip Kearns) and families (especially Sid's children, Clare, Isabella, and Emmett). Along family lines, we wish to thank all parents, sisters, and brothers, but in particular George Ray, one of the dedicatees, a careful and wise editor, and Sara Driver and Jim Jarmusch for their encouragement in our contacting Michael Almereyda.

We thank our colleagues at Pace University, especially Trisha Pender, Jonathan Silverman, Catherine Zimmer, and most particularly Tom Henthorne, a wonderful friend and editor, and Nancy Reagin, our indefatigable advocate. For offers of support, general kindness, and advice in completing the essay composed by Julia Briggs, we thank Marilyn Deegan, Tony Edwards, and especially Bill Raden. Thanks, too, to Mark Hussey, another English Department colleague and Julia's colleague in Woolf studies, who sent on so much precious information during her last illness.

Other thank-yous go out to Sloane Klevin and Linda Rafoss for the stills from *Heights*, to Gill Kent, and to current and former Pace University students, especially Amber Rodriguez, Lindsey Kerecz, and Lindsey Lee for their help and support. Without the generosity and kindness of Martin Humphries and Ronald Grant of the Cinema Museum in London, we would not have such a lavishly illustrated book. And we wish to thank our colleague and friend Terry Jones for first suggesting we contact that amazing archive. We also thank Michael Almereyda for bringing Dakin Matthews into the project. We wish to acknowledge the members of the Scholarly Research Committee at Pace and the Shakespeare Association.

Finally, we thank our wonderful contributors without whose scholarship there would not be the brave crossing of disciplines that has made this book a pleasure to edit and a joy to read.

Table of Contents

ACKNOWLEDGMENTS vi

FOREWORD: "THE SKELETON IN THE MIRROR"
Michael Almereyda and *Dakin Matthews* 1

GENERAL INTRODUCTION
Martha W. Driver and *Sid Ray* 7

Part I. "Abstract and Brief Chronicles of Time": The Histories

INTRODUCTION TO PART I
Martha W. Driver 21

"*Richard's* Himself Again": The Body of Richard III on Stage and Screen
Jim Casey 27

Falstaff in America
Catherine Loomis 49

Scoring the Fields of the Dead: Musical Styles and Approaches to Postbattle Scenes from *Henry V* (1944, 1989)
Linda K. Schubert 62

Part II. "Carnal, Bloody, and Unnatural Acts": The Tragedies

INTRODUCTION TO PART II
Martha W. Driver 81

"We're Everyone You Depend On": Filming Shakespeare's Peasants
Carl James Grindley 89

Medieval *Hamlet* in Performance
Patrick J. Cook 105

Finding Gruoch: The Hidden Genealogy of Lady Macbeth in Text and Cinematic Performance
Sid Ray 116

Part III. "Many Merry Men": The Comedies

INTRODUCTION TO PART III
Sid Ray 135

Reading *A Midsummer Night's Dream* through Middle English Romance
Martha W. Driver 140

"Chaucer ... the Story Gives": *Troilus and Cressida* and *The Two Noble Kinsmen*
    Julia Ruth Briggs 161

Shakespeare's Virgin Mother on the Modern Stage: *All's Well, That Ends Well* and the Madonna del Parto Tradition
    Gary Waller 178

Part IV. "Tragical-Comical-Historical-Pastoral": The Romances

INTRODUCTION TO PART IV
    Sid Ray 195

"The Quick and the Dead": Performing the Poet Gower in *Pericles*
    Kelly Jones 201

Shakespeare as Medievalist: What It Means for Performing *Pericles*
    R. F. Yeager 215

A Touch of Chaucer in *The Winter's Tale*
    Louise M. Bishop 232

Caliban's God: The Medieval and Renaissance Man in the Moon
    Kim Zarins 245

ABOUT THE CONTRIBUTORS 263

INDEX 267

Foreword: "The Skeleton in the Mirror"

MICHAEL ALMEREYDA *and* DAKIN MATTHEWS

To introduce readers to this volume, Dakin Matthews, perhaps best known as the adapter and dramaturge of the 2003 Lincoln Center production of Henry IV, *one of the finest productions of Shakespeare in recent memory, talks with filmmaker Michael Almereyda.*

Dakin Matthews: In the late winter of 1598, Shakespeare and his colleagues, in the dead of night and more than a little surreptitiously, dismantled their theatre, which stood on a plot of ground whose lease was about to expire, and carted or ferried the wood across the Thames to a new spot south of the river where they would later re-assemble the timbers into the framework of the first Globe.

I often think of Shakespeare's plays that way, as new constructs built on old frameworks. The new part, the part so new that it changed theatre forever, is not just Shakespeare's amazing gift for language, but the fact that he uses that facility to capture his equally amazing insight into the workings of the individual human heart and mind. His emphasis on complex characterization fits well with the Renaissance's unique focus on the individual. The plots, however, are most of them old and borrowed, and in many cases even the most radically modern of his plays continue to display what might be called a medieval footprint.

And because so often that "footprint" usually reveals something about the structure of the plays — about their frameworks or even their foundations — directors and producers would do well to refer to it. In other words, I tend to think that the medievalism in Shakespeare plays is most often embedded in the deep structure, and therefore it is at one and the same time more essential yet easier to overlook. Because Shakespeare's language and characterization are so overwhelming and original, we may miss what underlies them and at times holds them up, as the skeleton supports the body.

Michael Almereyda: I appreciate your points about frameworks, structure, skeletons, *scaffolding*; but let's assume that two or three readers of this book are not scholars or students. Aside from the Renaissance's "unique focus on the individual," what are the chief things that distinguish the medieval worldview from the cultural situation that Shakespeare was writing in? What are some specific medieval frames, skeletons, or ghosts, lurking within the plays?

DM: As I say, I think they're mostly structural. For example, the great mystery plays (as they are called) — which were still being performed in Shakespeare's youth — were sweeping cycles of mostly biblical plays, which dramatized the history of salvation from creation through final judgment. In these, Shakespeare may have found models for certain characters and a way of mixing comic and serious elements, but I suspect their greatest influence was in providing him a long view of historical events — in some cases, not very pleasant events — still being guided by an essentially providential plan. Shakespeare's two great tetralogies on English history, even though they were written out of sequence, still show something of that vision, tracing the ups and down of the

English monarchy from the dethronement of Richard II through the establishment of Richmond (Henry VII) to the monarchy. My own appreciation of this long view, in fact, moved me to tell the longer story of Henry IV and his son by combining the two Shakespeare plays on his reign into a single evening.

MA: I saw your adaptation of *Henry IV*, parts one and two, performed at Lincoln Center. Kevin Kline played Falstaff; Ethan Hawke was Hotspur; Jack O'Brian directed. The production had great fluidity, clarity and power. I'd say it's one of the best stage productions of Shakespeare I've ever seen. At any rate, as we've been called upon to conjure a foreword for a volume concerning "Medieval Shakespeare," perhaps we should bear down and identify Shakespeare's other plays that seem carpentered, more or less explicitly, from medieval planks.

DM: In my view, other obvious candidates are *Macbeth*, which is set in a medieval era and draws in part on medieval theologies of sin and diabolism; *Hamlet*, also set in a medieval era and drawing on both the Roman Catholic theology of purgatory and scholastic philosophy; *Othello*, for the culmination of the Vice character from medieval moralities; *Troilus and Cressida*, because of the Chaucer and Henryson sources; *The Two Noble Kinsmen* for its use of Chaucer's "The Knight's Tale" from *Canterbury Tales*; and *Pericles*, because of its connection with Gower. *Pericles* is in this way unique, because it includes an actual medieval poet and moralist among its cast members, and to some extent, therefore, incorporates, at least in his choral pronouncements, a medieval point of view as well. It is, perhaps because of this, one of the most moralistic and least psychologically complex plays in the canon. (In this regard, I particularly enjoyed — and learned a lot from — R. F. Yeager's article in this volume.)

MA: Back to *Henry IV*, parts one and two. As you adapted and combined the plays, what did you come to recognize as "medieval"? Was there an attempt to highlight these elements?

DM: I think our most important task was to avoid the gravitational pull of Falstaff and to maintain the dramaturgical balance among the characters. For both Jack O'Brian and me, Hal's story was the central narrative and driving force. And for Jack I think the most important "thematic" element of that journey was the father/son relationship. My focus was slightly different, and more specifically medieval. I worked hard to protect Shakespeare's broader structure, which I felt was heavily in debt to the medieval morality play.

MA: What's the difference between a medieval mystery play and a morality play?

DM: Simply put, the mystery plays — or better, mystery cycles of plays — were dramatizations of what is popularly called "salvation history." The morality plays were allegorical dramatizations, originally, of one person's battle to achieve his own salvation. *Everyman* is perhaps the best known example. That battle is, however, not exactly one that he fights, but that is fought over him. And the battlers are the personified virtues or vices that encourage or tempt him. Later that same form was also used to dramatize not only a religious theme, but a secular one as well. The Everyman character might be a student, for example; and the virtues might be "Study" and "Discipline" and the vices "Laziness" and "Drunkenness." Or the Everyman might be a king fought over by "Good Government" and "Evil Advice." Something like this, I think, underlies the two parts of *Henry IV*. Hal is both a student and a king in the making; and he must, in the time he is given, work out his future by self-education; he is offered models of behavior in his father, his rival, and his friend, and he must make the right choices. I'm not saying the play is a morality play; rather that Shakespeare grafted onto the morality structure not just the history of a particular English king of a medieval era, but also the very Renaissance theme of the "education of a prince."

MA: So are the King and Hotspur and Falstaff allegorical figures? Vices or virtues?

DM: I would say the Lord Chief Justice in Part Two comes close to allegory; but, no, Bolingbroke, Hotspur and Falstaff are characters, not allegories; yet even there, there is something of the morality characterization, something we might also call medieval, though it is far older than that, stretching back through Dante and Aquinas to Plato and Aristotle. They are, in short, characters each of whom embodies both the virtuous and vicious sides of a certain human temperament — for want of a better word.

MA: You mean like the choleric, sanguine or melancholic temperaments? Like that?

DM: Actually I probably shouldn't have used the word "temperament" — although in other plays Shakespeare did, I think, explore characterization through the theory of humors and temperaments. "Personality types" would be more accurate. The types I think he used in *Henry IV* were based on a quite common model of human nature, in which the person is viewed as having three centers of energy or activity — the head, the heart, and the gut. You can find this schema in Plato's *Republic*, so it's not strictly medieval. Aquinas organized his theory of human appetite around it, and Dante structures his vision of hell upon it. It underlies the very medieval concept of the world, the flesh, and the devil — which you do find in the moralities. Shakespeare uses it to structure the Malcolm/MacDuff scene in *Macbeth*. Falstaff organizes the entire sack speech in part two of *Henry IV* on the same tripartite division.

In the two plays Shakespeare creates around Prince Hal three fully rounded characters who are at the same time models of people who act from the head, the heart, and the gut: Bolingbroke, his father; Hotspur, his rival; and Falstaff, his friend. They are neither solely virtuous nor vicious, so they are not allegorical; but they present the young man with images of those parts of himself he must master if he is to become a great king. Each has positive qualities and each has negative qualities; Hal must imitate the positive and reject the negative. From his father he must learn intelligence but avoid the kind of duplicity that brought Bolingbroke to the throne. From Hotspur he must learn courage but avoid rashness. From Falstaff he must learn vivacity and the common touch but avoid indulgence and lawlessness.

When Hal vanquishes Hotspur, he demonstrates his mastery of courage, of the heart; so then the second half becomes more a battle between the head, eventually personified by the Lord Chief Justice, and the gut, represented by a Falstaff who grows more and more lawless and more and more self-indulgent, because of which the play, I think, moves even closer to a pure morality in structure. This is the "medieval" structure that I was determined to retain in the adaptation; even though the audience may not have been aware of it, and even though Jack O'Brian may not have focused his directing work on it, I firmly believe it helped to keep the production in balance and coherent.

MA: Even though, or especially because, the audience may not have been conscious of it?

DM: I think a lot of artistry works without the audience being consciously aware of it. In fact, I suspect that's what makes it art. But what about your *Hamlet*? Many people think there are strong medieval elements in that play: it is about a medieval era and medieval politics; it has a ghost; it deals with specifically Catholic concerns like purgatory, which to Shakespeare's audience might raise the spectre of medievalism. Did any of that affect your updated film?

MA: I'll sidestep the question, for a moment, by admitting that I don't see Shakespeare's plays as refurbished building materials, or skeletons to be clothed in performance, but rather, if we have to assign an encompassing metaphor, as *mirrors*. Mistakenly or not, I'm taking Shakespeare at his word when he has Hamlet tell us an actor/artist's "purpose" is to hold a mirror up to nature, and thereby to "show the very age and body of the time his form and pressure." This is an ambitious, tantalizing job description. It has scope and mystery. So I tend to regard Shakespeare's plays as magically durable, versatile mirrors. Mirrors that travel through time, that reflect the world in which they were written just as surely as they include glimpses of the medieval era that preceded and influenced them, and just as surely as they project conditions and concerns of succeeding times in which they've been (and will continue to be) performed. In every new production, the mirrors get polished, reframed, tilted at new angles. Inevitably, at the very least, we see ourselves. But, as Jan Kott insists in *Shakespeare, Our Contemporary*—a particularly exciting and rich book—the major plays reflect a larger picture, including all sorts of shifting cultural conditions, ideological imperatives and ideals. Shakespeare is always urgent, always contemporary; his characters, his concerns, are always alive in the moment. I take this to be a big part of what's meant when he's routinely called a genius.

DM: Okay, but back to the question: Were there specific medieval elements that got translated into your contemporary *Hamlet*?

MA: Early on, I took a shine to a hat Ethan Hawke was wearing—a peaked black cap with earflaps—because it looked like medieval headgear. But this was nearly a year before we commenced shooting; by the time the start date rolled around, Ethan had lost the hat, so our resourceful wardrobe designer bought a cheap surrogate from a street vendor. The replacement was a bit goofy—less sober, less noble—than Ethan's original. I noticed that a good many critics found the hat irritating—as Hamlet's parents would have. So what began as a kind of visual pun evolved into a more particular, eye-catching indication of Hamlet's character—a young man's insecurity, his willingness to hide, pose, play a part. When he returns from England with a new resolve, the hat is gone.

DM: And that's the extent of your medieval gloss?

MA: There were a few other references. It doesn't take a lot of imagination to suggest an equivalence between a brutal medieval feudal empire and the triumphant rise of capitalism and corporate culture in pre-millennial New York. We filmed in the fall, and indulged the idea that Halloween was in the air—a pagan holiday, you know, when the line between the living and dead starts to dissolve, a good time to set a ghost story. But that's not really medieval, is it? Also, as I recall, some shots of New York skyscrapers feature crenellated architectural ornament, vestiges of the medieval mingling with the modern. But when Ophelia gears up to shuffle off this mortal coil, I staged her breakdown in the Guggenheim, not the Cloisters.

The idea, as Martha Driver graciously elucidates elsewhere, is not just to score referential points, but to find connections, to try to come to terms with fragments of meaning within history, to gather a sense of continuity while dealing with the here and now.

In any case, can you name an example, in your experience, when the medieval skeleton got crammed into unfit performing flesh? A particular case when a mismanaged medieval structure or reference crippled the play?

DM: That's a tough question—because bad productions can be bad for so many different reasons, like Tolstoy's unhappy families. But take *Macbeth*. Most of the recent successful productions I've read about have emphasized the gore quotient. As if the less psychology and the more splatter, the better. Now I happen to think that if Shakespeare wanted to kill more people onstage, he could have, but in fact a fair number of the deaths in *Macbeth* are offstage—Macdonald, Cawdor, Duncan, Lady Macduff, and both the Macbeths themselves. I think the play's essential storyline is a mental journey rather than a physical killing spree. And there are two elements strongly informed by medievalism that help to trace that journey: a theology of sin inherited from the scholastics; and a belief in demonic temptation which, by King James's time, was strongly associated with the Old Faith. If you honor those elements, you are less likely to turn the enterprise into some kind of slasher play.

MA: It sounds like your ideal version might have been Travis Preston's 2006 production featuring Stephen Dillane as Macbeth and, in fact, every other character — a single actor channeling the entire text. The stage was strewn with sand; there was a musician playing a steel cello off to the side, but that was it — you watched the whole play storming through one man's head, one man's body, *Macbeth* as haunted house. I'm not sure if that got at the medieval root of things, but it was distinctly a "mental journey," and terrifically stirring.

But your negative remarks may refer, unfairly, to Rupert Goold's more recent staging of the play, with Patrick Stewart in the title role, set in a quasi–Stalinist totalitarian nightmare world, and cited by Martha Driver on page 86 of this book. I also found this production pretty thoroughly exciting. The killing was often explicit — the basic set was a kitchen, which started to seem like an abattoir, with blood flowing and flying — but implicit medieval elements were also foregrounded. Macbeth's attendant, Seyton, was conjoined with the role of the porter and played as a sadistic demon, a partner in damnation. And when Macbeth repeatedly calls out for Seyton towards the end, it seems plain Shakespeare knew and intended for his audience to be hearing a cry for *Satan*.

Sam Shepard (left, Ghost) and Michael Almereyda on the set of *Hamlet* (2000).

DM: It's in the nature of the beast — or the skeleton — that Shakespeare's words, meanings and emotions are layered, double-sided, double-jointed, as are the challenges built into staging the plays. The contents of this volume testify to the ever-unfolding richness of the texts, their roots in various traditions as well as their essential wildness. At any rate, it's time, I think, to turn the mirror over to scholars and specialists. Readers can hereby brace themselves for a journey into a particularly vast, multi-faceted looking glass.

General Introduction

Martha W. Driver *and* Sid Ray

> For out of olde feldes, as men seyth,
> Cometh al this newe corn from yer to yere,
> And out of olde bokes, in good feyth,
> Cometh al this newe science that men lere.
> — Chaucer, *The Parliament of Fowls*

> For 'tis your thought that now must deck our kings,
> Carry them here and there, jumping o'er times,
> Turning th' accomplishment of many years
> Into an hour-glass: for the which supply,
> Admit me Chorus to this history.
> — Shakespeare, *Henry V*

In Al Pacino's *Looking for Richard* (1996), Pacino as director sets his version of William Shakespeare's *Richard III* in the Cloisters, a beloved New York City museum built in the 1930s with materials from five medieval French monasteries and, like Pacino's film, a pastiche of old and new. The Cloisters houses about five thousand works of art from medieval Europe, the most famous of which are perhaps the Unicorn Tapestries, woven about a decade after the fall of the historic Richard III on Bosworth Field. In Michael Almereyda's *Hamlet* (2000), starring Ethan Hawke, Hamlet as the prince of postmodern New York still retains vestiges of that older Hamlet, Prince of Denmark, who dates from the twelfth-century chronicle accounts of Saxo Grammaticus. The Ghost may emerge from a vending machine and the action may be played in twentieth-century dress, but Hamlet is still recognizably Hamlet, a medieval character now transported to the dark and threatening corporate world of Manhattan.[1] Like these, *Henry V*, one of Shakespeare's best-known history plays, has undergone several transformations in its twentieth-century renderings, in which there are still attempts — notably by Laurence Olivier in his 1944 film, with its visual nods to the Limbourg brothers, painters of the *Très Riches Heures*, and by Kenneth Branagh's film of 1989, with his costume and prop choices — to retain the medieval flavor of the original story. It has been observed that for medieval and early modern chroniclers there was often no sense of narrative closure; the strands of history were traced through the authors' own lifetimes, while subsequent chronicle editions published posthumously were taken up and continued by others. After the same fashion, Shakespeare's medieval narratives continue to be reshaped and replayed by each generation.

This volume brings together medieval and early modern scholars to discuss films, television productions, and staged productions of Shakespeare's plays, specifically those that derive from medieval sources or are set in the Middle Ages. The essays consider Shakespeare's realization of his medieval sources in the language and drama of his day, drawing on medieval chronicles and important medieval authors such as John Gower, Geoffrey Chaucer, and John Lydgate whose works Shakespeare knew. Comparative readings shed light on the ways source texts have been used

Al Pacino in *Looking for Richard* (1996), directed by himself.

to create literary and national histories as well as to inform their dramatic representation in a variety of modern media. The book serves as an introduction to reading Shakespeare's plays through the lens of the medieval works that inform them and serves also as a guide to Shakespeare and medievalism in popular culture.

Our initial idea was to bring together medievalists and early modernists, who are often acquainted with differing bibliographies, to consider the primary texts from the perspective of their separate (though intrinsically linked) disciplines. The assignment was to select and examine medieval elements, to explore their filtering through Shakespeare, and then to discuss their impact (or not) on performance; this exercise proved to be quite difficult but rewarding for all of the contributors. By including essays that consider various and complementary subjects or that consider the same plays from varying angles, the volume creates tensions and dialogues not only between medievalists and early modernists but also between historians, literary scholars, and, in one case, a musicologist. Because Shakespeare continues to enjoy a lively career onstage and onscreen, our main examples are drawn from recent performance history in those venues.

We aim, in other words, to transcend disciplinary boundaries of rigid periodization and to emphasize the value of medievalists talking to early modernists as well as the importance of looking at drama not only as text but as performance. Because of the traditionally strict boundaries between the periods of literary studies (and indeed between disciplines such as history and music), Shakespeare has tended to remain separate from his medieval sources.[2] Recent collections such as *Reading the Medieval in Early Modern England*, edited by Gordon McMullan and David Matthews, the seminar on "Medieval Shakespeare" sponsored in 2007 by the Shakespeare Association of America, and anthologies such as Derek Pearsall's *Chaucer to Spenser: An Anthology of Writing in English 1375–1575* suggest that the boundary between fields is becoming more perme-

Romeo (Leonardo DiCaprio) in pseudo-medieval armor with a winged Juliet (Claire Danes) in Baz Luhrman's *Romeo + Juliet* (1996).

able from both sides of the breach.³ This trend has gained traction from biographies that explore Shakespeare's Roman Catholic roots and leanings and from recent studies of the shaping of Chaucer as proto–Protestant by his Renaissance printers.⁴

Shakespeare, though undoubtedly an admirer of medieval literature, was no medieval historiographer; some productions of his plays have even set out to correct his misrepresentations of the medieval period. Roman Polanski justified the nudity of his Lady Macbeth in the sleepwalking scene of his 1972 film *Macbeth* because his team of researchers had discovered that medieval Scotswomen did not wear nightgowns. In this case, Polanski's medievalism neatly dovetailed with the vision of the film's executive producer, Hugh Hefner. Polanski rectified this minor costuming anachronism of previous productions, yet turned a blind eye to the play's grander historical inaccuracies: the condensed time frame (Macbeth ruled for seventeen years, most of it peacefully), the tanist tradition of royal succession, the invented characters (Banquo and Fleance), and Malcolm's coronation (instead of Lulach's—Lady Macbeth's son). As this example suggests, when examining medieval Shakespeare in performance, we are not only dealing with Shakespeare's medievalism but also with that of the play's or film's director. In the early 1970s, Polanski may have wanted his rather selective medievalism, or "finicky historical exactness," as stage director John Barton characterizes such productions, to be more accurate than Shakespeare's, but today directors appear to be more interested in postmodern Shakespeare than in medieval Shakespeare, as Almereyda's *Hamlet* and Baz Luhrmann's *Romeo + Juliet* (1996) seem at least superficially to suggest, though these films, too, draw on notions of older social hierarchy, or the medieval estates, to account for the main characters' uncomfortable placement in the worlds they inhabit.⁵

Shakespeare's medieval plays include those set in the Middle Ages or those drawing directly on medieval sources, criteria that include almost every play. Of Shakespeare's histories, for example, only *Henry VIII* (*All Is True*) does not describe a medieval king. It is worth noting that though Henry VIII is treated as an early modern king, his father, the earl of Richmond, later Henry VII, who defeats Richard III, is treated as a medieval king, a difference that raises the question about the fixedness of the boundary between medieval and early modern. Much of what separates Henry VIII's epoch from that of his father is that England broke from its feudalist past and became a modern nation-state during Henry VIII's reign when monarchical power was officially centralized through the Act of Supremacy in 1534. But that is only one reason for drawing the line between medieval and early modern at that point in time. The emergence of modern English was one contributing factor, as were the Protestant Reformation and advances in science and technology. The movement from medieval to the modern in the early Tudor period was a subtle transition, promoted by new advances in a variety of media, including printed books, pamphlets, and theatrical performance.

Shakespeare's plays, then, give us an early modern perspective on the medieval world, full of inaccuracies and anachronisms, idealizations and demonizations that differentiate the two eras. The early modern interpretation of the medieval world, particularly Shakespeare's, has been highly influential and tenacious despite the efforts of medievalists to set the record straight. The exaggerated story of Richard III is a prime example of enduring early modern disinformation about medieval history, but there are many others as well. For example, Richard II, the patron of Chaucer and a king who seems to have valued human life and culture very highly, is rendered effete and materialistic for his preference for words over action and cash over courtliness in the first half of Shakespeare's play about him.[6]

Shakespeare's histories focus on two periods of medieval history: the reigns of Richard the Lionheart (1157–1199) and his brother John (1167–1216) in *King John*, in which John and his nephew Arthur (who significantly dies) contend for legitimate rule; and the convoluted regnal history of the fourteenth and fifteenth centuries, including the reigns of Richard II (1367–1400), patron of Chaucer and other important poets of the Middle Ages, Henry IV (1366–1413), Henry V (1386/7–1422), Henry VI (1421–1471) and Richard III (1452–1485). The historical arc Shakespeare traces from *Richard II*, a play that famously looks backward to an even more ideal time, to *Richard III*, a play that looks ahead by depicting a proto–Renaissance or at least Machiavellian king, suggests a rather grim outlook for the future. Though Shakespeare ends the second tetralogy with Henry V's dazzling victory at Agincourt, the author cannot help reminding us that tragedy came quickly thereafter during the reign of Henry V's son, Henry VI, "Whose state so many had the managing / That they lost France and made his English bleed, / Which oft our stage hath shown" (Epi. 11–13).[7] Likewise, though the defeat of Richard III at Bosworth Field ushered in the powerful Tudor monarchs represented by the God-fearing and dashing Richmond, we are left with the inexorability of the individualism, capitalism, nationalism, and absolutism that characterized the early modern period. Notably, *Henry V* and *Richard III* have been the most successful, both commercially and with audiences, of the histories to be filmed.

Among Shakespeare's tragedies that use medieval sources and/or settings are *Romeo and Juliet*, *Hamlet*, *King Lear*, *Macbeth*, and *Othello*, while the comedies include *A Midsummer Night's Dream*, *Two Noble Kinsmen*, *All's Well, That Ends Well*, and *Troilus and Cressida*. Like the history plays, these texts project the present onto the past, and they do so knowingly. Shakespeare had a well-developed sense of anachronism; as the Fool says in *Lear*, "This prophecy Merlin shall make, for I live before his time" (3.2.95). Lear's error in dividing his kingdom among his daughters speaks to the unification of England, Scotland, and Wales that so preoccupied King James early in his reign when the play was written. Reformation social attitudes come to the fore in the comedies, in which convents, for example, are so often cited as unhappy alternatives to marriage. When Hermia defies her father's attempt to arrange a marriage for her in *A Midsummer Night's Dream*, she is given the alternatives of facing life as a nun or condemnation to death (which seem to be about the same). And at the end of *All's Well*, nobody thinks Helena will really find happiness in

Modern Meets Early Modern Meets Medieval: Salvador Dalí sketches Laurence Olivier as Shakespeare's Richard III. Courtesy of the Cinema Museum, London.

her marriage with the cad Bertram, but marriage to him is her best option in the post–Reformation era. Shakespeare's medievalism extends to imagery, setting, characters, plots, even language, but the plays also reaffirm contemporary early modern values, whether regnal or domestic.

Though written at the end of Shakespeare's career, the romances or tragicomedies, like the histories, draw liberally from medieval sources: *Pericles* includes as one of its central characters the medieval poet John Gower; *Cymbeline* takes its title from King Cymbeline, who ruled England during the time of Augustus Caesar and who, like another legendary British king, King Arthur, refused to pay Roman tribute; *The Winter's Tale* harks back to Chaucer's *Canterbury Tales*, especially those of Patient Griselda and Melibee; and even *The Tempest*, which seems contemporary with Shakespeare, inspired as it was by a shipwreck of 1609, employs inescapably medieval allusions.

This volume cannot begin to address all of these plays, especially as this is intended to be an overview and an introduction to reading and teaching Shakespeare through his sources and simultaneously in production. Our essayists focus on one play, for example, *Troilus and Cressida* or *Pericles* (Briggs and Yeager), or one main character, such as Falstaff (Loomis) or Lady Macbeth (Ray), or on more general themes like the portrayal of Shakespeare's peasants (Grindley). We have grouped essays by subgenre with brief introductions to each section.

Writing recently in the *Huntington Library Quarterly*, Paulina Kewes observes that the power of early modern drama in its contribution "to transformations in the way history was written and used has gone largely unrecognized."[8] Distinctions between history and fiction were not clear-cut in Shakespeare's time. John Stow (d. 1605), early modern antiquarian and Chaucer editor, embodies the kind of conflation that could occur; Stow produced not only key histories of London and Britain, publishing his *Summarie of Englyshe Chronicles* in 1565, the *Chronicles of England* in 1580, the *Annales* of England in 1592, and his most famous history, *A Survey of London*, in 1598, but also the 1561 edition of the works of Chaucer, which was the edition most accessible to Shakespeare.[9] Shakespeare himself extracted large segments, sometimes verbatim, from the few chronicles available to him when writing his plays. But the histories he consulted were not informed by objective research or by what we consider today to be historiography. Raphael Holinshed's voluminous *Chronicles of England, Scotlande, and Ireland* (1577), one of Shakespeare's three preferred sources—the others being Ovid's *Metamorphoses* and Plutarch's *Lives*—invents "historical" figures, most notably Banquo and Fleance in its narrative on the Scottish king, Macbeth. The other books on England's past that Shakespeare consulted were *The Union of the Two Noble and Illustre Families of Lancaster and York* (1548) by Edward Hall, a Tudor apologist, and *A Mirror for Magistrates* (1559), a kind of conduct book for political rulers; both of these, of course, had strong biases. Shakespeare's knowledge of the medieval period is based on what Russ McDonald calls "piggyback history"—books that borrowed from other like-minded books and supported each other's claims.[10] Holinshed took information from Hall and from Hector Boece's *Scotorum historia* (1572), and Shakespeare, we are fairly certain, knew all three sources.

Another factor contributing to the imaginative historicizing of the early modern period was the increasing differentiation of history and theology. Phyllis Rackin explains that "Medieval chronicles, often written in monasteries, were informed by the religious perspective that viewed all human actions under the aspect of eternity." Meanwhile, early modern historians began to see history in terms of "second causes" rather than "first causes," or God's will; these second causes were human rather than divine. As a result, according to Rackin, early modern histories "cheerfully mingled providential and Machiavellian explanations, with no apparent sense of contradiction."[11] Performances of playtexts reimagining the past therefore become funhouse mirrors of history; they are representations of representations and appropriations of appropriations with a skewed or mixed sense of causation. The result is an alienation from the past; the Renaissance developed, as medievalist James Simpson notes, a philological relationship to the medieval era.[12] The past became an artifact to be studied. Unfortunately, that rigid differentiation of the medieval (a dead, dark past) from the early modern (Renaissance or rebirth) has stubbornly endured. Changes in conceptions of history make it difficult, therefore, to discern medieval elements in Shakespeare. Further, the problems of separating the medieval inheritance from early modern innovation leave us with the question of why we care so much to do so.

Indeed, the hard boundary set at 1534 has become more and more permeable as medievalists and early modernists "write across" the Act of Supremacy. As Simpson points out, "Scholars are breaking free of the habit of centuries of historiography that posits the shift from the medieval to early modern as an inevitable, natural historical break.... They are, in short, historicizing both the break and, more profoundly, the forms of understanding that flow from it."[13] This boundary crossing had been prevented by careful differentiation of the two periods that began in the mid-to-late sixteenth century. For example, the 1598 edition of Chaucer's works, edited by Thomas Speght, marks its difference from the earlier editions of Stow and Thynne by including editorial additions and scholarly notations, including a glossary of more than two thousand words. Speght's glossary, wherein "Old and obscure words [are] explained [sic]," may have helped early modern readers through the Middle English text, but it also marked Chaucer's work as antiquated and old-fashioned.[14]

Shakespeare, of course, participates in the differentiation of the medieval and early modern, but as this volume suggests, he also bridges the difference, especially when his appropriation of medieval source material is political. In her consideration of medieval and early modern penitential practice in *Measure for Measure*, Sarah Beckwith argues that Shakespeare's medievalism is politically radical rather than "nostalgic, conservative, or both," an analysis that is convincing for this play though perhaps not so directly for others, such as *Pericles*, for instance, where the spirit of the poet John Gower, Chaucer's contemporary, is summoned to narrate "a song that old was sung" (1.0.1), calling up a nostalgic past of strange and unlikely adventures that comes to be called romance.[15] Certainly, Shakespeare's deployment of the material had a different aim from that of the chroniclers. The chronicler Hall wrote to buoy the queen's claims to the throne, but there is much in Shakespeare's renderings of the Yorks and the Lancasters that would have made Elizabeth I uncomfortable about her own tenuous hold on power. The earl of Essex paid the Lord Chamberlain's Men to put on a production of *Richard II* on the eve of his attempted coup against the queen. It seems that medieval stories could be marshaled against as well as used in the service of early modern power structures.

The collection begins with essays on Shakespeare's histories. Jim Casey's "'*Richard's* Himself Again': The Body of Richard III on Stage and Screen" examines a range of depictions of Richard in one specific scene: his wooing of Lady Anne. Beginning with analysis of Shakespeare's medieval sources, Casey then interprets Richard's demonizing on stage in the contexts of contemporary political imaginings (culminating with Richard's portrayal by Colley Cibber) and concludes with an examination of several modern renderings of Richard on stage and screen. Catherine Loomis's "Falstaff in America" addresses the tradition of portraying Falstaff in the United States, a tradition that differs significantly from that of the United Kingdom. In "Scoring the Fields of the Dead: Musical Styles and Approaches to Postbattle Scenes from *Henry V* (1944, 1989)," musicologist Linda K. Schubert analyzes the sound tracks for filmed representations of the Battle of Agincourt and its aftermath, focusing on music composed by William Walton for Olivier's film (which draws on medieval plainchant and the fifteenth-century "Agincourt Carol") and Patrick Doyle's modern composition "Non nobis," created to accompany the scene of the dead and wounded lying on the battlefield. Giving us further background, Schubert provides several influential precedents for scoring Shakespeare's plays and battle scenes, most particularly music composed for Sergei Eisenstein's *Alexander Nevsky* (1938) by Sergei Prokofiev.

Essays on three of the tragedies follow. Shakespeare's representation of class, particularly of peasants, as drawn from medieval social-estates satire is the main subject of Carl James Grindley's "'We're Everyone You Depend On': Filming Shakespeare's Peasants." Grindley examines the ways in which lower-class or supporting characters are represented in films of *Romeo and Juliet* (Luhrmann, Zeffirelli) and in John Madden's *Shakespeare in Love*. Patrick J. Cook's "Medieval *Hamlet* in Performance" studies a range of *Hamlets* in imagined medieval settings, including the productions of Laurence Olivier (1948) and Franco Zeffirelli (1990), in which Ophelia is shown embroidering the Bayeux tapestry and Hamlet is portrayed as a Renaissance man seeking to burst forth from the confines of the medieval castle of Elsinore. Sid Ray's "Finding Gruoch: The Hidden Genealogy of Lady Macbeth in Text and Performance" explores both the genealogy of the historical Lady Macbeth, the eleventh-century Queen Gruoch, whose story has been suppressed, and the story of Lady Macbeth as rendered by Shakespeare and adapted by recent filmmakers.

Martha W. Driver's "Reading *A Midsummer Night's Dream* through Middle English Romance" begins the section on comedies. Her essay traces several medieval influences in the play, including its allusions to Chaucer's "Knight's Tale," *Legend of Good Women*, and "Sir Thopas" and to English folktale and the ways in which medieval imagery is exploited or ignored in recent film and concert productions, concluding with an analysis of productions of Benjamin Britten's opera. Julia Ruth Briggs's essay, "'Chaucer ... the Story Gives': *Troilus and Cressida* and *The Two Noble Kinsmen*," considers two of Shakespeare's plays, the latter cowritten with John Fletcher, which are adaptations of two of Chaucer's greatest poems. In Shakespeare's rewriting of the poems as plays, Chaucer's delicate ironies are transformed by a sense of disillusionment with war, love, heroism, and class, also reflected more broadly in changing social attitudes toward warfare in the early modern period. Gary Waller's "Shakespeare's Virgin Mother on the Modern Stage: *All's Well, That Ends Well* and the Madonna del Parto Tradition" focuses on the medieval background and modern stagings of the culminating scene of *All's Well, That Ends Well*. The momentary tableau of Helena's reappearance in Act 5 links the play with a very specific medieval miracle and an artistic tradition that are powerful reminders of the rich ideological contradictions in the ways medieval and early modern women were represented.

The romances are replete with medieval references. In "'The Quick and the Dead': Performing the Poet Gower in *Pericles*," Kelly Jones explores the role of Gower as choric commentator, tracing this figure back to medieval personifications of Vice in early drama. The performance function of Gower is then described in examples of staging from Shakespeare's day to contemporary theater. R. F. Yeager examines Gower's influence on Shakespeare in his "Shakespeare as Medievalist: What It Means for Performing *Pericles*," which comprehensively considers Shakespeare's other Gowerian sources for the composition of his play, along with popular productions that have tended to omit the figure of Gower the poet-narrator altogether, an ironic meditation on the excision of medieval elements that Shakespeare studied so carefully to put in. Louise M. Bishop's "A Touch of Chaucer in *The Winter's Tale*" reads Shakespeare's play through the lens of Chaucer's *Melibee*, in which Dame Prudence instructs her husband in morality and right action, and examines several recent stagings as feminist rereadings. Finally, in "Caliban's God: The Medieval and Renaissance Man in the Moon," Kim Zarins explores medieval and early modern images of the Man in the Moon from manuscript to print, arguing that Caliban finds in the moon man not only inspiration but a soul mate.

As these essays suggest, *Shakespeare and the Middle Ages* raises critical questions for scholars and students of early literature, including periodicity, historiography, intertextuality, and appropriation, among many others. It also suggests Shakespeare's enormous, inordinate, and misleading influence on the ways in which nonmedievalists regard the Middle Ages, an influence that is replayed again and again in modern stage and film productions of the plays. In this respect, *Shakespeare and the Middle Ages* illustrates how history is made: knowledge (if not the record) of a given time period derives from compelling but mostly exaggerated stories that are told and retold until they are made indelible through performance. Richard III may not have been the deformed, calculating killer Shakespeare depicts, but performances of that part by Olivier, Ian McKellen, and Al Pacino on film and by Richard Burbage, Edmund Kean, Olivier, and McKellen on stage have cast a long and unshakable shadow over our understanding of that particular maligned medieval king. It turns out that our misunderstanding of the history of the Middle Ages does not wholly originate from the biased reports of battlefield victors, as many would have it. Much of it comes from the son of a glover born in an unassuming farming town in central England writing centuries later. This abiding influence reminds us not only of Shakespeare's lasting power as an author but also of his deification by scholars and teachers and his usefulness to those supporting religious (Catholic or Protestant), political (monarchical or republican), and social (individualist or communal) ideologies. Shakespeare's plays on screen or on stage have had a profound impact on the historical memory, functioning, like the actors described by Hamlet, as "the abstract and brief chronicles of the time" (2.2.520).

Though Shakespeare was neither a stickler for accuracy nor an enemy of anachronism, these essays also indicate that we can learn much of value about the Middle Ages through his plays. Lady Macbeth tells us that royal Scottish women were assertive, political, and literate in the Middle Ages; they also nursed their babies in the hope of endowing their children with their passionate blood. We can deduce that feminine virtues were thus not limited to passivity and silence in the medieval period and that femininity could encompass both nurturing and aggression. Macbeth also reminds us that primogeniture and succession of power through sons has not always been the standard. Tanistry, though never actually mentioned in the play, was the established way in which the medieval Scots transferred royal power. *A Midsummer Night's Dream* celebrates medieval folk belief and the misunderstandings also commonly found in medieval fabliaux as joyfully as does any comic tale by Giovanni Boccaccio or Chaucer. And *King Lear* gives us insight into notions of the politics and economics of medieval inheritance, vividly presenting the shift from feudalism to protocapitalism and the will of the powerful to bequeath their property to whom they chose. The Wheel of Fortune, a central motif in many medieval English works from Chaucer's *Troilus and Criseyde* to John Lydgate's *Troy Book* and Sir Thomas Malory's *Morte Darthur*, makes a regular and often poignant appearance in a range of Shakespeare's plays, from *Romeo and Juliet* to *King Lear*, as do the figures of Constance (from Chaucer's "Man of Law's Tale") and Patient Griselda. The Wheel of Fortune even appears in Billy Morrissette's modernized film version of *Macbeth, Scotland, PA* (2001) in the form of a Ferris wheel at a 1970s carnival.

In fact, as these examples of Shakespeare's sometimes errant, sometimes elucidative medievalism suggest, early modernists and medievalists have plenty to discuss and to teach each other as they explore the plays. Not surprisingly, these essays, half of them written by early modernists and half by medievalists, vary remarkably in approach and conclusion, and yet the variations do not fall neatly on one side or the other of the dividing line between the two periods. We are pleased to report that there is as much disagreement within the historical fields of study as without. In the end, we are left in awe of the richness and open-endedness of the Shakespearean text.

Notes

1. For analysis of the urban and corporate setting of Almereyda's *Hamlet*, see Douglas M. Lanier, "Shakescorp *Noir*," *Shakespeare Quarterly* 53.2 (2002): 157–180, esp. 169–180.

2. There are, of course, notable exceptions: Carolyn Spurgeon, *Five Hundred Years of Chaucer Criticism and Allusion 1357–1900* (Cambridge, UK: Cambridge University Press, 1925); Geoffrey Bullough, *Narrative and Dramatic Sources of Shakespeare*, 8 vols. (New York: Columbia University Press, 1957); Alice S. Miskimin, *The Renaissance Chaucer* (New Haven, CT: Yale University Press, 1975); Ann Thompson, *Shakespeare's Chaucer: A Study in Literary Origins* (Liverpool: Liverpool University Press, 1978); E. Talbot Donaldson, *The Swan at the Well: Shakespeare Reading Chaucer* (New Haven, CT: Yale University Press, 1985), to name a few.

3. See Gordon McMullan and David Matthews, eds., *Reading the Medieval in Early Modern England* (Cambridge, UK: Cambridge University Press, 2007); James Simpson, *Reform and Cultural Revolution: The Oxford English Literary History: Volume II, 1350–1547* (Oxford: Oxford University Press, 2002); and Derek Pearsall, *Chaucer to Spenser: An Anthology of Writing in English 1375–1575* (Oxford: Blackwell, 2002), among other recent explorations and anthologies. David Wallace claims that "most of the running has been made by medievalists reading forward rather than by Renaissance scholars reading back," in *Reading the Medieval in Early Modern England*, ed. Gordon McMullan and David Matthews (Cambridge, UK: Cambridge University Press, 2007), 220.

4. See, e.g., Stephen Greenblatt's biography of Shakespeare, *Will in the World: How Shakespeare Became Shakespeare* (New York: W. W. Norton, 2004), esp. chap. 3. As Anne Hudson, *The Premature Reformation: Wycliffite Texts and Lollard History* (New York: Oxford University Press, 1988), 392, points out, Chaucer alludes to "contemporary interest in the ideas that Wyclif had advanced"; Derek Pearsall, *The Life of Geoffrey Chaucer: A Critical Biography* (Oxford: Blackwell, 1992), 182, comments, however, that "we are unlikely to get any explicit comments on Lollardy from Chaucer: he will be his usual cautious and evasive self, and make a joke of what might be very important to him or dangerous." For the reshaping of Chaucer as proto–Protestant by early printers, see Martha W. Driver, "A False Imprint in Chaucer's *Workes*: Protestant Printers in London (and Zurich?)," *Trivium* 31 (1999): 131–154, discussing the printer Nicholas Hill, who produced Chaucer's *Workes* (STC 5074) printed between 1542 and 1550 as well as Protestant polemical works; Alexandra Gillespie, *Print Culture and the Medieval Author: Chaucer, Lydgate, and Their Books 1473–1557* (Oxford: Oxford University Press, 2006), 195–206, outlining some Protestant additions to early printed editions of Chaucer; Simpson, *Reform and Cultural Revolution*, 40–42; Miskimin, *Renaissance Chaucer*, 253–257.

5. John Barton, *Playing Shakespeare: An Actor's Guide* (New York: Anchor Books, 1984), 233. Medieval sources for Hamlet and their realization in Almereyda's *Hamlet* are discussed further in Driver's introduction to Part 2 and in Patrick J. Cook, "Medieval *Hamlet* in Performance"; Luhrmann's film is treated in Carl James Grindley, "'We're Everyone You Depend On': Filming Shakespeare's Peasants," all in this volume.

6. Compare the treatment of Richard II in Michael Bennett, *Richard II and the Revolution of 1399* (Stroud, UK: Sutton, 1999).

7. William Shakespeare, *Henry V*, in *The Riverside Shakespeare*, ed. G. Blakemore Evans, et al. (Boston and New York: Houghton Mifflin, 1997), Epi. 11–13. All quotations from Shakespeare's plays are from this edition and are hereafter cited parenthetically in the text.

8. Paulina Kewes, "History and Its Uses: Introduction," in *The Uses of History in Early Modern England*, ed. Paulina Kewes, *Huntington Library Quarterly* 68.1–2 (2005): 1–30, 4–5.

9. STC 23319, 23333, 23334, 23341, 5076. Anne Hudson, "John Stow (1525?–1605)," in *Editing Chaucer: The Great Tradition*, ed. Paul G. Ruggiers (Norman, OK: Pilgrim Books, 1984), 53–70, 53, comments that "many Elizabethan authors, including Spenser and Shakespeare, knew Chaucer through the medium of [Stow's] imperfect edition." See Ian Gadd and Alexandra Gillespie, eds., *John Stow (1525–1605) and the Making of the English Past: Studies in Early Modern Culture and the History of the Book* (London: British Library, 2004).

10. STC 13568b, 13568.5, 12721, 1247. Russ McDonald, *The Bedford Companion to Shakespeare: An Introduction with Documents*, 2nd ed. (New York: Bedford/St. Martin's, 2001), 150.

11. Phyllis Rackin, *Stages of History: Shakespeare's English Chronicles* (Ithaca, NY: Cornell University Press, 1990), 6–7.

12. James Simpson, "Diachronic History and the Shortcomings of Medieval Studies," in *Reading the Medieval in Early Modern England*, ed. Gordon McMullan and David Matthews (Cambridge, UK: Cambridge University Press, 2007), 23.

13. *Ibid.*, 17–30, 29.

14. STC 5077. Jackson Campbell Boswell and Sylvia Wallace Holton, *Chaucer's Fame in England: STC Chauceriana 1475–1640* (New York: Modern Language Association of America, 2004), item 600, 158–174. According to Eleanor Hammond, *Chaucer: A Bibliographical Manual* (New York: Peter Smith, 1933), 506–507, Speght's glossary is arranged over seven leaves, "three columns to a page, with brief explanations of each; a little over 2000 are thus treated.... In a few cases the editor honestly left the explanation unattempted."

15. Sarah Beckwith, "Medieval Penance, Reformation Repentance and *Measure for Measure*," in *Reading the Medieval in Early Modern England*, ed. Gordon McMullan and David Matthews (Cambridge, UK: Cambridge University Press, 2007), 193–204, 194.

Works Cited

Barton, John. *Playing Shakespeare: An Actor's Guide*. New York: Anchor Books, 1984.

Bennett, Michael. *Richard II and the Revolution of 1399*. Stroud, UK: Sutton, 1999.

Boswell, Jackson Campbell, and Sylvia Wallace Holton. *Chaucer's Fame in England: STC Chauceriana 1475–1640*. New York: Modern Language Association of America, 2004.

Bullough, Geoffrey. *Narrative and Dramatic Sources of Shakespeare*. 8 vols. New York: Columbia University Press, 1957.

Donaldson, E. Talbot. *The Swan at the Well: Shakespeare's Reading Chaucer*. New Haven, CT: Yale University Press, 1985.

Driver, Martha W. "A False Imprint in Chaucer's *Workes*: Protestant Printers in London (and Zurich?)." *Trivium* 31 (1999): 131–154.

Gadd, Ian, and Alexandra Gillespie, eds. *John Stow (1525–1605) and the Making of the English Past: Studies in Early Modern Culture and the History of the Book*. London: British Library, 2004.

Gillespie, Alexandra. *Print Culture and the Medieval Author: Chaucer, Lydgate, and Their Books 1473–1557*. Oxford: Oxford University Press, 2006.

Greenblatt, Stephen. *Will in the World: How Shakespeare Became Shakespeare*. New York: W. W. Norton, 2004.

Hammond, Eleanor. *Chaucer: A Bibliographical Manual*. New York: Peter Smith, 1933.

Hudson, Anne. "John Stow (1525–1605)." In *Editing Chaucer: The Great Tradition*, ed. Paul G. Ruggiers. Norman, OK: Pilgrim Books, 1984. 53–70.

Hudson, Anne. *The Premature Reformation: Wycliffite Texts and Lollard History*. New York: Oxford University Press, 1988.

Kewes, Paulina. "History and Its Uses: Introduction." In *The Uses of History in Early Modern England*, ed. Paulina Kewes. *Huntington Library Quarterly* 68.1–2 (2005): 1–30.

Lanier, Douglas M. "Shakescorp *Noir*." *Shakespeare Quarterly* 53.2 (2002): 157–180.

McDonald, Russ. *The Bedford Companion to Shakespeare: An Introduction with Documents*. 2nd edition. New York: Bedford/St. Martin's, 2001.

McMullan, Gordon, and David Matthews, eds. *Reading the Medieval in Early Modern England*. Cambridge, UK: Cambridge University Press, 2007.

Miskimin, Alice S. *The Renaissance Chaucer*. New Haven, CT: Yale University Press, 1975.

Pearsall, Derek. *Chaucer to Spenser: An Anthology of Writing in English 1375–1575*. Oxford: Blackwell, 2002.
_____. *The Life of Geoffrey Chaucer: A Critical Biography*. Oxford: Blackwell, 1992.
Rackin, Phyllis. *Stages of History: Shakespeare's English Chronicles*. Ithaca, NY: Cornell University Press, 1990.
Spurgeon, Caroline Frances Eleanor. *Five Hundred Years of Chaucer Criticism and Allusion 1357–1900*. Cambridge, UK: Cambridge University Press, 1925.
Simpson, James. *Reform and Cultural Revolution: The Oxford English Literary History: Volume II, 1350–1547*. Oxford: Oxford University Press, 2002.
Thompson, Ann. *Shakespeare's Chaucer: A Study in Literary Origins*. Liverpool: Liverpool University Press, 1978.

FILMOGRAPHY

1938 *Alexander Nevsky*, d. Sergei Eisenstein and D. I. Vasiliev, with Nikolai Cherkasov. USSR: Mosfilm.
1944 *Henry V*, d. Laurence Olivier, with Laurence Olivier. UK: Rank/Two Cities.
1948 *Hamlet*, d. Laurence Olivier, with Laurence Olivier. UK: Rank/Two Cities.
1954 *Richard III*, d. Laurence Olivier, with Laurence Olivier. UK: London Film Productions.
1968 *Romeo and Juliet*, d. Zeffirelli, with Olivia Hussey and Leonard Whiting. USA: Paramount.
1972 *Macbeth*, d. Roman Polanski, with Jon Finch and Francesca Annis. UK: Playboy/Columbia.
1989 *Henry V*, d. Kenneth Branagh, with Kenneth Branagh. UK: Curzon/Renaissance Films.
1990 *Hamlet*, d. Franco Zeffirelli, with Mel Gibson. USA: Warner Brothers.
1995 *Richard III*, d. Richard Loncraine, with Ian McKellan. UK: United Artists.
1996 *Looking for Richard*, d. Al Pacino, with Al Pacino. USA: Twentieth Century–Fox.
1996 *Romeo + Juliet*, d. Baz Luhrmann, with Claire Danes and Leonardo DiCaprio. USA: Twentieth Century–Fox.
1999 *Shakespeare in Love*, d. John Madden, with Joseph Fiennes. USA: Miramax.
2000 *Hamlet*, d. Michael Almereyda, with Ethan Hawke. USA: Miramax.
2001 *Scotland, PA*, d. Billy Morrissette, with Maura Tierney. USA: Abandon Pictures.

Part I. "Abstract and Brief Chronicles of Time": The Histories

Introduction to Part I

Martha W. Driver

> We are always simultaneously making gestures that are archaic, modern, and futuristic.[1]

In a conversation about perceptions of historical time, the philosopher Michel Serres illustrates time's complexity, pointing out the difficulty of determining which attitudes or thoughts or practices are inherited from the past and which might be contemporary or even "futuristic." In the same interview, Serres compares the movement of time to an ironed handkerchief on which one might mark several points. When the handkerchief is crumpled, some points that seem distant are close together; if the handkerchief is torn, points originally close together are separated. An analogy might be made to the ways in which history is received and reported, particularly through an artistic medium like drama and, to add another layer, through its performance in the theater or on film.

Writing about historical film in his 1987 essay on Abel Gance's *Napoleon* (1927), film critic Marc Ferro comments:

> With distance, one version of history replaces another but the work of art remains. And so, with the passage of time, our memory winds up by not distinguishing between, on the one hand, the imaginative history of [Sergei] Eisenstein or Gance, and on the other, history such as it really happened, even though historians seek to make us understand and artists seek to make us participate.[2]

As we learn from Ferro and know from our own experience, drama provides a vivid immediacy, appealing to the imagination, engaging the viewer in the past, and involving him emotionally as well as intellectually with the action. But whose past is it? The ways in which Shakespeare's history plays are shaped to their perceived audience comprise one thread linking the essays in this section; the authors further consider how ideas about the Middle Ages are filtered through Shakespeare and then through later production. Among the questions raised are: What are the older elements informing the plays? Are medieval themes ignored, highlighted, or exploited? How successfully have the plays been translated to stage and film?

"Spot the anachronism," also known as "find the historical errors," is perhaps a pastime in which all critics, to some extent, are engaged. The classic example is described by the writer and film critic James Agee. Discussing Laurence Olivier's *Henry V*, Agee notes in his review of the film's U.S. release in 1946 that when the film was previewed by "a group of Oxford's impassive Shakespeare pundits, there was only one murmur of dissent. A woman specialist insisted that all the war horses which take part in the Battle of Agincourt should have been stallions."[3]

Though Agee points to the pettiness of such criticism (and does not reveal whether the lone woman scholar was in this instance correct or not), finding errors in the record, whether that record is written, played, or filmed, is part of talking about history and its reception. Ferro says:

There are several ways to look at a historical film. The most common of these, inherited from the tradition of scholarship, consists in verifying if the reconstruction is precise (are the soldiers of 1914 mistakenly wearing the helmets which were introduced only after 1916?), seeing that the décor and the location is [sic] faithful and the dialogue is authentic.[4]

A slippery term, authenticity can be another central issue when discussing relationships between history and fictional texts. As film critic Jonathan Rosenbaum commented to me some years ago, "It doesn't matter if the historical details of the film are authentic. They just have to look authentic to the audience."[5] Authenticity is a convention of costume drama, part of the visual language in the recreation of the historical past on stage or screen, and part of the process of recovery of the historical elements underlying that fiction, should one wish to explore them; a feeling of authenticity (which may be ahistorical in other words) or of familiarity with a recognizable past can also be created by association.

Commenting on his film *Chimes at Midnight* (1965), Orson Welles's adaptation of the several Shakespeare plays that feature Falstaff, Welles said: "It mustn't seem *perfectly* real. It doesn't mean anything unless it makes poetry possible."[6] The compilation of Falstaff stories has a long history in America, as Catherine Loomis illustrates; in the patchwork productions of Falstaff plays, some of the original elements and tensions are lost from Shakespeare's texts as the focus shifts to Falstaff as the central character. Yet in *Chimes at Midnight*, at the poignant moment of Falstaff's rejection, Welles places the viewer at the parting scene and shows "through the pain in the young King's eyes, that he understands what he is giving up; the look that Welles returns, mixing paternal pride and stunned sorrow, makes this exchange of glances one of Shakespeare's greatest moments, even if Shakespeare never wrote it."[7]

Orson Welles as Falstaff in *Chimes at Midnight* (1965).

Of Shakespeare's history plays, *King Henry VIII (All Is True)* is the only one that is not set in the Middle Ages, or not precisely, instead "dealing directly with events of Reformation history," one of the great markers of the movement from the medieval to the early modern periods.[8] The Middle Ages was clearly of great interest to Shakespeare's first audiences. Discussing in particular Shakespeare's *Henry VI* and *Richard* plays, Paul Strohm points to their political layering which must have appealed directly to early modern tastes: "Rather than simply wishing to see fifteenth-century disturbances overcome by Tudor statecraft, the Elizabethan audience might have discovered an intrinsic interest in the representation of an earlier and highly fragmented political situation."[9]

Politics, personal or global, also inform modern renderings of Shakespeare's histories. The first Shakespeare film, *King John* (1899), "was clearly made to record a historic performance by the actor Herbert Beerbohm Tree."[10] Tree made several emendations to Shakespeare's play onstage, reducing it to three acts and adding several tableaux vivants including a scene of the signing of the Magna Carta, "the latter not even mentioned by Shakespeare but conforming to the theatrical dictates of an increasingly historicist approach to staging Renaissance plays."[11] Only a fragment of this film remains.

The politics underpinning Laurence Olivier's 1944 film of *Henry V* are well known. Brought to the screen by Olivier and "dedicated to 'the commando and airborne troops of Great Britain,'" Olivier's film is one of the most influential films ever made.[12] Part of its power derives from allusions to other forms of cinema, most notably the "narrative and visual codes of the western, and the film's use of Technicolor [which] also linked it to American Hollywood pictures."[13] Much of the film was shot on a sound stage and includes scenes reminiscent of medieval manuscript miniatures. Agee describes the Battle of Agincourt, for example, in Olivier's *Henry V* as "not realistic. Olivier took great care not to make it so."[14] The beauty of this notably bloodless battle scene, "with its knights in silver armor, its deep-blue sky, its bright-green grass … [and] a visual poetry equivalent to Shakespeare's language" has been observed by many critics,[15] and there are specific agendas informing it, as Linda Schubert points out, that contrast with the motivations that come into play with the later Kenneth Branagh version (1989); Schubert here explores the scores of these films, explaining the music's history and metaphors as well as giving context for nonexperts by supplying several important examples of scores for historical films composed before 1944.

The famous art historian Erwin Panofsky praised Olivier's *Henry V* especially for its "shifts between three levels of archaeological reality: a reconstruction of Elizabethan London, a reconstruction of the events of 1415 as laid down in Shakespeare's play, and the reconstruction of a performance of this play on Shakespeare's own stage."[16] Panofsky more generally compares the film medium to "the development of line engraving, which started out as a cheap and handy substitute for book illumination and culminated in the purely 'graphic' style of Dürer." Like Shakespeare's plays, to which Panofsky also alludes, film is a form of commercial art:

> If commercial art be defined as all art not primarily produced in order to gratify the creative urge of its maker but primarily intended to meet the requirements of a patron or a buying public, it must be said that noncommercial art is the exception rather than the rule, and a fairly recent and not always felicitous exception at that.[17]

While many Shakespeare films (and some staged productions) have died at the box office, others struggled along, several to be recognized later as masterpieces. For *Chimes at Midnight*, Welles found a Spanish producer and financier but he had only enough money to pay John Gielgud for two weeks of work "and used a double for the rest; at times, all the major actors (except) Welles were doubles." Nonetheless, Welles "managed to impart an astoundingly rich physical texture to every scene," seeming merely to "have photographed a world miraculously found."[18] Olivier's *Richard III* (1955) was marketed aggressively. The film was released in theaters and shown on national television on the same day: "Tens of millions of people watched the NBC broadcast

Olivier as Henry V (1944).

Olivier as Richard III (1955). Courtesy of the Cinema Museum, London.

that Sunday afternoon, more than had seen 'Richard III' during all the previous centuries combined."[19] Though it reached a very wide audience, the film lost money; Olivier later said "the film's initial flop made it impossible for me to get the money to make *Macbeth*."[20] However, Olivier's film version created a Richard that has influenced all subsequent staged and filmed representations of Richard, the subject of the essay by Jim Casey, the third contributor to this section. The historical Richard has accrued layers of disinformation; his character has been fictionalized to fit received notions of the historical past. Like Beerbohm Tree's version of *King John*, Olivier's *Richard III* is a streamlined text, omitting characters included by Shakespeare and reducing the lines spoken by others: "Every ounce of linguistic fat is removed, leaving a lean, swiftly moving plot (slightly rearranged to make it more comprehensible and effective ...) with its central characters still intact."[21] Like Serres's handkerchief, the true history of Richard III has been crumpled and torn (and further emended in production), yet it is the version of history that most people remember.

Robert A. Rosenstone distinguishes between data, or the facts of history, and a larger impression or vision of the past that affects "how we look at and think about and remember and make meaningful what remains of people and events. This is the vision that explains why historians like Edward Gibbon, Jules Michelet, and George Bancroft affect our sense of the past long after their data has been superseded."[22] While Shakespeare is not history, he has shaped our reception of it, as the history plays so ably demonstrate.

Notes

1. Michel Serres and Bruno Latour, *Conversations on Science, Culture, and Time*, trans. Roxanne Lapidus (Ann Arbor: University of Michigan Press, 1995), 60. Serres further tells the story of elderly brothers who bury their thirty-year-old father, a mountaineer lost many years before whose body was found almost a half-century later perfectly preserved in ice. Serres comments, "his children, having grown old prepare to bury a body that is still young. That's the source of this alpine scene, which is ... often

observed — between a writer and his critics. Art, beauty, and profound thought preserve youth even better than a glacier" (61).

2. Marc Ferro, *Cinema and History*, trans. Naomi Greene (Detroit, MI: Wayne State University Press, 1988), 73.

3. James Agee, *Agee on Film: Criticism and Comment on the Movies*, series ed. Martin Scorsese, intro by David Denby (New York: Modern Library, 2000), 347.

4. Ferro, *Cinema and History*, 159.

5. Conversation with Jonathan Rosenbaum, author and film critic, also cited in Martha Driver, "Introduction," in *Special Focus: Medieval Period on Film*, special issue of *Film & History* 29, no. 1–2 (1999): 9; and in Martha W. Driver and Sid Ray, eds., *The Medieval Hero on Screen: Representations from Beowulf to Buffy* (Jefferson, NC: McFarland, 2004), 20.

6. Quoted in Claudia Roth Pierpont, "The Player Kings," *New Yorker*, November 19, 2007, 70–79, 78. *Chimes at Midnight* is listed under its original title, *Campanadas a medianoche*, in the Internet Movie Database, which also credits two writers, "William Shakespeare (plays)" and "Raphael Holinshed (book)," but not Welles (except as director). The original release date was 1965; the film was released in the United States in 1967. See "*Campanadas a medianoche* (1965)" at http://www.imdb.com/title/tt0059012/.

7. Pierpont, "Player Kings," 78.

8. Thomas Healy, "History and Judgement in *Henry VIII*," in *Shakespeare's Late Plays: New Readings*, ed. Jennifer Richards and James Knowles (Edinburgh: Edinburgh University Press, 1999), 158–175, 164.

9. Paul Strohm, *Politique: Languages of Statecraft between Chaucer and Shakespeare* (Notre Dame, IN: University of Notre Dame Press, 2005), 236.

10. Deborah Cartmell, "Film as the New Shakespeare and Film on Shakespeare: Reversing the Shakespeare/Film Trajectory," *Literature Compass* 3, no. 5 (2006): 1150–1159, 1155.

11. Anthony R. Guneratne, "'Thou Dost Usurp Authority': Beerbohm Tree, Reinhardt, Olivier, Welles, and the Politics of Adapting Shakespeare," in *A Concise Companion to Shakespeare on Screen*, ed. Diana E. Henderson (Oxford: Blackwell, 2006), 31–76, 34.

12. Sue Harper, *Picturing the Past: The Rise and Fall of the British Costume Film* (London: British Film Institute, 1994), 86. Harper further says that though "there is no direct evidence of government sponsorship, there are plenty of suggestions that the film enjoyed official support. Certainly the French government saw the film as the expression of official views."

13. Emma Smith, ed., *King Henry V* (Cambridge, UK: Cambridge University Press, 2002), 51.

14. Agee, *Agee on Film*, 350. Olivier is said to have been visually inspired by reproductions of the twelve calendar illustrations of *Les très riches heures du Duc de Berri* that he and his set designer, Paul Sherriff, had seen in a French magazine. Linda A. Kissler, "'Upon the King': A Comparative Analysis of England's King Henry V in History, Shakespearean Drama and Film," unpublished Ph.D. thesis, Duquesne University, 1995, 141, citing Dale Silviria, *Laurence Olivier and the Art of Film Making* (East Rutherford, NJ: Fairleigh Dickinson University Press, 1985), 75.

15. Pierpont, "Player Kings," 72. See also Agee, *Agee on Film*, 350–353, who comments that Olivier's "was the whole anti-naturalistic conception of the film — a true Shakespearean's recognition that man is greater, and nature less, than life" (353).

16. Erwin Panofsky, "Style and Medium in the Motion Pictures," in *Three Essays on Style*, ed. Irving Lavin (Cambridge, MA: MIT Press, 1997), 102.

17. Panofsky, "Style and Medium," 108, 120.

18. Pierpont, "Player Kings," 78.

19. Pierpont, "Player Kings," 77.

20. Ace G. Pilkington, *Screening Shakespeare from Richard II to Henry V* (Newark, NJ: University of Delaware Press, 1991), 160. Pilkington further notes that when Charlton Heston made a version of *Antony and Cleopatra* in 1972, his budget was so limited that he had to buy "outtakes from the galley footage of *Ben Hur*," while Playboy Enterprises never recouped its losses from Polanski's *Macbeth* (1971).

21. Constance A. Brown, "Olivier's *Richard III* — A Re-evaluation," *Film Quarterly* 20, no. 4 (1967): 23–32, 23.

22. Robert A. Rosenstone, ed., *Revisioning History: Film and the Construction of a New Past* (Princeton, NJ: Princeton University Press, 1995), 6.

WORKS CITED

Agee, James. *Agee on Film: Criticism and Comment on the Movies*. Series ed. Martin Scorsese, intro by David Denby. New York: Modern Library, 2000.

Brown, Constance A. "Olivier's *Richard III* — A Re-evaluation." *Film Quarterly* 20, no. 4 (1967): 23–32.

Cartmell, Deborah. "Film as the New Shakespeare and Film on Shakespeare: Reversing the Shakespeare/Film Trajectory." *Literature Compass* 3, no. 5 (2006): 1150–1159.
Driver, Martha. "Introduction." In *Special Focus: Medieval Period on Film.* Special issue of *Film & History* 29, no. 1–2 (1999): 9.
Driver, Martha W., and Sid Ray, eds. *The Medieval Hero on Screen: Representations from Beowulf to Buffy.* Jefferson, NC: McFarland, 2004.
Ferro, Marc. *Cinema and History.* Trans. Naomi Greene. Detroit, MI: Wayne State University Press, 1988.
Guneratne, Anthony R. "'Thou Dost Usurp Authority': Beerbohm Tree, Reinhardt, Olivier, Welles, and the Politics of Adapting Shakespeare." In *A Concise Companion to Shakespeare on Screen*, ed. Diana E. Henderson, 31–76. Oxford: Blackwell, 2006.
Harper, Sue. *Picturing the Past: The Rise and Fall of the British Costume Film.* London: British Film Institute, 1994.
Healy, Thomas. "History and Judgement in *Henry VIII.*" In *Shakespeare's Late Plays: New Readings*, ed. Jennifer Richards and James Knowles, 158–175. Edinburgh: Edinburgh University Press, 1999.
Kissler, Linda A. "'Upon the King': A Comparative Analysis of England's King Henry V in History, Shakespearean Drama and Film." Unpublished Ph.D. thesis, Duquesne University, 1995.
Panofsky, Erwin. "Style and Medium in the Motion Pictures." In *Three Essays on Style*, ed. Irving Lavin, 91–128. Cambridge, MA: MIT Press, 1997.
Pierpont, Claudia Roth. "The Player Kings." *New Yorker*, November 19, 2007, 70–79, 78.
Pilkington, Ace G. *Screening Shakespeare from Richard II to Henry V.* Newark, NJ: University of Delaware Press, 1991.
Rosenstone, Robert A., ed. *Revisioning History: Film and the Construction of a New Past.* Princeton, NJ: Princeton University Press, 1995.
Serres, Michel, and Bruno Latour. *Conversations on Science, Culture, and Time.* Trans. Roxanne Lapidus. Ann Arbor: University of Michigan Press, 1995.
Silviria, Dale. *Laurence Olivier and the Art of Film Making.* East Rutherford, NJ: Fairleigh Dickinson University Press, 1985.
Smith, Emma, ed. *King Henry V.* Cambridge, UK: Cambridge University Press, 2002.
Strohm, Paul. *Politique: Languages of Statecraft between Chaucer and Shakespeare.* Notre Dame, IN: University of Notre Dame Press, 2005.

Filmography

1899 *King John*, d. Walter Pfeffer Dando, William K. L. Dickson, with Herbert Beerbohm Tree.
1927 *Napoléon*, d. Abel Gance, with Gance, Antonin Artaud, Suzanne Bianchetti, Marguerite Gance. France: Films Abel Gance.
1944 *Henry V*, d. Laurence Olivier, with Olivier, Leslie Banks. UK: Rank/Two Cities.
1955 *Richard III*, d. Laurence Olivier, with Olivier, Cedric Hardwicke, Ralph Richardson, John Gielgud, Claire Bloom. UK: Laurence Olivier Productions.
1965 *Campanadas a medianoche* (*Chimes at Midnight*), d. Orson Welles, with Jeanne Moreau, John Gielgud, Margaret Rutherford. Spain: Alpine Films.
1971 *Macbeth*, d. Roman Polanski, with Jon Finch, Francesca Annis. US: Caliban.
1972 *Antony and Cleopatra*, d. Charlton Heston, with Heston, Hildegarde Neil. UK: Folio Films.
1989 *Henry V*, d. Kenneth Branagh, with Branagh, Derek Jacobi, Ian Holm, Robbie Coltrane, Judi Dench, Emma Thompson. UK: Curzon/Renaissance Films.

"*Richard's* Himself Again": The Body of Richard III on Stage and Screen[1]

Jim Casey

Richard III is perhaps the most notorious monarch ever to sit on the throne of England. He is remembered primarily as a hunchback and a murderer, despite the incessant campaigning of numerous Richard III societies. Members of these societies will tell anyone who will listen that Richard was not such a bad king, that he did not kill his nephews, and that he was not deformed. In fact, most historians agree that "Good King Richard" was quite different from the monster of popular tradition.[2] We imagine him as a demonic, kin-killing Quasimodo not because of the work of historians but because of the work of Shakespeare.

Shakespeare did not create the humpbacked monster, of course; that (in)famous depiction evolved from Tudor propaganda and earlier literary models, and Shakespeare was merely adapting his source material.[3] Yet Shakespeare's cultural influence is such that most people envision the playwright's character when they think of Richard III. This is particularly true of Richard's physical appearance, despite contrary historical evidence. As Peter Saccio notes, it is "quite unlikely" that the historical Richard's supposed physical deformity actually existed: "No contemporary document or portrait attests to it, and the fact that he permitted himself to be stripped to the waist for anointing at his own coronation suggests that his torso could bear public inspection."[4] Paul Kendall enumerates myriad historical sources that describe "no noticeable bodily deformity,"[5] and X-ray analysis of various portraits has shown that the crookbacked shoulders in many paintings were added later.[6] Nevertheless, we usually imagine Richard with a hunchback, due in large part to Shakespeare and the later performance tradition of his play.

The quotation in my title is not actually derived from Shakespeare's play but rather from Colley Cibber's 1699 revision. After his nightmare, immediately before the battle at Bosworth, Cibber's Richard rejects any feelings he may have of regret or contrition, crying, "Hence, Babling dreams, you threaten here in vain: / Conscience avant; *Richard's* himself again" (5.5.84–85).[7] This openly defiant, remorseless Richard greatly contributed to Cibber's success and even more to the success of later actors. As Janis Lull notes, "While Cibber's adaptation played 84 times in the 40 years after it was written, it was performed 213 times in the 29 years between 1747 and 1776, when [David] Garrick managed the Drury Lane Theatre."[8] Many critics have disparaged Cibber's alterations, but the adaptation was so popular that some of Cibber's lines were even retained by Laurence Olivier, who describes *Richard III* as "a rare Shakespeare event, when the part's the thing and not the play."[9]

Yet the part has been coveted not only for the opportunity to interpret Richard's lines but also for the opportunity to interpret his body. More agonizing has gone into considerations of Richard's appearance and corporeal representation than perhaps with any other character in Shakespeare, and as we shall see, the physical presence of the actor greatly impacts the efficacy of the

role. Robert Weimann argues that in Shakespeare's plays, "the stage's dual capacity could be projected between an imagined *locus* of verisimilitude and the *platea* materiality of 'this unworthy scaffold,'" where the physical and material "platea-like" dimension of the stage "privileged the authority not of what was represented (in historiographical and novelistic narrative) but of what was representing and who was performing."[10] On stage, Richard *becomes* himself only through the body that performs him. At the same time, the *platea* of performance privileges the actor's body over that of the historical or dramatic Richard.

Actors' bodies form and inform every dramatic role, but this is particularly true of Richard, whose body *is* much of the role. This essay examines the embodiment of Richard III in six Royal Shakespeare Company (RSC) stage productions and four film adaptations, beginning with Olivier's "definitive" incarnation.[11] For each Richard, I want to consider how the physical attributes of the actor affect the larger performance and in particular the wooing of Lady Anne.

Olivier's Richard

May 22, 2007, marked Laurence Olivier's centenary. His *Richard III*, although filmed more than fifty years ago, is still one of the most viewed and influential Shakespeare films ever, and his Richard is still one the world's most imitated and recognizable Shakespearean performances.

The film opened in the United Kingdom on April 16, 1955, with Queen Elizabeth II in attendance. It premiered in the United States on March 11, 1956, the first film to be shown simultaneously both in theaters and on TV. Although its NBC telecast was in the afternoon rather than during prime time, several million people saw the program.[12] Alice Griffin believes that "in insisting on clarity for the benefit of the millions who will see the film, [Olivier] has sacrificed the larger significance of the work."[13] The plot had been simplified, characters cut, and as Hugh Richmond observes, the film "consistently conforms more to the tradition founded on Cibber's script than on Shakespeare's."[14] Olivier even retained non–Shakespearean lines, such as the famous "Off with his head. So much for Buckingham" (4.4.188).[15] The result is a caricature of Shakespeare's Richard. This is not surprising, considering the fact that Olivier's performance itself was a kind of character-sketch. Olivier claims to have based his Richard on "the American theater director Jed Harris, the most loathsome man [he had] ever met" and, according to Olivier, the model for the Big Bad Wolf in Walt Disney's *Three Little Pigs*.[16] Nevertheless, many critics have come to regard the role as Olivier's greatest accomplishment, and the ghost of his Richard haunts every subsequent major production of the play.

Famously, Olivier claims to have "cut the wooing-of-Lady-Anne scene in two, in an attempt to make it more credible and possible."[17] In *On Acting*, he admits that dividing the scene "let time pass and gave Richard two glorious climaxes": "I'll have her, but I will not keep her long" (1.2.215) and "Was ever woman in this humour wooed? / Was ever woman in this humour won?" (1.2.213–214).[18] The first section ends after Richard announces his fitness for the young widow's bedchamber. She spits at him and leaves without another word. When Richard observes matter-of-factly that he will have her, his tone is cold and calculating. Olivier describes the voice he used for the part as "the thin reed of a sanctimonious scholar," comprised of "a mixture of honey and razor blades," with "a touch of a sexual smile."[19]

This combination of cutting wit and confident sexuality is integral to Olivier's character and perhaps the most imitated aspect of his performance. Returning to Weimann's distinction between the imagined *locus* of verisimilitude and the *platea* of materiality, we might consider how film, like the stage, privileges the authority of the performers over their roles, especially in the case of celebrities. Olivier was a well-known movie star by the time he filmed *Richard III*: he had already

Opposite: Poster for *Richard III*, dir. Laurence Olivier (1955). Courtesy of the Cinema Museum, London.

Olivier as Richard III with Claire Bloom (1955). Courtesy of the Cinema Museum, London.

played Heathcliff in *Wuthering Heights* (1939), Mr. Darcy in *Pride and Prejudice* (1940), and the leads in both *Henry V* (1944) and *Hamlet* (1948). Representationally, he supplants Richard onscreen in that his own body supercedes the humpbacked body of the king. Thus, when James Phillips suggests that Richard overwhelms Anne with "sheer sexual appeal,"[20] we should acknowledge that much of that sex appeal is Olivier's rather than Richard's.

The film emphasizes Olivier's sexual attractiveness by downplaying the king's deformity.

Although he limps noticeably, Richard's arm does not appear to be withered and his hunchback is hardly visible. Except for the long prosthetic nose, this Richard looks remarkably like the historical king in the various portraits, including the painting at the National Portrait Gallery. Richard may descant on his deformity, but we see no clear evidence that he is "deformed, unfinished, sent before [his] time / Into this breathing world scarce half made up" (1.1.20–21). Nor do we hear Richard's conclusion that his "rudely stamped" body makes him an inappropriate suitor:

> And therefore, since I cannot prove a lover
> To entertain these fair well-spoken days,
> I am determinèd to prove a villain,
> And hate the idle pleasures of these days [1.1.28–31].

Olivier claims to have removed these lines because he simply does not "believe them. Even Shakespeare makes [Richard] a 'credible' lover."[21] But by deemphasizing the character's deformity and cutting over half the wooing scene's lines, the film suggests that Anne is won not by the power of Richard's words but by the force of his personality. As Roy Walker notes, Anne is "a young woman hypnotized by the serpent that destroys her."[22]

Hugh Richmond, like many critics, protests the "savagery of the simplifying cuts" but points out that they illustrate "the tendency of film to substitute visual for verbal imagery."[23] In the wooing scenes, the visual imagery transmits meaning through sartorial opposition. Olivier is dressed all in black, while Claire Bloom's Anne is all in white. This color scheme is traditional, but here it figures Olivier's Richard as a kind of mesmerizing vampire, seducing Anne through his hypnotic charisma. The contrasting colors not only represent the characters' respective moral positions, they also illustrate Anne's submission to the bottled spider's web of words. The interaction of the black- and white-clad bodies produces a physical tableau that is visually analogous to the play's rhetorical wooing; as Chris Hassel observes, "Their physical intertwining is particularly effective as a symbol of [Richard's] increasing success."[24]

In their first encounter, Olivier has replaced the corpse of Henry VI with that of Prince Edward, Anne's husband. Walker argues that the substitution of Anne's husband for her father-in-law and king makes the wooing less believable,[25] but almost all film versions have adopted this alteration. Hugh Richmond concedes that the change "certainly heightens the outrageous nature of the courtship ..., but brings it dangerously near to melodrama, not to say farce."[26] Of course, much of what is risible and histrionic in these scenes may be attributed to what Harry Schein describes as "Claire Bloom's painfully bad acting."[27]

By their second confrontation, Anne is already half-won. H. R. Coursen notes that she "has taken off her wedding ring before her second meeting with Richard. It is as if she is waiting for him to ask 'Is not the causer of the timeless deaths.... As blameful as the executioner?'"[28] She may declare, "Never hung poison on a fouler toad" (1.2.145), but even as she calls him a toad, she leans in as if to kiss him. As Hassel describes her, "She is swaying, almost swooning, incredulous, but too tired and too hypnotized to resist or understand."[29] Clearly, Richard may speak of his own "infected" eyes, but she is the only one bewitched by the other's gaze. When she calls him a "dissembler," the word is spoken almost seductively, like a sobriquet. She tells him "To take is not to give" (1.2.188) only after she has already accepted his ring, and when he observes how his ring encompasses her finger, she allows his arms to encompass her body. His line about her breast enclosing his poor heart makes the audience particularly aware of how close his hand is to enclosing her breast. When they kiss, she is the one who reaches up to him. Her departure is slow, allowing him to pull her back for the additional, theatrical kiss she so obviously desires. Her hands linger on him as she exits, and when he opens the portal after his final lines, we see that she has not gone far.

Phillips suggests that Olivier "sacrificed something of Shakespeare's more extended and more credible analysis of the complex relationship between Richard and Anne."[30] As we shall see, Olivier's influence has been so great that others have repeated that sacrifice.

Stage Richards

In 1963, *Richard III* was performed as Part 3 of *The Wars of the Roses*, adapted by John Barton and directed by Peter Hall.[31] Ian Holm played Richard and Janet Suzman played Anne. As part of the Barton and Hall "watershed production," this *Richard* was placed self-consciously "in opposition to the Cibber tradition of individualist melodrama," opening the play, as Lull suggests, to "explorations of Richard's motives and political readings."[32] It was the first major modern production of *Richard III* staged within the context of the larger tetralogy. As with the two subsequent RSC productions of the histories, *The Wars of the Roses* was very well received. According to John Jowett, "The project was immediately acclaimed as one of the most monumental and significant treatments of Shakespeare ever."[33] Influenced by Jan Kott's idea of the Grand Mechanism, "It generated an epic sense of history as a horrific process. Richard's deeds, far from appearing as gratuitous crimes, were the final retributive throes of a sequence of events starting far back in the murder of Richard II."[34] Yet despite nearly universal praise for the production's intelligence and scope, Holm's depiction of the hunchbacked king garnered mixed reviews.

Emrys Jones notes that "the audiences that nowadays go to see *Richard III* presumably take it as a lurid, sometimes hilarious melodrama, which is fortunately still a great vehicle for a star actor."[35] By mounting the play as an interconnected piece within an ensemble season, the production presented Richard as a player within the larger history. Holm's solid characterization was simply one among many rather than a wicked, winking, virtuosic performance. Audiences looking for what Robert Speaight calls a "one-man, or rather one-monster play"[36] were disappointed. But the avoidance of melodrama alone does not account for the ambivalent reception. Two years earlier, Christopher Plummer had played what Harold Hobson described as "a subtler Richard than we have grown accustomed to."[37] Eric Johns noted that "there is nothing melodramatic about [Plummer's] Richard, no overacting of the blood and thunder approach."[38] Nevertheless, the performance was "widely celebrated."[39]

The difference, I believe, was in the embodiment of the part. Holm's diminutive stature may be perfectly suited for the part of a hobbit,[40] but his body could not sustain the horror required for the role of Richard. As Speaight observes, "the merely monstrous, the purely Satanic, does not seem to me to lie within Mr. Holm's very flexible range."[41] When Holm wryly shrugged his hump to illustrate his "rudely stamped" form, the effect was cute, almost endearing. This boyish Richard provided a juvenile, psychotic threat but failed to project a sense of power or sexual predation. As a result, the heartfelt seduction lacked plausibility. Suzman's Anne may have kissed Richard over the dead body of her kinsman, but she seemed to succumb neither through seduction nor fear. Of course, this may have been the point. The production was heavily influenced by Kott, who argues, "Lady Anne does not give herself to Richard out of fear…. Lady Anne goes into Richard's bed to be destroyed."[42]

The next production of note did not come until 1984, when Bill Alexander directed Antony Sher in a performance that Hassel argues "will almost certainly be remembered as the most impressive Richard since Olivier."[43] As Bernard Beckerman notes, Sher's innovative Richard was memorable for his use of crutches in the role:

> After all the many efforts actors have made to depict Richard's deformities, it hardly seems possible that an actor could invent something new. But this is what Sher has done with an unusual portrayal that has transformed the leading character and thereby the play. Sher uses arm crutches to show Richard supporting his shriveled legs. On one level, the effect is to make Richard more of a cripple than is commonly done. But on another level, the crutches give the actor enormous freedom. This is the result of two contradictory impressions. The crutches enable Sher to create the contrasting silhouette of spindly limbs and overdeveloped torso. That image, promising tortuous and labored locomotion, is belied by Sher's skillful manipulation of the crutches. Instead of confining his movements, they allow for him to scuttle across the stage with amazing

speed. This extraordinary and indeed thrilling mobility completely transforms the action, making it deft and sinister in a thoroughly novel fashion.[44]

Not all critics enjoyed the novelty. Clive Hirschorn described the action as "a Monty Python contest to find the fastest hunchback on crutches"; J. C. Trewin was decidedly unimpressed by the acrobatics; and Michael Ratcliffe imagined Sher as a "daddy longlegs on speed."[45] Hugh Richmond describes Sher's portrayal as "representative of our era's deliberate rejection of tradition — for it needed only a hint that Olivier had used a bit of business for Sher to reject it outright."[46] But Sher himself articulated the desire to avoid only Olivier, not tradition: "Olivier's interpretation *is* definitive and so famous that all around the world people can get up and do impersonations of it."[47] Sher even suffered nightmares about Olivier.[48] Nevertheless, most reviews, even favorable ones, compared Sher's performance to that of Olivier.[49]

In his memoir, *Year of the King*, Sher chronicles his exploration into the complex psychology of the character, quoting Bill Alexander's remark that "we can see Richard either as an Antichrist figure, or in Jung's words, as 'modern man in search of a soul.'"[50] Yet for all his elaborate psychological analysis of the character, Sher's actual performance was, as Jowett asserts, "a performance of the body."[51] All the internal richness and complex psychology hinted at in *Year of the King* was lost on stage. As S. P. Cerasano suggests, "There are no hidden depths the audience strained to see into. [Richard] was, flat out, a man obsessed with power, a man who wanted to attain the throne as quickly as possible, and a man who wanted to have fun along the way."[52] Instead of presenting a probing psychological study, Sher's gymnastic performance, delivered with what James Loehlin depicts as "hammy bravado,"[53] emphasized the "relentless theatricality" of the production.[54]

Sher delivered the play's famous opening speech as a soliloquy, with his crutches concealed behind him. At "But I that am not shaped for sportive tricks" (1.1.14), he spread his arms and crutches to the sides, forming a wide-winged T. He then darted forward with alarming dexterity. As Loehlin notes, Sher used the crutches throughout the performance "as natural extensions of his own body: holding them above his head as a cross, plucking a coronet from Margaret, probing in Lady Anne's skirts, closing them like mandibles around the neck of the doomed Hastings."[55] The swinging appendages provided a daunting physical presence that Holm's performance lacked. The warlike Richard pummeled his adversaries with violent and frightening attacks, using his crutches as weapons. Despite the enormous hump and the withered legs, this Richard was entirely convincing as a warrior, if not as a wooer.

Sher, in fact, eschewed the Olivier-style sexuality of Richard's character: "Making Richard sexy seems to me the same as making him funny; it avoids the issue, avoids the pain."[56] Instead, Sher emphasized the atrocity of Richard's horribly deformed body and played the courting of Anne (Penny Downie) as corporeal intimidation rather than rhetorical persuasion. Maintaining a semi-military motif, Sher's Richard won Anne almost as a martial rather than romantic conquest. When she spat on him, he did not move until "Never came poison from so sweet a place" (1.2.144), at which point, he wiped the spittle from his lips to hers, then scuttled off backwards, away from her anger. Julie Hankey attributes sexual significance to the gesture,[57] but Sher imbued the act with a lewdness that is more akin to the threat of rape than the promise of rapture. When Richard spoke of Anne's bedchamber, he slammed his crutches down around her like a cage, and when his arms enclosed her to force the ring on her finger, she was sobbing. Within the context of the action, Richard's prophetic assertion that he would not keep her long was wholly believable. He was a black widower. He would eat his wife. The black strips of cloth that depended from the shoulders of Sher's costume added to the impression of Richard as a "bottled spider" (1.3.242), with Anne trapped like a fly in the prison of his many spider legs. Hugh Richmond describes Anne in similar terms, as a victim in Richard's web: "Richard advances on Lady Anne as if with pincers raised to administer a poisonous bite. He grasps Anne with his crutches like pincers around his prey—Anne falls passive, as if paralysed by venom, and he can force the ring on her immobile finger."[58]

For me, the second half of the play was markedly less compelling. Without the gimmick of the crutches, the end of the play limped along like its crippled king. Cerasano reports that the final act was later "re-blocked to give even greater exposure to Richard's 'crutchery'" and to mitigate the "lassitude" of the second half.[59] Even without the revisions and improvements, however, Sher's spidery hunchback was one of the most dynamic and memorable Richards ever. Stanley Wells's initial review claimed that Sher's performance "aims at, and achieves, brilliance,"[60] and, if anything, the reputation of the production has only improved in the intervening years.

Despite Sher's conscious distancing of Olivier, the two performances were similar in their overall tone. Both presented the play as a grotesque, darkly humorous melodrama. Anton Lesser, who played the crookback in 1988, wanted to confound audiences' preconceptions by creating a Richard of greater "psychological nuance."[61] Like Holm's interpretation, Lesser's rendition developed out of performances contained within a larger history cycle, as Part 3 of Adrian Noble's *The Plantagenets*. According to Lesser, his goal in constructing the role was to "build a real person, not a two-dimensional figure of evil."[62] Unfortunately, Lesser's subtle nuance was not particularly wellsuited for what Robert Smallwood calls "the grand scale of main stage ostentation."[63] In his review of the season, Smallwood noted that the expectations of audiences were perhaps a bit too confounded by the understated delivery of this Richard: "Many will look for a more flamboyant performance than this one, for all its intelligence and thoughtfulness, particularly if they see the play on its own."[64]

Commenting on his approach to the role, Lesser explained that he perceived Richard as "primarily a fighter"; on the battlefield "he is the fastest, moves with the greatest alacrity, is the most lethal, and yet the effort takes less toll of him than of anyone else."[65] In *The Plantagenets*, Richard's hump was disguised by the enormous pauldrons of his armor, and in the winning of Anne, the soldierlike wooer based "his strategy on attack."[66] Unlike Sher, however, Lesser's Richard relied on verbal bullying rather than physical intimidation. Playing the consummate actor, he capitalized on the young widow's Christian guilt and compassion, implying that Geraldine Alexander's Anne was motivated by "guilt about her own sexuality, rather than any particular attraction towards his."[67] He did not hold her when proffering his ring and did not dominate her physically or erotically in the scene, but when he jammed the ring on her finger she gasped as if entered. Clearly, however, this Anne was not overwhelmed by Richard's sexual advances. He may have overcome her defenses in this particular skirmish but appeared to have lost the war. When he asked her to "Bid [him] farewell" (1.2.208) and quickly moved to kiss her, she leaned away, perhaps out of embarrassment or remorse. Ultimately, although Lesser's thoughtful performance was a fine one, his corporeal depiction of Richard was neither novel enough nor powerful enough to distinguish itself and seems to have faded in the collective memory.

This has not been the case with Simon Russell Beale's Richard. In 1992, Beale played the hunchbacked king opposite Annabelle Apsion's Anne in director Sam Mendes's disturbing version of the play.[68] I expect that anyone who saw Beale's "lump of foul deformity" (1.2.55) has found the performance difficult to forget. As Loehlin recounts, "Simon Russell Beale, in a gray overcoat, had a powerful and original physical presence: a large uneven hump exaggerating his fatness, a shaved but bristly head and face, a thick roll of fat at his neck."[69] He was so deformed and unfinished that dogs yapped at him whenever he entered, literalizing the lines of his opening soliloquy (1.1.23). Smallwood describes him as "a most disturbing mixture of lumpish stillness and sudden reptilian agility," suggesting that the actor was "clearly going in a big way for the 'poisonous bunch-backed toad' look—and achieving it with disturbing exactness."[70] With his cane, leather overcoat, shaved head, and supercilious sneer, Beale's Richard was a bizarre combination of aristocratic snob and pugnacious skinhead.

For Smallwood, the performance was "a profoundly intelligent and searching exploration of the play,"[71] but there were numerous crowd-pleasing touches, such as the booming Conan the Barbarian drums throughout. And although Loehlin, who also admires the intelligence of the production, claims that Beale "resists overplaying the laugh lines,"[72] there was, as Smallwood contends, "much to laugh at" in this production, such as "Richard's wide-eyed goggling of the audience in splendidly camp disbelief at the gullibility of his victims."[73] Ultimately, however, the humor was peeled back to reveal a "genuine evil moving beneath the comic overlay."[74] It is interesting that we have come to expect, even demand, that this historic "tragedy" should be comedic. For this production, most of the humor was sly and vicious. In fact, of all the performances discussed here, Beale's Richard struck me as the meanest (in the senses of both *malice* and *pettiness*). As Peter Holland notes, the play was marked by an unrelenting nastiness:

> Indeed the production found throughout a remarkable mode of theatrical brutality. I have never seen anything as brutal and callous as Richard's statement to Catesby, "Rumour it abroad / That Anne, my wife, is very grievous sick" [4.2.50–51], spoken so calmly over Anne seated next to him and his casual explanation, not in an aside but directly to her, as if to a child, "I must be married to my brother's daughter, / Or else my kingdom stands on brittle glass" [4.2.60–61].[75]

Apsion's devastated Anne was played with both pathos and dignity. She was not moved by Richard's wooing but rather duped by his shameless mendacity. As Smallwood notes, Beale "eschewed the recently perhaps rather overworked idea of the mesmerizing irresistibility of Richard's sexuality and presented instead a smoothly accomplished performance (transparently a performance) of penitence and of pitiable lumpish deformity."[76] When Richard offered her his dagger, there appeared to be a real danger that she might kill him, but like the various other characters in the play, she instead showed pity on the lame and unfashionable cripple. In the end, Beale's striking embodiment added weight and symbolic power to the role, as Richard's physical ugliness mirrored the deformity of his soul.

David Troughton, who played Richard in Stephen Pimlott's 1995 staging, adopted a similar understanding of the character. He not only had Richard tell Anne (Jennifer Ehle) to her face that she was "like to die" (4.2.51), as Beale did, he also imagined the king's deformity to be an external manifestation of his internal state. As Troughton says, his Richard was "not just an ambitious, embittered soldier but also an extraordinarily witty gargoyle of a man, who by his very immorality and shape seemed not human at all."[77] Delivering his initial lines in a jester's cap and bells, carrying a two-headed jester's bauble, Troughton reminded me of a medieval vice character, but Holland argues that the honest vulnerability of the Bosworth soliloquy "suggests a strongly psychologistic reading of character, not a devil or a vice but a man at the limit of his mental strength."[78] In an interview for the radio program *Kaleidoscope*, Troughton claimed to have constructed his Richard by working backwards from the Bosworth soliloquy,[79] and both the director's note and the quotation from Freud in the program support the psychoanalytical reading. But Troughton also admits to "wholeheartedly embracing the innate black humour in the play"[80] and presenting Richard as a demonic monster who can "seem a saint when most [he plays] the devil" (1.3.338):

> The whole idea of Richard being possessed by the devil can be introduced in performance, as I whisper the word with an evil grimace and take up an extremely deformed body posture. It is as if Satan himself rises out of his body for a brief instant and then slips silently back into his host — a nightmare vision which helps to establish the religious metaphors of the play, leading to its rather unusual ending.[81]

Troughton's grimacing, exaggerated posturing transformed Richard into an evil clown, a grinning caricature of the devil. But this may have been appropriate. After all, for most audiences, this is exactly what Richard has become.

Yet Troughton appears to have wanted it both ways. Having consulted an orthopedic surgeon, he decided that there was "one very simple explanation for Richard's malevolence": having been a breech birth, Richard would have suffered from an agonizing hip dislocation and would have endured tremendous pain all his life.[82] As Smallwood notes, the incessant pain, combined with Richard's dysfunctional "relationship with his mother, provided a kind of psychological explanation for his behavior."[83] This extrapolated history may have helped to explain Richard's psyche and account for what Troughton has described as the character's "undoubted misogynistic nature,"[84] but it seemed out of place alongside the production's diabolical imagery. Troughton recalls that "with Lady Anne, the idea of the tempting of Eve was uppermost: at first, the image of a devilish gargoyle, with a writhing snake-like gait of obsequiousness developing into the upright romantic hero professing undying love."[85]

Holland suggests that Troughton created "a thoroughly convincing lover,"[86] but the persona's malformed, contorted body made him more convincing in intent than effect. Because of the supposed hip displacement, Richard's limp was especially pronounced, with his knee almost hyperextended, and his withered arm was held awkwardly in front of him, small and useless, like the tiny front claw of Tyrannosaurus Rex. His body made him pitiable, and he exploited Anne's sympathy. Capitalizing on her apparent fear that he would kill himself, Richard did not pull the sword away until after she had accepted his ring. Then, after urging her to wear both his heart and the ring, "for both of them are thine" (1.2.191), he delivered a shocking eight-second kiss. He kissed her three more times in the scene, but when he tried to kiss her again at the end of the encounter, she avoided him, saying, "Imagine I have said farewell already" (1.2.210).

Throughout the wooing, Troughton's verse was unnatural and affected, with his metrical feet limping along as badly as his physical feet, yet his passion appeared genuine until the cynical concluding lines. In the end, however, his callous dismissal seemed to erode any last pity Anne may have felt for him. Richard may have won her, but he did not have her long. As Smallwood notes, Anne betrayed him at the long "Last Supper table," when she confirmed "her endorsement of Richmond with energetic kisses as she leaned across her husband's figure slumped at the table."[87]

The final stage version of *Richard III* discussed here was directed by Michael Boyd as part of the *This England* series in 2001. Aidan McArdle played Richard and Aislin McGuckin played Anne. Like the productions in 1963 and 1988, the play was richer and more resonant for having been placed alongside the other histories. The entire tetralogy was deeply invested in familial bonds— Keith Bartlet and Sam Troughton, for example, had various roles as one another's father and son throughout—and Richard's identity was powerfully constructed in relation to his father, Richard Plantagenet (Clive Wood). Richard's crimes took on new meaning after the butcheries of the preceding three plays, and the deaths of Henry and Edward and even the slaying of the two princes, were reframed against the slaughter of young Rutland and the mocking murder of Richard's father. As Michael Billington notes, "In isolation, the play becomes an individualistic study of a satanic joker," but in the context of *This England*, "it becomes something entirely different: a continuation of his late father's throne-lust and an extension of the de facto approach to power."[88]

Henry VI, Part 3 concluded with Richard alone on stage, uttering one word: "Now ..." (as Anton Lesser did in *The Plantagenets*). The thrill in the theater afterwards was electric. The first three plays of the series comprised some of the most compelling theater I have ever attended, and *Richard III* promised to be the best of the four. Sadly, that promise was never realized, and I was forced to agree with Georgina Brown, who lamented, "Alas, Aidan McArdle's Crookback Dick is a disappointing anticlimax."[89] Of course, I saw the play at the Young Vic in London, at the very end of *This England*'s exhausting run.[90] In fact, although I had seen the *Henry VI* plays at various times in Stratford-upon-Avon, I did not see *Richard III* until its final performance, when the company presented the entire tetralogy in one day. My main problems with the production, however, should not be attributed to fatigue. Charles Spencer found McArdle's performance lacking authority and menace, so that "though McArdle is an excellent Richard, he just misses greatness."[91] For me, the performance lacked only originality. In the earlier plays, McArdle's Richard was his father's brawler, clearly shaped for war, not sportive tricks. In the conclusion, however, McArdle's unpolished, violent, smoldering character was usurped by a gleefully wicked, Olivier-like caricature.

This reduced the wooing scene to a rerun of all we have seen before. As Russell Jackson describes it, McArdle's "wooing of Anne had the character of a spell—combined with outright sexual assault as he pushed her up against the bronze doors."[92] Like Olivier, McArdle portrayed Richard as a sexually mesmerizing stalker. Without Olivier's star power, however, the performance became a poor copy, an inferior version, Olivier lite (or even, after his ferocious potency in the *Henry* plays, McArdle lite). As Brown suggests, Anne's capitulation became incomprehensible: "McArdle's darkly handsome features and glossy black curls [made] a nonsense of his declaration that he isn't 'made to court an amorous looking-glass'"; yet at the same time, McArdle did not have "the charisma, the dangerous charm, the cruel humour or the megalomania ... to successfully seduce a weeping widow over the corpse of her husband, whom Richard has just murdered."[93] Much of the wooing was played for laughs, and the entire play suffered as a result.

In February of 2008, the RSC revived the play as part of their histories cycle. Once again, Boyd directed the entire tetralogy, which was performed at the Courtyard, the RSC's new temporary theatre in Stratford-upon-Avon. Jonathan Slinger replaced McArdle in the titular role, but as before, the performance was the weakest of the four plays, perhaps haunted by the ghosts of Richards Past. Separated from the three Henry plays by more than just the modern-dress costuming, the play again sacrificed the interesting complexity of the earlier plays for the facile demonization of the main character.

Screen Richards

Since Olivier's film, there have been surprisingly few Richards onscreen, perhaps because so many consider Olivier's portrayal to be definitive. In addition to the 1965 recording of Barton and Hall's stage production, *Richard III* has been filmed in two versions for the BBC: Jane Howell's in 1983 and Michael Bogdanov's in 1989 (as part of his seven-part epic, *The Wars of the Roses*). The play has been filmed in France, Hungary, and the Soviet Union and has been adapted or alluded to in movies such as Roger Corman's 1962 *Tower of London*, with Vincent Price (a remake of Rowland Lee's 1939 *Tower of London*, starring Boris Karloff and Basil Rathbone), and Neil Simon's *The Goodbye Girl* (1977), which featured Richard Dreyfus as aspiring actor Elliot Garfield, playing the hunchback as a homosexual. Yet it was not until December of 1995, when Richard Loncraine and Ian McKellen released their stylish *Richard III*, that Shakespeare's play was once again available at the English-speaking cinema.

In the years since its release, the film has gained mixed reviews. Philip French, for example, celebrates McKellen's "bravura performance,"[94] but Charles Marowitz dismisses the film as simply the "most recent and most egregious *Richard III*."[95] Developed from McKellen's production for the Royal National Theatre (directed by Richard Eyre), the film has drawn particular condemnation from critics who saw McKellen in the role on stage, such as Samuel Crowl, who suggests that "McKellen is a bravura stage actor whose brilliance dissolves on film."[96] Douglas Brode is one among many who contend that the film is enjoyable only if "one ignores Shakespeare,"[97] but this is a bit unfair. As Kevin Jackson argues, "This is not, perhaps, the most delicate Shakespearian film on record, but it's a powerful contender for the title of most entertaining."[98]

Peter Holland praises the film for avoiding the "fake medievalism of conventional representation" and creating a "precise cinematic analogy to the Shakespearean play" by setting the film in a 1930s alternate-reality Britain.[99] Other critics, however, have questioned the precision of Loncraine and McKellen's analogy. Marowitz, for instance, points out that "if you put a fifteenth-century warrior-king who believes in the Great Chain of Being into a modern political context charged with territorial expansionism and notions of ethnic cleansing, you are mixing history in such a way as to falsify the past and hopelessly fudge the present."[100] But this is true of any

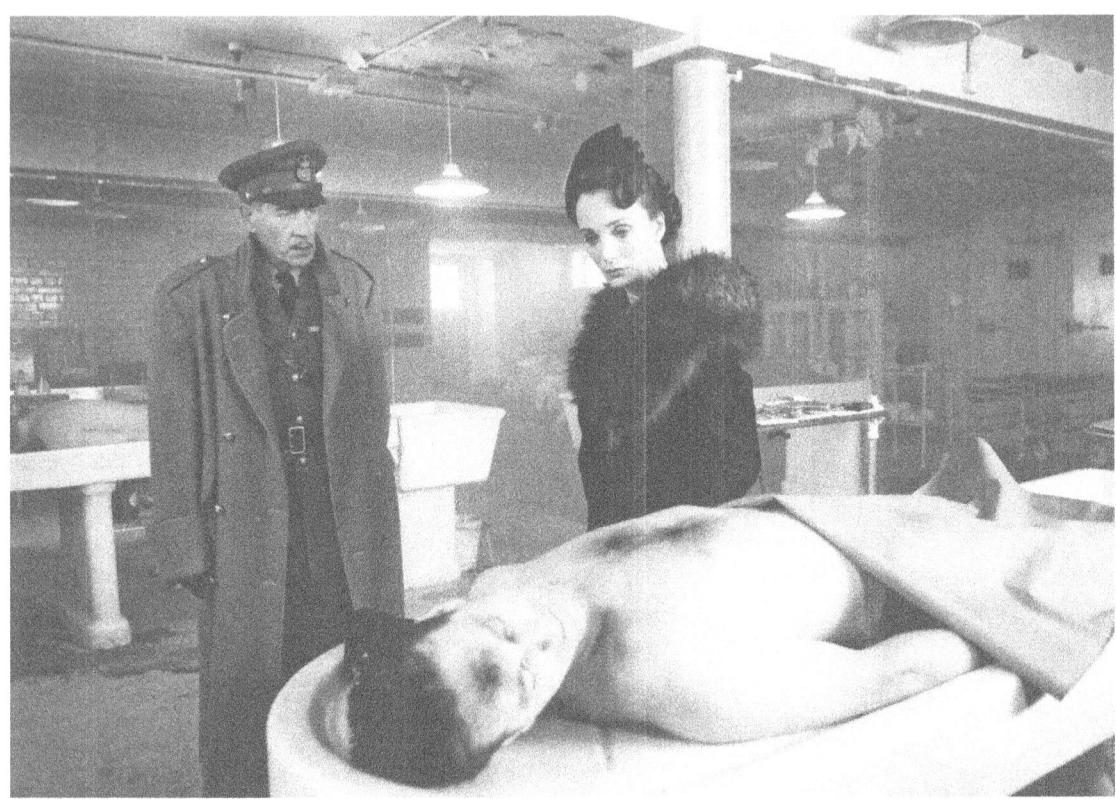

Richard (Ian McKellen) and Lady Anne (Kristen Scott Thomas) in Richard Loncraine's *Richard III* (1995). Courtesy of the Cinema Museum, London.

modernized production, and rather than quibbling over inexact analogues—Oswald Mosley or Adolf Hitler, blackshirts or Schutzstaffel—we might simply enjoy *Richard III* as a rich alternate history, similar to Bertolt Brecht's adaptation of the play, *The Resistible Rise of Arturo Ui*. As Loehlin asserts, the "primary level of meaning" may be a "retelling of the Richard III story in the context of modern British fascism, against the background of the 1930s and World War II," but the film operates on multiple levels, employing the cinematic codes of the slasher film, the Western, the British "heritage film," and the American gangster movie.[101]

Many critics still see *Richard III* as a black comedy, and several have complained that the film is not funny enough. Coursen, for example, claims that "This production has almost no humour," providing instead a "sheer and unrelenting grimness."[102] I disagree. There is an element of camp to the film, prompting critics such as Stephen Holden to read certain moments as "tongue-in-cheek."[103] Indeed, as Crowl suggests, even the serious scenes, such as when Richard learns of Hasting's death, appear "more Chaplinesque than chilling."[104] At the same time, however, our postmodern sensibilities accommodate the film's ironic commentary on the interconnectedness of death and media. As Peter Donaldson, observes, this *Richard III* can be understood through the "trope of cinema as necropolis or kingdom of death ... framing the story of Richard as an allegory of the role of cinema and other modern media in the institution and maintenance of death-dealing social regimes."[105]

For audiences, associations with the death-dealing media and regimes of modern dictators help to counteract much of Richard's charm, despite Rosenthal's assertion that McKellen "creates a more human anti-hero than Olivier."[106] Barbara Freedman notes that McKellen, gauging public response to his far less sympathetic stage portrayal, expected audiences to identify with Richard and to want him to succeed. But feelings for Richard have not been warm, and Freedman declares, "McKellen's confidence regarding a fixed audience response to his character underlines his innocence regarding the control of the camera over performance."[107]

Yet, as Forest Whitaker has shown as Ugandan dictator Idi Amin in *The Last King of Scotland* (2006), charismatic death-dealers may still enthrall today's audiences. I would suggest that viewers were not seduced by Richard because McKellen's body is not seductive,[108] not because the character suffered from intimations of despotism or genocide. Crowl depicts McKellen's Richard as "a repressed, tightly coiled cobra: a very different animal from Olivier's bird of prey, Antony Sher's bottled spider, Simon Russell Beale's pop-eyed toad, or David Troughton's court jester"; but he also points out that McKellen's "Richard delights in (and delights us by) poking ironic humor at his own physical deformity."[109] By aligning himself with the Bakhtinian grotesque body, McKellen distances Richard from the appellation "lover." Brode argues that the wooing "doesn't come across" because "McKellen is quite devoid of the sex appeal Olivier projected," and Terence Rafferty suggests that "as the charmless McKellen and the wan Kristin Scott Thomas play it, Anne's capitulation is wholly incomprehensible, not a breath of sexual passion is visible."[110] But McKellen's own body has already obviated any convincing "sexual passion" in the scene.

Commenting on McKellen's desire to "look a little like Clark Gable and a little like Vincent Price," Brode remarks, "Gable is Burbage, the sexy villain; Price is Kean, the king of horror-movie heavy," with McKellen "more in line with Kean, a horrifying figure of disgust."[111] My students would agree with the description of McKellen's appearance as disgusting; according to them, he is "too old and ugly" to play the part of a lover (he was fifty-six when he filmed *Richard III*). When he silently appears behind Anne in the morgue, they see him as "creepy" and associate him with the "black magician" (1.2.32) of Anne's lines. Later in the scene, when he makes the sexually suggestive gesture of removing the ring from his hand by sliding his finger into his mouth, my students always squirm, seeing the movement as an obscenity. They are uncomfortable with the idea of an old man wooing an attractive, much younger woman, and they certainly do not want to think of Gandalf having sex.[112]

McKellen, perhaps anticipating objections to his physical appearance, plays Richard not as a seducer but as a suppliant. He never attempts to kiss Anne and utters the audacious "your bedchamber" line to the camera rather than to her. With almost two-thirds of the wooing lines removed,[113] his words confuse rather than convince her. He skillfully manipulates his gloves, money, wallet, documents, and buttons with only one hand; similarly, he manipulates Anne as a pitiable, crippled war veteran. Ian Moulton demonstrates that by positioning himself on his knees before Anne as her "poor devoted suppliant" (1.2.192), Richard proffers the dispossessed widow a fantasy of masculine power: "By offering Anne his sword, he stages a calculated (and illusory) gender reversal, offering her an opportunity to exercise phallic power which he assumes in advance she will be incapable of accepting."[114] But McKellen's Richard gives Anne the metaphorical sword, and the illusion of control, throughout the entire scene. He dutifully hunches away, for example, when she exclaims, "Out of my sight, thou dost infect my eyes" (1.2.145), yet he does not actually leave. Ultimately, after she has been won, Anne must resort to drugs to tolerate her relationship with Richard.

While McKellen and Loncraine were filming their *Richard III*, Al Pacino was working on his labor-of-love documentary *Looking for Richard*, released in 1996. Although Jowett describes it as "perhaps the most intriguing late twentieth-century American response to *Richard III*," Marowitz sees the film as "a kind of 'Shakespeare for Dummies,' with actors shouting 'Eureka' as they stumble on to every cliché and banality thrown up in over four centuries of remorseless Richardizing."[115] Both are correct to some degree. For me, the body politics of the film are particularly interesting, especially alongside McKellen's Richard. Although only a year younger than McKellen, Pacino still exudes sex-symbol charisma in the film. In addition, fellow actor and collaborator Frederic Kimball verbalizes Pacino's agenda to establish actors as the "proud inheritors of the understanding of Shakespeare." In opposition to the film's handsome thespians Pacino placed the academic scholar Emrys Jones, looking stuffy and pedantic and physically unattractive.

Discussing Rosalind's "a good play needs no epilogue" (*As You Like It*, epilogue 4), Weimann notes that as the actor proceeds with the epilogue, "He gradually distances the assimilated fiction [of his role within the play], making his own cultural and sexual em-bodi-ment supersede whatever representation overlapped with the public dissolution of the play's illusion."[116] By constantly stepping out of character, Pacino similarly stresses his own "cultural and sexual em-bodi-ment." Of course, with famous actors, this is already the case. When relating the plot of *Braveheart*, for example, most people refer to the main character as Mel Gibson rather than William Wallace. In the case of the documentary's wooing scene, Coursen maintains that Anne, alone and bereft, "buys into Richard's sexuality,"[117] but I would argue that both Anne and the audience buy into Pacino's sexuality. As Emily Bartels observes:

> Pacino attempts to pull us under Richard's sway, to overpower us with Richard's seductive language and passion, his awesome command over intricacies of plot and character, his alluring displays of intimacy, self-awareness, and assurance, all features which Richard himself spotlights and Pacino, as mediator, shares.[118]

But actors are more than merely mediators; their bodies themselves *generate* the characters they play. This is true of Pacino and is also true of Winona Ryder, who plays Anne.

Brode believes that "tinged with 1990s feminism via Ryder's liberated-lady image, Lady Anne is anything but a frightened, pliable, weak person,"[119] but Pacino himself admits in the film that Ryder was chosen as Anne for her youth and vulnerability. More than thirty years younger than Pacino, Ryder presents an Anne deceived by the experience and guile of an older Richard. Exploiting Pacino's own masterful presence, the film stresses the seductive nature of Shakespeare's language. Richard leans forward on "your bedchamber" and provides erotic emphasis to words such as "beauty, " "bosom," and "lips." When he says "breast," Richard's hand touches or almost touches Anne's breast, and Richard ends the speech nestled against her stomach. He may appear to be, as Anne says, "so penitent" (1.2.206), but like the earlier intercut "I'll have her," Pacino's "*Ha!*" here lets the audience into Richard's head, belying his seeming sincerity. The two say farewell as would-be lovers, with a very seductive kiss, and Anne's closing lines are almost playful. For Brode, Anne's reaction here suggests "some heretofore unacknowledged dark side in this seemingly nice woman," implying that she is interested in both "the dangerous excitement of succumbing to sex with a man who murdered her father and husband and the kinky charms of a grotesque figure whose innate charisma allows him one triumph of will after another."[120]

The final *Richard III* I discuss here is Scott M. Anderson's recent independent film, starring Anderson as Richard and Sung Hi Lee as Anne Neville.[121] The flashy "update" is pure Hollywood, and what better location for a Hollywood adaptation than Hollywood itself? Set in a modern-day Los Angeles where guns are outlawed and the rich and powerful settle their disputes in the dueling arena, the film chronicles the battle between the Yorks and the Lancasters, rival branches of the former England Studios, for entertainment-industry supremacy. As a modernized *Richard*, the film suffers from all the banes of McKellen's version but without the blessing of seasoned Shakespearean actors: Anderson is a veterinarian, Sung Hi Lee is a *Playboy* model, and even the veteran actors, such as David Carradine, Danny Trejo, and Maria Conchita Alonso, are known for their decidedly non–Shakespearean roles. It seems somehow appropriate, however, that Carradine plays Buckingham, since the film is more interested in martial than metrical arts.[122] Lee, in particular, mutilates Shakespeare's words. Her emotion in the wooing scene peaks early, and she maintains an almost feedbacklike squeal throughout, with her voice alternately breathless and squeaky-high. It is difficult to tell here whether Anne is struggling to think or Lee is struggling just to speak the verse. The actress seems to forget her lines, for example, when she asserts that poison never hung "on a fouler ... *toad!*" Similarly, "homicide" sounds less like an appellative than an exclamation or non sequitur.

Clearly, this piece typifies what Judith Buchanan terms the "Roguish Interventions" of American offshoots. Unlike their tentative British counterparts, these radical adaptations are not "over-respectful" of the text and offer at least the potential for more vibrant, dynamic readings of the play.[123] Anderson's *Richard III* is not museum-piece Shakespeare, but the film's strength is also its greatest weakness: the film privileges its own authority over Shakespeare's. The dueling arena, for instance, may work within the logic of the film (although I am not certain that it does) but it in no way correlates to the complexity of the English civil war. As with McKellen's film, witty allusions and cinematic shorthand displace the intricacy of the original, often in confusing or contradictory ways. Thus, although a Hollywood executive, Richard dresses in purple and, like the rest of the city's plutocracy, maintains the aristocratic titles of the original play.

By retaining the early modern language yet modernizing the setting, Anderson creates a world that seems distant, foreign, and unreal. This disjunctive effect may be why so many critics believe that entirely translated adaptations, such as those by Grigori Kozintsev or Akira Kurosawa, constitute the best filmic Shakespeare. In English, James Gavin Bedford and Jon Seda have also adapted *Richard III* in *The Street King*.[124] Set in Los Angeles like Anderson's version, but located within the violent milieu of drug and gang warfare, the film adopts the strategy of recent teen–Shakespeare adaptations — *10 Things I Hate About You* (1999), *She's the Man* (2006), *O* (2001) — and abandons Shakespeare's text altogether. Such an approach avoids some of the pitfalls of adapting Shakespeare to a modern context, such as the difficulty described by Terry Hands: "The problem is, down that road lies 'A tank, a tank — my kingdom for a tank!'"[125] On the other hand, when adaptations retain the original Shakespearean lines, they are forced to innovate in order to render the lines comprehensible to a modern audience. This often leads to interesting (some might say cheeky) new readings. In Anderson's film, for example, rather than converting Richard's horse to a tank, the director has cleverly contrived to make "A horse, a horse! My kingdom for a horse!" (5.6.13) refer to the horse-symbol key chain for Richard's Ferrari. For me, however, by far the most interesting aspect of this production is Richard's body: Anderson plays the humpback without a hump.

Anderson believes that Richard may be handicapped, but not physically. He submits that the character may have been abused as a child, perhaps psychologically (and thus evidences great anger toward his mother), but does not consider himself handicapped and has no physical markers of deformity. Anderson keeps many of the lines that refer to Richard's physical body but recasts them as alluding to the man's internal state alone. A modern, politically correct audience might pity or excuse a disabled Richard; Anderson has maintained the medieval aversion to Richard's deformity by making his hunchback entirely one of character — a moral disfigurement, a deformity of the psyche. This permits an unequivocal loathing of Richard as the film progresses, but it also allows for greater ambivalence at the beginning of the story, particularly in the wooing scene.

Like Olivier, Anderson has Richard woo Anne over the body of her husband, an audacious gesture set up by the slightly altered lines, "For then I'll marry Lancaster's widow. What though I killed her husband and his father?" Rather than Warwick's daughter, Anne is introduced as Edward's widow. The two characters are backlit throughout the scene, and Richard is difficult to read. His cracking voice is low and husky, as if he may have been weeping, and his words sound potentially sincere. Anne is clearly confused by both his declarations and his demeanor, and he uses this to his advantage. Instead of admitting to the killings or claiming that Edward was "slain by Edward's hand" (1.2.90), Richard accuses Anne herself of the murder, stating that the former king's son was "slain by his wife's hands." This attempt to blame Anne for the death of her husband baffles her, for she saw the murder with her own eyes (rather than hearing of it from Margaret, as in the original play), as Richard well knows. When she spits at him, Richard wipes the "poison" from his hand with a smoochy kiss. Neither we nor Anne can tell if the kiss signals heartfelt sincerity or sardonic scorn.

The wooing is interspersed with scenes from the dueling-arena knife fight, and the bright reds and yellows of the stained-glass window (reminiscent of the colors of the ring) frame the two characters, implying that the threat of violence may still be present. Anne's "Well, well," when she tells him to put up his sword has been altered to a frightened "No! No!" as if she fears he might kill himself. Richard, too, is breathing hard, as if he fears she might do it. He puts his forehead on her hand in what appears to be a gesture of submission and relief. Yet we might mistrust the honesty of his emotion by how smoothly he removes her wedding ring and replaces it with his own. Anderson highlights Richard's manipulation by his emphasis in the line, "Vouchsafe to wear *this* ring," and although Anne says, "To take is not to give," she holds out her hand as if accepting a proposal of marriage. When she departs, she leaves with an "almost coquettish look."[126]

The film script concludes with an eerie echo of Cibber, asserting twice that "Richard's himself again."[127] Of course, this Richard is not Cibber's Richard. He is not Shakespeare's Richard, or even the historical Richard. Instead, he is an entertaining, malicious, modern, unhunched Richard. But as with all physical embodiments of the part, the thrill of watching this character comes not from what has been retained of the old Richard but from what has been made exciting and new. We should not lament the fact that Richard is not "himself" again. After all, he never really was.

NOTES

1. This essay has been improved by the perceptive comments of Jim Bulman and the editors of this volume, Sid Ray and Martha W. Driver. Special thanks to them and to the librarians at the Shakespeare Birthplace Trust, who allowed me to view archival footage of several Royal Shakespeare Company stage productions.

2. For more information, see the following: Peter Saccio, *Shakespeare's English Kings: History, Chronicle, and Drama*, 2nd ed. (Oxford: Oxford University Press, 2000); Alison Weir, *The Princes in the Tower* (New York: Ballantine, 1992); Keith Dockray, *Richard III: A Reader in History* (Wolfboro, NH: Sutton, 1988); Alison Hanham, *Richard III and His Early Historians, 1483–1535* (Oxford: Oxford University Press, 1975); Paul Murray Kendall, *Richard III* (New York: Norton, 1955); Jeremy Potter, *Good King Richard? An Account of Richard III and His Reputation* (London: Constable, 1983); and Anne F. Sutton and P. W. Hammond, eds., *The Coronation of Richard III: The Extant Documents* (Gloucester, UK: Sutton, 1983).

3. Shakespeare himself was influenced not only by the works of Polydore Virgil, Thomas More, Edward Hall, and Raphael Holinshed but also, as Scott Colley notes, by "literary sources, including writings of Seneca, Lyly, Kyd, Spenser, Marlowe" and others; in addition, More's *History of Richard III*, the basis for Hall and Holinshed, was "greatly influenced by the writings of Tacitus, Suetonius, and Plutarch" (Colley, "*Richard III* and Herod," *Shakespeare Quarterly* 37, no. 4 [1986]: 451–458; 451).

4. Saccio, *Shakespeare's English Kings*, 159.

5. Kendall, *Richard III*, 537n.

6. Weir, *Princes in the Tower*, 32.

7. Colley Cibber, *The Tragical History of Richard III*, in *Shakespeare Made Fit: Restoration Adaptations of Shakespeare*, ed. Sandra Clark (London: Dent, 1997), 377–459; 451. The line would fall somewhere after 5.4.198 in Shakespeare. Unless otherwise noted, all quotations from Shakespeare's play are from the Oxford Shakespeare's edition of William Shakespeare, *The Tragedy of King Richard III*, ed. John Jowett (Oxford: Oxford University Press, 2000).

8. Janis Lull, "Introduction," in William Shakespeare, *King Richard III*, ed. Janis Lull (Cambridge, UK: Cambridge University Press, 1999), 1–41; 25.

9. Laurence Olivier, *On Acting* (New York: Simon and Schuster, 1986), 122.

10. Robert Weimann, "Representation and Performance: The Uses of Authority in Shakespeare's Theatre," in *Materialist Shakespeare: A History*, ed. Ivo Kamps (London: Verso, 1995), 198–217; 207–208. For more on embodiment and dual representation in Shakespeare, see Robert Weimann, "Bifold Authority in Shakespeare's Theatre," in *Shakespeare in Performance*, ed. Robert Shaughnessy (New York: St. Martin's, 2000), 78–99; especially 86–97.

11. For a more complete history of the play's performance, see Scott Colley, *Richard's Himself Again: A Stage History of* Richard III (Westport, CT: Greenwood Press, 1992).

12. Critics differ on the actual numbers. In his essay for Criterion's 2004 digitally restored and reconstructed film, movie and music historian Bruce Eder suggests that 62.5 million people saw the broadcast (see http://www.criterion.com/asp/release.asp?id=213&eid=344&section=essay&page=2); Michael Brooke, writing for the British Film Institute, estimates 25 to 40 million (see http://www.screenonline.org.uk/film/id/467017/index.html); and Daniel Rosenthal puts the number at 25 million (Rosenthal, *Shakespeare on Screen*

[London: Hamlyn, 2000], 113). Perhaps as a result of the simultaneous U.S. theater and TV release, the film did poorly financially, but it still won several nominations and awards, including an Academy Award nomination for Best Actor, two BAFTA Best Film Awards, a BAFTA Best British Actor Award, a Berlin International Film Festival Silver Bear Award, the David di Donatello Award for Best Foreign Production, the Jussi Award for Best Foreign Actor, and a Golden Globe Award for Best English-Language Foreign Film.

13. Alice Griffin, "Shakespeare through the Camera's Eye: III," *Shakespeare Quarterly* 7, no. 2 (1956): 235–240; 235.

14. Hugh M. Richmond, *King Richard III* (Manchester, UK: Manchester University Press, 1989), 59.

15. Cibber, *Tragical History of Richard III*, 441; if the line were in Shakespeare's play, it would come after 4.4.448.

16. Olivier, *On Acting*, 125.

17. Alan Dent, "*Richard III*: A Disclaimer," *Illustrated London News* 228 (1956): 228–230; 230.

18. Olivier, *On Acting*, 297.

19. *Ibid.*, 119.

20. James E. Phillips, "Some Glories and Some Discontents," *Quarterly of Film Radio and Television* 10, no. 4 (1956): 399–407; 405.

21. Olivier, *On Acting*, 307.

22. Roy Walker, "Bottled Spider," *Twentieth Century* 159 (1956): 58–68; 63.

23. Richmond, *King Richard III*, 59.

24. R. Chris Hassel, Jr., *Songs of Death: Performance, Interpretation, and the Text of* Richard III (Lincoln: University of Nebraska Press, 1987), 13.

25. Walker, "Bottled Spider," 68.

26. Richmond, *King Richard III*, 60.

27. Harry Schein, "A Magnificent Fiasco?" *Quarterly of Film Radio and Television* 10, no. 4 (1956): 407–415; 411.

28. H. R. Coursen, "Filming Shakespeare's History: Three Films of *Richard III*," in *Cambridge Companion to Shakespeare on Film*, ed. Russell Jackson (Cambridge, UK: Cambridge University Press, 2000), 99–116; 99.

29. Hassel, *Songs of Death*, 13.

30. Phillips, "Some Glories and Some Discontents," 405.

31. The production combined the three *Henry VI* plays with *Richard III*, forming three parts from the four plays (similar to what Adrian Noble would do in 1988 with *The Plantagenets*). The production would later evolve into the 1965 BBC miniseries, *The Wars of the Roses*.

32. Lull, "Introduction," 34.

33. John Jowett, "Introduction," in William Shakespeare, *The Tragedy of King Richard III*, ed. John Jowett (Oxford: Oxford University Press, 2000), 1–132; 101.

34. *Ibid.*, 101.

35. Emrys Jones, "Bosworth Eve," *Essays in Criticism* 25, no. 1 (1975): 38–54; 53.

36. Robert Speaight, "Shakespeare in Britain," *Shakespeare Quarterly* 14, no. 4 (1963): 419–432; 430.

37. Harold Hobson, *Sunday Times*, May 28, 1961.

38. Eric Johns, *The Stage*, January 16, 1961.

39. Jowett, "Introduction," 101.

40. In addition to playing Bilbo Baggins in Peter Jackson's *The Lord of the Rings: The Fellowship of the Ring* (2001) and *The Lord of the Rings: The Return of the King* (2003), Holm also portrayed Frodo Baggins in the 1981 BBC Radio adaptation of *The Lord of The Rings*.

41. Speaight, "Shakespeare in Britain," 430.

42. Jan Kott, *Shakespeare Our Contemporary*, trans. Boleslaw Taborski (New York: Norton, 1964), 45.

43. Hassel, *Songs of Death*, 145.

44. Bernard Beckerman, "The Odd Business of Play Reviewing," *Shakespeare Quarterly* 36, no. 5 (1985): 588–593; 589.

45. Clive Hirschorn, *The Sunday Express*, May 5, 1985; J.C. Trewin, *Birmingham Post*, June 20, 1984; Michael Ratcliffe, *Observer*, June 24, 1984.

46. Richmond, *King Richard III*, 109.

47. Antony Sher, *Year of the King: An Actor's Diary and Sketchbook* (London: Chatto & Windus, 1985), 67.

48. *Ibid.*, 135.

49. For descriptions of the various reviewers' reactions, see R. Chris Hassel, Jr., "Context and Charisma: The Sher-Alexander *Richard III* and Its Reviewers," *Shakespeare Quarterly* 36, no. 5 (1985): 630–643; and S. P. Cerasano, "Churls Just Wanna Have Fun: Reviewing *Richard III*," *Shakespeare Quarterly* 36, no. 5 (1985): 618–629, esp. 626–628.

50. Sher, *Year of the King*, 169.
51. Jowett, "Introduction," 104.
52. Cerasano, "Churls Just Wanna Have Fun," 624.
53. James Norris Loehlin, "Playing Politics: *Richard III* in Recent Performance," *Performing Arts Journal* 15, no. 3 (1993): 80–94; 83.
54. Peter McGarry, "Richard III," *Coventry Evening Telegraph*, June 20, 1984.
55. Loehlin, "Playing Politics," 83.
56. Sher, *Year of the King*, 158.
57. William Shakespeare, *Richard III*, ed. Julie Hankey (Bristol, UK: Bristol Classical, 1988), 111.
58. Richmond, *King Richard III*, 114.
59. Cerasano, "Churls Just Wanna Have Fun," 629.
60. Stanley Wells, "Richard III," *Times Literary Supplement*, June 29, 1984.
61. Anton Lesser, "Richard of Gloucester in *Henry VI* and *Richard III*," in *Players of Shakespeare 3*, ed. Russell Jackson and Robert Smallwood (Cambridge, UK: Cambridge University Press, 1993), 140–159; 142.
62. *Ibid.*, 141.
63. Robert Smallwood, "Introduction," in *Players of Shakespeare 3*, ed. Russell Jackson and Robert Smallwood (Cambridge, UK: Cambridge University Press, 1993), 1–20; 10.
64. Robert Smallwood, "Shakespeare at Stratford-upon-Avon, 1988," *Shakespeare Quarterly* 40, no. 1 (1989): 83–94; 91.
65. Lesser, "Richard of Gloucester," 143.
66. *Ibid.*, 152.
67. *Ibid.*, 152.
68. Mendes's *Richard III* was originally staged by the RSC in 1992 at the Other Place; I saw the 1993 version at the Swan.
69. Loehlin, "Playing Politics," 90.
70. Robert Smallwood, "Shakespeare at Stratford-upon-Avon, 1992," *Shakespeare Quarterly* 44, no. 3 (1993): 343–362; 359.
71. *Ibid.*, 362.
72. Loehlin, "Playing Politics," 90.
73. Smallwood, "Shakespeare at Stratford-upon-Avon, 1992," 359.
74. *Ibid.*, 359.
75. Peter Holland, *English Shakespeares: Shakespeare on the English Stage in the 1990s* (Cambridge, UK: Cambridge University Press, 1997), 118.
76. Smallwood, "Shakespeare at Stratford-upon-Avon, 1992," 361.
77. David Troughton, "*Richard III*," in *Players of Shakespeare 4*, ed. Robert Smallwood (Cambridge, UK: Cambridge University Press, 1998), 71–100; 77.
78. Holland, *English Shakespeares*, 241.
79. *Kaleidoscope*, BBC Radio 4, September 7, 1995.
80. Troughton, "*Richard III*," 89.
81. *Ibid.*, 80.
82. *Ibid.*, 74.
83. Robert Smallwood, "*Richard III* at Stratford," *Shakespeare Quarterly* 47, no. 3 (1996): 326–329; 327.
84. Troughton, "*Richard III*," 87.
85. *Ibid.*, 75.
86. Holland, *English Shakespeares*, 241.
87. Smallwood, "*Richard III* at Stratford," 329.
88. Michael Billington, "Henry VI/Richard III," *Guardian*, April 27, 2001.
89. Georgina Brown, "A Bloodfest that Leaves You Drained," *Mail on Sunday*, April 29, 2001.
90. The company performed all four plays back-to-back on a number of occasions, and each of the plays was very physical and vigorous, featuring myriad battles and a lot of ropework.
91. Charles Spencer, "RSC Burrow to the Heart," *Daily Telegraph*, April 27, 2001.
92. Russell Jackson, "'This England': Shakespeare at Stratford-upon-Avon, Winter 2000–2001," *Shakespeare Quarterly* 52, no. 3 (2001): 383–392; 388.
93. Brown, "A Bloodfest that Leaves You Drained."
94. Philip French, "Richard the Iron Heart," *Observer*, April 28, 1996.
95. Charles Marowitz, "Cinematizing Shakespeare," *Shakespeare Bulletin* 22, no. 2 (2004): 67–78; 69.
96. Samuel Crowl, *Shakespeare at the Cineplex: The Kenneth Branagh Era* (Athens, OH: Ohio University Press, 2003), 117.
97. Douglas Brode, *Shakespeare in the Movies: From the Silent Era to* Shakespeare in Love (Oxford: Oxford University Press, 2000), 36.

98. Kevin Jackson, "More than a Touch of Evil in McKellen's Malevolent Monarch," *Independent*, April 28, 1996.
99. Peter Holland, "Richard III," *Times Literary Supplement*, May 10, 1996.
100. Marowitz, "Cinematizing Shakespeare," 70.
101. James Norris Loehlin, "'Top of the World, Ma': *Richard III* and Cinematic Convention," in *Shakespeare, the Movie: Popularizing the Plays on Film, TV, and Video*, ed. Lynda E. Boose and Richard Burt (London: Routledge, 1997), 67–79; 71.
102. Coursen, "Filming Shakespeare's History," 104.
103. Stephen Holden, "An Arch-Evil Monarch, Updated to the 1930s," *New York Times*, December 29, 1995.
104. Crowl, *Shakespeare at the Cineplex*, 117.
105. Peter S. Donaldson, "Cinema and the Kingdom of Death: Loncraine's *Richard III*, *Shakespeare Quarterly* 53, no. 2 (2002): 241–259; 244.
106. Rosenthal, *Shakespeare on Screen*, 114.
107. Barbara Freedman, "Critical Junctures in Shakespeare Screen History: Three Films of *Richard III*," in *The Cambridge Companion to Shakespeare on Film*, ed. Russell Jackson (Cambridge, UK: Cambridge University Press, 2000), 47–71; 63.
108. At least not in close-up. On the stage, McKellen is incredibly attractive, and his bodily presence continually procures the admiration of critics and audience alike.
109. Crowl, *Shakespeare at the Cineplex,* 106, 108.
110. Brode, *Shakespeare in the Movies*, 37; Terence Rafferty, "Richard III," *New Yorker*, January 22, 1996.
111. Brode, *Shakespeare in the Movies*, 36–37. Brode consistently separates performances of Richard into two categories: the sexually irresistible, "terrifyingly charming Jekyll" of Richard Burbage and the "utterly repulsive Hyde" of Edmund Kean (*ibid.*, 29). We might note, however, that Edmund Kean's Richard was not as physically revolting as Brode would suggest. Samuel Drummond's 1814 portrait of Kean in the role, for example, depicts an attractive actor of smoldering sexuality.
112. McKellen played Gandalf in all three of Peter Jackson's *Lord of the Rings* films.
113. The film retains only sixty-nine of the wooing scene's 192 lines—from Richard's entrance to Anne's exit—including six of the twelve lines added to the Folio.
114. Ian Frederick Moulton, "'A Monster Great Deformed': The Unruly Masculinity of Richard III," *Shakespeare Quarterly* 47, no. 3 (1996): 251–268; 267.
115. Jowett, "Introduction," 109; Marowitz, "Cinematizing Shakespeare," 71.
116. Weimann, "Representation and Performance," 212–213.
117. Coursen, "Filming Shakespeare's History," 112–113.
118. Emily C. Bartels, "Shakespeare to the People," *Performing Arts Journal* 19, no. 1 (1997): 58–60; 59.
119. Brode, *Shakespeare in the Movies*, 39.
120. *Ibid.*, 39.
121. Special thanks to Scott Anderson for letting me view portions of his film three months before its premiere (on April 27, 2007, at Worldfest in Houston, TX). All of Anderson's observations regarding the character of Richard are from a phone interview, December 12, 2006.
122. Carradine not only gained fame playing Kwai Chang Caine in the early 1970s TV show *Kung Fu* and the mid–1990s revival *Kung Fu: The Legend Continues*, he also portrayed the master assassin Bill in Quentin Tarantino's two volume *Kill Bill*.
123. Judith Buchanan, *Shakespeare on Film* (London: Pearson, 2005), 90.
124. Also released under the titles *Rikki the Pig* and *King Rikki*.
125. Quoted in Michael Billington, ed., *Approaches to Twelfth Night* [with Director Bill Alexander] (London: Hern, 1990), 33.
126. Page 19 in the unpublished script.
127. Pages 102 and 108 in the unpublished script.

Works Cited

Bartels, Emily C. "Shakespeare to the People." *Performing Arts Journal* 19, no. 1 (1997): 58–60.
Beckerman, Bernard. "The Odd Business of Play Reviewing." *Shakespeare Quarterly* 36, no. 5 (1985): 588–593.
Billington, Michael, ed. *Approaches to Twelfth Night* [with Director Bill Alexander]. Royal Shakespeare Company's Director's Shakespeare Series. London: Hern, 1990.
Brode, Douglas. *Shakespeare in the Movies: From the Silent Era to* Shakespeare in Love. Oxford: Oxford University Press, 2000.
Buchanan, Judith. *Shakespeare on Film*. Inside Film Series. London: Pearson, 2005.

Cerasano, S. P. "Churls Just Wanna Have Fun: Reviewing *Richard III*." *Shakespeare Quarterly* 36, no. 5 (1985): 618–629.
Cibber, Colley. *The Tragical History of Richard III*. In *Shakespeare Made Fit: Restoration Adaptations of Shakespeare*, edited by Sandra Clark, 377–459. London: Dent, 1997.
Colley, Scott. "*Richard III* and Herod." *Shakespeare Quarterly* 37, no. 4 (1986): 451–458.
_____. *Richard's Himself Again: A Stage History of* Richard III. Westport, CT: Greenwood Press, 1992.
Coursen, H. R. "Filming Shakespeare's History: Three Films of *Richard III*." In *Cambridge Companion to Shakespeare on Film*, edited by Russell Jackson, 99–116. Cambridge, UK: Cambridge University Press, 2000.
Crowl, Samuel. *Shakespeare at the Cineplex: The Kenneth Branagh Era*. Athens, OH: Ohio University Press, 2003.
Dent, Alan. "*Richard III*: A Disclaimer." *Illustrated London News* 228 (1956): 228–230.
Dockray, Keith. *Richard III: A Reader in History*. Wolfboro, NH: Sutton, 1988.
Donaldson, Peter S. "Cinema and the Kingdom of Death: Loncraine's *Richard III*." *Shakespeare Quarterly* 53, no. 2 (2002): 241–259.
Freedman, Barbara. "Critical Junctures in Shakespeare Screen History: Three Films of *Richard III*." In *The Cambridge Companion to Shakespeare on Film*, edited by Russell Jackson, 47–71. Cambridge, UK: Cambridge University Press, 2000.
Griffin, Alice. "Shakespeare through the Camera's Eye: III." *Shakespeare Quarterly* 7, no. 2 (1956): 235–240.
Hanham, Alison. *Richard III and His Early Historians, 1483–1535*. Oxford: Oxford University Press, 1975.
Hassel, R. Chris, Jr. "Context and Charisma: The Sher-Alexander *Richard III* and Its Reviewers." *Shakespeare Quarterly* 36, no. 5 (1985): 630–643.
_____. *Songs of Death: Performance, Interpretation, and the Text of* Richard III. Lincoln: University of Nebraska Press, 1987.
Holland, Peter. *English Shakespeares: Shakespeare on the English Stage in the 1990s*. Cambridge, UK: Cambridge University Press, 1997.
Jackson, Russell. "'This England': Shakespeare at Stratford-upon-Avon, Winter 2000–2001." *Shakespeare Quarterly* 52, no. 3 (2001): 383–392.
Jones, Emrys. "Bosworth Eve." *Essays in Criticism* 25, no. 1 (1975): 38–54.
Jowett, John. "Introduction." In William Shakespeare, *The Tragedy of King Richard III*, edited by John Jowett, 1–132. Oxford Shakespeare. Oxford: Oxford University Press, 2000.
Kendall, Paul Murray. *Richard III*. New York: Norton, 1955.
Kott, Jan. *Shakespeare Our Contemporary*. Trans. Boleslaw Taborski. New York: Norton, 1964.
Lesser, Anton. "Richard of Gloucester in *Henry VI* and *Richard III*." In *Players of Shakespeare 3*, edited by Russell Jackson and Robert Smallwood, 140–159. Cambridge, UK: Cambridge University Press, 1993.
Loehlin, James Norris. "Playing Politics: *Richard III* in Recent Performance." *Performing Arts Journal* 15, no. 3 (1993): 80–94.
_____. "'Top of the World, Ma': *Richard III* and Cinematic Convention." In *Shakespeare, the Movie: Popularizing the Plays on Film, TV, and Video*, edited by Lynda E. Boose and Richard Burt, 67–79. London: Routledge, 1997.
Lull, Janis. "Introduction." In William Shakespeare, *King Richard III*, edited by Janis Lull, 1–41. Cambridge, UK: Cambridge University Press, 1999.
Marowitz, Charles. "Cinematizing Shakespeare." *Shakespeare Bulletin* 22, no. 2 (2004): 67–78.
Moulton, Ian Frederick. "'A Monster Great Deformed': The Unruly Masculinity of *Richard III*." *Shakespeare Quarterly* 47, no. 3 (1996): 251–268.
Olivier, Laurence. *On Acting*. New York: Simon and Schuster, 1986.
Phillips, James E. "Some Glories and Some Discontents." *Quarterly of Film Radio and Television* 10, no. 4 (1956): 399–407.
Potter, Jeremy. *Good King Richard? An Account of Richard III and His Reputation*. London: Constable, 1983.
Richmond, Hugh M. *King Richard III*. Shakespeare in Performance. Manchester, UK: Manchester University Press, 1989.
Rosenthal, Daniel. *Shakespeare on Screen*. London: Hamlyn, 2000.
Saccio, Peter. *Shakespeare's English Kings: History, Chronicle, and Drama*. 2nd ed. Oxford: Oxford University Press, 2000.
Schein, Harry. "A Magnificent Fiasco?" *Quarterly of Film Radio and Television* 10 no. 4 (1956): 407–415.
Shakespeare, William. *The Tragedy of King Richard III*. Edited by John Jowett. Oxford Shakespeare. Oxford: Oxford University Press, 2000.
_____. *Richard III*. Edited by Julie Hankey. Plays in Performance. 2nd ed. Bristol, UK: Bristol Classical, 1988.
Sher, Antony. *Year of the King: An Actor's Diary and Sketchbook*. London: Chatto & Windus, 1985.

Smallwood, Robert. "Introduction." In *Players of Shakespeare 3*, edited by Russell Jackson and Robert Smallwood, 1–20. Cambridge, UK: Cambridge University Press, 1993.
_____. "*Richard III* at Stratford." *Shakespeare Quarterly* 47, no. 3 (1996): 326–329.
_____. "Shakespeare at Stratford-upon-Avon, 1988." *Shakespeare Quarterly* 40, no. 1 (1989): 83–94.
_____. "Shakespeare at Stratford-upon-Avon, 1992." *Shakespeare Quarterly* 44, no. 3 (1993): 343–362.
Speaight, Robert. "Shakespeare in Britain." *Shakespeare Quarterly* 14, no. 4 (1963): 419–432.
Sutton, Anne F., and P. W. Hammond, eds. *The Coronation of Richard III: The Extant Documents*. Gloucester, UK: Sutton, 1983.
Troughton, David. "*Richard III*." In *Players of Shakespeare 4*, edited by Robert Smallwood, 71–100. Cambridge, UK: Cambridge University Press, 1998.
Walker, Roy. "Bottled Spider." *Twentieth Century* 159 (1956): 58–68.
Weimann, Robert. "Bifold Authority in Shakespeare's Theatre." In *Shakespeare in Performance*, edited by Robert Shaughnessy, 78–99. New Casebooks. New York: St. Martin's, 2000.
_____. "Representation and Performance: The Uses of Authority in Shakespeare's Theatre." In *Materialist Shakespeare: A History*, edited by Ivo Kamps, 198–217. London: Verso, 1995.
Weir, Alison. *The Princes in the Tower*. New York: Ballantine, 1992.

STAGE PRODUCTIONS

1963 *Richard III* [*The Wars of the Roses, Part 3*], d. Peter Hall, adapted by John Barton, with Ian Holm and Janet Suzman. Stratford-upon-Avon.
1984 *Richard III*, d. Bill Alexander, with Antony Sher and Penny Downie. Stratford-upon-Avon.
1988 *Richard III* [*The Plantagenets, Part 3*], d. Adrian Noble, with Anton Lesser and Geraldine Alexander. Stratford-upon-Avon.
1992 *Richard III*, d. Sam Mendes, with Simon Russell Beale and Annabelle Apsion. Stratford-upon-Avon.
1995 *Richard III*, d. Stephen Pimlott, with David Troughton and Jennifer Ehle. Stratford-upon-Avon.
2001 *Richard III* [*This England, Part 4*], d. Michael Boyd, with Aidan McArdle and Aislin McGuckin. London.

FILMOGRAPHY

1939 *Tower of London*, d. Rowland Lee, with Boris Karloff and Basil Rathbone. USA: Universal.
1939 *Wuthering Heights*, d. William Wyler, with Lawrence Olivier and Merle Oberon. USA: Samuel Goldwyn.
1940 *Pride and Prejudice*, d. Robert Leonard, with Lawrence Olivier and Greer Garson. USA: MGM.
1944 *Henry V*, d. Lawrence Olivier, with Lawrence Olivier, Leslie Banks, and Renée Asherson. UK: Two Cities Films.
1948 *Hamlet*, d. Lawrence Olivier, with Lawrence Olivier and Jean Simmons. UK: Two Cities Films.
1955 *Richard III*, d. Laurence Olivier, with Laurence Olivier, Ralph Richardson, John Gielgud, and Claire Bloom. UK: London Film Productions.
1962 *Tower of London*, d. Roger Corman, with Vincent Price. USA: United Artists.
1977 *The Goodbye Girl*, d. Herbert Ross, with Richard Dreyfus and Marsha Mason. USA: MGM.
1983 *The Tragedy of Richard III*, d. Jane Howell, with Ron Cook. UK: BBC.
1989 *The Wars of the Roses*, d. Michael Bogdanov, with Andrew Jarvis, Michael Pennington, and Janet Suzman. UK: BBC.
1995 *Richard III*, d. Richard Loncraine, with Ian McKellen, Jim Broadbent, and Kristen Scott Thomas. UK: United Artists.
1996 *Looking for Richard*, d. Al Pacino, with Al Pacino, Kevin Spacey, and Winona Ryder. US: 20th Century–Fox.
1999 *10 Things I Hate About You*, d. Gil Junger, with Julia Stiles and Heath Ledger. USA: Touchstone.
2001 *The Lord of the Rings: The Fellowship of the Ring*, d. Peter Jackson, with Ian McKellen, Viggo Mortensen, and Elijah Wood. New Zealand: New Line Cinema.
2001 *O*, d. Tim Blake Nelson, with Mekhi Phifer, Julia Stiles, and Josh Hartnett. USA: Rhulen Entertainment.
2002 *The Lord of the Rings: The Two Towers*, d. Peter Jackson, with Ian McKellen, Viggo Mortensen, and Elijah Wood. New Zealand: New Line Cinema.
2002 *The Street King*, d. James Gavin Bedford, with Jon Seda, Mario Lopez, and Tonantzin Carmelo. USA: Mistral Pictures.
2003 *Kill Bill: Vol. 1*, d. Quentin Tarantino, with Uma Thurman and David Carradine. USA: Miramax.
2003 *The Lord of the Rings: The Return of the King*, d. Peter Jackson, with Ian McKellen, Viggo Mortensen, and Elijah Wood. New Zealand: New Line Cinema.

2004 *Kill Bill: Vol. 2*, d. Quentin Tarantino, with Uma Thurman and David Carradine. USA: Miramax.
2006 *The Last King of Scotland*, d. Kevin Macdonald, with Forest Whitaker and James McAvoy. UK: Fox Searchlight.
2006 *She's the Man*, d. Andy Fickman, with Amanda Bynes and Channing Tatum. USA: Dreamworks.
2007 *Richard III*, d. Scott Anderson, with Scott Anderson, David Carradine, and Sung Hi Lee.

Falstaff in America

Catherine Loomis

Sir John Falstaff officially arrived in the American colonies on December 17, 1761, when an advertisement in the *New York Gazette* announced his imminent appearance at the Chapel Street Theater in New York City in a performance of Shakespeare's *1 Henry IV*. David Douglass, who had taken over management of the touring company of British players when he married the widow of theatrical entrepreneur Lewis Hallam, played Falstaff. As he does on the battlefield at Shrewsbury, Falstaff then appeared to die and revive: Douglass's British players, who by 1763 had named themselves the American Company, are not recorded as performing *1 Henry IV* again until 1768, when the play began to appear once every few months in their repertory with advertisements that enticed ticket buyers with the promise that "the humours of Sir John Falstaff" would be part of the show. This pattern has continued: Falstaff and his peculiar brand of medievalism disappear, then reappear in significant productions at moments in American history when a "reverent Vice"[1] is of particular cultural use. This essay will look at Falstaff as an embodiment of—and as an antibody to—Shakespeare's medievalism by examining the character as performed at three points in American history: the first half of the nineteenth century, the Great Depression, and the mid–1960s.

Shakespeare's Falstaff is medieval in the historical sense—he is loosely based on the Lollard martyr Sir John Oldcastle (d. 1417)—and in the literary sense—he is the love child of the Wife of Bath and Jack Juggler. But the character also embodies the same misconception of medieval appetites that is responsible for the appearance of roast turkey legs and quart-sized tankards of ale at twenty-first-century Renaissance fairs. To focus exclusively on Falstaff's excesses, even his excess of wit, is to lose sight of his value as a subtle chorus reminding the audience to ask for itself "Is not the truth the truth?" (*1 Henry IV* 2.4.229–230) when presented with events or texts that claim to be historical.

That the role of deconstructing history is handed to an ostensibly medieval figure and that this figure has proved popular in American adaptations of Shakespeare is not surprising: as Bernard Rosenthal and Paul Szarmach note in the introduction to their 1989 collection *Medievalism in America*, "The symbiosis between America and the medieval world grows from the central fact that each has been invented and that neither in its mythic form corresponds very closely to historical scrutiny."[2] Falstaff's appeal to American audiences is in part a function of his mythic status—analyses of the carnivalesque in Shakespeare routinely identify Falstaff as the most Dionysian of Shakespeare's characters[3]—and in part a function of the fact that he calls medieval ideals into question by mocking many of the same English feudal values America's European settlers rejected.

Although his theatrical roots are found in the disruptive Vice or Iniquity figures of the medieval morality plays, Falstaff's idiom, his beverage of choice—sherris-sack—and his ability to commit "The oldest sins the newest kind of way" (*2 Henry IV* 4.5.126) are thoroughly early modern, making the fat knight a disruptive anomaly in the two parts of *Henry IV*, a pair of plays that otherwise closely follow historical accounts as they dramatize the reign of Henry Bolingbroke

(1367–1413; reigned 1399–1413) and examine the king's contribution to events leading to the Wars of the Roses.

Shakespeare's Falstaff is present on the fifteenth-century battlefields at Shrewsbury and Gaultree Forest but also comfortably governs a late-sixteenth-century tavern, the Boar's Head, where he contributes to the education of King Henry's son Prince Hal and in the process, as A. Elizabeth Ross contends, illustrates "the volatility of a commonwealth composed of debased versions of the Tamburlanian ideal of 'aspiring minds.'"[4] Like Marlowe's Tamburlaine, Falstaff does not have modest ambition — he assures Hal that to "banish plump Jack" is to "banish all the world" (*1 Henry IV* 2.44.479–480)— and his aspiring mind imagines a court in which he is king, judge, and seller of offices, a form of misrule that, in its violation of the social hierarchy, was a source of terror for early modern aristocrats. But Falstaff is also an intensely delightful presence who relieves the tensions created by Henry IV's attempts to hold onto and legitimize his shaky claim to the throne and to discipline his son Prince Hal.

Falstaff's misrule of the Boar's Head's staff and patrons provides an often bitter commentary on Henry IV's attempts to quell the rebellions that threaten his kingdom and his relationship with his son. By moving between the medieval and modern worlds of the court and the Boar's Head, Falstaff and Hal enact a pedagogical function of history that Shakespeare describes in the second part of *Henry IV* in lines given to the Earl of Warwick:

> There is a history in all men's lives,
> Figuring the natures of the times deceas'd,
> The which observed, a man may prophesy,
> With a near aim, of the main chance of things
> As yet not come to life [3.1.80–84].

Using Henry, Hal, and Falstaff as a way to prophesy the main chance of things makes the *Henry IV* plays into an Elizabethan early-warning system against political rebellion.

The history plays in which Falstaff appears are ensemble pieces that depict the development of an eventually well-governed political community; they are less allegorically virtuous than the three parts of *Henry VI* and less personality-driven than the historical tragedies *Richard II* and *Richard III* and the historicomedy *Henry V*. In their depiction of honor-obsessed antagonists and Machiavellian monarchs, the two parts of *Henry IV* present a view of fifteenth-century England that is in keeping with Morton W. Bloomfield's definition of medievalism as "the idealization of medieval life and culture, with an emphasis upon a rich, mysterious and imaginary world of nobility, honor, class-consciousness, defenders of women, battles and so forth that, it was believed, flourished in the Middle Ages."[5] But no matter how seriously the feuds and feudalism of either part of *Henry IV* are depicted on stage or in film, Falstaff's importation of morality-play comedy, his conscious anachronisms, his wandering nights, intoxicated queans, and damsels causing distress remind the audience of the gap between historical fact and rich, mysterious, and imaginary theatrical representation.

On stage, Falstaff is an enormous presence whose habit of dominating the play is an outward and visible sign of the temptations presented by rebellion and misrule, temptations in which Hal indulges but which he must eventually overcome in order to succeed as King Henry V. Actors who succumb to Falstaff's considerable charms have sometimes compiled a Falstaff play made up of the fat knight's scenes from the two parts of *Henry IV* and the more farcical bits of *Merry Wives of Windsor*, thus further isolating the morality-play set pieces depicting Vice in the tavern from the far uglier battles and political manipulations of the history plays' kings, prelates, and rebels. As in medieval mystery plays, in which scripture-speaking angels mingle with thieving shepherds and shrewish wives, the Falstaff plays emerge from the intersection of reverence for an ancient text — the providential history of the origin of the Tudor dynasty — and irreverence in interpreting that text.

The *Henry IV* plays themselves question the honor associated with medievalism by exposing the dishonorable political realities and self-serving quests behind the chivalrous surfaces of Henry Bolingbroke and Henry Percy, but that questioning becomes less intensive in non–British productions of the play that emphasize Falstaff at the expense of the politicians. I will illustrate this by using three of Falstaff's American incarnations: James Henry Hackett's nineteenth-century performances; the Falstaff play that was offered at the 1935 World's Fair; and Orson Welles's 1966 film *Chimes at Midnight*. In each of these examples, as has been and continues to be the case when the play is staged, the more romantic aspects of medievalism are overshadowed by Falstaff, transforming *Camelot* into *Spamalot* and leading to the terrifying "social indifferentiation" that Jean Howard and Phyllis Rackin rightly note "hangs heavy over the heterogeneous world of the Henriad."[6] When the focus is on Falstaff, what is lost is Shakespeare's chilling demonstration of the ways in which honor and chivalry become "a mere scutcheon" (*1 Henry IV* 5.1.140) behind which monarchs, nobles, and prelates hide their desire for power and wealth.

The records of performances of Shakespeare plays in the American colonies are sparse and often maddening: both George Washington and Thomas Jefferson attended the theater assiduously but recorded only the price of the ticket and not the name of the play; other records are dominated by cities such as New York, Philadelphia, Charleston, Annapolis, and Williamsburg, which had purpose-built theaters and widely circulating newspapers.[7] According to the records that do survive, the most frequently performed of Shakespeare's medieval plays were *Richard III* and *Macbeth*. These plays, like the state of Virginia and John Wilkes Booth, share a commitment to the motto *sic semper tyrannis*,[8] but *Richard III* is a tragedy more interested in examining Richard's evil nature than depicting medieval history, and *Macbeth*'s medievalism is more a function of costume than a question of which eleventh-century Scots values survive in a world in which "violent sorrow seems / A modern ecstasy" (4.3.169–170).

The plays were performed by companies made up of professional actors from London, beginning with Lewis Hallam's troupe, whose performance of *The Merchant of Venice* in Williamsburg, Virginia, in September 1752 is usually identified as the first professional production of Shakespeare in America. Although the London companies were not of the freshest — theater historian Charles Shattuck characterizes them as being comprised of "actors who could never make the grade at home or who were too fretful to wait their turn on the London ladder"— they brought Shakespeare's plays to an apparently eager audience, promising, according to Hallam's advertisement in the *Virginia Gazette*, that patrons could "depend on being entertain'd in as polite a Manner as at the Theatres in London."[9] Under Hallam's successor, David Douglass, *1 Henry IV* was an occasional addition to a repertory composed largely of Restoration comedies and eighteenth-century melodramas that the company performed throughout the colonies. In 1774, the Continental Congress banned "Exhibitions or Shews, Plays, and other expensive Diversions and Entertainments" in order to "discountenance and discourage every Species of Extravagance and Dissapation" in the years leading up to the American Revolution.[10] The ban was repeated in 1778 with a more detailed description of the dangers the theater posed to the country:

> Whereas frequenting play houses and theatrical entertainments has a fatal tendency to divert the minds of the people from a due attention to the means necessary for the defence of their country and the preservation of their liberties: Resolved, That any person holding office under the United States, who shall act, promote, encourage, or attend such plays, shall be deemed unworthy to hold such office, and shall be accordingly dismissed.[11]

Falstaff easily evaded this law: on March 25 and 30, 1778, as Washington's troops were encamped at Valley Forge, an amateur company of British soldiers, "Howe's Thespians," performed *1 Henry IV* in Philadelphia at the Southwark Theatre to benefit "the Widows and Orphans of those who have lost their lives in his Majesty's service, as well as for such other generous charities as their funds may enable them to perform."[12] Unfortunately no account of the production survives to indicate if Hotspur and his fellow northern rebels were given American accents, but colonial claims on Shakespeare were undeterred: that same year, an anonymous American author defended the playwright as "Old Shakespeare, a poet who would not be spit on, / Although he was born in an island called Britain."[13]

After the war's end, American productions of Shakespeare began to function as markers of cultural independence. The first American edition of Shakespeare's complete works appeared in 1795; although the text was pirated from an Irish edition, it was given a new preface justifying the study of "a poet as yet but imperfectly known on the western shore of the Atlantic" and defending the scarcity of annotations by asserting footnotes are out of keeping with the American character: "An American reader is seldom disposed to wander through the wilderness of verbal criticism." The anonymous American author of the preface offers an elaborate defense of Falstaff's moral character. Reading Shakespeare's plays as morality plays, the author of the preface notes that Shakespeare's fools are "always despised" and his villains "always hated," but adds that Shakespeare wisely used "cynical pleasantry" to make his villains tolerable without "overbalanc[ing] their guilt," thus permitting sensitive readers and theater patrons to "without disgust attend to [the villains] to the completion and punishment of their crimes." The character who complicates this scheme is Falstaff, but the author notes that Shakespeare is careful to provide Sir John with a suitably awful fate:

> If any one of the vicious characters in this writer can be termed seductive, it must be Falstaff; yet he is, on every occasion, overwhelmed with such ridicule and contempt, that no reader can envy his situation, and Shakespeare, in the sequel, dismisses him to an excess of neglect and ignominy, that may hurt the sensibility even of the severest moralist.

Readers received particular assurance that Falstaff's whorish consorts Mistress Quickly and Doll Tearsheet were no threat to public morals:

> In Farquhar and other writers of his kind, the laws of marriage are universally despised; their violation is a common jest; and from an attendance on such scenes, young people of both sexes must retire with the most unsuitable impressions. But in no part of Shakespeare will such depravity be found. Doll Tearsheet and Falstaff's hostess are no formidable advocates of corruption.[14]

Thus the potentially disruptive Falstaff was declared safe for American audiences. Maurice Morgann, the secretary to the British Commission that negotiated the peace treaty that ended the Revolutionary War, had made a similar attempt to redeem Falstaff in his still-anthologized 1777 *Essay on the Dramatic Character of Falstaff*, and these reassurances that comic characters could serve a moral function prepared the way for the arrival of the first American Falstaff, an arrival perhaps assisted by the hints about the fat knight's character offered by the inclusion of his "Encomium to Sack," a lavish tribute to wine's power to produce "excellent wit" (*2 Henry IV* 4.3.86–125), in William Scott's 1795 *Lessons in Elocution* and the publication in that same year of *Funny Stories*, whose title page bore the blurb "'I love funn!' Falstaff."[15]

James Henry Hackett (1800–1871) is usually acknowledged as the first native-born professional American actor. He began his career playing Yankee characters but eventually made a specialty of Falstaff, playing the role for over forty years. Hackett prided himself on his meticulous attention to textual details; a London critic credited the actor with having "studied the speeches of the fat knight with … a carefulness worthy of a commentator on Sophocles."[16] Hackett's promptbook for *1 Henry IV*, now at the Folger Shakespeare Library, includes a note from the actor offering an elaborate defense for putting Falstaff on stage. Hackett presents the actor's side of the debate over whether Shakespeare is best understood on the page or on the stage, and although he focuses on performance as a means of self-improvement rather than as a means of improving his audience, he anticipates the arguments of late-twentieth-century performance historians when he argues that it is only through enacting the play that scholars' interpretations can be tested for their validity:

Even provided [the actor] possesses every intellectual requisite to conceive, & physical qualification to embody [the role]; be it never so well studied in the *closet*; it is only as the performer's effects upon the *stage* are reflected upon his own mind by his audience, that he, who undertakes to personate this part, can confirm the value of his own Conceptions, learn to correct his errors in taste, judgment or execution, acquire the necessary ease, give unrestrained vent to his humour, & thus gradually approach the perfection of his own capability.[17]

Hackett's description of his commitment to hard work and self-improvement helped Americanize Falstaff and made it clear why it would not be as a king that an American actor would make his mark as a Shakespearean.

Hackett began playing Falstaff in *1 Henry IV* in 1828, *Merry Wives* in 1838, and *2 Henry IV* in 1841, performing the role "from Boston to New Orleans, from New York to San Francisco, in almost every American town that had a proper theatre," playing the part in London in 1833, 1839, 1845, and 1851, and capping his career with "a month-long stand of Falstaff at Booth's Theatre" in New York in 1869.[18] Borrowing from Maurice Morgann and the anonymous author of the preface to the first American edition, Hackett created a moral Falstaff whose purpose, the actor claimed, was to help his audience to avoid "becoming corrupted by intimacy with old and vicious company" or "ministering to the vices of great patrons."[19] As divided as the new nation itself about his ties to England and his American exceptionalism, Hackett cultivated a reputation for American authenticity while at the same time claiming ties to the British aristocracy: he was, or pretended to be, the descendent of "a Norman knight" and the "heir to the title long held by the Barons Hackett of Hackett's Court in Ireland,"[20] although he also liked it known that "he does not claim the title because being a recognized gentleman, the equal of any in America, a British Barony of the third degree in the peerage, would degrade him, and make his rank relatively below what it is at present," a sentiment which a critic noted "Sir John Falstaff would have treated ... with sovereign contempt."[21] Hackett's characterization of Falstaff was important enough to be exported to England, where his Falstaff was attentively watched, professionally reviewed, and turned into a piece of Staffordshire pottery.[22]

In costumes inauthentic for any period except nineteenth-century America, Hackett created a Falstaff suitable for a nation attempting to free itself of its ties to Merry Olde England: he played the part as a "huge, hulking, rollicking gentleman gone to seed"[23] with a "cynical temperament, with the infirmity of age already weighing upon him [so] that he has a kind of mental as well as bodily obesity."[24] One American reviewer claimed Hackett's characterization "lacked a universal and constant unctuousness. There were hard moments; impressions of dryness: the face was not always jolly."[25] Even complaints about Hackett's performance emphasized its Americanness: an anonymous review of an 1838 New York performance derided Hackett's "nasal twang" and claimed "his attempt to personate Falstaff reminds us only of a fat Yankee tavern-keeper."[26] Hackett delivered Falstaff's shocking battlefield catechism on honor—"What is honor? A word.... Who hath it? He that died a' Wednesday" (*1 Henry IV* 5.1.129–141)—in such a way that a London critic was convinced the soliloquy, "though comic, is deeply reflective, and involves the destruction of the whole life of the middle ages,"[27] a painful recognition that these lines, properly read, are capable of deconstructing Hotspur's genuine if misguided chivalry, loyalty, and commitment to honor, virtues his family used to give their attempted coup moral legitimacy and virtues Prince Hal believes he can acquire in a modern economic "exchange" in which he uses Hotspur as his "factor" (*1 Henry IV* 3.2.145–147).

The extent of Hackett's theatrical tours, his account of Falstaff in his 1863 *Notes and Comments upon Certain Plays and Actors of Shakespeare*, his widely publicized correspondence with John Quincy Adams about Shakespeare's art, and the availability of prints of Hackett costumed as Falstaff[28] made his interpretation visible and available to a wide audience. By attending to Shakespeare's text and avoiding the temptation to be overly jolly, Hackett disabled any efforts to use Falstaff to create an ideal medieval world of sack, women, and song. An American audience eager to prove that "Shakespeare is ours as truly as he is England's poet ... by reason of the very variety, complexity, and fullness of the cosmopolite forces which have gone and go to the making up of our national character, taste, and training,"[29] would find an intellectual model in a Falstaff who had the audacity to ask whether adhering to a code of honor was feudal or futile.

As Hackett was beginning his career, Charles Kemble was introducing a vogue for period costumes in Shakespeare productions in London. Beginning with *King John* in 1823 and eventually including *1 Henry IV*, Kemble produced Shakespeare plays that in their meticulous efforts to duplicate authentic medieval costumes and to suggest medieval architecture in their sets, necessarily made the productions of the history plays more English. Kemble brought some of his reconstructed costumes to America during a two-year tour that began in 1832 in New York, and interest in historicized productions continued, taking on a new intensity when Shakespeare plays began to be filmed.

In the early 1930s, however, the Falstaff plays once again took on a specifically American form. The occasion was the Pacific National Exhibition, which became known as the World's Fair, held in San Diego, California, in 1935 and 1936. The previous World's Fair, held in Chicago in 1934, had featured a reconstruction of the Globe Theatre based on the dimensions described in the 1600 construction contract for the Fortune Theater. Those attending the Chicago World's Fair could tour the reconstructed Globe and could for an additional fee see a play there. The plays were forty- to fifty-minute abridgments of Shakespeare's greatest hits, with the quick turnover designed to permit as many visitors as possible to see a play. The Chicago repertory included *Comedy of Errors, Midsummer Night's Dream, Taming of the Shrew, All's Well that Ends Well, Julius Caesar, Macbeth*, and *King Lear*. The abridged texts, some of which are still in print, were edited by Thomas Wood Stevens, and the plays were directed by Ben Iden Payne.

The concept proved so popular that it was repeated in San Diego during both the 1935 and the 1936 seasons of the Fair. In 1935 the repertory expanded to include under-an-hour versions of *Hamlet, Much Ado, Winter's Tale, As You Like It, Twelfth Night, Merry Wives*, and Marlowe's *Dr. Faustus*. Those who wished to see the plays had to pay an extra charge for the tickets; nevertheless the Old Globe and its nearby Falstaff Tavern proved immensely popular. In 1936, still more plays were added: *Two Gentlemen of Verona, Romeo and Juliet, The Tempest, Henry VIII*, and the only purpose-built play in the repertory, *The Life and Death of Falstaff*, a pastiche that combined the Falstaff scenes from *1* and *2 Henry IV* and *Merry Wives*.[30] Tens of thousands of visitors saw the abridged plays, and the reconstructed Globe was turned into a permanent structure, San Diego's Old Globe Theater, which is still in operation. Similar theaters were built in Dallas and Cleveland in the 1930s.

The Pacific National Exhibition must at times have resembled a Hieronymus Bosch painting. Among its features were a nudist colony, complete with a knot-hole-filled wooden fence, and a village staffed by midgets.[31] The Shakespeare plays presented at the reconstructed Globe were noticeably short of medieval kings, but the spirit was certainly in keeping with other events in which culture is commodified, including medieval fairs and pilgrimages, in which difficult paths are made smooth and snacks and souvenirs are sold. The Shakespeare abridgments performed in Chicago and San Diego are notable for their thoroughly modern efficiency in reducing complex and dilatory plots to a coherent, consumable form; decades before the appearance of television, the plays' producers had cut them down to the perfect length for commercial broadcast. The companies that performed the plays were young and apparently inexhaustible, and the result of their efforts was that an unusually large and diverse audience now knew something about Shakespeare, at least to the extent of being able to quote important lines from the plays and to identify the source of the names for the moons of Uranus or of commercial products such as Falstaff beer.[32]

In 1930s America, the abridged plays performed a cultural role similar to that of mystery plays: valuable texts were reduced to their essence in memorable productions meant to reinforce a limited set of values. In the versions of Shakespeare's plays performed at the World's Fairs, the absence of kings and the abundance of romance enhanced Shakespeare's relevance to a twentieth-century American audience while rewriting Shakespeare's links to British history.

In 1939, not long after the San Diego *Life and Death of Falstaff* made its debut, Orson Welles wrote and directed *Five Kings*, a two-part compression of all eight of Shakespeare's Wars of the Roses plays. Although not particularly well reviewed, Welles's play was performed in New York, Boston, Washington, Philadelphia, Belfast, and Dublin. The play emphasized Prince Hal's evolution into King Henry V; Welles characterized the Prince as "a demagogue who plans to become a great popular hero.... His good nature, his good angel, was Falstaff, and his bad angel was the king."[33] Welles played the role of Falstaff, "the best role that Shakespeare ever wrote,"[34] in *Five Kings*, then used his play as the basis for his 1966 film *Chimes at Midnight* (released in the United States as *Falstaff*), which also incorporated excerpts from *Richard II* and *Henry V* and included narrative bridges derived from Shakespeare's primary source for the plays, Raphael Holinshed's 1587 *Chronicles*.

Although the film was not initially popular or profitable, it remained Welles's favorite, and he spoke about it frequently in interviews.[35] For Welles, who admitted to having a "strong affinity" for "the high Middle Ages,"[36] Falstaff represented Shakespeare's nostalgic conception of medieval England, a conception that the playwright realized could not survive in a modern world. Falstaff's domination of the film demonstrates, as Welles confirms in interviews,[37] that the director identified very closely with Falstaff as a good man struggling in a postlapsarian world. England, with its cold and Machiavellian kings, rejects the warmth and wit of Falstaff, a situation with which Welles, as a misunderstood, or at least underfunded, artist, could identify. *Chimes at Midnight* includes a shocking and much-imitated combat scene: the Battle of Shrewsbury is depicted in dozens of short shots of the death and mutilation of soldiers, whose nationalities quickly become indistinguishable as they and their horses are butchered, intercut with shots of Falstaff hiding in the forest and watching the battle.

Although *Chimes at Midnight* does include scenes between Henry IV and the northern rebels and between the king and his son, Shakespeare's text is severely cut, with the separate rebellions of Shakespeare's two plays condensed into a single battle. The low-budget period costumes and weapons mark the film as medieval, but the film places a much higher value on Falstaff's antics and excesses than it does on the conduct of lords and knights. Unusually for a production of these hypermasculine plays, there are many women in the tavern scenes, and Doll Tearsheet and Mistress Quickly receive sophisticated interpretations from Jeanne Moreau and Margaret Rutherford. But Falstaff remains the film's focus.

As Laurence Olivier had discovered in 1944, and as Kenneth Branagh would discover in 1989, it is difficult to resist the impulse to put Falstaff into a history play; despite the fact that Shakespeare carefully leaves Falstaff out of his account of Henry V's victory over France, except to allow a brief narration of Sir John's death by Mistress Quickly, Olivier and Branagh include flashback scenes of the fat knight in their film adaptations of *Henry V*.[38] Welles made no effort to hide the centrality of his Falstaff; *Chimes at Midnight* opens with the character trudging through a snowy landscape as a means of reinforcing Falstaff's connection with cyclical rather than linear time and with Dionysian rather than Apollonian magic, and Welles associates Falstaff with the sound of bells, enabling the character and his connection with time to be recalled aurally even when he does not appear in a scene. Although the play ends with a victorious Henry V making plans to invade France and a chastised Falstaff on his way to an enforced reformation, Welles's film closes with the funeral of Falstaff, a scene whose shots center on what critic Samuel Crowl notes is "the largest coffin in the history of film."[39]

Both before and after he filmed *Chimes at Midnight*, Welles described Shakespeare as painfully trapped between the medieval and modern worlds. In a 1958 print interview published in *Cahiers*

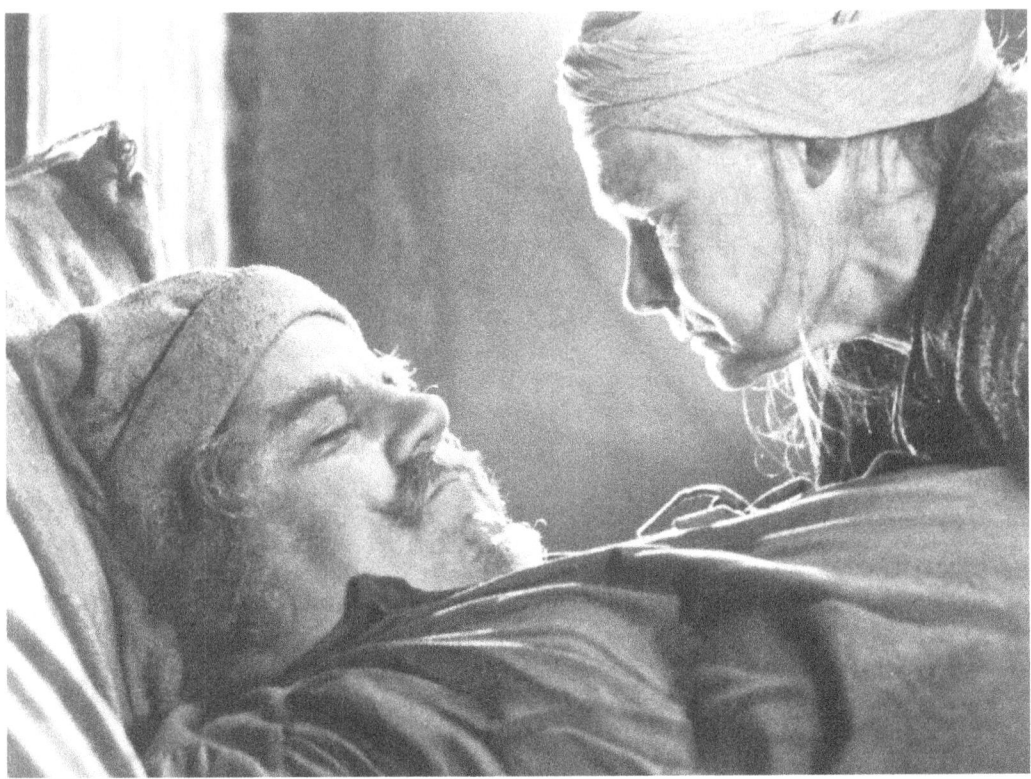

Falstaff (Robbie Coltrane) on his deathbed as Mistress Quickly (Judi Dench) looks on in Branagh's *Henry V* (1989).

du Cinéma, Welles explains his theory in terms that perhaps inadvertently expose a link between the playwright and Welles, who was himself living in a culture that had undergone a recent and major cultural shift:

> Shakespeare was very close to the origin of the culture he was in. The language he wrote had just been formed, the old England of the Middle Ages was still alive in the memories of all the people of Stratford. He was very close indeed to another age.... He was standing in the door which opened onto the modern age and his grandparents, the old people in the village, the countryside itself, still belonged to the Middle Ages, to the Old Europe.[40]

Having been born in 1915, Welles was a witness to the destruction of "Old Europe" in World War II; as a filmmaker, Welles was producing art in a language that "had just been formed." When Welles goes on to assert that Shakespeare's "lyricism, his comic verve, his humanity" were medieval while "his pessimism, his bitterness ... belong to the modern world, the world which has just been created, not the world as it existed for eternities, but *his* world,"[41] the filmmaker is using the categories "medieval" and "modern" imprecisely and nostalgically to describe his own combination of a painterly visual lyricism of the sort that enlivens Pieter Brueghel's 1559 "The Fight between Carnival and Lent" and a modern cinematic pessimism, illustrated by the near-documentary chaos of the *Chimes at Midnight* battle scene. He is also explicating a line Shakespeare gives to the Archbishop of York in *2 Henry IV*: "Past and to come seems best; things present worst" (1.3.108).

In a filmed 1982 interview with Leslie Megahey, Welles expands on his characterization of Falstaff, using the fat knight as a way to talk about his own status as a cultural refugee. Welles identifies Falstaff with "Merrie England" and notes that he and Shakespeare share an artistic pre-

Orson Welles impersonates Falstaff in *Chimes at Midnight* (1965).

occupation with "the loss of innocence," specifically the loss of the pastoral vision of "an older England, which was sweeter and purer, where the hay smelt better and the weather was always springtime, and the daffodils blew in the gentle, warm breezes." Unable to find this England even in the sixteenth century, Shakespeare turned "profoundly against the modern age," an attitude Welles, at the end of his career, now shares: "I am against my modern age, he was against his." Castigating the "modern" and "Continental" who destroyed Old England, Welles finds comfort in what he sees as Shakespeare's promotion of Arthurian values:

> I think [Shakespeare] was a typically English writer, archetypically, the perfect English writer, in that very thing, that preoccupation with that Camelot which is the great English legend.... [Falstaff] is a kind of refugee from that world. And he has to live by his wits, he has to be funny. He hasn't a place to sleep if he doesn't get a laugh out of his patron. So it's a rough modern world that he's living in.[42]

Welles's conception of Falstaff as an essentially good man surrounded by crowned thieves and schemers was not the final American incarnation of Falstaff,[43] but it remains the most permanently visible one. By creating a film that "laments the death of chivalry" and the loss of "the old England of the greenwood and Maytime" in favor of "a new kind of England that Shakespeare deplored — an England that ended up as the British Empire,"[44] Welles rejects the cultural weight of medievalism and uses Shakespeare's play, as Shakespeare himself used Holinshed, to question received authority.

By celebrating Falstaff but reducing the roles of the Henrys, James Henry Hackett, the World's Fair producers, and Orson Welles limit Falstaff's usefulness as an antidote to more pious incar-

William Richert as Bob Pigeon, the Falstaff figure, with River Phoenix as Mike Waters in Gus Van Sant's *My Own Private Idaho* (1991).

nations of medievalism[45] because those more pious incarnations are not part of the show. In the Falstaff-centered productions, the fat knight's tale begins with the verbal and physical comedy of Eastcheap, Gadshill, and sometimes Herne's Oak and ends with the pathetic rejection and banishment by Henry V and Mistress Quickly's solemn narration of Sir John babbling of green fields until he becomes "as cold as any stone" (*Henry V* 2.3.9–26). By overshadowing the political and paternal struggles of Henry, Hal, and Hotspur, by editing out the self-serving corruption of nobles and prelates, and by eliding the complexities of Falstaff's attempted seduction of Windsor's merry wives, the reduced or compiled texts strip Falstaff of much of his political weight while adding to his mythological status: each of his scenes save the last one is a high-calorie comic feast, and this causes Hal's fear of the consequences of unbelted rule to be realized: "If all the year were playing holidays / To sport would be as tedious as to work" (*1 Henry IV* 1.2.204–205).

In the absence of careful attention to the way medieval stage kings raise questions about the distribution of power, and in a nation not noted for its lean and hungry look, these three American Falstaffs perform another kind of cultural work: arriving shortly before the social and political upheavals of the Civil War, World War II, and the Vietnam War, eras in which the old gods would be overthrown, Falstaff offers a theogony explaining the origins of a deity who combines the attributes of the Trickster figure, the Green Man, Santa Claus, and Dionysus, thereby creating the god that many Americans needed and that Puritan theology could not provide. Let loose in America, this Falstaff reappears in the comic excesses of John Belushi, Roseanne Barr, Eddie Murphy in his fat suits, or *My Own Private Idaho*'s Bob Pigeon but denies us the luxury of being able to compare Shakespeare's modern conception of honor to that embodied by his medieval kings.

Notes

1. William Shakespeare, *1 Henry IV*, in *The Riverside Shakespeare*, ed. G. Blakemore Evans et al. (Boston and New York: Houghton Mifflin, 1997), 2.4.453. All quotations from Shakespeare's plays are from this edition and will be cited parenthetically.

2. Bernard Rosenthal and Paul E. Szarmach, "Introduction," in *Medievalism in American Culture: Papers of the Eighteenth Annual Conference of the Center for Medieval and Early Renaissance*, ed. Rosenthal and Szarmach (Binghamton, NY: Medieval & Renaissance Texts & Studies, 1989), 4.

3. See, e.g., C. L. Barber, *Shakespeare's Festive Comedy: A Study of Dramatic Form and its Relation to Social Custom* (Princeton, NJ: Princeton University Press, 1959), 67–73 and 192–221; David Wiles, *Shakespeare's Clown: Actor and Text in the Elizabethan Playhouse* (Cambridge, UK: Cambridge University Press, 1987), 116–135; and Kristen Poole, "Saints Alive! Falstaff, Martin Marprelate, and the Staging of Puritanism," *Shakespeare Quarterly* 46 (1995): 47–75.

4. A. Elizabeth Ross, "Hand-Me-Down Heroics: Shakespeare's Retrospective of Popular Elizabethan Heroical Drama in *Henry V*," in *Shakespeare's English Histories: A Quest for Form and Genre*, ed. John Velz (Binghamton, NY: Medieval & Renaissance Texts & Studies, 1996), 177.

5. Morton W. Bloomfield, "Reflections of a Medievalist: America, Medievalism, and the Middles Ages" in Bernard Rosenthal and Paul E. Szarmach, eds., *Medievalism in American Culture: Papers of the Eighteenth Annual Conference of the Center for Medieval and Early Renaissance*, ed. Rosenthal and Szarmach (Binghamton, NY: Medieval & Renaissance Texts & Studies, 1989), 14.

6. Jean Howard and Phyllis Rackin, *Engendering a Nation: A Feminist Account of Shakespeare's English Histories* (London and New York: Routledge, 1997), 175.

7. Sources for eighteenth-century American theater history include Odai Johnson, *The Colonial American Stage 1665–1774: A Documentary Catalog* (Madison, NJ: Farleigh Dickinson University Press, 2001); Jared Brown, *Theater in America during the Revolution* (Cambridge, UK: Cambridge University Press, 1995); Esther Dunn, *Shakespeare in America* (New York: Macmillan, 1939); and Charles Shattuck, *Shakespeare on the American Stage: From the Hallams to Edwin Booth* (Washington: Folger Shakespeare Library, 1976). George Washington's theatergoing is described in Paul Leicester Ford, *Washington and the Theater* (New York: Dunlap Society, 1899); Thomas Jefferson's visits to the theater are documented in James A. Bear, Jr., and Lucia C. Stanton, eds., *Jefferson's Memorandum Book: Accounts, with Legal Records and Miscellany 1767–1826*, 2 vols. (Princeton, NJ: Princeton University Press, 1997).

8. *Sic semper tyrannis* is the state motto of Virginia; Booth shouted the phrase from the stage of Ford's Theater after assassinating Lincoln.

9. Shattuck, *Shakespeare on the American Stage*, 4 and 8.

10. Ford, *Washington and the Theater*, 24.

11. Ibid., 27.

12. "Preface to a Prologue," *Philadelphia Ledger*, February 11, 1778. The performances of *1 Henry IV* are advertised in the *Ledger* on March 25 and March 28.

13. Quoted in Esther Dunn, *Shakespeare in America* (New York: Macmillan, 1939), 112.

14. Preface to William Shakespeare, *The Plays and Poems of William Shakespeare*, 8 vols. (Philadelphia: Bioren & Madan, 1795), iv; x; vi.

15. *Funny Stories: or The American Jester: Being a Companion for a Merry Goodfellow* (Worcester, MA: [Isaiah Thomas, Jr.] 1795).

16. Quoted in Shattuck, *Shakespeare on the American Stage*, 61; biographical details on 56–62.

17. James Henry Hackett, prefatory remarks in his prompt copy of William Shakespeare, *1 Henry IV* (Boston: Welles and Lilly; and New York: A. T. Goodrich & Co., 1823), Folger Shakespeare Library F4/15/41 (21).

18. Shattuck, *Shakespeare on the American Stage*, 59.

19. Quoted in *ibid.*, 59.

20. James Henry Hackett, *Notes and Comments upon Certain Plays and Actors of Shakespeare* (New York: Carleton, 1863), 333–334.

21. *Ibid.*, 334; a more complimentary anonymous account of "Baron Hackett, The Comedian" appeared in the October 15, 1836, edition of the periodical *Spirit of the Times*: "The attempt to ferret out his connexion with a title family was so repugnant to the stern republican principles which had been instilled into his mind from boyhood, that without a thought upon the matter, except to smile at the incredulous hopes of partial friends, he returned from his first professional tour no wiser, so far as his 'baronetcy' was concerned, than when he left his native land."

22. Two examples of Hackett as pottery can be found in the Folger Shakespeare Library (Acc. 255864 and Acc. ART 231735). Hackett quotes extensively from his London reviews and answers some of their criticism in Hackett, *Notes and Comments*, passim.

23. "The Editor's Easy Chair," *Harper's New Month Magazine* 35 (August, 1867): 394.
24. Quoted from the London *Times*, February 7, 1845, in Hackett, *Notes and Comments*, 324.
25. "The Editor's Easy Chair," 395.
26. Anonymous review, *The New-Yorker*, December 1, 1838.
27. Quoted from the London *Times*, February 7, 1845, in Hackett, *Notes and Comments*, 324.
28. Shattuck, *Shakespeare on the American Stage*, 60 and 61.
29. Anonymous, "Shakespeare in America," *Round Table. A Saturday Review*, February 20, 1864.
30. Newspaper accounts remain the primary source for information regarding the repertory and the popularity of the World's Fair Globes. See the archives of the *Chicago Tribune* and the *San Diego Union* for 1933–1936.
31. An illustrated account of the fixed and movable features of the California Pacific Exposition can be found in Richard Amero, "History of the Exposition," http://www.sandiegohistory.org/calpac/35expo11.htm.
32. Most of the twenty-one known moons of Uranus are named after Shakespeare characters; Ariel, Titania, and Oberon were among the moons discovered before 1935. Falstaff Beer was registered as a trademark by Lemp Brewery of St. Louis, Missouri, in 1903.
33. Orson Welles, 1974 filmed interview with Richard Marienstras, in *Orson Welles: Interviews*, ed. Mark W. Estrin (Jackson, MS: University Press of Mississippi, 2002).
34. Orson Welles, 1964 print interview with Juan Cobos et al., in Estrin, *Interviews*, 118.
35. See Estrin, *Interviews*, 116–118; 131–133; 159–162; 201–203.
36. Orson Welles, 1974 filmed interview with Richard Marienstras, in Estrin, *Interviews*, 170.
37. See, for instance, Welles's characterization of himself as melancholic, slothful, and gluttonous in his 1967 print interview with Kenneth Tynan in Estrin, *Interviews*, 140.
38. 1944 *The Chronicle History of King Henry the Fift with His Battell Fought at Agincourt in France*, d. Laurence Olivier, photography by Jack Hildyard and Robert Krasker, with Laurence Olivier. UK: Two Cities Films, Ltd.; 1989 *Henry V*, d. Kenneth Branagh, photography by Kenneth MacMillan, with Kenneth Branagh. UK: BBC Films and Renaissance Films.
39. Samuel Crowl, "The Long Goodbye: Welles and Falstaff," *Shakespeare Quarterly* 31 (1980) 380. Shakespeare's play ends with Hal, now Henry V, rejecting and banishing Falstaff (5.5.41–71) and with Prince John and the Lord Chief Justice exchanging compliments about Henry's "fair proceeding" and anticipating the war with France (5.5.97–109). Shakespeare reports Falstaff's death in *Henry V* 2.3.5–44.
40. Estrin, *Interviews*, 58.
41. *Ibid.*, 58.
42. *Ibid.*, 202.
43. In 2006, the Chicago Shakespeare theater company performed both parts of *Henry IV* as part of the Royal Shakespeare Company's complete works festival. Although critics admired the audacity of an American company performing the history plays at Stratford-upon-Avon, the production was a traditional one, emphasizing the relationship between Prince Hal and King Henry.
44. Orson Welles, print interview with Kenneth Tynan, in Estrin, *Interviews*, 132–33.
45. They also launched a trend that continues in American productions of Shakespeare's history plays: a 2003 Lincoln Center production with Kevin Kline as Falstaff conflated the two Henry plays, as did Ralph Alan Cohen's *The Most Lamentable Comedy of Sir John Falstaff* at the American Shakespeare Center's Blackfriars Theater in 2004.

Works Cited

Bloomfield, Morton W. "Reflections of a Medievalist: America, Medievalism, and the Middle Ages." In *Medievalism in American Culture: Papers of the Eighteenth Annual Conference of the Center for Medieval and Early Renaissance*. Edited by Bernard Rosenthal and Paul E. Szarmach. Binghamton, NY: Medieval & Renaissance Texts & Studies, 1989.

Dunn, Esther. *Shakespeare in America*. New York: Macmillan, 1939.

"The Editor's Easy Chair." *Harper's New Monthly Magazine* 35 (August, 1867): 393–397.

Estrin, Mark. *Orson Welles: Interviews*. Jackson, MS: University Press of Mississippi, 2002.

Ford, Paul Leicester. *Washington and the Theater*. New York: The Dunlap Society, 1899.

Funny Stories. Worcester, MA: 1795.

Hackett, James Henry. *Notes and Comments upon Certain Plays and Actors of Shakespeare*. New York: Carleton, 1863.

Howard, Jean and Phyllis Rackin. *Engendering a Nation: A Feminist Account of Shakespeare's English Histories*. London and New York: Routledge, 1997.

Ross, A. Elizabeth. "Hand-me-Down Heroics: Shakespeare's Retrospective of Popular Elizabethan Heroical

Drama in *Henry V*." In *Shakespeare's English Histories: A Quest for Form and Genre*. Edited by John Velz. Binghamton, NY: Medieval & Renaissance Texts & Studies, 1996.

Rosenthal, Bernard and Paul E. Szarmach. *Medievalism in American Culture: Papers of the Eighteenth Annual Conference of the Center for Medieval and Early Renaissance*. Binghamton, NY: Medieval & Renaissance Texts & Studies, 1989.

Shakespeare, William. *1 Henry IV*. Boston: Welles and Lilly and New York: A. T. Goodrich & Co., 1823.

_____. *1 Henry IV*. In *The Riverside Shakespeare*. Edited by G. Blakemore Evans et. al. Boston and New York: Houghton Mifflin, 1997.

_____. *The Plays and Poems of William Shakespeare*. 8 vols. Philadelphia: Bioren & Madan, 1795.

Shattuck, Charles. *Shakespeare on the American Stage: From the Hallams to Edwin Booth*. Washington, D.C.: The Folger Shakespeare Library, 1976.

Filmography

1944 *The Chronicle History of King Henry the Fift with His Battell Fought at Agincourt in France*, d. Laurence Olivier, photography by Jack Hildyard and Robert Krasker, with Laurence Olivier. UK: Two Cities Films.

1966 *Chimes at Midnight (Campanadas a Medianoche)*, d. Orson Welles, photography by Edmond Richard, with Orson Welles, Keith Baxter, John Geilgud. Spain and USA: Internacional Films Espanola and Alpine Productions.

1989 *Henry V*, d. Kenneth Branagh, photography by Kenneth MacMillan, with Kenneth Branagh. UK: BBC Films and Renaissance Films.

1991 *My Own Private Idaho*, d. Gus Van Sant, photography by John Campbell and Eric Alan Edwards, with River Phoenix and Keanu Reeves. USA: New Line Cinema.

Scoring the Fields of the Dead: Musical Styles and Approaches to Postbattle Scenes from *Henry V* (1944, 1989)[1]

LINDA K. SCHUBERT

One of the well-known advantages of a filmed play is that one can show elaborate events and actions difficult to present onstage. The two film versions of *Henry V,* Laurence Olivier's of 1944 and Kenneth Branagh's of 1989, include such events and actions. In these films we see not only the Battle of Agincourt but also the dead and wounded lying on the field afterward, though the latter are not explicitly included in Shakespeare's original play.

In addition to showing the bloody consequences of fighting, these "field of the dead" scenes in particular allow directors to offer interpretations and blunt opinions about war in general. Olivier's film, made during World War II with the support of the British Ministry of Information, has long been recognized as a successful propaganda effort as well as a work of high artistic merit. It was a powerful, morale-boosting picture that invited audiences to interpret the British victory against impossible odds in 1415 as the precursor to a future British victory against Nazi Germany in the 1940s. Branagh's film, on the other hand, was based on a stage production performed soon after the Falkland Islands War and consequently has a very different viewpoint, showing the English victory in painful rather than glorious detail.

The music supporting these postbattle scenes considerably heightens their impact. The power of William Walton's music in Olivier's film — particularly for the charge into battle — was noted at the time of its release, and the excerpts of early music that accompany the declaration of victory followed by brief views of the dead create an atmosphere of reverence and respect. In Branagh's work, Patrick Doyle's originally composed, intentionally contemporary-sounding "Non nobis" provides the framework and impetus for perhaps the most memorable scene in the film.

The purpose of this essay is to bring a musicologist's perspective to a larger discussion of the use of medieval elements in film performances of Shakespeare's *Henry V,* particularly in the musical scores and most particularly in the music heard during the postbattle scenes. After describing the cues given for music found in Shakespeare's original play, I briefly discuss the scores for several historical sound films made before 1944, including *Alexander Nevsky*, which provided important models for later Shakespeare films. The essay then further focuses on how music is used in both versions of *Henry V* to help project particular interpretations and opinions about war in the postbattle scenes.

Shakespeare's Play

Shakespeare's original *Henry V* (probably completed in 1599) tells how the English king Henry V claimed the French throne and conquered vastly superior French forces at the Battle of Agincourt (1415) to establish a foothold on the Continent. The play describes and interprets a historical event that had occurred almost two hundred years before — it is, in other words, a powerful construct in which the audience is asked to participate by the narrating Chorus:

> Can this cockpit hold the vasty fields of France? ... On your imaginary forces work.... Piece out our imperfections with your thoughts.... Think, when we talk of horses, that you see them.... For 'tis your thoughts that now must deck our kings.[2]

Shakespeare, writing during the reign of Elizabeth Tudor, took most of his information for the Lancaster history plays from sixteenth-century chroniclers Edward Hall and Raphael Holinshed.[3] By the beginning of the sixteenth century, however, Henry V was already a popular figure in English literature. Young Henry VIII was especially inspired by his predecessor's exploits in France and had probably read the *Gesta Henrici Quinti, or Deeds of Henry V*, which was published in 1513 and had existed in several manuscripts before that.[4] By the end of the century, the victor of Agincourt had become a popular subject of Elizabethan theater, and in the late 1580s and early 1590s there had been at least three other plays about Henry's reign.[5]

Henry V was popular and often performed in Shakespeare's day. It has remained in the active theater repertory, though as Kenneth Branagh notes, it was rarely performed in the twentieth century.[6] It has, not surprisingly, become more widely known through the two film versions. At first glance, the play appears to be a glorification of war. But it also offers other voices, characters who, in Michael Neill's words, are skeptical of or even satirize "the heroic values and high rhetoric that glamorize King Henry's conquests."[7] The aristocratic traitors (particularly the Earl of Cambridge), the mostly lower-class Eastcheap company (Pistol, Bardolph, Nym, Nell Quickly, and Sir John Falstaff), the Irish Captain MacMorris, and the French Princess Katherine all offer opinions and attitudes conflicting with Henry's nationalistic, heroic perspectives on warfare. As Neill comments: "In all of Shakespeare's histories, moreover, we are repeatedly made aware of competing schemes of explanation that undercut the public certainties of official history. Nowhere are such conflicting explanations more apparent than in *Henry V*."[8]

After the announcement of the victory at Agincourt in the original play, Shakespeare (following Holinshed and Hall) provided cues for music appropriate to the immediate situation. Henry says, "Let there be sung *Non nobis* and *Te deum*, the dead with charity enclosed in clay" (4.8.128–129). These were Latin songs of praise to God and would have been appropriate music for the characters themselves to sing and hear at this point in the story (see Example 1, page 64).

The medieval Latin plainchant "Te Deum" was part of the Roman Catholic Divine Office, specifically Matins, but was also sung in other situations. It could be used, for example, to conclude a liturgical drama, to express thanksgiving during important occasions such the canonization of a saint, and even to thank God for victory on the battlefield. There is a tradition going back to the eighth century that it was composed by St. Augustine and St. Ambrose during the former's baptism; at present the identities of neither the author nor composer have been settled. The words may have been composed before the middle of the fourth century; the earliest source currently available for published transcriptions of the melody is from the twelfth century.[11] Later it became one of two originally Roman Catholic hymns to be included in the Anglican service by Thomas Cranmer in *The Book of Common Prayer* of 1549; it continues to be used, mainly at Evensong by Anglicans.[12]

"Non nobis" are the opening words of Psalm 115 in *The Book of Common Prayer* (*BCP*) of Shakespeare's (and our) time. The Roman Catholic Vulgate of Henry V's day, however, presented

EXAMPLE 1. TEXTS AND TRANSLATIONS OF "TE DEUM" AND "NON NOBIS"

Non nobis

Non nobis, Domine,	Not to us, O Lord,
Non nobis,	Not to us,
Sed nomini	But to Your Name
Tuo da Gloria.	Give glory.[9]

Te Deum (opening lines only)

Te Deum laudamus:	O God, we praise Thee:
te Dominum confitemur.	We acknowledge Thee to be the Lord
Te aeternum Patrem omnic terra veneratur.	Everlasting Father, all the earth doth worship Thee.
Tibi omnes Angeli; tibi Caeli et universae Potestates;	To Thee all the Angels, the Heavens and all the Powers;
Tibi cherumbim et Seraphim incessabili voce proclamant:	all the Cherubim and Seraphim unceasingly proclaim:
Sanctus, sanctus, sanctus, dominus Deus Sabaoth.	Holy, Holy, Holy, Lord God of Hosts.[10]

---

the "Non nobis" as part of the psalm "In exitu Israel" (Psalm no. 113 in the Vulgate, Psalm no. 114 in the *BCP*).[13] Richmond Noble, and later on T. W. Craik, editor of the Arden Shakespeare edition of *Henry V*, observed that Holinshed reported Henry to have ordered the psalm "In exitu Israel" to be sung after the victory at Agincourt:

> Holinshed relates that ... the King "gaue thanks to almightie god for so happie a victorie: cau[s]ing his prelats and chapleins to sing this psalme: 'In exitu Israel de Aegypto'; and commanded euerie man to kneele downe on the ground at this verse: '*Non nobis*, Domine, non nobis, sed nomini tuo da gloriam.' Which doone, he caused *Te Deum*, with certeine anthems to be soong."[14]

Noble points out that Shakespeare, knowing "In exitu Israel" and "Non nobis" were separate psalms in the Anglican Psalter, had Henry ask specifically for the psalm "Non nobis" to be sung. Shakespeare did this, Noble believed, as a corrective to Holinshed, but Craik suggests the change was made because Shakespeare thought using the "Non nobis" would be more "immediately comprehensible" to his audience since it was easily identified in the *BCP* and used during Morning Prayer throughout the year.[15]

Olivier and Branagh both include Henry's spoken orders for music in their films. In Olivier's film, both pieces are then sung in already-existing early versions (the "Non nobis" as a polyphonic work, the "Te Deum" in its plainchant form), followed by a performance of the "Agincourt Carol" with choir and orchestra. In Branagh's film, however, only the "Non nobis" is sung, and in an originally composed, contemporary setting. Whereas Shakespeare's cues in the original play called for music appropriate to the immediate situation that characters as well as audience would hear, the film scores provide both this kind of music (called "source" or "diegetic" music) and also background (or "nondiegetic") music. The background music for these films—which only the audience hears, not the characters—establishes mood and atmosphere and reminds viewers of people, ideas, and events through the use of recurring themes (called "leitmotifs"). Like the characters who contradict or interrogate Henry's heroic, nationalistic view of warfare in the original play, the background music in the films also offers commentary and can even contradict the implications of the visuals with accompaniments using unexpected styles and elements. One example of this, to be explored later, is the gentle, increasingly triumphant "Non nobis" from Branagh's film mentioned above, which plays as weary, miserable people wander the gory battlefield.

Scoring Shakespeare Films: Precedents and Models

With hindsight we now know that Olivier's *Henry V* was the first successful sound film version of a Shakespeare work. Many silent and several sound film versions of Shakespeare plays preceded it, however,[16] and some featured notable approaches to the music. *A Midsummer Night's Dream* (1935), for example, was scored by Erich Wolfgang Korngold and is best remembered for the cues based on selections from Felix Mendelssohn's incidental music for the play and arranged by Korngold for the film.

Herbert Stothart's music for MGM's *Romeo and Juliet* (1936) also stands out, for he created a score that used not only originally composed music but also versions of early pieces from the sixteenth and seventeenth centuries, including works by Giovanni Pierluigi da Palestrina, Thomas Morley, and Thoinot Arbeau. Unfortunately, he was later ordered to alter the score drastically and incorporate the love theme from Pyotr Ilich Tchaikovsky's concert overture *Romeo and Juliet* as a main theme. A good deal of early music, however, remained in the final score.[17]

Historical films set in sixteenth-century England, such as *The Private Life of Henry VIII* (1933), *Fire over England* (1937), and *The Prince and the Pauper* (1937), were also popular in the 1930s. These kinds of films were often accompanied by originally composed scores in musical styles not contemporary with the time period of the stories, though occasional references were made to historical early music. Even *The Adventures of Robin Hood* (1938), with its original "swashbuckling" music by Korngold that drew strongly upon late-nineteenth-century German Romanticism, included a brief quotation from the late-medieval "Sumer is icumen in."[18]

Like *The Adventures of Robin Hood,* Sergei Eisenstein's *Alexander Nevsky* (1938) offered a powerful score made up of originally composed cues. Unlike Korngold, however, composer Sergei Prokofiev deliberately avoided using period music in this most famous of medieval films, later explaining that ancient works such as medieval church music no longer held meaning for contemporary audiences.[19] (More pragmatically, it would have been unwise to use Roman Catholic church music in a film certain to be personally scrutinized by Joseph Stalin.) *Nevsky* provided powerful combinations of images and music that are still imitated, and cues such as the "aria" that accompanies a woman searching for loved ones on the battlefield also influenced Olivier and probably Branagh.

The musical conceptions represented by the examples above—arrangements of previously composed incidental music, performances and/or arrangements of early music, use of originally composed music, and various combinations of these—all provided models and ideas for scoring later Shakespeare films.

Two Films of *Henry V*

In the canon of "great scores" for historical films, one of the most frequently mentioned is Walton's score for Olivier's *Henry V*. Following the lead of the images that move fluidly from the sixteenth-century Globe Theatre to increasingly realistic settings in fifteenth-century France, the score combines pieces of music from Shakespeare's day and the period of Agincourt within the composer's own twentieth-century idiom.[20]

Shot in 1943 and premiered in London in 1944, Olivier's film had special meaning for British viewers enduring the ravages of World War II.[21] Film music specialist Christopher Palmer described the movie as a powerful piece of propaganda for the British war effort:

Olivier's rousing speech in *Henry V* (1944).

Olivier's *Henry V* was as much a propaganda play in 1943 as Shakespeare's had been in 1600.... Uppermost in the minds of those making and viewing the Agincourt scenes would have been the heroism of the British at Dunkirk, in the Battle of Britain, and latterly, in the Allied invasion of Europe.[22]

This bent toward propaganda (somewhat controversial among scholars)[23] is especially noticeable in the Battle of Agincourt, a battle difficult to show on stage and therefore all the more effective on film. But Olivier's role in the film as producer-director-actor is complicated. His twentieth-century version of a sixteenth-century play about a fifteenth-century event is rich, frustrating, involved, and quite self-conscious. Film allowed Olivier to explore ways of moving fluidly between realistic and stylized representations of the fifteenth and sixteenth centuries, embedding them within each other and within a twentieth-century framework. By deliberately making the audience conscious of these shifts between time periods, Olivier shatters the impression of a seamless reality, an effect the classic Hollywood film sought to preserve and which is still usually expected in historical films today. Such shifts continually break the narrative flow to remind members of the audience that they are watching illusions of the past. Viewers today may find the stylized settings distracting, even irritating, but the technique forces them to recognize they are watching a constructed and fictionalized past, not witnessing history as it actually happened.

Olivier's experiments with realism and stylization begin immediately with the opening "aerial shot"—obviously a model—of the City of London in the sixteenth century.[24] We then move into the Globe Theatre to watch a performance of *Henry V.* The film audience watches the actors and the theater audience until Henry sets sail for France, at which point the action "opens out" and the theater audience disappears. Yet, even in a new land, the backgrounds still resemble props and imply containment on a stage. The views of the French countryside are not real landscapes but pictures based on illustrations from *Les Très Riches Heures du Duc de Berry*, a famous early-fifteenth-century illuminated manuscript, used as backdrops for the scenes at the French court.[25]

Olivier's decision to make a twentieth-century film framing the fifteenth-century story of Henry V within a sixteenth-century setting in the Globe Theatre complicated Walton's task. Hubert Clifford noted that "the form of the film posed an awkward problem for the composer — the conflict between three periods. With the resources of 1944 (for the ears of 1944), the composer had to encompass a musical atmosphere of the days of Queen Elizabeth and those of Henry V."[26]

Walton's solution was to rely on his own contemporary style, using an orchestra, abstract forms (including a passacaglia and a fugue), and sometimes distantly related key areas while remaining essentially tonal.[27] In the Globe Theatre setting we hear "pseudo-Elizabethan music"[28] — an originally composed cue by Walton not based on early music texts but emulating a sixteenth-century style.[29] He also integrated actual early music and folk songs into the score, and pieces from several time periods can be identified, including medieval plainchant (the "Te Deum"). Walton is concerned, however, not with accurately recreating performance practices of early music but with evoking a general impression of the time.

Christopher Palmer identified the borrowed music in the score, tracing it back to three main sources, namely *The Fitzwilliam Virginal Book*, a seventeenth-century collection of keyboard music and the source of "Rosa Solis" and "Watkin's Ale;"[30] the *Chants d'Auvergne*, a collection of French folk songs compiled, transcribed, and arranged by Joseph Canteloube, from which Walton used "Obal, dinlou Limouzi, " "Bailèro," and "L'Antouèno" for scenes set at the French court;[31] and fellow composer Ralph Vaughan Williams, who suggested using the sixteenth-century pieces "Reveillez-vous Piccars" and the "Agincourt Carol" (Vaughan Williams had himself used these pieces in earlier works, including in his own *Henry V*, a composition for brass band written between 1933 and 1934.)[32]

Alexander Nevsky, mentioned above, was also an important visual and aural model for Olivier's film, especially the Battle of Agincourt, as it was a source for some of the very few large-scale medieval battle scenes available on sound film at the time. Olivier studied it closely[33] and did not hesitate to give Eisenstein credit. In his autobiographical *Confessions of an Actor*, Olivier mentions that his (Olivier's) Agincourt battle scene "was littered with petty larcenies from our Master of All, Eisenstein."[34]

Walton may have also modeled some of his cues on the montage of music and images for *Nevsky*'s Battle on the Ice, which involved, in Walton's own words, "an unusually complex and close collaboration of sound and screen from one bar or visual movement to the next."[35] Among other approaches, the composer used the well-established technique, found in *Nevsky* but used earlier in classical music, of assigning musical themes to each side, then alternating or combining them to give an aural impression of battle.

Olivier's *Henry V* was an innovative work meant to help strengthen English morale, so it is no surprise that the Battle of Agincourt is the centerpiece of the film. Little screen time is given to the dead and dying after the battle, though there are two respectful, if brief, shots. But before discussing these shots, it will be helpful first to consider Branagh's later approach to the play.

Henry V was not filmed again until 1989. Funding was difficult to find, as many felt another version was not necessary. Kenneth Branagh recalled hearing the same thing everywhere he went: "People said, 'How dare you make this film? Who do you think you are? Don't you know there's another version with a rather remarkable actor?'"[36]

As we know, of course, Branagh did make the picture, with music by Patrick Doyle, and the film received mostly positive critical attention. *Henry V* was nominated for three Academy Awards and was a popular hit, as the director had hoped it would be. Making a pointed reference to

Olivier's overshadowing work, Branagh wrote that he wanted the film to be relevant and accessible to contemporary audiences: "The more I thought about it ... the more convinced I became that here was a play to be reclaimed from jingoism and its World War Two associations."[37]

Branagh had first played Henry V in the Royal Shakespeare Company production of 1984, which was powerfully influenced by the 1982 Falklands War. Branagh later formed his own Renaissance Theatre Company, and later, Renaissance Films. Patrick Doyle was music director for the theater company as well as an actor and composer, and he decided to approach Branagh about writing the music for the film *Henry V* during their first UK tour with *Hamlet* (he had previously worked as a composer with Branagh for a stage production of *Twelfth Night*).[38] After hearing some of Doyle's musical ideas formulated during rehearsals for the film, Branagh agreed to the collaboration.

These days it is important to remember that the earlier Olivier film was not "just" propaganda supporting a British war effort, nor was the Branagh film just a left-leaning film protesting another. With his stylized, even experimental approach, Olivier and his staff — many of whom came out of the theater, not the movie business — continually reminded viewers that they were watching a construction and that they were being quite deliberately steered toward particular interpretations. Branagh, on the other hand, harked back to a more old-fashioned, "realistic" style whose mark of success was that viewers became so absorbed in the story that they forgot it was a story and came away feeling they had just witnessed history itself taking place — rather like *Alexander Nevsky*, in fact (though one can argue that the twentieth-century-style score heard throughout *Nevsky* may have helped remind viewers they were watching a construct).

One's first impression on viewing *Henry V* is that Branagh seems determined to make a war film that refuses to glorify war. But as Graham Holderness has pointed out, labels like "post–Falklands film" can be deceptive: "post" does not necessarily mean "anti." He stresses that the "post–Falklands" stage play and the film may be "antiwar," but they also frequently display a fascination with war as a theater for human drama.[39] My own view is that Branagh's "fascination with war as theater" leads to mixed messages in his version of *Henry V*, and that this can be seen perhaps most clearly and powerfully in the combination of music and images in the postbattle scene.

Olivier's production had a profound, if negative, impact on Branagh's film — negative in that many of Branagh's choices, including musical ones, are deliberately the opposite of those informing Olivier's movie. Where Walton, for example, incorporated a good deal of early music into the earlier score, Branagh made it abundantly clear that embroideries upon medieval carols and plainchant were not for him:

> From my very first conversations with Pat Doyle I encouraged him to be as bold as possible. The film was taking what I believed to be legitimate historical license with costumes, sets and military detail. I wanted the musical approach to be equally uninhibited. I required no authentically "medieval" sounds; the score needed to be of our time, classically rich in tone but instantly accessible.[40]

Consequently, almost all of Doyle's music is in his own contemporary style. Except for a flashback scene with Falstaff, there is not so much as a peep from a recorder.

It is difficult to know just how much advice Olivier gave Walton concerning the music — the composer seems to have often worked independently and may have even orchestrated his own cues.[41] We know that Doyle, though, regularly consulted with the director. Branagh's desire to oversee the music was understandable: this was not only his own first directing effort, but Doyle's first film score. The composer emphasized accessibility over classical craftsmanship — though he produced, in his own words, "neatly rounded pieces that [can] ultimately stand on their own."[42] Doyle preferred to connect short, immediately understandable motifs and ideas into longer cues. Like many film composers, he described his approach as "operatic" — probably referring to his use of leitmotifs, recurring melodies or shorter figures assigned to represent people and events (these were used and described as a specific technique by Richard Wagner for his opera dramas). Incidentally, Doyle did not orchestrate his own cues. This was done by Lawrence Ashmore and was not necessarily a reflection on Doyle's musicianship, since even the most experienced and skilled film composers use orchestrators because of time constraints, and Doyle was also acting in the film.[43]

The Postbattle Scenes

The scenes immediately following the news of the English victory at Agincourt are crucial to both films, for they show how Henry responds to his victory, what the director thinks of the situations, and how audiences should respond. With Olivier, the victory is mostly positive, though the terrible loss of war is acknowledged with the brief shots of the dead. With Branagh, however, the message is mixed, with images and sound track giving conflicting impressions.

In Olivier's film, a particularly striking musical action occurs when Henry learns the battle is won. He says "Then call we this the field of Agincourt, fought on the day of Crispin Crispianus" (4.7.95). At this point we hear a stirring arrangement of the famous fifteenth-century "Agincourt Carol" which accompanies a shot of an English banner flying victoriously over the field (see Example 2).[44]

EXAMPLE 2. THE AGINCOURT CAROL

When Henry commands "Let there be sung *Non nobis*, and *Te Deum*" (4.8.128), which are Shakespeare's original music cues, Olivier's film then presents early music versions of these pieces: a polyphonic "Non nobis" followed by the plainchant "Te Deum."[45] During each work we see a shot of the dead on the battlefield, the chant especially setting a solemn tone, as though in a church. Nevertheless, it is still the Agincourt Carol and the victory it represents that viewers are encouraged to remember, for not only does Walton's powerful cue ring out at the conclusion of the battle, but the complete piece is repeated under the end titles, finishing the film as a whole on a note of triumph.

Branagh, on the other hand, expresses obviously mixed feelings about the battle: there is no glorious rendering of carols here. After commanding "Non nobis" and "Te Deum" to be sung, Henry picks up the dead body of a young boy, carrying it across the battlefield as the camera tracks along in one continuous shot. The shot is accompanied not by an excerpt of early music, but by a single, complete, originally composed setting of the "Non nobis," a theme and variations. There is no dialogue.

It is possible that the "Field of the Dead" scene from *Alexander Nevsky* mentioned earlier may have influenced Branagh's approach: as with *Nevsky*, we hear an entire musical piece, complete with vocalists, as we walk with Henry through another Field of the Dead. Here, too, we watch loved ones seeking the dead and dying as the music expresses intense emotion. But though the combination of images and music in *Henry V* is riveting, unlike *Nevsky*, it is highly conflicted.

The music, a song of praise to God, is joyous. It is set originally in B♭ major; we hear the full tune first as source music sung by a single soldier standing alone. The soldier is, in fact, Patrick Doyle himself, who is established visually as the originator of the piece, which he is also literally, being the composer.[46] A new element is added to the melody with each repeat, and by the second

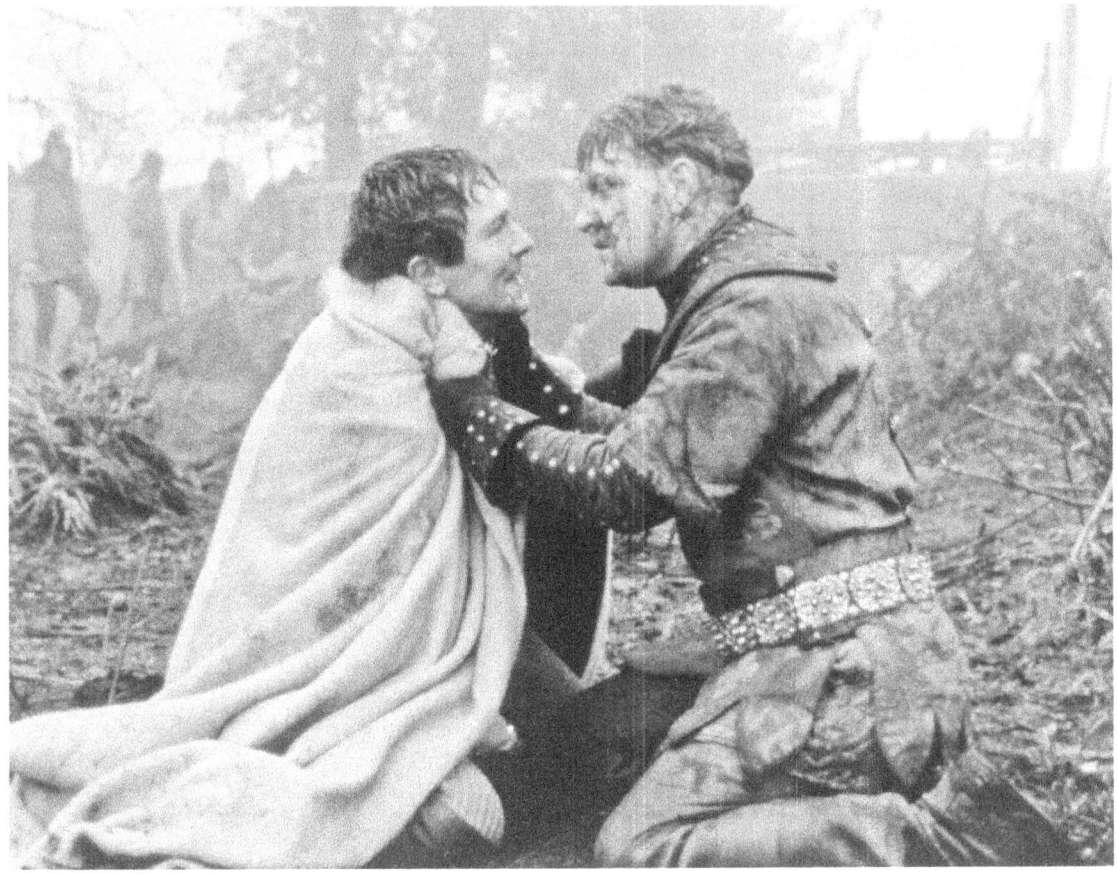

King Henry (Branagh) with the French herald (Christopher Ravenscroft) in *Henry V* (1989).

variation — when the strings enter — we know that this is no longer "just" source music. The music has become a more abstract background score as well, not only operating in the immediate present but projecting how the victory will be remembered by others.

The music and images are carefully coordinated, which was possible because — as Doyle recalled later — the music was prerecorded and played as the scene was shot (a technique known as "playback") in order to "instill as much emotional assistance and atmosphere as possible for the actors on the set."[47] Each time the melody repeats with a new musical element, a new action is shown visually: the camera changes panning speed or position, various people enter or leave the frame, and so forth. Table 1 describes the on-screen action that occurs with each variation of the melody:

TABLE 1. BREAKDOWN OF MUSIC AND VISUALS FOR "NON NOBIS" IN BRANAGH'S HENRY V

Music (theme and six variations)	Visuals
Theme in Bb major:	
(1) Solo male voice	One man sings. Henry begins to walk carrying body of boy
Variations:	
(2) Men's voices added, music becomes a more abstract, formal "choir"	Henry walks, camera pulls back and ahead of him

Field of the dead in Branagh's *Henry V* (1989). Boy (Christian Bale) with Fluellen (Ian Holm) and Gower (Danny Webb).

(3) Choir sings with strings added	Camera pulls back further, pans faster
(4) Upper voices sing countermelody	Pan slows, Henry walks on left side of frame
(5) Key change to F major, winds enter	Camera moves to face Henry, then up; Henry disappears from frame
(6) Full orchestra dominates, voices continue; trumpet obbligato	Camera pans to Exeter, slows when Henry appears. Henry begins walking

Interlude:

(6a) Orchestral interlude with trumpets (no voices), key modulations	Camera follows Henry to French herald. French women run to attack Henry, herald pulls them back; red puddle

Final variation in D major:

(7) Full orchestra and choir, with women's voices added	Henry sets body down beside tattered French flag. Close-up of Henry

End on plagal ("amen") cadence

There is almost too much going on here to catch in a single viewing. In one way, the scene serves as a visual summary of the king's life, bringing many of the important people in that life together in one place to greet Henry as he passes in his moment of glory. But in contrast to the joyous music, the images show the horror and tragedy of war: not only are the dead bodies of the French and English lying everywhere (nationality is not important to whose those who are dead), but there are also women robbing bodies and other women — presumably French widows, mothers, and sweethearts— angrily trying to mob Henry as he walks by, oblivious.[48] In an ironic touch that may not be accidental, women's voices enter the musical texture for the first time in the final, triumphant variation that begins soon after. Though we have just witnessed the angry despair of the French women, we may be hearing the joyous response of English women to the victory.

For the last musical variation, the audience sees a torn French banner lying on the ground, perhaps recalling the contrasting tattered English flag that fluttered bravely over Olivier's Agincourt. The music ends on a plagal cadence, the familiar "amen" cadence moving from the subdominant (IV) chord to the tonic (I) chord heard at the end of church hymns.[49] We seem to be hearing the end of a hymn — an inspiring conclusion, except that we are staring at Henry's anguished face.

This soul-searching is absorbing to watch and provocative in its implications: true to the production's "post–Falklands" origins, the scene provides a strong indictment of war. But the critical stance is considerably softened by the end titles. Here, for once, Branagh and Doyle do exactly what Olivier and Walton did: of all the cues available, they, too, use the large-scale, "positively-charged" music from the postbattle scene to end the film. In Branagh's case, a somewhat abridged and slightly subdued version is heard as the credits roll by. But there are no mixed messages in the concluding scene — only triumphant music without anguished visuals to contradict it.

Shakespeare himself chose to end the play with the wedding of the French princess Katherine to Henry, and in the tradition of happy movie endings, both Olivier and Branagh provide upbeat music through the final credits. Still, given Branagh's determination to rescue the play from Olivier's "World War II jingoism," it is a little odd to see the "antiwar" version end so similarly. But though this musical choice appears to draw the teeth from Branagh's critique, it also contrasts with — and therefore may heighten the effect of — the battle scenes and does most certainly offer a necessary respite from them. Like Shakespeare, both directors end the story on a happy note, which allows the viewer to come back to fight — and consider the issues of fighting — another day.

Notes

1. This essay is based on a paper given at the *Film and History* conference "War in Film, Television, and History," for the section "Heroes and Heroism in Medieval Films at War," Friday, November 12, 2004, Dallas/Fort Worth, Texas. I especially wish to thank Martha W. Driver and Sid Ray for their very helpful comments, information, and suggestions for the present text.

2. Prologue, 12–30, *The New Folger Library Shakespeare: Henry V*, ed. Barbara A. Mowat and Paul Werstine (New York: Washington Square Press, 1995), 7–8.

3. Michael Neill, "*Henry V*: A Modern Perspective," in *The New Folger Library Shakespeare: Henry V*, 253–254; see also Tanja Weiss, *Shakespeare on the Screen: Kenneth Branagh's Adaptations of Henry V, Much Ado about Nothing, and Hamlet* (New York: Peter Lang, 1999), 45.

4. Peter Ackroyd, *The Life of Thomas More* (New York: Anchor Books, 1998), 157–158.

5. William Shakespeare, *Henry V*, ed. G. Taylor (Oxford: Clarendon Press, 1982), 3.

6. Kenneth Branagh, *"Henry V" by William Shakespeare: Screenplay and Introduction* (New York: W. W. Norton, 1989), xiv.

7. Neill, "*Henry V*," 255.

8. *Ibid.*, 254–255. For further discussion of the views opposing Henry's within the play, see *ibid.*, 262–273.

9. Translation from *The Book of Common Prayer According to the Use of the Episcopal Church* (New York: Seabury Press, 1979), 757.

10. Translation from *Thesaurus Precum Latinarum*, copyrighted by Michael Martin. http://www.preces-latinae.org/thesaurus/Trinitas/TeDeum.html (May 15, 2006).

11. Some ascribe the chant to Niceta of Remesiana, but there is no general agreement on this. See Ruth Steiner, Keith Falconer, and John Caldwell, "Te Deum," *Grove Online*, ed. L. Macey. http://www.grove

music.com/shared/views/article.html?from=search&session_search_id=565523034&hitnum=1&section=music.27618 (February 19, 2007). See also H. T. Henry, "The Te Deum," The Catholic Encyclopedia. http://www.newadvent.org/cathen/14468c.htm (February 19, 2007).

12. See "Te Deum laudamus," *Hymnology*. http://www.smithcreekmusic.com/Hymnology/Latin.Hymnody/Te.Deum.html (January 22, 2007). For more about the 1549 *Book of Common Prayer*, see esp. John N. King, *English Reformation Literature: The Tudor Origins of the Protestant Tradition* (Princeton, NJ: Princeton University Press, 1982), 134–138.

13. See "Latin Vulgate, Book of Psalms," in *The ARTFL Project: Multilingual Bibles*. http://artfl.uchicago.edu/cgi-bin/philologic/getobject.pl?c.18:1:112.vulgate (February 19, 2007).

14. Richmond Noble, *Shakespeare's Biblical Knowledge* (New York: Macmillan, 1935), 80–81. See also William Shakespeare, *The Arden Shakespeare: Henry V*, ed. T. W. Craik, 332, n. 124 (New York: Routledge, 1995).

15. Noble, *Shakespeare's Biblical Knowledge*, 81; *Arden Shakespeare*, 332, n. 124.

16. For more information, see Kenneth S. Rothwell and Annabelle Henkin Melzer, *Shakespeare on Screen: An International Filmography and Videography* (New York and London: Neal-Schuman, 1990).

17. See Linda K. Schubert's article about Stothart's score for *Romeo and Juliet* in a forthcoming issue of *Journal of Film Music*.

18. The swashbuckling quality certainly includes the theme for Robin Hood himself, which was marked to be played "sweepingly" in Hugo Friedhofer's original orchestration of the opening titles music. See Fred Karlin, *Listening to the Movies: A Film Lover's Guide to Film Music* (New York: Schirmer Books, 1994), 93–99. The words of "Sumer is icumen in" are the most famous of Middle English lyrics, while the music to which they are set is the only known piece of six-part polyphony before the fifteenth century. The complete piece, about the coming of spring, is found in a monk's commonplace book originally compiled at Reading Abbey and now in the British Library (MS. Harley 978, fol. 11v). There has been some debate about the date of the work; musicologist now believe the music was composed around 1250, probably in Reading. As Burkholder points out, though the lyrics are in English, the music is far too complex to be folk or popular music — it was probably composed as "entertainment music intended to be performed by those learned in church polyphony." For the score and discussion, see J. Peter Burkholder and Claude V. Palisca, eds., *The Norton Anthology of Western Music*, 5th ed., vol. I (New York: W. W. Norton, 2006), 116–120.

19. "The temptation to make use of the actual music of the period was naturally great. But a brief acquaintance with Catholic 13th-century choral singing was enough to show that this music has in the past seven centuries become far too remote and emotionally alien to us to be able to stimulate the imagination of the present-day film spectator." Sergei Prokofiev, "Music for *Alexander Nevsky* (February 16, 1939)," in *Sergei Prokofiev: Materials, Articles, Interviews*, trans. Rose Prokofieva, compiled by Vladimir Blok (Moscow: Progress, 1978), 34.

20. Roger Manvell and John Huntley, *The Technique of Film Music*, revised and enlarged by Richard Arnell and Peter Day (New York: Focal Press, 1975), 93–107, 126–127; Stephen Lloyd, *William Walton: Muse of Fire* (Woodbridge, UK: Boydell Press, 2001); and also Susana Walton, *William Walton: Behind the Façade* (New York: Oxford University Press, 1988), 87–99.

21. According to Geduld, the film was dedicated at the time to the commandos and airborne troops of Great Britain — "the spirit of whose ancestors it has been humbly attempted to recapture." Quoted in Harry M. Geduld, *Filmguide to Henry V* (Bloomington: Indiana University Press, 1973), 2.

22. Christopher Palmer, "Notes," *Henry V* from "Sir William Walton's Film Music," vol. 3; Orchestra and Chorus of the Academy of St. Martin in the Fields; Sir Neville Marriner, conductor; Christopher Plummer, narrator. Chandos ABTD 1503, cassette recording, 1990.

23. Pilkington argues that Olivier did not see the film "as dealing primarily with war and violence." Ace G. Pilkington, *Screening Shakespeare from "Richard II" to "Henry V"* (Newark, NJ: University of Delaware Press, 1991), 102. But see Anthony Davies, *Filming Shakespeare's Plays* (Cambridge, UK: Cambridge University Press, 1988), 27. See also Laurence Olivier, *Confessions of an Actor* (New York: Simon & Schuster, 1982), 123.

24. The model is based on J. C. Visscher's early seventeenth-century map view of the city. Geduld, *Filmguide*, 23.

25. See Patrick J. Cook, "Medieval Hamlet in Performance," in this volume, 109, 114n35. The manuscript *Les Très Riches Heures du Duc de Berry* was started in 1409 and completed in 1478. Geduld reports that the original manuscript was in the Condé Museum in Chantilly, France, and was not accessible to Olivier and his art director Paul Sherriff in 1943, so the reproductions they used were probably the twelve calendar pages published in the art journal *Verve* 2, no. 7 (April–July 1940); Geduld, *Filmguide*, 18–19. See also Martha W. Driver's discussion of *Henry V*'s visual sources in Driver, "'We Band of Brothers': Rousing Speeches from *Robin Hood* to *Black Knight*," in *Medieval Cultural Studies: Essays in Honour of Stephen Knight*, ed. Ruth Evans, Helen Fulton, and David Matthews, 103 (Cardiff: University of Wales Press, 2006).

26. Hubert Clifford, "Walton's 'Henry V' Music," *Tempo* 9 (December 1944): 13–14.

27. A passacaglia is a musical genre from the Baroque period (1600–1750) consisting of variations occurring over a repeated bass line (sometimes called a "ground bass") or a repeated harmonic progression. The fugue, also associated with the Baroque era, is "a composition or section of a composition in imitative texture that is based on a single subject (theme) and begins with successive statements of the subject in voices." These definitions are taken from J. Peter Burkholder, Donald J. Grout, and Claude Palisca, *A History of Western Music*, 7th ed. (New York: W. W. Norton, 2006), A8, A14.

28. Graham Holderness, *Shakespeare Recycled* (New York: Harvester Wheatsheaf, 1992), 186.

29. Kennedy, however, has described this music as "a successful example of pastiche Byrd," possibly suggesting a basis in early music. Michael Kennedy, *Portrait of Walton* (New York: Oxford University Press, 1989), 125.

30. "Rosa Solis" by Giles Farnaby, no. CLXIII, in *The Fitzwilliam Virginal Book*, vol. 2, ed. Blanche Winogron, 148 (New York: Dover, 1979); "Watkin's Ale" (anonymous), no. CLXXX, in *Fitzwilliam Virginal Book*, vol. 2, 236. See also Linda Schubert, "Hearing Illusions: A Problem of Using Early Music in Period Films," in *Mittelalter-Sehnsucht? Proceedings of the Interdisciplinary Conference on Medieval Music Reception at the University of Heidelberg, April, 1998*, ed. Annette Kreutziger-Herr and Dorothea Redepenning, 57–70 (Kiel, Germany: Wissenschafts Verlag Vauk, 2000).

31. Palmer, "Notes." Canteloube's collection is published as Joseph Canteloube, compiler and harmonizer, *Chants d'Auvergne*, series one (Paris: Heugel, 1924), 20–21.

32. Vaughan Williams' *Henry V* was not published, however, until 1979. See Palmer, "Notes."

33. Bruce Eder, "Commentary Accompanying *Henry V*," *Henry V* (1944), Criterion edition, HEN030, DVD 1999.

34. Olivier, *Confessions*, 162.

35. Walton, quoted in Geduld, *Filmguide*, 23.

36. Kenneth Branagh, quoted in Jack Kroll, Review of *Henry V*, in *Newsweek*, November 20, 1989, 80; repr. *Film Review Annual 1990* (Englewood, NJ: Film Review Publications, 1990), 582.

37. Geoff Brown, Review of *Henry V*, *Monthly Film Bulletin*, October 1989, 302; repr. *Film Review Annual 1990*, 578.

38. Patrick Doyle, "Notes," *Henry V*, original soundtrack recording, EMI 4DS 49919 (1989) cassette; and Patrick Doyle interviewed in David Morgan, *Knowing the Score* (New York: HarperCollins, 2000), 41.

39. Holderness, *Shakespeare Recycled*, 201–210.

40. Kenneth Branagh, "Notes," *Henry V*, original soundtrack recording, EMI 4DS 49919 (1989) cassette.

41. Kennedy, *Portrait of Walton*, 125. The Internet Movie Database, however, cites Roy Douglas as the uncredited orchestrator. "Henry V," Internet Movie Database. http://www.imdb.com/title/tt0036910/fullcredits#cast (June 30, 2006).

42. See Doyle, "Notes."

43. Orchestrators assist composers in the film scoring process and serve in a variety of roles, ranging from writing out individual instrumental or vocal parts based on the composer's specific instructions to being the person who actually makes the main decisions about instrumentation. Composers normally have very little time to write a score once a film has been edited — if they have six weeks, they are fortunate. Under these circumstances, orchestrators provide invaluable support. From the 1930s to the 1950s and later, film composers often sketched out their music in the form of a piano score (two staves) and then wrote detailed notes alongside the music indicating what instruments should play. The orchestrator then took this material and fleshed out the parts so that each member of the ensemble had his or her own part to read from. Most of Hollywood's finest composers worked with orchestrators; in the 1930s, for example, Max Steiner and Erich Wolfgang Korngold at Warner Brothers regularly worked with orchestrator Hugo Friedhofer to get scores out on time. (Friedhofer himself was a fine composer, later winning an Academy Award for his score to *The Best Years of Our Lives* in 1946.) These days one cannot assume that a composer has been trained in the skill of orchestration, and in that case the orchestrator becomes even more essential to the process, literally deciding who plays what. However, because the orchestrator's duties vary so widely and the process and decisions involved in making a score are not public and therefore difficult to ascertain, one should never make assumptions about a composer's musicianship based only on the fact that an orchestrator worked on the score.

44. The tune as it appears here is in the key of D, the key in which it is heard an octave lower in the trailer for Olivier's film. See the trailer for *Henry V*, Internet Movie Database. http://imdb.com/title/tt0036910/trailers-screenplay-E12901-10-2. John Stevens describes a carol as a medieval song with an English or Latin text "of uniform stanzas beginning with a refrain called a 'burden' that is repeated after each stanza." The subjects tended to be about the Virgin Mary, saints, or Christmas. The Agincourt Carol, also called "Deo gracias Anglia" (No. 7 of Cambridge, Trinity College Library MS. 0.3.58, known as the "Trinity Roll"), is the earliest surviving carol with two burdens, one for soloists and one for a choir. Stevens points out that though the Agincourt Carol is popularly believed to have been sung on the battlefield, it is "an elaborate and sophis-

ticated piece of responsorial music"—music composed to alternate, as mentioned, between soloists and a chorus. He suggests that the work may have been performed by the Chapel Royal during the lavish civic reception given Henry V upon his return to London after the battle. See John Stevens and Dennis Libby, "Carol," *Grove Online*, ed. L. Macey. http://www.grovemusic.com/shared/views/article.html?from=search&session_search_id=1090034616&hitnum=3&section=music.04974 (February 19, 2007). Today one can still find the tune in church hymnals, such as *The Hymnal 1982* of the American Episcopal Church (New York: Church Hymnal Corporation, 1985), nos. 218 and 449. Here it is described simply as "*Deo gracias*, English ballad melody."

45. The "Non nobis" in the Olivier film is a canon, a multivoice work in which one musical line is strictly imitated by the others. The original composer is now disputed, though the piece was once misattributed to William Byrd. See Philip Brett, "Did Byrd Write 'Non Nobis, Domine'?" *Musical Times* 113, no. 1555 (September 1972): 855–857. There is essentially one plainchant melody for the *Te Deum*, with variants among sources. The chant sung in the Olivier film is very similar to a version published by the monks of Solesmes. See *Liber Brevior* (New York: Desclee, 1954), 540.

46. Doyle, quoted in Morgan, *Knowing the Score*, 45.

47. Ibid.

48. Medieval descriptions of the robbing of bodies on the battlefield offer a horrific picture. One such scene occurs near the end of Sir Thomas Malory's *Morte Darthur* after the last battle: "Then heard they people cry in the field. Now go thou, Sir Lucan, said the king, and do me to wit what betokens that noise in the field. So Sir Lucan departed, for he was grievously wounded in many places. And so as he yede, he saw and hearkened by the moonlight, how that pillers and robbers were come in to the field, to pill and to rob many a full noble knight of brooches, and beads, of many a good ring, and of many a rich jewel; and who that were not dead all out, there they slew them for their harness and their riches. When Sir Lucan understood this work, he came to the king as soon as he might, and told him all what he had heard and seen." Sir Thomas Malory, *Le Morte Darthur: Sir Thomas Malory's Book of King Arthur and of his Noble Knights of the Round Table*, vol. 2, book 21, chap. 4. Electronic Text Center, University of Virginia Library. http://etext.lib.virginia.edu/etcbin/toccer-new2?id=Mal2Mor.sgm&images=images/modeng&data=/texts/english/modeng/parsed&tag=public&part=256&division=div2 (February 23, 2007).

49. In traditional Western music theory and composition, each note in a scale is assigned a Roman numeral, a name, and a hierarchical status. The chord that can be built on each note also receives this number and status. For example: in the C major scale, the first note is C; the chord built on C (C, E, and G) is assigned the Roman numeral "I" and is called the "tonic" chord. It is the most important chord in the scale. The next most important is the note and its chord a fifth above C, namely G, and is the V chord, called "dominant." The next most important is the note and chord a fourth above C, namely F, which is the IV chord and called "subdominant." The other scale notes and chords are also assigned places in this system. The chordal movement V to I is traditionally considered the strongest ending, or "cadence," to a musical thought; IV to I is also quite strong and is often heard at the end of church hymns. The phrase "plagal cadence," referring to this IV-I movement, is an anachronistic holdover from the terminology of the Middle Ages, when a scale or "mode" (different from the major/minor scales of today) could take one of two forms, "authentic" or "plagal," depending on range and other factors.

Works Cited

Ackroyd, Peter. *The Life of Thomas More.* New York: Anchor Books, 1998.
The Book of Common Prayer According to the Use of the Episcopal Church. New York: Seabury Press, 1979.
Branagh, Kenneth. *"Henry V" by William Shakespeare: Screenplay and Introduction.* New York: W. W. Norton, 1989.
———. "Notes." *Henry V*, original soundtrack recording, EMI 4DS 49919 (1989) cassette.
Brett, Philip. "Did Byrd Write 'Non Nobis, Domine'?" *Musical Times* 113, no. 1555 (September 1972): 855–857.
Brown, Geoff. Review of *Henry V*. *Monthly Film Bulletin* (October 1989): 302; reprinted *Film Review Annual 1990*. Englewood, NJ: Film Review Publications, 1990, 578.
Burkholder, J. Peter, Donald J. Grout, and Claude Palisca. *A History of Western Music.* 7th ed. New York: W. W. Norton, 2006.
Burkholder, J. Peter, and Claude V. Palisca, eds. *The Norton Anthology of Western Music.* 5th ed., vol. 1. New York: W. W. Norton, 2006.
Canteloube, Joseph, compiler and harmonizer. *Chants d'Auvergne*, series one. Paris: Heugel, 1924.
Clifford, Hubert. "Walton's 'Henry V' Music." *Tempo* 9 (December 1944): 13–14.
Davies, Anthony. *Filming Shakespeare's Plays.* Cambridge, UK: Cambridge University Press, 1988.
Doyle, Patrick. "Notes." *Henry V*, original soundtrack recording, EMI 4DS 49919 (1989) cassette.

Driver, Martha W. "'We Band of Brothers': Rousing Speeches from *Robin Hood* to *Black Knight*." In *Medieval Cultural Studies: Essays in Honour of Stephen Knight*, edited by Ruth Evans, Helen Fulton, and David Matthews, 91–106. Cardiff: University of Wales Press, 2006.

Eder, Bruce. "Commentary Accompanying *Henry V.*" *Henry V* (1944). Criterion edition, HEN030, DVD 1999.

Edgerton, Ellen. "Non nobis, Domine." http://web.syr.edu/~ebedgert/pd/non-nobis.html (January 22, 2007).

Geduld, Harry M. *Filmguide to Henry V.* Bloomington: Indiana University Press, 1973.

Henderson, Diana E., ed. *A Concise Companion to Shakespeare on Screen.* Oxford: Blackwell, 2006.

Henry, H. T. "The Te Deum." *The Catholic Encyclopedia.* http://www.newadvent.org/cathen/14468c.htm (February 19, 2007).

Holderness, Graham. *Shakespeare Recycled.* New York: Harvester Wheatsheaf, 1992.

The Hymnal 1982 of the American Episcopal Church. New York: Church Hymnal Corporation, 1985.

Karlin, Fred. *Listening to the Movies: A Film Lover's Guide to Film Music.* New York: Schirmer Books, 1994.

Kennedy, Michael. *Portrait of Walton.* New York: Oxford University Press, 1989.

King, John N. *English Reformation Literature: The Tudor Origins of the Protestant Tradition.* Princeton, NJ: Princeton University Press, 1982.

Kroll, Jack. Review of *Henry V. Newsweek*, November 20, 1989, 80. Reprinted *Film Review Annual 1990.* Englewood, NJ: Film Review Publications, 1990, 582.

"Latin Vulgate, Book of Psalms." In *The ARTFL Project: Multilingual Bibles* http://artfl.uchicago.edu/cgi-bin/philologic/getobject.pl?c.18:1:112.vulgate (February 19, 2007).

Lloyd, Stephen. *William Walton: Muse of Fire.* Woodbridge, UK: Boydell Press, 2001.

Malory, Sir Thomas. *Le Morte Darthur: Sir Thomas Malory's Book of King Arthur and of his Noble Knights of the Round Table.* Vol. 2. Electronic Text Center, University of Virginia Library. http://etext.lib.virginia.edu/etcbin/toccer-new2?id=Mal2Mor.sgm&images=images/modeng&data=/texts/english/modeng/parsed&tag=public&part=256&division=div2 (February 23, 2007).

Manvell, Roger, and John Huntley. *The Technique of Film Music.* Revised and enlarged by Richard Arnell and Peter Day. New York: Focal Press, 1975.

Morgan, David. *Knowing the Score.* New York: HarperCollins, 2000.

Neill, Michael. "*Henry V*: A Modern Perspective." In *The New Folger Library Shakespeare: Henry V.* New York: Washington Square Press, 1995.

Noble, Richmond. *Shakespeare's Biblical Knowledge.* New York: Macmillan, 1935.

Olivier, Laurence. *Confessions of an Actor.* New York: Simon & Schuster, 1982.

Palmer, Christopher. "Notes." *Henry V* from "Sir William Walton's Film Music," vol. 3. Orchestra and Chorus of the Academy of St. Martin in the Fields; Sir Neville Marriner, conductor; Christopher Plummer, narrator. Chandos ABTD 1503, cassette recording, 1990.

Pilkington, Ace G. *Screening Shakespeare from "Richard II" to "Henry V."* Newark, NJ: University of Delaware Press, 1991.

Prokofiev, Sergei. "Music for *Alexander Nevsky* (February 16, 1939)." In *Sergei Prokofiev: Materials, Articles, Interviews*, translated by Rose Prokofieva, compiled by Vladimir Blok, 34. Moscow: Progress, 1978.

Rothwell, Kenneth S., and Annabelle Henkin Melzer. *Shakespeare on Screen: An International Filmography and Videography.* New York and London: Neal-Schuman Publishers, 1990.

Schubert, Linda. "Hearing Illusions: A Problem of Using Early Music in Period Films." In *Mittelalter-Sehnsucht? Proceedings of the Interdisciplinary Conference on Medieval Music Reception at the University of Heidelberg*, April 1998, edited by Annette Kreutziger-Herr and Dorothea Redepenning, 57–70. Kiel, Germany: Wissenschafts Verlag Vauk, 2000.

Shakespeare, William. *The Arden Shakespeare: Henry V.* Edited by T. W. Craik. New York: Routledge, 1995.

———. *The New Folger Library Shakespeare: Henry V.* Edited by Barbara A. Mowat and Paul Werstine. New York: Washington Square Press, 1995.

———. *Henry V.* Edited by G. Taylor. Oxford: Clarendon Press, 1982.

Solesmes, Monks, eds. *Liber Brevior.* New York: Desclee, 1954.

Steiner, Ruth, Keith Falconer, and John Caldwell. "Te Deum." *Grove Online.* Edited by L. Macey. http://www.grovemusic.com (February 19, 2007).

Stevens, John, and Dennis Libby, "Carol." *Grove Online.* Edited by L. Macey. http://www.grovemusic.com (February 22, 2007).

"The Te Deum." *Thesaurus Precum Latinarum.* Copyrighted by Michael Martin. http://www.preces-latinae.org/thesaurus/Trinitas/TeDeum.html (May 15, 2006).

"Te Deum laudamus." *Hymnology.* http://www.smithcreekmusic.com/Hymnology/Latin.Hymnody/Te.Deum.html (January 22, 2007).

Walton, Susana. *William Walton: Behind the Façade.* New York: Oxford University Press, 1988.

Weiss, Tanja. *Shakespeare on the Screen: Kenneth Branagh's Adaptations of Henry V, Much Ado about Nothing, and Hamlet.* New York: Peter Lang, 1999.
Winogron, Blanche, ed. *The Fitzwilliam Virginal Book.* Vol. 2. New York: Dover, 1979.

FILMOGRAPHY

1933 *The Private Life of Henry VIII,* d. Alexander Korda, music by Kurt Schroeder, with Charles Laughton. UK: London Films.
1935 *A Midsummer Night's Dream,* d. Max Reinhardt, music by Felix Mendelssohn, arranged by Erich Wolfgang Korngold, with James Cagney, Olivia de Havilland, Mickey Rooney. USA: Warner Brothers.
1936 *Romeo and Juliet,* d. George Cukor, music by Herbert Stothart, with Norma Shearer, Leslie Howard. USA: MGM.
1937 *Fire over England,* d. William K. Howard, music by Richard Addinsell, with Flora Robson, Laurence Olivier. UK: London Film/Pendennis.
1937 *The Prince and the Pauper,* d. William Keighley, music by Erich Wolfgang Korngold, with Errol Flynn. USA: Warner Brothers.
1938 *The Adventures of Robin Hood,* d. Michael Curtiz, music by Erich Wolfgang Korngold, with Errol Flynn, Olivia de Havilland. USA: Warner Brothers.
1938 *Alexander Nevsky,* d. Sergei Eisenstein, music by Sergei Prokofiev, with Nikolai Cherkasov. USSR: Mosfilm.
1944 *Henry V,* d. Laurence Olivier, music by William Walton, with Laurence Olivier. UK: Rank/Two Cities.
1989 *Henry V,* d. Kenneth Branagh, music by Patrick Doyle, with Kenneth Branagh. UK: Curzon/Renaissance Films.

Part II. "Carnal, Bloody, and Unnatural Acts": The Tragedies

Introduction to Part II

Martha W. Driver

> Would you lend me that "Macbeth"? I'd like to look it over tonight. I don't feel, somehow, as if I'd ever really read it.[1]

In "The Macbeth Murder Mystery," James Thurber tells of a comic encounter while on vacation in the Lake District with an American lady mystery buff who finds she has purchased a copy of *Macbeth* instead of the latest Agatha Christie; her analysis of the play's action ("'Oh Macduff did it, all right,' said the murder specialist. 'Hercule Poirot would have got him easily'") parodies the plots of British detective fiction, and the murderer is finally pegged as Lady Macbeth's (oddly elusive) father. Thurber's short story gives new insights into the resolution of the play that are humorously intended and rather more radical than any emendations in the dramatic productions under consideration here. Though *Macbeth* is reduced in this case to a formulaic murder mystery, the story illustrates the tendency to read our modern interests and concerns into Shakespeare, to make Shakespeare relevant to our own experience, which often enlarges rather than minimizes the scope of the plays.

In order to make Shakespeare's tragedies set in the Middle Ages meaningful to modern audiences, directors cut text, sometimes scrap medieval settings and recast medieval elements, opt in some famous cases for a film *noir* approach and in others for transposition of action and character to another time and place. However, a brief overview of a range of productions of Shakespeare's tragedies from the films of *Hamlet* by Laurence Oliver and *Macbeth* by Orson Welles (both 1948) to Michael Almereyda's *Hamlet* (2000) and recent stagings of *Macbeth* indicates that fragments of an older history informing the plays, as well as ideas about that history, are not entirely lost in translation.

Akira Kurosawa's *Throne of Blood* (*The Castle of the Spider's Web*, 1957), his version of *Macbeth*, and *Ran* (1985), his version of *King Lear*, are perhaps the most interesting in this regard. The action of Shakespeare's plays has been transposed to the samurai culture of feudal Japan. Both films are thoroughly Japanese in language, style and setting, yet both engage profoundly with the Shakespeare plays as retold through medieval Japanese history, samurai epic and Noh drama. Developed in the fourteenth century, Noh theater was patronized by samurai lords. It employs stylized performance, musical instruments (especially the flute), masks worn by actors, and stereotypes, such as the old man, wife, warrior, to teach moral lessons.[2] Informed by traditional Buddhist practice and belief, Noh drama examines causality across generations rather than looking specifically at how actions determine immediate outcomes.[3] This seems a distant world from Shakespeare's plays, but the shape of the dramatic action remains similar in Kurosawa's Japanese transpositions of Shakespearean sources. Like *Macbeth*, the action of which occurs in eleventh-century Scotland during a period of civil war, *Throne of Blood* has a medieval context; the plot is set sometime during Sengoku Jidai (the "Age of the Country at War"), a tumultuous hundred-year period, starting in 1477, characterized by murderous wars between rival clans.[4] The action of *Ran* also takes place during this period.

Interestingly, Nogami Teruyo, script supervisor for *Throne of Blood*, recalls that Kurosawa did not consult *Macbeth* "while shaping the story within Japan's organic, linguistic, and dramatic traditions," and in a 1985 interview discussing *Ran*, Kurosawa comments: "My original intention was not to make *King Lear* in Japanese. I told the story of Hidetora. And that was then, suddenly, the story of King Lear arose — and the two stories merged with each other, in a certain way that I can't even explain to myself."[5] Yet these two films, perfect in themselves and enjoyable on their own terms, are instantly recognizable as shaped by Kurosawa's reading of Shakespeare as well as by traditional Japanese influences; in both films, the director "negotiates the distance between reading and seeing, literature and performance."[6]

Asaji, the Lady Macbeth character in *Throne of Blood*, is shown as "highly conventionalized and shaped within the choreographic discipline of the Noh drama." Her face has been whitened to resemble a Noh mask, and her "'hand-washing scene' [is] wholly stylized within Noh conventions."[7] Kurosawa makes a direct connection between his Lady Macbeth and fate: through costuming and the white makeup, Asaji is visually connected to the eerie forest witch, a Japanese version of the future-telling weird sisters, "the strange, ambiguously gendered spirit in the forest, who spins her wheel and knows, perhaps even controls, the fates of vain and mortal men who 'end in fear.'"[8] With her still composure and ritualized gestures, Asaji may be the most frightening representation of Lady Macbeth to date.

Designer helmets and crown (with plaid) in Orson Welles's *Macbeth* (1948).

Olivier as *Hamlet*, wall and column paintings just visible (1948).

The daughters in *King Lear* have become in *Ran* sons of the self-destructive emperor Hidetora; the youngest, Saburo, is faithful to his father as Cordelia is, though, as in *Lear*, even the loyal child is destroyed. In this story, again set in feudal Japan, women act through the men, as Anthony Davies points out: "the most vicious action against Hidetora (the Lear figure) is motivated by the eldest son's wife, Kaede, through her husband."[9] Michael Wilmington, former film critic for the *Chicago*

Kaede (Mieko Harada) threatens to strike in *Ran*, dir. Akira Kurosawa (1985).

Tribune, comments that "*Ran*'s events are pitiless toward Saburo as they are toward everyone else, the wicked ... as well as the good," and in a 1985 interview, the director explains that the secret subject of *Ran* "is the threat of nuclear apocalypse."[10] Kurosawa's films are powerful Shakespeare adaptations, yet they were not "produced merely as acts of reverence to Shakespeare or as a means of enhancing the cultural value of film" but are rooted in Japanese tradition.[11] Moreover, they have become part of our thinking about Shakespeare's plays, making "Western scholarship more aware of the universal appeal of Shakespeare's dramatic material."[12] As Anthony Dawson so succinctly points out, Kurosawa's Shakespeare films are both "Unabashedly Japanese" and "profoundly Shakespearean." Dawson draws a parallel between Shakespeare's reading of his sources and Kurosawa's that is quite apt:

> Kurosawa, it might be said, reads Shakespeare rather as Shakespeare read some of his authors, Plutarch, Ovid, Chaucer; that is, not just for stories, as he did the chronicles or some of the pulp romances of his day, but from the inside, responding to the complex dynamics of the original work. At the same time, both filmmaker and playwright made their precursors' work their own, adapting it in relation to their own imaginative apprehensions as artists and linking it to contemporary cultural concerns.[13]

This linking of Shakespeare with contemporary interests is reflected on film as early as 1948 in Laurence Olivier's *Hamlet*, which was shot in black and white "as though it were a nineteen-forties mystery — what the French were just beginning to call film noir — edged in darkness and soaked in paranoia. At times, the camera seems nearly sick with emotion as it leads us through the narrative maze," a style of filming that also to some extent characterized Orson Welles's *Othello* (1952).[14] A more or less direct descendant of *noir* style informs Michael Almereyda's *Hamlet* (2000), deftly dissected by Douglas M. Lanier, who points to various *noir* elements in the film, including its

Macbeth/Taketoki Washizu (Toshiro Mifune) in Kurosawa's *Throne of Blood* (*The Castle of the Spider's Web*, 1957).

brooding atmosphere; its use of the city as a character; its images of an oppressive, urban nightworld of blue-lit neon, chrome, and asphalt; its emphasis on systematic corruption, surveillance, and violence behind a façade of benign normalcy; and its characterization of the protagonist as a fallen innocent who struggles against his own impotence, alienation, and complicity with the system he resists.[15]

Almereyda's consciousness of the manipulation of mass media by corporate interests motivates these emphatic choices in which *noir* has "become a powerful icon and model for the contemporary independent-film movement."[16] This Hamlet is pointedly self-reflexive, caught up with his memories and their meaning, shown brooding over his home videos, which "look at first like what Pierre Nora would call the 'sifted and sorted historical traces' of a lost past."[17] These traces include details of medieval paintings, which are also pinned to a board above Hamlet's desk, fragments of an historical past put together as a collage, not only pointing, perhaps, to the medieval sources of the play but indicating this twenty-first-century Hamlet's attempts to make meaning of history in relation to himself, to store and order his memories. As Thomas Cartelli and Katherine Rowe point out, "Hamlet's obsessive replays serve not to slow the rush of present into the past but to organize memory records for meditation and self-reflection."[18] This Hamlet seems to ask: Can history be found, stored, or simply replaced through adept manipulation of the media?

Almereyda's Hamlet is particularly haunted not only by his father's ghost but by ghosts of dead actors, dead relationships, old footage of dead soldiers; the term "ghost in the machine" seems to take on new meaning as the viewer considers Hamlet's attempts to become his own historian and archivist. In the original screenplay of Almereyda's film, Fortinbras is characterized,

Ethan Hawke broods as *Hamlet* in Michael Almereyda's 2000 film.

like Hamlet, as an indy filmmaker; at the play's climax, when Fortinbras speaks the play's last line ("Go, bid the soldiers shoot," 5.2.347), "his final act is to pull out his videocam and photograph the scene of carnage and the audience that has witnessed it."[19] The film ends, in fact, with the announcement of Fortinbras's ascension by real-life newscaster Robert MacNeil; the lines between fiction, reality, and the manipulation of historical memory by the media are once more shown as malleable.[20] This intelligent and playful staging is everywhere evident in Almereyda's brilliant reconceiving of *Hamlet* for contemporary viewers.

Video has recently come into use in Shakespearean theater as well. The production of *Macbeth* created at the Chichester Festival Theater in 2007, which starred Patrick Stewart in the leading role and had successful runs at London's Gielgud Theatre, Brooklyn Academy of Music, and on Broadway, was staged "in cinematic terms designed to establish a mood of dread as Macbeth and his wife bloody their hands in order to become rulers of an unruly state."[21] Reviewer Sam Marlowe in the London *Times* describes the "stark, creepily abattoir-environment that becomes flooded with resonances ... video imagery shows Soviet-style military parades, while a torture scene arrestingly suggests the videoing of kidnap victims."[22] This production employed a video and projection designer, Lorna Heavey, described in the playbill as a "Multi-disciplinary artist and filmmaker."[23] Her specialty is video for theater, and her work has appeared in productions of *The Tempest* for the Royal Shakespeare Company and *Phaedra* for the Donmar Warehouse and in set designs for *Titus Andronicus* for the Battersea Arts Center, among others. Her videos for *Macbeth* contribute to the atmosphere of anxiety and fear, emphasizing the relentless pacing and raw violence of the production, perhaps the only similarity to the version filmed in 1952 by Orson Welles, which has been described as "unrelenting, one long intensifying shriek."[24]

The productions under discussion here are enjoyable in their own right and retain an internal integrity no matter the setting or context, yet they remain recognizable as Shakespeare, who chose the Middle Ages as an Otherwhere, an alternative space in which to set his dramas as well as a resource for some of his greatest stories. The chapters that follow engage in a process of historical recovery, looking at some of Shakespeare's sources and their realization (or not) in the plays and in their representation in modern productions. Like Thurber's murder mystery fan — or theater and film directors, for that matter — scholars bring their own perspectives to these texts. Class in Shakespeare's *Romeo and Juliet* concerns Carl Grindley, while Sid Ray considers gender in one possible historical model and in later representations of Lady Macbeth. Patrick Cook closes this section with a discussion of national identity and its development in *Hamlet*.

NOTES

1. James Thurber, "The Macbeth Murder Mystery," in *My World and Welcome to It* (New York: Harcourt Brace, 1942; repr. 1969), 33–39, 37.
2. Stephen Prince, *The Warrior's Camera: The Cinema of Akira Kurosawa* (Princeton, NJ: Princeton University Press, 1991), 17–20, 34, 47–50; Anthony Davies, *Filming Shakespeare's Plays: The Adaptations of Laurence Olivier, Orson Welles, Peter Brook and Akira Kurosawa* (Cambridge, UK: Cambridge University Press, 1988), 153–154, 160, 164–166, 265–266, 185; Donald Keene, *Noh: The Classical Theatre of Japan* (Tokyo and Palo Alto, CA: Kodansha International; distrib. New York: Harper & Row, 1973).
3. Marsha Kinder, "Throne of Blood: A Morality Dance," *Literature Film Quarterly* 5, no. 4 (1977): 339–345. Davies, *Filming Shakespeare's Plays*, 153.
4. Prince, *Warrior's Camera*, 204–205, 284, 352.
5. Kiyoshi Watanabe, "Interview with Akira Kurosawa on *Ran*," *Positif* 296 (October 1985); repr. trans. from French by Dorna Khazeni in booklet accompanying *Ran: A Film by Akira Kurosawa*, DVD, The Criterion Collection, 2005.
6. Anthony Dawson, "Reading Kurosawa Reading Shakespeare," in *A Concise Companion to Shakespeare on Screen*, ed. Diana E. Henderson (Oxford: Blackwell, 2006), 155–175, 158.
7. Davies, *Filming Shakespeare's Plays*, 160.
8. Dawson, "Reading Kurosawa Reading Shakespeare," 167.
9. Davies, *Filming Shakespeare's Plays*, 152.
10. Michael Wilmington, "Apocalypse Song," in booklet accompanying *Ran: A Film by Akira Kurosawa*, DVD, The Criterion Collection, 2005, 6–9, 7 (both quotations in text appear on 7).
11. Deborah Cartmell, "Film as the New Shakespeare and Film on Shakespeare: Reversing the Shakespeare/Film Trajectory," *Literature Compass* 3, no. 5 (2006): 1150–1159, 1155.
12. Davies, *Filming Shakespeare's Plays*, 154.
13. Dawson, "Reading Kurosawa Reading Shakespeare," 172.
14. Claudia Roth Pierpont, "The Player Kings," *New Yorker*, November 19, 2007, 70–79, 74.
15. Douglas M. Lanier, "Shakescorp *Noir*," *Shakespeare Quarterly* 53, no. 2 (2002): 157–180, 169–170.
16. Ibid., 171.
17. Thomas Cartelli and Katherine Rowe, *New Wave Shakespeare on Screen* (Cambridge, UK: Polity Press, 2007), 60. For Pixelvision, the format in which Hamlet creates his media in Almereyda's film, see Peter S. Donaldson, "Hamlet among the Pixelvisionaries: Video Art, Authenticity, and 'Wisdom' in Almereyda's *Hamlet*," in *A Concise Companion to Shakespeare on Screen*, ed. Diana E. Henderson (Oxford: Blackwell, 2006), 216–237, 218–225.
18. Cartelli and Rowe, *New Wave Shakespeare*, 65.
19. Lanier, "Shakescorp *Noir*," 177.
20. Discussed by e-mail with Michael Almereyda (June 27, 2008), who kindly clarified for me the distinction between the published screenplay and the final film, which were blurred in my own memory of reading and seeing *Hamlet*.
21. Ray Bennett, "Patrick Stewart Gives 'Macbeth' New Life," Reuters UK/*Hollywood Reporter*, October 1, 2007: http://uk.reuters.com/article/entertainmentNews/idUKN0124949720071001 (May 15, 2008).
22. Sam Marlowe, "Macbeth," *The Times* (London), June 5, 2007: http://entertainment.timesonline.co.uk/tol/arts_and_entertainment/stage/theatre/article 1884152.ece (May 15, 2008).
23. "Who's Who," *Macbeth*, BAMbill, *Encore: The Performing Arts Magazine*, February 2008, n.p.
24. Pierpont, "Player Kings," 75.

WORKS CITED

Bennett, Ray. "Patrick Stewart Gives 'Macbeth' New Life." Reuters UK/*Hollywood Reporter*, October 1, 2007. http://uk.reuters.com/article/entertainmentNews/idUKN0124949720071001. (May 15, 2008).

Cartelli, Thomas, and Katherine Rowe. *New Wave Shakespeare on Screen*. Cambridge, UK: Polity Press, 2007.
Cartmell, Deborah. "Film as the New Shakespeare and Film on Shakespeare: Reversing the Shakespeare/Film Trajectory." *Literature Compass* 3, no. 5 (2006): 1150–1159.
Davies, Anthony. *Filming Shakespeare's Plays: The Adaptations of Laurence Olivier, Orson Welles, Peter Brook and Akira Kurosawa*. Cambridge, UK: Cambridge University Press, 1988.
Dawson, Anthony. "Reading Kurosawa Reading Shakespeare." In *A Concise Companion to Shakespeare on Screen*, ed. Diana E. Henderson, 155–175. Oxford: Blackwell, 2006.
Donaldson, Peter S. "Hamlet among the Pixelvisionaries: Video Art, Authenticity, and 'Wisdom' in Almereyda's *Hamlet*." In *A Concise Companion to Shakespeare on Screen*, ed. Diana E. Henderson, 216–237. Oxford: Blackwell, 2006.
Keene, Donald. *Noh: The Classical Theatre of Japan*. Tokyo and Palo Alto, CA: Kodansha International; distrib. New York: Harper & Row, 1973.
Kinder, Marsha. "Throne of Blood: A Morality Dance." *Literature Film Quarterly* 5.4 (1977): 339–345.
Lanier, Douglas M. "Shakescorp *Noir*." *Shakespeare Quarterly* 53, no. 2 (2002): 157–180.
Marlowe, Sam. "Macbeth." *The Times* (London), June 5, 2007. http://entertainment.timesonline.co.uk/tol/arts_and_entertainment/stage/theatre/article1884152.ece (May 15, 2008).
Pierpont, Claudia Roth. "The Player Kings." *New Yorker*, November 19, 2007, 70–79.
Prince, Stephen. *The Warrior's Camera: The Cinema of Akira Kurosawa*. Princeton, NJ: Princeton University Press, 1991.
Thurber, James. "The Macbeth Murder Mystery." In *My World and Welcome to It*, 33–39. New York: Harcourt Brace, 1942; reprint 1969.
Watanabe, Kiyoshi. "Interview with Akira Kurosawa on *Ran*." *Positif* 296 (October 1985); repr. trans. from French by Dorna Khazeni in booklet accompanying *Ran: A Film by Akira Kurosawa*. DVD. The Criterion Collection, 2005.
"Who's Who." *Macbeth*, BAMbill. *Encore: The Performing Arts Magazine*, February 2008.
Wilmington, Michael. "Apocalypse Song." In booklet accompanying *Ran: A Film by Akira Kurosawa*. DVD. The Criterion Collection, 2005.

Performances

1948 *Hamlet*, d. Laurence Olivier, with Olivier, Felix Aylmer, Stanley Holloway, Eileen Herlie, Jean Simmons. UK: Two Cities.
1948 *Macbeth*, d. Orson Welles, with Welles, Jeanette Nolan, Roddy McDowall. UK: Mercury Productions.
1952 *Othello*, d. Orson Welles, with Welles, Suzanne Cloutier. USA/UK: Mercury Productions.
1957 *Throne of Blood (The Castle of the Spider's Web)*, d. Akira Kurosawa, with Toshiro Mifune, Isuzu Yamada. Japan: Toho Productions.
1985 *Ran*, d. Akira Kurosawa, with Tatsuya Nakadai, Mieko Harada. Japan: Greenwich Film Productions.
2000 *Hamlet*, d. Michael Almereyda, with Ethan Hawke, Bill Murray, Sam Shepard, Julia Stiles. USA: Double A Films.
2007 *Macbeth*, d. Rupert Goold, with Patrick Stewart. Chichester Festival Theatre; London, Gielgud Theatre; New York, Brooklyn Academy of Music.

"We're Everyone You Depend On":
Filming Shakespeare's Peasants

Carl James Grindley

> "Remember this," Tyler said. "The people you're trying to step on, we're everyone you depend on. We're the people who do your laundry and cook your food and serve your dinner. We make your bed. We guard you while you're asleep. We drive the ambulances. We direct your call. We are cooks and taxi drivers and we know everything about you ... So don't fuck with us."[1]
> — Chuck Palahniuk, *Fight Club*

Shakespeare lived at the very close of the transition between the medieval and the modern and he wrote his plays during a time when, although the old feudal orders were incontestably moribund, the Elizabethan state and its aristocracy had not yet finished negotiating a new social order. Many of Shakespeare's plays navigate through these issues, and in particular, the plays with medieval settings frequently address social distinction and hierarchy. In this paper I examine this complex subject from a single perspective — the role of the medieval peasant — and I approach my topic through the study of a single play, *Romeo and Juliet*, as it moves from the stage to three specific filmed versions, Franco Zeffirelli's *Romeo and Juliet* (1968), Baz Luhrmann's *Romeo + Juliet* (1996), and John Madden's *Shakespeare in Love* (1998).

In general, there are three basic observations to be made: first, the role of the medieval peasant tends to contribute not to a definition of peasantry but rather to the characterization of a play's aristocrats; second, the peasantry is, on the whole, first shown to be dramatically impotent and then summarily discarded from the action; and third, the representation of peasants provides an opportunity for different aristocratic characters to assume new relationships and new power dynamics and to address more serious although subtle challenges to their authority from the rising merchant class. As Jerald Spotswood argues, "In leveling status distinctions among commoners and in denying individuality to them, Shakespeare both denigrates collective action and heightens the tragic individuality of elites, fashioning a world in which aristocratic values are privileged."[2] These subtle features, although present in Shakespeare's plays, become exaggerated when those plays are adapted for the screen and in many ways have left persistent legacies in our culture.

As more than a few have noted, Shakespeare's sympathies may be complex but they usually side with a noble (but responsible) aristocracy — usually at the expense of the peasantry[3] and certainly at the expense of the rising merchant class — an aristocracy usually sobered by the knowledge that "the sacred trust of feudal rule has been replaced by the modern state founded on an ethic of self-interest, calculation and betrayal."[4] Indeed, in those plays that are even remotely posited as representing historicized moments, Shakespeare was not only able to craft compelling dramas and fashion believable three-dimensional characters out of their historically distant antecedents but was also able to forward a wide variety of comments on the class dynamics of his own time through a multifaceted depiction of the collapse of the late-medieval social estates. Of these estates, the commoners most often find themselves locked in some of Shakespeare's most enigmatic dramatic spaces. Unfortunately, Shakespeare's themes are sometimes subject to significant dilution when presented on the stage or in other performative spaces; but although contemporary cinema has sometimes approached Shakespeare's peasantry with a significant level of disregard that borders on the critically oblivious, it has also made some extraordinarily complex statements on the subject.

One particularly useful way to observe this dynamic is to focus on the representation of servants in *Romeo and Juliet*. To this end, I look at four specific scenes: Romeo's and Benvolio's encounter with the illiterate Capulet servant (1.2); the servants discussing the Capulet feast (1.5); the stage direction calling for mob intervention in the first confrontation between Capulets and Montagues (1.1); and the general failure of Prince Escalus, as the play's premier aristocratic voice, to make an appropriate transition from feudal to Renaissance values.

At first glance, it does not seem too convenient to side with the play's Chorus and blame the familial and societal prolapse of *Romeo and Juliet* on an emotionally distant, unavoidable chain of fate — almost an Anglo-Saxon notion of *wyrd*— and attribute the outcome of the main action to an unknowable and impossibly distant prime mover. There are almost too many compellingly plausible factors that could be the one invariably leading to the Prince's final ironic sestet (a feeble attempt to bring resolution to a situation he has helped to create). Indeed, Jerry Weinberger provides an excellent list of the seemingly random events responsible for the tragedy:

> The sword thrust that kills Mercutio; the immediacy of Juliet's arranged wedding to the County Paris; Friar Laurence's carelessness in not telling Friar John that the letter to Romeo was important; Friar John's detention by the quarantine; Friar Laurence's slowness in getting to the tomb when he realizes that Romeo has not been informed of the plot; Romeo's failure to recognize Paris in the tomb; Romeo's suicide just moments before Juliet wakes up; Friar Laurence's further carelessness in abandoning her in the tomb. This air of fantastic chance is heightened by the play's frantic pace, which grounds the split-second accidents on which the tragedy depends.[5]

To this list I might add at least five other factors: first is Romeo's laudably inept understanding of the *stilnuovistic* poetics of Guido Guinizelli and Francesco Petrarca, which somehow manages to warp the young man's comprehension of the interplay of literature and life and leads him to fall in love — in the real world — with Rosaline, a would-be nun, and later the daughter of his family's mortal enemies. Romeo confuses the homosocial literary competition of the sonneteer, driven toward an anagogic understanding of salvation through the mechanism of an imaginary affair with an idealized blonde-haired beauty, with a world where real sleepless lovers attempt to have actual sex with the women who live across town (cf. 1.1.179–186 and 2.1.6–21).

Second is the virtually one-sided collision between Continental and English aesthetic values, a collision that Mercutio valiantly attempts to redress with comic verse (2.4.108) and an aversion to the latest in Continental swordplay (3.1.74). Mercutio never realizes for a moment that he is imprisoned in a thick armor of continentally-inspired verse and a thoroughly Continental plot — one that will, regardless of Mercutio's fate and similarity of intent, ultimately ridicule its young protagonists' relentlessly bourgeois formalized poetics.

Third is the image of the plague, an ever-present factor in Shakespeare's life, which is presumably responsible not only for delaying the critical missive from Friar Lawrence but also for carrying off Juliet's dead siblings.

Fourth is the nearly inescapably poisonous internecine politics of the historical Guelphs and Ghibellines, two groups who, as both Shakespeare and his audience would have known, continued to battle long after the deaths of the historical antecedents of Romeo and Juliet (the Montecchi and the Cappelletti, whose warring families were familiar enough to Dante for him to use as a symbol of Italian feuds in *Purgatorio* VI).[6]

Fifth, the play contains a hero and a heroine willing to make the "beast with two backs" after four hundred or so shared words, which indicates at the very least that the two young protagonists are prone to making extremely rash decisions without much regard for any possible consequences.

The play is riddled with potential causalities, including both the abstract and the concrete. Certainly, there is the notion that a mutual idolatry is to blame for the deaths of the protagonists, who seemingly worship one another to the exclusion of all else (2.2 *passim*), but there are also a destitute apothecary who knows full well that he is contributing to either a murder or a suicide, meddling servants who confuse Romeo and Juliet with their masters, and an almost satanically possessed friar who dabbles in alchemy, randomly and illegally performs Church sacraments, and hatches a plot so ludicrous as to stagger the imagination — at times, it almost seems as if Friar Lawrence must have *known* his scheme would fail. It is compellingly easy simply to give up and side with the Chorus: it was all written in the stars.

Romeo and Juliet is awash in book imagery. Paris is described as a book: "Read o'er the volume of young Paris' face, / And find delight writ there with beauty's pen" (1.3.82–83); Romeo "kisses by the book" (1.5.113), and so on.[7] But it is one servant's illiteracy that contributes to the movement of the plot. In 1.2.57–89, Romeo and Benvolio encounter an unlettered Capulet servant who, unable to understand his master's note, inadvertently requests assistance from the two Montagues:

> SERVANT: Go gi' go-den. I pray, sir, can you read?
> ROMEO: Ay, mine own fortune in my misery.
> SERVANT: Perhaps you have learned it without book. But, I pray, can you read anything you see?
> ROMEO: Ay, if I know the letters and the language.
> SERVANT: Ye say honestly. Rest you merry.
> ROMEO: Stay, fellow; I can read [57–63].

The scene is important in that it explains Romeo's attendance at the Capulet party and reinforces Romeo as typical sonnet-sequence lover. Following a simple enough request, at line 58, Romeo apes a Petrarchan conceit, speaking a paradox, in this case, fortune in misery. The Servant is having none of it, and as he prepares to take his leave, Romeo decides to give him a real answer.

Benvolio, playfully enough, suggests a homosocial ritual of comparing the relative merits of a variety of would-be sonnet ladies, but it is a task rejected by Romeo, who predictably decides to attend the party merely to be near his lady, Rosaline. Had the Servant known how to read, Romeo's attendance would have been doubtful and the tragedy could have been avoided.

For such an important dramatic moment, it is interesting to note its haphazard nature. The Servant, although illiterate, is not depicted as being in any way subservient. His responses to Romeo — at first playful and then resigned to apparent failure — although respectful, are not deferential. Although the Servant speaks formally, he is willing, after only two sarcastically answered questions, to give up good-naturedly and continue looking for assistance elsewhere. And although the Servant is able to identify Romeo as being Benvolio's social superior — and hence more likely to be literate — the Servant is also willing to pay Romeo's initial playfulness back with interest, for the Servant likewise offers Romeo three sarcastic replies before delivering a straight answer.

This servant figure, although not of Romeo's class and certainly subject to some social constraints, is not so low on the social ladder that he cannot reply saucily to two gentlemen. Neither Romeo nor Benvolio comment on the encounter as it occurs nor offer an autopsy of it after the scene has played out.[8] Nor does it seem from the Servant's remarks that his illiteracy is a matter of shame. The scene does not appear to argue for the increased literacy of the peasant class but instead presents a muted difference between the two classes. In the context of *Romeo and Juliet*, such a lack of distinction can be seen as problematic, similar to some of the conflicts arising in

The Merchant of Venice, which include "a disruption or blurring of distinctions between superior and inferior, master and subordinate, that the former in each pairing can only resolve through an appeal to radical differentiations of the kind to which the hierarchies of a class system respond."[9]

Thomas Moisan here argues that the aristocracy is able to resolve challenges to the social order only by reasserting some form of innate privilege and that any disruption to social boundaries is inherently dangerous. In *Romeo and Juliet,* this "blurring" of the social order also occurs in 1.5.1–17:

> FIRST SERVANT: Where's Potpan that he helps not to take away? He shift a trencher? he scrape a trencher!
> SECOND SERVANT: When good manners shall lie all in one or two men's hands, and they unwashed too, 'tis a foul thing.
> FIRST SERVANT: Away with the joint-stools, remove the court-cupboard, look to the plate. Good thou, save me a piece of marchpane; and, as thou lovest me, let the porter let in Susan Grindstone and Nell-Antony, and Potpan!
> SECOND SERVANT: Ay, boy, ready.
> FIRST SERVANT: You are looked for and called for, asked for and sought for, in the great chamber.
> SECOND SERVANT: We cannot be here and there too. Cheerly, boys! Be brisk awhile, and the longer liver take all.

In this scene, Capulets' servants simultaneously complain about their position as guardians, as it were, of the social graces, plan to save food for themselves, arrange to have women brought into the estate, and champion the merits of their own service. Initially, the Second Servant's lament that it is regrettable "when good manners shall lie all in one or two men's hands, and they unwashed too" (1.5.4–5) appears as if he is simply criticizing his comrades for being tardy when it comes to cleaning the plates and presenting new dishes. In addition to making his complaint, he is also implying that "good manners" are *not* in the hands of the Capulets themselves but are a function of those who serve them, thereby reinforcing the notion that the Capulets have a debased societal position. Likewise, the plans to secure the tastiest of treats—the marzipan of line 9—and arrange for the entry of women into the estate reveal that these servants have their own agenda which runs at best parallel to that of their masters. The servants' compact is good-natured, and solidarity is maintained among the staff, who apparently view their employers' demands with a fair bit of cynicism, as if service to the Capulets is more of an inconvenience to be overcome than anything else.

Seeing the Capulets and the Montagues as an inconvenience is par for the course in *Romeo and Juliet*—their inexplicable feud causes tremendous hardship for every single level of Verona's social hierarchy. The two families, at least to me, are not representative of aristocratic values but instead appear to be bourgeois intrusions into an older and rapidly disintegrating social order. They are not directly allied with the Prince and are therefore not of the ruling class. Escalus, for example, never addresses either family with a feudal title. The Capulets' servants describe their masters merely as "rich" (1.2.81), and according to the invitations to the party, most of the Capulet guests are referred to as "signior" (which Shakespeare used frequently as a nonspecific courtesy title in his Italian plays, giving it, for example, to Baptista in *The Taming of the Shrew*, Antonio in *The Merchant of Venice*, and Benedick in *Much Ado about Nothing*). There is nothing about the Capulets or the Montagues that is remarkable other than their wealth and shared hatred. That Escalus's family has sought an alliance with the Capulets could be attributed more to their wealth than to the desire of Paris and his family to associate with one of the principal parties in Verona's civil unrest.

The people of Verona certainly do not have much respect for either the Capulets or the Montagues, and as Weinberger points out:

> The people's interest is civil peace, not honor, dignity, virtue, or even justice—they take no sides in the quarrel between the houses. They are of course shocked by the deaths of the innocents, but they cry out the slain characters' Christian names, not their surnames with their reference to party interests.[10]

Weinberger further states that the Prince owes the people more than they owe him and argues that Escalus's role as keeper of the peace has been largely usurped by a makeshift "citizen militia."[11] This is illustrated particularly by the armed response to the initial brawl between representatives of the Montague and Capulet families in the first act, a particular dramatic moment that seems to have been important to both Shakespeare and his various editors and copyists. The stage direction and associated dialogue are fairly specific across the quartos and folios:

Q1: *They draw, to them enters Tybalt, they fight, to them the Prince, old Mountague, and his wife, old Capulet and his wife, and other Citizens and part them.*

Q2: *Enter three of foure Citizens with Clubs or partysons.*
   Offi. Clubs, Bils and Partisons, strike, beate them downe,
   Downe with the Capulets, downe with the Mountagues.

F1: *Enter three or foure Citizens with Clubs.*
   Offi. Clubs, Bils, and Partisons, strike, beat them down
   Downe with the Capulets, downe with the Mountagues.[12]

The scene is constructed to show spontaneous civic anger at the warring families, to ensure that the audience understands that the families are equally to blame, and to reinforce the notion that neither family is representative of Verona itself. If either the Montagues or the Capulets were aristocratic, the public would see them as being emblems of Verona — and this, I think, holds true even if the status of a royal house is under threat. In Arthurian mythology, for example, it is typical to link a sick land with an inept ruler, but no such relationship exists in *Romeo and Juliet* between the warring clans and the city. It is perhaps attractive to want to celebrate the civic-mindedness of the commoners in Verona, but that they are willing to take up arms seems to suggest that Escalus is not an effective prince and that commoners like Capulet and Montague must be stopped from taking the law into their own hands. Shakespeare is no fan of peasant uprisings— even though he may be sympathetic to their complaints. In *Romeo and Juliet*, the crisis of authority must be resolved from within by negotiating a new power structure with an upstart bourgeoisie.

To Spotswood, a Shakespearean mob scene usually comes undone, with the crowd being revealed as animalistic or impotent and the play's aristocrats— usually the central characters— being showcased for their inherent nobility, individuality, or tragedy. Paul Delany explains the broad class divisions in Shakespeare's plays by noting that Shakespeare "lived at a time when an uncertain balance had been struck in the transition from the feudal-aristocratic society of medieval England to the emergent bourgeois state."[13] Wayne Rebhorn, following a similar line of reasoning, remarks:

Aristocratic self-definition was of vital interest in Elizabethan culture and was in good measure the result of the dislocations caused by the social mobility and the ontological insecurity that mobility produced for Englishmen used to living in a seemingly immutable, intensely hierarchial [*sic*] society. Aristocratic identity was a problem, and writers responded to it with a vast outpouring of courtesy books, poetry, essays, and even epics.[14]

It is a commonplace that distinctions between the estates— especially when the estates are under outside threat — should be preserved and reinforced. Of the appearance of these class distinctions on the stage, Spotswood claims that "Renaissance drama reinforces symbolic boundaries between gentlemen and commoners, even as it reveals the performative aspects of both roles."[15] Shakespeare's mob is never the direct agent of dramatic resolution, but its aims can at times be satisfied.

Initially, Escalus reacts with words and little else. He offers a mild rebuke, one that, as Weinberger notes, was probably delivered on two other occasions, but he saves his more pointed words for private consultations offstage with the two families. Escalus is impotent to assert any public demonstration of will and, indeed, never gains any sort of agency. Shakespeare arguably used this conflict and Escalus's characterization to offer his usual nostalgic criticism of princely figures:

> An aristocratic protagonist ... undermined by a naïve confidence in the potency of his own magnanimous imaginings; becoming more histrionic as he loses touch with the realities of power.... This, then, is the basic mode in which Shakespeare apprehends the crisis of the aristocracy in his time and the decline of feudal-heroic values.[16]

A similar situation seems to exist in Mantua, where the Apothecary — a commerce-minded foil for Friar Lawrence, Verona's alchemical hobbyist — adamantly asserts the vigor of the city's laws. However, the Apothecary not only is willing to sell deadly poison to a complete stranger but also makes the exchange at a moment's notice, showing as little respect for civil authority as Lawrence shows for sound ecclesiastical practice.

As a tragedy by its very definition, *Romeo and Juliet* culminates in the death of its protagonists, and Weinberger — more optimistically than I do — reads its ending as a sort of hollow victory for the Prince and the people of Verona:

> In this Verona the people's interest is ultimately served by the sacrifices of the nobility, the deeds and sacrifices of the Prince, and the machinations of the priest. The play's outcome is certainly consistent with popular interests. The people want peace and quiet, and they get it at no cost to themselves.[17]

The play's ending seems forced, with Escalus resorting to poetic "histrionics" in an attempt to bring a false closure to the action. His final words, a sestet solution to the play's overall octave, are weak and fall into the same facile romanticizing that caused so much trouble for Romeo. Escalus still refuses to perform any public acts of justice or even to give judgment, preferring to single out a vague "some" between whom he cannot even distinguish. This is a portrait of a prince who, when confronted by a new social order, is unable to adapt. He can envision the obedience of the old social order but little else.

The three films of *Romeo and Juliet* present startlingly different approaches to the situations and themes raised in Shakespeare's play and range in their treatment of his work from the conventional to the contemporary to the analogue. Franco Zeffirelli's version is a costume drama, filmed on location in Italy, using actors who were close to the ages Shakespeare indicates for his characters. A creature of the late 1960s, Zeffirelli's work appears today to be slightly dated but is, nevertheless, a favored teaching resource. The film has been called both "melodramatic and linear" and focuses on the "impertinence and naivete" of the two central characters, sacrificing much of the play's other concerns to keep the spotlight on Romeo and Juliet.[18]

Baz Luhrmann's film is operatic and expansive, with wildly exaggerated acting, and features a seventeen-year-old Claire Danes opposite a twenty-one-year-old Leonardo DiCaprio — actors only slightly older than the characters described in the play. The film is controversial for some of its readings — in particular for casting Mercutio's Queen Mab speech as a paranoid drug reaction. Luhrmann moves the action to the present day and sets the conflict in "Verona Beach," California. This striking setting presents "an inner city gang culture with a bizarre blend of wealth and barbarism," according to Sarah L. Lorenz.[19] To her astute observation, I would add that Luhrmann has managed to translate the background gangsterism of the source conflict between the Guelphs and the Ghibellines into a believable modern equivalent.

John Madden's *Shakespeare in Love*, regardless of what the credits say, is primarily the work of Tom Stoppard, and Stoppard's familiarity with the material is apparent throughout the script; the writing is witty and knowing. Joseph Fiennes plays William Shakespeare (who stands in for Romeo), and Gwyneth Paltrow plays Viola de Lesseps (who stands in for Juliet). Stoppard relates Marc Norman's story of William Shakespeare's efforts to write *Romeo and Juliet* and does so in such a way that Shakespeare's experiences nearly mirror the events of his play.

With regard to the origins of Romeo's attendance at the Capulet party, Zeffirelli's version omits

Romeo (Leonardo DiCaprio) is transfixed in Baz Luhrman's *Romeo + Juliet* (1996).

the dialogue between the illiterate servant and Romeo altogether and leads the characters to the Capulet estate directly, relying on reordered dialogue from 1.4. Instead of offering an explanation of why the characters should be attending the party, Zeffirelli's script merely provides them with the necessary excuses should they be discovered. Although this change is a minor one, it does remove an instance of class conflict from the play and condenses the action (Zeffirelli is, after all, making a film and so is limited in the number of lines of dialogue he can include). More important, Zeffirelli's change removes Benvolio's comments on the nature of Romeo's love for Rosaline, thereby lessening the impact that Romeo's spontaneous change of affections might have on the suspension of disbelief. Romeo is no longer assuming a risk in attending the party in order to catch a stray glimpse of his beloved but is simply engaging in homosocial bonding with his friends.

Luhrmann, on the other hand, preserves Benvolio's teasing of Romeo and focuses on the Servant's illiteracy, turning the sequence into a moment of social commentary. Instead of using a street confrontation between Benvolio, Romeo, and a Capulet servant, Luhrmann has Benvolio and Romeo relaxing in a decrepit pool hall. During their game, a television program announces the Capulet party, with one newsreader announcing the party and the other reading the guest list. The use of the television is inspired commentary, and like the interactions between the Servant and Romeo in Shakespeare's version, the interaction between Romeo and Benvolio and the television passes without other comment. Like Zeffirelli, Luhrmann is also concerned to provide his characters with a plausible excuse for attending the party, and in the film's equivalent of 1.4, Mercutio provides each Montague with an invitation that reads "Mercutio and his friends."

Madden's *Shakespeare in Love* represents the furthest departure from Shakespeare's original but also preserves much of the original's intent. Stoppard's script introduces several competing Rosaline figures (a seamstress named Rosaline, the unseen Ann Hathaway, prostitutes named Black Sue, Fat Phoebe, and Aphrodite, and presumably a host of also unsuccessful candidates), thereby preserving Romeo's fickle nature as a failed Petrarchan lover who in this case is incapable of both love and poetry. The sequence also introduces its Romeo (Shakespeare) to its Juliet (Viola

Elite women in John Madden's *Shakespeare in Love* (1998). From left, Bridget McConnell, Judi Dench (Queen Elizabeth) and Georgie Glen. Courtesy of the Cinema Museum, London.

de Lesseps) by a serendipitous chain of events that includes Shakespeare's crashing a party to which he was not invited and having a confrontation with the film's Tybalt/Paris analogue, the Duke of Wessex (played by Colin Firth). The film even addresses the notion of the servant and the invitation but reverses expectations by having Shakespeare deliver a letter to one of Viola's servants.

Both the Zeffirelli and the Luhrmann versions cut the scene between the Capulet servants as they prepare for the party, although Luhrmann does provide a hint of their work by having Juliet's mother encounter the bustling servants at the start of 1.3. Self-centeredly, she bypasses her servants in order to talk to Juliet about marriage. Madden's film, on the other hand, although not preserving the original scene, does provide a close analogue. Shakespeare, on entering the de Lesseps estate, finds his way into the great hall with a group of hired musicians. At the de Lesseps's party, Shakespeare takes an hors d'oeuvres from a passing tray and is berated: "Musicians don't eat ... Sir Robert's orders."[20] Of the three versions, Madden's is the only version to feature at least a hint of the social conflict between classes at this point in the story.

The ongoing attempts of the citizens of Verona to intervene in the affairs of the Capulets and the Montagues are muted in Zeffirelli, more or less respected if not exaggerated by Luhrmann, and handled with great subtlety by Madden. Zeffirelli preserves the general tone of the scene by showing the effects that the brawl has on the ordinary citizens of Verona: they run for their lives as the town square is reduced to chaos. Women scream, carrying their children; shopkeepers' stands are overturned; and some citizens seem to be at least trying to impede the battle by hurling garbage and debris at the combatants (although it is not entirely clear if these figures could be simply minor members of either family). The Officer's part is cut, including his lines advising the citizens to take up arms against both sides. No citizen militia materializes with poleaxes and clubs. When the Prince arrives, it is on horseback with armed knights—in the original play, there

Peasant girls selling wares, *Shakespeare in Love*, dir. John Madden (1998). Courtesy of the Cinema Museum, London.

is merely a vague stage direction calling for a "train." In Zeffirelli, similar to what we have already seen, the role played by Verona's commoners is also cut: Zeffirelli's interests focus primarily on the play's two lovers and little else. Likewise, as far as the play's other great peasant intervention is concerned — when Benvolio is seized by the mob at 3.1.142–143 — Zeffirelli has chosen to omit the scene but has not done so to save screen time, for he has transferred the action to a sequence showing both the Capulets and the Montagues carrying the dead to the Prince in an attempt to seek justice.

The destruction caused to the citizens of Verona in the initial confrontation between the Capulets and the Montagues is preserved and somewhat elaborated upon in Luhrmann's film. Verona is portrayed as being rundown and poverty-stricken, with only the Capulets and the Montagues possessing any overt wealth. The film commences with the prologue being delivered via a television news story, which then cuts to show images of the burning city and newspaper and magazine headlines.[21] The opening battle occurs at a gas station, which is set ablaze during the near-riot. During the fight, Tybalt points his gun at a child's face. Other commoners are shown as being in harm's way. Innocent bystanders attempt to bring the two parties under control, but their efforts are limited to one old woman beating Sampson on the head with her handbag while he attempts to use her car door as a shield. When the authorities do arrive, it is by air, and the attempt to bring order to the city includes mass arrests and police snipers shooting from helicopters. Although the Officer and his line advising mob justice are once again cut, Luhrmann's film is far more interested in the civic effects of the dispute between the Capulets and the Montagues than Zeffirelli's version and more forcefully depicts the psychological and physical effects that the disorder has on the city.

Similarly, although the scene showing Benvolio's arrest does not appear in Luhrmann's film, its aftermath does, and Benvolio is shown handcuffed in the back of a police car, literally surrounded by the city's police force. Luhrmann presents neither the Capulets nor the Montagues as aristocratic and instead preserves some of the play's more interesting class commentary, showing the two families as members of a powerful merchant class. The film does, however, clearly link Escalus's character with the commoners, which, as we have seen, is not quite the case in Shakespeare's text. The Prince in Luhrmann's version is the Chief of Police, who is not a member of the aristocracy—unlike this film's Paris, who is the son of the state's governor. Chief Prince, at least in terms of our world, must himself be a commoner, a conflation of the Officer and the Prince in *Romeo and Juliet*.

Although Madden does not present an opening conflict of the sort where intervention by a citizen militia would make dramatic sense, he does outline the power dynamics of Stoppard's script in a way that is both clear and complex. As an aside, it is interesting to note that 3.1.139–143, the Citizen's and the Prince's interrogation of Benvolio following Tybalt's death, has the potential to be presented three times in *Shakespeare in Love*, twice in reasonably distant analogues—once concerning a conflict between Burbage and Shakespeare and once concerning a conflict between Wessex and Shakespeare—but also during the final staged performance of *Romeo and Juliet*. In the first analogue, the conflict is resolved without intervention from the authorities—indeed, in this internecine theatrical dispute, witnesses initially confuse the fight with a scripted one. In the second analogue, the role of public arrest is performed twice. In this first instance, the arresting statement is delivered by Shakespeare, who, having subdued Wessex at the point of a broken stage sword, proclaims: "This is the murderer of Kit Marlowe."[22] The second arrest is made by the Master of Revels' guards, and the playhouse is closed for the indecency of having a woman on stage. Finally, when the play itself is acted, although 3.1.139–143 does not appear on screen, it can be heard offstage. These repetitions explore different possibilities for governance but interestingly refuse to choose one form as superior to any other and instead draw out the problems with each style of intervention—whether by mob, personal justice, or through the agency of the Crown.

As far as a more general discussion of the political landscape of *Romeo and Juliet* is concerned, of the three filmed versions, only Madden's draws a clear line between Escalus, the Capulets and Montagues, and the commoners. The action opens with a vision of Elizabethan London as a vibrant hub of commerce commingled with the residue of fifteen hundred years of history. The streets are filled with commoners, and although the city is dirty and chaotic, it is not impoverished but appears to represent a healthy state. The conflicts that rage occur, as they do in Luhrmann, entirely between various factions of the newly minted urban bourgeoisie—as Stoppard's nurse claims: "well-monied is the same as well-born."[23] The Rose's impresario, Philip Henslowe, is in conflict with a moneylender, Hugh Fennyman. Shakespeare competes, albeit ineptly, with Kit Marlowe. The de Lesseps compete with the preexisting class system and attempt through marriage to align themselves with the bankrupt but titled Duke of Wessex—the one character who is most direct about his motivations. When Sir Robert says of Viola, "She is a beauty, my lord, as would take a king to church for a dowry of a nutmeg," Wessex replies, "My plantations in Virginia are not mortgaged for a nutmeg. I have an ancient name that will bring you preferment when your grandson is a Wessex."[24]

Observing these conflicts are two forces both at least vaguely invested in the possible outcomes: the commoners of London and the monarchy. At the start of the film, the story's commoners are comprised of two competing subsets. One subset is the traditional stock of England, in this case seemingly cribbed from Shakespeare's Second Tetralogy: the denizens of London's underbelly of alehouses, brothels, and playhouses. The second subset is comprised of more dangerous forces, ones who wish to subvert the current political system for their own ambitions. This group is embodied in *Shakespeare in Love* by Makepeace the Puritan preacher, a figure who campaigns aggressively against the theater: "The players breed lewdness in your wives, rebellion in your servants, idleness in your apprentices and wickedness in your children."[25] The irony of Makepeace's name is completely in keeping with *Romeo and Juliet's* initial instinct toward peasant rebellion, the historicity of such an impulse tempered in Stoppard's script by the knowledge that Makepeace's ideology will one day at least temporarily succeed. Makepeace's hatred of the theater presents a clear challenge to the Queen's will — as she is portrayed throughout the script as a supporter of the dramatic arts.

Balanced against the commoners is the monarchy. Like the commons, the forces that support and comprise the monarchy lack a sense of political harmony. Part of the machine of state is still invested in the absolute rule of the old feudal system, where privilege comes from name. Wessex may have already come to the conclusion that his world has changed, but the Master of the Revels, Tilney, has not. Tilney is an important character in that he is able to interpret the will of the Crown seemingly without constraint. Tilney initially seems inadvertently sympathetic to Makepeace's politics, but his motivations merely run in parallel. Tilney is obsessed with personal power, opening and closing the playhouses not only on grounds of morality but also to guarantee himself sexual access to Burbage's seamstress. The Queen, on the other hand, does not have a secure grip on her subjects. Granted, she has the goodwill of the general population, but her rule is threatened not only by Makepeace but also by Tilney's abuses and the changing world represented by the play's other conflicts. Before the end of the drama, she has to fashion a relationship with the new middle class, reassert control over her traditional aristocratic power base, and maintain order in her kingdom.

Of the three films, Zeffirelli's work presents a vision of the text where Shakespeare's commoners have been almost completely silenced, the play's political meaning abridged, and its action more or less reduced to a parenthetical romantic exemplum written into the middle of an incomplete sonnet. Indeed, as far as dramatic resolution is concerned, the film's final scene is greatly truncated. Instead of a general crowd of miscellaneous figures, the scene is populated entirely by Capulets and Montagues, who take up the whole of the public square outside the Prince's palace. Gone are the consolatory gestures shared by the Capulets and the Montagues, and absent, too, are the Prince's attempts to determine any causalities behind the disaster and the Friar's self-serving and long-winded explanation. Likewise, Escalus's final lines have been awarded to Laurence Olivier's narrator, who provides a voice-over as the film ends. In Zeffirelli, the blood feud offers little final resolution, and the drama focuses entirely on Romeo and Juliet. The Prince, never leaving the liminal space of the palace threshold, is seemingly lost in thought, unable to comprehend the tragedy that has transpired. His final act is to abandon his subjects symbolically as he turns and walks away into the gloom. It seems as though Escalus has learned little and the feud will continue to fester.

Luhrmann, oddly enough, structures 5.3 almost exactly the same as Zeffirelli did thirty years earlier, using almost the same choice of lines — he too, for example, awards the Prince's sestet to the Chorus (a television newsreader), but he does not omit lines 308–309, as Zeffirelli does, and in retaining them, Luhrmann provides an intact sestet. Like Zeffirelli, Luhrmann denies his Montagues and Capulets any attempt at reconciliation, but unlike Zeffirelli, the play's conclusion is populated by the full spectrum of Verona's citizens: Capulets, Montagues, the police, and the general public. Instead of walking into his palace — the analogue here being the police headquarters, which, by necessity, is a far more public space — the Prince walks out into the public square. He turns his back on the Capulets and Montagues and walks toward his people. Although the two films use similar dialogue, the emphasis of the scene in the latter case moves away from the central story of tragic love to take up Luhrmann's theme of the damage the feud has caused to the larger society. Luhrmann's Prince may have learned some lessons but also seemingly has recognized his absolute powerlessness in the face of a new order. This is a prince who will probably establish order not through a new compact with the various competing forces in Verona but through brute force.

The one version of *Romeo and Juliet* that most closely reflects Shakespeare's political subtext is Madden's *Shakespeare in Love*. Like the scene of Benvolio's arrest, the play's conclusion is performed twice: once on stage in the internal *Romeo and Juliet*, and once in the story's main plot. The onstage *Romeo and Juliet* is concluded by the Prince, but the part is played by the same actor who plays the Chorus—the roles noted in Stoppard's script. The role of the Chorus/Escalus is played for the stage by Wabash, Henslowe's stuttering tailor, who wears the same costume for both roles. Wabash is the one of two characters in *Shakespeare in Love* who is capable of provoking astonishment in Shakespeare (the other being the seemingly base moneylender Fennyman, who likewise reveals himself as having considerable emotional depth and significant acting talent). Wabash, who has only been seen stuttering pathetically, is undeniably brilliant on stage and delivers his lines on the stage's apron, successfully mediating the landscape between the other actors and the audience. His character straddles a middle position; on the one hand, he is by class a commoner, but on the other, he is filled with an internal nobility. In this regard, Wabash shares much with Shakespeare's commoners as seen in other plays, for example, the rustics in *A Midsummer Night's Dream* and Dogberry and his men in *Much Ado about Nothing*.

On stage with Wabash during the final speech are Juliet's parents and Romeo's father, as well as the corpses of Paris, Romeo, and Juliet. Unlike in Zeffirelli's and Luhrmann's versions, the scene is set at the Capulet tomb. At first glance, the onstage version is more intimate and cut off from the population of Verona than in Zeffirelli's and Luhrmann's versions, except that the immediacy of the play's audience creates the illusion of a totalizing public space, making it more rather than less effective. This is a Prince who has become sadder and wiser, and instead of walking either into the crowd or offstage, he freezes the play's action by bowing. It is as if the Prince has assumed the ultimate authority in the play, for he both introduces and ends its action.

In the main plot of *Shakespeare in Love*, the Prince figure, Queen Elizabeth, is able to renegotiate her regnal position forcefully while at the same time satisfying all of her subjects, both her traditional base and the newer elements of her society. In particular, she is able to reward each of them, specifically Wessex, Shakespeare, Tilney, and Makepeace, according to his deserts. Wessex is humbled by his experiences. Previously, and although his social position carries with it a formal relationship to the Crown requiring him to obtain royal consent prior to marriage, his status has given him an attitude of entitlement that carries over even into his relationship with his intended bride. He not only describes himself as her "six day lord and master"[26] and tells Shakespeare that she is "my property,"[27] but announces their engagement by saying: "Your father should keep you better informed. He has bought me for you. He returns from his estates to see us married two weeks from Saturday.... You are allowed to show your pleasure."[28]

When Viola objects that she does not love him, Wessex appears to be baffled, and testily responds: "How your mind hops about! Your father was a shopkeeper, your children will bear arms, and I will recover my fortune. That is the only matter under discussion today. You will like Virginia."[29] Wessex understands that Viola's father wants the social capital that can be obtained only by aligning his family of wealthy commoners with an ancient but bankrupt aristocratic family—his grandchildren will be heirs to both the prestige inherent in the Wessex dukedom and the power provided by the de Lesseps's fortune.

Wessex spends the majority of *Shakespeare in Love* relying on his physical power but also watching it slowly erode. When he originally arrives at the de Lesseps estate, he rides through a crowd of musicians, scattering them like leaves, secure in his hereditary position. He accosts Shakespeare at knifepoint and promises a later revenge.[30] Early in their relationship, Viola warns Shakespeare that Wessex will kill him if they are to duel,[31] but contrary to her warning, Wessex's power continues to subside. By the time he confronts Shakespeare, the two are on equal footing, and Shakespeare is able to overpower Wessex. Eventually, Wessex is reduced to a virtual public cuckold, forced to watch his wife repeatedly kiss Shakespeare and then forced to pay the playwright fifty pounds for the honor.

The only way that Wessex manages to retain any dignity is to remember his ties to the Crown. He mistakenly believes that he can be purchased by Viola's family and lend his ancient name to the merchant class without any inherent loss of prestige, but the film makes it clear that as the middle class buys into Wessex, he buys into them. Queen Elizabeth is able to set the matters straight, restore Wessex's wife to him, provide him with some face-saving comments, and give him the opportunity to exit London safely.

The Queen's intervention also allows Shakespeare a new position in her kingdom. One of the story's main concerns has been the quest — mirrored in the historical record — that Shakespeare undertook to "gentle his condition." In *Shakespeare in Love*, this quest focuses on leaving the ranks of hired actor or hired playwright and purchasing a stake in a theater company — on becoming a gentleman of property.

The Queen has been savvy enough to recognize that in the new political landscape, her dim-witted "gaggle" of courtiers—favored members of ancient families— offers her less than they used to. Instead, she is able to grant Shakespeare a type of legitimacy that he could never obtain strictly through commerce. She is able to commission a play from him, and her status transfers to him in the process; but at the same time her public recognition of Shakespeare's gift also increases her prestige, and, aware of the new landscape, she publicly shames her courtiers as she leaves the film.

Elizabeth, both in *Shakespeare in Love* and in the historical record, understood the usefulness of public spectacle and entertainment — provided the subject matter was controlled. As long as the greater public is kept placated, it will be less likely to rebel. The Queen makes it clear that open theaters are important to her reign when she publicly decides that Shakespeare has won his wager with Wessex, inviting Shakespeare by name into her world at Greenwich. The commoners in essence get a glimpse of a possible future meritocracy, one based on sheer ability and political agility and one that can make aristocrats out of the worthy.

Shakespeare in Love is not *Romeo and Juliet*. In many ways, Stoppard's script and Madden's film are the play's antithesis. The film invokes a world where civic unrest is successfully curtailed, where Rosaline is not unseen "baggage"[33] but a figure aggressively sought by three of the major characters, where no one dies, where its dual Romeo and Juliet figures achieve immortality, and where its monarch triumphs, managing through shrewd governance to reconcile all of her subjects with one another. But the film also includes fragments of the play *Romeo and Juliet*, presenting Shakespeare's text as moving tragedy, with many seemingly hard-hearted characters "openly weeping," and "involuntarily" responding to its drama.[34]

Throughout his plays, Shakespeare used a variety of mostly undifferentiated commoners and peasants to fill a number of important dramatic roles—for example, it is impossible to envision the First and Second Tetralogy or *Coriolanus* or *Midsummer Night's Dream* without their assortment of peasants, commoners, thieves, drunkards, and bumbling rustics. Consequently, Shakespeare, generally speaking, established some conventions for these parts, and his "base, common and popular" characters behave with a certain degree of consistency.

These characters are usually distanced from his more aristocratic characters— sometimes linguistically through differences in formal versus informal pronouns and grammar, sometimes through being dramatically segregated to their own scenes or subscenes, and sometimes through the physical space of their own locations— and are kept that way, sometimes, as is the case at the close of the Second Tetralogy, by violent means. Further, Shakespeare's peasants often find themselves in curious dramatic spaces, cut off from the greater action, often mimicking or aping the larger dramas around them. The rustics in *Midsummer Night's Dream* provide a duplicate plot, as do the players in *Hamlet*, whereas Pistol's progress through *Henry V* provides the picaresque mirror of Henry's growth.

Although his more base characters are used to present social commentary, Shakespeare's peasants do not have much agency. Although their concerns are usually addressed, it is not by them. Other forces act to bring resolution to the types of crises that affect the general public. Shakespeare, for obvious reasons, can never be seen as advocating a revolution or uprising. Even with these caveats, however, it is an error to minimize these roles — after all, without the players, Hamlet has no plan.

The commoners in *Romeo and Juliet* are indelibly keyed into the play's overall concern with good governance and the end of feudal rule. Without their common good in mind, Escalus's reaction to the tragedy would lack dramatic motivation — and, presumably, he would only be moved to take revenge on both the Capulets and the Montagues for the deaths of Mercutio and Paris. Likewise, his seeming lack of concern for the public earlier in the play — who have suffered through two unseen public brawls even before the events of the stage unfold — practically guarantees that his "brace of kinsmen" will end up in their graves. The poor behavior of the Capulets and the Montagues is of course noticed by the townspeople, who at least hint at revolt, and eventually it becomes clear to the Prince that he should have acted. The commoners similarly are part of Verona's greater existence, and they perform many of the roles and have many of the concerns echoed by Tyler Durden in *Fight Club*.

Fight Club's peasant revolt, like the one in *Henry VI*, is brutally suppressed and its leader eliminated, but the points made by Tyler and his associates are nevertheless valid. Powerful elites abuse their privileges, and the working class is extremely dissatisfied. Likewise, Shakespeare understood the political concerns of the commoners, and although his plays usually present purely aristocratic solutions or cynical laments, the peasants and their concerns are at least addressed.

With this observation in mind, therefore, it is interesting to see how three different filmmakers came to an understanding of a subtle and important part of Shakespeare's *Romeo and Juliet*. Of the three, Zeffirelli, with his ambition to put the failed romance of the eponymous characters at the forefront of his film, has lost track of the play's political meaning; his treatment's reliance on the innocence of young love not only lacks support in the original but is dated, trapped forever in a specific moment in the 1960s. He has cut his peasant roles, transferring their dramatic contributions to their social superiors — the one notable exception being the Nurse, whose part remains intact.

Luhrmann, on the other hand, has recognized the political situation beneath the feet of *Romeo and Juliet*'s star-crossed lovers but has misunderstood the subtlety of Shakespeare's worldview, ironically foregrounding the citizens of Verona and their Prince of the people. Luhrmann's Prince acts with too much force against the warring Capulets and Montagues, but in his defense, Luhrmann has correctly read the two families not as aristocrats but as upstarts. Although Luhrmann has reduced the speaking parts and actions of the commoners, their intent seems preserved but exaggerated beyond what can be supported by the original text.

Finally, *Shakespeare in Love* — at first consideration merely an analogue of *Romeo and Juliet* more distantly removed from its source text than either of the other two films — has managed to read the political landscape of *Romeo and Juliet* accurately and understands Shakespeare's play in a way that was beyond either Zeffirelli or Luhrmann. The peasants remain and retain their dramatic function. Oddly enough, the further one appears to have moved away from the source text, the closer one has actually come.

Notes

1. Chuck Palahniuk, *Fight Club* (New York: Owl Books, 1997), 166.
2. Jerald W. Spotswood, "'We Are Undone Already': Disarming the Multitude in *Julius Caesar* and *Coriolanus*," *Texas Studies in Literature and Language* 42, no. 1 (Spring 2000): 73.
3. Stephen Greenblatt, "Murdering Peasants: Status, Genre, and the Representation of Rebellion," *Representations* 1 (February 1983): 1–29.
4. Nina Levine, "Extending Credit in the Henry IV Plays," *Shakespeare Quarterly* 51, no. 4 (Winter 2000): 403.

5. Jerry Weinberger, "Pious Princes and Red-Hot Lovers: The Politics of Shakespeare's *Romeo and Juliet*," *Journal of Politics* 65, no. 2 (May 2003): 352.
6. In *Purgatorio* VI, Dante offers a critique of Italian politics, showing how the political system has decayed from Roman times, destroying an empire he describes as a "garden" (105). Dante singles out the Capulets and the Montagues, claiming that they "live in grief" (108).
7. See also 2.2.156–157 ("Love goes toward love as schoolboys from their books") and 3.2.83–84 ("Was ever book containing such vile matter So fairly bound?") for further examples.
8. Cf. Hamlet's remarks to Horatio (*Hamlet* 5.1.137–141).
9. Thomas Moisan, "'Knock Me Here Soundly': Comic Misprision and Class Consciousness in Shakespeare," *Shakespeare Quarterly* 42, no. 3 (Autumn 1991): 276.
10. Weinberger, "Pious Princes and Red-Hot Lovers," 363.
11. *Ibid.*
12. STC 22322, 22323, 22273. Texts available at http://ise.uvic.ca/Library/Texts/Rom/.
13. Paul Delany, "King Lear and the Decline of Feudalism," *PMLA* 92, no. 3 (May 1977): 429.
14. Wayne A. Rebhorn, "The Crisis of the Aristocracy in *Julius Caesar*," *Renaissance Quarterly* 43, no. 1 (Spring 1990): 81.
15. Jerald W. Spotswood, "Maintaining Hierarchy in *The Tragedie of King Lear*," *Studies in English Literature, 1500–1900* 38, no. 2 (Spring 1998): 266.
16. Delany, "King Lear and the Decline of Feudalism," 439.
17. Weinberger, "Pious Princes and Red-Hot Lovers," 370.
18. Jennifer L. Martin, "Tights vs. Tattoos: Filmic Interpretations of *Romeo and Juliet*," *English Journal* 92, no. 1 (September 2002): 41.
19. Sarah L. Lorenz, "*Romeo and Juliet:* The Movie," *English Journal* 87, no. 3 (March 1998): 50.
20. Marc Norman and Tom Stoppard, *Shakespeare in Love* (New York: Hyperion, 1998), 41.
21. These headlines comprise a fascinating feature of the mise-en-scène with reference to a variety of Shakespeare's plays: "Feigned Ecstasies" from *Titus Andronicus*, 4.4.21; "Brawl," and "A Rash Fierce Blaze of Riot" from John of Gaunt's "scepter'd isle" speech, *Richard II*, 2.1.33; and "Riot and Dishonor" from Henry IV's characterization of his out-of-control son in *1 Henry IV*, 1.1.84.
22. Norman and Stoppard, *Shakespeare in Love*, 119.
23. *Ibid.*, 21.
24. *Ibid.*, 42.
25. *Ibid.*, 8.
26. *Ibid.*, 58.
27. *Ibid.*, 44.
28. *Ibid.*, 59.
29. *Ibid.*, 60.
30. *Ibid.*, 44.
31. *Ibid.*, 89.
32. *Ibid.*, 149.
33. *Ibid.*, 36.
34. *Ibid.*, 144.

Works Cited

Delany, Paul. "King Lear and the Decline of Feudalism." *PMLA* 92, no. 3 (May 1977): 429–440.
Greenblatt, Stephen. "Murdering Peasants: Status, Genre, and the Representation of Rebellion." *Representations* 1 (February, 1983): 1–29.
Levine, Nina. "Extending Credit in the Henry IV Plays." *Shakespeare Quarterly* 51, no. 4 (Winter 2000): 403–431.
Lorenz, Sarah L. "*Romeo and Juliet:* The Movie." *English Journal* 87, no. 3 (March 1998): 50–51.
Machiavelli, Nicolo. *The Prince*. http://www.fordham.edu/halsall/basis/machiavelli-prince.html.
Martin, Jennifer L. "Tights vs. Tattoos: Filmic Interpretations of *Romeo and Juliet*." *English Journal* 92, no. 1 (September 2002): 41–46.
Moisan, Thomas. "'Knock Me Here Soundly': Comic Misprision and Class Consciousness in Shakespeare." *Shakespeare Quarterly* 42, no. 3 (Autumn 1991): 276–290.
Norman, Marc, and Tom Stoppard. *Shakespeare in Love*. New York: Hyperion, 1998.
Palahniuk, Chuck. *Fight Club*. New York: Owl Books, 1997.
Rebhorn, Wayne A. "The Crisis of the Aristocracy in *Julius Caesar*." *Renaissance Quarterly* 43, no. 1 (Spring 1990): 75–111.

Shakespeare, William. Editions of Q1, Q2, F1, F2, F3 and F4 of *Romeo and Juliet* on "Romeo and Juliet." *Internet Shakespeare Editions*. University of Victoria. http://ise.uvic.ca/Library/Texts/Rom/ (September, 15, 2006).
Spotswood, Jerald W. "'We Are Undone Already': Disarming the Multitude in *Julius Caesar* and *Coriolanus*." *Texas Studies in Literature and Language* 42, no. 1 (Spring 2000): 61–73.
_____. "Maintaining Hierarchy in *The Tragedie of King Lear*." *Studies in English Literature, 1500–1900* 38, no. 2 (Spring 1998): 265–280.
Weinberger, Jerry. "Pious Princes and Red-Hot Lovers: The Politics of Shakespeare's *Romeo and Juliet*." *Journal of Politics* 65, no. 2 (May 2003): 350–375.

FILMOGRAPHY

1968 *Romeo and Juliet*, d. Franco Zeffirelli, with Olivia Hussey, Leonard Whiting, Milo O'Shea, Michael York, and John McEnery. USA: Paramount.
1996 *William Shakespeare's Romeo + Juliet*, d. Baz Luhrmann, with Leonardo DiCaprio, Claire Danes, Brian Dennehy, John Leguizamo, Pete Postlethwaite, and Paul Sorvino. USA: Twentieth Century–Fox.
1998 *Shakespeare in Love*, d. John Madden, with Gwyneth Paltrow, Joseph Fiennes, Geoffrey Rush, Colin Firth, Ben Affleck, and Judi Dench. USA: Miramax.

Medieval *Hamlet* in Performance

Patrick J. Cook

Among Shakespeare's evocations of the Middle Ages, that of *Hamlet* may be the most elusive and strange. The English history plays with medieval settings contain anachronisms conspicuous to a modern audience accustomed to standards of historical authenticity different from Shakespeare's, but such discrepancies are not central to the plays' meanings. Of the great tragedies located in the Middle Ages, *Macbeth* represents an extension of the method of the history plays to a broader British scope occasioned by the succession of a Scottish king. Even *King Lear*, despite its murky chronology and the interpretive problems occasioned by its status as a Christian play about a pagan world, is a drama, rooted like *Macbeth* in Holinshed's *Chronicles*, about a British past familiar to Shakespeare's contemporaries and relatively unproblematic for the modern audience as well as for the scholar. History in *Hamlet*, I wish to suggest, is more problematic. This essay will attempt to describe the Danish play's unique medievalism and trace some of the ways this medievalism has been staged.

What is the historical setting of *Hamlet*? If we follow Saxo Grammaticus, the Danish cleric whose twelfth-century Latin history contains the earliest surviving version of the story, the young prince "Amlethus" who feigns madness and avenges the murder of his father by his uncle is the grandson of Roricus, who is probably the Viking king Rorik, a fierce pagan who warred savagely on both Slavs and Christians in the ninth century. If we follow Saxo's sixteenth-century French translator, François de Belleforest, whom scholars generally favor as Shakespeare's direct source, we simply learn that "Hamblet" lived "a long time before the kingdome of Denmark received the faith of Jesus Christ, and imbraced the doctrin of the Christians."[1]

When we turn to the play itself, the issue of Hamlet's historical milieu grows more difficult. On the one hand, Hamlet is the quintessential man of the Renaissance, a courtier shaped by Castiglione in a world governed by Machiavellian realities, an early modern humanist fascinated by classical exemplars and the Piconian promise of man as "the beauty of the world, the paragon of animals."[2] He has studied philosophy and much else at the University of Wittenberg, "the first and most famous of Protestant universities," and puns on the Diet of Worms (4.3.20), at which Martin Luther, a professor at the university, was banned for refusing to recant his challenges to the Roman Church in 1521.[3] Hamlet experiences a tension between Stoicism and skepticism that is very specific to late Renaissance thought.[4] A list of his Renaissance attributes could be extended at will by noting the endless scholarly attempts to view Hamlet as his author's breakthrough into modernity.

On the other hand, *Hamlet* is arguably the most Roman Catholic of Shakespeare's works and therefore in important ways the most medieval. This dimension of the play has received less attention than its Renaissance dimension but it has hardly gone unnoticed. As Jan Blits writes, "Virtually all the characters in *Hamlet* still believe in purgatory, angels, saints, and ghosts, and take very seriously the rites of the Catholic church. Denmark is still a Catholic country."[5] Cherrell Guilfoyle demonstrates Shakespeare's use — unquestionably more pervasive in *Hamlet* than in other plays—of "scenic forms" drawn from the mystery plays, whose performance had been suppressed by the English Reformation but which lived on in the memory of Shakespeare's audience.[6] Stanislaus Kozikowski argues that "implicit in the perspective, theme, and plot of *Hamlet* are three fixtures of medieval consciousness common to English morality drama—the *psychomachia*, the *ars moriendi*, and the *memento mori*."[6] Very little specific to ninth-century Denmark remains in the play, but doctrines and artistic forms from the Middle Ages are not minor residuals casting a shadow of an early modern plot; rather, they pervasively and persistently evoke a medieval world view.

What prompted Shakespeare to insert his emphatically Renaissance hero into this emphatically medieval world? One part of the answer, I suggest, is that he was participating in a rising wave of English interest in Denmark and that this interest found expression in representations of the pre–Norman domination of England by the Danes. Denmark, a major power that controlled Norway and Iceland as well as its Jutland homeland, had recently regained prominence in English minds as trade expanded to the east and geopolitical tensions surged between Catholic southern Europe and the largely Protestant north. Kronborg Castle at "Elsinore," or Helsingor, was completed in 1583. This advanced example of military architecture, the most formidable artillery platform in the world, commanded the narrow Sound of Denmark and solidified Danish control over the burgeoning Baltic trade. As Keith Brown observes, Danish enforcement of the infamous toll on all ships passing through the Sound "made the name of Elsinore not only well known but symbolic: it was the place where the King of Denmark manifested not only his authority within his own domains, but also his ability to impose his will upon a wide range of surrounding states."[8] The marriage in 1589 of James VI of Scotland to the sister of the Danish king meant that the inheritor of Mary Stuart's claim to the English throne was now allied with England's major geopolitical competitor in northern Europe while war continued against Spain. Throughout the 1590s, English relations with Denmark were in flux. Rumors circulated about secret Danish alliances with the Spanish enemy, and English Catholics regularly passed through Denmark en route to Continental Jesuit seminaries which the English feared as dens of subversion.[9] One intelligence missive of the time from Antwerp even stoked fears that the Danes were plotting to reimpose the "Danegeld," the tribute last exacted from England in the eleventh century.[10]

Such fears gained plausibility from the fact that, as Brown writes, for the Elizabethans the Anglo-Saxon "struggles with the Danish invaders were still surprisingly alive in their minds."[11] The period's proliferating chronicles and chorographies kept the memory of these struggles alive. Samuel Purchas wrote of the folk tradition of Hocktide, commemorating the defeat of Hardecnut and the final expulsion of the Danes and involving the taking of hostages and "compelling them to some ransom."[11] Numerous locations vividly recalled the period of Danish oppression. Holinshed's *Chronicles*, which dwells at length upon Danish abuses, notes the "sundrie places, sundrie ruines" associated with the Danes, "upon the which whensoever a man of a relenting spirit casteth his eie, he can not but enter into a dolefull consideration of former miseries."[13]

Playwrights responded to this combination of a rising interest in contemporary Denmark and a vividly remembered past of Danish oppression. The end of the sixteenth century witnessed a veritable boom of Danish plays. In addition to *Hamlet*, two with Danish settings have survived. *Sir Clyomon and Sir Clamydes* (printed 1599) and *Faire Em, the Miller's Daughter* (printed circa 1593) are worth considering in comparison to *Hamlet* because both reach back to the Middle Ages, the former to facilitate a chivalric quest plot, the latter to introduce William the Conqueror as an English hero who overcomes a fictional Danish invasion and claims the Danish throne.[14] Perhaps even more common were plays set in England during the Danish domination. The two surviving examples, the anonymous *Edmund Ironside* and Anthony Brewer's *The Love-Sick King*, feature English-Danish conflict during the eleventh-century reign of Cnut, the last great Danish ruler of English territory. Henslowe's diary also mentions a *Cutlack* staged in 1594, a *Hardicute* and a *Knewtus* staged in 1597, a *Hardicanewtes* purchased in 1598, and a 1598 *Earl Godwin and His Three Sons*. All of these titles clearly indicate pre–Norman settings and English struggles against the Danes.¹⁵

Awareness of Shakespeare's participation in a theatrical trend in which medieval Englishmen struggled against medieval Danes, a trend that reinforced long-held stereotypes about Danish cruelty and drunkenness, helps us to understand the unusual nature of *Hamlet*'s medievalism.¹⁶ Claudius, with his war preparations, his odd fondness for cannon fire, his insistence on English tribute, and his embodiment of anti–Danish stereotypes, bears the villainous weight of a long threat of foreign oppression. Hamlet, the Protestant-educated prince suffering usurpation, may comically be sent to recover his wits in a land where "the men are as mad as he" (5.1.150), but he is also associated more heroically with English liberty and with the Reformed modernity not yet achieved by the Roman Catholic forces aligned in Europe against militantly Protestant England. Patriotic audiences must have cheered at the thought of an English executioner's ax descending on the necks of Rosencrantz and Guildenstern, the play's only characters with genuine Danish names.¹⁷

Spatial configurations on stage could recall the mystery plays, but for Shakespeare's virtually property-less theater the principal means of evoking *Hamlet*'s ties to the Middle Ages was verbal. Ironically, when elaborate pictorial scenery suddenly became fashionable after the Restoration, and a medieval past could have been evoked visually, compensating for increasing historical distance, there was no interest in doing so. *Hamlet*, in William Davenant's "improved" version, was the first Shakespearean play staged in the new scenic manner. Exactly what Samuel Pepys saw before recording that the 1661 production was "done with Scenes very well" is unknown, but there is no doubt that Davenant's visual improvements, no less than his verbal ones, did not communicate an historically grounded vision of the past.¹⁸ Symptomatic is Davenant's "excision or dilution of oaths and other expressions offensive to piety."¹⁹ Removing references to heaven, the devil, and praying obscured the play's religious context. Painted backdrops were used to produce a generic, nonhistorical setting that recalled the grandeur witnessed by the largely Royalist audience during the Interregnum French exile among the extravagant Bourbons. For over a hundred years after the Restoration, Richard Southern concludes, "any conception of scenery as factual background to action was wholly unmeaningful and indeed alien" on the English stage.²⁰

Hamlets invariably strode the eighteenth-century stage in a "modern black velvet court dress" in front of painted panels of conventionalized rooms, gardens, and outdoor walkways that suggested no period in particular and that could be reused efficiently for play after play, no matter where or when the action occurred.²¹ Even in *Macbeth*, whose setting would later inspire much scenic exoticism and which increasingly joined *Hamlet* in crowding the other tragedies out of English theaters, the eleventh-century Scotsman strutted his hour within a vaguely modern space-time essentially the same as that of the medieval Dane. Perhaps the repeated implied comparison had an effect, for in 1773 Charles Macklin stunned audiences with a Macbeth in medieval costume, though the scenery was not adjusted to fit the Highland chieftain.²² Period costumes, including full armor, soon graced a number of Shakespearean heroes.

William Macready finally added period backdrops to period costume in his productions, including *Hamlet*, at Covent Garden beginning in 1837. His innovation seems to have been quickly imitated at Drury Lane, where Charles Kean played *Hamlet* and *Othello*, though the only evidence for period settings lies in the fact of their design by the Grieve family of scenarists, who were known for their historical panoramas.²³ The era of full-scale "archaeological" stagings, based on meticulous research and sparing no expense in the quest for authenticity, was soon to follow.

The theatrical revolution launched during Charles Kean's nine-year managerial tenure at the Princess's Theatre in London has been extensively studied, most recently in Richard Schoch's *Shakespeare's Victorian Stage*. As Schoch ably demonstrates, Kean's "chief legacy undoubtedly resides in his grand revivals of Shakespeare's English (and in one case Scottish) chronicle plays:

King John (1852), *Macbeth* (1853), *Henry VIII* (1855), *Richard II* (1857), and *Henry V* (1859)."[24] Kean expended unprecedented resources to feed the enormous appetite for Victorian medievalism, indeed to transform theater into a full partner in this movement, along with architecture, painting, literature, and the crafts. He set a new standard of spectacular historical staging in such scenes as the interpolated arrival of Henry V at old London Bridge after Agincourt, featuring hundreds of extras, and the masque at York Palace in *Henry VIII*, which left a critic "captive to the intoxication produced by such a *tout ensemble*."[25] The theater, it seemed, had reached its limits in bringing history to life.

Hamlet's important role in Kean's project has been neglected in the scholarship. Schoch observes that "*Hamlet* presented something of a quandary":

> But for actor-managers who wanted to produce the tragedy with historically accurate stage accessories, *Hamlet* offered no reliable or consistent clues as to the precise historical period in which its action supposedly took place.... Although Hamlet was the Shakespearean role for which Kean was most famous, he never produced *Hamlet* with the antiquarian splendor he lavished not only upon Shakespeare's history plays, but also upon such non-historical plays as *The Merchant of Venice, The Winter's Tale,* and even *A Midsummer Night's Dream*.[26]

Kean's *Hamlet* certainly lacked the extravagant splendor of his other productions, but it decidedly did not lack their antiquarian attention to period. Kean privately printed his edited performance texts along with annotations and prefaces, selling these volumes to theater patrons to explain and justify his choices. He includes the following explanation in the preface to his *Hamlet* text:

> Saxo has placed his history about 200 years before Christianity, when barbarians, clothed in skins, peopled the shores of the Baltic. The poet, however, has so far modernised the subject as to make Hamlet a Christian, and England tributary to the "sovereign majesty of Denmark." A date can therefore be easily fixed, and the costume of the tenth and eleventh centuries may be selected for the purpose. There are but few authentic records in existence, but these few afford reason to believe that very slight difference existed between the dress of the Dane and that of the Anglo-Saxon of the period.[27]

Set drawings reveal the architectural quest for authenticity, which located the action in the Norman period. The painted castle on a promontory behind the battlement scenes is not merely crenellated and moated but features as well a quadruple set of pilasters that recalls the White Tower of the Tower of London, the building a London audience would associate most immediately with the Normans. The graveyard scene was played in front of a modest stone chapel, the round arches of its door and window and the leaning tombstone recalling the hundreds of parish churches in England that date to the Norman period.

Most noteworthy are the interior scenes, all eleven of which consist of variations on the theme of massive, low, round, stone arches, the foremost architectural signifier of the Romanesque style that replaced the Saxon after 1066. In all but two instances, these arches loom with stark symmetry horizontally across the entire stage. Kean's most famous spectacles, including those from *Henry V* and *Henry VIII* mentioned above, draw the eye in with superabundant detail deployed along striking diagonals, inviting the spectator to feel present at a historic celebration. In contrast, Kean's repeated Norman arches visually support Hamlet's sense that "Denmark's a prison" (2.2.243). The stage sets imply that Hamlet is a man seeking release but contained within structures representing his time. These structures would have felt all the more oppressive against the background of the Victorian Gothic Revival, which favored the pointed arches and soaring spaces of the great cathedrals as symbols of transcendence.[28]

The repeated runs of *Hamlet* over nine years at the Princess's Theatre had a lasting effect on theatrical practice, for they made Norman archways, no less than Yorick's skull, a standard visual association for the Danish prince. Variations on the setting were made. Charles Fechter in London and Edwin Booth in America created fully researched "archaeological" but less oppressive versions. Henry Irving recreated Shakespeare's temporal complexity by combining the Norman arch with a Hamlet in Renaissance costume.[29] But eventually, as the author *The Hamlet of Edwin Booth* writes, pursuit of historical accuracy came to appear "a grand delusion and a dangerous one.... Not indeed until the art of the cinema took 'historical accuracy' for its special province would the theatre be able to put its whole mind upon its proper kind of art."[30]

Historical authenticity found a new impetus and new resources in the early years of cinema. The drive for respectability by early studios led to an emphasis on "classic" stories set in the past, and as one early attempt to define such art films noted, historicized productions "demand an expensive outlay of costumes and scenic effects, deep and careful research into the manners and costume of the era depicted."[31] The first feature-length *Hamlet* (1913) was originally conceived as a memorializing record of the long-running stage version starring Johnston Forbes-Robertson as he retired from the stage. The filmmakers, however, were not content with merely preserving a cherished performance for posterity. The desire for correct period detail led the production company to claim they were building "an exact replica of the famous old castle still standing in Denmark," but Elsinore in the completed film is a collection of by-now familiar architectural details, varied and expanded in the way that cinema allows.[32] To the interior sets modeled on the stage production were added "huge carved Norman columns" as "special cinematographic scenery."[33] Especially impressive are the battlements, framed by large stone arches and including a small crenellated tower. Forbes-Robertson attempted to retain the nuances of his character that he had developed on stage, which had prompted one reviewer to ask if his civilized "Florentine courtier" Hamlet could be the "wildly whirling Northman that Shakespeare drew."[34] Within the film's more elaborate and varied medieval scenery, he must have seemed even more out of his time.

Like Kean's archaeological theater, the obsessive periodizing of early film gave way over time to more flexible and nuanced approaches. The first great sound films of *Hamlet* eschew a definable period setting. Laurence Olivier's *Henry V* (1944), with its reconstructed Globe Theatre and its scenery inspired by a Book of Hours, evoking both the time of its original performance and the time of its action, is an innovative extension of Victorian archaeological theatrics into cinema.[35] To set his *Hamlet* (1948), in contrast, within what Olivier calls "some time, any time, in the remote past," Olivier's set and costume designers labored to avoid "pinning down the action to any historical period."[36] Elsinore's conventional Norman arches combine with costumes that are a "fusion" of Holbein and Titian to create a slight sense of temporal incongruity, but Olivier does not use this incongruity to signify Hamlet's imprisonment in the manner of Henry Irving. Olivier's Elsinore is less a historical setting than a psychological one, a fluid grouping of spaces "suggestive," as Jack Jorgens observes, "of the mind's labyrinths."[37]

The temporality of the great Russian filmmaker Grigori Kozintsev's *Hamlet* (1964) is even more mixed. Jorgens describes the layering of period styles at Kozintsev's Elsinore:

> The Medieval style includes the massive fortress, armor, Laertes' family sword, and the stone faces, friezes, and coats of arms. The Renaissance style includes the frescoes, tapestries, maps, books and sextant. The ugly Modern style is dominated by Claudius' garish trappings—the gilded goblets and lions, smiling statues and portraits.[38]

The result is a vaguely modern setting that allows reference to lost values, the Renaissance curiosity of Hamlet that has been quenched by modern oppression, the chivalric values of Ophelia's unicorn wall hanging which contrast with the Stalinesque trappings of Claudius's regime.

With Franco Zeffirelli's 1990 *Hamlet,* medieval Shakespeare in performance reaches a degree of development unmatched since Charles Kean. Zeffirelli developed his passion for historical authenticity while working as a theatrical set designer for Luchino Visconti. He recalls in his autobiography:

> His way, and this was another lesson I learned from him, was to be faithful to the setting of a play as its author had conceived it and to render it in the most precise detail, probably with more

Ophelia embroidering the Bayeux Tapestry in Zeffirelli's *Hamlet* (1990).

attention and fidelity than when the play was first done. He could never have staged a modern Hamlet with actors holding umbrellas and wearing tracksuits. If he was doing a Goldoni play, he would find out everything about Goldoni's Venice in the eighteenth century — or I would do so for him. Then we would spend evenings in the library looking at engravings or books of paintings, at objects found in junk shops, at anything that could help us absorb that particular period.[39]

Zeffirelli continued applying this lesson when he turned to filmmaking, creating sumptuously detailed Italian Renaissance settings for *The Taming of the Shrew* (1966) and *Romeo and Juliet* (1968) and depicting medieval Tuscany with remarkable fidelity in *Brother Sun, Sister Moon* (1973), his story of young St. Francis of Assisi. For *Hamlet*, he wished to create a setting characterized by his production designer, Dante Feretti, as "more medieval, more strong, more wild" than one usually sees in modern productions.[40] To do so, he created a Norman *Hamlet* that richly evokes its period but also subtly redefines it.

The film was shot at three castles — Dunnottar and Blackness in Scotland and Dover Castle in England — as well as on interior and exterior sets. Great care was taken to make the settings consistently Norman: no cannons are to be seen in this age before artillery, for example, and the arch moldings innovatively combine zigzag and "billet" forms, the two most common Norman styles. Older sections of the castles were used exclusively, and the studio set was built to match these precisely, even to the extent of using molds cast from ancient stone walls.[41] The result is an Elsinore that continually communicates its period materially, through rough stone surfaces, unfinished wood, forged metal, coarse cloth, and geometrical ornamentation that visually connects the full range of human artifact, from jewelry to clothing to architecture.

Even though *Hamlet* lacks the urban setting that Zeffirelli used effectively in his previous films to create the impression of a vibrant community of interacting people and commodities, his composite castle is expansive enough to include the life of a medieval town. Around the enormous winged dragon that guards the palace entrance everyday life goes on, the preponderance of which is concerned with foodstuffs: women carrying jugs of water and baskets of food, men bearing sacks of grain and rolling casks. This economic activity culminates in the enormous banquet that fills the hall while Hamlet awaits the ghost, implying that the community is a unified organism of production, transport, and consumption. For Hamlet the revelry is a sign of the court's corruption, but it also provides verisimilitude to the audience and conveys an authentically medieval sense of commensality. The society is hierarchical and focused on the king but it is also a functioning system of exchange.

Within this richly detailed, fundamentally Norman environment, Zeffirelli departs somewhat from the archaeological approach through details that broaden temporal reference. Armor is less rigorously authentic than the architecture, ranging across several centuries to create such effects as placing Ophelia next to a shinily plated knight (ca. 1400) at the Mousetrap, signifying a conventionally "chivalric" presence that distinguishes her companion from grittier mailed soldiers and from Hamlet, whose cruelty is played up in the scene. Wall decorations, at their most lavish in Gertrude's chamber, reach back to four centuries before the Norman invasion. Their stylized figures and colorful interlace patterns provide contrast with Hamlet's private room, where maps, an hourglass, and most notably an armillary sphere support the idea of his relative modernity and visually compensate for the use of Mel Gibson as an action hero less tormented than many Hamlets by "the pale cast of thought" (3.1.85).

In the nineteenth century, Kean's archaeological project provided assurances of authenticity for the entire audience. It offered additional pleasures for those in the audience who could not only appreciate authenticity but perceive how this authenticity was being achieved. Understanding that Kean was authentically dressed and accessorized as Richard II at the Princess's Theatre in 1857 supported the experience of bringing the past to life, but there was added pleasure for those who recognized the careful recreation of meaningful details from Richard's Jerusalem Chamber portrait in Westminster Abbey. Similarly, Zeffirelli's stated aim was to popularize, to make Shakespeare "available to as many people as possible," but he also offers added delights to students of the Middle Ages.[42] The most startling example is the collective project of the castle's women, whom we first meet when Laertes bids his sister farewell. Ophelia is one of seven women gaily singing as they sew in the castle's weaving room. Recognition dawns when Ophelia evades her brother's remarks about the "trifling" of Hamlet's favor (1.3.5) by fingering a phallic plant form on an uncompleted fabric panel. We enter the weaving room again when Ophelia encounters Hamlet while, according to the play, sewing in her closet (2.1.77). This time she is preparing to work on another panel, which she holds before the camera, again inviting the viewer's gaze. Yes, it is the Bayeux Tapestry, the Norman period's most famous textile, which narrates and offers ideological support for the Norman Conquest of 1066.

Recognition converts an authenticating detail into a provocative, multidimensional allusion. As the women pursue a traditional woman's craft, playing an economic role in a tightly knit community, their project is the pictorial celebration of the Norman Conquest "fashioned to promote the idea that the invasion was an indisputably legal and divinely sanctioned affair."[43] Divine sanction is an especially prominent theme in the two frames selected for highlighting, which are also two of the tapestry's best known and most closely analyzed. The banquet scene, which shows Odo, bishop of Bayeux and brother of William the Conqueror, offering benediction before the invasion, "carries both social and sacramental associations of commensality."[44] Halley's comet soars over the second scene during the English King Harold's coronation, an omen of his imminent defeat by the Norman conqueror. At the very least, the most elaborate example of visual political propaganda from the Middle Ages, which asserts William's right to the throne that it implies has been usurped by Harold, might be seen as a commentary on the fate of Claudius's usurpation.

The closet scene with tapestry in Zeffirelli's *Hamlet* (1990).

The Bayeux Tapestry contains additional parallels with the film. Its world, filled with a variety of medieval people, animals, and things that range from the real to the emblematic and fantastic, is very much the world that the film's details attempt to reproduce. The tapestry expresses its period's fascination with "communalism and unity of group purpose." The banquet scene, for example, "is preceded by energetic preparations of the meal. Sheep, cows, and pigs are rounded up as wood is chopped for roasting the animals," much as Zeffirelli places similar processes in the background of his royal story.[45] Even more surprising, perhaps, is the way the tapestry comments on the very art of film. Anne Prah-Perechon marvels at the tapestry's "*présentation quasi cinématographique*": "From its first to its last scenes, the Bayeux Tapestry represents the work of a large crew, conceived and realized like a film in the selection of episodes, the development of a scenario and its division into scenes, visual realization, and finally editing."[46] Creatively imitating Shakespeare's inclusion of a play-within-the-play, Zeffirelli includes protofilm within the film.

Those who recognize the Bayeux Tapestry might also recognize the decorations of Gertrude's chamber. A wall hanging behind her bed is closely modeled on the page depicting St. Matthew in the exquisitely illuminated *Book of Durrow*, a Gospel manuscript dating from around A.D. 675.[47] Even more prominent is the lion symbol of John from the same book, which dominates the arras through which Hamlet thrusts his sword into Polonius. The queen's incest, we wryly conclude, has taken place under evangelical eyes. Since the Bayeux Tapestry and the *Book of Durrow* have not previously entered into the scholarly discourse on the film, were such sly allusions vain labors by a filmmaker fond of spending evenings in the library looking at engravings or books of paintings? Not entirely, I can say, for at least another Hamlet seems to have noticed. In Michael Almereyda's 2000 film version, Hamlet has conspicuously posted on the collage wall above his desk the calf of St. Mark, another evangelical image from the *Book of Durrow*. The Middle Ages remain relevant to *Hamlet* even in the corporate world of Almereyda's modern Manhattan.

NOTES

1. Geoffrey Bullough, ed., *Narrative and Dramatic Sources of Shakespeare* (London: Routledge and Kegan Paul, 1973), vol. 7, 83. Bullough reprints the Hamlet materials from the anonymous English translation of 1608, the earliest known. Whether Shakespeare used an earlier version of the translation, the French original, or indeed Saxo's text remains unknown.
2. William Shakespeare, *Hamlet*, ed. Harold Jenkins (London: Methuen, 1982), 2.2.307. Citations of *Hamlet* by line number refer to this Arden edition.
3. Roland Mushat Frye, *The Renaissance* Hamlet: *Issues and Responses in 1600* (Princeton, NJ: Princeton University Press, 1984), 19. Frye's book is the most ambitious attempt to place Hamlet within his author's cultural setting.
4. Rosalie Colie, *Paradoxica Epidemica: The Renaissance Tradition of Paradox* (Princeton, NJ: Princeton University Press, 1966), 396–429. On Hamlet's Renaissance Stoicism, see also Jan H. Blits, *Deadly Thought:* Hamlet *and the Human Soul* (Lanham, MD: Lexington Books, 2001).
5. Blits, *Deadly Thought,* 3.
6. Cherrell Guilfoyle, *Shakespeare's Play within Play: Medieval Imagery and Scenic Form in* Hamlet, Othello, *and* King Lear (Kalamazoo, MI: Medieval Institute Publications, 1990).
7. Stanislaus J. Kozikowski, "The Three Medieval Plots of *Hamlet*: Psychomachia, Ars Moriendi, Memento Mori," *Hamlet Studies* 20, 1–2 (Summer-Winter 1998): 163–170.
8. Keith Brown, "*Hamlet*'s Place on the Map," *Shakespeare Studies* 4 (1969): 160.
9. Edward Cheyney, "England and Denmark in the Later Days of Queen Elizabeth," *Journal of Modern History* 1 (1929): 31.
10. Cay Dollerup, *Denmark, Hamlet, and Shakespeare* (Salzburg: Universität Salzburg, 1975), 37.
11. Brown, "*Hamlet*'s Place on the Map," 180.
12. Samuel Purchas, *Hakluytus Posthumus, or Purchas his Pilgrimes* (Glasgow: J. MacLehose and Sons, 1905–1907), vol. 13, 442.
13. Raphael Holinshed, *Holinshed's Chronicles,* ed. Henry Ellis (London: J. Johnson, 1807–1808), vol. 1, 186.
14. Betty J. Littleton, ed., *Clyomon and Clamydes: A Critical Edition* (The Hague: Mouton, 1968) [STC 5450a]; Standish Henning, ed., *Faire Em: A Critical Edition* (New York: Garland, 1980) [STC 7675]. On *Clyomon and Clamydes,* see also the essay in this volume by Martha Driver, and C. R. Baskerville, "Some Evidence for Early Romantic Plays in England — Concluded," *Modern Philology* 14.8 (1916): 467–512.
15. Eric Sams, ed., *Shakespeare's Lost Play, Edmund Ironside* (New York: St. Martin's Press, 1985). I am not persuaded by Sams's argument for Shakespeare's authorship. Anthony Brewer, *The Love-Sick King* (London: Rob Pollard, 1655) [Wing B4426]; Philip Henslowe, *Henslowe's Diary,* ed. R. A. Foakes (Cambridge, UK: Cambridge University Press, 2002).
16. For the stereotypes and actual habits of Danish drinking, see Dollerup, *Denmark, Hamlet, and Shakespeare,* 122–127.
17. For the Danish background of Rosencrantz and Guildenstern, see *ibid.,* 211–212.
18. Samuel Pepys, *The Diary of Samuel Pepys,* ed. Robert Latham and William Matthews (Berkeley: University of California Press, 1995), vol. 2, 161.
19. Hazelton Spencer, *Shakespeare Improved: The Restoration Versions in Quarto and on the Stage* (Cambridge, MA: Harvard University Press, 1927), 178.
20. Richard Southern, *Changeable Scenery: Its Origin and Development in the British Theatre* (London: Faber and Faber, 1952), 357.
21. John A. Mills, *Hamlet on Stage: The Great Tradition* (Westport, CT: Greenwood Press, 1985), 56. On scenery, see Ernest Reynolds, *Early Victorian Drama: 1830–1870* (Cambridge, UK: W. Heffer and Sons, 1936), 34.
22. George C. Odell, *Shakespeare from Betterton to Irving* (New York: Charles Scribner's Sons, 1920), vol. 1, 452–454.
23. Richard W. Schoch, *Shakespeare's Victorian Stage: Performing History in the Theatre of Charles Kean* (Cambridge, UK: Cambridge University Press, 1998), 43.
24. *Ibid.,* 6.
25. An illustration of the scene from *Henry V* can be found in *ibid.,* 48, an illustration of the scene from *Henry VIII* in *ibid.,* 96.
26. *Ibid.,* 153.
27. A copy of the Kean prompt book using the privately printed volume is available at the Folger Shakespeare Library in Washington, D.C.
28. Illustrations of the sets for Kean's *Hamlet* can be found in Raymond Mander and Joe Mitchenson, *Hamlet through the Ages* (London: Salisbury Square, 1952), 4, 12, 19, 30, 51, 72, 97, 124, 140.
29. On Fechter's productions, see Odell, *Shakespeare from Betterton to Irving,* vol. 2, 358–360. On Irv-

ing's, see *ibid.*, vol. 2, 396–398, 418–421. On Booth's, see Charles H. Shattuck, *The Hamlet of Edwin Booth* (Urbana: University of Illinois Press, 1969).

30. Shattuck, *Hamlet of Edwin Booth*, 57–58.

31. Quoted in William Urichhio and Roberta E. Pearson, *Reframing Culture: The Case of the Vitagraph Quality Films* (Princeton, NJ: Princeton University Press, 1993), 50.

32. Robert Hamilton Ball, *Shakespeare on Silent Film* (London: George Allen and Unwin, 1968), 188.

33. *Ibid.*, 190.

34. Quoted in Mills, *Hamlet on Stage*, 175.

35. Olivier's *Henry V* not only includes both periods but contrasts the realistically rendered Globe Theatre with the stylized spaces of the fifteenth-century action in England and France. For the sources and methods of Olivier's scenic innovations, see Dale Silviria, *Laurence Olivier and the Art of Film Making* (East Rutherford, NJ: Fairleigh Dickinson University Press, 1985), 75–77.

36. Laurence Olivier, "An Essay in *Hamlet*," in *The Film* Hamlet: *A Record of Its Production*, ed. Brenda Cross (London: Saturn Press, 1948),12; Roger Furse, "Designing the Film *Hamlet*," in Hamlet: *The Film and the Play*, ed. Alan Dent (London: World Film Publications, 1948), 32.

37. Jack Jorgens, *Shakespeare on Film* (Bloomington: Indiana University Press, 1977), 210.

38. *Ibid.*, 228.

39. Franco Zeffirelli, *Zeffirelli: An Autobiography* (New York: Weidenfeld and Nicolson, 1986), 93.

40. Cyndi Stivers, "*Hamlet* Revisited," *Premiere* 4.6 (February 1991): 52.

41. DVD extras on *Hamlet*, d. Franco Zeffirelli, with Mel Gibson, US: Warner Brothers. Dunnottar Castle is a ruined complex in which the earliest remaining structures date to the thirteenth century. Zeffirelli used the location for its stunning seaside cliffs, erecting crenellated structures to represent Elsinore at a distance. He used two sections of the fifteenth-century fortress at Blackness largely unaffected by its sixteenth-century reconstruction as an artillery fortification: the hall interior, in which were shot the weaving room scenes, and the exterior courtyard, whose picturesque natural stone outcropping lies outside the entrance to the weaving room. The remaining structures at Dover Castle date for the most part to the twelfth and thirteenth centuries. The great twelfth-century square keep at Dover Castle's center is the inspiration for the constructed front façade of Zeffirelli's Elsinore. Hamlet leads the players and Laertes returns over the moat into the impressive Constable's Gate, built in the 1220s. See the fine photographs of Dover in Colin Platt, *Dover Castle* (London: English Heritage, 1988).

42. John Tibbetts, "Breaking the Classical Barrier: Franco Zeffirelli Interviewed by John Tibbetts," *Literature/Film Quarterly* 22 (1994): 138–139.

43. Martha Rampton, "The Significance of the Banquet Scene in the Bayeux Tapestry," *Medievalia et Humanistica* 21 (1994): 40. As I learned after completing this essay, Richard Burt notes the presence of the Bayeux Tapestry in Zeffirelli's *Hamlet* in "Re-embroidering the Bayeux Tapestry in Film and Media: The Flip Side of History in Opening and End Title Sequences," *Exemplaria* 19.2 (2007) (no pagination).

44. Rampton, "Significance of the Banquet Scene," 42.

45. *Ibid.*, 40.

46. Anne Prah-Perochon, "Le film animé de la Tapisserie de Bayeux," *Stanford French Review* 1.3 (1977): 357; my translation.

47. For analysis and reproductions from this Gospel book, see Bernard Meehan, *The Book of Durrow: A Medieval Masterpiece at Trinity College Dublin* (Dublin: Town House and Country House, 1996). A reproduction of Matthew's symbol, the man, is on p. 35. A reproduction of the calf of St. Mark is on p. 56. A reproduction of the lion of St. Luke is on p. 63. The *Book of Durrow* follows the correlation of symbols to evangelists used by Irenaeus rather than the more commonly found correlation favored by St. Jerome.

Works Cited

Baskerville, C. R. "Some Evidence for Early Romantic Plays in England — Concluded." *Modern Philology* 14.8 (1916): 467–512.

Blits, Jan H. *Deadly Thought:* Hamlet *and the Human Soul.* Lanham, MD: Lexington Books, 2001.

Brewer, Anthony. *The Love-Sick King.* London: Robert Pollard, 1655.

Brown, Keith. "*Hamlet*'s Place on the Map." *Shakespeare Studies* 4 (1969): 160–182.

Bullough, Geoffrey, ed. *Narrative and Dramatic Sources of Shakespeare.* Vol. 7. London: Routledge and Kegan Paul, 1973.

Burt, Richard. "Re-embroidering the Bayeux Tapestry in Film and Media: The Flip Side of History in Opening and End Title Sequences." *Exemplaria* 19.2 (2007) (no pagination).

Cheyney, Edward. "England and Denmark in the Later Days of Queen Elizabeth." *Journal of Modern History* 1 (1929): 9–39.

Colie, Rosalie. *Paradoxica Epidemica: The Renaissance Tradition of Paradox*. Princeton, NJ: Princeton University Press, 1966.
Dollerup, Cay. *Denmark, Hamlet, and Shakespeare*. Salzburg: Universität Salzburg, 1975.
Frye, Roland Mushat. *The Renaissance* Hamlet: *Issues and Responses in 1600*. Princeton, NJ: Princeton University Press, 1984.
Furse, Roger. "Designing the Film *Hamlet*." In Hamlet: *The Film and the Play*, edited by Alan Dent, 25–32. London: World Film Publications, 1948.
Guilfoyle, Cherrell. *Shakespeare's Play within Play: Medieval Imagery and Scenic Form in* Hamlet, Othello, *and* King Lear. Kalamazoo, MI: Medieval Institute Publications, 1990.
Henning, Standish, ed. *Faire Em: A Critical Edition*. New York: Garland, 1980.
Henslowe, Philip. *Henslowe's Diary*. Edited by R. A. Foakes. Cambridge, UK: Cambridge University Press, 2002.
Holinshed, Raphael. *Holinshed's Chronicles*. Edited by Henry Ellis. Vol. 1. London: J. Johnson, 1807–1808.
Jorgens, Jack. *Shakespeare on Film*. Bloomington: Indiana University Press, 1977.
Kozikowski, Stanislaus J. "The Three Medieval Plots of *Hamlet*: Psychomachia, Ars Moriendi, Memento Mori." *Hamlet Studies* 20.1–2 (Summer-Winter 1998): 63–70.
Littleton, Betty J., ed. *Clyomon and Clamydes: A Critical Edition*. The Hague: Mouton, 1968.
Mander, Raymond, and Joe Mitchenson. *Hamlet through the Ages*. London: Salisbury Square, 1952.
Meehan, Bernard. *The Book of Durrow: A Medieval Masterpiece at Trinity College Dublin*. Dublin: Town House and Country House, 1996.
Mills, John A. *Hamlet on Stage: The Great Tradition*. Westport, CT: Greenwood Press, 1985.
Odell, George C. D. *Shakespeare from Betterton to Irving*. 2 vols. New York: Charles Scribner's Sons, 1920.
Olivier, Laurence. "An Essay in *Hamlet*." In *The Film* Hamlet: *A Record of Its Production*, edited by Brenda Cross, 11–15. London: Saturn Press, 1948.
Pepys, Samuel. *The Diary of Samuel Pepys*. Edited by Robert Latham and William Matthews. Vol. 2. Berkeley: University of California Press, 1995.
Platt, Colin. *Dover Castle*. London: English Heritage, 1988.
Prah-Perochon, Anne. "Le film animé de la Tapisserie de Bayeux." *Stanford French Review* 1.3 (1977): 339–365.
Purchas, Samuel. *Hakluytus Posthumus or Purchas his Pilgrimes*. Vol. 13. Glasgow: J. MacLehose and Sons, 1906.
Rampton, Martha. "The Significance of the Banquet Scene in the Bayeux Tapestry." *Medievalia et Humanistica* 21 (1994): 33–53.
Reynolds, Ernest. *Early Victorian Drama: 1830–1870*. Cambridge, UK: W. Heffer and Sons, 1936.
Sams, Eric, ed. *Shakespeare's Lost Play, Edmund Ironside*. New York: St. Martin's Press, 1985.
Schoch, Richard W. *Shakespeare's Victorian Stage: Performing History in the Theatre of Charles Kean*. Cambridge, UK: Cambridge University Press, 1998.
Shakespeare, William. *Hamlet*. Edited by Harold Jenkins. London: Methuen, 1982.
Shattuck, Charles H. *The Hamlet of Edwin Booth*. Urbana: University of Illinois Press, 1969.
Silviria, Dale. *Laurence Olivier and the Art of Film Making*. East Rutherford, NJ: Fairleigh Dickinson University Press, 1985.
Southern, Richard. *Changeable Scenery: Its Origin and Development in the British Theatre*. London: Faber and Faber, 1952.
Spencer, Hazelton. *Shakespeare Improved: The Restoration Versions in Quarto and on the Stage*. Cambridge, MA: Harvard University Press, 1927.
Stivers, Cyndi. "*Hamlet* Revisited." *Premiere* 4.6 (February 1991): 51–56.
Tibbetts, John. "Breaking the Classical Barrier: Franco Zeffirelli Interviewed by John Tibbetts." *Literature/Film Quarterly* 22 (1994): 135–140.
Urichhio, William, and Roberta E. Pearson. *Reframing Culture: The Case of the Vitagraph Quality Films*. Princeton, NJ: Princeton University Press, 1993.
Zeffirelli, Franco. *Zeffirelli: An Autobiography*. New York: Weidenfeld and Nicolson, 1986.

FILMOGRAPHY

1913 *Hamlet,* d. Cecil Hepworth, with Johnston Forbes-Robertson. USA: Gaumont.
1944 *Henry V,* d. Laurence Olivier, with Laurence Olivier. UK: Two Cities.
1948 *Hamlet,* d. Laurence Olivier, with Laurence Olivier. UK: Two Cities.
1964 *Hamlet,* d. Grigori Kozintsev. Russia: Lenfilm.
1973 *Brother Sun, Sister Moon,* d. Franco Zeffirelli. Italy: Euro International Film.
1990 *Hamlet,* d. Franco Zeffirelli, with Mel Gibson. USA: Warner Brothers.
2000 *Hamlet,* d. Michael Almereyda, with Ethan Hawke. USA: Miramax.

Finding Gruoch: The Hidden Genealogy of Lady Macbeth in Text and Cinematic Performance

SID RAY

> ORSINO: And what's her history?
> VIOLA: A blank, my lord.
> —*Twelfth Night* 2.4.109–110

When the Gentlewoman watching over the suicidal Lady Macbeth says about her charge, "Heaven knows what she has known" (5.1.41), she seems to refer to the Queen's knowledge of the bloody events of the play: Duncan's and Banquo's murders, and the Macduff massacre.[1] But the line also raises an important epistemological question: What does anyone really know about Lady Macbeth? What exactly *has* she known? The Gentlewoman says that she "will not report after" her lady (5.1.12), which suggests loyalty or, more probably, fear that her report will not be believed or will be understood as treason. Suggestions that there is more to the story, particularly Lady Macbeth's story, abound in *Macbeth*. Among the moments indicative of an untold but rich and intriguing history are Lady Macbeth's reference to her father, "Had he not resembled / My father as he slept, I had done't" (2.2.12–13), and to a child Lady Macbeth once suckled, "I have given suck, and know / How tender 'tis to love the babe that milks me" (1.7.54–55). There is also the enigmatic question she poses to Macbeth, "What beast was't then, / That made you break this enterprise to me?" (1.7.47–48), a question that suggests Macbeth first proposed Duncan's murder to her.[2] Lady Macbeth's fainting after Duncan's murder is another mystery—is she trying to distract the investigators or is she overcome by her part in the deed?[3] Less often cited is Macbeth's reflection to the Doctor that his wife has "a rooted sorrow, "written troubles of the brain," and a "bosom "stuffed ... of that perilous stuff / Which weighs upon the heart" (5.3.42–46), remarks that suggest some trauma that has occurred in Lady Macbeth's preplay life.

Shakespeare tells us twice in the play to "Look to the Lady" (2.3.112; 118), and this essay follows that directive: it attempts a fresh look at Lady Macbeth as she has been chronicled in history and analyzed as a character in the play and in four film treatments of it. Though films have tended to offer a fiendish yet also somewhat diminished Lady Macbeth, two recent films, *Heights* (2005), a modern meditation on the Scottish play, and *Macbeth* (2006), an updated Australian rendition, show how the lacunae in Lady Macbeth's story can be used to reimagine and reframe this maligned character.

In the two most prominent, most often taught films (in English) of *Macbeth*, the productions by Orson Welles (1948) and Roman Polanski (1971), Lady Macbeth does not fare well.[4] In the Welles film script, Lady Macbeth is a supporting character, subordinate to and overshadowed by Welles's Macbeth. Indeed, the film suggests that she is not worth knowing or examining thoroughly. In the Polanski film, Lady Macbeth is played by a young and sexy actor, and though she is lovely to look at, she seems rather insubstantial — on display and alluring but presented with very little depth. In contrast, the recent Australian *Macbeth*, directed by Geoffrey Wright and set in twenty-first-century Melbourne, is more progressive and insightful, disclosing from the outset that Lady Macbeth is in deep mourning for a dead son, providing her with a history that mitigates or at least explains her actions. Taking a related but broader stance on questions of history, the recent *Macbeth* offshoot, *Heights*, directed by Chris Terrio, draws attention to the lost genealogy of Lady Macbeth, to the collective oversights of and inattentions to the character of Lady Macbeth, and to the secrets and obfuscations of storytellers. But before examining the films, this essay outlines the ways in which Lady Macbeth has been read by scholars and teachers and attempts to recover what we do know about the historical figure on whom she is based.

Shakespeare seems to want to tell Lady Macbeth's whole story but, like the Gentlewoman in the play, does not. His sources provide some background on her — she is named Gruoch in Hector Boece's *Scotorum Historiae* (1527) — but the information is scanty and some of it manufactured.[5] Medieval and early modern chronicles placed little importance on facts and tended toward moral didacticism.[6] Based on regnal lists, the chronicles also privileged the stories of kings over those of their wives. Olga Valbuena observes:

> With regard to Lady Macbeth and women generally, it must be noted that [Raphael] Holinshed, like his predecessors Boece (in [John] Bellenden's translation) and [George] Buchanan, customarily organizes his narrative of early history around the career and fortunes of individual kings so that the actions and influence of their wives or other significant women become subordinated to the central male narrative.[7]

As the epigraph that opens this essay suggests, Shakespeare seems to realize and acknowledge that women's history, "a blank," was unfairly subordinate to men's. But did Shakespeare leave Lady Macbeth's story untold for the same reasons as the chroniclers? We do know that he was prevented by the lack of information from providing her with much history, but even so, he left tantalizing glimpses of a hidden past. To an actor-playwright such as Shakespeare, such glimpses, or lacunae, would function as openings for actors to develop performances of characters. Players of Lady Macbeth have to create a backstory from the hints dropped in the text and, if they are thorough, from descriptions of the historical character in the sources.[8] Actors preparing a role often write detailed biographies of their characters constructed from equal parts textual information and imagination. Method actors in particular develop a backstory for their characters to find the motivation for action.[9] Constructing a backstory would be a formidable exercise for any actor intent on learning about eleventh-century Scottish queens, and this is made more difficult by the textual lacunae. Edith Evans, an acclaimed actor of the 1930s, supposedly declined the part of Lady Macbeth precisely because of the gaps, claiming, "there's a page missing."[10]

But the missing pieces — the lack of a motive for Lady Macbeth's complicity in the murder of Duncan in act 2 and the contrast between her strength in the banquet scene in act 3 and her decline into madness in act 5 — could well be deliberate, giving an actor room to imagine or research motives. Indeed, Lady Macbeth's radical psychological shift from act 3 to act 5 has sent some actors to the history books. The 1888 performance of the play acted by Henry Irving and Ellen Terry and the 1955 performance by Laurence Olivier and Vivian Leigh both insinuated that many years passed between act 3 and act 5. They filled in the notable gap by suggesting the passage of time, "more or less following Holinshed's account" that Macbeth ruled for seventeen years.[11] Both Terry's and Lee's Lady Macbeths were softer, more conventionally feminine, and more admirable than she is represented in most other productions.[12] As these portrayals suggest, performances of *Macbeth* can allow for more of that latent content to surface and provide us a view of a Lady Macbeth much more multifaceted than scholars or students focused on reading rather than on performance might acknowledge.

Despite Shakespeare's leaving compelling gaps about Lady Macbeth for us to fill in, scholars and teachers of the play have, like the chronicles, left Lady Macbeth's backstory unexplored even as they have plumbed the chronicles for any historical detail that will mitigate Macbeth's crimes. Scholars regularly observe that tanistry, the quasi-elective system of determining kings from alternating rival clans in medieval Scotland, gives Macbeth reason to kill.[13] Tanistry, however, is never actually mentioned in the play. Nevertheless, in teaching guides such as *Understanding Macbeth: A Student Casebook to Issues, Sources, and Historical Documents*, we are told, "Historically, Scotland's laws of succession gave Macbeth a legitimate claim to the throne, as well as reason to be troubled when Duncan named Malcolm as heir," but there is no mention of Gruoch's status as a princess nor of her own compelling reasons for revenge.[14] In a play that hangs on notions of history, lineage, and dynasty, it is negligent not to include Lady Macbeth's history in our interpretations of the play. Valbuena articulates this point best:

> I believe it is one thing for the play itself to repeat blithely the effacement and demonization of women's motives practiced among early Scottish and English historiographers; it is quite another for critics to remain incurious about the effects of that choice. It is particularly significant that historicist critics examining the conflict of succession have not addressed the historical Lady Macbeth's dynastic claims and revenge motive lurking at the margins of historical and dramatic master texts or the public transcript.[15]

Beyond ignoring Shakespeare's hints that this central female figure has an important story to tell, critics like to use Lady Macbeth as a scapegoat for Macbeth's crimes—the standard reading is that she goads him into murder by threatening his manhood, which, by some logic, makes her worse than he is. One of the earliest critics, Samuel Johnson, writing in 1765, stated what has become a commonplace: "Lady Macbeth is merely detested; and though the courage of Macbeth preserves some esteem, yet every reader rejoices at his fall."[16] Critics who follow Johnson tend to admire Macbeth for his great imagination, his courage, and what they perceive to be his innate innocence, but revile Lady Macbeth for her lack of maternity and non-normative femininity;[17] as we shall see, both of these supposedly missing qualities are accounted for in the historical record. Learning from followers of Johnson, students tend to lay the blame for Macbeth's bloody rampage squarely at his wife's feet, despite her limited involvement in only one of his many murders. They reject the idea that Macbeth is a "butcher" but embrace the claim that Lady Macbeth is a "fiend-like queen," both of which are Malcolm's (the succeeding king's) self-interested and prejudiced assessments. Not only actors, then, but also teachers should try to reconstruct history to gain a more complete picture of Lady Macbeth and resist relying on limited, prejudiced points of view.

Medieval historians still debate what happened between the years 1040 and 1057 in tribal Scotland. The story remains a patchwork pieced together from Scottish and English chronicles, Irish annals, Icelandic sagas, regnal lists, genealogies, poems of flyting bards, and charters. We know that Macbeth reigned for seventeen years mainly unchallenged by the rival dynasty—that of Duncan's son, Malcolm Cranmor (later Malcolm III of Scotland). While it seems clear that Macbeth was mortally wounded at the battle of Lumphanan in 1057, his side may have won the day, which would explain why his stepson (and Lady Macbeth's son), Lulach, succeeded Macbeth as king, if only briefly. In 1058, Malcolm III claimed the throne of Scotland, but only after ruthless killings, one of them Lulach's, and unholy compromises, launching two centuries of hereditary, Anglo-inflected rule that left many of the traditions of old Scotland behind. In the defeat of the Macbeth dynasty, Malcolm III ushered in the beginnings of modern Anglicized Scotland.

Though we can never know how deeply Shakespeare researched this female queen from medieval Scotland, we can assume that with a Scottish king on the English throne at the time of play's composition, stories about the north country's fascinating past were circulating widely in early modern London. Shakespeare could have consulted a number of available chronicles, including those of Raphael Holinshed (1577, 1587), George Buchanan (1582), and Hector Boece (1526, 1575, translated by John Bellenden ca. 1540). However inventive, contradictory, and biased they may be, these records do provide answers to many of our questions about Lady Macbeth. The massacre of Gruoch's family in 1032 by Malcolm II (Duncan's grandfather) gives Lady Macbeth a motive for murdering the killer's grandson, King Duncan. As Valbuena puts it, "This woman, Gruoch by name, had lost her grandfather, her uncles, her brother, and her first husband to Malcolm II's purge. Such a loss would be sufficient, one would think, to fill her 'from the crown to the toe topful / Of direst cruelty.'"[18] Beyond this family tragedy, we also learn from the medieval chronicles of Gruoch's royal lineage, which suggests that through his marriage to her, Macbeth solidified his right to be king. That Gruoch was a princess before she married gives her character's actions political rather than personal resonance. One of the rare mentions of Gruoch in the source texts comes when she is credited for endowing the monastery at Loch Levin, an act of philanthropy befitting a diplomatic and beneficent queen, which is at odds with her depiction in the play and reception by critics and students. Her politics are important: Gruoch may have been the last bona fide Celtic Scottish queen; true to the English connections that enabled him to overthrow Macbeth, Malcolm III, Duncan's son, married an Anglo-Saxon wife, Margaret, who was responsible for Englishing the Scottish court and church — and was praised for her influence.[19]

The chronicles also answer that notorious and recurring question about the number of children Lady Macbeth had — one, a son, Lulach.[20] Lulach was not the biological son of Macbeth, which may explain why Macbeth becomes excited when his wife makes reference to killing her child in the play (1.7.56–59). The very possibility of Lulach's claiming the throne of Scotland may be what ultimately rankles Shakespeare's Macbeth when he laments that the witches foresee "no son of mine succeeding" (3.1.65). Certainly he is envious of Banquo's ability to "get kings" but also of his wife's ability to do the same, her obvious fertility an implicit criticism of Macbeth's apparent sterility. Perhaps most importantly, Lulach's close proximity to the crown could explain why Lady Macbeth is, according to Holinshed, "verie ambitious, burning in unquenchable desire to beare the name of a queene": she wants the crown not only for her husband and herself but also for her son.[21] As historian Lois L. Huneycutt observes, medieval queens "channel[ed] their ambitions and secure[d] their power through sons."[22] In this regard, Lady Macbeth has not denied her maternity at all; in fact, her actions are predicated on a desire to see her own child on the throne. Though in the play she claims she would have dashed his brains out had she promised her husband to do so, historically, she somehow managed to get her son by another man to succeed her husband as king of Scotland.

Queen Gruoch's own status and safety would have been in jeopardy if she could not secure a successor to the throne who was obligated to her. As historian Janet Nelson writes, "The queen's position during her husband's lifetime necessarily carried a disadvantage — dependence on his favor and concomitant vulnerability should that favor be withdrawn or the husband die without a son (or sons) to offer the widow a substitute power base."[23] Actions that appear to be driven by ambition might also be driven by the survival instinct. Lady Macbeth has been vilified for abusing the position of hostess when she entertains King Duncan only to oversee his murder "under [her] battlements" (1.5.38). But if we consider the unorthodox elevation of the king's son, Malcolm, to Prince of Cumberland as a threat to her husband's and son's claims to the throne and recall that the king's grandfather massacred her family, she might have regarded Duncan's visit as a kind of siege. One central role of a medieval royal woman was to fortify and guard the home as a "battlement."

As Nelson puts it, the medieval queen held a tenuous position that oddly empowered her: "The power to straddle, to intercede, to set personal influence against official authority, was the queen's defining trait. It empowered her yet at the same time limited her scope. Her unique influence made her unpredictable, wild, like the chessboard queen."[24] While this assessment squares with Shakespeare's depiction, Lady Macbeth should not be demonized for behaving the

Orson Welles strikes a pose as Macbeth in *Macbeth* (1948).

very way the medieval system of monarchy molded her to behave.²⁵ Nevertheless, demonized she has been, as many onscreen depictions of her bear witness.

In Welles's 1948 colonialist production of *Macbeth*, medieval Scotland is more barbaric and less Christian than medieval England. The Scottish characters are differentiated from the English by their animal-skin attire and their cartoonlike guttural stage brogues. Though Michael Anderegg, André Bazin, and others claim that Welles creates a timelessness in his *Macbeth*, depicting a colo-

Welles as Macbeth in the foreground; Jeanette Nolan as Lady Macbeth in the background in *Macbeth* (1948).

nial setting as ahistorical is a strategy designed to dehistoricize and render it uncivilized. The colonialist ahistoricity of Welles's Scotland dovetails with his antifeminist portrayal of Lady Macbeth. As played by Jeanette Nolan, then thirty-seven, Lady Macbeth embodies the "fiend-like queen" reading. Nolan's interpretation was so repulsive to the film's producer, Charles Feldman, that he tried to excise her opening scene and wrote in a memo, "I think she looks horrible and frightening, and everyone ... was appalled at the looks of the girl."[26] Making her "horrible and frightening" was, however, part of Welles's design. Welles resisted the cut but removed other bits, many of them Lady Macbeth's, reducing the movie by nearly a third. He even appropriated some of Lady Macbeth's key lines for his own character, including the powerful and damning one uttered before the murder, "Leave all the rest to me" (1.5.71). As J. Lawrence Guntner comments, "This film certainly celebrates Orson Welles, who is at once the producer, director, adaptor and star actor, omnipresent before and behind the camera."[27] But the result of the director's megalomania was a diminished but severe Lady Macbeth.[28]

The producers insisted that Welles redub the entire film to make it more commercial by giving the characters American accents, and his frustration at the interference was leveled at Nolan.[29] Welles blamed her for the failure of the redub and for his own character's onscreen dominance over hers, even though he was the one who had reduced her role both verbally and visually; his staging placed her in the background of many shots. Welles observed:

Nolan is not a large woman; her personality is not commanding. She lacks what the French call "presence." Her success in the role of Lady Macbeth was entirely based on her intelligence and on the vocal authority which informed and underlined the playing of her big scenes. The unfortunate Montana whine, wheeze, and scrape completely nullify this authority.[30]

Now that her Scottish accent has been restored to the DVD version (2003), it is plain that Nolan had more than the question of accent to contend with. She had to endure Welles's legendary misogyny, his cutting and appropriation of her lines, his imposing himself in some of her scenes, and the unflattering, colonialist portrait of medieval Scotland that her character, in this version of the play, was made to represent.

Nolan's Lady Macbeth, shrill and demonic but still rather inconsequential in this film, suggests that medieval Scotswomen were, paradoxically, impotent harpies, which, of course, was not the case for Scottish queens historically.[31] Thus Welles widens Shakespeare's lacunae instead of filling them in, further marginalizing and belittling the character of Lady Macbeth.

The Polanski *Macbeth* evinces the same incuriousness about Lady Macbeth's backstory as the Welles film does. Infamous for its bloodiness and for its debt to executive producer Hugh Hefner, the film includes unflinching scenes of violence and nudity and lives up to *Playboy*'s tagline, "Entertainment for Men," without irony. As Lady Macbeth, twenty-seven-year-old Francesca Annis is young and beautiful, looking remarkably like Ellen Terry in John Singer Sargent's portrait of her as the Scottish queen, yet she brings little of Terry's reputed gentleness to the role.[32] Polanski was cowriter of the screenplay with Kenneth Tynan, a *Playboy* contributing editor, and, like Welles, they cut many of Lady Macbeth's lines, including the "I have given suck" speech, deliberately erasing the most significant hint Shakespeare leaves about the character's past.

Lady Macbeth and her husband (played by Jon Finch) appear to be newlyweds, and she acts

The gorgeous Macbeths (Jon Finch and Francesca Annis) in *Macbeth*, dir. Roman Polanski (1971).

as his accessory in all senses—the body of this Lady Macbeth is constantly on display. Whereas Macbeth broods, spying on people from darkened recesses and peering from the shadows as he contemplates Duncan's murder, Lady Macbeth is front and center, reciting her "unsex me" speech through a voice-over as she displays herself from the castle ramparts, her gown and hair billowing behind her. Polanski has her wearing bright colors and using her long, strawberry-blonde tresses as a means of drawing attention to herself. She appears to be all surface and no substance, carefree and unencumbered by guilt or fear, until the murders of Lady Macduff and her children. During the sleepwalking scene, Annis's Lady Macbeth is stark naked, a reminder that her past is bare—a blank—and her present barren. She is merely an object. Polanski justified the nudity by claiming that eleventh-century Scots did not wear nightgowns, but the scene nevertheless seems gratuitous rather than edifying.[33] Moreover, Polanski's use of history was selective: the fact of women sleeping naked in the eleventh century took precedence over the fact of Lady Macbeth's royal lineage and maternity. At the end, when Lady Macbeth's dead body is discovered on the ground by Malcolm and the English, they lift for a mere second the blanket placed over her body and casually walk away. Their disregard serves as a visual representation of her persona's overall treatment by the chronicles, historians, scholars, students, and directors such as Welles and Polanski.

Polanski's portrayal of Lady Macbeth is at one with the executive producer's—Hugh Hefner's—portrayal in *Playboy* of his Playmates of the Month. Akin to the thin backstory of Polanski's Lady Macbeth, *Playboy* Playmates' biographies, called "Playmate Data Sheets," include only

Lady Macbeth (Francesca Annis) feasting with Duncan (Nicholas Shelby) in *Macbeth*, dir. Roman Polanski (1971).

the following details of their lives: birth date, measurements, likes, and dislikes. Despite A. R. Braunmuller's assertion that this film is "the most distinguished cinematic version of the play," in Polanski's treatment such surface information is all we get of Lady Macbeth, whose costumes accentuate her figure, and whose youth and unlined face belie personal history, such as childbirth or family tragedy.[34]

In contrast to the shallow depictions of Lady Macbeth by Welles and Polanski are two films, *Macbeth* (2006) and *Heights* (2005), that deepen the character by suggesting that Lady Macbeth has a history worth revealing. In both cases, the film scripts were written or cowritten by women — *Heights* was originally a roundelay playlet written by Amy Fox, who authored the film script, and *Macbeth* was coadapted by the film's director, Geoffrey Wright, and the actor who plays Lady Macbeth, Victoria Hill. The Aussie *Macbeth*, though set in contemporary times with Ipods, flat-screen TVs, and high-tech surveillance devices, takes pains to give Lady Macbeth a tragic past; specifically, it imagines that she has lost her infant son.

The film, shot in twenty-five days on high-definition cameras, opens in a Melbourne cemetery in broad daylight. The witches are redheaded Goth girls in school uniforms reciting the play's opening poetry as they desecrate tombstones, gouging out the eyes of female statues. The camera eventually finds a couple hovering around one grave — that of a "beloved son." The mother (Lady Macbeth, we soon discover) weeps uncontrollably while the father (Macbeth) stands slightly detached, watching the Goth girl witches. From the outset the film gives Lady Macbeth a reason for her subsequent reckless and destructive behavior. The director, Geoffrey Wright, explains, "Victoria and I had a discussion about whether Lady Macbeth had any children or not. In the end we decided to set it up so there has been a death of her child and that she is still grieving the loss of this child. This makes Lady Macbeth a lot more vulnerable. She becomes more ruthless in the mind, but desperate as a person."[35] The second time we see Lady Macbeth is when her husband finds her asleep in the bathtub and is clearly afraid that she has killed herself. As he takes her to bed, she is unresponsive to his embraces, remaining listless and glassy-eyed even as he delivers the information that Duncan will be visiting their home this very night. Hill's Lady Macbeth is a mother enduring the most tragic loss imaginable. She has nothing more to lose.

Later, when Duncan (head of an Australian mob) arrives at the Macbeths' heavily fortified gabled manor house, "Dunsinane," to celebrate the defeat of the Macdonwald clan (Asian gangsters with machine guns), Lady Macbeth is able to put on a happy face as Macbeth's wife with the aid of some lines of cocaine. Still, as she gazes into the backyard at the empty infant swing swaying slightly in the breeze, she delivers a haunting "unsex me" speech filled with despair for the lost baby. Though she entertains Duncan and crowd for her husband's advancement, she already seems to know that it will be a hollow achievement.

Duncan's murder is a bloodbath worthy of a Quentin Tarantino film, and Lady Macbeth plays her part — urging her husband to do the deed, planting the daggers on the bodyguards, and washing her and her husband's hands of bloodstains. She is in the manic phase of what appears to be a bipolar condition and remains at this high level of energy until the aftermath of the banquet scene, when she realizes her husband is out of control. At this point, we see her maternity and sense of loss reemerge. When she happens to catch news coverage of the murders of Lady Macduff and her son, she focuses on the murdered boy. Here she is able to bridge the "missing pages" noted by Edith Evans that would explain how her character moves from cool, calculated behavior in act 3 to madness in act 5. Toward the end of this film, Lady Macbeth returns to the suicidal state we found her in at the film's start, a state triggered by the murder of Lady Macduff's little boy which reminds her of her own unspeakable loss.

From the production notes of the film, we learn "that working with Hill meant [director Geoffrey Wright] could trust her to give a more female point of view overall, and more especially when it came to the character of Lady Macbeth. 'I think Lady Macbeth has been short changed in a lot of productions. I think this is the most sympathetic version of that character that I've seen, and that is largely due to Victoria's input as a writer and an actress.'"[36] While all this seems true, the film is not exactly a feminist interpretation of the play. The Goth girl witches reinforce our culture's disturbing fetish for schoolgirls, and their exploitation is made more troubling in the second prophecy scene, staged as an orgy, when the witches deliver their equivocal promises as they orgasm: "Macbeth, Macbeth, *Macbeth*!" The film acknowledges and outdoes the Polanski film in matters of blood and flesh.

The last film considered here, *Heights*, is not a production of *Macbeth* but a contemporary urban drama that makes abundant reference to *Macbeth*; the title refers in part to the theme of ambition shared by the film and its Shakespearean intertext.[37] Written by Amy Fox, *Heights* focuses our attention on Lady Macbeth as a character and, through the screenplay's analogies, reminds us that the role has been marginalized and the backstory left undiscovered. Since *Heights* departs from the Macbeth narrative, I will spend some time summarizing the film's story line.

One of the central characters, Diana Lee (played by Glenn Close), is a renowned actor rehearsing the part of Lady Macbeth for a Broadway production of the play. Drawing from *Macbeth* on a number of levels, the film begins with Diana Lee guest-coaching two students in a master class at Juilliard; they are performing lines of act 1, scene 7, 47–72 which begin "What beast was't then, / That made you break this enterprise to me?" It is the critical line suggesting that Macbeth masterminded the regicide and reducing Lady Macbeth's part in it. Diana interrupts the scene to chide the actors for pulling out a gun—"What? And wake the guards?" Having thought through the logic of the scene, Diana lectures the audience of students about understanding the Macbeths' passion: "These people are on fire ... we are tap water ... if I should find out my husband is sleeping with someone else, what would I do?—nothing." She ends the class with: "And, for Christ's sake, take a risk sometime this weekend."

We soon learn that Diana's husband is openly sleeping with Diana's own understudy, the woman playing Lady Macduff, the character often idealized by scholars and directors as a mother willing to sacrifice her life for her son's. The philandering husband, too, is in the cast, though we never find out which part he plays. As Diana bluntly puts it, her husband is "humping Lady Macduff in the lighting booth ... she's my goddamn understudy." Since Lady Macduff has been praised as an exemplar of maternity, Diana's replacement in her husband's affections by Lady

Diana Lee (Glenn Close) rehearsing the role of Lady Macbeth in *Heights*, dir. Chris Terrio (2005).

Where is Macbeth? The marquis for the production of *Macbeth* in *Heights*, dir. Chris Terrio (2005).

Macduff is particularly ironic, made more so when we later witness moments of great tenderness between Diana and her daughter. Like Lady Macbeth herself, Diana seems unfairly caught between wielding power and exhibiting emotion. When she catches her husband and her understudy together in the makeup room, we see just how difficult it is for her to maintain a strong front. To their faces Diana pretends to be archly amused, but then we see her weeping bitterly behind a pillar.[38]

It is not obvious why the film, which is about secret pasts and women being cheated, makes reference so boldly to *Macbeth*—billboards with Close as Lady Macbeth dominate the background and we see not only the master class on *Macbeth* but also Diana rehearsing the "unsex me" speech in full costume. Yet we never even glimpse the actor who plays Macbeth himself; the many billboards advertising the play in the film feature only Diana in close-up, as if it is Lady Macbeth's show and her show only—the opposite of the Welles film production. Through its erasure of Macbeth the character and its illumination of his queen, *Heights* calls attention to the editing of Lady Macbeth's lines in film and stage productions, the unexplored latent content of her character, and the suppression of that content. As Diana explains in describing her interpretation of *Macbeth*, "Everything you thought about the play will be reversed in an instant."

In a further twist, we eventually discover that Diana Lee is not the film's central character but that it is instead her daughter Isabel (Elizabeth Banks), a photojournalist, who is preparing for her wedding to her fiancé, Jonathan (James Marsden). In their first scene together, Jonathan lies to Isabel, claiming there is no access to the roof of their building—we learn later that he does not want her to go there because that is where he meets his male lover, Alec (Jesse Bradford), also a resident of their building. In that scene, Jonathan also hides cigarettes from Isabel, denies that they have any, and then, when she leaves, takes one out and smokes it. Just as the tryst between the actor playing Lady Macduff and Diana's husband suggests the speciousness of idealizing the Lady Macduff character, the hidden cigarettes delineate the hidden recesses or lacunae of the text, suggesting that they were deliberately made. Diana, standing for Lady Macbeth, is unfairly compared to her understudy, who stands in for the ever-praised Lady Macduff; and her daughter, a surrogate for misled or incurious readers of *Macbeth*, has been denied information critical to draw conclusions about the man she is planning to marry. The film seems to suggest that audiences and readers of the play have been duped by hidden information, unsound comparisons, and constructions of normative femininity.

Like Diana, both Isabel and Jonathan face crises during the film, which takes place in post–9/11 New York City during a twenty-four-hour period. Jonathan, we learn, is about to be exposed as a nude model and former lover of a famous photographer, Benjamin Stone, and Isabel is offered the journalism assignment of a lifetime by an old boyfriend, an assignment that would postpone her marriage indefinitely. Jonathan, a lawyer, is trying to suppress the photographs of himself and the story; the pictures, he claims "were never meant to be shown in public." We are led to believe that this emerging secret past is Jonathan's conflict, but we find out at the end that his real conflict with Isabel is his ongoing secret relationship with Alec. Just as there are hints about Lady Macbeth's past in Shakespeare's play, the film constantly drops hints about Alec and Jonathan and about all the characters' unexplored histories: Diana may have slept with Benjamin Stone, too; she appears to have negotiated an "open" marriage but is unhappy with it; and Isabel had a serious relationship before the one with Jonathan.

When Jonathan meets with the rabbi (George Segal) about the upcoming marriage, he tells him, "There's some stuff that I haven't told Isabel ... she almost found out about it tonight," an echo, perhaps of act 5, scene 3, lines 45–46, in which Macbeth describes "the stuff'd bosom of that perilous stuff / Which weighs upon the heart." The rabbi responds, "You can't change the past ... tell her what happened, and then you both can move on." Meanwhile, Isabel, miserable about having turned down the photojournalist assignment, goes to her mother's birthday party, where she meets a Welsh artist who encourages her to look behind a door on her mother's roof that has always been locked. "What's behind the door?" he asks, "... It could be Narnia back there." Breaking through locked doors is a lesson Isabel needs to learn — she discovers that there are literal and metaphorical hidden recesses in her personal life that she has resisted exploring. When Isabel and her new acquaintance break through the door, she is awestruck by the rather banal hidden room, a place to hide the building's water tank: "It's like a church," she whispers, suggesting not only her religious conflict with Jonathan (she is Christian and he is Jewish) but also her frustration at his preference for keeping doors, both literal and metaphoric, closed and locked.

The Welsh artist, still nameless, leaves the party with Isabel. On the subway platform, as he chides her for not asking his name, someone attempts to mug Isabel, and her new friend suffers a knife wound while trying to protect her. Isabel follows the ambulance to the hospital but is unable to thank the hero because she cannot enter the ER treatment room without knowing the name of the person she wants to see. Much like many scholars writing about Lady Macbeth, she has not discovered the name that would open doors for her.

When she returns to the apartment she shares with Jonathan, Isabel finds the deliberately hidden cigarettes, washes her hands (highly significant in a *Macbeth*-referencing text, but here suggesting disgust rather than guilt), and, proceeding to the roof of the building, discovers Jonathan with Alec. She does not throw herself from the parapet, however. Isabel is both saddened and relieved to know the relationship is over and goes in search of the Welsh artist. Once again, the emergency room receptionist will not let her pass unless she can provide the name of the person she wants to see. But Isabel has learned. She pushes through the doors anyway, probing into the unknown despite the prohibitions against it, and finds her new friend: "Ian," she says, looking at his chart. And the film ends.

The film's concluding with this final discovery — the Celtic name of an unexamined but chivalrous character from Wales (land of King Arthur) — points back to medieval sources, further suggesting the importance of looking beyond the surface, of mining the past to uncover, at the very least, a person's name, and through that name to discover the details of a person's life, whether for good or for ill.

With so much emphasis on hidden names, stories, and pasts of characters who are hiding emotions and secrets, *Heights* functions as a feminist reading of *Macbeth*. Indeed, director Chris

Terrio, a literature major at Harvard and Cambridge, studied Virginia Woolf, along with phenomenological philosophy and how it "has affected ideas of time and subjectivity."[39] What happens off-camera in *Heights* suggests to some degree what happens offstage in *Macbeth* and also what happens in the lacunae of history. Significantly, in Terrio's and Fox's interpretation of the play, Macbeth is nowhere to be found. Even in that first scene with the Juilliard students, Macbeth has very few lines — Lady Macbeth dominates. None of the recurring billboards of the Broadway production features the play's titular character. Through Diana Lee and her daughter, the film centralizes the hidden, suppressed story of Lady Macbeth. Moreover, the film suggests that Lady Macbeth may be weeping behind pillars though she puts on a mocking and defiant public face.

Partly through this tension between the public and private performances of female characters, *Heights* draws attention to the lost genealogy of Lady Macbeth and other marginalized personas from literature and history; the film underscores the importance of breaking through obstacles — whether they be erected by the author, the sources, or the scholarship on them both — and peering into recesses to discover what has been lost. That so much rests on the real name of a Celtic character, the hero of *Heights*, reminds us also of Lady Macbeth, whose name was mentioned in Boece but occluded by Holinshed, and indicates that we have been prevented from discovering her lost story.

Knowledge of that single name, though, is where we can begin to research her character. As Valbuena notes, it is from a single mention of Gruoch's name in an eleventh-century chartulary of St. Andrew's Church that the trail begins: "*Machbet filius Finlach ... et Gruoch filia Bodeh, Rex et Regina Scottorum.*"[40] With Terrio's and Fox's emphasis on hidden Celtic names, omitted information, and the centrality of Lady Macbeth in contrast to the chronicles, the critics, and the Welles and Polanski films, *Heights* goes some way toward finding Gruoch and uncovering "that perilous stuff / Which weighs upon [her] heart." It may in fact be a watershed moment for depictions of the lady in films. Indeed, *Heights* not only rehabilitates Lady Macbeth from the depictions in the Welles and Polanski film productions of *Macbeth* and paves the way for more progressive interpretations such a Wright's *Macbeth*, it also offers a welcome change from the way in which many Shakespearean women have historically been portrayed in scholarship and film.

Notes

1. All quotations from *Macbeth* are from the Cambridge edition, William Shakespeare, *Macbeth*, ed. A.R. Braunmuller (Cambridge, UK: Cambridge University Press, 2001).
2. For a comprehensive examination of the critical debates about this line, see Kenneth Muir's introduction to the Arden edition of *Macbeth* (London: Methuen, 1955), xlviii-xlix.
3. As Muir notes, the fainting "may be real or pretended"; Shakespeare, *Macbeth*, ed. Muir, 67n.
4. Because it is a film of a staged production, I am not considering the Trevor Nunn production of *Macbeth* for the BBC (1978) starring Judi Dench and Ian McKellen, though it is taught frequently.
5. There are no mentions of Macbeth's wife in the earlier Scottish chronicles; neither Andrew of Wytoun nor John of Fordun makes reference to her. The first mention comes in Boece, and she is further elaborated in Holinshed's *Chronicles of England, Scotlande, and Ireland*. See Geoffrey Bullough, ed., *Narrative and Dramatic Sources of Shakespeare*, vol. 8 (New York: Columbia University Press, 1973), 423–469. Banquo and Fleance are entirely fictional characters with no basis in history.
6. As Glenn Burgess writes, history in the Middle Ages was "to provide moral lessons for the present, and that was its basic function." It was not what we would consider objective. Burgess, *The Politics of the Ancient Constitution: An Introduction to English Political Thought, 1603–1642* (Philadelphia: University of Pennsylvania Press, 1992), 8–9. Historian Janet Nelson writes, "Partiality and prejudice in literary texts of all kinds, including histories, is what historians expect and allow for. Thus the queens of the Old Testament, whose images so strongly influenced medieval writers (including female ones), were models of virtue (Esther) or vice (Jezebel, Athaliah)." Nelson, "Medieval Queenship," in *Women in Medieval Western European Culture*, ed. Linda Mitchell (New York: Garland, 1999), 181.
7. Olga Valbuena, *Subjects to the King's Divorce: Equivocation, Infidelity, and Resistance in Early Modern English Literature* (Bloomington: Indiana University Press, 2003), 107.

8. The open-ended quality of the character of Lady Macbeth has encouraged some actors to do some profitable imagining. When Derek Jacobi remembers his preparation for the 1993 Adrian Noble *Macbeth*, he notes that he and his co-star, Cheryl Campbell, had to come up with a history to explain the reference to the suckled child: "We had decided that somewhere in the past of their relationship they had lost a child. There are many other possible interpretations but you have to decide for one. It's something that really needs a programme note: you can't act it, really, though you can think it." Derek Jacobi, "Macbeth," in William Shakespeare, *Macbeth*, ed. Robert S. Miola (New York: W.W. Norton, 2004), 335. Sinead Cusack mentions making a similar decision with Jonathan Pryce in a 1983 production also directed by Noble: "we decided that the Macbeths had had a child and that the child had died." Quoted in Carol Rutter, *Clamorous Voices: Shakespeare's Women Today* (London: Women's Press, 1989), 56.

9. Though Method acting, a "technique [that] combines work on the role, with an emphasis on researching and experiencing the character's life, and work on the self" (David Krasner, ed., *Method Acting Reconsidered: Theory, Practice, Future* [New York: St. Martin's Press, 2000], 4), is a modern practice, its roots can be found in early modern acting. Hamlet himself discusses the actors finding "the motive and the cue for passion" in performance (2.2.561). He later instructs the actors "to show ... the very age and body of the time his form and pressure" (3.2.23–24). While Konstantin Stanislavski (developer of Method acting) encouraged actors to create an imagined past, Shakespeare in *Hamlet* might have been suggesting a more scholarly approach to investigating the hints of the past left in the text. Actors Michael York and Adrian Brine write that Shakespeare "is ... a man of the theater writing material for actors, and leaving them space.... He does not treat actors as his instruments, but as his colleagues. He opens the door, and points the way along the road, but he does not know the journey's end"; Brine and York, *A Shakespearean Actor Prepares* (Lyme, NH: Smith and Kraus, 2000), 268–269). As actor Fiona Shaw has said, "It's not my right or the right of any actress to define what women are. We are merely trying to understand the circumstances that bring about what they are"; quoted in Penny Gay, *As She Likes It: Shakespeare's Unruly Women* (New York: Routledge, 1994), 5.

10. Reported in the introduction to William Shakespeare, *Macbeth*, ed. A. R. Braunmuller (Cambridge, UK: Cambridge University Press, 2001), 66.

11. See *ibid.*, 80 n. 3. Vivian Lee's hair had changed to gray by act 5 in the 1955 Stratford production.

12. One review of Ellen Terry's Lady Macbeth held that her depiction, "though beautiful, is 'the whitewashing of Lady Macbeth'"; quoted in *ibid.*, 78. Director Glen Byam Shaw of the 1955 production found Lady Macbeth to be quite admirable: "Her loyalty to her husband is magnificent. The way she behaves in the banquet scene is beyond praise. In spite of her complete lack of compassion & goodness of heart one cannot but have the greatest admiration for her courage & loyalty"; quoted in *ibid.*, 81.

13. Peter Ellis, *Celtic Women: Women in Celtic Society and Literature* (Grand Rapids, MI: William B. Eerdmans, 1996), claims that Gruoch "must in no way be confused with the Shakespearian image of 'Lady Macbeth'" (quoted in Valbuena, *Subjects to the King's Divorce*, 99), and few have objected to such injunctions. Marjorie Garber, *Shakespeare After All* (New York: Anchor Books, 2004), consults Shakespeare's sources selectively in her analysis of *Macbeth*; she discusses how tanistry explains Macbeth's aggression against Duncan but does not consider how Gruoch's genealogy might explain Lady Macbeth's.

14. Faith Nostbakken, *Understanding Macbeth: A Student Casebook to Issues, Sources, and Historical Documents* (Westport, CT: Greenwood Press, 1997), 7.

15. Valbuena, *Subjects to the King's Divorce*, 81.

16. Quoted in Harold Bloom, ed., *Macbeth: Major Literary Characters* (New York: Chelsea House Publishers, 1991), 7–8.

17. See *ibid.*, in particular Kay Stockholder's claim that Lady Macbeth has "denied maternity" (226) and Lisa Low's belief that we are drawn to Macbeth "because, like us, he moves within breathing distance of innocence" (211). Frank Kermode, in *The Riverside Shakespeare*, ed. G. Blakemore Evans, et al. (New York: Houghton Mifflin, 1997), 1357, calls Macbeth an Everyman.

18. Valbuena, *Subjects to the King's Divorce*, 97.

19. Gordon Donaldson, *Scottish Kings* (London: B.T. Batsford, 1967), 13.

20. The question is notorious. In 1933, L. C. Knights published "How Many Children Had Lady Macbeth? An Essay in the Theory and Practice of Shakespeare Criticism" (reprinted in *Explorations*, London: Chatto and Windus, 1946), that did not answer the question referred to in its title but instead criticized the school of character-focused criticism such as that of A. C. Bradley that would seek to answer such a question. Attempting to answer the question has remained controversial; Bradley himself thought it irrelevant. Nevertheless, over the last century scholars have continued to raise the question. Marvin Rosenberg writes, "Of course Lady Macbeth has at least one child; she reminds her husband that she has 'given suck,' and knows 'How tender 'tis to love the babe that milks me.' History may insist that the child was not sired by Macbeth; but Shakespeare carefully censored Lady Macbeth's earlier marriage.... Shakespeare begins with a loving pair, and tells us, unequivocally — in a play full of equivocation — that they have had a

child"; Rosenberg, *Educational Theatre Journal* 26, no. 1 (March 1974): 14. See also Elizabeth Nielsen, "Macbeth: The Nemesis of the Post-Shakespearian Actor," *Shakespeare Quarterly* 16, no. 2 (Spring 1965): 193–199.

21. Raphael Holinshed, *The Chronicles of England, Scotlande, and Ireland*, quoted in Bullough, *Narrative and Dramatic Sources of Shakespeare*, 496.

22. Lois L. Huneycutt, *Matilda of Scotland: A Study in Medieval Queenship* (Woodbridge, UK: Boydell Press, 2003), 44. See also Nelson, who writes, "The most important kind of power sought and wielded by an earlier medieval queen was the power to secure the royal succession of her favored candidate, usually her own son"; Nelson, "Macbeth," 195.

23. Nelson, "Macbeth,"198.

24. *Ibid.*, 205.

25. While Lady Macbeth is not queen of Scotland at this point in the play, as the wife of the Thane of Cawdor she is a kind of queen. As Edward J. Cowan puts it, "There was also in eleventh century Scotland some form of gradation of kingship similar to that of Ireland where there were three grades—the *ri* king of a single *thuath* or tribe, the *ruiri*, a superior king recognized as such by the kings of two or more other tribes and a 'king of kings,' the *ri ruirech*"; Cowan, "The Historical Macbeth," in *Moray: Province and People*, ed. W. D. H. Sellar (Edinburgh: Scottish Society for Northern Studies, 1993), 119. Macbeth was *mormaer* of Moray, which Cowan argues is a *ruiri*.

26. Quoted in Michael Anderegg, *Orson Welles, Shakespeare and Popular Culture* (New York: Columbia University Press, 1999), 78.

27. J. Lawrence Guntner, "Hamlet, Macbeth and King Lear on Film," in *The Cambridge Companion to Shakespeare on Film*, ed. Russell Jackson (Cambridge, UK: Cambridge University Press, 2000), 124.

28. Welles's reluctance to allow Nolan a voice in decisions about the production is somewhat typical of how directors have treated female actors. Sinead Cusack, who played Lady Macbeth in the 1986 Stratford production directed by Adrian Noble and starring herself and Jonathan Pryce, describes how she was left out of production planning meetings. She says, "But Adrian and I didn't really talk about the play until the evening of the first rehearsal. That wasn't a good idea. I kept asking to be involved in discussion; Jonathan Pryce was allowed to participate but not me"; quoted in Rutter, *Clamorous Voices*, 57. As a result, when Cusack arrived on the set, she discovered that they had adopted her "nightmare": a black stage and black costumes. As Cusack puts it, "Don't predispose the audience right from the beginning of the play to the tragedy and horror and evil. That'll come. But *let* it come" (57).

29. The redubbed version was released in 1950; the executives at Republic, the studio, also encouraged Welles to make significant cuts, editing some twenty-six minutes from the original 1948 production; Anderegg, *Orson Welles, Shakespeare*, 92–93.

30. Quoted in *ibid.*, 93.

31. Margaret of Scotland, for example, "discussed even the most subtle questions with the learned men of her circle." Joan M. Ferrante, "The Education of Women in the Middle Ages in Theory, Fact, and Fantasy," in *Beyond Their Sex: Learned Women of the European Past*, ed. Patricia H. Labalme (New York: New York University Press, 1984), 11.

32. When cast, Annis was the same age as Polanski's deceased wife, Sharon Tate, who, eight months pregnant, had been murdered in 1969 by the members of the Charles Manson cult. Annis was known for her beauty, and her nude scenes were particularly remarked upon by film critics.

33. See "The Making of '*Macbeth*': Behind the Scenes of Roman Polanski's Latest Film — the First Release under the Playboy Banner," *Playboy*, February 1972.

34. William Shakespeare, *Macbeth*, ed. Braunmuller, 86. In some ways, however, the film is careful to be true to its medieval sources. Lady Macbeth walks barefoot, perhaps a nod to Bellenden's translation of Boece, which notes that medieval Scotswomen "traveled barefooted." In other places, it is clear that Polanski knew Holinshed, for example when he has Duncan formally elevate Malcolm to the position of Prince of Cumberland at court rather than on the battlefield. Polanski was reputedly devoted to reenacting eleventh-century Scotland as accurately as possible.

35. See thecia.com.au/reviews/m/m.shtml the link on that page for macbeth-production-notes.rtf (August 16, 2007).

36. *Ibid.*

37. Amy Fox wrote the one-act play that inspired the Merchant-Ivory production team to commission her to write a full-length film script.

38. Not only does this scene suggest that we miss Lady Macbeth's complexities, it also seems to comment wryly on the one-sided femme fatale characters Close is notorious for playing (Alex Forrest in *Fatal Attraction* [1987] and Marquise Isabelle de Merteuil in *Dangerous Liaisons* [1988]). These characters represent ugly stereotypes of strong women; they are the wicked cinematic daughters of Lady Macbeth as interpreted in the limited way described here.

39. Walter Chaw (Film Freak), "*Heights* Director Chris Terrio Isn't Afraid of Virginia Woolf," interview with Chris Terrio, July 10, 2005, filmfreakcentral.net/notes/cterriointerview.htm (June 28, 2007).
40. Valbuena, *Subjects to the King's Divorce*, 102.

WORKS CITED

Anderegg, Michael. *Orson Welles, Shakespeare and Popular Culture*. New York: Columbia University Press, 1999.
Bloom, Howard, ed. *Macbeth: Major Literary Characters*. New York: Chelsea House Publishers, 1991.
Brine, Adrian, and Michael York. *A Shakespearean Actor Prepares*. Lyme, NH: Smith and Kraus, 2000.
Bullough, Geoffrey, ed. *Narrative and Dramatic Sources of Shakespeare*. Vol. 8. New York: Columbia University Press, 1973.
Burgess, Glenn. *The Politics of the Ancient Constitution: An Introduction to English Political Thought, 1603–1942*. Philadelphia: University of Philadelphia Press, 1992.
Chaw, Walter. "*Heights* Director Chris Terrio Isn't Afraid of Virginia Woolf." Interview with Chris Terrio, July 10, 2005. http://filmfreakcentral.net/notes/cterriointerview.htm (June 28, 2007).
Cowan, Edward J. "The Historical Macbeth." In *Moray: Province and People*, edited by W. D. H. Sellar. Edinburgh: Scottish Society for Northern Studies, 1993.
Donaldson, Gordon. *Scottish Kings*. London: B. T. Batsford, 1967.
Ellis, Peter. *Celtic Women: Women in Celtic Society and Literature*. Grand Rapids, MI: William B. Eerdmans, 1996.
Ferrante, Joan M. "The Education of Women in the Middle Ages in Theory, Fact, and Fantasy." In *Beyond Their Sex: Learned Women of the European Past*, edited by Patricia H. Labalme. New York: New York University Press, 1984.
Garber, Marjorie. *Shakespeare after All*. New York: Anchor Books, 2004.
Gay, Penny. *As She Likes It: Shakespeare's Unruly Women*. New York: Routledge, 1994.
Guntner, J. Lawrence. "Hamlet, Macbeth and King Lear on Film." In *The Cambridge Companion to Shakespeare on Film*, edited by Russell Jackson. Cambridge, UK: Cambridge University Press, 2000.
Holinshed, Raphael. *The Chronicles of England, Scotlande, and Ireland*. Quoted in *Narrative and Dramatic Sources of Shakespeare*, vol. 8, edited by Geoffrey Bullough, 496. New York: Columbia University Press, 1973.
Huneycutt, Lois L. *Matilda of Scotland: A Study in Medieval Queenship*. Woodbridge, UK: Boydell Press, 2003.
Jacobi, Derek. "Macbeth." In William Shakespeare, *Macbeth*, ed. Robert S. Miola. New York: W. W. Norton, 2004.
Knights, L. C. "'How Many Children Had Lady Macbeth': An Essay in the Theory and Practice of Shakespeare Criticism." 1933. Reprinted in *Explorations*, London: Chatto and Windus, 1946.
Krasner, David, ed. *Method Acting Reconsidered: Theory, Practice, Future*. New York: St. Martin's Press, 2000.
"The Making of *Macbeth*: Behind the Scenes of Roman Polanski's Latest Film — the First Release under the Playboy Banner." *Playboy*, February 1972.
Nelson, Janet. "Medieval Queenship." In *Women in Medieval Western European Culture*, edited by Linda Mitchell. New York: Garland Publishing, 1999.
Nielsen, Elizabeth. "Macbeth: The Nemesis of the Post-Shakespearian Actor." *Shakespeare Quarterly* 16, no. 2 (Spring 1965): 193–199.
Nostbakken, Faith. *Understanding Macbeth: A Student Casebook to Issues, Sources, and Historical Documents*. Westport, CT: Greenwood Press, 1997.
Rosenberg, Marvin. "Lady Macbeth's Indispensable Child." *Educational Theatre Journal* 26, no. 1 (March 1974): 14–19.
Rutter, Carol. *Clamorous Voices: Shakespeare's Women Today*. London: Women's Press, 1989.
Shakespeare, William. *Macbeth*. Edited by A. R. Braunmuller. Cambridge, UK: Cambridge University Press, 2001.
_____. *Macbeth*. Edited by Kenneth Muir. London: Methuen, 1955.
_____. *Macbeth*. Edited by Robert S. Miola. New York: W. W. Norton, 2004.
_____. *The Riverside Shakespeare*. Edited by G. Blakemore Evans, et al. New York: Houghton Mifflin, 1997.
Valbuena, Olga L. *Subjects to the King's Divorce: Equivocation, Infidelity, and Resistance in Early Modern English Literature*. Bloomington: Indiana University Press, 2003.

FILMOGRAPHY

1948 *Macbeth*, d. Orson Welles, with Orson Welles and Jeanette Nolan. USA: Mercury/Republic.
1971 *Macbeth*, d. Roman Polanski, with Jon Finch and Francesca Annis. UK: Playboy/Columbia.

1987 *Fatal Attraction*, d. Adrian Lyne, with Glenn Close and Michael Douglas. USA: Paramount Pictures.
1988 *Dangerous Liaisons*, d. Stephen Frears, with Glenn Close and John Malkovich. USA: Lorimar.
2005 *Heights*, d. Chris Terrio, with Glenn Close and Elizabeth Banks. USA: Sony Pictures Classics.
2006 *Macbeth*, d. Geoffrey Wright, with Sam Worthington and Victoria Hill. Australia: Arclight Films.

Part III. "Many Merry Men": The Comedies

Introduction to Part III

Sid Ray

The Middle Ages have been played for laughs since, of course, the Middle Ages began. In following "The Knight's Tale" with "The Miller's Tale" in *The Canterbury Tales*, Chaucer mandates that renderings of the Middle Ages be both sincere and silly, romantic and ribald, earnest and ironic. Like Chaucer, Shakespeare adds to and celebrates medieval tropes and clichés even as he pokes fun at them. This mixture of nostalgia for and parody of the Middle Ages emerges fully in the history plays, but it is also detectable in Shakespeare's comedies. Though *As You Like It*, for one, is in many ways an early modern comedy "rooted in its place and time," as James Shapiro says, it is chock-full of sly and witty references to medieval romance and fabliaux.[1]

When Celia teases Rosalind with an account of seeing Orlando in the forest under a tree, she describes, "There lay he stretched along like a wounded knight," in prose dangerously close to mocking a classic medieval tableau (3.2.235–236). Celia later goes further in her playful assessment of Orlando as not quite living up to romantic notions of knighthood:

> O, that's a brave man; he writes brave verses, speaks brave words, swears brave oaths, and breaks them bravely, quite traverse, athwart the heart of his lover, as a puny tilter, that spurs his horse but on one side, breaks his staff like a noble goose [3.5.37–41].

Likened here to a "puny tilter," Orlando is a throwback to medieval clichés, prefiguring the overdone Arthurian hero Luke Skywalker, especially when Orlando says such things as "The spirit of my father grows strong in me" (1.1.65–66) and stands there "a mere lifeless block," dumbstruck by Rosalind's beauty (1.2.238).

Orlando's name is the Italianate version (and an almost perfect anagram) of Roland, the name of his father, Sir Rowland de Boys, and, not coincidentally, the name of the popular medieval hero Sir Roland of the eleventh-century poem *Chanson de Roland*, which spawned a long line of Rolandic literary works.[2] Shakespeare changed the name of this hero from the Rosader of his source, Thomas Lodge's prose narrative *Rosalynde*, based on "The Tale of Gamelyn," which was believed at the time to have been written by Chaucer. Living up to his name, Orlando, a mixed-up Roland, yearns for the recent medieval past, the "antique world," as he calls it (2.3.57). The third son, abused by his eldest brother, he matures from boy to man by performing a series of heroic stunts with medieval analogues, and he rises in status with each.

Like Chaucer's Miller, Orlando excels at "wrastlynge," and it is his prowess at the sport that wins him Rosalind's affections. A favorite sport of the Middle Ages, wrestling was depicted in early book illustrations and mentioned in Geoffrey of Monmouth as the sport at which Corineus, founder and first duke of Cornwall, defeated the Cornish giant Gogmagog.[3] Talk of the wrestling match reminds Celia of "an old tale" (1.2.124), and Orlando's winning of Rosalind in this fashion recalls tournaments of the Middle Ages. Orlando evokes the heroic defeat of Gogmagog in ancient Britain in his match against Charles, "the Duke's wrestler" (1.1.89), but Corineus is only one of the medieval heroes Orlando evokes in the play.

Rosalind (Bryce Dallas Howard) and Orlando (David Oyelowo) in *As You Like It*, dir. Kenneth Branagh (2006). Courtesy of the Cinema Museum, London.

Duke Senior lives, as Charles tells us, with "many merry men ... like the old Robin Hood of England" (1.1.110–111). But rather than the duke, it is Orlando who most resembles Robin Hood when he demands food from the royal table at sword-point to feed Adam, his aged and starving servant. As with Orlando's anagrammatic kinship with Sir Roland, this allusion to medieval England's native hero cuts two ways: it is both nostalgic for a romantic past and ironic about it. The "of England" qualifier on Robin Hood makes the hero alien in his Englishness to these quasi-French courtiers, but as a historical figure his motivations are also foreign to the burgeoning individualism and capitalism of the play's early modern English audience.

Fighting the lioness, of course, finally elevates Orlando to a level worthy of Rosalind, the heir to a duke. Though he does not reach into the lioness's throat and extract her heart, he at least survives the battle. This last evocation of a medieval hero, Richard the Lionheart, not only gives Orlando the stature he needs to be a husband to his Rosalind but also reveals Rosalind's own "good heart" for Orlando (4.3.171), which Orlando has metaphorically reached and seized.

Ever the good sport, Rosalind plays along with both Orlando's chivalric performance and Celia's gentle mocking of it. She is no passive lady waiting for her knight. She cross-dresses as a kind of knight herself, with "a gallant curtal ax upon [her] thigh, / A boarspear in [her hand]" (1.3.116–115); she is in fact as much a descendant of Sir Roland as Orlando is. The letters of Rosalind's name rearranged spell "is Roland" (and nearly "Sir Roland"), one of the clever ways in which Shakespeare creates a twinship between Rosalind and her beloved Orlando and links them to the medieval romance tradition.

Rosalind herself plays on the themes of medieval romance. She takes the lead in the courtship when, cross-dressed as Ganymede, she pretends to be Rosalind and teaches Orlando that the "chroniclers of that age," that is, the age that celebrated the hero-knight, were "foolish." She takes a jaundiced view of Orlando's medieval ideals: "Men have died from time to time, and worms have eaten them, but not for love" (4.1.99–100). The joke is on both of them, however, in that, as

Rosalind (Bryce Dallas Howard) crossdressing as Ganymede in Branagh's *As You Like It* (2006). Courtesy of the Cinema Museum, London.

Shakespeare plainly recognized, medieval romance is inescapable; Orlando nearly does die for love when, channeling the legend of Richard the Lionheart, he fights the lioness to protect his villainous brother, and Rosalind faints like any common or garden damsel in distress when she hears the news.[4]

While Chaucer may have pioneered comedic takes on the medieval tradition, Shakespeare added some music and brokered them into an industry. *As You Like It*, with its five songs, may have been a very early prototype for musical theater, although the first true musical, John Gay's *The Beggar's Opera*, was not written until 1728.[5] One song from *As You Like It*, "It was a lover and his lass," appeared in Thomas Morley's *The First Book of Ayres* (1600), an early modern songbook. The first adaptation of a Shakespeare play to musical did not come to fruition until 1938 in the form of Rogers and Hart's *The Boys from Syracuse,* a reinterpretation of *The Comedy of Errors*. *Errors* has since been adapted again as *A Bomb-itty of Errors*, a hip-hop exploration of the play billed as an "ad-rap-tation." Cole Porter's *Kiss Me, Kate* (first produced in 1948) is a wildly popular and award-winning musical take on *The Taming of the Shrew*. Perhaps inspired by these successful adaptations, Kenneth Branagh exploited the musical theater qualities of Shakespearean comedy in his refiguring of *Love's Labour's Lost* as musical film (1999).

While none of these musical adaptations is particularly medieval, Shakespeare's overall debt to the music of the Middle Ages is deep. As any first-year medievalist (or French student) knows, the *Chanson de Roland* is itself musical, and so music, comedy, and the Middle Ages have always traditionally gone together. On the page or in performance, as Shakespeare well knew, medievalism sells, and as Rogers and Hart, Cole Porter, and others have discovered, Shakespeare's comedies seem highly adaptable to ironic power ballads and witty choruses.

As the essays in this section suggest, the medieval world is in the marrow of Shakespeare's

(From left) Berowne (Kenneth Branagh), Longaville (Matthew Lillard), King Ferdinand of Navarre (Alessandro Nivola) and Dumaine (Adrian Lester) in Branagh's musical version of *Love's Labour's Lost* (2000). Courtesy of the Cinema Museum, London.

funny bone, even though the comedies also focus on such early modern themes as the rising merchant class (*The Merchant of Venice*), the crisis of the aristocracy (*Twelfth Night*), the conditions of the working class (*A Midsummer Night's Dream*), and compulsory marriage (all of them). Gary Waller's examination of medieval vestiges of the Virgin and how they are staged in *All's Well, That Ends Well* demonstrates that the religion and iconography of medieval England resonated for Shakespeare in protofeminist ways. Martha W. Driver's exploration of medieval sources in *A Midsummer Night's Dream* sheds new light on Shakespeare's debt to medieval folklore, Chaucer's "Knight's Tale," *Legend of Good Women*, and "Sir Thopas" and finds in her reading of Benjamin Britten's opera that fertile grouping of the medieval, the musical, and the comical. Finally, in an implicit but fitting critique of war in general, Julia Ruth Briggs examines the medieval elements in *Troilus and Cressida* and *The Two Noble Kinsmen* that suggest the bard's disillusionment with violence and warfare. This is Julia's own Shakespearean chanson, a swansong in all senses of the word.

NOTES

1. James Shapiro, *A Year in the Life of William Shakespeare 1599* (New York: HarperCollins, 2005), 216.
2. Some of these include Ariosto's *Orlando Furioso*, Boiardo's *Orlando Innamorato*, and Woolf's *Orlando*.
3. Thanks to Martha W. Driver for sharing her knowledge of wrestling in early book illustrations. Geoffrey of Monmouth, *Historia Regum Britanniae* (ca. 1136–1139). A further allusion in *As You Like It* to Geoffrey of Monmouth's chronicle emerges with the lovesick shepherd Silvius. In Geoffrey, Silvius is Aeneas's grandson and the father of Brutus, legendary founder of Britain.
4. Patricia Parker's wonderful book on early romance is titled *Inescapable Romance: Studies in the Poetics of a Mode* (Princeton, NJ: Princeton University Press, 1979).

5. See Shapiro, *Year in the Life*, 224, who considers *As You Like It* an "embryonic musical" and notes that by 1824 a production of the play at Drury Lane also included songs from *A Midsummer Night's Dream, Twelfth Night, The Passionate Pilgrim,* and *Venus and Adonis*, with an original piece appended to the end: "An Allegorical Dance and Chorus of Aeriel Spirits."

Works Cited

Parker, Patricia. *Inescapable Romance: Studies in the Poetics of a Mode.* Princeton, NJ: Princeton University Press, 1979.
Shapiro, James. *A Year in the Life of William Shakespeare 1599.* New York: HarperCollins, 2005.

Performances

1938 *The Boys from Syracuse*, d. George Abbott, with Eddie Albert. New York, Alvin Theater, Broadway.
1948 *Kiss Me, Kate*, d. John C. Wilson, with Alfred Drake and Patricia Morison, New York, New Century Theatre, Broadway.
1999 *The Bomb-itty of Errors*, d. Andy Goldberg, with Jordan Allen Dutton, New York, 45 Bleecker, Off-Broadway.
2000 *Love's Labour's Lost*, d. Kenneth Branagh, with Kenneth Branagh and Natascha McElhone. UK/USA: Arts Council of England/Miramax.
2007 *As You Like It*, d. Kenneth Branagh, with Bryce Dallas Howard and David Oyelowo. UK: BBC Films.

Reading *A Midsummer Night's Dream* through Middle English Romance

Martha W. Driver

> Who may been a fool but if he love?
> —"The Knight's Tale," 1.1799

This essay provides a brief overview of the several medieval sources that inform William Shakespeare's play *A Midsummer Night's Dream* (*MND*) and looks at their rendering (or not) in past and contemporary performance. Modern memory retains some vestigial sense of the underlying sources of Shakespeare's play, though the main intention of modern directors is to make Shakespeare relevant to present-day audiences. It is fascinating, however, to observe how many of the medieval underpinnings remain, even in modern production.[1] The influence of medieval romance, in particular, on *MND* seems clearly evident. While the many Chaucerian references in *MND* are well known, much discussed, and will be briefly summarized, this essay focuses on the influence of Middle English romance on Shakespeare's play, especially of the romance *Huon of Burdeux*[2] in shaping the supernatural characters and of Geoffrey Chaucer's comic masterpiece "Sir Thopas" on Shakespeare's representation of Bottom and on the Pyramus and Thisbe play.

Though the medieval sources are themselves not precisely fixed, their characters, plots, and to some extent their language are appropriated and transformed in Shakespeare's drama, influencing (perhaps often unconsciously) modern performance, which is also malleable, shifting shape each time the play is staged or filmed. "Like textual variants, historical subtexts cannot easily be performed," as Diana E. Henderson has pointed out, but understanding more about the medieval texts influencing Shakespeare's plays "may lead us back not solely to the remembrance of things past but also to historically informed analogies within the present, a careful use of history that adds more drama."[3] This, then, is a reading of the play primarily through the lens of medieval romance, with which Shakespeare and several of his famous contemporaries seem to have been quite familiar, a reading that further examines several aspects of "late modern collaborations with an early modern Englishman's vision of his country's late medieval past."[4]

Overview

It seems that the more one studies a Shakespeare play, the more sources one finds. The Theseus-Hippolyta frame of *MND* has been taken from Chaucer's "Knight's Tale," as John W. Hales noted in 1873, and further source hunters have found references to Chaucer's "The Merchant's Tale," "The Tale of Sir Thopas," *Legend of Good Women*, "Parliament of Fowles," and "Book of the Duchess."[5] In her important survey of Chaucer's influence on Shakespeare, Ann Thompson comments that in *MND* "The borrowings are of every kind, from substantial parallels of plot to the briefest of one-line references."[6] Writing in 1957, Kenneth Muir found ten probable sources for the play, most of them for Pyramus and Thisbe.[7] Muir asserts, along with several other critics, that the rivalry of the young lovers, Demetrius and Lysander, for Hermia was suggested by the rivalry of Palamon and Arcite for Emily in "The Knight's Tale," an idea also put forward by Dorothy Bethurum in 1945, who comments that Shakespeare heightens "the satire he found in Chaucer. The plots of the tales are not the same, of course, but the situation is, that of two lovers contending for a girl. Shakespeare raises the comedy to farce by having them contend, not for one girl, but for two. He makes Emily two girls, leaves Palamon and Arcite as they are, and allows the extravagances of love and youth full play."[8] While Muir is rather dismissive of the fairies, saying "most of the fairy matter seems to have been derived from folk-lore," Bethurum elaborates on the suggestion made by Thomas Tyrwhitt in the eighteenth century (and later by Otto Ballmann in 1902 and many others) that the quarrel of the fairy king and queen was suggested by the debate between Pluto and Proserpyna in Chaucer's "Merchant's Tale," where the gods of the underworld are described as fairies in typical medieval fashion.[9] Again, as many critics have, Bethurum compares Bottom's infatuation with the fairy queen to the love of Chaucer's Sir Thopas for his elf queen.[10] "Sir Thopas" is Chaucer's spoof of medieval romance, and its ties to Shakespeare's play, while often cited in passing, have not been closely examined. Perhaps most importantly, Bethurum aptly identifies *MND* as a satire of medieval romance.[11] Bethurum seems most on the pulse of the play when she writes "that the story of the four lovers was conceived in the spirit of parody on mediaeval romance" and that in *MND* "it is literary forms which are being satirized."[12] As this exercise and summary suggest, it seems Shakespeare read his copy of Chaucer well.[13] This paper argues further that Shakespeare was more closely familiar with Middle English romance than has been noted previously and that this familiarity influenced his portrayal not only of the lovers but of the fairies and the "rude mechanicals."

Medieval Romance

What elements typical of Middle English romance might Shakespeare have incorporated when drafting *MND*? According to John Finlayson, knightly adventure is "the real core of *romance*," and among its elements are various standard "'characteristics,' such as the love motif, the encounter with the supernatural, and the elaborate *descriptio personae*." But, even by Chaucer's day, medieval romance was a bit tired, if still read and much loved, the point of the wild satire in Chaucer's "Sir Thopas, " "a parody," says Finlayson, that "depends on the audience's recognition of the standard pattern of romance."[14] Carol Fewster has noted further distinctive elements of Middle English romances: the story is often told in rhymed couplets, and paralleling, or doubling, is a regular feature. In this "diptych structure," characters and/or story elements are doubled "to create two sets of parallel events." Other components that create a sense "of artificial self-containedness" include "recapitulation, verbal repetition, [and] thematic patterning."[15] In addition, medieval romance is self-referential, often describing itself as performative, which is very probably a literary conceit rather than a statement of actual fact.[16] The stories are placed in distant times, and adventures occur in exotic foreign lands, while the concept of the knight in these stories "is a literary play-space, without closely mapped-social reference."[17] Medieval romance also employs fantastic elements, such as "magic, grateful lions, dragons and giants, foolproof disguises: many of the devices and incidents in romance suggest their own separateness from the real."[18]

Several of the same elements are found in *MND*: Chaucer's Emily, loved by two men in "The Knight's Tale," is doubled to become two young women, Hermia and Helena. The concept of "diptych structure" might be further expanded to include the parallel plots, themes, and allusions in the Theseus-Hippolyta frame, the fairies' quarrel, the lovers' chase, and the play performed by the mechanicals. *MND* alludes to the idea of knighthood several times, usually satirically. The mechanicals, for example, are apparently aware of medieval romance as a type of story. "What is Thisbe, a wandering knight?" asks Flute (1.2.41) when Quince first assigns him his role, a naive reference to tales of knight errantry, and in the Pyramus and Thisbe play, Bottom, as Pyramus discovering the bloodied mantle, refers to himself as a "poor knight" (5.1.266). In the quarrel between Titania and Oberon over the Indian boy, "jealous Oberon would have the child Knight of his train" (2.1.24–25), that is, to serve the fairy lord as a member of his preternatural court, while the deluded, fickle Lysander under the influence of love-in-idleness turns all his vows from Hermia to Helena, vowing to honor her "and to be her knight!" (2.2.143). Like the supernatural elements in medieval romances, the enchanted wood of *MND* provides an otherworldly setting, and the fairies are the catalyst for the lovers' misadventures. Even the gentle lion, so familiar from medieval romances of *Yvain*, *Perceval*, and *Sir Lanval*, makes a comic appearance in Shakespeare's play. As Fewster points out, elements of medieval romance "can be moved around, re-quoted, ironised and used in a whole series of economical and creative ways."[19]

Oberon as Fairy King: Sources and Performance

Writing in 1904, H. R. D. Anders traced Shakespeare's Oberon to a character of the same name who appears in *The Boke of Duke Huon of Burdeux*, translated from a French chivalric prose romance by Sir John Bourchier, Lord Berners (*c.* 1467–1533), an important early Tudor author and translator.[20] According to entries in Philip Henslowe's Diary, a play of Huon's adventures ("hewen of burdoche") was performed during the 1593–1594 Christmas season, though this play is now lost.[21] Oberon appears briefly in *James IV* (1590?, printed 1598), a play by "England's first celebrity author," Robert Greene (*c.* 1558–1592).[22] Oberon is also briefly named as king of fairies by Edmund Spenser in Book 2, Canto 1, of the *Faerie Queene* (1596), where he is linked with Huon, and again in the fairyland genealogy provided in Canto 10.[23] The romance of *Huon of Burdeux* seems to have been known by Christopher Marlowe and was used as a source by Ben Jonson in a late play called *The Magnetic Lady, or Humors Reconciled* (licensed Oct. 12, 1632, printed 1641).[24]

That Shakespeare drew the character of his fairy king from the Oberon who figures largely in the Middle English romance of *Huon* has been suggested (in passing) for about a century.[25] The fairy king in the medieval romance comes from India, is interested in the affairs of Athens, and haunts the wood through which the hero, Huon, must travel on his way to Babylon: "in that wood abydyth a kynge of ye fayrey namyd Ober*on* / he is of heyght but of .iii. fote, and crokyd shulderyd, but yet he hathe an aungelyke visage."[26] Fathered by Julius Caesar, this Oberon is only three feet tall because of a fairy curse — the one fairy who was overlooked at the party celebrating his birth condemns Oberon to remain the size of a three-year-old child forever, but then remorsefully makes him "the fayreste creature that euer nature formyd." The other fairies ensure that Oberon will never age and that he can tame all birds and beasts, and they give him the gifts of instant travel anywhere and anything he wants simply by wishing.[27]

Riding through the woods wearing a rich gown "so garnyshyd w*ith* precy*ous* stones that the clerenes of them shone lyke the sone," this Oberon is a master illusionist; with his magic horn, he can summon fantastic rain, wind, hail, snow, marvelous tempests with thunder and lightning so it will seem "that all the worlde shoulde pereshe," and he can also create, so Huon is told, "a grete rynnynge riuer, blacke and depe. But ye may passe it at your ease, and it shall not wete the fete of your horse / for all is but fantesey and enchauntment*es*."[28] Huon is warned not to speak with Oberon, despite his beautiful face and frightening phantasms, as then Huon will be lost forever. But, curious to meet the dwarf fairy king, Huon does not heed this advice; he rides through

Oberon's woods and experiences the predicted illusions.[29] Oberon then befriends Huon and helps him through his many adventures.

Throughout this rather lengthy romance, Huon does not follow Oberon's advice either and regularly gets himself into situations from which he needs rescue by the fairy king, who functions as a magical father figure to the hero knight.[30] Finally, as Oberon is dying, he summons Huon and his wife, Esclaramonde, to his palace, where he sits upon "a ryche trone garnyshed & borderyd with fyne golde and precyous stones" and entertains Morgan le Faye, among other fairies.[31] A flying monk transports Huon and Esclaramonde to fairyland, and Huon is proclaimed Oberon's successor: "I ordeyne that Huon who is here presented be your kynge and lorde, & Esclaramonde quene and lady / and fro hensforthe I put my realme and dyngnyte into his handes ... none shal haue it but alonly Huon of Burdeaux, who is here present, whom I wyl crowne kynge in all your presences." As with the deaths of medieval saints (and Sir Lancelot in Sir Thomas Malory's *Morte Darthur*), Oberon dies in the odor of sanctity: "there was so swete a smell *tha*t euery man thought they had bene rauysshed in to paradise."[32]

In the Middle English romance Oberon is described as child-sized with the face of an angel. He can create illusions and leads human wanderers astray in the woods, but ultimately his purpose is to bless human endeavors. Oberon in *Huon of Burdeux* is, in effect, a composite of Puck and Oberon in Shakespeare's play. In creating two characters out of one, Shakespeare is again employing the doubling or twinning element that is also typically found in medieval romance, similar to the twinning of Emily in the persons of Hermia and Helena. Puck might thus be read as a projection of Oberon, or as an aspect of Oberon, with additions from English folklore in his dual representation as Robin Goodfellow.[33]

In nineteenth- and twentieth-century productions, this idea of duality, or "diptych structure," has been realized by casting the same actors to play two roles; in several famous modern versions of the play, Theseus and Oberon are played by the same actor, as are Hippolyta and Titania, characters who are never on stage at the same time, a practice that may go back to earliest Elizabethan productions, as David Bevington, among others, has suggested.[34] The recent stage production and subsequent film by Adrian Noble (1996) push this doubling almost to the limit. The invented boy dreamer who provides another frame for the plot in Noble's film is also the Indian

Oberon (Rupert Everett) and Titania (Michelle Pfeiffer) contend in *A Midsummer Night's Dream*, dir. Michael Hoffman (1999).

boy of the quarrel between the fairy king and queen. Theseus and Oberon are played by the same actor, as are Titania and Hippolyta; Puck is played by the same actor who plays Philostrate; the fairies under Titania's command (Peaseblossom, *et al.*) are played by the same actors as play the mechanicals.[35]

On stage, Oberon, the director of the central action in Shakespeare's play, has been variously played by women or as a rather menacing dark male figure wearing a crown of antlers or twigs; in Benjamin Britten's opera, the role of Oberon is sung by a countertenor. In the 1840s, when Victoria was on the throne, the role of Oberon was acted and sung on the London stage by Lucia Elizabeth Vestris, a sultry brunette contralto, and "after Vestris, the role of Oberon was played by a woman in every major English and American production of the play until 1914, with one exception,"[36] which puts a curious spin on perceptions and representations of female power in patriarchal Victorian culture, as well as upon the gender dynamics within the play itself. The production in London and New York of 1914–1915 directed by Harley Granville Barker made perhaps an even stranger familial connection between maternal and paternal Oberons, casting in the part Dennis Neilson-Terry, whose mother, Julia, had played the role of Oberon in Sir Herbert Beerbohm Tree's production of 1900.[37] In the 1925 German Expressionist film of Shakespeare's play (*Ein Summernachtstraum*), Oberon was played by the Russian ballerina Tamara Geva, who was also the first wife of the celebrated choreographer George Balanchine.[38]

In the staged productions by Max Reinhardt which began to be seen in 1905 (and were played some 587 times between 1905 and 1919) and culminated in Reinhardt's 1935 film, Oberon sometimes wore "a rather imposing rack of antlers; in the film, Oberon (Victor Jory) wears a crown of silver and antlerlike twigs and rides a black horse."[39] Reinhardt's Oberon becomes one model for the character's subsequent more manly representation on stage and screen. A great showman legendary for his extravagant outdoor presentations of *A Midsummer Night's Dream* in Florence, Oxford, and Hollywood, Reinhardt drew his fairies from German folk tradition, including "trolls, dwarfs, gnomes, and pixies," and the main focus of his stage set was the forest.[40] Reinhardt's first set for the production opening at Berlin's Neues Theatre am Schiffbauerdamm in 1905 "featured a revolving, shadowy, three-dimensional forest," and one commentator, Heinz Herald, remarked upon the centrality of the wood, which is almost a character itself in Reinhardt's reading of the play: "It breathes, it is alive," wrote Herald.[41]

Victor Jory as Oberon in *A Midsummer Night's Dream*, dir. Max Reinhardt and William Dieterle (1935).

Oberon's enchanted wood has

a similar function in Benjamin Britten's romantic chamber opera, the 1960 adaptation of Shakespeare's play by Britten and Peter Pears, with music by Britten.[42] The opera opens with the music and setting of the forest; much of the action occurs there, and the wood itself is personified, again almost seeming to breathe through the music: "The wood indeed is virtually a character — a musical character — in the opera; no mere background to the action but a living, breathing entity that affects all who enter it."[43] In the Glyndebourne Festival Opera production, the trees are shown as swaying and embodied, some portrayed by actors dressed in greenery with branches; the music seems to sigh and moan like the wind.[44] Oberon, the king of this eerie place, is a countertenor, and while his duets with Titania ("Tytania" in the libretto) are as beautiful and transcendent as any baroque song featuring a countertenor and a coloratura soprano by George Frideric Handel, for example, much has been made of this Oberon's perhaps unnatural relationship to Puck and the boy fairies.[45] But Britten's Oberon is not so far from his female forebears, the women who impersonated the fairy king onstage in the nineteenth and early twentieth centuries, and he becomes more understandable still when he is read through the Oberon in the medieval romance of *Huon*, who has been split by Shakespeare into two entities, the king Oberon and the sprite Puck.

While Shakespeare's Oberon, like the fairy king in *Huon*, has a protective and paternal role toward both fairies and humans, Puck retains the qualities of shape-shifter and illusionist; like Oberon in *Huon*, Puck travels swiftly, is often child-sized or played by children, and misleads humans in the forest, a trait that is probably the source of Shakespeare's other identification of Puck with Robin Goodfellow.[46] In Britten's opera, Puck is a speaking part played by a boy acrobat.[47] Reinhardt famously cast the diminutive fourteen-year-old Mickey Rooney in the role of Puck in his Hollywood Bowl production in September 1934 and again in his 1935 film, in which fairies are played by both adults and children. Reinhardt's film version also shows Puck shifting shape in Act 3 after the transformation of Bottom: as Puck chases the mechanicals from the wood, he is literally shown onscreen becoming a hound, a hog, and a fire.[48] Even when played by adults, Puck tends to be of small size; one thinks of Ian Holm in the role in the Peter Hall film (1968). There may also be some faint recollection of the child-sized fairy king of *Huon* in the casting of children in the roles of fairies, the history of which seems very old.[49] The hairy, randy Robin Goodfellow of broadside and ballad does not seem to be quite the same figure portrayed in Shakespeare's text, as several scholars have noted, though he is sometimes played that way.[50] Puck in Noble's production is shown as very sexually charged, for example, simulating sex with a sleeping Helena and kissing Oberon on the lips just before he flies off to "put a girdle round the earth in 40 minutes."[51]

In *Robin Good-Fellow, His Mad Prankes, and Merry Jests* (1628), a text that postdates *MND* and probably draws upon Shakespeare's play for some of its material, Oberon "impregnates a country maid, the result of which union is the rough and hairy Robin Goodfellow."[52] In this version of the story, Oberon has become an actual parent, which seems to literalize the parental and guiding roles that Oberon plays both in *Huon* and in Shakespeare's play. As for Puck and Oberon in *A Midsummer Night's Dream*, whether they are played by women, children, or strangely attired men, the Oberon in *Huon of Burdeux* is their "parent and original," in whom qualities of both Shakespearean characters are combined.

Medieval Romance and the Mechanicals

Bottom's encounter with Titania and the play of Pyramus and Thisbe seem also to have roots in medieval romance, perhaps most particularly in Chaucer's hilarious burlesque of the genre in his "Tale of Sir Thopas." As Derek Pearsall has remarked, Chaucer's poem "almost seems to have been made up by a latter-day Peter Quince from some list of instructions on 'How to write a romance,'" and the tone of "Sir Thopas" is similar to that found in the Pyramus and Thisbe play:

"There too there is the lovingly absurd burlesque of a style and a literary art that Shakespeare had absorbed, learnt from and outgrown."[53]

Dieter Mehl further points to Chaucer's satire "as exaggerated, brilliantly precise, and detached imitation," in which the "poet seizes on certain characteristic examples from the wealth of formulas and motifs in the romances, ... and transforms them by his art, an art that is very different from the spirit of the romances."[54] The final section of this essay examines the poets' (and directors') transformative power more fully.

Chaucer's Sir Thopas is a young knight, described "as fair and gent In bataille and in tourneyment" (715–716), who rides into "a fair forest" (754) to seek adventure. When he hears birdsong in the woods, particularly the notes of the thrush, a bird twice mentioned ("The thrustelcok made eek hir lay," 769; "whan he herde the thrustel synge," 774), Sir Thopas falls immediately "in love-longynge" (771) and decides to seek the fairy queen of whom he has dreamed "al this nyght" (787). Thopas then seeks "An elf-queene for t'espye" (799), and enters "The contree of Fairye So wilde" (802–803). He quickly comes to the dwelling place of the fairy queen, which is full of magical music ("Heere is the queene of Fayerye, With harpe and pipe and symphonye, Dwellynge in this place," 814–816). Sir Oliphaunt ("elephant"), a three-headed giant and protector of the fairy bower, then challenges Thopas to fight. Thopas agrees to meet him the next day on the battlefield when he is properly armored, after which Thopas fortifies himself for the fight with "sweete wyn" and "gyngebreed" (851, 854). Wearing "cote-armour As whit as is a lilye flour," the hero-knight is armored with several unlikely weapons along with a shield "al of gold" (866–867, 869), impractical in battle for all sorts of reasons. Chaucer's description of the knight's armoring is as precious and self-conscious as the opening physical description of Sir Thopas, who is "a doghty swayn" with pink cheeks and face as white "as payndemayn" (724–725), or fine white bread. With his lips "rede as rose" (727), "a semely nose" (729), and beard and hair "lyk saffroun" (730) growing down to his waist, Sir Thopas is a storybook knight, as pretty as a pastry cut from gingerbread.

When Chaucer the narrator exclaims that the story of Sir Thopas is a romance "of prys," worthy to be told alongside the great romances "Of Horn child, and of Ypotys, Of Beves and Sir Gy" (897, 898–899), Harry Bailey, the host and self-appointed director of the storytelling, interrupts Chaucer's story, calling it "rym dogerel" and exclaiming emphatically, "Thy drasty rymyng is nat woth a toord!" (925, 929). Harry misses the joke of Chaucer's playful satire on knightly romance into which "Chaucer has crammed ... almost more stock elements than are to be found in any but the worst Middle English romances."[55]

Like Thopas, Bottom finds himself in an enchanted wood haunted by fairies. Newly translated into an ass, Bottom, too, invokes the romantic power of the thrush's song ("The throstle, with his note so true," 3.1.122). Both heroes are fascinated by a fairy queen, the theme of mortals transformed by otherworldly monarchs being a staple of medieval romances like *Sir Lanval* and *Sir Orfeo*. In both cases, the haunts of the fairy queen are enlivened with a supernatural music. Both story and drama include the upending of conventional beauty descriptions typically found in medieval romance, which, in the cases of Thopas and of Bottom as Pyramus, are applied to men in comic fashion.[56]

Another stylistic similarity is found in the repetitive and silly verses of "Sir Thopas" and in the Pyramus and Thisbe play. The couplet is the "basic unit" of Middle English romance (including the stanzaic romances),[57] and the couplet form is exploited to comic effect both in "Sir Thopas" and in the play performed by Shakespeare's mechanicals. The jangling internal rhymes of Thopas, as he wonders at his newfound love for the fairy queen ("O Seinte Marie, benedicite! What eyleth this love at me To bynde me so soore? Me dremed al this nyght, pardee, An elf-queene shal my lemman be And slepe under my goore," 784–789), also appear in the Pyramus play, for example when Pyramus discovers the bloodied mantle ("But stay! O spite! But mark, poor knight? What dreadful dole is here? Eyes, do you see? How can it be? O dainty duck! O dear!" 5.1.265–270).

The verses of the Pyramus and Thisbe play also echo the language and meter of "dramatizations of medieval romances which remained popular through the sixteenth century," as C. R. Baskervill, among other critics, has pointed out.[58] The prologue of the Pyramus play, with its dumb show, further suggests an earlier form of drama found in mummings, pageants, and festival plays. Dieter Mehl has traced "examples of attempts to illustrate the spoken word by simultaneous silent action, or, conversely, of a pantomime explained to the audience by a commentary" to the poetry of John Lydgate, especially his *Mumming at Windsor,* and to Lydgate's description in *Troy Book* of a dumb show performed during a reading of poetry, along with pantomimes related to "'mummings' or 'disguisings,' festive parades, usually in allegorical guise, which were frequently presented on special occasions, such as after a solemn banquet."[59] The dumb show may also have been drawn from dramatized medieval romances, which are known mainly through town records and allusions; its existence in *MND* is strongly suggested by the role of Prologue performed by Peter Quince.[60]

In modern productions, these older elements may be retained or discarded. For example, in Reinhardt's film, the dumb show and most of the prologue are cut. Britten's opera is more careful in its presentation of the Pyramus play, termed "a burlesque metaopera," enhancing its credibility "by the excision of Philostrate's contemptuous preview" and retaining its prologues, which "are characterized more richly in the opera by parodic music."[61] Britten includes Quince's initial prologue (5.1.109–117), which is sung by all the rustics; then Quince introduces the players as the dumb show is performed, with each mechanical defined by "literal equivalences for the text: hence such jokes as Flute/Thisby's flute, the trombone lion, and the percussion chink in the cello/double bass wall…. [T]his relationship between representation and reality is one that the Rustics in both Shakespeare and Britten insist on interpreting in a singularly literal way."[62] Britten's musical parodies in the play-within-a-play are wonderfully funny, even to those who might be unfamiliar with the *bel canto*–style ariettas that Britten playfully mocks.

In Peter Hall's film, the prologue is used mainly to introduce the characters of the Pyramus play with minimal pantomime, though the audience is shown Lion gnawing on Thisbe's mantle, Pyramus finding the bloodied mantle and stabbing himself, and Thisbe's suicide. For Peter Brook, however, the centerpiece of *MND* "is the Pyramus and Thisbe play, which doesn't come at the end of a highly organized work just for comic relief. The actor's art is truly celebrated in this episode,"[63] and the book for Brook's production contains elaborate stage directions to the players in the performance of the dumb show.[64] David Selbourne, who observed the development of Brook's production from first rehearsal to first performance, recounts that Brook asked his actors

> to "introduce something new and surprising into these poses on each night of performance," "something genuinely comic and fresh," for the benefit both of their courtly and box-office audiences…. Pyramus and Thisby, stopped in their tracks before us, exchange transfixed but loving glances; whisper (in silence) through Wall's frozen fingers; to Moonshine's unmoving lantern and Lion's noiseless roaring. The lovers' death, as the tableau rearranges, is both mute and bloodless. Stabbed, Pyramus and Thisby expire without a murmur, eyes staring.[65]

In Adrian Noble's stage and film versions, the dumb show is treated as an introduction of the characters in the Pyramus play, the action then acted out at top speed in the style of the Reduced Shakespeare Company, while in Michael Hoffman's film (1999), as in the Reinhardt versions, the prologue is completely cut; the Pyramus and Thisbe play begins with Wall, and there is no bergomask to complete the action.[66]

The bergomask proposed in the play by Bottom and graciously accepted by Duke Theseus (5.1.340, 346) was a type of folk dance related to morris dancing. Morris dances were performed not only by "the folk" but for entertainments at the courts of Henry VII and Henry the VIII.[67] Shakespeare's collaboration *Two Noble Kinsmen* (also drawn from Chaucer's "Knight's Tale") includes a morris dance performed before Duke Theseus, which Harley Granville Barker inserted into his 1914 production of *MND*, with the lines of the wedding song sung for Theseus and Hip-

Titania (Sarah Kestelman) woos Bottom (David Waller) in Peter Brook's *MND* production (1970). David Farrell.

polyta set by Cecil Sharp, the pioneer folklorist and collector of English folk songs and traditional dances. The bergomask in Barker's production was danced to the tune of "Greensleeves," and the dance itself was "an authentic folk dance known as the Wryesdale dance."[68]

In Reinhardt's film, the bergomask is just about to begin when the mechanicals, noting for the first time that Theseus and the noble company have fled the hall, literally freeze in action, a rather cruel end to their performance. In Britten's opera, conversely, the bergomask concludes and completes the action, "notable among the many set forms with musical associations in the

The bergomask about to begin in *MND*, dir. Reinhardt and Dieterle (1935). (Left to right) Starveling/Moon (Otis Harlan); Epilogue (Arthur Treacher); Bottom/Pyramus (James Cagney); Snout/Wall (Hugh Herbert); Flute/Thisbe (Joe E. Brown); Peter Quince (Frank McHugh); and Snug/Lion (Dewey Robinson).

play."⁶⁹ In Britten's opera, the dance is performed by all six rustics using figures familiar from English country dancing; the figures of this dance were first described by John Playford in *The English Dancing Master*, published in the seventeenth century, then were repopularized by Cecil Sharp in the early twentieth century, and are still danced today.⁷⁰ While the bergomask in Peter Brook's production was translated into a high-wire acrobatic display, Peter Hall's version presents it as a morris dance between Pyramus and Thisbe with two waving hankies and the other mechanicals performing a rudimentary music, mainly through the nose. In Noble's version, the bergomask is performed as clogging, another (later) traditional form of dance.

Unlike the Pyramus play itself and "Sir Thopas," both of which contain loving (and relentlessly silly) imitations of elements found in medieval romance, the dumb show and the dance that concludes it are not simply satires of earlier forms of performance, given to the workmen to interject the "folk world into the court of Theseus" or "to characterize the crude dramatic style of the craftsmen."⁷¹ The pantomimes of John Lydgate and the records of morris dancing performed at the courts of Henry VII and Henry VIII suggest that dumb shows and dance were widely enjoyed by a range of social classes, just as medieval romances were still widely read in Shakespeare's day, their stories known by workmen as well as by playwrights and princes. Shakespeare's last plays—*Pericles, Henry VIII,* and *The Tempest*—seriously employ pantomime, looking backward to this earlier dramatic form to supply visual narration, or in the case of *The Tempest*, transcendent and

Thisbe (Joe E. Brown) and Pyramus (James Cagney) strike a pose in *MND*, dir. Reinhardt and Dieterle (1935).

celebratory resolution.[72] In modern performances of *MND*, Britten's opera comes closest to interpreting the Pyramus play with its pantomime and dancing most fully and satisfactorily, though Brook's and Hall's thoughtful productions are not far behind.

For Peter Brook, the central problem of *A Midsummer Night's Dream* is that Shakespeare is "writing very clearly and consciously for adults a play about fairies. It's quite clear, however, that this line which runs throughout the play cannot be presented convincingly through dead or second-hand imagery."[73] In medieval romance, fairies often appear as powerful and manipulative spirits bound by rules other than those that govern mortals; fairies are frightening but usually benevolent, though they have since lost many of those associations, which is one problem for the modern director. Middle English romance also provides a model for diptych structure, or doubling, which Shakespeare realizes in his creation of two young women from one and of two supernatural figures from one, with Puck as a projection or one aspect of the fairy king Oberon as first presented in *Huon of Burdeux*. Other romance elements that appear in *A Midsummer Night's Dream* include the magical forest, so wonderfully represented in the productions of Reinhardt and Britten, the shifting and parodic conception of the knight, the gentle lion of the Pyramus and Thisbe play, and perhaps even the dumb show that may have been drawn from fifteenth- and sixteenth-century dramatizations of medieval romance, among other available sources.

Shakespeare's play, at least in part, satirizes earlier literary forms, as Bethurum points out, but it also makes somehow more of them; the play is larger than the sum of its parts. Modern productions remarkably and variously retain many of the medieval elements apparent in *MND*. In negotiating between past and present performances, between earlier sources and the dramatic text, the modern director "may be like Shakespeare himself, picking up pieces of history from chronicle and stage, reshaping them to fit his own dramatic patterns," and including enough of the source material, whether consciously or instinctively, to please even the most discerning medievalist.[74]

NOTES

1. All quotations are taken from Larry D. Benson, ed., *The Riverside Chaucer*, 3rd ed. (Oxford University Press, 1988), unless otherwise indicated; and from Harold F. Brooks, ed., *A Midsummer Night's Dream*, in *The Arden Edition of the Works of William Shakespeare* (London: Methuen, 1979; repr. 1983). In an interview with Ronald Bryden, drama critic for the *Observer*, director Peter Brook indicated his awareness of the influence of medieval texts on *MND* (admittedly in somewhat garbled fashion), when Brook "talked about a recent trip to Iran on which he'd seen some marvellous ancient Persian folk-plays, like Old English sagas played by the medieval mummers." Quoted in *Peter Brook's Production of William Shakespeare's* A Midsummer Night's Dream *for the Royal Shakespeare Company: The Complete and Authorized Acting Edition*, ed. and with interviews by Glenn Loney (Chicago: Dramatic Publishing Company, 1974), 16. David Selbourne, *The Making of* A Midsummer Night's Dream: *An Eye-Witness Account of Peter Brook's Production from First Rehearsal to First Night* (London: Methuen, 1982), 73, further quotes Brook discussing 3.2.407–418: "There is a bare and plangent tone, unheard before, in Lysander's 'Come, thou gentle day,' and the sound of an odd melancholy reaching to the crux of the play, at 'fallen am I in dark uneven way.' At this deeply resonating echo of an Anglo-Saxon ... saga, or of a cadence from Gawain, Brook himself ... describes the moment of Lysander's thraldom as ... 'almost going into tragedy.' Each of the four lovers in the enchanted wood seems to speak with the exhausted despair of the old Christian hero lost in a medieval world of wonders, and assailed by temptation."

2. S. L. Lee, ed., *The English Charlemagne Romances*, part VII, *The Boke of Duke Huon of Burdeux Done into English by Sir John Bourchier, Lord Berners*, 3 vols. (London: EETS Trübner & Co., 1882). *Huon* was translated in the late fifteenth or early sixteenth century, most probably from a French edition printed by Michel le Noir (1513, 1514). There is some confusion about the original number of English printed editions, which are said to have been printed by Wynkyn de Worde (c. 1515?, now lost), Julian Notary (c. 1515, STC 13998.5), and Thomas Purfoot (1601, STC 13999). According to the *Short Title Catalogue*, the Notary edition is in "private collections." See also Edward Hodnett, *English Woodcuts 1480–1535, Additions & Corrections* (London: Bibliographical Society, 1973), xii, 36–39; Joyce Boro, "The Textual History of *Huon of Burdeux*: A Reassessment of the Facts," *Notes and Queries* n.s. 48 (2001): 233–237; and James P. Carley, "Bourchier, John, Second Baron Berners (ca. 1467–1533)," *Oxford Dictionary of National Biography* (Oxford University Press, 2004), http://www.oxforddnb.com/view/article/2990 (December 9, 2006).

3. Diana E. Henderson, *Collaborations with the Past: Reshaping Shakespeare across Time and Media* (Ithaca, NY: Cornell University Press, 2006), 238, 258.

4. Henderson, *Collaborations*, 239.

5. John W. Hales, "Chaucer and Shakespeare," *Quarterly Review* 134 (1873): 225–255. Among sources and analogues that have been identified for this play are "The Knight's Tale," ll. 859–930; 1056–1184; 2483–2532; 2565–2603; *The Life of Theseus*, in *Plutarch's Lives of the Noble Grecians and Romans*, trans. Sir Thomas North (1579); *Huon of Burdeux*, trans. Lord Berners (c. 1534); *The Discoverie of Witchcraft*, by Reginald Scot (1584), Bk. 4, Chap. 10; Bk. 5, Chap. 3; Bk. 7, Chap. 2, 15, Bk. 8, Chap. 19; *Thesaurus Linguae Romanae et Britannicae* (1573 ed.), T. Cooper (Midas, Pyramus); *The XI Bookes of the Golden Asse Conteininge the Metamorphoses of Lucius Apuleius*, trans. William Adlington, Bk. 3, Chap. 17; Ovid, *Metamorphoses*, Bk. 4, trans. Arthur Golding (1575); ll. 67–201 from *A Handefull of Pleasant Delites*, by Clement Robinson and divers others (1584); *The Tragedy of Pyramus and Thisbe* (from BM Add. MS. 15, 227), cited in Geoffrey Bullough, ed., *Narrative and Dramatic Sources of Shakespeare*, vol. 1, *Early Comedies, Poems, Romeo and Juliet* (London: Routledge and Kegan Paul; New York: Columbia University Press, 1964), xvi–xvii, 377–422. An ingenious identification of one source for "Bottom's Dream" in Chaucer's *Book of the Duchess* has been made by David G. Hale, "Bottom's Dream and Chaucer," *Shakespeare Quarterly* 36, no. 2 (Summer 1985): 219–220.

6. Ann Thompson, *Shakespeare's Chaucer: A Study in Literary Origins* (Liverpool, UK: Liverpool University Press, 1978), 88. Thompson includes a useful summary of Chaucerian reference found by critics in *MND*. In *The Swan at the Well: Shakespeare Reading Chaucer* (New Haven, CT: Yale University Press, 1985), 2, medievalist E. Talbot Donaldson, however, rightly cautions that "Shakespeareans are naturally interested in showing how the Chaucerian background can illuminate the plays, but this perfectly proper interest often has the effect of assuming that, although the play is a puzzle requiring answers, the Chaucerian works that may help provide answers have settled — one might almost say static — meanings that are available to any reader."

7. Kenneth Muir, *Shakespeare's Sources: Comedies and Tragedies* (London: Methuen, 1957; repr. 1961), 31–47, 255, 32.

8. Dorothy Bethurum, "Shakespeare's Comment on Mediaeval Romance in *Midsummer-Night's Dream*," *Modern Language Notes* 60 (1945): 85–94, 88.

9. Muir, *Shakespeare's Sources*, 31; Bethurum, "Shakespeare's Comment on Mediaeval Romance," 89–90; Ballmann, cited in Thompson, *Shakespeare's Chaucer*, 92; Wendy Wall, "Why Does Puck Sweep? Fairylore, Merry Wives, and Social Struggle," *Shakespeare Quarterly* 52 (Spring 2001): 67–106, says that by the sixteenth century fairies were representative of "the pastoral life endangered by the social ills of the present world" (73), an idea earlier expressed by Chaucer's Wife of Bath. Wall cites Minor White Latham, *The Elizabethan Fairies: The Fairies of Folklore and The Faires [sic] of Shakespeare* (New York: Columbia University Press, 1930), who "argues that in English literature there were few references to fairies before mid-sixteenth century but abundant allusions in Scottish literature" (73, n. 12). In Middle English romance, however, fairies are often stock characters. In her analysis, Wall says further that "the folk fairy tradition underwent a change in late-sixteenth- and early-seventeenth-century England. Country fairylore blended into classical mythology, with the result that demonic spirits were rehabilitated and became less sinister" (74), but there are many medieval examples to be found, for example, in Chaucer's "Merchant's Tale" and in the romance of "Sir Orfeo" in the Auchinleck MS (National Library of Scotland MS 19.2.1), produced in London in the 1330s. Bibliography on fairies in "Sir Orfeo" includes D. R. Baldwin, "Fairy Lore and the Meaning of *Sir Orfeo*," *Southern Folklore Quarterly* 41 (1977): 129–142; John B. Friedman, "Eurydice, Heurodis, and the Noon-Day Demon," *Speculum* 41 (1966): 22–29; Patrizia Grimaldi, "Sir Orfeo as Celtic Folk-Hero, Christian Pilgrim, and Medieval King," in *Allegory, Myth, and Symbol*, ed. M. W. Bloomfield (Cambridge, MA: Harvard University Press, 1981), 147–161.

10. Bethurum, "Shakespeare's Comment on Mediaeval Romance," 90.

11. *Ibid.*, 86. Nevill Coghill, "Shakespeare's Reading in Chaucer," in *Elizabethan and Jacobean Studies Presented to Frank Percy Wilson in Honour of His Seventieth Birthday*, ed. Herbert Davis and Helen Gardner (Oxford: Clarendon Press, 1959), 91, remarks, "Miss Bethurum suggests that Chaucer himself, in his *Rhyme of Sir Thopas*, had given Shakespeare a hint for Bottom's dream and Titania's infatuation," citing Chaucer's lines about the "elf-queene shal my lemman be And slepe under my gore." See also Larry S. Champion, "*A Midsummer Night's Dream*: The Problem of Source," *Papers on Language and Literature*, Southern Illinois University, 4 (1968): 13–19, who identifies twelve potential sources for *MND* and comments further on the play as an adaptation of Chaucer's "Knight's Tale."

12. Bethurum, "Shakespeare's Comment on Mediaeval Romance," 93, 94.

13. Donaldson identifies the edition of Chaucer known to Shakespeare this way: "Shakespeare read Chaucer ... in Thynne's edition of Chaucer's works of 1532, or one of its reprintings of 1542 or 1550, in Stow's edition of 1561, or in Speght's edition of 1598" (75). Donaldson, the great medievalist, himself uses as his exemplar for his commentary on Shakespeare's reading of Chaucer John Stow's 1561 printing with modernized punctuation and line numbers from "standard modern texts" (Donaldson, *Swan at the Well*, 141, n. 1).

14. John Finlayson, "Definitions of Middle English Romance," *Chaucer Review* 15 (1980–1981): 44–62, 168–181, 57, 47. See also Derek Pearsall, "The Development of Middle English Romance," *Mediaeval Studies* 27 (1965): 91–116; Paul Strohm, "The Origin and Meaning of Middle English *Romaunce*," *Genre* 10 (1977): 1–28; Paul Strohm, "*Storie, Spelle, Geste, Romaunce, Tragedie*: Generic Distinctions in the Middle English Troy Narratives," *Speculum* 46, no. 2 (1971): 348–359, 354; Dieter Mehl, *The Middle English Romances of the Thirteenth and Fourteenth Centuries* (New York: Barnes & Noble, 1969), vii, 22.

15. Carol Fewster, *Traditionality and Genre in Middle English Romance* (Woodbridge, UK: D. S. Brewer, 1987), 18, 21.

16. *Ibid.*, 24–27. See also A. C. Baugh, "The Middle English Romance: Some Questions of Creation, Presentation, and Preservation," *Speculum* 42 (1967): 1–31, 4–5: "Whoever were the authors of the English romances, and however surely these romances were intended for a listening audience, they were originally literary creations devised by poets with their parchment or wax tablets before them"; and Mehl, *Middle English Romances*, 10: "We can find in many romances striking instances of an oral formulaic technique.... Nevertheless, the extant romances appear to be for the most part 'literary' creations, composed with some care at the desk, not just memorized reproductions of some improvised recital by wandering minstrels."

17. Fewster, *Traditionality and Genre*, 35.

18. *Ibid.*, 36.

19. *Ibid.*, 50.

20. H. R. D. Anders, *Shakespeare's Books: A Dissertation on Shakespeare's Reading and the Immediate Sources of His Works* (1904; repr. New York: AMS Press, 1965), 162–163. See also Joyce Boro, "Lord Berners and His Books: A New Survey," *Huntington Library Quarterly* 67 (2004): 236–250, 239, 237; Carley, "Bourchier," n.p.

21. Anders, *Shakespeare's Books*, 162; Boro, "Lord Berners and His Books," 239; Bullough, *Narrative and Dramatic Sources*, 371.

22. Bethurum, "Shakespeare's Comment on Mediaeval Romance," 90, n. 9: "Greene had put Oberon, the king of the fairies, into his play *James the Fourth*, but Oberon's function in the play is not at all comparable to his namesake's in *MND*." The full title of Greene's play is fairly explanatory of its plot(s): *The Scottishe story of James the Fourthe slayn at Fflodden intermixed with a pleasant Comedie presented by Oboron kinge of ffayres* (STC 12308). L. H. Newcomb points out that: "the posthumous *Greene's Groats-Worth of Witte* ... is the first contemporary reference to Shakespeare: 'there is an upstart Crow, beautified with our feathers, that with his *Tygers heart wrapt in a Players hide, supposes he is as well able to bumbast out a blanke verse as the best of you: and being an absolute Johannes fac totum*, is in his owne conceit the onely Shake-scene in a countrie,'" but that Greene's work was influential on Shakespeare's: "Both writers may have contributed (not necessarily at the same time) to the *Henry VI* plays or *Titus Andronicus*. Certainly Shakespeare drew affectionately on *Pandosto* [STC 12285] and the coney-catching pamphlets in *The Winter's Tale* (1610–11), and Autolycus, his ballad-selling rogue, may memorialize Greene himself"; L.H. Newcomb, "Greene, Robert (bap. 1558, d. 1592)," *Oxford Dictionary of National Biography* (Oxford: Oxford University Press, 2004), http://www.oxforddnb.com/view/article/11418 (December 11, 2006). For more on Greene, see Louise M. Bishop, "A Touch of Chaucer in Shakespeare's *Winter's Tale*," this volume, 236–238, 242–243n25–31, and Robert F. Yeager, "Shakespeare as Medievalist: What It Means for Performing *Pericles*," this volume, 217, 226n18–21.

23. Jefferson B. Fletcher, "*Huon of Burdeux* and *The Fairie Queene*," *Journal of English and Germanic Philology* 2 (1899): 203–212; John R. MacArthur, "The Influence of *Huon of Burdeux* upon *The Fairie Queene*," *Journal of English and Germanic Philology* 4 (1902): 215–238. MacArthur argues for "an undoubted influence, though limited, of Huon of Burdeux upon the Fairie Queene," especially "the account of the Red Cross Knight's fight with the Dragon, and secondly, a part of the account of Guyon's voyage before he comes to the Bower of Bliss" (223). In *Faerie Queene*, Book 2, Canto 1, 6 (STC 23082), Sir Guyon is described as an "Elfin borne of noble state.... Well could he tourney and in lists debate, And knighthood tooke of good Sir Huons hand, When with king Oberon he came to Faerie land." Oberon recurs in the genealogy provided in Book 2, Canto 10, 75–76: "He left two sonnes, of which faire Elferon/ The eldest brother did vntimely dy;/Whose emptie place the mightie Oberon /Doubly supplide, in spousall, and dominion." In Spenser's version, Oberon then dies, leaving "the fairest Tanaquill." Edmund Spenser, *The Faerie Queene*, Book Two, ed. and with an intro. by Erik Gray (Indianapolis: Hackett, 2006), 7, 180.

24. For Marlowe's reading of romances, see Ethel Seaton, "Marlowe's Light Reading," in *Elizabethan and Jacobean Studies Presented to Frank Percy Wilson in Honour of His Seventieth Birthday*, ed. Herbert Davis and Helen Gardner (Oxford: Clarendon Press, 1959), 17–35. Seaton finds verbal echoes and imagery drawn from *Huon* in Marlowe's *Tamburlaine* and *Dido, Queen of Carthage* (19–23, 24). John W. Draper, "A Reference to 'Huon' in Ben Jonson," *Modern Language Notes* 35, no. 7 (November 1920): 439–440, cites Ben Jonson's play *Magnetic Lady* (STC 14754) as containing references not only to *Guy of Warwick* but also to *Huon* (440).

25. In his 1905 Arden Shakespeare edition of the play, Henry Cuningham, *A Midsummer Night's Dream* (London: Methuen, 1905; repr. 1922), xxxix, cites references to the griffin (*MND* 2.1.232) and to the "fearful wild fowl" (*MND* 3.1.31), both of which are marvelous creatures in *Huon*. See Harold F. Brooks, ed., *A Midsummer Night's Dream: The Arden Edition of the Works of William Shakespeare* (London: Methuen, 1979; repr. 1983), 41, n. 232; 53, n. 30–31. Anders, *Shakespeare's Books*, 163, identifies a further reference to *Huon* in *Much Ado About Nothing* (2.1.247–254), when Benedick describes the impossible tasks he will undertake, including fetching "a hair off the great Cham's beard" before he will speak three words to Beatrice, seen as drawn from Huon's quest to take a "handfull of the here" from the head of the Admiral, father of the fair Esclaramonde (Lee, *English Charlemagne Romances*, 1: 50).

26. Lee, *English Charlemagne Romances*, 1: 73.

27. Ibid., 73.

28. Ibid., 64, 65. The magic horn has four main properties, which are healing the sick, feeding and giving fine wines to the hungry and thirsty, causing the sick and feeble to dance, and calling anyone from far or near: "that who so euer harde it, yf he were a .C. iornyes of, he sholde come at the pleasure of hym that blew it, farre or nere" (66). Elsewhere in the text, Oberon is described as "rychely aparellyd in cloth of golde & the border therof was fret with ryche precyous stonnes; goodly it was to behold" (259).

29. Ibid., 67–68: "suche a wynde a and tempest so horryble to here that it bare downe trees, and therwith came suche a rayne & hayle that semyd that heuen and the erthe hade fought together, and that yᵉ worlde shulde haue ended / the beestys in the wodes brayed and cryed / and *t*hou foules of the eyre fell doune deed for feer that they were in / ther was no creature but he wolde haue bene / afrayed of that tempeest / then sodenly aperyd before them a grete ryuer / that ran swyfter than the byrdes dyde flye / and the water was so blacke and so pe*r*relous, & made such a noyse that it myght be herde .x. leges of / 'Alas,' quod Huon, 'I se well now we all be all loste ; we shall here be oppressyd without god haue pyte of vs / I repent me that euer I enteryd in to this wode; I had ben better a traueyled a hole here [yeere] than to haue come hether.'" When Gareyn says this is just the work of fairies, Huon replies, "I thynke it beste to alyght fro our horse, for I thynke we shall neuer skape fro hense, but that we shall be all oppressyd."

30. After Huon conquers the Admiral, cuts off his beard, takes out "hys .iiii. grete teth" (*ibid.*, 153), and cuts off his head, he woos and wins his daughter, Esclaramonde. Oberon commands Huon not to have intercourse with her until they are married at Rome: "that ye be not so hardy to company with her bodely tyll ye be maryed together in ye cyte of Rome" (*ibid.*, 154). Being heedless of advice throughout the story, Huon cannot keep this promise. He and Esclaramonde are then shipwrecked on an island, which is invaded by ten Saracen pirates, and Esclaramonde has various separate adventures, plots which may contain the seeds of both *A Winter's Tale* and *The Tempest*.

31. Lee, *English Charlemagne Romances*, 2: 536. In a recent review of Carolyne Larrington, *King Arthur's Enchantresses: Morgan and Her Sisters in Arthurian Tradition* (London: Tauris, 2006), Elizabeth Archibald says that "In *Huon of Bordeaux*, [Morgan] even has a son by Julius Caesar, who becomes Oberon, king of the fairies" ("Magic School," *Times Literary Supplement*, February 2, 2007, 9), which is perhaps misleading. In *King Arthur's Enchantresses*, Larrington describes only the French text of *Huon* (95, 217, n. 90), not the English translation. In the translation of *Huon* by Lord Berners, Morgan is never identified as the mother of Oberon. Oberon's mother is said only to be a lady of the secret island (named Chyfalonnye) who was formerly the lover of Florimont. She later marries and has a son who was the father of Alexander the Great. She also meets Caesar and has Oberon with him (Lee, *English Charlemagne Romances*, 1: 72–73). In the English translation, Morgan appears at Oberon's court; she is named as Arthur's sister and as part of his entourage, and she accompanies Clariet (Lee, *English Charlemagne Romances*, 2: 536, 601, 648). I thank Joyce Boro for double-checking and confirming this for me.

32. Lee, *English Charlemagne Romances*, 2: 595, 599, 605. King Arthur is Huon's rival as king of fairyland and complains about the succession. The child Merlin is also introduced (601). Oberon proclaims that if Arthur does not obey Huon as King of the Fairies, he will "condempne hym parpetually to be a warwolfe ... and to ende his dayes in payne and mysery" (602).

33. Katharine Briggs, *An Encyclopedia of Fairies: Hobgoblins, Brownies, Bogies and Other Supernatural Creatures* (New York: Pantheon, 1976), explains that "in folk tradition emphasis is perhaps most laid on Puck as a misleader" (337). Puck's character as Robin Goodfellow is discussed in Mary Ellen Lamb, "Taken by the Fairies: Fairy Practices and the Production of Popular Culture in *A Midsummer Night's Dream*," *Shakespeare Quarterly* 51, no. 3 (Autumn 2000): 277–312, 295.

34. David Bevington, *From Mankind to Marlowe* (Cambridge, MA: Harvard University Press, 1962), 104–113 and *passim*; William A. Ringler, Jr., "The Number of Actors in Shakespeare's Early Plays," in *The Seventeenth Century Stage: A Collection of Critical Essays*, ed. Gerald Eades Bentley (Chicago: University of Chicago Press, 1968), 130–134. Dual roles were one highlight of the 1971 Peter Brook production (Alan Howard was Theseus and Oberon; Sara Kestelman played Hippolyta and Titania; John Kane was both Puck and Philostrate; and Philip Locke took the roles of Egeus and Quince). See Loney, *Peter Brook's Production*, cast list (n.p.). For doubling in other modern productions, see also Gary Jay Williams, "*Our Moonlight Revels*": *A Midsummer Night's Dream in the Theatre* (Iowa City: University of Iowa Press, 1997), 216–217, 236, 242, 251, 252, 254.

35. The Royal Shakespeare Company version directed by Adrian Noble was first performed on stage in Stratford and New York in 1994–1995. The stage production, which I saw in New York, used several special effects seemingly derived from Brook (which I also saw), fairies spiraling down wires over the stage, and much use of umbrellas, but this was preferable to the film, which is almost uncomfortably surreal. See also Williams, "*Our Moonlight Revels*," 255–257. A recent production of *MND* at the Roundhouse, Camden Town, reviewed by Lucy Munro, "Translated from Top to Bottom," *Times Literary Supplement*, March 23, 2007, 20, describes overt doubling of character with "costumes overlaid and exchanged on stage. In Act Five, Titania's flowing hair may have been contained by Hippolyta's elaborate head-dressing, but the fairy queen's costume is still visible beneath Hippolyta's robe. As Philostrate, Ajay Kumar sets up the stage for the mechanicals' play, then sweeps it away again as Puck."

36. Williams, "*Our Moonlight Revels*," 93, see also 94–97, figs. 12, 23.

37. *Ibid.*, 153. See also Andrew Porter, "Spells and Shadows," *Times Literary Supplement*, July 14, 2006, 20: "In 1914, Harley Granville-Barker sought to rescue the *Dream* from Victorian scenic elaboration, with patterned curtains instead of naturalism, Elizabethan music instead of Mendelssohn, and fairy rulers 'based on Cambodian idols.'"

38. Anthony R. Guneratne, "'Thou Dost Usurp Authority': Beerbohm Tree, Reinhardt, Olivier, Welles, and the Politics of Adapting Shakespeare," in *A Concise Companion to Shakespeare on Screen*, ed. Diana E. Henderson (Malden, MA: Blackwell, 2006), 31–53, 43. For the Balanchine reference, see Deborah Jowitt, *Time and the Dancing Image* (Berkeley: University of California Press, 1988), 265–266. Balanchine later created a ballet of *A Midsummer Night's Dream* (1962) set to Felix Mendelssohn's score.

39. Williams, "*Our Moonlight Revels*," 165, 168. Julia Briggs suggested to me that the antlers worn by Oberon might also be an allusion to Herne the Hunter, described by Mrs. Page in *Merry Wives of Windsor* (4.4.28) as a supernatural figure said to haunt oaks in Windsor Forest. In the last act of *Merry Wives*,

Falstaff wearing buck's horns (or perhaps the whole head of a buck) is pinched by fairies (children in disguise) and humiliated. The antlers may also refer possibly to the stag horns used in the Abbotts Bromley horn dance. This is a traditional English folk dance (which is still performed) that dates from the medieval era and includes six dancers with horns, a fool, a hobbyhorse, a Maid Marian who collects money in a ladle, a boy with a bow and arrow, a musician, and a boy with a triangle. Reinhardt's film met with various critical responses. Writing in 1935, Franz Werfel commented on the film's "unique faculty to express by natural means and with incomparable persuasiveness all that is fairylike, marvelous, supernatural"; cited in Walter Benjamin, *Illuminations: Essays and Reflections*, ed. and with intro. by Hannah Arendt (1955; reprint, New York: Schocken Books, 1978), 228 n. In his essay "Style and Medium in the Motion Pictures" (1936), in *Three Essays on Style*, ed. Irving Lavin (Cambridge, MA: MIT Press, 1997), the art historian Erwin Panofsky was less than thrilled by Reinhardt's cinematic magic, commenting, "Reinhardt's *Midsummer Night's Dream* is probably the most unfortunate major film ever produced" (102).

40. When invited to stage the play at Oxford, Reinhardt supposedly sent a telegram that requested "eighty extras and a lake" (Williams, "*Our Moonlight Revels*," 175). See also ibid., 167–168: "Reinhardt's wood belonged to Teutonic elves and Grimm's fairy tales." Guneratne, "'Thou Dost Usurp Authority,'" comments, "other German films of *A Midsummer Night's Dream* from the 1910s and 1920s, with which [Reinhardt] must have been familiar, emphasized the play's ... fairies who became associated with the forest spirits of Central European folklore" (42–43).

41. Williams, "*Our Moonlight Revels*," 166, 168.

42. Benjamin Britten and Peter Pears, *A Midsummer Night's Dream: An Opera in Three Acts Adapted from William Shakespeare*, opus 64 (London: Boosey and Hawkes, 1960). Pears and Britten cut about one third of the play, opening the opera in the wood instead of at Theseus's court and doing away with Egeus altogether. See William H. L. Godsalve, *Britten's* A Midsummer Night's Dream: *Making an Opera from Shakespeare's Comedy* (Madison, NJ: Fairleigh Dickinson University Press, 1995), 11, who describes Britten's version as "a mid-twentieth-century romantic chamber opera in English" and later as "a highly refined chamber opera" (208). Godsalve discusses the cuts made by Britten and Pears to Shakespeare's play in great detail. Britten's interest in medieval and early modern texts is reflected as well in his *Noye's Fludde* (1957), envisioned as an operatic miracle play, drawn from the medieval Chester cycle plays, and sung primarily by children, and in his *Ceremony of Carols* (1948), which took its lyrics from medieval and early modern sources.

43. Christina J. Burridge, "'Music, Such as Charmeth Sleep': Benjamin Britten's *A Midsummer Night's Dream*," *University of Toronto Quarterly* 51 (1981–1982): 149–160, 151. Peter Brook's stage production also featured moving trees: a stage direction specifies that the trees move in the scene in which Hermia awakes from her dream and elsewhere; Loney, *Peter Brook's Production*, 35a. The moving trees might allude to the myth of the Green Man, a medieval image often found painted on the walls or in the carving of English churches. Andrew Porter, "Dreaming of the 'Dream,'" *Stagebill / JFK Center*, April 1973, 7, critic for the *Financial Times*, the *New Yorker*, and the *Times Literary Supplement*, described the staging of Britten's opera at Covent Garden by the Royal Opera in 1961: "It opened with soft warm sighs from the orchestra that portrayed the breathing of the enchanted midsummer wood, and in that wood three very different kinds of people — well-born young lovers, fairies, and rustic tradesmen, sharply characterized by three very different kinds of music — dreamt their dreams, until Theseus's horns heralded the new day, and all misunderstandings seemed to have been swept away by the healing power of music."

44. Porter, "Spells and Shadows," comments that Peter Hall's staging for Glyndebourne in 1981 "has lasted for decades. At each revival the spell is cast afresh."

45. Williams, "*Our Moonlight Revels*," 201–202, says Britten's Oberon's "relationship with the virile, younger Puck, and his desire for the Indian boy" echo "disturbing motifs in several other Britten operas, notably *Peter Grimes* and *The Turn of the Screw*, in which an older man is sexually attracted to a very young boy." In an interview with British tenor Ian Bostridge by Alex Ross, "Songs of Experience: Ian Bostridge Sings Benjamin Britten," *New Yorker*, March 27, 2006, 88, "Bostridge also mentions the continuing unease over Britten's personality, his psychology, and, above all, his sexuality, which expressed itself in one enduring relationship, with the tenor Peter Pears, and in a series of sexless infatuations with boys." John Bridcut, *Britten's Children* (London: Faber, 2006), delineates Britten's love for thirteen-year-old male muses, who were projections of his younger self and served for a time (until they grew older) as Britten's surrogate children, which further suggests a particularly poignant reading of the relationship between Oberon and Puck in Britten's opera. In a review of *Britten's Children*, David Matthews ("Lucky Thirteen," *Times Literary Supplement*, November 10, 2006, 6) points out that "the special nature of Britten's obsession with young male beauty and intelligence is nevertheless easily misunderstood." Williams, "*Our Moonlight Revels*," 202, cites a review of the 1996 Britten staging by the Metropolitan Opera in which "*New York Times* critic Anthony Tommasini wrote of both the opera's 'thinly veiled pederasty' and of the 'homoerotic undertones' in the conception of Oberon, suggesting that Britten 'did not have to contort Shakespeare much to uncover this implicit [homosexual] theme.'"

46. Lamb, "Taken by the Fairies," 295, cites a reference in William Tyndale's translation of the Bible (1531) to Robin Goodfellow as one who misleads: "The scripture is become a maze unto them, in which they wander as in a mist, or (as we say) led by Robin Goodfellow." Lamb then examines descriptions of Robin Goodfellow in ballads, but according to the STC, all extant copies were printed after c. 1625, well after the writing, performance, and publication of *MND* (STC 12018.3, 12016, 12017, etc.). Wall, "Why Does Puck Sweep?" explains that "Oberon has roots in German folklore, Oberon and Titania in classical mythology; the miniature floral fairies come from Welsh tradition; and Robin Goodfellow is a native English hobgoblin" (86, n. 48). She cites no source for this confusing information but is probably drawing on Katharine Mary Briggs, *The Anatomy of Puck: An Examination of Fairy Beliefs among Shakespeare's Contemporaries and Successors* (London: Routledge and Paul, 1959), or Briggs, *Encyclopedia of Fairies*.

47. Godsalve, *Britten's A Midsummer Night's Dream*, says Britten was inspired to cast Puck as a speaking acrobat after "watching some Swedish child acrobats with extraordinary agility and powers of mimicry," 156–157, citing Christopher Palmer, ed., *The Britten Companion* (Cambridge, UK: Cambridge University Press, 1984), 179.

48. Williams, "*Our Moonlight Revels*," quotes the *New York Times* reviewer who "praised the Puck of Mickey Rooney, who 'revealed a greater comprehension of his role than almost anyone in the cast'" (177).

49. In Christine Edzard's film *The Children's Midsummer Night's Dream* (2001), the play is performed entirely by children ranging in age from eight to twelve years old. Williams, "*Our Moonlight Revels*," discusses fairies as played by child actors, especially 131, 135, and passim. Porter, "Spells and Shadows," 20, has commented on Baz Luhrmann's Raj production at the 1994 Edinburgh Festival, in which the fairies were transformed into "gopies," or Krishna companions. Loney, *Peter Brook's Production*, 111, says the young Margaret Drabble played a fairy in the 1962 Stratford-upon-Avon production directed by Peter Hall. Hall's 1968 film is set mainly outdoors at Compton Verney, a mansion designed by Robert Adam in the 1760s with landscaping by Lancelot "Capability" Brown, in Warwickshire, England (e-mail from British Film Institute, March 10, 2006). Warwickshire is the setting for the well-known Guy of Warwick romances, popular from the fourteenth through sixteenth centuries.

50. Lamb, "Taken by the Fairies," 309, comments, "The play's unlikely conflation of a priapic Robin Goodfellow with a courtly and Cupid-like Puck would seem to obliterate a subversive folk source to suit an aristocratic agenda."

51. Williams, "*Our Moonlight Revels*," 257: "When Puck kissed Oberon fully and sensually on the mouth before 'I fly...,' the audience was surely being tantalized with a suggestion of gay sexual behavior." Puck and Oberon are later shown holding hands. The fairies also wear feathers in their hair (wigs) that might call to mind not only birds but the bird headdresses worn by Oberon and Titania in the 1954 production directed by George Devine at the Shakespeare Memorial Theatre, Stratford-upon-Avon (plate 11 in Williams).

52. Wall, "Why Does Puck Sweep?," 75, discusses the representation of Robin Goodfellow in the 1628 and later texts at some length (75–83 and passim); the text postdates publication of *MND* (1600). See also Briggs, *Encyclopedia of Fairies*, 342, "The black-letter pamphlet of 1628, *Robin Goodfellow, his mad Pranks and Merry Jests*, first reprinted by Collier as the *Life of Robin Goodfellow*, makes him a half-fairy, the son of Oberon by a country wench."

53. Derek Pearsall, *The Canterbury Tales* (London: Unwin Hyman, 1985), 162–163.

54. Dieter Mehl, *Middle English Romances*, 255, comments further that Chaucer parodies medieval romances "not only in Sir Thopas, where it seems most obvious, but also in the tales of the Squire, the Franklin, and the Man of Law, parody being here not so much understood as derision, but as exaggerated, brilliantly precise, and detached imitation." Donaldson, *Swan at the Well*, 9–18, includes a convincing argument that Shakespeare is rewriting Chaucer's "Tale of Sir Thopas."

55. Finlayson, "Definitions of Middle English Romance," 47. In the "Prologue of the Tale of Sir Thopas," Harry Bailey, the host, spots Chaucer the pilgrim among the company and comments on his diminutive stature, "This were a popet in an arm t'enbrace For any womman, smal and fair of face" (701–702), and on his face, which "semeth elvyssh" (703), allusions perhaps picked up in different contexts in *MND*.

56. Comic inversions of conventional attributes are also found in several verses appended by John Stow to his Chaucer edition, which Stow supplied from Trinity College, Cambridge, MS R.3.19. The poem "I Haue a Ladie" describes several unbeautiful features of the mistress: "Face and all, she hath enough fairnesse // Her iyen been holow, and grene as any grasse // And Rauinish yelowe is her founitresse." Another verse "O Mossie Quince" is powerful as invective: "Your uglie chere deinous and forward // Your grene iyen frownyng and not glad // Your chekes enbolned like a melowe Costard // Colour of Orenge your brestes Satournad." The green eyes and yellow complexions of both medieval ladies may have provided one inspiration for the wonderful lines of the lady's lament in the Pyramus and Thisbe play: "These yellow cowslip cheeks, Are gone, are gone! Lovers, make moan. His eyes were as green as leeks" (5.1.328–332).

57. A. C. Baugh, "Improvisation in the Middle English Romance," *Proceedings of the American Philosophical Society* 103 (1959): 418–454, 428, observes that romances typically use a "predictable complement": "Cer-

tain statements seem to call up automatically in the mind of the poet or reciter a conventional way of completing the thought. It was as though he were subject to a kind of conditioned reflex. Generally the statement and its predictable complement form a couplet and this feature of the composition is the result of the fact that the couplet is the basic unit of most Middle English romances, even the stanzaic romances."

58. Laura A. Hibbard, *Mediaeval Romance in England: A Study of the Sources and Analogues of the Non-Cyclic Metrical Romances* (1924; rev. ed. New York: Burt Franklin, 1963), cites a drama of Robert of Cisyle, a legend popular in England in the late fourteenth and fifteenth centuries (60–61), that in 1452–1453 was "acted at Lincoln and in the time of Henry VII another play on the same subject was given at Chester." Hibbard says, "The play of *Eglamour and Degrebelle* was given at St. Albans in 1444 (its production recorded in Trinity College, Dublin, MS. E. 5.9), and in 1580 Sidney's satirical formula for a popular play so strikingly parallels the plot of *Eglamour* that it is not improbable that he was familiar with some dramatization of the romance." See Sir Philip Sidney, *An Apology for Poetry*, ed. Forrest G. Robinson (Indianapolis: Bobbs-Merrill, 1970), 75–76. C. R. Baskervill, "Some Evidence for Early Romantic Plays in England—*Concluded*," *Modern Philology* 14, no. 8 (December 1916): 467–512, 500, comments that the meter of *Sir Eglamour*, "The Nut Brown Maid," and *Sir Clyomon and Sir Clamydes* is similar to that of the Pyramus and Thisbe play: "A point is very obviously made of it in Shakspere's [*sic*] satire on folk productions in the 'Pyramus and Thisbe.'" For brief further mention of *Sir Clyomon and Sir Clamydes*, see Patrick J. Cook, "Medieval *Hamlet* in Performance," this volume, 106, 113n14. Baskervill further points out (507) that several Breton dramas based on *Huon of Burdeux* still survive. See also Michael L. Hays, "A Bibliography of Dramatic Adaptations of Medieval Romances and Renaissance Chivalric Romances First Available in English through 1616," *Research Opportunities in Renaissance Drama* 28 (1985): 87–109.

59. Dieter Mehl, *The Elizabethan Dumb Show: The History of a Dramatic Convention* (Cambridge, MA: Harvard University Press, 1966), 3–4.

60. *Ibid.*, 109: "The pantomime in this play is not explicitly described and can therefore only be conjectured from the text. I feel, however, fairly certain that the play performed by the craftsmen was to be preceded by a brief dumb show in which the plot of the play was acted while the Prologue gave his account of it."

61. Godsalve, *Britten's* A Midsummer Night's Dream, 188, 90.

62. Burridge, "'Music, Such as Charmeth Sleep,'" 158.

63. Williams, "*Our Moonlight Revels*," 230. As Williams elsewhere notes, a version of the *Pyramus and Thisbe* play was performed on television in 1964 by the Beatles (212–213). Sid Ray forwarded to me the URL for this segment on YouTube http://youtube.com/watch?v=psATFlmUpUU&mode=related&search=Shakespeare/.

64. Stage directions for Brook's production of the dumb show are included in Loney, *Peter Brook's Production*, beginning at Quince's speech "Gentles, perchance you wonder," 74b: 74b, "This man is Pyramus" (74a, stage direction—"Bottom stands up straight."); 74b, "This beauteous lady Thisbe is" (74a, stage direction—"Flu flutters eyelashes."); 74b, "This man with lime and roughcast doth present Wall" (74a, stage direction—"Sno holds out arms."); 74b, "through Wall's chink, poor souls, they are content to whisper" (74a, stage direction—"Bot + Flu whispering at Sno's hands"); 74b, "This man with lantern, dog, and bush of thorn Presenteth Moonshine" (74a, stage direction—"All back in line."); 75b, "To meet at Ninus' tomb, there, there to woo" (75a, stage direction—"Flu, Sno, Bot cross arms."); 75b, "This grisly beast—which Lion hight by name—"(75a, stage direction—"Snug between Sno's legs."); 75b, "Did scare away, or rather did affright," (75a, stage direction—"Flu: running movement to SL."); 75b, "He bravely broached his boiling bloody breast" (75a, stage direction—"Bot stabs himself, goes down on knees."); 75b, "And Thisbe, ... His dagger drew, and died" (75a, stage direction—"Flu takes Bot's sword, stabs himself, on knees."); 75b, "For all the rest, Let Lion..." (75a, stage direction—"As names mentioned, each stands to attention."); 75b, "Moonshine, Wall, and lovers twain" (75a, stage direction—"Bot + Flu kneel up."); 75b, "At large discourse while here they do remain." (75a, stage direction—"All bow, get up and cross USL. Applause. Block to USC.")

65. Selbourne, *Making of* A Midsummer Night's Dream, 279.

66. In his cuts and some of his emphases, Michael Hoffman tends (perhaps unconsciously) to mirror Reinhardt. Set in Tuscany at the end of the nineteenth century, Hoffman's version adds to his film the character of Bottom's shrewish wife, who only speaks Italian. Her abusive behavior provides some motivation for Bottom's romance with Titania (see further Courtney Lehmann, "Crouching Tiger, Hidden Agenda: How Shakespeare and the Renaissance Are Taking the Rage out of Feminism," *Shakespeare Quarterly* 53, no. 2 [2002]: 260–279, 266). The discovery by Russell Jackson in the Birmingham Public Library in 1998 of Reinhardt's final shooting script containing several scenes not included in the released film, including "narrative intrusions by Bottom's 'virago' wife," is cited by Guneratne, "'Thou Dost Usurp Authority,'" 31–53, 42.

67. Williams, "*Our Moonlight Revels*," 26, says the bergomask "was a country dance, a cousin to the morris." John Forrest, *The History of Morris Dancing, 1458–1750* (Toronto: University of Toronto Press, 1999), 49, cites a reference "to the Drapers' guild sponsoring a dance at the Midsummer Watch in 1477 [as] the first

source to mention a specific dance event categorically identified as 'morris.'" Morris dancing is recorded in the 1494 court accounts paid by Henry VII to dancers at Christmas revels (*ibid.*, 51). Lords of Misrule are recorded for Christmas 1491 in Henry VII's accounts (*ibid.*, 112), and references continue throughout the reigns of Henry VII and Henry VIII. A letter detailing the Christmas festivities of 1552–1553 describes "the Lord of Misrule accompanied by musicians dressed in 'turkes garmen*tes*' and 'a challeng p*er*formed with hobbie horsis'" (*ibid.*, 113).

68. Williams, "*Our Moonlight Revels*," 146, 150.
69. Godsalve, *Britten's* A Midsummer Night's Dream, 59.
70. Playford's *The English Dancing Master* (November 7, 1650) appeared in ten editions between 1651 and 1698 and included descriptions of dance figures with their melodies. In 1651, Playford published *A Musical Banquet* with music, dances, and a collection of catches, and in 1653, he issued *A catalogue of all the musickbookes that have been printed in England*, a comprehensive list of extant historical music texts (BL, Harleian MS 5936, no. 421). His *Introduction to the Skill of Musick*, including music by Thomas Campion and Christopher Simpson, "first published in 1654, was still available in 1730, the twelfth edition of 1694 having been revised by Henry Purcell." Discussed in Robert Thompson, "Playford, John (1622/3–1686/7)," in *Oxford Dictionary of National Biography* (Oxford: Oxford University Press, 2004), http://www.oxforddnb.com/view/article/22374 (December 12, 2006).
71. Williams, "*Our Moonlight Revels*," 26; Mehl, *Elizabethan Dumb Show*, 110.
72. See Mehl, *Elizabethan Dumb Show*, 157, who comments, "with the return to an earlier form of drama the pantomime also plays a more important part again and the influence of the earlier pageants as well as that of the court masque, just becoming fashionable again, is more prominent. In all of the 'last plays' are masque-like elements, impressive processions, and other visual effects." For further discussion of Shakespeare's use of dumb shows, see Robert F. Yeager, "Shakespeare as Medievalist: What It Means for Performing *Pericles*," this volume, 218–219.
73. Loney, *Peter Brook's Production*, 24.
74. Henderson, *Collaborations with the Past*, 258.

Works Cited

Anders, H. R. D. *Shakespeare's Books: A Dissertation on Shakespeare's Reading and the Immediate Sources of His Works*. 1904. Reprint, New York: AMS Press, 1965.
Archibald, Elizabeth. "Magic School." *Times Literary Supplement*, February 2, 2007, 8–9.
Baldwin, D. R. "Fairy Lore and the Meaning of Sir Orfeo." *Southern Folklore Quarterly* 41 (1977): 129–142.
Baskervill, C. R. "Some Evidence for Early Romantic Plays in England — Concluded." *Modern Philology* 14, no. 8 (December 1916): 467–512.
Baugh, A. C. "Improvisation in the Middle English Romance." *Proceedings of the American Philosophical Society* 103 (1959): 418–454.
_____. "The Middle English Romance: Some Questions of Creation, Presentation, and Preservation." *Speculum* 42 (1967): 1–31.
Benjamin, Walter. *Illuminations: Essays and Reflections*. Edited and with an introduction by Hannah Arendt. 1955. Reprint, New York: Schocken Books, 1978.
Benson, Larry D., ed. *The Riverside Chaucer*. 3rd ed. Oxford: Oxford University Press, 1988.
Bethurum, Dorothy. "Shakespeare's Comment on Mediaeval Romance in *Midsummer-Night's Dream*." *Modern Language Notes* 60 (1945): 85–94.
Bevington, David. *From Mankind to Marlowe*. Cambridge, MA: Harvard University Press, 1962.
Boro, Joyce. "Lord Berners and His Books: A New Survey." *Huntington Library Quarterly* 67 (2004): 236–250.
_____. "The Textual History of *Huon of Burdeux*: A Reassessment of the Facts." *Notes and Queries* n.s. 48 (2001): 233–237.
Bridcut, John. *Britten's Children*. London: Faber, 2006.
Briggs, Katharine M. *The Anatomy of Puck: An Examination of Fairy Beliefs among Shakespeare's Contemporaries and Successors*. London: Routledge and Paul, 1959.
_____. *An Encyclopedia of Fairies: Hobgoblins, Brownies, Bogies and Other Supernatural Creatures*. New York: Pantheon, 1976.
Britten, Benjamin, and Peter Pears. *A Midsummer Night's Dream: An Opera in Three Acts Adapted from William Shakespeare*. Opus 64. London: Boosey and Hawkes, 1960.
Brooks, Harold F., ed. *A Midsummer Night's Dream, The Arden Edition of the Works of William Shakespeare*. 1979. Reprint, London: Methuen, 1983.
Bullough, Geoffrey, ed. *Narrative and Dramatic Sources of Shakespeare*. Vol. 1. *Early Comedies, Poems, Romeo and Juliet*. London: Routledge and Kegan Paul; and New York: Columbia University Press, 1964.

Burridge, Christina J. "'Music, Such as Charmeth Sleep': Benjamin Britten's *A Midsummer Night's Dream*." *University of Toronto Quarterly* 51 (1981–1982): 149–160.
Carley, James P. "Bourchier, John, Second Baron Berners (c. 1467–1533)." *Oxford Dictionary of National Biography*. Oxford: Oxford University Press, 2004. http://www.oxforddnb.com/view/article/2990 (December 9, 2006).
Champion, Larry S. "*A Midsummer Night's Dream*: The Problem of Source." *Papers on Language and Literature* (Southern Illinois University) 4 (1968): 13–19.
Coghill, Nevill. "Shakespeare's Reading in Chaucer." In *Elizabethan and Jacobean Studies Presented to Frank Percy Wilson in Honour of His Seventieth Birthday*, edited by Herbert Davis and Helen Gardner, 86–99. Oxford: Clarendon Press, 1959.
Cuningham, Henry, ed. *A Midsummer Night's Dream*. 1905. Reprint, London: Methuen, 1922.
Davis, Herbert, and Helen Gardner, eds. *Elizabethan and Jacobean Studies Presented to Frank Percy Wilson in Honour of His Seventieth Birthday*. Oxford: Clarendon Press, 1959.
Draper, John W. "A Reference to 'Huon' in Ben Jonson." *Modern Language Notes* 35, no. 7 (November 1920): 439–440.
Donaldson, E. Talbot. *The Swan at the Well: Shakespeare Reading Chaucer*. New Haven, CT: Yale University Press, 1985.
Fewster, Carol. *Traditionality and Genre in Middle English Romance*. Woodbridge, UK: D. S. Brewer, 1987.
Finlayson, John. "Definitions of Middle English Romance." *Chaucer Review* 15 (1980–1981): 44–62, 168–181.
Fletcher, Jefferson B. "*Huon of Burdeux* and *The Fairie Queene*." *Journal of English and Germanic Philology* 2 (1899): 203–12.
Forrest, John. *The History of Morris Dancing, 1458–1750*. Toronto: University of Toronto Press, 1999.
Friedman, John B. "Eurydice, Heurodis, and the Noon-Day Demon." *Speculum* 41 (1966): 22–29.
Godsalve, William H. L. *Britten's* A Midsummer Night's Dream: *Making an Opera from Shakespeare's Comedy*. Madison, NJ: Fairleigh Dickinson University Press, 1995.
Grimaldi, P. "Sir Orfeo as Celtic Folk-Hero, Christian Pilgrim, and Medieval King." In *Allegory, Myth, and Symbol*, edited by M. W. Bloomfield, 147–161. Cambridge, MA: Harvard University Press, 1981.
Guneratne, Anthony R. "'Thou Dost Usurp Authority': Beerbohm Tree, Reinhardt, Olivier, Welles, and the Politics of Adapting Shakespeare." In *A Concise Companion to Shakespeare on Screen*, edited by Diana E. Henderson, 31–53. Oxford: Blackwell, 2006.
Hale, David G. "Bottom's Dream and Chaucer." *Shakespeare Quarterly* 36, no. 2 (Summer 1985): 219–220.
Hales, John W. "Chaucer and Shakespeare." *Quarterly Review* 134 (1873): 225–255.
Hays, Michael L. "A Bibliography of Dramatic Adaptations of Medieval Romances and Renaissance Chivalric Romances First Available in English through 1616." *Research Opportunities in Renaissance Drama* 28 (1985): 87–109.
Henderson, Diana E. *Collaborations with the Past: Reshaping Shakespeare across Time and Media*. Ithaca, NY: Cornell University Press, 2006.
Hibbard, Laura A. *Mediaeval Romance in England: A Study of the Sources and Analogues of the Non-Cyclic Metrical Romances*, rev. ed. New York: Burt Franklin, 1963 [1924].
Hodnett, Edward. *English Woodcuts 1480–1535, Additions & Corrections*. London: Bibliographical Society, 1973.
Jowitt, Deborah. *Time and the Dancing Image*. Berkeley: University of California Press, 1988.
Lamb, Mary Ellen. "Taken by the Fairies: Fairy Practices and the Production of Popular Culture in *A Midsummer Night's Dream*." *Shakespeare Quarterly* 51, no. 3 (Autumn 2000): 277–312.
Larrington, Carolyne. *King Arthur's Enchantresses: Morgan and Her Sisters in Arthurian Tradition*. London: Tauris, 2006.
Lee, S. L., ed. *The English Charlemagne Romances, Part VII. The Boke of Duke Huon of Burdeux Done into English by Sir John Bourchier, Lord Berners*. 3 vols. London: EETS Trübner & Co., 1882.
Lehmann, Courtney. "Crouching Tiger, Hidden Agenda: How Shakespeare and the Renaissance Are Taking the Rage out of Feminism." *Shakespeare Quarterly* 53, no. 2 (2002): 260–279.
Loney, Glenn, ed. *Peter Brook's Production of William Shakespeare's* A Midsummer Night's Dream *for The Royal Shakespeare Company: The Complete and Authorized Acting Edition*. Chicago: Dramatic Publishing, 1974.
MacArthur, John R. "The Influence of *Huon of Burdeux* upon *The Fairie Queene*." *Journal of English and Germanic Philology* 4 (1902): 215–238.
Matthews, David. "Lucky Thirteen." *Times Literary Supplement*, November 10, 2006, 6.
Mehl, Dieter. *The Elizabethan Dumb Show: The History of a Dramatic Convention*. Cambridge, MA: Harvard University Press, 1966.
_____. *The Middle English Romances of the Thirteenth and Fourteenth Centuries*. New York: Barnes & Noble, 1969.
Muir, Kenneth. *Shakespeare's Sources: Comedies and Tragedies*. 1957. Reprint, London: Methuen, 1961.

Munro, Lucy. "Translated from Top to Bottom." *Times Literary Supplement*, March 23, 2007, 20.
Newcomb, L. H. "Greene, Robert (bap. 1558, d. 1592)." *Oxford Dictionary of National Biography*. Oxford: Oxford University Press, 2004. http://www.oxforddnb.com/view/article/11418 (December 11, 2006).
Palmer, Christopher, ed. *The Britten Companion*. Cambridge, UK: Cambridge University Press, 1984.
Panofsky, Erwin. "Style and Medium in the Motion Pictures." In *Three Essays on Style*, edited by Irving Lavin. Cambridge, MA: MIT Press, 1997.
Pearsall, Derek.*The Canterbury Tales*. London: Unwin Hyman, 1985.
_____. "The Development of Middle English Romance." *Mediaeval Studies* 27 (1965): 91–116.
Porter, Andrew. "Dreaming of the 'Dream.'" *Stagebill/JFK Center*, April 1973, 7–9.
_____. "Spells and Shadows." *Times Literary Supplement*, July 14, 2006, 20.
Ringler, William A. "The Number of Actors in Shakespeare's Early Plays." In *The Seventeenth Century Stage: A Collection of Critical Essays*, edited by Gerald Eades Bentley, 130–134. Chicago: University of Chicago Press, 1968.
Ross, Alex "Songs of Experience: Ian Bostridge Sings Benjamin Britten." *New Yorker*, March 27, 2006, 87–90.
Selbourne, David. *The Making of* A Midsummer Night's Dream: *An Eye-Witness Account of Peter Brook's Production from First Rehearsal to First Night*. London: Methuen, 1982.
Sidney, Sir Philip. *An Apology for Poetry*. Edited by Forrest G. Robinson. Indianapolis: Bobbs-Merrill Educational, 1970.
Spenser, Edmund. *The Faerie Queene. Book Two*. Edited by Erik Gray. Indianapolis: Hackett, 2006.
Strohm, Paul. "The Origin and Meaning of Middle English Romaunce." *Genre* 10 (1977): 1–28.
_____. "Storie, Spelle, Geste, Romaunce, Tragedie: Generic Distinctions in the Middle English Troy Narratives." *Speculum* 46, no. 2 (1971): 348–359.
Thompson, Ann. *Shakespeare's Chaucer: A Study in Literary Origins*. Liverpool, UK: Liverpool University Press, 1978.
Thompson, Robert. "Playford, John (1622/3–1686/7)." *Oxford Dictionary of National Biography*. Oxford: Oxford University Press, 2004. http://www.oxforddnb.com/view/article/22374 (December 12, 2006).
Wall, Wendy. "Why Does Puck Sweep? Fairylore, Merry Wives, and Social Struggle." *Shakespeare Quarterly* 52 (Spring 2001): 67–106.
Williams, Gary Jay. *"Our Moonlight Revels":* A Midsummer Night's Dream *in the Theatre*. Iowa City: University of Iowa Press, 1997.

FILMOGRAPHY AND PERFORMANCES

1913 *Ein Sommersnachtstraum in unserer Zeit* (A Midsummer Night's Dream in our Time), d. Stellan Rye, script by Rye and Hanns Heinz Ewers, with Grete Berger, Carl Clewing, Grete Reinwald. Germany: Deutsche Bioscop.
1913 *Ein Sommersnachtstraum*, d. Max Reinhardt. Germany: Berlin, Deutsches Theater.
1925 *Ein Sommersnachtstraum*, d. Hans Neumann, with Charlotte Ander, Theodor Becker, Valeska Gert, Tamara Geva. Germany: Neumann-Filmproduktion.
1935 *A Midsummer Night's Dream*, d. Max Reinhardt and William Dieterle, with James Cagney, Joe E. Brown, Dick Powell, Victor Jory, Olivia de Havilland, and Mickey Rooney. USA: Warner Brothers.
1960 *A Midsummer Night's Dream: An Opera in Three Acts Adapted from William Shakespeare by Benjamin Britten and Peter Pears*, d. Peter Hall. UK: Glyndebourne Festival Opera.
1962 *A Midsummer Night's Dream*, d. Peter Hall, with Judi Dench, Ian Holm, Ian Richardson, Helen Mirren, and Diana Rigg. UK: Stratford-upon-Avon.
1968 *A Midsummer Night's Dream*, d. Peter Hall, with Judi Dench, Ian Holm, Ian Richardson, Helen Mirren, and Diana Rigg. UK: Water Bearer Films (DVD).
1970 *A Midsummer Night's Dream*, d. Peter Brook, with Frances de la Tour, Alan Howard, John Kane, Sara Kestelman, Ben Kingsley, Philip Locke. UK: Stratford-upon-Avon.
1994–1995 *A Midsummer Night's Dream*, d. Adrian Noble, with Alex Jennings, Lindsay Duncan, and Barry Lynch. UK: Stratford-upon-Avon.
1996 *A Midsummer Night's Dream*, d. Adrian Noble, with Alex Jennings, Lindsay Duncan, and Barry Lynch. UK: Capitol Films (DVD).
1999 *William Shakespeare's A Midsummer Night's Dream*, d. Michael Hoffman, with Rupert Everett, Kevin Kline, Michelle Pfeiffer, Stanley Tucci. USA: Fox Searchlight Pictures.
2001 *The Children's Midsummer Night's Dream*, d. Christine Edzard, with Dominic Haywood-Benge, Leane Lyson, Rajouana Zalal. UK: Sands Films.

"Chaucer ... the Story Gives":
Troilus and Cressida and *The Two Noble Kinsmen*

Julia Ruth Briggs

William Shakespeare, like all great writers, was also an avid reader — attentive, selective, and retentive. In his day the works of Geoffrey Chaucer, in the editions of William Thynne, John Stow, and Thomas Speght, were widely read and enjoyed, and it is evidently no accident that the playwright, during the course of a consciously commercial career, dramatized Chaucer's two best-loved masterpieces, *Troilus and Criseyde* and *The Knight's Tale* (as *The Two Noble Kinsmen*).[1] Nor was Shakespeare the only dramatist to do so: Philip Henslowe's diary records a play about Troy performed by the Admiral's Men in 1596, and in 1599 Henslowe made payments to Henry Chettle and Thomas Dekker for a "Troyeles & creasse daye," since lost.[2] Richard Edwards presented a play of Palamon and Arcite before Queen Elizabeth in 1566, and Henslowe's company apparently produced a play on the same subject in 1594.[3] But Shakespeare's adaptations always go far beyond mere dramatization: they interrogate, challenge, and recast their sources. Substantial changes are, of course, inevitable in the process of adapting a long poem for the stage, but humanist rereadings of the old tales of Troy and Thebes had introduced new perspectives, triangulating classical legend and Renaissance responses to it with the medieval interpretations of Chaucer and, in the case of *Troilus and Cressida*, those of Robert Henryson in the *Testament of Cresseid* and of Caxton's *Recuyell of the Historyes of Troye* as well.[4]

Neither of Shakespeare's two major adaptations from Chaucer was performed as he wrote them until the twentieth century; though both plays are now better understood and appreciated, they offer contrasting performance histories. In the context of Shakespeare's medievalism, it is perhaps ironic that his *Troilus and Cressida* and *The Two Noble Kinsmen*, the two plays that most directly and overtly use Chaucer's work as sources, tend to be performed without much awareness of earlier source texts. This paper considers first Shakespeare's emendation and expansion of his medieval sources and then the ways in which medieval elements are played (or, more often, not) in contemporary performance.

In the process of dramatizing Chaucer, Shakespeare largely abandons the older poet's philosophy, his Boethean vision of a Providence stoic yet consoling that softens the sharp edges of suffering and loss in the two poems; Shakespeare replaces them with a bleaker and more skeptical outlook. For the critic Philip Edwards, "*The Two Noble Kinsmen* seems to me to give the most cynical assessment of the progress of life since the writing of *Troilus and Cressida*."[5] His adjective "cynical" may perhaps be more appropriately applied to the views of particular characters than to a sense of the play as a whole;[6] but both plays question Providence, and *The Two Noble Kinsmen* ends with Theseus doubting how far we can grasp the meaning of human actions and events:

> Oh, you heavenly charmers,
> What things you make of us! For what we lack
> We laugh, for what we have are sorry, still
> Are children in some kind. Let us be thankful
> For that which is, and with you leave dispute
> That are above our question [5.4.131–136].

One factor in their prevailing sense of disillusion is that both plays take war as their background — ancient, mythical wars, it is true, yet their very mythic status lends them a universal application and not only for modern audiences but also for Shakespeare and perhaps for Chaucer as well. While Chaucer recognized the devastation war brought, Shakespeare seems to have felt an altogether deeper revulsion. This was partly, no doubt, a reaction to its developing technology: with the use of gunpowder on the battlefield and the possibility of killing at a distance, older ideals of chivalry and heroism became increasingly irrelevant, confined to aristocratic games and pastimes. Renaissance warfare was increasingly a matter of bitter religious struggles, not merely against remote "infidels" but against fellow countrymen in civil wars; the beginnings of national, colonial, and class conflicts were changing its character. As Erasmus had pointed out, war brought all other evils in its wake — starvation and epidemics, the terrible Horsemen of the Apocalypse.[7] And indeed it was at a Renaissance siege — that of Naples by the army of the French Emperor Charles VIII in 1495 to 1496 — that syphilis had first appeared, and in a peculiarly virulent form that spread rapidly across Europe, particularly affecting the upper classes.[8] This is the disease that threatens both Greeks and Trojans in *Troilus and Cressida* and acts as a figure for the political, commercial, and sexual exchanges that deliver Cressida to the Greek camp and return the traitor Antenor to Troy.

War is scarcely less sordid in *The Two Noble Kinsmen*, where the wedding pageant that opens the play is interrupted by three mourning queens whose husbands' bodies lie unburied on the battlefield.[9] As in *Troilus and Cressida*, love in wartime is continuously interrupted and crossed. Both plays acknowledge the destructive force of time as the "eater of things" ("*tempus edax rerum*"), as Shakespeare's sonnets also do:

> Oh, grief and time,
> Fearful consumers, you will all devour! [*TNK*, 1.1.69–70][10]

In 1980, Glynne Wickham argued that *The Two Noble Kinsmen* was most closely connected with another play of crossed lovers: it should be read, he claimed, as a sequel to *A Midsummer Night's Dream*.[11] There are certainly some notable points of resemblance: both plays begin with the imminent wedding of Theseus and Hippolita, a contract made upon the battlefield. Their central scenes take place in a wood near Athens where rival lovers are fighting for the same woman and a group of locals are preparing an entertainment for the aristocracy. Both the mechanicals of the earlier play and the rustics of the later perform versions of the morris dance, traditionally a celebration of sexuality and fertility. Yet in *A Midsummer Night's Dream* the darker aspects of passion are ultimately dismissed as bad dreams, remaining undeveloped, whereas those of *The Two Noble Kinsmen* turn the play decisively toward tragicomedy, so that it is more closely linked to the moral dilemmas and political disillusion of *Troilus and Cressida*.

Both *Troilus and Cressida* and *The Two Noble Kinsmen* treat love and war as sources not of heroic joy but of inevitable suffering, and this, combined with their note of disillusion, gives these plays a curiously contemporary atmosphere, though, except in terms of their Chaucerian (and ultimately ancient Greek) origins, there has been little critical analysis in the way of comparisons between them.[12] This is largely due to the marginal position occupied by *The Two Noble Kinsmen* within the Shakespearean canon. It is, in point of fact, Shakespeare's last known work, written in collaboration with John Fletcher (as the 1634 Quarto records), though several critics (notably Paul Bertram)[13] have considered it essentially Shakespearean in conception and structure. Unlike

Ralph Fiennes as Troilus and Amanda Root as Cressida in the 1990 production of the play directed by Sam Mendes, Swan Theatre, Stratford-upon-Avon. Courtesy of John Haynes, London.

Pericles, another late collaborative play based upon a medieval source, *The Two Noble Kinsmen* never appeared in any of the seventeenth-century Shakespeare Folios but was reprinted in the second Beaumont and Fletcher Folio of 1679.[14] In particular, there has been a widespread reluctance to acknowledge it as Shakespeare's last play, his final account of the human condition. Instead, *The Tempest* continues to occupy that position in preference to the two late collaborations with John Fletcher (the other being *Henry VIII*).[15] This lack of canonical status has drastically diminished the play's performance history.

By contrast, *Troilus and Cressida*, though initially neglected and possibly never performed in its original version from its first publication in 1609 until the end of the nineteenth century, has since come into its own. Hailed by Polish theatre critic Jan Kott in the 1960s as "Amazing and Modern," by the end of the twentieth century *Troilus and Cressida* had become one of the most frequently performed. As Anthony Dawson points out, the play "was given four major British productions in the 1990s, three at the RSC and one at the National, which made it the single most frequently performed Shakespeare play of the decade at those venues."[16] Twentieth-century performances of the play have emphasized its Elizabethan character (as did William Poel's 1912 production), its contemporary aspects (from Michael Macowen's 1938 production onwards), or its ancient Greek origins (John Barton's productions of 1960 and 1968), but its medieval sources have nearly always been ignored. Thus, though for entirely different reasons, Shakespeare's two major adaptations from Chaucer were not performed as he wrote them until the twentieth century, and even today, when they are better understood and appreciated, they offer complex and contrasting performance histories.[17]

Cressida — and Troilus

The largest differences between Chaucer's narrative of *Troilus and Criseyde* and Shakespeare's play can, of course, be accounted for simply in terms of generic difference: the slow unfolding of the several stages of a love affair is a subject ideally suited to a long poem, whose sustained rhythms can accommodate fluctuating moods and feelings. Chaucer's poem has great psychological inwardness; its narrative viewpoint is primarily that of Troilus, and as the action progresses and Criseyde is exiled to the Greek camp, the narrator and the reader lose touch with her and she becomes an increasingly mysterious figure — and thus the focus for a great deal of later critical controversy.

With no equivalent to a narrative viewpoint, drama might be seen as a more explicit medium, but its determination typically takes place at the level of performance rather than of text. Shakespeare's Cressida is arguably quite as enigmatic as Chaucer's, but the director and the actor must decide how to represent her — how experienced, how loving, how timid she is to be — questions that Chaucer's text poses but does not resolve. And Shakespeare follows Chaucer's example, so that Cressida's words and actions provide a series of small surprises, and the text refuses to resolve whether she is the instigator or the victim of her tragedy. Like the text itself, she is open to multiple interpretations: as Claire Tylee puts it, "[i]n a sense Cressida *is* the text." Heather James goes a step further, seeing Shakespeare as constructing Cressida from "the least reputable versions of her," so that she becomes "a creature of intertextuality."[18]

As an enigma that cannot be resolved, Cressida has affinities with another Shakespearean character from the same phase of his work — Hamlet's mother, Queen Gertrude. She is angrily accused by her son yet touchingly protected by the ghost of her former husband, and her innocence or complicity with Claudius remains an unanswered question, one oddly linked with *Troilus and Cressida* through the allusions to Hecuba in both plays. After the First Player's account of the sack of Troy, Hamlet contrasts the Player's histrionic display of grief with his own failure to respond to his situation, but the further subtext is an unspoken contrast between Hecuba, as a mythically devoted wife and mother, and the failures, as Hamlet sees them, of his own mother:

> What's he to Hecuba or Hecuba to him
> That he should weep for her? [2.2.553–554].[19]

Hecuba does not actually appear in *Troilus and Cressida*, but Troilus, watching with incredulity the encounter between Cressida and Diomedes, also invokes his mother as a standard to judge by:

> Let it not be believed, for womanhood!
> Think, we had mothers [5.2.135–136].

To which the puzzled Ulysses replies:

> What hath she done, Prince, that can soil our mothers? [5.2.140].[20]

This scene (5.2), in which Troilus and Ulysses look down upon Cressida and Diomedes and are in turn watched by Thersites while all five are, of course, watched by the audience, is one of Shakespeare's major additions to the story of Cressida, an addition that exploits a popular stage convention, familiar not only from his own work but from Elizabethan drama as a whole: a key example occurs in Thomas Kyd's *Spanish Tragedy*, when Lorenzo and Balthazar overlook their sister Bellamira's assignation with Horatio, commenting with sinister irony on its outcome.[21] Overlooking or overhearing scenes were typically played in early modern productions with the onlookers on the gallery above the stage, so that Troilus and Ulysses would probably have stood where Pandarus and Cressida had done in Act 1, scene 2, as they watched the return of the Trojans warriors in a scene inspired by Chaucer.[22]

The effect of showing Cressida's betrayal of Troilus onstage and beneath his gaze seems, on the face of it, to preclude further doubt as to her guilt, yet just as Chaucer's Criseyde was gradually exonerated from the condemnation of generations of misogynist critics by C. S. Lewis's argument that she was not so much fickle as "slyding of courage,"[23] so feminist criticism of the 1970s and 1980s has pointed to Cressida's vulnerability as a lone woman among the sex-hungry Greeks and more generally to the suffering and victimization of women in wartime.

Another of Shakespeare's major additions is also a crucial scene for the interpretation of Cressida within the play — that of her welcome at the Greek camp, where she is kissed "in general" (4.5.21) and where her sharp repartee can be read either as evidence for an innate hardness or else as a desperate reaction to a dangerous situation. Both these scenes can be performed in a variety of ways, depending on how Cressida is interpreted. Hurried to the Greek camp the morning after her first and only night with Troilus, she may be in a state of shock, still wearing her nightdress (as was Juliet Stevenson in Howard Davies's 1985 production),[24] or she may be revealed in provocative décolletage (as in Ian Judge's 1996 version).[25] And the kissing can vary from a comparatively disciplined queue to near-gang rape, from which Cressida is rescued by the intervention of Diomedes. Thus the range of possibilities offered by a dramatic text is quite as wide as those of a poem — and Shakespeare's heroine remains as elusive and unknowable as Chaucer's.

James's observation that Shakespeare's Cressida is "a creature of intertextuality" is particularly apt.[26] Shakespeare's play forms part of a sequence of narrative treatments that extend beyond Chaucer to his sources in Benoît de Sainte-Maure's *Roman de Troie* (c. 1160) and in Giovanni Boccaccio's poem *Il Filostrato* (c. 1338), where the poet's identification with Troilus creates a tone of reproach, even of resentment. Shakespeare was also influenced by Robert Henryson's homage to Chaucer, *The Testament of Cresseid*, a poem regularly reprinted in sixteenth-century editions of Chaucer's work.[27]

Chaucer's poem ends with Troilus's death and his translation to the eighth sphere, where he looks back at the earth with contempt and even amusement at "The blynde lust, the which that may nat laste" (5.1824). Henryson gives his version of Cresseid's end: after a terrible prophetic dream, she awakes to find that the gods have afflicted her with leprosy as a punishment for her infidelity. Exiled to a lazar house, she is reduced to begging for alms. In a reversal of the traditional *anagnorisis*, Troilus rides past her, but neither recognizes the other, although Troilus is painfully reminded of her and so gives her his girdle, jewels, and a gold purse. Horribly disfigured by leprosy, Cresseid then speaks her "Testament," or will, in which she bequeaths the ring "with this Ruby reid" that Troilus has given her "in drowrie" (582, 583, 592). She dies soon afterwards, having discovered the identity of Troilus. The ring is taken by "ane Lipper man" to Troilus, to whom the leper recounts the sad end of Cresseid.[28]

Shakespeare was evidently familiar with Henryson's poem and made several references to it, notably in *Twelfth Night*, where Feste, begging coins from the disguised Viola, observes that "Cressida was a beggar" (3.1.47).²⁹ Leprosy was mistakenly thought to be sexually transmitted and so an appropriate punishment for sexual promiscuity. Shakespeare's *Troilus and Cressida* does not include the lovers' deaths, but he may have thought of Cressida as a potential victim of syphilis (which was sometimes confused with leprosy in the late-medieval and early modern periods), since syphilis, the great pox, is the disease that haunts the play: "the Neapolitan bone ache; for that methinks is the curse depending in those that war for a placket" (2.3.19–21). By the end, Cressida's uncle Pandarus, dying of the pox, bequeaths it to the audience (5.10.45–56).³⁰

The tale of Troilus and Cressida was familiar enough for Shakespeare to give his characters some presentiment of their own literary future and thus of the multiple sources that would come to constitute the Troy legend. He creates a little ritual around its familiarity, registering its power to predetermine the plot: as the lovers prepare for bed, they vow constancy, while Pandarus adds that if they fail their vows, "[l]et all constant men be Troiluses, all false women Cressids, and all brokers-between panders! Say 'Amen'" (3.2.197–199). Shakespeare composed a comparably metatheatrical moment after Caesar's assassination in *Julius Caesar* (3.1.111–113).³¹ Yet there the prolepsis reminds audiences of how often Caesar's death would be reenacted upon the stage, whereas in *Troilus* the lines serve to emphasize the way its characters are trapped by what the audience already knows of their destinies.

That scene, set in a distant past, anticipates a future when Cressida's faithlessness will be proverbial, yet when John Dryden came to adapt Shakespeare's play for the Restoration stage in *Troilus and Cressida, or, Truth Found Too Late* (1679),³² he exonerated her. In Dryden's view, Shakespeare composed the play in "the Ap[p]renticeship of his Writing," evidenced by the cardinal mistake of leaving the main characters alive at the end of the tragedy. Dryden therefore "undertook to remove that heap of Rubbish, under which many excellent thoughts lay wholly bury'd."³³ He pared down the plot and completely rewrote the ending; in his version, Cressida's father, Calchas, persuades her to pretend to accept Diomede in order to allay Troilus's suspicions, so that they can escape together to Troy. But Troilus distrusts her, and Diomede increases Troilus's jealousy by producing her ring. Cressida, faithful but misjudged, kills herself, and Troilus, having learned the truth too late, kills Diomede and is then slain in battle himself.

A comparably misjudged Cressida turns up unexpectedly in a mid-twentieth-century version: William Walton's opera *Troilus and Cressida* of 1954.³⁴ His librettist, Christopher Hassall, rewrote her story according to operatic conventions (which were not so different from those of John Dryden). Hassall consulted a range of sources, including Dryden and Chaucer, for his version of the plot, and he reinstated Chaucer's careful buildup to the lovers' consummation by having Pandarus invite an innocent Cressida to his house, where she plays chess and is checkmated by Horaste (Troilus's supposed rival in Chaucer's version). She is then obliged to stay the night because of the bad weather. Pandarus brings Troilus to her room and, as in Chaucer's poem, goes to fetch a cushion for him to kneel on. This second act (which Walton composed first) ends with a musical interlude in which "the ecstasy of their lovemaking is juxtaposed with the violent foreboding of the storm outside," variously recalling the "Royal Hunt and Storm" music of Hector Berlioz's *The Trojans*, the erotic act 1 climax of Richard Wagner's *Die Walküre*, and the sea interludes of Benjamin Britten's 1945 opera *Peter Grimes*.³⁵

In the third act of Walton's opera, Hassall, like Dryden before him, exonerates Cressida: at the Greek camp, Calkas has instructed Cressida's maid, Evadne (a mezzo-soprano and an entirely new character), to burn all letters from Troilus. In despair Cressida has agreed to marry Diomede and become Queen of Argos, when Troilus and Pandarus arrive. In the confusion that follows, Troilus attacks Diomede and is fatally stabbed by Calkas (another new twist). Cressida escapes enslavement to Diomede by falling on Troilus's sword:

> Open the gates. We are riding together into Troy.
> And by this sign I am still your Cressida.
> *She stabs herself.*³⁶

Greeks — and Trojans

In accordance with theatrical convention, Shakespeare speeds up and foreshortens Chaucer's leisurely paced poem, which takes two and a half books to get the lovers into bed; thereafter they remain devoted until fortune parts them in Book Four. He also greatly reduces the lovers' importance by presenting the war as a whole and introducing a far larger cast of Greeks, including Agamemnon, Menelaus, Nestor, Ulysses, Ajax, Achilles, Patroclus, and the railing Thersites, whose role as commentator counterbalances that of Pandarus among the Trojans. The debates among the Trojans and the Greeks, and in particular Ulysses' efforts to draw the sulking Achilles back into battle, become as important as the story of Troilus.

For these episodes, Shakespeare drew on Homer in George Chapman's translation (c. 1611) as well as William Caxton's *Recuyell of the Historyes of Troye* and perhaps John Lydgate's *Troy Book*.[37] Shakespeare's sense of the destructive effects of war probably derives originally from Homer, for although the *Iliad* celebrates the glory of its heroes, it never underestimates the human cost of war.[38] The resulting widening of focus sets the tragedies of *Troilus and Cressida* in a more obviously war-torn world in which Cressida and Helen are both seen as objects of male exchanges and testosterone fuels sex and war alike: "Lechery, lechery, still wars and lechery; nothing else holds fashion. A burning devil take them!" (5.3.201–203).

In modern representations, the play's military ethos dominated John Barton's two productions in 1960 and 1968, where warriors in leather thongs and birdlike helmets engaged in a series of homoerotic duals.[39] In 1968, Barton's Achilles appeared in drag, though other productions have reserved this for "mistress Thersites," as did Jonathan Miller's 1981 TV film, or even for Pandarus, as in Ian Judge's 1996 production.[40] In the 1912 production by William Poel, the part of Thersites was taken by the actress Elspeth Keith, who played him as a medieval jester with a Scots brogue.[41]

Shakespeare's wider action invites comparison between his Trojans and his Greeks. Ensconced in their own city, the Trojans are still part of a family structure that includes Priam's numerous children (Cassandra, Hector, Paris, Deiphobus, Helenus, Troilus, and Margareton) and the marriages of Hector and Paris. The Trojans observe the traditional chivalric code and value honor achieved through single combat (hence Hector's challenge). The Greeks pay lip service to honor but are more interested in reputation, and in act 5, scene 2, Achilles has his Myrmidons murder an unarmed Hector in a notable departure from Homer's narrative (though this action is found in some medieval versions of the Troy story).[42] Yet the Trojans also fail to maintain the moral high ground: Hector points out that in keeping Helen they are breaking a natural law, yet for him the claims of honor override even those of natural law. Once the war has begun, there is no way out without losing face and betraying those who have already died for it — a double bind as potent now as then.

The British had identified themselves with the Trojans since Geoffrey of Monmouth's claim that Britain had been founded by Aeneas's grandson Felix Brutus. This legend of descent, of empire succeeding empire, though dismissed by serious historians such as Polydore Vergil (c. 1470–c. 1555), was still employed in poetry, transforming Elizabeth's London into "Troy-Novant." Whether or how that identification affected early performances of the play is uncertain — but then so are those performances themselves: the preface to the 1609 quarto claimed that the play had never been "staled with the stage, never clapper-clawed with the palms of the vulgar," and this could well be true. There are certainly no records of any contemporary performances, though the records themselves are very far from complete.[43]

Today, when empires are more commonly seen as evil oppressors and the British are ashamed of their colonial past, recent productions have reversed that traditional alignment, identifying the British with the conquering Greeks, while the defeated Trojans become the "other." Thus in Michael Boyd's 1998 Royal Shakespeare Company production, the Trojans were Roman Catholic, probably Irish, while the Greeks became their British oppressors, a configuration also adopted in

Troilus (Anton Lesser) and Cressida (Suzanne Burden) in the BBC production of *Troilus and Cressida* (1981).

Dominic Dromgoole's production for the Oxford Stage Company at the Old Vic in 2000. In Trevor Nunn's version for the National Theatre in 1999, all the Trojans apart from Pandarus were played by black actors and the Greeks by white ones, creating powerful tensions around a blonde Helen among the Trojans and a black Cressida among the pallid Greeks. This interestingly complicated the kinship ties between Ajax and Hector and (probably unconsciously) interrogated the play's assumption that both camps share the same military culture. Peter Stein's production at Stratford-upon-Avon in 2006 responded to the Iraq War by representing the Trojans as Middle Eastern, resisting a Western invasion.

Over the last forty years, *Troilus and Cressida* has been presented in a range of wartime settings, including the Crimean War (in Howard Davies's version of 1985) and the American Civil War,[44] as well as in terms of contemporary conflicts, but the play's Chaucerian source has been consistently overlooked. One exception is Jonathan Miller's 1981 production for BBC TV. Prompted by Jan Kott's reading of the play, Miller decided that Shakespeare had achieved his "*buffo* tone" by reducing Homer's legendary heroes to the stature of his own contemporaries. Miller therefore deliberately set the play in "a period which hovered between the medieval Gothic of Chaucer and Henryson and the Renaissance of Shakespeare," giving it late fifteenth- or early sixteenth-century costumes inspired by Albrecht Dürer and Lucas Cranach.[45] Anxious to avoid reproducing a stage production, Miller exploited to the full the tracking and close-up effects available on film. His production provides some memorable shots as well as some good verse-speaking, notably by John Shrapnel as Hector and Benjamin Whitrow as Ulysses, but the total effect remains conscientious rather than inspired, struggling to pull together the play's disparate moods and characters. It fails to assimilate the play's drive toward chaos, so essential a part of its delicate balancing of competing forms, genres, and values. As Heather James puts it, *Troilus and Cressida* is "a totality menaced by its various parts."[46]

The Two Noble Kinsmen

This absence of a medieval dimension in performances of *Troilus and Cressida* is ultimately due to the nature of Shakespeare's adaptation: by speeding up Chaucer's action, Shakespeare effectively eliminates the courtly love element, and his Greeks, who seem contemporary, reflect the practical, end-directed attitudes to warfare of his own day, even as his more antiquated Trojans hark back to more chivalric times. By contrast, *The Two Noble Kinsmen* plays up its medieval features. It has even been claimed that the chivalric code, one central concern of Chaucer's "Knight's Tale," with its twin themes of love and honor, prompted Shakespeare and John Fletcher to dramatize it. As Roy Strong shows, in Shakespeare's later days a nostalgic cult of chivalry grew up around Prince Henry, the young heir to the throne—a cult of jousting, tournaments, and Accession Day tilts—linked earlier, during Queen Elizabeth's reign, with Protestant militancy.[47] That cult is vividly reflected in Ben Jonson's masques of *Prince Henry's Barriers* (1610) and *Oberon* (1611).[48] In the former, King Arthur and Merlin summon Meliadus (played by Prince Henry) to awaken English knighthood from its long sleep by reviving the practice of single combat at the barriers, the main action of the masque and a self-conscious harking back to idealized medieval courtly entertainments.

In 1613, the themes of an interrupted wedding and a young man's sudden death were painfully topical, since the sudden death of Prince Henry in November 1612 had temporarily delayed the marriage of his sister, Princess Elizabeth, to Count Frederick V, Elector Palatine of the Rhine. The marriage was finally celebrated on St. Valentine's Day, 1613, and among the various wedding masques was that of the Inner Temple and Grey's Inn, performed on February 20 and written by Francis Beaumont, John Fletcher's usual collaborator. The second antimasque within this play presented traditional May games in the form of a morris dance performed by a "pedant" or schoolmaster, the Lord and Lady of May, two "bavians" or baboons, and several other couples, all of whom reappear in act 3, scene 5 of *The Two Noble Kinsmen*. At the masque's original performance in February, the antimasque would have been danced by the King's Men, Shakespeare's company, and in all likelihood the players would have reused the music and possibly also the costumes of Beaumont's antimasque. Glynne Wickham further identifies Arcite with Prince Henry and Palamon with the Elector Palatine, while the Olympian Knights who dance the main sequence of the masque have been associated with the kinsmen's supporters in the play's culminating tournament.[49] Certainly the various rituals of wedding and funeral processions, morris dance and May games, the duel, sacrifices, and tournament determine the rhythm of the play, and its theatrical impact depends to a large extent on how effectively these ritual elements are played out.

The main changes made by Shakespeare and Fletcher to Chaucer's *Knight's Tale* are to integrate the morris dance and May games derived from Beaumont's antimasque and to introduce a crucial new character, the (unnamed) Gaoler's Daughter. She releases Palamon from prison, having fallen in love with him, and her passion counterbalances Emilia's reluctance but also challenges courtly assumptions concerning the exclusively aristocratic nature of tragic and unrequited love. At the outset, the Gaoler's Daughter admits, with painful realism, the hopelessness of her position:

> Why should I love this gentleman? 'Tis odds
> He never will affect me: I am base,
> My father the mean keeper of his prison,
> And he a prince. To marry him is hopeless;
> To be his whore is witless [2.4.1–5].

After she has lost Palamon in the Athenian woods, and fearful that he has been eaten by wolves, she slips into madness.

Unlike *Troilus and Cressida*, it is clear that *The Two Noble Kinsmen* was performed on stage in 1613, probably at the indoor theatre at Blackfriars (where songs, music, and masquelike effects were popular) as well as at the Globe. Some evidence suggests that it was acted again between 1619 and 1620 and around 1625; the quarto text was published in 1634. It was then adapted for the restoration stage by William Davenant (or D'Avenant) in a version entitled *The Rivals* (1664) that cuts free of its Chaucerian and Theban contexts, setting the tale in Arcadia. Davenant tips the play firmly toward comedy by omitting the first act, with its "rotten kings" and "blubbered queens" and the kinsmen's talk of Thebes' moral degeneracy under Creon's regime. The scenes in the Athenian woods are expanded to include "a hunt in music." In most productions, the Gaoler's Daughter steals the show: Davenant dissolves the rest of the play's disagreeables by naming her Celania and raising her status to that of the Provost's Daughter so that she can finally marry Philander (i.e., Palamon) in a double wedding with Heraclia/Emilia and Theocles/Arcite. The actress Mary (Moll) Davis, who played Celania, was herself further elevated when her performance attracted the attention of Charles II, who made her his mistress.[50] Two eighteenth-century adaptations survive in manuscript, as Lois Potter records: Richard Cumberland's *Palamon and Arcite* (1779) and Francis Godolphin Waldron's *Love and Madness* (1795).[51] Both retain the improved status of the Gaoler's Daughter, but the former ends in partial tragedy, as does Shakespeare's play, while the latter ends with a double wedding.

From the outset, the play's lack of canonicity told against it. The first professional revival to use the original text of the *Two Noble Kinsmen* had to wait until 1928. It was performed at the Old Vic with a program note explaining that the play was "a dramatic version of 'The Knights Tale'" and was "essentially a story of medieval chivalry rather than of Greek legend. We are, therefore, presenting it in the costume of Chaucer's time as being in keeping with the hunting and maying, the morris dancing and tilting with which the play abounds." The significance of the dances was acknowledged by their being choreographed by Dame Ninette de Valois, founder of London's Royal Ballet.[52] The play's dances not only connect it with Beaumont's antimasque and the masque form more generally but are also part of the range of rituals that dignify and universalize the instincts to make love and war. Set at the center of the play, the morris dance gives physical expression to these atavistic impulses. For Hugh Richmond, "[t]his ritual recognition of biological forces is another continuity with the elaborate festival references of [*A Midsummer Night's*] *Dream*."[53]

Forty-five years later, in 1973, Richard Digby Day directed *The Two Noble Kinsmen* for the New Shakespeare Company at the York Theatre Royal. Perversely, he cut the rustics and the morris dance itself, yet his production was otherwise deliberately stylized, and the battles were performed in the morris-dance tradition. He also set up an apron stage that included members of the audience, as at the original Globe. The following summer, the same company performed the play at the Regent's Park Open Air Theatre, this time in repertory with *A Midsummer Night's Dream*. The same actors played Theseus and Hippolyta, and the *Dream*'s mechanicals played the *Kinsmen*'s rustics, thus bringing out connections between the two plays originally noticed by Muriel Bradbrook and later developed by Glynne Wickham.[54] As at York, dancing featured importantly. Another memorable production of *The Two Noble Kinsmen*, this time at the Berkeley Shakespeare Festival of 1985, also played it in repertory with *A Midsummer Night's Dream*. Directed by Julian López-Morillas, these productions doubled not only Theseus and Hippolyta but also the lovers: Hermia and Lysander also played Emilia and Arcite, while Nancy Carlin acted Helena and a touchingly young Gaoler's Daughter. Dakin Matthews, who performed Oberon, took the small but interesting role of the Doctor who restores the Daughter to her former Wooer in disguise.[55]

Played back to back, *A Midsummer Night's Dream* and *The Two Noble Kinsmen* reveal striking structural parallels, not least in their use of class comedy to comment on a spectrum of attitudes to love, from the idealism of courtly love to the more urgent desires of the lower orders. Such comedy is thoroughly Chaucerian, recalling *The Parliament of Fowles* or the parodic juxtaposition of "The Knight's Tale" with "The Miller's Tale" and "The Reeve's Tale"; Chaucer, too, challenges class distinctions, raising the question of the nature of true nobility in "The Franklin's

Tale," where the Clerk competes in courtesy with the Squire and the Knight, and the Franklin asks us, "Which was the moooste fre?" (l.1622), and through the perfect obedience of patient Griselda in "The Clerk's Tale."

Similarly, the Gaoler's Daughter threatens to complicate easy social assumptions in ways that seemed unacceptable to the play's seventeenth- and eighteenth-century adapters. In Shakespeare and Fletcher's version, the Daughter's fate remains uncertain. The Doctor packs her off to bed with her Wooer, disguised as Palamon, but the text does not reveal (though individual productions must decide) how far she realizes what is going on and finds it acceptable. This resolution of the subplot parallels the substitution of Palamon for Arcite in the main plot, commenting on the strategies by which comic closure is achieved. In the 1994 Oregon Festival production at Ashland, the Daughter reentered the stage at the end, still evidently mad. She and Emilia, though hot and cold respectively, are both victims of the arbitrary social rules that they resist as far as they may, and their critical views of events correspond closely to that of a modern audience. In the 1986 production by the RSC, the two women encountered one another silently onstage in the play's closing moments.[56]

The Two Noble Kinsmen was a surprising choice to open the new Swan Theatre at Stratford in 1986. Since then, this delightful wooden theater, with its galleries and apron stage, has come to seem an ideal location for performing Shakespeare and his contemporaries, at once intimate yet formal. But in directing *The Two Noble Kinsmen* for the Swan's opening, Barry Kyle felt he must bring out the play's ritual qualities: the main plot was performed in a medieval Japanese style that was rather oddly paired with the English morris dancers; these arrived with a maypole that shot out its ribbons in all directions (referred to as "the ejaculation" in the production notebook), suggesting a lack of inhibition that contrasted sharply with the refined deportment of the main characters.[57]

In both *Troilus and Cressida* and *The Two Noble Kinsmen*, the atavistic forces of love and war are closely linked, even though the codes of chivalry and courtly love seek to constrain them. The rape of Helen and the exchange of Cressida disempower and commodify women, as does, though somewhat differently, the helplessness of Emilia and the Gaoler's Daughter. In the later play, the primitive connections between love and war are emphasized from the opening scene, where the mourning queens warn Theseus that if he proceeds, their suit will be forgotten in the immediacy of nuptial pleasure:

> Oh, when
> Her twinning cherries shall their sweetness fall
> Upon thy taste-full lips, what wilt thou think
> Of rotten kings or blubbered queens? What care
> For what thou feel'st not, what thou feel'st being able
> To make Mars spurn his drum? [1.1.177–182].

And though the play concludes with Emilia's wedding, it can only be achieved at the cost of a life:

> Is this winning?
> Oh, all you heavenly powers, where is your mercy?
> But that your wills have said it must be so, ...
> I should and would die too [5.3.138–140, 143].

The histories of these two plays in performance provide a contrast that reflects Shakespeare's very different handling of his sources: in dramatizing *Troilus and Cressida* he contextualizes it in such a way as to reduce the specifically medieval aspects of his Chaucerian source, or at any rate to assimilate them into a wider narrative. His account of the Trojan War concentrates on the misery and degradation of war itself, reducing its cast of heroes to deluded Trojan idealists and callous Greek machiavels. *The Two Noble Kinsmen* is no less darkened by its death-driven masculine rivalries, but here the critique is articulated not by the warrior patriarchs—by Hector or

Thersites—but by its female characters, by the mourning queens, Emilia, and the Gaoler's Daughter. So productions of *Troilus and Cressida* are continuously drawn toward disillusion and disgust with warfare, an exasperation that we can recognize and share today, while productions of *The Two Noble Kinsmen* must evolve for themselves a style that can lend conviction to the reenactment of ancient rites that lies at the heart of the dramatic text.

NOTES

1. The title quotation, "Chaucer, of all admired, the story gives: There constant to eternity it lives," is from John Fletcher and William Shakespeare, *The Two Noble Kinsmen*, ed. Lois Potter, The Arden Shakespeare (Walton-on-Thames, UK: Thomas Nelson and Sons, 1997), 1, Prologue, 13–14. Other Shakespeare editions consulted for this essay include William Shakespeare, *Troilus and Cressida*, ed. Anthony B. Dawson (Cambridge, UK: Cambridge University Press, 2003); and William Shakespeare, *Troilus and Cressida*, ed. David Bevington, The Arden Shakespeare (Walton-on-Thames, UK: Thomas Nelson and Sons, 1998). The editors wish to thank independent scholar Bill Raden for his help with the notes and production list left unfinished at the author's death in 2007. Gill Kent supplied the Works Cited list, drawing on the notes compiled by the editors and Raden. STC 5068, 5077, 5078, 22331, 22332, 11075.

2. Shakespeare, *Troilus and Cressida*, ed. Bevington, 375, 393–394.

3. Fletcher and Shakespeare, *Two Noble Kinsmen*, 46, 47, 327.

4. STC 13165, 15375.

5. Philip Edwards, "On the Design of *The Two Noble Kinsmen*," *Review of English Literature* 5 (1964): 89–105, 105. See also Mary Beth Rose, *The Expense of Spirit: Love and Sexuality in English Renaissance Drama* (Ithaca, NY: Cornell University Press, 1988), 212–230, who comments that "the dislocations of the traditional emphases of chivalric sexuality transform idealistic lovers and their treasured object of desire and source of inspiration into three ambivalent narcissists, for whom love becomes an isolated, compulsive experience" (222).

6. In finding the play inherently cynical, Fenwick agrees with the director Jonathan Miller, who says, "I think it's thought to be cynical because it's about a subject that invites cynicism, but any social institution you care to look at is riddled with hypocrisy and falls below the ambitions people set themselves.... I think it's an entertaining, rather frothily ironic play. It's got a bitter-sweet quality, rather like black chocolate"; Henry Fenwick, "The Production," in William Shakespeare, *Troilus and Cressida*, The BBC TV Shakespeare, intro. by John Wilders, notes by Henry Fenwick (London: British Broadcasting Corporation, 1981), 18–28.

7. Desiderius Erasmus, *The Education of a Christian Prince*, trans. Lester K. Born (New York: Columbia University Press, 1965), 192. See also Phillip Dust, *Three Renaissance Pacifists: Essays in the Theories of Erasmus, More and Vives* (New York: American University Studies, 1987); and Desiderius Erasmus, *The Complaint of Peace* (Querela Pacis), in *The Essential Erasmus*, selected and newly trans. with intro. and commentary by John P. Dolan (New York: New American Library, 1964), 174–204.

8. See Greg W. Bentley, *Shakespeare and the New Disease: The Dramatic Function of Syphilis in Troilus and Cressida, Measure for Measure, and Timon of Athens* (New York: Peter Lang, 1989), 12. For his analysis of the effects of the disease in Shakespeare's *Troilus*, see ibid., 41–100.

9. Compare the opening scene of Chaucer, "The Knight's Tale" (KT 1.898–911), in which black-clad ladies accost Duke Theseus riding beside his new bride, Hippolyta, seize the reins of his horse, and ask him to avenge the death of their husbands in the battle for Thebes (1.931–951) and restore to the widows "The bones of hir freendes that were slayn" (1.992) for proper burial. All Chaucer citations are from *The Riverside Chaucer*, ed. Larry D. Benson, 3rd ed. (New York: Oxford University Press, 1988).

10. For time as an "eater of things," see John Bayley, "Time and the Trojans," in *Shakespeare: Troilus and Cressida: A Casebook*, ed. Priscilla Martin (London: Macmillan, 1976), 219–238; originally published in *Essays in Criticism* 25 (1975): 55–73.

11. Glynne Wickham, "*The Two Noble Kinsmen* or *A Midsummer Night's Dream, Part II*?" in *The Elizabethan Theatre VII: Papers Given at the Seventh International Conference on Elizabethan Theatre Held at the University of Waterloo, Ontario, in July 1977*, ed. and intro. by G. R. Hibbard (Hamden, CT: Archon Books in collaboration with the University of Waterloo, 1980), 167–196. For *Midsummer Night's Dream*, see STC 22302, 22303, both dated 1600.

12. For the most extensive treatment of their Chaucerian sources, see Ann Thompson, *Shakespeare's Chaucer: A Study in Literary Origins*, Liverpool English Texts and Studies (New York: Barnes and Noble, 1978), 110–215; E. Talbot Donaldson, "Love, War, and the Cost of Winning: *The Knight's Tale* and *The Two Noble Kinsmen*," in *The Swan at the Well: Shakespeare Reading Chaucer* (New Haven, CT: Yale University Press, 1985), 50–71; Donaldson, "Criseyde Becoming Cressida: *Troilus and Criseyde* and *Troilus and Cressida*," in

The Swan at the Well, 74–118; and Donaldson, "Lovers' Problems: *Troilus and Criseyde* and *Troilus and Cressida*" in *The Swan at the Well*.

13. Paul Bertram, *Shakespeare and "The Two Noble Kinsmen"* (New Brunswick, NJ: Rutgers University Press, 1965), puts forth the argument that the whole play was Shakespeare's, though very few scholars accept this. See also Shakespeare, *Two Noble Kinsmen*, ed. Potter, 19, where Potter comments, "Paul Bertram, arguing that the play is wholly by Shakespeare, claims that Fletcher was too busy writing and collaborating on other plays in 1613 to have been involved."

14. STC 22334, 22335, 22336, 11075.

15. STC 22273, 22274; see further Julia Briggs, "Tears at the Wedding: Shakespeare's Last Phase," in *Shakespeare's Late Plays: New Readings*, ed. Jennifer Richards and James Knowles (Edinburgh: Edinburgh University Press, 1999), 210–227, esp. 210–216.

16. Jan Kott, "*Troilus and Cressida*—Amazing and Modern," in *Shakespeare Our Contemporary*, trans. Boleslaw Taborski (London: Methuen, 1964), 75–83; Shakespeare, *Troilus and Cressida*, ed. Dawson, 59.

17. For more on twentieth-century performance, see Fletcher and Shakespeare, *Two Noble Kinsmen*, 78–110; in Shakespeare, *Troilus and Cressida*, ed. Dawson, 46–66, Dawson comments, "In 1912, William Poel staged an amateur production at King's Hall in Covent Garden, a space associated, appropriately enough, with boxing.... His *Troilus* introduced Edith Evans to the English stage; Evans played Cressida as 'amoral, that was all,' a 'sexually experienced' court lady who, while Troilus pressed her for oaths of fidelity, was 'manifestly preoccupied with pinning on her hat'" (47). In Macowan's modern-dress production for the London Mask company at London's Westminster Theatre (Fall 1938), the Trojans wore British khaki and the Greek generals were dressed in blue uniforms that reminded some of Germany or the Balkans. Barton's production with Peter Hall in 1960, as described by Bevington in Shakespeare, *Troilus and Cressida*, ed. Bevington, 101, featured "Dorothy Tutin, dressed in a classical robe slit in front to the hip, [who] played Cressida for sensual allure." Other Barton productions (all at Stratford-on-Avon) showed Achilles and Patroclus as lovers while "Hector and Ajax stripped for their combat to loin-cloths"; ibid., 102.

18. Claire M. Tylee, "The Text of Cressida and Every Ticklish Reader: *Troilus and Cressida*, the Greek Camp Scene," in *Shakespearian Stages and Staging*, ed. Stanley Wells, Shakespeare Survey 41 (Cambridge, UK: Cambridge University Press, 1989), 63–76, 67; Heather James, *Shakespeare's Troy: Drama, Politics, and the Translation of Empire* (Cambridge, UK: Cambridge University Press, 1997), 95; see also 107, 111.

19. William Shakespeare, *Hamlet*, ed. Harold Jenkins, The Arden Shakespeare (London: Methuen, 1982).

20. See further Janet Adelman, *Suffocating Mothers: Fantasies of Maternal Origin in Shakespeare's Plays, Hamlet to The Tempest* (New York: Routledge, 1992), 31–34, 42–45, 54, who comments (54): "Troilus immediately associates the infidelity of his beloved with the infidelity of his mother. Ulysses's puzzled question insists on the association and clarifies the fantasy that shapes it: for Troilus, Cressida has the power to soil a mother figure so universal that she becomes 'the general sex,' all 'our mothers.'"

21. STC 15086, 15093a.

22. Compare Chaucer, *Troilus and Criseyde*, 2.598–651. In this scene Criseyde is alone and views Troilus triumphantly riding from the battlefield from her window.

23. C. S. Lewis, *The Allegory of Love: A Study in Medieval Tradition* (Oxford: Oxford University Press, 1936; repr. 1953), 185–190.

24. In Shakespeare, *Troilus and Cressida*, ed. Dawson, 56, Dawson says about Davies's 1985 Stratford production that "the attempt to make a statement about male sexual brutality ended up reproducing some of the attitudes it apparently sought to dislodge," while in Shakespeare, *Troilus and Cressida*, ed. Bevington, 108–109, Bevington comments, "Juliet Stevenson's sympathetic portrayal of Cressida in Howard Davies's 1985 production by the Royal Shakespeare Company was ... something of an event," elaborating that "Davies appears to have been at odds with Juliet Stevenson; he wanted to create a threesome of Pandarus, Troilus and Cressida, whereas Stevenson understood Cressida to be wary of her uncle and of her prospective lover from the start."

25. Dawson says of Ian Judge's production that while Cressida was shown as "ardent and earnest with Troilus" she was also "fascinated by the carnal"; Shakespeare, *Troilus and Cressida*, ed. Dawson, 61.

26. James, *Shakespeare's Troy*, 95, quoting L. C. Knights's description of Cressida as "a creature of intertextuality, of Chaucer, Lydgate, Caxton, Henryson and others ... endowed with self-consciousness," from L. C. Knights, "The Theme of Appearance and Reality in *Troilus and Cressida*," in *Some Shakespearean Themes* (Stanford, CA: Stanford University Press, 1959), 69.

27. STC 13165; also included in Chaucer's *Works*, STC 5068 ff.

28. Robert Henryson, *The Testament of Cresseid and Other Poems* (New York: Penguin Books, 1973), 19–42, 41.

29. William Shakespeare, *Twelfth Night or What You Will*, ed. Elizabeth Story Donno (Cambridge, UK: Cambridge University Press, 1985; repr. 2003).

30. Thompson, *Shakespeare's Chaucer*, 121, suggests the possibility "that the disease imagery of the play

and the references to divine retribution were partially suggested by [Henryson's] *Testament.*" Bentley, *Shakespeare and the New Disease*, 94–95, says the final text implies that "many of those attending the performance, like Pandarus himself, are presumed to have advanced cases of syphilis."

31. William Shakespeare, *Julius Caesar*, ed. Martin Spevack (Cambridge, UK: Cambridge University Press, 1988; repr. 2003), spoken by Cassius, "How many ages hence Shall this our lofty scene be acted over In states unborn and accents yet unknown!"

32. John Dryden, *Troilus and Cressida, or, Truth Found Too Late* (London: Abel Swall and Jacob Tonson, 1679), first edition examined in the Morgan Library and Museum.

33. Following Dryden's dedication "To the Right Honourable Robert Earl of Sunderland, Principall Secretary of State, One of His Majesties most Honourable Privy Council, &c." comes "The Preface to the Play"; Dryden, *Troilus and Cressida*, sig. A 4v. Dryden cites several earlier versions of the story, including that told by "Lollius a Lombard, in Latin verse, and Translated by Chaucer into English: intended I suppose as a Satyr on the Inconstancy of Women: I find nothing of it among the Ancients.... Shakespear, (as I hinted) in the Aprenticeship of his Writing, model'd it into that Play, which is now call'd by the name of Troilus and Cressida"; *ibid.*, sig. A4v.

34. William Walton, *Troilus and Cressida: Opera in Three Acts,* with libretto by Christopher Hassall (London: Oxford University Press, 1954). Hassall, 4, explains, "As I lifted the story out of the Middle Ages and retold it in a setting of legendary Troy, all that was essentially Chaucerian fell away"; he then says the opening scene of the opera and many of the subsequent events were suggested by Chaucer's poem, though some events were rearranged. Echoes of Chaucer's poem are heard in Cressida's solo "How Can I Sleep?" in act 2, scene 1 (38), for example. He comments, "There is nothing of Shakespeare in the libretto" (4–5), but further investigation may prove fruitful. In this version of the story, Troilus sings tenor, Pandarus is tenor buffo, Cressida, soprano, and Diomede, baritone.

35. Various libretti for the Berlioz are held in the Morgan Library, including *La Prise de Troie: Opera en trois actes*, lyrics and music by Hector Berlioz (Paris: Choudens, *c.* 1864); and *Les Troyens à Carthage: Opera en cinq actes*, with a prologue, lyrics, and music by Hector Berlioz (Paris: Calmann-Lévy, *c.* 1892). Also in the Morgan collections are programs for performances of Richard Wagner's *Die Walküre* in London, Buenos Aires, New York, Boston, and Bayreuth between 1897 and 1977, along with the musical score for the opera (Heineman MS 231) penned by Wagner in manuscript around 1864. The program for the first performance of Benjamin Britten's *Peter Grimes* by Sadler's Wells Opera (June 7, 1945), with soloists Peter Pears and Joan Cross, is in the Morgan collections, along with Benjamin Britten, *Peter Grimes: An Opera in Three Acts*, with a Prologue derived from the poem of George Crabbe (op. 33), words by Montagu Slater, music by Benjamin Britten, vocal score by Erwin Stein (New York: Boosey & Hawkes, *c.* 1945).

36. Walton, *Troilus and Cressida*, 71.

37. STC 13634, 15375, 5579–5581.

38. As Simone Weil, *The Iliad, or, The Poem of Force* (New York: Politics, 1946), 24, argues: "It is in this that the *Iliad* is absolutely unique, in this bitterness that proceeds from tendernes [sic] and that spreads over the whole human race.... Nothing precious is scorned, whether or not death is its destiny; everyone's unhappiness is laid bare without dissimulation or disdain; no man is set above or below the condition common to all men; whatever is destroyed is regretted. Victors and vanquished are brought equally near us; under the same head, both are seen as counterparts of the poet, and the listener as well."

39. In Shakespeare, *Troilus and Cressida*, ed. Dawson, 52, Dawson describes John Barton's three RSC productions between 1960 and 1976 as reflecting "the widening cultural awareness in the 1960s and '70s of the subterranean relations between sex and violence." Dawson includes photographs of scenes from the 1968 staging in which "nearly all the actors appeared semi-nude" (fig. 8, 53). A caption to fig. 9 (54) alludes to the headdresses worn by the nearly naked actors as creating a "beaked dance of metallic-crested birds" (citing R. Bryden, *Observer*, August 11, 1968).

40. In Shakespeare, *Troilus and Cressida*, ed. Dawson, 61, Dawson says that in Judge's 1996 version, "Pandarus was a desperate old queen with heavy make-up and long black wig, whose final disease carried with it dark resonances of AIDS."

41. *Ibid.*, fig. 6, 48, a reproduction of a photograph of the actress Elspeth Keith shown as a court jester in the role of Thersites.

42. Geoffrey Bullough, ed., *Narrative and Dramatic Sources of Shakespeare*, vol. 6 (New York: Columbia University Press, 1966), 107, comments that "Achilles (as in Lydgate and Caxton against *Troilus*) plans to use his Myrmidons to overcome Hector (V.7), and kills the latter unchivalrously when he is unarmed (V.8), and maltreats his corpse." See also *ibid.*, 142–150, quoting "The Slaying of Hector," in *The Iliad of Homer*, trans. George Chapman (London, J. Windet, 1598).

43. In Shakespeare, *Troilus and Cressida*, ed. Dawson, 7. See also Shakespeare, *Troilus and Cressida*, ed. Bevington, 18–19, for the notion that *Troilus* might have been banned from the stage early on. The "never clapper-clawed" quotation is also cited by Wilders in Shakespeare, *Troilus and Cressida*, *BBC TV*, 8.

44. Shakespeare, *Troilus and Cressida*, ed. Bevington, 100–101, describes a Stratford, Connecticut, staging of 1961 that celebrated "the centennial of the American Civil War in a production that featured Priam as Robert E. Lee, Agamemnon as Ulysses S. Grant, Cressida (Jessica Tandy) as a flirtatious southern belle and Troilus (Ted van Griethuysen) as a naively idealistic Confederate officer. Pandarus entertained the lovers on the mandolin as they met in the wisteria-draped garden of his home, visibly a mansion of the Old South." Bevington draws this from a review by Judith Crist, *New York Herald Tribune*, July 25, 1961.

45. Fenwick, "The Production," in Shakespeare, *Troilus and Cressida, BBC TV*, 18–19, comments on various visual sources informing the BBC production of the play, including "woodcuts of Cranach, Dürer, Altdorfer, all of whom spent a lot of their time in their graphic work representing sieges and curious medieval palaces which are taken in the pictures to be representations of classical antiquity."

46. James, *Shakespeare's Troy*, 89.

47. Roy C. Strong, *Henry, Prince of Wales, and England's Lost Renaissance* (New York: Thames and Hudson, 1986), 65–67, and passim.

48. Ben Jonson's *Oberon* and *Prince Henry's Barriers* are discussed in *ibid.*, 141–146, 160–174.

49. Glynne Wickham, "Two Noble Kinsmen?" 188–190.

50. Sir William D'Avenant, *The Rivals* (London: William Cademan, 1668), Wing D337. The play was staged in 1664 by the Duke's Company, and a revival production in 1667 included Thomas Betterton as Philander and Mary "Moll" Davis as Celania.

51. Fletcher and Shakespeare, *Two Noble Kinsmen*, 76–77.

52. *Ibid.*, 78, and further, "The 1928 Old Vic production, with its medieval setting, was described (favourably on the whole) as 'an experiment in prettiness' (Birrell).... This revival had a strong cast — Ernest Milton and Eric Portman as Palamon and Arcite, Jean Forbes-Robertson as the Jailer's Daughter."

53. Hugh Richmond, "Performance as Criticism: *The Two Noble Kinsmen*," in *Shakespeare, Fletcher and The Two Noble Kinsmen*, ed. Charles Frey (Columbia, MO: University of Missouri Press, 1989), 174.

54. For further description of the production, see Fletcher and Shakespeare, *Two Noble Kinsmen*, 79–80; M. C. Bradbrook, "Shakespeare and his Collaborators," in *Shakespeare 1971: Proceedings of the World Shakespeare Congress, Vancouver, August 1971*, ed. Clifford Leech and J. M. R. Margeson (Toronto: University of Toronto Press, 1972), 21–36. See also M. C. Bradbrook, "What Shakespeare Did to Chaucer's *Troilus and Criseyde*," *Shakespeare Quarterly* 9 (1958): 311–319; Wickham, "Two Noble Kinsmen?" passim.

55. In Fletcher and Shakespeare, *Two Noble Kinsmen*, 81, Potter comments on the "significant cross-casting: the same Theseus and Hippolyta appeared in both plays; Hermia and Lysander were Emilia and Arcite, with Helena (Nancy Carlin) reappearing as the Jailer's Daughter. In a particularly interesting cameo, the role of the Doctor was taken by Dakin Matthews, who had previously played Oberon." The costuming for the López-Morillas production gestured toward the Middle Ages. See also Phyllis Brooks, "Berkeley Shakespeare Festival Summer 1985," *Shakespeare Quarterly* (1985): 393–399.

56. Fletcher and Shakespeare, *Two Noble Kinsmen*, 81–82. Lois Potter discusses the Ashland Shakespeare Festival staging further in "Shakespeare Performed: *The Two Noble Kinsmen* in 1993–94," *Shakespeare Quarterly* (1994): 197–203. The director, Nagle Jackson, "set the play in the time of Chaucer, whose portrait hung above the stage throughout" (200).

57. Fletcher and Shakespeare, *Two Noble Kinsmen*, 82; the sexual aspects of the plot were made plain both in the morris dance and in the several references to horses: "the Jailer's Daughter rode in upon a phallic maypole that spewed out long, white silk ribbons (referred to in rehearsal as the 'ejaculation' [RSC, 'Promptbook']) and was later seen in a bridle which served as her straitjacket."

WORKS CITED

Adelman, Janet. *Suffocating Mothers: Fantasies of Maternal Origin in Shakespeare's Plays, Hamlet to The Tempest*. New York: Routledge, 1992.

Bayley, John. "Time and the Trojans." In *Shakespeare: Troilus and Cressida: A Casebook*, edited by Priscilla Martin, 219–238. London: Macmillan, 1976. Originally published in *Essays in Criticism* 25 (1975): 55–73.

Bentley, Greg W. *Shakespeare and the New Disease: The Dramatic Function of Syphilis in Troilus and Cressida, Measure for Measure, and Timon of Athens*. New York: Peter Lang, 1989.

Bertram, Paul. *Shakespeare and "The Two Noble Kinsmen."* New Brunswick, NJ: Rutgers University Press, 1965.

Bradbrook, M. C. "Shakespeare and His Collaborators." In *Shakespeare 1971: Proceedings of the World Shakespeare Congress, Vancouver, August 1971*, edited by Clifford Leech and J. M. R. Margeson. Toronto: University of Toronto Press, 1972.

———. "What Shakespeare Did to Chaucer's Troilus and Criseyde." *Shakespeare Quarterly* 9 (1958): 311–319.

Briggs, Julia. "Tears at the Wedding: Shakespeare's Last Phase." In *Shakespeare's Late Plays: New Readings*, edited by Jennifer Richards and James Knowles, 210–227. Edinburgh: Edinburgh University Press, 1999.

Britten, Benjamin. *Peter Grimes: An Opera in Three Acts.* With a Prologue derived from the poem of George Crabbe (op. 33), words by Montagu Slater, music by Benjamin Britten, vocal score by Erwin Stein. New York: Boosey & Hawkes,1945.
Brooks, Phyllis. "Berkeley Shakespeare Festival Summer 1985." *Shakespeare Quarterly* (1985): 393–399.
Bullough, Geoffrey, ed. *Narrative and Dramatic Sources of Shakespeare* Vol. 6. New York: Columbia University Press, 1966.
Chaucer, Geoffrey. *The Riverside Chaucer.* Edited by Larry D. Benson. 3rd edition. New York: Oxford University Press, 1988.
D'Avenant, Sir William. *The Rivals.* London: William Cademan, 1668.
Donaldson, E. Talbot. *The Swan at the Well: Shakespeare Reading Chaucer.* New Haven, CT: Yale University Press, 1985.
Dryden, John. *Troilus and Cressida, or, Truth Found Too Late.* London: Abel Swall and Jacob Tonson, 1679.
Dust, Phillip. *Three Renaissance Pacifists: Essays in the Theories of Erasmus, More and Vives.* New York: American University Studies, l987.
Edwards, Philip. "On the Design of *The Two Noble Kinsmen.*" *Review of English Literature* 5 (1964): 89–105, 89.
Erasmus, Desiderius. *The Complaint of Peace* (Querela Pacis). In *The Essential Erasmus.* Selected and translated with introduction and commentary by John Dolan, 174–204. New York: New American Library, 1964.
_____. *The Education of a Christian Prince.* Translated by Lester K. Born. New York: Columbia University Press, 1965.
Fenwick, Henry. "The Production." In William Shakespeare, *Troilus and Cressida, The BBC TV Shakespeare,* introduction by John Wilders, notes by Henry Fenwick. London: BBC, 1981.
Fletcher, John, and William Shakespeare. *The Two Noble Kinsmen.* Edited by Lois Potter. The Arden Shakespeare. Walton-on-Thames, UK: Thomas Nelson and Sons, 1997.
Henryson, Robert. *The Testament of Cresseid and Other Poems.* New York: Penguin Books, 1973.
Homer, *The Iliads of Homer.* Translated by George Chapman. London, J. Windet, 1598.
James, Heather. *Shakespeare's Troy: Drama, Politics, and the Translation of Empire.* Cambridge, UK: Cambridge University Press, 1997.
Knights, L. C. "The Theme of Appearance and Reality in Troilus and Cressida." In *Some Shakespearean Themes.* Stanford, CA: Stanford University Press, 1959.
Kott, Jan. "Troilus and Cressida — Amazing and Modern." In *Shakespeare Our Contemporary,* translated by Boleslaw Taborski, 75–83. London: Methuen, 1964.
Lewis, C. S. *The Allegory of Love: A Study in Medieval Tradition.* Oxford: Oxford University Press, 1936. Reprinted 1953.
Potter, Lois. "Shakespeare Performed: *The Two Noble Kinsmen* in 1993–94." *Shakespeare Quarterly* (1994): 197–203.
Richmond, Hugh. "Performance as Criticism: *The Two Noble Kinsmen.*" In *Shakespeare, Fletcher and* The Two Noble Kinsmen, edited by Charles Frey. Columbia, MO: University of Missouri Press, 1989.
Rose, Mary Beth. *The Expense of Spirit: Love and Sexuality in English Renaissance Drama.* Ithaca, NY: Cornell University Press: 1988.
Shakespeare, William. *Hamlet.* Edited by Harold Jenkins. The Arden Shakespeare. London: Methuen, 1982.
_____. *Julius Caesar.* Edited by Martin Spevack. Cambridge, UK: Cambridge University Press, 1988. Reprinted 2003.
_____. *Troilus and Cressida.* Edited by Anthony B. Dawson. Cambridge, UK: Cambridge University Press, 2003.
_____. *Troilus and Cressida.* Edited by David Bevington. The Arden Shakespeare. Walton-on-Thames, UK: Thomas Nelson and Sons, 1998.
_____. *Troilus and Cressida, The BBC TV Shakespeare.* Introduction by John Wilders and notes on the production by Henry Fenwick. London: British Broadcasting Corporation, 1981.
_____. *Twelfth Night or What You Will.* Edited by Elizabeth Story Donno. Cambridge, UK: Cambridge University Press, 1985. Reprinted 2003.
Strong, Roy C. *Henry, Prince of Wales, and England's Lost Renaissance.* New York: Thames and Hudson, 1986.
Thompson, Ann. *Shakespeare's Chaucer: A Study in Literary Origins.* Liverpool English Texts and Studies. New York: Barnes and Noble, 1978.
Tylee, Claire M. "The Text of Cressida and Every Ticklish Reader: *Troilus and Cressida,* the Greek Camp Scene." In *Shakespearian Stages and Staging,* edited by Stanley Wells, 63–76. Shakespeare Survey 41. Cambridge, UK: Cambridge University Press, 1989.
Walton, William. *Troilus and Cressida: Opera in Three Acts.* Libretto by Christopher Hassall. London: Oxford University Press, 1954.

Weil, Simone. *The Iliad, or, The Poem of Force.* New York: Politics, 1946.
Wickham, Glynne. "*The Two Noble Kinsmen* or *A Midsummer Night's Dream, Part II?*" In *The Elizabethan Theatre VII: Papers Given at the Seventh International Conference on Elizabethan Theatre Held at the University of Waterloo, Ontario, in July 1977*, edited and with an introduction by G. R. Hibbard. Hamden, CT: Archon Books in collaboration with the University of Waterloo, 1980.

PERFORMANCES

1912 *Troilus and Cressida*, d. William Poel, with Esmé Percy, Edith Evans, William Poel, Hermione Gingold. London, King's Hall, Covent Garden.
1938 *Troilus and Cressida*, d. Michael Macowen, with Ruth Lodge, Robert Speaight, Max Adrian, Stephen Murray. London, Westminster Theatre, Mask Theatre Company.
1954 *Troilus and Cressida* by William Walton, libretto by Christopher Hassall, with Frederick Dalberg, Geraint Evans, Barbara Howitt, Richard Lewis. Conductor Sir Malcolm Sargent. London, Covent Garden, Royal Opera House.
1960 *Troilus and Cressida*, d. Peter Hall and John Barton, with Denholm Elliott, Ian Holm, Dorothy Tutin, Diana Rigg, Peter O'Toole. Stratford-upon-Avon, Royal Shakespeare Theatre, Royal Shakespeare Company.
1968 *Troilus and Cressida*, d. John Barton, with Helen Mirren, Ben Kingsley, Patrick Stewart, Michael Williams. Stratford-upon-Avon, Royal Shakespeare Theatre, Royal Shakespeare Company.
1976 *Troilus and Cressida*, d. John Barton and Barry Kyle, with Mike Gwilym, Francesca Annis, John Nettles, David Waller, Robin Ellis. Stratford-upon-Avon, Royal Shakespeare Theatre, Royal Shakespeare Company.
1981 *Troilus and Cressida*, d. Jonathan Miller, with Anton Lesser, Suzanne Burden, Kenneth Haigh, John Shrapnel, Charles Gray, Jack Birkett. Royal Shakespeare Company. UK: British Broadcasting Corporation.
1985 *Troilus and Cressida*, d. Howard Davies, with Anton Lesser, Juliet Stevenson, Alan Rickman, Alun Armstrong. Stratford-upon-Avon, Royal Shakespeare Theatre, Royal Shakespeare Company.
1990 *Troilus and Cressida*, d. Sam Mendes, with Ralph Fiennes, Amanda Root, Simon Russell Beale, Norman Rodway. Stratford-upon-Avon, Swan Theatre, Royal Shakespeare Company.
1996 *Troilus and Cressida*, d. Ian Judge, with Joseph Fiennes, Victoria Hamilton, Richard McCabe, Philip Voss. Stratford-upon-Avon, Royal Shakespeare Theatre, Royal Shakespeare Company.
1998 *Troilus and Cressida*, d. Michael Boyd, with William Houston, Jayne Ashbourne, Lloyd Hutchinson, Roy Hanlon. Stratford-upon-Avon, Pit Theatre, Royal Shakespeare Company.
1999 *Troilus and Cressida*, d. Trevor Nunn, with Sophie Okenedo, David Bamber, Roger Allam, Jasper Britton. London, National Theatre, Olivier Theatre.
2000 *Troilus and Cressida*, d. Dominic Dromgoole, with Jordon Murphy, Eileen Walsh, Matt Lucas, Darragh Kelly. London, Old Vic Theatre, Oxford Stage Company.
2006 *Troilus and Cressida*, d. Peter Stein, with Annabel Scholey, David Yelland, Henry Pettigrew, Paul Jessor. Edinburgh, Scotland, King's Theatre, Edinburgh International Festival.
1928 *Two Noble Kinsmen*, d. Andrew Leigh, with Eric Portman, Ernest Milton, Barbara Everest, Jean Forbes-Robertson. Choreographer, Ninette de Valois. London, Old Vic Theatre.
1973 *Two Noble Kinsmen*, d. Richard Digby Day, with Malcolm Armstong, Philip Bowen, Lea Dregorn, Elizabeth Tyrell. York, York Theatre Royal, York Festival of the Arts, New Shakespeare Company.
1974 *Two Noble Kinsmen*, d. Richard Digby Day, London, Open Air Theatre, Regent's Park, New Shakespeare Company.
1985 *Two Noble Kinsmen*, d. Julian Lopez-Morillos, with Chiron Alston, Nike Doukas, Louis Lotorto, Nancy Carlin. Berkeley, CA, John Hinkel Park, Berkeley Shakespeare Festival.
1986 *Two Noble Kinsmen*, d. Paul Barry, with J. C. Hoyt, Rick Parks, Robin Leary, Margaret Emory. Madison, New Jersey, Drew University, New Jersey Shakespeare Festival.
1986 *Two Noble Kinsmen*, d. Barry Kyle, with Peter Guinness, Roberta Taylor, Gerard Murphy, Imogen Stubbs, Amanda Harris. Stratford-upon-Avon, Swan Theatre, Royal Shakespeare Company.
1993 *Two Noble Kinsmen*, d. Nagle Jackson, with Jay Karnes, Robin Goodrin Nordli, Ray Chapman, Corliss Preston. Ashland, Oregon, Ashland Shakespeare Festival.

Shakespeare's Virgin Mother on the Modern Stage: *All's Well, That Ends Well* and the Madonna del Parto Tradition

GARY WALLER

The Riddle

The climactic scene of *All's Well, That Ends Well* provides us with a striking medieval moment. The Florentine virgin Diana announces to the scene's onlookers a "riddle" involving an apparent impossibility:

> for this lord...
> He knows himself my bed he hath defiled,
> And at that time he got his wife with child.
> Dead though she be, she feels her young one kick,
> So there's my riddle: one that's dead is quick [5.3.295–303].

Diana then announces the entrance of the riddle's answer: "And now," she proclaims, "behold the meaning" (5.3.304). Helena enters. Helena has just been nostalgically recalled as a "remembrance dear" (5.3.20) — a young virgin, a compelling though somewhat disturbing interloper into the court of France, who has cured the King of a fistula, whose surprising marriage to Bertram, Count of Rousillion, remained unconsummated, and who subsequently died. Her (supposedly) widower husband is about to be remarried at the instigation of the King. But this carefully constructed conclusion is now disturbed by a group of Florentine women, claiming that Bertram has seduced Diana and promised marriage to her; and now, even more disruptively, Helena herself enters, alive, claiming her husband — and clearly pregnant. The King voices the sense of wonder the shocked spectators feel: "Is there no exorcist / Beguiles the truer office of mine eyes? / Is't real that I see?" (5.3.304–306).

In my description of the scene, I deliberately stress the play's links with the medieval romance traditions on which it draws: Helena evokes the resurrected heroine, miraculously restored wife, unexpectedly returning virtuous healer, her reappearance momentarily hovering between fairy story and miracle play. In particular, as Regina Buccola shows, these characteristics evoke the many facets of the medieval Fairy Bride tradition.[1] Giovanni Boccaccio, probably through Painter's English translation, provided Shakespeare with his "realistic" main narrative; but it is these stories drawn from medieval fairy and folk material that erupt through the narrative and produce the climactic affect to which the French lord Lafew draws attention: "Mine eyes smell onions, I shall weep anon" (5.3.318).[2]

All's Well has been seen as displaying Shakespeare's affinities not only with medieval cultural remnants but specifically with the "old" religion, the Catholicism to which England had been the most faithful adherent — England was known as the "Virgin's dowry"— until Henry VIII's divorce, the Royal Supremacy Act of 1534, the abolition of the monasteries in 1538, and what turned out to be the final Elizabethan religious Settlement of 1559. By Shakespeare's time, state Protestantism had been the established religion for fifty years, and Catholics were a persecuted minority. But there was an increasing fashion for looking back to the Catholic Middle Ages, not least in the theater, and Shakespeare's plays betray significant signs of a nostalgia for at least the mystery and theatricality of the lost Catholic world.

One of the major points of contention between Catholic and Protestant remained the Virgin Mary: the Reformers had directed particularly hostile (and violently gynophobic) disapproval of the cult of the Virgin. R. G. Hunter therefore correctly notes that given the religious paranoia of Jacobean England, "a straightforward reference to the Virgin as intercessor is too Popish to be probable."[3] But the momentary tableau of Helena's reappearance links the play with a very specific medieval mariological reference: Helena is the Pregnant Virgin. Behind her appearance is the tradition of the Madonna Gravida, exemplified most famously by Piero della Francesca's fresco, the Madonna del Parto (ca. 1467).[4] In this essay, I relate the dramatic entrance of Shakespeare's pregnant virgin to this tradition and survey some modern productions that highlight it in their staging.

Shakespeare is (to put it mildly) unlikely to have seen Piero's work, but he would have been aware of the tradition of the pregnancy of the Virgin Mary, which was, even in Protestant theology, part of the verification of the genuine humanity of Christ and had scriptural basis. But the very fact that Shakespeare alludes so obviously to the *del parto* iconology lends weight to those who highlight his religious knowledge of (if not allegiance to) Catholicism, since, as Gail Gibson shows in relation to English late-medieval devotion and drama, the *del parto* tradition constituted a major stand of English devotion to the Virgin.[5] Piero's is the most spectacular piece of art in the tradition and serves to bring out its ideological contradictions as well as its artistic (and theatrical) possibilities. As Elena Bonelli notes, his rendition brings out the inherent theatricality of the event, showing a maternal body anticipating birthing, caught in exaltation but tinged with anxiety — precisely the combination no doubt felt by many of the women who came to pay their devotions to Piero's fresco in a chapel in Monterchi. The Virgin's body thrusts itself dramatically at the spectator, with a striking combination of naturalism and ritual symbolism. Two identical angels open a damask canopy through which she emerges; they gaze at us as they gesture (like Diana in *All's Well*) that we should "behold the meaning." The Virgin herself is stately, calm, and triumphant, her body arranged formally in a grill of triangles that marks a perfect star of David, with its center on the Virgin's hand as it rests on the vent or slit in her robe (of which detail, more below).

Some recent speculation suggests connections to either Piero's desire to see the Madonna as uniting Christianity and Judaism or the embodiment of some secret knowledge associated with the Knights Templar and possibly (shades of the *Da Vinci Code?*) even "really" a reproduction of the "other" Mary, the Magdalene. Independent of any "secret" knowledge, the overall effect is toward emotional realism: a mixture of hope, rebirth, and anxiety, all conveyed by the angle of the Virgin's body, which is slightly awkward, as if adjusting for the strain of the additional weight she carries.[6]

Virginity and Motherhood

Mary the Virgin Mother focused the central paradox of medieval Christianity: the Incarnation. Mary, said St. Augustine, "had in her flesh two things worthy of honor, virginity and fruitfulness; inasmuch as she both continued a virgin and bore."[7] What the orthodox Catholic theology behind the *gravida* tradition tried to bypass, however, was what all women and probably most men recognized as the origins and consequences of pregnancy — sexual intercourse and its details of interpenetrating genitalia, exchange of bodily fluids, aromas, and complicated feelings, not to mention the physical accompaniments of pregnancy, like morning sickness, weight gain, and exhaustion. From its beginning, the fresco was part of a local birthing cult aimed "at the protection and support of mothers of the local peasantry during difficult periods of pregnancy and birth." By contrast, the Virgin, as St. Bernard put it, "conceived her son without sin and bore him without heaviness, and gave birth to him without pain." The Virgin's independence from sexuality was a subject of centuries of discussion and dogma. Mary's hymen remained intact, the Church decided in the Councils of Constantinople (553) and Lateran (640): Mary remained a virgin before, during, and after childbirth; she was thus a "miraculous anomaly," detached by dogma from sexual desires, menstruation, and the physicality of human life.[8]

Yet medieval Christianity paradoxically presented itself as the religion of the Incarnation — the embracing of flesh, and specifically Mary's flesh. Bodies undergo change and feel pain. Many artistic representations of the pregnancy and nativity did represent the pain, exhaustion, and what a contemporary Catholic theologian calls a "genuine childbirth, with the mother's customary pains and post-partum blues and the child's pollution." Or, more radically, to quote the queer theologians Lisa Isherwood and Marcella Althaus-Reid, "not the genetically modified metaphysical Son of God ... but the screaming baby born amidst the cow shit and fleas, covered in his birthing blood and received into the arms of his child/mother."[9]

At the heart of Christian dogma, therefore, is a contradiction that many late-medieval artistic representations of the Nativity, the Virgin and Child, made explicit. The story of the two midwives in attendance at the Nativity, traditionally named Salome and Zalome, brings these contradictory traditions together. The midwife Salome examines the mother and is astounded that her hymen remains intact; Zalome, however, is punished for doubting that Mary remains a virgin by having her hand wither — before it is miraculously restored. But the midwives do not simply test Mary's intact hymen and proclaim her ever virgin; they aid and comfort the mother and they bathe and care for baby and mother after the pains of birth.[10] Mary was supposed, according to medieval gynotheology, to have been untouched by the physicality of pregnancy; but the midwives aid her by doing what midwives do for real postpartum mothers.

There lay deep in the history of Christianity, therefore, a battle with the Docetic heresy, that Jesus was divine but not fully human, with the bodily reality of the scene subverting the theological purity of the concept. The theologians too often drifted toward that heresy; it is as if the artists pulled them back.

The tableau of the Virgin surrounded by supportive women is also part of the emotive power of *All's Well*, with the Florentine women, the Widow, Diana, Marianna, and Violentia, rallying around Helena and supporting her quest. They are her midwives in many senses. The emotionally powerful concurrence of virginity and pregnancy of course constitutes the momentary shock of Helena's entrance. The script does not mention her pregnancy until that moment. Some productions have deliberately had Helena not showing her pregnancy until her entry; others have suggested, through her weariness or swollen midriff, that she is indeed pregnant. But unlike Mary, Helena is of course decidedly no longer a virgin, let alone perpetually virgin.

The wonder of her appearance, both alive and pregnant, immediately makes us switch attention to Bertram — as the husband and now the father. Helena has experienced the emotional and physical complexities of what she terms the "sweet" (4.4.22) uses of her body with Bertram — in which discovery, she now reminds him, he was "wondrous kind" (5.3.310). Her pregnancy has come about not by impregnation through the ear, which the *Protevangelium*, the major source for nonbiblical stories about the Virgin, recounts and which we see in so many medieval Annunciations, but in the natural way and very much through the affirmation of her sexuality and her own sexual choice.[11]

Historically, therefore, Helena manages to combine aspects of both old medieval Catholic veneration of the Virgin and "new" Protestant reduction of the Virgin to a humble exemplum of obedience, with marriage as the ideal vocation for a woman. Shakespeare's virgin also remains an object of veneration, not least in the resurrection scene I am considering, though it is the veneration due to a mortal woman, not the Mother of God.

Theologically, Protestants saw Catholic devotion to the Virgin and her body as idolatrous. But the cultus and the images and relics they reviled—for example, the vial of the Virgin's milk at the shrine of Our Lady of Walsingham — were more repulsive to them precisely because they were female.[12] The reformers were appalled by the physicality and what they accurately perceived as the syncretism of Mariology—that despite a thousand-year battle, pagan goddess cults which affirmed rather than repressed sexuality had still managed to permeate the Church's devotional life. In triumphing over the pagan goddess religions, early Christianity had still absorbed sufficient from them to permit subversion. As Barbara Newman observes, "the God or gods worshipped within any tradition are not only those that its doctrinal formulas proclaim, but those that its devotees address in prayer, its artists paint or sculpt, its poets celebrate in hymns, and its mystics encounter in ecstasy."[13] The reformers saw such slippage as unacceptable—false to the truths of the Gospel and what they saw as its revolutionary break from such blasphemous paganism.

"When you hear of Our Lady of Walsingham," thundered the protracted Elizabethan *Homily on Idolatry*—years after the shrine at Walsingham, undoubtedly the most powerful place of Marian pilgrimage in England and centered on Mary's mothering function—had been destroyed, "what is it but an imitation of the Gentiles idolators?"[14] That primitive pagan substratum — what the modern Catholic theologian Maria Kassel terms the "fundamental experience that all life, both psychologically and physically, derives from the female"[15]— is what reformers sensed was still present in the Catholic devotion to the Virgin and what they tried to eliminate in a century of focused iconoclasm from the 1530s until the Civil War.

In fairness, there was some truth to the reformers' suspicions of the sexualization of Mary and the Virgin's cult. However they may have been transfigured by theological dogma, her womb, breasts, hymen, and closed birth canal and vaginal entrance became obsessively fetishized objects of attention in late-medieval devotion and theology. The reformers were objecting to a real phenomenon, devotion centered on "the infused sexuality of the sacred mother's vaginality," exemplified in a vast range of cultural artifacts, devotional practices, and theological concepts, and no more so than in the cult of Mary's pregnancy and motherhood.[16]

Mystics' use of highly erotic imagery for their devotion to (and imagined responses by) the Virgin and the prevalence of female symbols in medieval church architecture and representations of her have long been noted by scholars. Madeline Caviness argues that the increasing realism of later medieval depictions of the Virgin increased the level of potential eroticism as "subjects that were not erotic in the abstract modes of representation of Romanesque art became disturbingly sado-erotic in the more and more graphic representations of physicality."[17]

In England, once again, the shrine at Walsingham embodied a peculiarly female source of power that was rooted in the female body. The pilgrims' route from the south to the shrine in Norfolk became known as the "Milky Way," in part because of the vial of the Virgin's milk awaiting them at the shrine. It was not an ironic phrase, nor was the Virgin's milk just a piece of superstition that Calvinists attacked. Walsingham was associated with women's experiences of pregnancy and childbirth. Susan Morrison has reconstructed how women pilgrims "traveled spatially" from one wayside shrine related to childbearing to another on the way to Walsingham.[18] All the more fascinating that in *All's Well*, the central character is a woman, a pregnant woman, a virgin — and a pilgrim. Shakespeare's "reformed" virgin, who will affirm the vocation of motherhood, carries with her strong echoes of the medieval Madonna.

At the start of the play, Helena and Parolles have a battle of wits over the uses of virginity. "Loss of virginity," argues Parolles "is rational increase," and "to speak on the part of virginity" is "to accuse your mothers ... your virginity, your old virginity, is like one of our French withered pears, it looks ill, it eats drily; marry, 'tis a withered pear; it was formerly better; marry, yet 'tis a withered pear" (1.1.109–161). But Helena wins the debate rhetorically: she does not disagree on the right uses of virginity but rather she affirms her right to choose to lose her virginity on her own terms, as she asks the play's key question: "How might one do, sir, to lose it to her own liking?" (1.1.149).

While in medieval religious ideology virginity had special status as a symbol of women's noncirculation in the secular world of bargaining and marriage negotiations, female virginity was commodified by Protestants as part of the accrued capital of marriage, property acquisition, and civic duty. Helena and Parolles agree that virginity is but one stage of a woman's life that, in accord with Protestant doctrine, directs her to marriage; and further, that the responsibility for the proper use of virginity falls heavily on women themselves. But Helena's question adds another, unexpected dimension to the issue — and that is a woman's affirmation of her own sexuality.

Sexuality

The most prominent visual aspect of Piero's Virgin is her touching the half-opened straining gusset in her blue robe, her right hand revealing a shadowy slit, indirectly displaying the bodily orifice by which, in the natural way of things, conception and birthing normally occur. Piero's representation therefore thrusts (if I may draw that metaphor from the midwives' story) the sexuality of the Virgin Mary into the center of the picture.

The sexuality of divine personages was an uneasy though perpetual topic during the Middle Ages and became a matter of grave concern to the Council of Trent just as it was for iconoclastic Protestant attacks on the Church — and, as Leo Steinberg points out, for their embarrassed descendants, the modern arbiters of good taste in art. Steinberg focuses on medieval representations of Christ's sexuality, specifically on the penis. He quotes Augustine's remarks that Christ was "complete in all the parts of a man," arguing that from the thirteenth century, painters and sculptors "asked intimate questions that do not translate well into words."[19] The result was a tradition of painting stressing the masculinity of Christ, showing his circumcised penis, often erect, and sometimes clearly held, displayed, and seemingly manipulated by his mother.

But however theologians obsessed over the issue verbally, the genital sexuality of the Virgin Mother does not get represented directly in art, though there are multiple representations of the *Virgin lactans*, including extravagances like the Madonna's squirting milk to extinguish purgatorial fires or to heal or suckle St. Bernard.[20] What is represented, explicitly in the Piero mural, are indirect representations of the female organs of pleasure and birthing. Architectural historians, anthropologists, and historians have referenced such instances as the shape of cathedrals, the Christian piscatorial symbol, the mandorla, the *vesica pisces*, the Order of the Garter, and the vulva-shaped, bleeding, or oozing wounds in Christ's side. In *Le Roman de la Rose*, the poem's pilgrim-lover draws back the curtain, like the angels in the Piero fresco, suggesting the opening of the vaginal labia — the much-sought-after Rose lies inside the sanctuary and in the final lines of the poem "opens up" after a few drops of "dew" are sprinkled on it.[21]

The relevance of these considerations of the *del parto* tradition and the eroticization of the Virgin to *All's Well* is that the uneasy contradictions of incarnational theology behind the pregnant Virgin and references to the Virgin's repressed sexuality are momentarily displayed in Helena's entrance. The woman whom all last saw alive as wedded yet unbedded is here miraculously returned, pregnant, confronting her husband, who has just sworn to us (and truthfully, as far as he knows) that he has not touched her sexually. Helena's pregnancy is no miracle — and in accord with conventional Elizabethan belief, she has conceived not passively, but through orgasm. Her initial reaction to having had sex with Bertram was to marvel at the psychological dislocations that sex can cause, but now, at the play's end, she affirms her wonder that sexual contact could be so pleasurable, so "wondrous kind" (5.3.310). She is the apparent Virgin transformed into a vision of sexual affirmation.

Staging Shakespeare's Pregnant (and Sexualized) Madonna

There is no record of any performance of *All's Well* before 1741—and then, for over 150 years, the sexually explicit scenes were often omitted or reduced. But since the 1950s there have been significant productions: by the Royal Shakespeare Company, directed by John Barton (1967), Trevor Nunn (1981), Barry Kyle (1989), and Peter Hall (1992), and a satisfying BBC TV version, directed by Elijah Mosinsky (1982); along with Richard Monette's at Stratford, Ontario (2002), such "establishment" productions culminate in the 2003-to-2004 Greg Doran Royal Shakespeare Company production starring Judi Dench, which was rapturously reviewed, primarily for her cameo performance as the Countess. But more significant than even these heartening and intense productions is the remarkable number of times *All's Well* has been staged in local, regional, and university theaters over the past decade. In part this reflects a search for a Shakespeare play not often seen, but the variety of productions also suggests that *All's Well* has become a play for our time.

In preparing this essay, I reviewed almost a hundred recent productions since the 1960s and surveyed a number of directors who had worked on the play since about 2000. My own direct experience in the play's ongoing history was as the teacher of a company of actors in a semester-long seminar on the play; I then acted as dramaturge for their Purchase Repertory Theatre production (2005), directed by David Bassuk. That production and other recent ones showed how powerfully the play's medieval and early modern characteristics can be effectively combined, even in productions that use a contemporary or eclectic and not just a period setting.[22]

The play's culminating moment can be staged variously. Some productions align the play's ending with romantic comedy, smoothing the potentially ironic and distasteful, compensating for the play's flaws and its arguably underscripted hero by skillful staging and textual additions; they stress the restored marriage and Bertram's maturation. In fact, most recent productions cannot resist the emotional impact of the restorative ending—not necessarily one to please those of us, including myself, who see the play as raising issues of gender, class, and personal choice, but certainly a delight to most audiences.

In the Yale Repertory production (2006), the audience only slowly warmed to Helena, who was gradually transformed into a romantic musical-comedy heroine, complete with schmaltzy 1950s Italian songs and an atmosphere reminiscent of the sentimental Broadway pseudo-Italian musical *Light on the Piazza*. Other productions have, however, chosen an ironical ending, leaving the audience dislocated, even indignant, at the reuniting of Helena with Bertram. A third approach has stressed the play's anticipation of the tragic-comic mixture of Shakespeare's late plays, often harking back to the mixed generic nature of medieval drama. Lafew's remark that Helena's curing of the King is "the rarest argument of wonder" (2.3.8) is echoed in the even greater "wonder" of the final scene; wonder is an affective quality generally associated with tragedy, and an effective romance ending incorporates as much pain as possible before producing the desired "wondrous" effects. A fourth reading is to stress that regardless of Bertram's moral or marital wishes, the outcome is a triumph of Helena's brilliance, sexual choice, and independence.

The staging of the entry of the Pregnant Virgin has been crucial to all these readings of the play. Yale Repertory provided a warm comic atmosphere, beautifully choreographed, with Helena announced and then emerging, fondly and forgiving, to help continue the education of the boy-husband she had desired and yearned for and had cleverly earned—encouraged by her jolly Italianate companions and an audience that had been wooed into mellow affection. Even Diana's

Female solidarity between Helena (Diana Hoyt) and Countess (Mindi Burnett) in *All's Well, That Ends Well*, dir. David Bassuk, Purchase Repertory Theatre (2005).

enthusiastic acceptance of the King's offer to provide her with a dowry, despite her previous vow of virginity, did not sound as self-betraying as some critics have asserted. The sentimental comic ending was reinforced not only by the music but by the setting and costumes—Europe after World War II, with a sense of new hope, soldiers going home, revived possibilities, optimism after oppression and death.

Darko Tresnjak's more ironic production by Theater for a New Audience in New York (2006) had, by contrast, Bertram and Helena eyeing each other warily, hardly touching, and thus restoring a sense of the uneasiness of the "problem play" taxonomy so beloved by critics fifty to a hundred years ago. But the entrance of Helena herself was triumphant as she moved serenely though a central cloister to an amazed court. The production's final irony came in the way the exiting couple tentatively picked up a child's toy on the stage — not so much an affirmation of sexual choice as the acceptance of the Protestant affirmation of marriage and bourgeois responsibility.

Helena (Diana Hoyt) and Bertram (Kenyan Burnett) reconciled in *All's Well, That Ends Well*, dir. David Bassuk, Purchase Repertory Theatre (2005).

In these productions, it was not clear to the audience that Helena was pregnant before her triumphant entry. In the BBC TV version, her return was brilliantly staged as triumphant comic romance without the "family values" emphasis, with the camera panning the faces of the astonished spectators before turning to the object of their admiration who, like Piero's Virgin, entered reveling in her transformative physicality. The pregnancy was therefore a revelation, presented as a triumph of Helena's own will and choice. By contrast, Bassuk in his Purchase production brought the theater audience into the secret by having Helena's pregnancy increasingly obvious in the scenes where she and the Florentine women go to search for the King, and finally, entering down a long rake to center stage to be met by the amazed Bertram and then, significantly, by the Countess. The miraculous return of her "daughter" emphasized continuity and, surrounded by her Florentine women friends, women's solidarity — pregnant, affirmative, triumphant, as an affirmation of motherhood as one of the great "miracles" of life.

She was greeted by her errant and now-repentant husband but also, more significantly, by the other women. In the sexual economy of the play, Bertram's pilgrimage has been to leave the Mother, only to be refound by her; but Helena's has been to find through choice and risk her own affirmation.[23] A complex medieval–early modern moment, with its contradictions and emergent ideologies, is re-created in a twentieth- and twenty-first-century idiom.

Comedy, either restorative or ironical, then, constitutes the majority of contemporary stagings of the scene. But seeing *All's Well* as anticipating Shakespeare's late romances, looking forward especially to *The Winter's Tale*, with its miraculous ending of resurrection and hard-won forgiveness, has become a more interesting recent critical approach to the play, and one uncannily in tune with its medieval roots.

The combination of intense pain and emergent joy for which Shakespeare draws from his medieval precedents may perhaps be best illustrated by the emotional riches of Peter Hall's 1992 Royal Shakespeare Company ending. The genius of this production was to have a seemingly cynical, even ruthless, Bertram, an obnoxious boy turning, on the surface, into a mean-spirited man — an anticipation of *Cymbeline*'s Posthumus or *The Winter's Tale*'s Leontes in the suffering he caused — until, abandoned by his mother, the King, and the court, and undone by his own confused lies, he collapses in despair. He looks up to find unexpected (however undeserved) rescue by the entering figure of the pregnant Helena, the woman he has abused and thought dead and who (as we in the audience know) has dedicated her life to fulfilling the conditions he has set, the only person who loves him wholeheartedly, without condition, and who now raises him from the floor in a miraculous, unlooked-for redemption that goes beyond desert or expectation.

Hall's Helena, Sophie Thompson, read the first few words of his letter renouncing his marriage and her, then ripped it up in passionate forgiveness. The interpretation of Bertram's cry for pardon and acceptance as he perceives Helena is crucial: "If she, my liege, can make me know this clearly / I'll love her dearly, ever, ever dearly" (5.3.313–314). Often read as a qualification of his acceptance of her return, on stage these lines can easily become an affirmation: if (as is now manifestly obvious from her visible presence and pregnancy, to which the actor can gesture) she has indeed shown her skill, ingenuity, and now love, then Bertram may be moved to respond positively — the repletion of "ever, ever dearly" emphasizing his acceptance and even conversion.

Bertram says no more in the scene. But as Wilbur Sanders points out on the equivalent scene in *The Winter's Tale*, if Bertram's response to Helena's reappearance seems anticlimactic, "there are anti-climaxes in literature richer than any climax can hope to be."[24] We may well argue that such a reading enacts an all-too-deeply-engrained male fantasy within our cultural history — medieval and modern alike — that however badly a man behaves, there will always be a woman waiting to rescue or redeem him. But it is certainly a fantasy structure that lay deep in the mariological contradictions of medieval Catholicism, to which Shakespeare returned over and over, and one that — as increasing numbers of feminist criticism and productions have shown — many of his plays worked to move beyond.[25]

Finally, there has been a handful of productions that drew on (or at least paralleled) feminist criticism that since the mid-1980s has heralded the play as the clearest affirmation in Shakespeare of women's sexual choice, arguing that Helena exemplifies the will, persistence, planning, and choice of an aggressive (and successful) outsider: as Helena asks in the play's key question, as she contemplates the uses of her virginity, "How might one do, sir, to lose it to her own liking?" (1.1.149). "To her own liking" becomes the central phrase of the play. The feminist director Helena Kaut-Howson staged the play twice in London in the 1990s, stressing how Helena was "a palpable outsider in a filthy rich society," triumphing over the play's more privileged men.[26] Bassuk likewise portrayed her as earnest but focused, an outsider in a corrupt world but very determined to get what she wanted. Both had the revelatory Pregnant Virgin scene as the triumph of a woman's choice and determination.

Among recent critics of the play, Michele Osherow writes forcefully of the irrelevance of Bertram, and indeed males generally, to the outcome and the staging of the scene. The choice has been Helena's. Like Joseph in the medieval York Annunciation and Nativity plays, Bertram is sidelined by the centrality of the Pregnant Virgin herself. Though with a surprisingly low-key entry from the side by Helena, the Cambridge Shakespeare Festival production (2004) deemphasized the reconciliation of the couple to emphasize Helena's control and choice of her pregnancy and generation, underlining the point by having Lavatch the clown (in this particular production, a woman) increasingly obviously pregnant as the play moved along, giving birth offstage during the final scene and entering at the play's end with a new infant. New mother and mother-to-be stood side by side, with Bertram almost forgotten.

While productions inevitably have to incorporate Bertram and the King into the final tableau, *All's Well* is remarkable for its affirmation of the hearts of women to embody literally what Osherow terms the continuity and "right" ordering of life. In such readings, Helena enters, like Piero's autonomous Virgin, without men, affirming her solidarity with the women who accompany her.[27]

Indeed, feminist critics in the past twenty years have embraced the play precisely because of its open affirmation of sexual choice. There is, observes Theodora Jankowski, "something distinctly queer about Helena's character" in her challenges to patriarchal control of a woman's body. *All's Well*, says Mary Bly in similar vein, is a "radical experiment — a bold effort to place on the comic stage women who show sexual desire, pursue consummation, have intercourse during the five acts, and are celebrated at the end."[28] The fact that the play's ending brings about the integration of the radical heroine into the reassuring structure of dominant heterosexuality, marriage, family, and property does not, Jankowski argues, negate the boldness of her resistance — and it makes the place of Diana, the play's more obvious militant virgin, even more important.

A satisfying feminist reading would have Diana refuse the King's patriarchal gesture at the play's end to find her a husband and would have her affirm her right to remain the resistant virgin. Yet there is far more to Shakespeare's (ex-)virgin than a celebration of the sexuality about which orthodox theology was so uneasy, however important a cultural shift that marks. Jankowski argues that in the activity that conventionally defines the virgin/nonvirgin boundary, the initiating actor is traditionally "[the penis of] a man, and the reason for the change (a man's wish to gain control, usually via impregnation, of a woman's body) are all male-controlled, male-initiated, and male-determined."[29] But Helena is not the virgin who announced, as Mary did in the Annunciation, "be it according to thy word," either to God or man; she announced her own determination to preserve her virginity in order to lose it only "to her own liking."

Under the surface of a story that can be read as the affirmation of procreative heterosexual marriage is another story — a woman's right to make sexual choices. Helena's entry is an affirmation of the pregnant subject who is not merely a container for a child but rather constitutes what the feminist philosopher Christine Battersby — in her attempt to think an identity that is fleshy, relational, and born — terms the "birthing self"; a self, Rosemary Betterton similarly argues, that is "depicted outside of the sexual economy of the male gaze."[30] Where medieval theology worked to constrain women's sexuality to either virginity or reproduction, and Protestants directed a woman to be a wife and mother, with both seeing a woman as firmly under patriarchal control, what Helena affirms is the primary importance of a woman's owned choice.

What is new, even radical, about *All's Well* is Helena's questioning of who may ultimately make the choice of person, time, and place in the "loss of virginity." Helena's provocative question to Parolles at the end of their debate strikes at the heart of hundreds, perhaps thousands, of years of patriarchal presumptions about the control of women's bodies by men. This is surely the major reason the play has been so well received by feminist criticism and why, in part, it has become such a popular play in the repertoire. As Irving Wardle claimed after seeing the Kyle production, it "comes as near as Shakespeare can to being a woman's play."[31] It does so by working both within and against one of the most oppressive icons of women in our history, that of the Virgin Mary, which paradoxically — especially as the Middle Ages lurched into Shakespeare's time and now into our own — is shown to carry in itself complexities and contradictions that allow it to be a subversive historical force, enacting its surprises on stage and, it is to be hoped, beyond.

Notes

1. Regina Buccola, "'As Sweet as Sharp': Helena and the Fairy Bride Tradition," in *All's Well, That Ends Well: New Critical Essays*, ed. Gary Waller, 71–84 (London: Routledge, 2006). For further discussion of the medieval background and an overview of the play, see Gary Waller, "From 'The Unfortunate Comedy' to 'This Infinitely Fascinating Play': The Critical and Theatrical Emergence of *All's Well, That Ends Well*," in *All's Well, That Ends Well: New Critical Essays*, 1–56. Quotations from the play are taken from the Penguin edition, ed. Barbara Everett (London: Penguin, 2005).

2. For the play's direct medieval sources in Boccaccio, see William Painter, *The Palace of Pleasure*, ed. Joseph Jacobs, vol. 1, 10–14, 171–179 (London: David Nutt, 1903). The story comes to Painter from Boccaccio, *The Decameron*, the Third Day, Ninth Story.

3. R. G. Hunter, *Shakespeare and the Comedy of Forgiveness* (New York: Columbia University Press, 1965), 129–130.

4. For the Madonna del Parto tradition, with reproductions of over one hundred examples, see *La Madonna nell'Attesa del parto: Capolavori dal patrimonio italiano del '300 e '400* (Milan: Libri Scheiwiller, 2000). Piero's Madonna del Parto is one of the most widely reproduced paintings of the Renaissance; see, e.g., Marco Busagli, *Piero della Francesca* (Florence: Giunti, 1998), 130; Jean-Luc Nancy, *The Ground of the Image*, trans. Jeff Fort (New York: Fordham University Press, 2005), 120. For a modern filmmaker's recreation of the making of the fresco, see Andrej Tarkovsky, *Sculpting in Time: Reflections on the Cinema*, trans. Kitty Hunter-Blair (Austin: University of Texas Press, 1989).

5. For Protestant hostility to the *del parto* tradition, see Mary Elizabeth Fissell, *Vernacular Bodies: The Politics of Reproduction in Early Modern England* (New York: Oxford University Press, 2005), chap. 1. For the late-medieval *del parto* tradition in England, see Gail MacMurray Gibson, *The Theater of Devotion: East Anglian Drama and Society in the Late Middle Ages* (Chicago: University of Chicago Press, 1989), chap. 6.

6. Elena Bonelli, "Maternity on Stage between Veils and Curtains," paper presented at the Nineteenth International Conference in Literature & Psychology, University of Siena, Arezzo, 2002, http://www.clas.ufl.edu/ipsa/abstr-02.htm. For current esoteric speculation, see John Hooper, "Catholic Dissent over Mystery of the Pregnant Madonnas" *The Guardian*, July 23, 2005 http://www.guardian.co.uk/arts/news/story/0,11711,1534682,00.html.

7. Augustine, *Of Virginity* [*De virginitate*], 7, http://www.well.com/user/aquarius/augustine-virginity.htm; Ronald Lightbrown, *Piero della Francesca* (New York: Abbeville, 1993), 193. For an orthodox theological overview of the physicality of Mary's pregnancy, see John Saward, *Redeemer in the Womb: Jesus Living in Mary* (San Francisco: Ignatius Press, 1993).

8. Lightbrown, *Piero*, 193; Jerome H. Neyrey, "Mary: Mediterranean Maid and Mother in Art and Literature," *Biblical Theology Bulletin* 20 (1990): 70.

9. Neyrey, "Mary: Mediterranean Maid," 70; Lisa Isherwood and Marcella Althaus-Reid, "Queering Theology," in *The Sexual Theologian* (London: T & T Clark 2004), 7.

10. *The Book of James, or Protevangelium*, trans. M. R. James (Oxford: Clarendon Press, 1924), 19–20.

11. Nicholas Constas, *Proclus of Constantinople and the Cult of the Virgin in Late Antiquity* (Leiden, Netherlands: Brill, 2003), 279; for examples of the many paintings depicting this legend, see, e.g., the Annunciations by Simone Martini, ca. 1330 (Uffizi, Florence), and Robert Campin, Triptych ca. 1425 (Metropolitan Museum, New York). For the theological tradition, see Mary M. Foskett, *A Virgin Conceived: Classical Representations of Virginity* (Bloomington: Indiana University Press, 2002), 205–207; Constas, *Proclus*, 274–285.

12. For Walsingham and the cult of the Virgin in pre–Reformation England, see (most reliably) J. C. Dickinson, *The Shrine of Our Lady of Walsingham* (Cambridge, UK: Cambridge University Press, 1956). More brief and somewhat (differently) partisan, though moderate in tone, are Colin Stephenson, *Walsingham Way* (London: Darton, Longman & Todd, 1970); and Elizabeth Ruth Obbard, ODC, *The History and Spirituality of Walsingham* (Norwich, UK: Canterbury Press, 1995). For the Virgin's milk, of many references, see, e.g., Desiderius Erasmus, "Pilgrimage for Religion's Sake," *Pilgrimages to Saint Mary of Walsingham and Saint Thomas of Canterbury*, ed. J. G. Nichols (London, 1849), 32; Margaret R. Miles, "The Virgin's One Bare Breast: Female Nudity and Religious Meaning in Tuscan Early Renaissance Culture," in *The Female Body in Western Culture: Contemporary Perspectives*, ed. Susan Rubin Suleiman (Cambridge, MA: Harvard University Press, 1986). For an overview of the symbology of the Virgin in pre–Reformation and contemporary Walsingham, see Gary Waller, "An Erasmian Pilgrimage to Walsingham," *Peregrinations* 2, no. 2 (March 2007).

13. Barbara Newman, *God and the Goddesses: Vision, Poetry, and Belief in the Middle Ages* (Philadelphia: University of Pennsylvania Press, 2002), 94.

14. *Certain Sermons or Homilies Appointed to Be Read in Churches in the Time of Queen Elizabeth* (London: John Griffiths, 1855), 202.

15. Maria Kassel, "Mary and the Human Psyche Considered in the Light of Depth Psychology," in *Mary in the Churches*, ed. Hans Kung and Jürgen Moltmann (New York: Seabury Press, 1983), 74.

16. Annette B. Weiner, *Inalienable Possessions: The Paradox of Keeping-While-Giving* (Berkeley: University of California Press, 1992), 59.

17. Madeline Caviness, *Visualizing Women in the Middle Ages: Sight, Spectacle, and Scopic Economy* (Philadelphia: University of Pennsylvania Press, 2001), 36.

18. Susan Signe Morrison, *Women Pilgrims in Late Medieval England: Private Piety as Public Performance* (London: Routledge, 2000), chap. 1.

19. Leo Steinberg, *The Sexuality of Christ in Renaissance Art and in Modern Oblivion*, 2nd ed. (Chicago: University of Chicago Press, 1996), 16.

20. For Calvin's classic critique of relics, including Mary's milk, see *A Treatise on Relics* [1543], trans. Valerian Krasinski (Edinburgh: Johnston and Hunter, 1854); Carlos Eire, *War against the Idols: The Reformation of Worship from Erasmus to Calvin* (Cambridge, UK: Cambridge University Press, 1989), 16.

21. For the sexual symbolism of the mandorla, see Elizabeth Blackledge, *The Story of V: Opening Pandora's Box* (London: Weidenfeld and Nicholson, 2003), 52–54; for vulva-like representations in art and architecture, see, e.g., Dan Cruickshank, *The Story of Britain's Best Buildings* (Buffalo, NY: Firefly Books, 2003), 57–69; Karma Lochrie, "Mystical Acts, Queer Tendencies," in *Constructing Medieval Sexuality*, ed. Karma Lochrie, Peggy McCracken, and James A. Schultz, 180–200 (Minneapolis: University of Minnesota Press, 1997).

22. The performances discussed are BBC TV, d. Elijah Moshinsky, 1980; Royal Shakespeare Company, d. Peter Hall, Swan Theatre, Stratford-upon-Avon, and London, 1992–1993; The New Shakespeare Company, d. Helena Kaut-Howson, London, 1997; Folger Theatre, d. Richard Clifford, Washington, D.C., 2003; Royal Shakespeare Company, d. Gregory Doran, Stratford-upon-Avon and London, 2003–2004; Cambridge Shakespeare Festival, d. David Crilly, Emmanuel College, Cambridge, 2004; Purchase College Repertory Theatre, d. David Bassuk, Purchase College, New York, 2005; Theatre for a New Audience, d. Darko Tresnjak, New York, 2006; Yale Repertory Theatre, d. James Bundy and Mark Rucker, New Haven, Connecticut, 2006.

23. For a Freudian reading of the sexual dynamics of the play, see Janet Adelman, *Suffocating Mothers: Fantasies of Maternal Origin in Shakespeare's Plays, Hamlet to The Tempest* (New York: Routledge, 1992), 78–81.

24. Wilbur Sanders, *The Winter's Tale* (Boston: Twayne, 1987), 121.

25. Coppélia Kahn, *Man's Estate: Masculine Identity in Shakespeare* (Berkeley: University of California Press, 1981); Gary Waller, "The Winter's Tale," in *Greenwood Companion to Shakespeare*, vol. 4 ed. Joseph Rosenblum, 964–968, 985–990 (Westport, CT: Greenwood, 2005).

26. Elizabeth Schafer, *Ms-Directing Shakespeare: Women Direct Shakespeare* (London: Palgrave, 2000), 113–117.

27. Michele Osherow, "She Is in the Right: Biblical Maternity and *All's Well, That Ends Well*," in Waller, ed. *All's Well*, 155–168.

28. Theodora A. Jankowski, *Pure Resistance: Queer Virginity in Early Modern English Drama* (Philadelphia: University of Pennsylvania Press, 2000), 5, 106–107; Mary Bly, "Imagining Consummation: Women's Erotic Language in Comedies of Dekker and Shakespeare," in *Look Who's Laughing: Gender and Comedy*, ed. Gail Finney (Langhorne, PA: Gordon and Breach, 1994), 37.

29. Theodora A. Jankowski, "Hymeneal Blood, Interchangeable Women, and the Early Modern Marriage Economy in *Measure for Measure* and *All's Well that Ends Well*," in *A Companion to Shakespeare's Works IV: The Poems, Problem Comedies, Late Plays*, ed. Richard Dutton and Jean E. Howard, 89–105 (Oxford: Blackwell, 2001).

30. See Christine Battersby, *The Phenomenal Woman: Feminist Metaphysics and the Patterns of Identity* (Cambridge, UK: Cambridge University Press, 1998); Rosemary Betterton, "Prima Gravida: Reconfiguring the Maternal Body in Representation," http://www.women.it/quarta/workshops/spectacles2/rbetterton.htm.

31. Irving Wardle, Review of *All's Well That Ends Well*, *The Times* (London), October 12, 1989, 20.

Works Cited

Adelman, Janet. *Suffocating Mothers: Fantasies of Maternal Origin in Shakespeare's Plays, Hamlet to The Tempest*. New York: Routledge, 1992.

Augustine. *Of Virginity* [*De virginitate*], 7. http://www.well.com/user/aquarius/augustine-virginity.htm.

Battersby, Christine. *The Phenomenal Woman: Feminist Metaphysics and the Patterns of Identity*. Cambridge, UK: Cambridge University Press, 1998.

Betterton, Rosemary. "Prima Gravida: Reconfiguring the Maternal Body in Representation." http://www.women.it/quarta/workshops/spectacles2/rbetterton.htm.

Blackledge, Elizabeth. *The Story of V: Opening Pandora's Box*. London: Weidenfeld and Nicholson, 2003.

Bly, Mary. "Imagining Consummation: Women's Erotic Language in Comedies of Dekker and Shakespeare."

In *Look Who's Laughing: Gender and Comedy*, edited by Gail Finney, 35–52. Langhorne, PA: Gordon and Breach, 1994.
Bonelli, Elena. "Maternity on Stage between Veils and Curtains." Paper presented at the Nineteenth International Conference in Literature & Psychology, University of Siena, Arezzo, 2002. http://www.clas.ufl.edu/ipsa/abstr-02.htm.
The Book of James, or Protevangelium. Translated by M. R. James. Oxford: Clarendon Press, 1924.
Buccola, Regina. "'As Sweet as Sharp': Helena and the Fairy Bride Tradition." In *All's Well, That Ends Well: New Critical Essays*, edited by Gary Waller. London: Routledge, 2006.
Busagli, Marco. *Piero della Francesca*. Florence: Giunti, 1998.
Calvin, John. *A Treatise on Relics*. Translated by Valerian Krasinski. Edinburgh: Johnston and Hunter, 1854 [1543].
Caviness, Madeline. *Visualizing Women in the Middle Ages: Sight, Spectacle, and Scopic Economy*. Philadelphia: University of Pennsylvania Press, 2001.
Certain Sermons or Homilies Appointed to Be Read in Churches in the Time of Queen Elizabeth. London: John Griffiths, 1855.
Cruickshank, Dan. *The Story of Britain's Best Buildings*. Buffalo, NY: Firefly Books, 2003.
Dickinson, J. C. *The Shrine of Our Lady of Walsingham*. Cambridge, UK: Cambridge University Press, 1956.
Eire, Carlos. *War against the Idols: The Reformation of Worship from Erasmus to Calvin*. Cambridge, UK: Cambridge University Press, 1989.
Erasmus, Desiderius. "Pilgrimage for Religion's Sake." In *Pilgrimages to Saint Mary of Walsingham and Saint Thomas of Canterbury*, edited by J. G. Nichols. London: Nichols, 1849.
Constas, Nicholas. *Proclus of Constantinople and the Cult of the Virgin in Late Antiquity*. Leiden, Netherlands: Brill, 2003.
Fissell, Mary Elizabeth. *Vernacular Bodies: The Politics of Reproduction in Early Modern England*. New York: Oxford University Press, 2005.
Foskett, Mary M. *A Virgin Conceived: Classical Representations of Virginity*. Bloomington: Indiana University Press, 2002.
Gibson, Gail MacMurray. *The Theater of Devotion: East Anglian Drama and Society in the Late Middle Ages*. Chicago: University of Chicago Press, 1989.
Hooper, John. "Catholic Dissent over Mystery of the Pregnant Madonnas." *The Guardian*, July 23, 2005. http://www.guardian.co.uk/arts/news/story/0,11711,1534682,00.html.
Hunter, R. G. *Shakespeare and the Comedy of Forgiveness*. New York: Columbia University Press, 1965.
Isherwood, Lisa, and Marcella Althaus-Reid. *The Sexual Theologian*. London: T & T Clark, 2004.
Jankowski, Theodora A. *Pure Resistance: Queer Virginity in Early Modern English Drama*. Philadelphia: University of Pennsylvania Press, 2000.
———. "Hymeneal Blood, Interchangeable Women, and the Early Modern Marriage Economy in *Measure for Measure* and *All's Well that Ends Well*." In *A Companion to Shakespeare's Works IV: The Poems, Problem Comedies, Late Plays*, edited by Richard Dutton and Jean E. Howard, 89–105. Oxford: Blackwell, 2001.
Kahn, Coppélia. *Man's Estate: Masculine Identity in Shakespeare*. Berkeley: University of California Press, 1981.
Kassel, Maria. "Mary and the Human Psyche Considered in the Light of Depth Psychology." In *Mary in the Churches*, edited by Hans Kung and Jürgen Moltmann, 74–82. New York: Seabury Press, 1983.
La Madonna nell'Attesa del parto: Capolavori dal patrimonio italiano del '300 e '400. Milan: Libri Scheiwiller, 2000.
Lightbrown, Ronald. *Piero della Francesca*. New York: Abbeville, 1993.
Lochrie, Karma. "Mystical Acts, Queer Tendencies." In *Constructing Medieval Sexuality*, edited by Karma Lochrie, Peggy McCracken, and James A. Schultz, 180–200. Minneapolis: University of Minnesota Press, 1997.
Miles, Margaret R. "The Virgin's One Bare Breast: Female Nudity and Religious Meaning in Tuscan Early Renaissance Culture." In *The Female Body in Western Culture: Contemporary Perspectives*, edited by Susan Rubin Suleiman. Cambridge, MA: Harvard University Press, 1986.
Morrison, Susan Signe. *Women Pilgrims in Late Medieval England: Private Piety as Public Performance*. London: Routledge, 2000.
Nancy, Jean-Luc. *The Ground of the Image*. Translated by Jeff Fort. New York: Fordham University Press, 2005.
Newman, Barbara. *God and the Goddesses: Vision, Poetry, and Belief in the Middle Ages*. Philadelphia: University of Pennsylvania Press, 2002.
Neyrey, Jerome H. "Mary: Mediterranean Maid and Mother in Art and Literature." *Biblical Theology Bulletin* 20 (1990): 65–75.
Obbard, Elizabeth Ruth, ODC. *The History and Spirituality of Walsingham*. Norwich, UK: Canterbury Press, 1995.

Osherow, Michele. "She Is in the Right: Biblical Maternity and *All's Well, that Ends Well*," in *All's Well, That Ends Well: New Critical Essays*, edited by Gary Waller, 155–168. London: Routledge, 2006.
Painter, William. *The Palace of Pleasure*. Edited by Joseph Jacobs. London: David Nutt, 1903.
Sanders, Wilbur. *The Winter's Tale*. Boston: Twayne, 1987.
Saward, John. *Redeemer in the Womb: Jesus Living in Mary*. San Francisco: Ignatius Press, 1993.
Schafer, Elizabeth. *Ms-Directing Shakespeare: Women Direct Shakespeare*. London: Palgrave, 2000.
Shakespeare, William. *All's Well That Ends Well*. Edited by Barbara Everett. London: Penguin, 2005.
Steinberg, Leo. *The Sexuality of Christ in Renaissance Art and in Modern Oblivion*. 2nd ed. Chicago: University of Chicago Press, 1996.
Stephenson, Colin. *Walsingham Way*. London: Darton, Longman & Todd, 1970.
Tarkovsky, Andrej. *Sculpting in Time: Reflections on the Cinema*. Translated by Kitty Hunter-Blair. Austin: University of Texas Press, 1989.
Waller Gary. "The Winter's Tale." In *Greenwood Companion to Shakespeare*. Vol. 4, edited by Joseph Rosenblum, 964–968, 985–990. Westport, CT: Greenwood, 2005.
_____. "From 'The Unfortunate Comedy' to 'This Infinitely Fascinating Play': The Critical and Theatrical Emergence of *All's Well, That Ends Well*." In *All's Well, That Ends Well: New Critical Essays*, edited by Gary Waller, 1–56. London: Routledge, 2006.
_____. "An Erasmian Pilgrimage to Walsingham." *Peregrinations* 2, no. 2 (March 2007).
Wardle, Irving. Review of *All's Well That Ends Well*. *The Times* (London), October 12, 1989, 20.
Weiner, Annette B. *Inalienable Possessions: The Paradox of Keeping-While-Giving*. Berkeley: University of California Press, 1992.

Filmography and Performances

1967 *All's Well That Ends Well*, d. John Barton, with Esther Kohler, Ian Richardson, Clive Swift, Helen Mirren. Royal Shakespeare Company, Stratford-upon-Avon.
1980 *All's Well That Ends Well*, d. Elijah Moshinsky, with Angela Down, Donald Sinden. BBC TV.
1981 *All's Well That Ends Well*, d. Trevor Nunn, with Harriet Walter, Peggy Ashcroft, Margaret Tyzack. Royal Shakespeare Company, Stratford-upon-Avon.
1989 *All's Well That Ends Well*, d. Barry Kyle, with Hugh Ross, Patricia Kerrigan, Gwen Watford. Royal Shakespeare Company, Stratford-upon-Avon.
1992–1993 *All's Well That Ends Well*, d. Peter Hall, with Barbara Jefford, Sophie Thompson. Royal Shakespeare Company, Swan Theatre, Stratford-upon-Avon, and London.
1997 *All's Well That Ends Well*, d. Helena Kaut-Howson, with Isabelle Pollen and Jonathan Elsom. The New Shakespeare Company, London.
2002 *All's Well That Ends Well*, d. Richard Monette, with William Hutt, Lucy Peacock, Bernard Hopkins, Sarah Topham. Stratford (Ontario) Festival.
2003 *All's Well, That Ends Well*, d. Richard Clifford. Folger Theatre, Washington, D.C.
2003–2004 *All's Well That Ends Well*, d. Gregory Doran. Royal Shakespeare Company, Stratford-upon-Avon and London.
2004 *All's Well That Ends Well*, d. David Crilly. Cambridge Shakespeare Festival, Emmanuel College, Cambridge.
2005 *All's Well That Ends Well*, d. David Bassuk. Purchase College Repertory Theatre, Purchase College, New York.
2006 *All's Well That Ends Well*, d. Darko Tresnjak. Theatre for a New Audience, New York.
2006 *All's Well That Ends Well*, d. James Bundy and Mark Rucker. Yale Repertory Theatre, New Haven, CT.

Part IV. "Tragical-Comical-Historical-Pastoral": The Romances

Introduction to Part IV

Sid Ray

> HERMIONE: Pray you sit by us, / And tell 's a tale.
> MAMILLIUS: Merry, or sad, shall't be?
> —*The Winter's Tale*, 2.1.22–23

Shakespeare did not apply the term *romance* to the four unique plays he wrote in the five-year period between 1606 and 1611: *Pericles, Cymbeline, The Winter's Tale*, and *The Tempest*. Even after his death, Shakespeare's actor colleagues John Heminge and Henry Condell classified them separately when they compiled the 1623 First Folio; *Cymbeline* fell under the heading of tragedy, and *The Tempest* and *The Winter's Tale* under comedy. *Pericles* was omitted from Heminge and Condell's Folio altogether and did not appear in a collection of works until the 1664 Third Folio. It was not until the nineteenth century that scholars began to apply the term *romance* to these plays; some editors and scholars still categorize them as *tragicomedies*.[1]

The difference is meaningful; the term *romance* recognizes that these plays are descendents of medieval romance—the adventure stories of wandering knights, of magic and princesses, of trials and quests, which are themselves descendents of classical adventure stories such as the epic poem *The Odyssey* and prose tales such as Heliodorus's *Aethiopica*. *Tragicomedy*, rather differently, suggests that these plays are a Renaissance playwriting innovation initiated by the Italian writer Giambattista Guarini (1538–1612), who applied the term to his play *Il Pastor Fido* (*The Faithful Shepherd*) and inspired Francis Beaumont and John Fletcher to write tragicomic plays such as *Philaster* (1608–1610) and *The Faithful Shepherdess* (ca. 1608–1609).[2] Unlike the term *romance*, *tragicomedy* elides rather than evokes the medieval elements of Shakespeare's four late magical plays. Not only are the plays very much in debt to the mode and style of medieval romances of all kinds—chivalric romance, exemplary romance, and miracle plays—they are also full of obvious and specific medieval allusions: the medieval poet Gower is a major figure in *Pericles*; *Cymbeline* begins in Roman-occupied Luds Town but alludes to later medieval moments such as the annexation of Wales (1284); the title of *The Winter's Tale*, evoking fairy tales, may be a play on and homage to *The Canterbury Tales*; and *The Tempest* has as its central character a wizard who is equal parts Sir Thomas Malory's Merlin and the medieval thinker Roger Bacon. Such allusions, coupled with a lack of realism, inspired Ben Jonson, Shakespeare's contemporary, to deride the plays as "mouldy" and to criticize the author for "mix[ing] his head with other mens heeles."[3] With the romances, as Jonson could see, Shakespeare was not breaking with the medieval past but rather bridging it.

Suspect not only for its medieval resonances, romance as a genre was derided by early modern humanists for its association with sexual license, lying, and fantasy. Women were to refrain from reading (much less writing) romance lest they fell into concupiscent imaginings and neglected their more banal Protestant marital duties. In *Instruction of a Christen Woman* (1524), humanist Juan Luis Vives reviled "bokes written in our mothers tonges, that be made but for idel men and women to rede, have non other matter, but of warre and love," and asked, "What shulde a mayde do with armour?" He believed that "therefore a woman shuld beware of all these bokes, likewise as of serpents or snakes."[4] According to Thomas Nashe, romance was a genre associated with Roman Catholicism, written by "those exiled Abbie-lubbers, from whose idle pens proceeded those worne out impressions of the feyned now where acts, of Arthur of the rounde table, Arthur of little Brittaine, sir Tristram, Hewon of Burdeaux, the Squire of low degree, the foure sons of Aymon, with infinite others."[5] Nashe regarded romance, Catholicism, and the medieval as inseparable.

Despite the post–Reformation backlash against romance, Shakespeare's experiments with the genre, like all of his plays, look forward and backward. Hermione of *The Winter's Tale* is a version of Chaucer's Patient Griselda, but she has more agency, in part because she has such a forceful advocate in Paulina. Through Paulina, the play moralizes against the husband's tyranny rather than praises the wife's obedience. *Cymbeline* likewise mixes medieval with early modern elements. While King Cymbeline's Britain is perched between the ancient and medieval periods, the Italy in which Posthumus finds exile seems quintessentially early modern with its protocapitalist rhetoric, its wagering and lawyering. Likewise, the evil queen with her poisons, reminiscent of so many wicked stepmothers and notorious Renaissance gynocrats such as Mary Queen of Scots, alludes also to Boudicca, the fierce and unruly queen of ancient English lore. As Michael Hattaway observes, in Shakespeare's romances "morality is based on feudal idealizations projected forward from medieval predecessors."[6] Common romance motifs such as queens on trial, ships set adrift, and lost heirs, according to Helen Cooper,

> were first developed in the twelfth century in romances written in French and the gradually diverging form of French spoken in England, Anglo-Norman; they moved across the language barrier into English in the thirteenth to fifteenth centuries, acquired a new and vibrant popularity when prints of medieval romances became the pulp fiction of the Tudor age, and underwent remarkable metamorphoses in the works of the great Elizabethan writers.[7]

Shakespeare was a dedicated adherent to medieval romance yet pushed the genre beyond its already generous boundaries.

Indeed, Shakespeare's romances are a mixed response to the past, and there is an awareness in them, despite Jonson's diatribe, that what the audience is seeing is something old-fashioned, refashioned. Shakespeare was innovating, to be sure; he wrote these plays for a specific enclosed modern theater with artificial lighting—Blackfriars—whose audience was on the whole more affluent and better educated than the audience at the Globe. Regarding the innovative qualities of the genre, Cooper writes, "Once the generic norms for romance were established, they invited exploitation and resistance, and writers from the Middle Ages forwards (Chaucer, Malory, Shakespeare) responded by producing works designed to question their own generic assumptions."[8] An emblem of this respect for yet challenge to medieval romance conventions would be Pericles' armor, which the hero prizes and requires for the tournament to win the princess, even though it is rusted through.

Romance as a term seems to be prevailing among Shakespeare editors. But among stage and screen directors, such categories may be more limiting than illuminating. Performance is where directors may choose whether to draw out the idea of romance and its medieval associations or of tragicomedy and Shakespeare's innovations in these plays. Prospero may wear a long white beard and conical hat, which has become the stereotypical image of the "Arthurian mage."[9] John Gielgud in Peter Greenaway's *Prospero's Books* (1991) appeals to this tradition with his short, white beard and assortment of astonishing, medievalesque hats, costuming choices that contrast with the garb of the shipwrecked crew from Milan who are dressed in outrageously large Elizabethan ruffs. But Gielgud also played Prospero in Peter Hall's 1974 stage production at the Old Vic

Creative haberdashery: John Gielgud as Prospero in Peter Greenaway's *Prospero's Books* (1991).

looking remarkably like the Droeshout portrait of Shakespeare himself.[10] Dr. Morbius, the Prospero figure of *Forbidden Planet* (1956) played by Walter Pidgeon, has silvery gray hair and a short beard, which, though less Merlin-like, still draws on a sorcerer's image. Or, as with John Cassavetes in the offshoot *Tempest* (1982), Prospero may be clean-shaven and robust, less typical of the popular image of Merlin. Likewise, a director may choose to play up the significance of the play's chess game, a sly reference to medieval feudal dynasties, or glide over Prospero's provocative reference to religious indulgences at the play's end.

The essays in this section of *Shakespeare and the Middle Ages* suggest that there is still much to uncover and analyze about the medieval elements of Shakespeare's romances. The two essays on *Pericles* examine in different ways the intriguing presence of Gower, the medieval author of *Confessio amantis*, as Chorus in the play. Demonstrating that "Shakespeare was a better and more subtle reader of Chaucer than we are," Louise M. Bishop explores *The Winter's Tale*'s indebtedness to Chaucer's *Tale of Melibee* and finds in Hermione and Paulina Melibee's wife, Prudence, split into two. Finally, Kim Zarins's essay on allusions to the "Man in the Moon" in *The Tempest* suggests that though scholars now tend to focus on the play's colonial context, England's pre–Christian history and folklore still carry deep significance. As Zarins argues, Caliban may represent equal parts colonial subject and abject English laborer.

Possibly because it is not often revived, there is no essay here on *Cymbeline*, the only romance set in England of old. It is worth noting that productions of *Cymbeline* often emphasize the fairy-tale aspects of the play but less so the medieval ones. Peter Hall's 1957 production of *Cymbeline* in Stratford incorporated a set of "impossibly ornate gothic architecture and some enormous trees," and Andrei Serban's 1998 Public Theater production in New York's Central Park, with its lovely outdoor setting and a ring of water circling the set, similarly emphasized a fairy forest-like

Prospero, in another hat, before abjuring his books in Greenaway's *Prospero's Books* (1991).

quality.[11] Bartlett Sher's cowboy *Cymbeline* in 2001–2002 with Theatre for a New Audience in New York City mixed Asian elements with western attire such as chaps and ten-gallon hats. Some productions have incorporated gothic, medievalesque imagery. According to Ros King, Dominic Cooke's rendition at the Swan Theatre in Stratford in 2003 had the Britons painted like "ancient Celts," and Dieter Dorn's 1998 production for the Munich Kammerspiele had "the Queen and her son, both gothically dressed and made up, together trying to push back an open crate containing an enormous sculpted head of Caesar, born by six hulking Romans in dinky skirts, breastplates and plumed helmets."[12]

Though *Cymbeline* has had varying degrees of success on the stage, like *Pericles* and *The Winter's Tale*, it has yet to be made into film. And no film production of *The Tempest* has truly succeeded. *Prospero's Books* comes closest, for film scholars anyway; to the everyday viewer, it is more strange than true. Perhaps the genre's experimental mixing of tragic and comic, medieval and modern, illusion and reality makes it singularly difficult to translate to the screen.

NOTES

1. Edward Dowden, *Shakespeare: A Critical Study of his Mind and Art* (London: Henry S. King and Co., 1875) seems to have been the first to apply the term *romance* to *Pericles, Cymbeline, The Winter's Tale,* and *The Tempest* as a group. The *Riverside Shakespeare* categorizes the four plays as romances and adds to them *The Two Noble Kinsmen*. The *Norton* resists categorization, and one of its editors, Jean Howard, observes the diverse placement of the four plays in the 1623 Folio "as suggestive of the mixed tragicomic nature of these particular dramas"; *The Norton Shakespeare*, ed. Stephen Greenblatt, et al. (New York: W.W. Norton, 1997), 2873. For application of the word *tragicomedy* to the romances, see Joan Hartwig, *Shakespeare's Tragicomic Vision* (Baton Rouge: Louisiana State University Press, 1972); Robert Henke, *Pastoral Transformations: Ital-*

ian Tragicomedy and Shakespeare's Late Plays (Cranbury, NJ: University of Delaware Press, 1997); and Nancy Klein Maguire, ed., *Renaissance Tragicomedy: Explorations in Genre and Politics* (New York: AMS Press, 1987).

   2. There is some debate about Beaumont and Fletcher's influence on Shakespeare's romances, which is covered thoroughly by J.M. Nosworthy in the Arden *Cymbeline*, xxxvii-xl. Nosworthy believes it more probable that the influence went the other way.

   3. The "mouldy tale" reference comes from Jonson's "Ode to Himself," and the latter quotation comes from the Induction to *Bartholomew Fair* (1614): "If ther bee never a Servant-monster I'the Fayre; who can helpe it? He sayes; nor a nest of Antiques? Hee is loth to make Nature afraid in his Playes, like those that beget Tales, Tempests, and such like Drolleries, to mixe his head with other mens heeles"; David Bevington, et al., eds., *English Renaissance Drama: A Norton Anthology* (New York: Norton, 2002), 125–129.

   4. The English translation of this text by Richard Hyde went to nine editions in the sixteenth century; Juan Luis Vives, *The Instruction of a Christen Woman*, ed. Virginia Walcott Beauchamp, et al. (Urbana and Chicago: Illinois University Press, 2002), 24–27.

   5. Thomas Nashe, *The Works of Thomas Nashe*, ed. Ronald B. McKerrow, rev. ed. F. P. Wilson (Oxford: Basil Blackwell, 1958), vol. 1, ii.

   6. Michael Hattaway, *Renaissance and Reformations: An Introduction to Early Modern English Literature* (Maldon, MA: Blackwell Publishing, 2005), 101.

   7. Helen Cooper, *The English Romance in Time: Transforming Motifs from Geoffrey of Monmouth to the Death of Shakespeare* (Oxford: Oxford University Press, 2004), 3.

   8. Ibid., 363.

   9. Michael Torregrossa, "The Way of the Wizard: Reflections of Merlin on Film," in *The Medieval Hero on Screen: Representations from Beowulf to Buffy*, ed. Martha W. Driver and Sid Ray (Jefferson, NC: McFarland, 2004), 167–168.

   10. For a discussion of Gielgud's Prospero in the Hall production of 1973, see Michael Neill, "'Noises, / Sounds, and sweet airs': The Burden of Shakespeare's *Tempest*," *Shakespeare Quarterly* 59.1 (Spring 2008): 36–59, esp. 59.

   11. Ros King, *Cymbeline: Constructions of Britain* (Aldershot, UK, and Burlington, VT: Ashgate, 2005), 31.

   12. Ibid., 33 and 168.

Works Cited

Bevington, David, et al., eds. *English Renaissance Drama: A Norton Anthology*. New York: Norton, 2002.
Cooper, Helen. *The English Romance in Time: Transforming Motifs from Geoffrey of Monmouth to the Death of Shakespeare*. Oxford: Oxford University Press, 2004.
Dowden, Edward. *Shakespeare: A Critical Study of his Mind and Art*. London: Henry S. King and Co., 1875.
Hartwig, Joan. *Shakespeare's Tragicomic Vision*. Baton Rouge: Louisiana State University Press, 1972.
Hattaway, Michael. *Renaissance and Reformations: An Introduction to Early Modern English Literature*. Maldon, MA: Blackwell Publishing, 2005.
Henke, Robert. *Pastoral Transformations: Italian Tragicomedy and Shakespeare's Late Plays*. Cranbury, NJ: University of Delaware Press, 1997.
King, Ros. *Cymbeline: Constructions of Britain*. Aldershot, UK, and Burlington, VT: Ashgate, 2005.
Maguire, Nancy Klein, ed. *Renaissance Tragicomedy: Explorations in Genre and Politics*. New York: AMS Press, 1987.
Nashe, Thomas. *The Works of Thomas Nashe*. 5 Vols. Ed. Ronald B. McKerrow, rev. ed. F. P. Wilson. Oxford: Basil Blackwell, 1958.
Neill, Michael. "'Noises, / Sounds, and sweet airs': The Burden of Shakespeare's *Tempest*." *Shakespeare Quarterly* 59.1 (Spring 2008): 36–59.
Shakespeare, William. *The Norton Shakespeare*. Ed. Stephen Greenblatt, et al. New York: W.W. Norton, 1997.
_____. *Cymbeline*. The Arden Shakespeare. Ed. J.M. Nosworthy. New York: Routledge, 1988.
Torregrossa, Michael. "The Way of the Wizard: Reflections of Merlin on Film." In *The Medieval Hero on Screen: Representations from Beowulf to Buffy*, ed. Martha W. Driver and Sid Ray. Jefferson, NC: McFarland, 2004. 167–168.
Vives, Juan Luis. *The Instruction of a Christen Woman*. Ed. Virginia Walcott Beauchamp, et al. Urbana and Chicago: Illinois University Press, 2002.

Filmography and Performances

1956 *Forbidden Planet*, d. Fred M. Wilcox, with Walter Pidgeon, Anne Francis, Leslie Nielsen. USA: MGM.
1957 *Cymbeline*, d. Peter Hall, with Peggy Ashcroft. Shakespeare Memorial Theatre, Stratford-upon-Avon.

1974 *The Tempest*, d. Peter Hall, with John Gielgud. National Theater, Old Vic, London.
1982 *Tempest*, d. Paul Mazursky, with John Cassavetes, Gena Rowlands, Susan Sarandon. USA: Columbia TriStar.
1991 *Prospero's Books*, d. Peter Greenaway, with John Gielgud. Netherlands/France: Allarts.
1998 *Cymbeline*, d. Andrei Serban, with Liev Schreiber. Delacorte Theater, New York.
1998 *Cymbeline*, d. Dieter Dorn. Munich Kammerspiele, Munich, Germany.
2001 *Cymbeline*, d. Bartlett Sher, with Michael Stuhlbarg and Erica N. Tazel. Theatre for a New Audience, Lucille Lortel Theater, New York.
2003 *Cymbeline*, d. Dominic Cooke, with Daniel Evans and Emma Fielding. Swan Theatre, Stratford-upon-Avon.

"The Quick and the Dead": Performing the Poet Gower in *Pericles*[1]

Kelly Jones

In the mystery play cycles of the late medieval period, the dramatic representation of Bible stories served as a method of sermonizing through show. Because of the high levels of illiteracy and because Church services were conducted in Latin, the visual and aural expression of the sacred chronicles through dramatic representation could be a substantially potent tool for the transmission of the holy word. While it is uncertain how much the medieval religious drama was punctuated by more secular forms of oral and performative entertainment such as minstrelsy, acrobatics, and vernacular forms of storytelling, the plays created a fundamental synthesis between dramatic, literary, and oral culture to bring the biblical narratives to life.[2]

However, some did not see the correlation between action and word as wholly beneficial. An antitheatrical tract entitled *The Tretise of Miraclis Pleyinge* appeared sometime between 1380 and 1425 (the tract survives only in one early fifteenth-century manuscript); in it the author rehearses arguments in defense of miracle cycle playing only to attack such dramatic entertainments as vehicles of moral corruption.[3] The writer considers the argument in favor of dramatic action and its powerful influence as opposed to what he calls "dead books":

> siþen it is leveful to han þe myraclis of God peyntid, why is it not as wel leveful to han þe myraclis of God pleyed, siþen men mowen bettere reden þe wille of God and His marvelous werkis in þe pleyinge of hem þan in þe peytynge, for þis is a deed bok, þe toþer a qu[i]ck [70–74].[4]

Since it is lawful to paint God's miracles, the author asks, why is it not lawful as well to see them dramatized ("played"), so that men can read God's will and his marvelous works in the drama? A play may make an even more lively impression than paintings, which the writer compares to a "dead book."

However, the anonymous author then expresses concern over the potentially subversive and anarchic tendencies of dramatic action: "miraclis pleyinge ... ben made more to deliten men bodily þan to ben bookis to lewid men. And þerefore, 3if þei ben quike bookis, þei ben quike bookis to shrewidnesse more þan to godenesse" (138–139).[5]

The dangers posed by the drama may be seen to lead unlearned men more to villainy ("shrewidnesse") than to virtue, and the author of *The Tretise* emphasizes a distinction between the competing modes of authority when he contrasts the trustworthy and entirely static authority of visual images ("dead" paintings) and (as is implied by the analogy) books, whereby the audience may better *read* the written word of God, with the unpredictable nature of "quick" or living performance of dramatic action (though again, significantly, the word "book" is used to describe the drama). In other words, the *Tretise* exhibits anxiety about the idea that the literary

THE LATE,
And much admired Play, Called
Pericles, Prince of Tyre.

With the true Relation of the whole History, aduentures, and fortunes of the sayd Prince:

As also,

The no lesse strange, and worthy accidents, in the Birth and Life, of his Daughter

MARIANA.

As it hath beene diuers and sundry times acted by his Maiestyes Seruants, at the Globe on the Banck-side.

By VVilliam Shakespeare.

Printed at London by S. S.
1611.

Title page of 1611 Third Quarto edition of *Pericles, Prince of Tyre*.

and moral authority mediated through static images or texts ("a deed bok") becomes vulnerable when translated into performed action.

The Tretise appeared a few years after the appearance of John Gower's poem *Confessio Amantis* in the 1390s. The poem describes the confession of the lover, Amans, to Genius, a priest figure who subjects Amans to tales of the perils and perversions of love to instruct both lover and reader to avoid such pitfalls themselves. In the eighth book of Gower's poem, Genius relates the story of Apollonius, the Prince of Tyre, whose dealings with the incestuous Antiochus and his daughter provided one of the major source materials for *Pericles*, a play that appeared in the repertory of Shakespeare's company, the King's Men, sometime in 1606 or 1607.[6] As well as having provided the source material for the play's narrative, the figure of Gower was resurrected from the dead, "assuming man's infirmities" (Prologue, 3), to serve as a chorus to the play, and in his opening lines the actor who represents Gower announces, "[t]o sing a song that old was sung, / From ashes, ancient Gower is come" (Prologue, 1–2).[7] The real Gower died in 1408, and although the poet was not literally raised from his final resting place in the nearby priory of St. Mary Ovarie (now St. Saviour's, Southwark Cathedral) for the space of an afternoon's entertainment, he would haunt a nearby playhouse as a ghostly author to "glad" the ears and "please" the eyes of the audience (Prologue, 4).[8]

As is the nature of ghosts, the Gower of *Pericles* is an explicitly liminal figure, occupying a fluctuating transience between the states of theatrical life and biological death both as a literary author of a "dead book" and in Shakespeare's rendering as an agent of "quick" theatrical performance.[9] This essay seeks to investigate the performance function of the dramatic representation of Gower in Shakespeare's *Pericles* and to assess how Gower's role as chorus was embedded within the theatrical and cultural practices of both the medieval and the Renaissance periods. Furthermore, it addresses how this theatrical positioning concurrently antagonized and complimented the representation of Gower as a literary authority. I hope to demonstrate how the liminality of Gower's role as the living agent of the play's performance exhibits a playful concern with the unstable, vulnerable, and unreservedly performative nature of authorship itself.[10]

The question surrounding the authorship of *Pericles* itself is notoriously ambiguous. Only the quarto version survives of what many scholars have decided is a deeply flawed and severely depleted literary text. The play, though assigned to William Shakespeare, is widely considered to be the product of his collaboration with at least one other contemporary author (although, as Barbara Everett argues, such a suggestion is deeply problematic, for, she insists, "no known Jacobean playwright writes badly enough to be the author of *Pericles*, and nothing suggests why the age's most successful dramatist should have chosen, or agreed, to collaborate with a writer so helplessly incapable").[11] Nevertheless, the strongest contender for the identity of the possible collaborator is George Wilkins, whose novel, *The Painfull Adventures of Pericles Prince of Tyre*, appeared in 1608, a year or so after the appearance of the King's Men's play. The title page of the novel asks the reader to "receive this Historie in the same manner as it was ... by the Kings Maiesties Players excellently presented," and there are striking similarities in select passages of both the novel and the play (so much so that in 1986 for *The Oxford Complete Works*, Gary Taylor constructed a text of the play from sections of the novel).[12] Many critics assert that the first two acts of the play were penned by Wilkins and the last three by Shakespeare. Regardless of the truth behind such claims, the play continues to occupy a marginalized position within the Shakespeare canon.

The play has not enjoyed the same recognition as other Shakespeare plays, and after the seventeenth century it suffered from considerable neglect that was largely caused by the play's omission from the 1623 Folio of Shakespeare's collected works. However, despite the supercilious reference to *Pericles* as a "mouldy tale" in 1629 by Ben Jonson, a contemporary playwright of Shakespeare and himself a vehement admirer of Gower's work, the play enjoyed immense popularity in the seventeenth century, especially, as several playwrights remarked (with an overtly derogatory tone), with the plebeian masses.[13] Ben Jonson criticized the play's esteem among "the common tub," and John Tatham, in his commendatory verse for Richard Brome's play *A Jovial*

Crew (1652), wrote of the playwright, "*Shakespeare* the *Plebean* Driller, was / Founder'd in's *Pericles*."[14] Despite its mixed reputation, the play clearly represented the epitome of popular culture in the theater of the day—a popularity that has since been lost.

A closer examination into the theatrical potency of Gower can perhaps unlock the dramatic energies of a play that in the modern age is often criticized as being static, dull, crude in composition, and lacking in aesthetic merit. In order to appreciate the theatrical potential of the play, it is necessary to turn our attention to Gower and to his dramatic function as a choric presenter and prologue to the play. In their collaborative study *Prologues to Shakespeare's Theatre*, Douglas Bruster and Robert Weimann provide a much-needed exploration of the theatrical function of the prologue figure in early modern English drama. Although Gower's role extends beyond the function of a prologue, as a chorus figure he shares much in common with it, and Bruster and Weimann's observations are extremely useful tools through which to explore Gower's role in the mediation of the play.

Throughout their study they examine the position of the prologue as an agent of transition "between the somewhat turbulent world of the playhouse and the equally energized but more focused representational world of the performed play."[15] Bruster asserts that in occupying the threshold between the world of the play and the world of the audience, the prologue figure manifests an ambivalent mode of authority. Despite exercising subservience to the audience, welcoming them to the play, courting their good will, and calling upon their complicity in the fabrication of the theatrical event, the prologue also asserts a degree of control and manipulation over the audience's reception of the play, and Bruster remarks that "given the task of quieting the assembled audience ... even as he needed to gain that audience's good will ... the early modern prologue could be—and often was—alternately deferential and commanding."[16]

Bruster proceeds to examine the authority associated with the pre–Shakespearean prologue in the English medieval morality plays, such as the vexilators who announce the banns in *The Castle of Perseverance* (ca. 1405–1425) and the figure of Mercy in *Mankind* (ca. 1464–1471). In each case, the prologue both embodies and exhibits a degree of moral authority, announcing the didactic purpose of the drama and the moral message to be mediated through performance. Furthermore, as Bruster contends, the ethical authority of the prologue can also be aligned to a literary authority: "wherever the orthodox prologue achieved its authority by subscription to firmly established norms and choices, the authorization of the play was literary in the twofold sense that the author's meaningful writing was grafted upon a scriptural message informed by Christian doctrine."[17]

Bruster and Weimann allege that the prologue's authority was usually allied with the moral and literary authority made flesh by the figure of Virtue in the morality play and that the Vice figures, although they usually interrupted the prologue with their anarchy and performative license, were, at least by the end of the play, defeated by the drama's moral agency.

The prologues of Shakespeare's theater retained a position of authority, yet it was perhaps no longer an explicitly moral authority but the literary authority of the playwright attempting to engage and manipulate the audience's "imaginary forces," as demonstrated par excellence by the Chorus in Shakespeare's *Henry V* (Prologue, 23). In a theatrical company, motivated not by moral concerns but by economic and cultural forces, the prologue or chorus figure stood between literary authority and theatrical agency, ushering the audience into the world of the play while reminding them that they were watching actors upon a stage involved in a fictional performance. To this end, the prologue or chorus figure worked on behalf of both playwright and theatrical company to rouse an audience's complicity in the act of performance.

It is also worth remembering that such prologue figures served to introduce the audience to the plays presented in the Elizabethan and Jacobean public playhouses, which were situated upon the city margins. Given the civic authorities' distrust of the players as masterless men, the theaters, as Steven Mullaney asserts in *The Place of the Stage*, were themselves spaces of ambivalent authority.[18] Consequently, Bruster claims, "both the experiential order of representation and geographical-political marginality were deeply assimilated and yet partially intercepted in many Elizabethan prologues."[19] Further, the prologue, while still located in the authoritative position of the Virtue figure of the medieval morality play, could potentially incorporate both the literary authority of the playwright who wrote his lines and the more subversive power of the player (the liminal and marginalized agent of performance) who spoke them.

The chorus figure embodied an ambivalent relationship with authority similar to that of the prologue — an ambivalence that could be incorporated into the presentation of the role itself. For example, Rumour opens *2 Henry IV* when, dressed in a cloak "painted full of tongues" to present an iconic motif, he addresses the audience rather abruptly, "Open your ears; for which of you will stop / The vent of hearing when loud Rumour speaks?" (Induction, 1–2). Rumour, by his very nature, shares strong affinities with the devilish Titivillus — the demon of transgressive speech acts and idle gossip who appears in the fifteenth-century morality play *Mankynde* as well as being recurrently cited as a corrupter of language in certain medieval sermon, poetic, and instructional texts.[20] The appearance of Rumour at the opening of the play challenges the conventional mediation of moral authority that was usually associated with the role of the prologue in the medieval morality plays and instead propounds a subversive immoral agency. In initiating the play with such a figure, Shakespeare was possibly inviting either laughter or indignation from his audience — an active response that would stimulate the playgoers and involve them in the action of the play.

Another such subversive authority is Machiavel, the infamous political philosopher, who, like Gower, is brought back from the dead to serve as prologue to Marlowe's *The Jew of Malta* (1589). Reveling in his theatrical license as prologue, the performer who speaks the lines can exploit and combine his playful freedom with the notorious dissident literary authority associated with the figure to challenge and affront the audience:

> Let me be envied, and not pitied!
> But whither am I bound? I come not, I,
> To read a lecture here in Britany,
> But to present the tragedy of a Jew,
> Who smiles to see how full his bags are crammed,
> Which money was not got without my means [Prologue, 27–32].[21]

Perhaps the ultimate subversive authority for the opening of a play is Shakespeare's antiheroic king who opens his own history play in *Richard III*. Although technically not a prologue in the formal sense, the character's soliloquy to the audience at the play's beginning serves to involve the audience in the projection of the play world and provides a bridge between the world of the audience and the fictional world of the play.[22]

In this respect, Shakespeare's Richard, like Marlowe's Machiavel, projects the complex hybridism of the authority of the "dead" historical or literary figure and the "quick" mediator of theatrical performance, under the command of the playwright's pen. It is with this complexity in mind that this essay now turns to examine the dramatic function of Shakespeare's Gower.

Like Mercy in *Mankind*, *Pericles*'s Gower boasts a moral and literary authority; he moralizes on as well as presents the play's action, and he makes it perfectly clear that there is a lesson to be learned from the examples of characters in the narrative, as the virtuous are rewarded and the wicked are duly and providentially punished. In his epilogue to the play, Gower muses:

> In Antiochus and his daughter you have heard
> Of monstrous lust the due and just reward.
> In Pericles, his queen and daughter, seen,
> Although assail'd with fortune fierce and keen,
> Virtue preserv'd from fell destruction's blast,
> Led on by heaven, and crown'd with joy at last [Epilogue, 1–6].

Like Shakespeare's Richard III, Gower is also a historical figure and subject to the same degree of visual iconicity, not merely as a prologue or chorus figure but as a historical character in the play that the actor must perform; presumably the actor who played Gower would have been shown to the audience in a costume that would have encouraged the audience's recognition of Gower's external form as a vision of literary authority. Members of the audience who attended ecclesiastic services at the nearby Southwark Cathedral would be familiar with the image of Gower's effigy. There are two further descriptions of Gower's appearance that may have had an impact upon the stage representation of the role. One portrayal is given in a poem called *Greene's Vision* (1592) by the London writer Robert Greene. It offers the following depiction of the poet:

> Large he was, his height was long;
> Broad of brest, his lims were strong;
> But culler pale, and wan his looke, —
> Such haue they that plyen their book:
> His head was gray and quaintly shorne,
> Neately was his bearde worne.
> His visage graue, sterne, and grim.[23]

Greene's description is one of a serious and solemn author that appositely reflects the grave moral message mediated through the *Confessio*. An illustration of the poet Gower also appears on the title page of George Wilkins's novel, *The Painfull Adventures of Pericles Prince of Tyre*. It shows a bearded figure with a long staff and a branch of laurel in his hand (an emblematic symbol of a poet) standing beside a desk on which an open book is placed. The representation of Gower, the medieval poet, as he appears in Shakespeare's play is further reinforced by the archaic octosyllabic lines and iambic tetrameters in which Shakespeare's Gower speaks, and the playwright and actor work together to show forth a figure both familiar in his iconic semblance and striking in his anachronistic alterity.

However, the control Shakespeare exercises over the projected idea of Gower serves to demonstrate the synthetic construction of Gower as a literary author. Furthermore, as the actor playing Gower addresses the audience directly, he draws attention to the performativity of the play and the instability of the fictional roles on the stage, including that of his own character of Gower. Standing upon the threshold between the world of the play and the world of the audience, the actor who represents Gower with the appropriate material and performative modes of signification (costume, speech patterns) can exploit his power to represent both the play and the play's author by drawing attention to the character's explicit theatrical fabrication. As simultaneously part of the theatrical performance and outside of it, and as concurrently theatrical creation and creator, Gower is ultimately a dramatic character upon the stage, a culturally, aesthetically, and theatrically constructed emblem of literary authority that is subject to representation through the voice and body of an actor. The figure of literary authority is a signified that is dependent upon his mediation through a highly ephemeral signifier — the player who performs Gower both is and is not Gower, exercising a liminal doubleness that Robert Weimann refers to as a "bifold authority" (an appropriation of a line from Shakespeare's *Troilus and Cressida*) as "two modes of signification — writing and playing — came together to multiply, and make dynamic, the theatrical process itself."[24] Bruster elaborates:

> The theatre was particularly suited to serve this function once its own generic structure had come to conjoin two socially and culturally distinct media and traditions: combining the authority of the word with the sensuous impact and validity of its bodily delivery, the theatre, as no other cultural institution of the time, harboured a twofold, contestatory mode of authorization.[25]

Shakespeare's Gower embodies this theatricality as a creature born of the fusion of both literary and performance culture, of the synthesis between "author's pen" and "actor's voice."[26]

In *The Place of the Stage*, Steven Mullaney asserts that the appearance of Gower in the play marks a transition toward a new authority attached to literary authorship with the rising status of print culture and that Gower, "presenting himself as an authoritative supplement to theatrical representation, ... serves in fact as an antitheatrical agent, an embodiment of the play's effort to divorce itself from the cultural grounds of theatricality in Jacobean London."[27] However, in centralizing the status of the author, Mullaney overlooks the unstable identity of the role, with its theatricality and its dependency upon its vehicle — the actor and his corporeal presence that perpetrates the somatic experience of storytelling through dramatic performance.

Gower himself was writing in a culture where perhaps the literary and performative modes of storytelling were not so entirely disparate entities. Although Gower lifted the story of Apollonius from a collection of literary sources—and when, in *Pericles*, he announces, "let me tell you what mine authors say" (Prologue, 20), he is possibly referring to Godfrey of Viterbo's *Pantheon* (ca. 1186) among his several other sources— it must be remembered that he emerges from a poetic culture wherein literary and oral narrative forms were not always clearly autonomous vehicles of mediation. The story itself was not confined to a single and static text but was an amalgamation of oral and textual sources. Hoeniger reminds us that in the Renaissance, "the story's appeal remained as great as ever, as new adaptations in many languages, in prose, verse, and drama, and the scholarly edition of the early romance, *Historia Apollonii Regis Tyrii*, by Velserius testify" and that even today "in some parts of the world the story of Apollonius of Tyre is still passed on from mouth to mouth."[28] It was by no means unusual for literary texts to have been read aloud, and as Brian Stock asserts, it is perhaps difficult for the modern critic to "understand orality as anything but the opposite of literacy."[29] John D. Niles, in his examination of the storytelling process found in the Anglo-Saxon poem *Beowulf* as a hybrid of literary manuscript and oral narrative, takes up Stock's argument to ask whether we, the modern critics, have been ideologically conditioned to view oral culture as inferior to and necessarily distinct from literary art.[30]

Scholars are beginning to examine the interrelationship between oral and literary culture with regard to the early modern text. In Shakespeare's play, the choral Gower himself relates the story to both oral and literary traditions when he remarks both that the tale had "been *sung* at festivals, / On ember-eves and holy days" (Prologue, 5–6; emphasis added) and that "lords and ladies in their lives / ... *read* it for restoratives" (Prologue, 7–8; emphasis added). The play must be seen as a fusion of performance and literary and visual culture, and as such, *Pericles* assimilates oral storytelling, dumb show, pageantry, actor's voice, and author's pen to relate its narrative. With its blend of literary, oral, and performance traditions, Shakespeare's play decenters any stable notion of the "author" while foregrounding the theatricality and the dispersed loci of authorial ownership. It is important to remember that the play text was deeply entrenched in the theatrical praxis of the day as both a product and a producer of performance. As William Worthen asserts: "The conditions of production in the Renaissance playhouse militate against the final ascription of an ideal, coherent work to a single animating *author*, and the texts of Shakespeare's plays are the result of dialogue and collaboration, of authorial and non-authorial demands of theatre practice."[31]

The interrelation between text and performance has steadily been lost as the author's pen has taken precedence. Furthermore, the play's reputation suffered because of its omission from the Folio, and its unstable origins of authorship caused diminishment of the status of the text. The scorn for the tainted authorial origins of the play is apparent in George Lillo's prologue to his unsuccessful adaptation of the play, *Marina* (1738):

> We dare not charge the whole unequal play
> Of Pericles on him; yet let us say,
> As gold though mix'd with baser matter shines,
> So do his bright inimitable lines
> Throughout those rude wild scenes distinguish'd stand,
> And shew he touch'd them with no sparing hand.[32]

Like many critics, Lillo attributes the play's imperfections to the contamination of Shakespeare's genius with "baser matter."

The play fell into further disregard in the eighteenth and nineteenth centuries—a disdain that was to some extent the result of contemporary embarrassment regarding the play's lewd subject material in the brothel scenes and the scenes of Antiochus's incest. The choral Gower also suffered, and when the play was finally revived by Samuel Phelps in 1854, the role was omitted altogether. Gower as poet and narrator was no longer seen as central to the play in performance, and his perceived importance as a medieval author was also diminished (though Gower's reputation was then somewhat recovered through the magisterial editions of his works by G. C. Macauley, published from the 1890s).[33]

During the twentieth century, when the play was finally accepted into the canon, it aroused the interest of theatrical opportunists who aimed to stage the entirety of Shakespeare's works, throwing in the apocryphal plays for good measure. However, over the past fifty years, a period that in literary studies has witnessed the postmodern fixation with the death of the author and a search for meaning beyond the canonized text, there has been a revived interest in the play on its own dramatic merits. The play's revivified stage life has possibly been the result of theatrical developments and a renewed interest in narrative form in theater that lies beyond the pale of naturalism — a move aided by the likes of Bertolt Brecht as well as by a willingness to explore multicultural forms of storytelling and performance.[34] Interestingly, the play has spawned only one televised production, which was filmed as part of the BBC Time-Life project (1984), directed by David Jones, despite the fact that the film medium seems particularly appropriate to a play that continually switches between locations.[35]

Significantly, in recent theatrical productions Gower's liminal and anachronistic otherness as a medieval author has been reappropriated to project a cultural and geographical disparity from the medieval English Gower that appeared in the seventeenth-century performances.[36] In Terry Hand's 1969 production at the Royal Shakespeare Theatre, Emrys Jones presented Gower as a Welsh bard, while in Tony Richardson's 1958 production at the Shakespeare Memorial Theatre in Stratford-upon-Avon, wherein the action was set aboard a rowing galley, West Indian actor Edric Connor played Gower as a calypso singer, singing his story to a group of sailors.[37] Rudolph Walker also sang in soothing calypso rhythms for David Thacker's 1990 production at The Pit, though Walker made an attempt to project the literary tradition of the story by clutching a book and he remained on stage constantly to remind the audience of his role as storyteller.[38] More recently, in Yukio Ninagawa's 2003 production at the National Theatre, in which the entire play was performed in Japanese with English subtitles, the role of Gower was divided between one female and one male performer who both manipulated Bunraku puppets to illustrate their tale visually.[39]

In 2005, Kathryn Hunter's production at the Globe cast Patrice Naiambana as a West African "grigot" who, relating Pericles's story both to the audience and to the elderly Pericles himself, demonstrated the power of healing through storytelling.[40] Appropriately, Naiambana also doubled as Cerimon, a witch doctor, who brings Thaisa, Pericles's dead wife, back to life — a casting choice that by virtue of association also extended the remedial effect of the play's choric figure. Significant as well was the fact that Naiambana's Gower attempted to create an extremely interactive relationship with the audience, hoisting them up onstage, ad-libbing, and at times dispensing with the text altogether. This Gower's theatrical energies met with an ambiguous response from the critics: there were those who praised Naiambana for investing the character and his story with such verve and those who attacked the performer and his willingness to extemporize as a boisterous attempt to conceal apologetically what was perceived to be essentially a "dull" play.[41]

These recent productions met with varying degrees of success, and despite the fact that the productions were sometimes attacked for projecting a gimmicky multiculturalism, at least such geocultural reappropriations of Gower's English medievalism attempt to recreate the fusion of literary, oral, and performance culture that the play so thoroughly both encompasses and celebrates. Such cultural relocations, despite their "otherness" from the implicitly English Gower, perhaps serve as a potent reminder of the loss of the synthesis between oral, literary, and performative storytelling in medieval and early modern English culture which Gower and Shakespeare were so much a part of.

If, as I have argued, Shakespeare's play projects Gower as a hybrid of archaic alterity and iconic familiarity, on the modern stage the character necessarily retains his alterity but not his iconic status, and the recent productions have created Gower as a figure of cultural otherness while neglecting his role as author, a recognizable icon of medieval literature. A cynic might contend that even if today's audiences were presented with Gower as Greene describes him appearing on the Globe stage four hundred years ago or as he appears on his effigy, they would not recognize him. Somewhere between the seventeenth century and the present day, Gower lost his prominence as an icon of English literary culture and regrettably is remembered in relation to his better-known contemporary Geoffrey Chaucer rather than for his own work.

Despite the relative obscurity that surrounds the character, several productions have attempted to represent Gower as a medieval English author: Edward Petherbridge's Gower as he appeared in the 1984 BBC Time-Life version is one of the representations closest to Greene's description of the author; Petherbridge presented a figure dressed in a long, plain robe with gray hair and beard and looking distinctly "pale" and "wan," as was Griffith Jones's portrayal in the Royal Shakespeare Company's production directed by Ron Daniels in 1979, in which Jones appeared in a long, "medieval-looking" garb.[42] However, whether an audience would necessarily and immediately interpret such portrayals as an honest and readily identifiable reflection of the poet is uncertain. Gower is certainly alive and well today among medieval scholars, though his poetry has yet to be taught or read on the same level as the works of Chaucer in high schools, colleges, and universities.[43]

Finally, does the visual iconicity that Gower still retained in Shakespeare's day now belong to the Bard himself? Having, in collaboration with his fellow playwrights and actors, exposed the vulnerable status of Gower's authorship, Shakespeare has become an authoritative symbol of insurmountable literary genius and authorship. As an emblematic image deeply entrenched in popular cultural consciousness, Shakespeare is a cultural icon that is as easily recognizable as Gower was in the seventeenth century. With recourse to his costume and archaic speech patterns, Shakespeare is extensively recognized, even by those who are unfamiliar with his plays, as a bald figure dressed in black with a prominent angular white collar, displaying a hint of, if not a full, moustache and beard and possibly clutching a quill in one hand. Should such a figure speak, archaic and anachronistically elaborate iambic rhythms would flow forth from his lips. The image is so well known that it can be subjected to caricature. If, as this essay argues, *Pericles* demonstrates the problematic authority of literary authorship divorced from its codependency upon performance culture, it is necessary to realize, too, that the literary and iconic authority of Shakespeare is itself a cultural construction and that the Bard himself participates in the unstable performance of authorship.

Furthermore, I would venture that despite, or perhaps because of, the play's literary imperfections, it may constitute the most perfectly theatrical text in the canon. Barbara Everett claims that the play is "almost always wonderful in the theatre," and I align my voice with that of Everett when she suggests that perchance the "badness" of *Pericles* was a conscious ploy on the part of Shakespeare.[44] Perhaps, seeing that the 1623 Folio addressed itself to "the Great Variety of Readers" with its aim of transforming theatrical play into the literary authority of Shakespeare's authorship, it would have been a formidable infringement on the status of the play for John Heminges and Henry Condell, when they compiled the Folio, to have incorporated into the collection *Pericles*, a play that portrays a character that so stoically resists the stability of his own literary authority. If this is the case, rather than trying to ascertain which parts of the play "belong" to

Shakespeare's hand, it may be more advisable to invest energy in realizing the demonstrable theatrical potency of the play, a theatrical energy epitomized in the representation of Gower.

Perhaps modern directors feel an inclination to dislocate the Englishness of Gower culturally and geographically in order to unleash this theatrical potential, reveling in the anachronism and inaccuracy of their projection of Gower as medieval author. In "Teaching the Middle Ages on Film," Martha Driver speaks of the film medium's capacity to offer audiences a way of engaging with an imagined historical past, however anachronistic and historically inaccurate such a representation maybe.[45] Driver's thesis certainly illuminates the power of performance in that whether it is mediated via film or theater, it can revel in its capacity to delight, entertain, and "quicken" the human imagination. Shakespeare's play must be seen not to disseminate the "dead" literary authority of a medieval poet nor to aspire to propound the playwright's own pretentious literary genius as a canonized author but instead to take an ostensible delight in storytelling itself as a pleasurable practice that shall only, as Shakespeare's Gower himself asserts, "for itself, itself perform" (3.0.54).

NOTES

1. The title is an appropriation of director Sam Raimi's film *The Quick and the Dead*, USA: Columbia, TriStar (1995). The title is also a reference to Christ's judgment of "the quick and the dead" in the Nicene Creed as it appears in the Book of Common Prayer as revised under Edward and Elizabeth I. The author is grateful to the editors for this observation.

2. For a more detailed exploration of the mystery plays and their dramatic function within medieval culture, see V. A. Kolve, *The Play Called "Corpus Christi"* (Stanford, CA: Stanford University Press, 1966); Clifford Davidson, *From Creation to Doom: The York Cycle of Mystery Plays* (New York: AMS Press, 1984); and Peter Happé, *English Drama before Shakespeare* (Harlow, UK, and New York: Longman, 1999).

3. The *Tretise* has attracted a significant amount of attention in recent years, most notably from Lawrence M. Clopper, "Miracula and *The Tretise of Miraclis Pleyinge*," *Speculum* 65, no. 4 (October 1990): 878–905, in which Clopper argues that the *Tretise* is not implicitly antitheatrical but is rather to be seen as a criticism of a certain kind of play that involved licentious parody and "tricks intended to delight and amuse people and which, in many cases, led people to devalue the truth of God's miracles" (902). Clopper's thesis hinges upon a reexamination of the contextual significance of the word "miracula," which has often (erroneously, Clopper contends) been applied to describe the medieval religious pageants. However, more recently Glending Olson has challenged Clopper's argument in "Plays as Play: A Medieval Ethical Theory of Performance and the Intellectual Context of the *Tretise of Miraclis Pleyinge*," *Viator* 26 (1995): 195–221. In an analysis of how the *Tretise* can illuminate certain scholastic formulations toward a theory of play and medieval performance by illustrating a distinction made between various kinds of performance and playing, Olson argues that Clopper fails to account for the moments in the *Tretise* that censor the more mimetic and serious forms of play. For Olson, as with Erick Kelemen, "Drama in Sermons: Quotation, Performativity, and Conversion in a Middle English Sermon on the Prodigal Son and in *A Tretise of Miraclis Pleyinge*," *English Literary History*, 69, no. 1 (Spring 2002): 1–19, the tract remains overtly antitheatrical in its attitudes toward dramatic performance.

4. Cited in Greg Walker, ed., *Medieval Drama: An Anthology* (Malden, MA, and Oxford: Blackwell Publishers, 2000), 198; cf. Clifford Davidson's 1993 edition of the text.

5. Cited in Walker, *Medieval Drama*, 200.

6. STC 22335. Another primary source for the play was Laurence Twyne's novel, *The Patterne of Painefull Adventures* (1594; repr. 1607). STC 709, 709.5, 710.

7. All citations from *Pericles* are taken from *Pericles, Prince of Tyre*, ed. Doreen DelVecchio and Antony Hammond, The New Cambridge Shakespeare (Cambridge, UK: Cambridge University Press, 1998). All other citations from the plays of William Shakespeare are taken from *The Oxford Shakespeare: The Complete Works*, 2nd ed., ed. John Jowett, William Montgomery, Gary Taylor, and Stanley Wells (Oxford: Oxford University Press, 2005).

8. See Robert F. Yeager, "Shakespeare as Medievalist" in this volume, 218.

9. The concept of liminality derives from Arnold van Gennep, *Rites of Passage*, trans. Monika B. Vizedom and Gabrielle L. Cafee (Chicago: University of Chicago Press, 1960), and is used to describe the unfixed mode of transition between two states of being. "Liminality" has been reappropriated in reference to theatrical performance through the work of the performance anthropologist Victor Turner. Douglas Bruster and Robert

Weimann draw upon Turner's definition and claim that their concept of the liminal properties of the prologue finds "confirmation in Turner's declaration that the transitional (or, in his phrase, 'midliminal') state is often marked by the paradoxical: 'the most characteristic midliminal symbolism is that of paradox, or being *both* this *and* that'"; Victor Turner, "Variations on a Theme of Liminality," in *Secular Ritual*, ed. Sally F. Moore and Barbara G. Myerhoff, 37 (Assen, Netherlands: Van Gorcum, 1997); Douglas Bruster and Robert Weimann, *Prologues to Shakespeare's Theatre: Performance and Liminality in Early Modern Drama* (London and New York: Routledge, 2004), 39. Also, for a discussion of the liminal role of the ghost on the sixteenth- and seventeenth-century stage, cf. Stephen Greenblatt, *Hamlet in Purgatory* (Princeton, NJ: Princeton University Press, 2002). Greenblatt aligns ghostly presence with theatrical presence and explores the theatricality of ghosts and the idea of the stage as a kind of Purgatory. Greenblatt's argument is directly pertinent to examination of the theatrical resurrection of the dead, and perhaps there is scope for future research to develop Greenblatt's argument with reference to the appearance of Gower in *Pericles*.

10. Explorations of the role of Gower in Shakespeare's play appear to be somewhat limited, but two important articles on the subject of the appearance of Gower in *Pericles* are F. David Hoeniger, "Gower and Shakespeare in *Pericles*," *Shakespeare Quarterly* 33 (1982): 461–479; and Richard Hillman, "Shakespeare's Gower and Gower's Shakespeare: The Larger Debt of *Pericles*," *Shakespeare Quarterly* 36 (1985): 427–437.

11. Barbara Everett, "By the Rough Seas Reft: How the 'Badness' of the *Pericles* Quarto May Be of Shakespeare's Making," *Times Literary Supplement*, August 11, 2006, 13.

12. STC 25638.5. Cited in Barbara Mowat, "The Theater and Literary Culture," in *A New History of Early English Drama*, ed. John D. Cox and David Scott Kastan (New York: Colombia University Press, 1997), 219. Mowat discusses the problems of the play's status as a literary text. For Taylor's version of the play, see *The Oxford Shakespeare*.

13. Ben Jonson, "Ode to Himselfe" (21), in *The Complete Poetry of Ben Jonson*, ed. William B. Hunter Jr. (New York: New York University Press, 1963) 386–388.

14. Jonson, "Ode to Himself" (25), 387: John Tatham, "To My Worthy Friend, Master Richard Brome, on his Excellent Play Called *A Jovial Crew: or, The Merry Beggars*," in Richard Brome, *A Jovial Crew*, ed. Ann Haaker (Lincoln: University of Nebraska Press, 1968), 10; emphasis in original.

15. Bruster and Weimann, *Prologues to Shakespeare's Theatre*, viii. Bruster and Weimann assert that the Prologue occupied a position on the *platea* space, a fluid area of the dramatic space that had no fixed locality assigned to it and where the stage could be seen for what it was: a stage and an area of performance. The *platea* space was distinct from the *locus*: the stage area integrated with the fictional world of the play and used symbolically to represent location. For a more detailed discussion of the interrelationship between the *platea* and *locus* and how this relationship extended into the English Renaissance theater, see Robert Weimann, *Shakespeare and the Popular Tradition in the Theater: Studies in the Social Dimension of Dramatic Form and Function*, ed. Robert Schwartz (Baltimore and London: Johns Hopkins Press, 1978).

16. Bruster and Weimann, *Prologues to Shakespeare's Theatre*, 33.

17. Ibid., 72–73.

18. Steven Mullaney, *The Place of the Stage: License, Play, and Power in Renaissance England* (Chicago and London: University of Chicago Press, 1988).

19. Bruster and Weimann, *Prologues to Shakespeare's Theatre*, 44.

20. For examples of this, see Susanna Greer Fein, "A Thirteen-Line Alliterative Stanza on the Abuse of Prayer from the Audelay MS," *Medium Aevum* 63 (1994): 61–74, 64, discussing references to Titivillus in the fifteenth-century Audelay manuscript.

21. STC 17412. Christopher Marlowe, *The Jew of Malta*, edited by N. W. Bawcutt (Manchester, UK: Manchester University Press, 1997), 66. Weimann also discusses Machiavel's role as prologue in Bruster and Weimann, *Prologues to Shakespeare's Theatre*, 95–97.

22. For further examination of the relationship between Richard III and the medieval Vice, see Lesley Wade Soule, *Actor as Anti-Character: Dionysus, the Devil, and the Boy Rosalind* (Westport, CT, and London: Greenwood Press, 2000), 104–107; and Weimann, *Shakespeare and the Popular Tradition*, 160.

23. STC 12261. Cited in *The Oxford Shakespeare: The Complete Works*, 2nd ed., 1060.

24. Robert Weimann, *Author's Pen and Actor's Voice: Playing and Writing in Shakespeare's Theatre*, ed. Helen Higbee and William West (Cambridge, UK: Cambridge University Press, 2000), 48. Cited in Bruster and Weimann, *Prologues to Shakespeare's Theatre*, 60.

25. Bruster and Weimann, *Prologues to Shakespeare's Theatre*, 60.

26. Weimann, *Author's Pen and Actor's Voice*, 62–70, both explores and exploits the terms used by the Prologue to Shakespeare's *Troilus and Cressida*, who announces that he has come "A Prologue armed, but not in confidence / Of author's pen or actor's voice" (Prologue, 23–24), to describe the two competing and sometimes complimentary modes of power of the textual authority of the playwright's text and the actor's performative authority. Such a relationship is highly pertinent in the context of *Pericles*, wherein Gower is reliant upon both forms of authority for his mediation as an integrated character, actor, author, and storyteller.

27. Mullaney, *The Place of the Stage*, 148–149.

28. F. D. Hoeniger, "Introduction," in *The Arden Shakespeare: "Pericles"* (London and New York: Methuen, 1963), xiv.

29. Brian Stock, *Listening for the Text: On the Uses of the Past* (Baltimore and London: Johns Hopkins University Press, 1990), 9. Cited in John D. Niles, *Homo Narrans: The Poetics and Anthropology of Oral Literature* (Philadelphia: University of Pennsylvania Press, 1999), 127.

30. Niles, *Homo Narrans*, 127.

31. William B. Worthen, *Shakespeare and the Authority of Performance* (Cambridge, UK: Cambridge University Press, 1997), 8; emphasis in original.

32. Cited in Hoeniger, "Introduction," liii.

33. G. C. Macaulay, ed., *The Complete Works of John Gower*, 4. vols. (Oxford: Clarendon Press, 1899–1901).

34. On the relationship between storytelling and the contemporary theater, see Michael Wilson, *Storytelling and Theatre: Contemporary Storytellers and Their Art* (Hampshire, UK, and New York: Palgrave, 2006).

35. 1984 *Pericles: Prince of Tyre*, d. David Jones, with Mike Gwilym, Edward Petherbridge, Amanda Redman, John Woodvine, Annette Crosbie and Juliet Stevenson, UK: BBC TV.

36. DelVecchio and Hammond, "Introduction," 23, also refers to Gower's "otherness" in the context of performance.

37. Samuel L. Leiter, ed., *Shakespeare around the Globe: A Guide to Notable Postwar Revivals* (New York, Westport, CT, and London: Greenwood Press, 1986): 555–560; DelVecchio and Hammond, "Introduction," 20. See list of productions for details.

38. Peter Holland, *English Shakespeares: Shakespeare on the English Stage in the 1990s* (Cambridge, UK: Cambridge University Press, 1997), 64–65; see also Lyn Gardner's review for *City Limits*, April 26, 1990, and Jim Hiley's review for *Listener*, April 26, 1990. Both reviews are reprinted in *Theatre Record*, April 9–22, 1990, 493.

39. Cf. Kate Bassett's review for *Independent on Sunday*, April 6, 2003; Alistair Macaulay's review for *Financial Times*, April 1, 2003; and Paul Taylor's review for *The Independent*, April 3, 2003. All reviews are reprinted in *Theatre Record*, March 26–April 8, 2003, 409–413.

40. Cf. Nicholas de Jongh's review for *Evening Standard*, June 3, 2005; Simon Edge's review for *Daily Express*, June 3, 2005; Michael Billington's review for *The Guardian*, June 6, 2005; Paul Taylor's review for *The Independent*, June 6, 2005, and Sarah Hemming's review for *Financial Times*, June 8, 2005. All reviews are reprinted in *Theatre Record*, May 21–June 3, 2005, 744–747.

41. In his review, Simon Edge wrote, "The point of the Globe is to make the Bard accessible by doing him in an engaging way. The director clearly thinks Pericles [sic] is too dull to show on its own terms, and she may be right." Edge, *Daily Express*, June 3, 2005, cited in *Theatre Record*, May 21–June 3, 2005, 744.

42. The author would like to thank David Rabey for this observation regarding Griffith Jones's performance.

43. Scholars are currently working on "The Gower Project," a hypertext scheme developed to create a forum for discussion for those interested in the poet's work (http://people.westminstercollege.edu/faculty/gdonavin/gower/). Hypertext, by its very nature, boasts an ephemeral theatricality of its own through which the individual reader will construct his or her own unique intertextual reading of Gower's "literary" authority. The site contains bibliographical lists that direct the reader to modern publications of Gower's work, scholarly articles about Gower's texts, details of future meetings for Gower enthusiasts, and links to other sources that appertain to Gower and his work. As in Shakespeare's play, the project must necessarily depart from the static "dead" authority associated with dusty old books to capture the audience's enthusiasm via an innovative and multimediated framework of presentation.

44. Everett, "By the Rough Seas Reft," 15.

45. Martha Driver, "Teaching the Middle Ages on Film: Visual Narrative and the Historical Record," *History Compass* 5, no. 1 (2007): 146–161.

Works Cited

Bassett, Kate. Review of *Pericles* at the Olivier Theatre. *Independent on Sunday*, April 6, 2003, repr. in *Theatre Record*, March 26–April 8, 2003, 409–410.

Billington, Michael. Review of *Pericles* at Shakespeare's Globe. *The Guardian*, June 6, 2005. Reprinted in *Theatre Record*, May 21–June 3, 2005, 744–747.

Brome, Richard. *A Jovial Crew*. Edited by Ann Haaker. Lincoln: University of Nebraska Press, 1968.

Bruster, Douglas, and Robert Weimann. *Prologues to Shakespeare's Theatre: Performance and Liminality in Early Modern Drama*. London and New York: Routledge, 2004.

Clopper, Lawrence M. "Miracula and *The Tretise of Miraclis Pleyinge*." *Speculum* 65, no. 4 (October 1990): 878–905.
Davidson, Clifford. *From Creation to Doom: The York Cycle of Mystery Plays*. New York: AMS Press, 1984.
_____. ed. *Tretise of Miraclis Pleyinge*. Kalamazoo, MI: Medieval Institute Publications, 1993.
de Jongh, Nicholas. Review of *Pericles* at Shakespeare's Globe. *Evening Standard*, June 3, 2005. Reprinted in *Theatre Record*, May 21–June 3, 2005, 744–747.
DelVecchio, Doreen, and Antony Hammond. "Introduction." In *The New Cambridge Shakespeare: "Pericles*,*"* by William Shakespeare. Cambridge, UK: Cambridge University Press, 1998, 1–80.
Driver, Martha. "Teaching the Middle Ages on Film: Visual Narrative and the Historical Record." *History Compass* 5, no. 1 (2007): 146–161.
Edge, Simon. Review of *Pericles* at Shakespeare's Globe. *Daily Express*, June 3, 2005. Reprinted in *Theatre Record*, May 21–June 3, 2005, 744–747.
Everett, Barbara. "By the Rough Seas Reft: How the 'Badness' of the *Pericles* Quarto May Be of Shakespeare's Making." *Times Literary Supplement*, August 11, 2006, 13–16.
Fein, Susanna Greer. "A Thirteen-Line Alliterative Stanza on the Abuse of Prayer from the Audelay MS." *Medium Aevum* 63 (1994): 61–74.
Gardner, Lyn. Review of *Pericles* at the Pit. *City Limits*, April 26, 1990. Reprinted in *Theatre Record*, April 9–22, 1990, 493.
Greenblatt, Stephen. *Hamlet in Purgatory*. Princeton, NJ: Princeton University Press, 2002.
Happé, Peter. *English Drama before Shakespeare*. Harlow, UK, and New York: Longman, 1999.
Hemming, Sarah. Review of *Pericles* at Shakespeare's Globe. *Financial Times*, 8 June 2005. Reprinted in *Theatre Record*, May 21–June 3, 2005, 744–747.
Hiley, Jim. Review of *Pericles* at the Pit. *Listener*, 26 April 1990. Reprinted in *Theatre Record*, April 9–22, 1990, 493.
Hillman, Richard. "Shakespeare's Gower and Gower's Shakespeare: The Larger Debt of *Pericles*." *Shakespeare Quarterly* 36 (1985): 427–437.
Hoeniger, F. David. "Gower and Shakespeare in *Pericles*." *Shakespeare Quarterly* 33 (1982): 461–479.
_____. "Introduction." In *The Arden Edition of the Works of William Shakespeare: "Pericles*,*"* by William Shakespeare. London and New York: Methuen, 1963, xiii–xci.
Holland, Peter. *English Shakespeares: Shakespeare on the English Stage in the 1990s*. Cambridge, UK: Cambridge University Press, 1997.
Jonson, Ben. "An Ode to Himselfe." In *The Complete Poetry of Ben Jonson*. Edited by William B. Hunter, Jr. New York: New York University Press, 1963.
Kelemen, Erick. "Drama in Sermons: Quotation, Performativity, and Conversion in a Middle English Sermon on the Prodigal Son and in *A Tretise of Miraclis Pleyinge*." *English Literary History* 69, no. 1 (Spring 2002): 1–19.
Kolve, V. A. *The Play Called "Corpus Christi."* Stanford, CA: Stanford University Press, 1966.
Leiter, Samuel L., ed. *Shakespeare around the Globe: A Guide to Notable Postwar Revivals*. New York, Westport, CT, and London: Greenwood Press, 1986.
Macaulay, Alistair. Review of *Pericles* at the Olivier Theatre. *Financial Times*, April 1, 2003. Reprinted in *Theatre Record*, March 26–April 8, 2003, 411.
Macaulay, G. C., ed. *The Complete Works of John Gower*. 4 vols. Oxford: Clarendon Press, 1899–1901.
Marlowe, Christopher. *The Jew of Malta*. Edited by N. W. Bawcutt. Manchester, UK: Manchester University Press, 1997.
Mowat, Barbara. "The Theater and Literary Culture." In *A New History of Early English Drama*. Edited by John D. Cox and David Scott Kastan, 213–230. New York: Columbia University Press, 1997.
Mullaney, Steven. *The Place of the Stage: License, Play, and Power in Renaissance England*. Chicago and London: University of Chicago Press, 1988.
Niles, John D. *Homo Narrans: The Poetics and Anthropology of Oral Literature*. Philadelphia: University of Pennsylvania Press, 1999.
Olson, Glending. "Plays as Play: A Medieval Ethical Theory of Performance and the Intellectual Context of the *Tretise of Miraclis Pleyinge*." *Viator* 26 (1995): 195–221.
Shakespeare, William. *The Oxford Shakespeare: The Complete Works*. 2nd ed. Edited by John Jowett, William Montgomery, Gary Taylor, and Stanley Wells. Oxford: Oxford University Press, 2005.
_____. Pericles, Prince of Tyre. Edited by Doreen DelVecchio and Antony Hammond. The New Cambridge Shakespeare. Cambridge, UK: Cambridge University Press, 1998.
Stock, Brian. *Listening for the Text: On the Uses of the Past*. Baltimore and London: Johns Hopkins University Press, 1990.
Taylor, Paul. Review of *Pericles* at the Olivier Theatre. *The Independent*, April 3, 2003. Reprinted in *Theatre Record*, March 26–April 8, 2003, 411–412.

———. Review of *Pericles* at Shakespeare's Globe. *The Independent*, June 6, 2005, Reprinted in *Theatre Record*, May 21–June 3, 2005, 744–747.
van Gennep, Arnold. *Rites of Passage*. Translated by Monika B. Vizedom and Gabrielle L. Cafee. Chicago: University of Chicago Press, 1960.
Wade Soule, Lesley. *Actor as Anti-Character: Dionysus, the Devil, and the Boy Rosalind*. Westport, CT, and London: Greenwood Press, 2000.
Walker, Greg, ed. *Medieval Drama: An Anthology*. Malden, MA, and Oxford: Blackwell Publishers, 2000.
Weimann, Robert. *Author's Pen and Actor's Voice: Playing and Writing in Shakespeare's Theatre*. Edited by Helen Higbee and William West. Cambridge, UK: Cambridge University Press, 2000.
———. *Shakespeare and the Popular Tradition in the Theater: Studies in the Social Dimension of Dramatic Form and Function*. Edited by Robert Schwartz. Baltimore and London: Johns Hopkins University Press, 1978.
Wilson, Michael. *Storytelling and Theatre: Contemporary Storytellers and Their Art*. Hampshire, UK, and New York: Palgrave, 2006.
Worthen, William. *Shakespeare and the Authority of Performance*. Cambridge, UK: Cambridge University Press, 1997.

FILMOGRAPHY AND PERFORMANCES

1958 *Pericles*, d. Tony Richardson, with Richard Johnson, Edric Connor, Stephanie Bidmead, and Geraldine McEwan. Stratford-upon-Avon.
1969 *Pericles*, d. Terry Hands, with Ian Richardson, Emrys James, and Susan Fleetwood. Stratford-upon-Avon.
1979 *Pericles*, d. Ron Daniels, with Peter McEnery, Griffith Jones, Emily Richard, and Julie Peasgood. Stratford-upon-Avon.
1984 *Pericles: Prince of Tyre*, d. David Jones, with Mike Gwilym, Edward Petherbridge, Amanda Redman, John Woodvine, Annette Crosbie, and Juliet Stevenson. UK: BBC TV (DVD).
1990 *Pericles*, d. David Thacker, with Nigel Terry, Rudolph Walker, Sally Edwards, and Suzan Sylvester, Stratford-upon-Avon.
1995 *The Quick and the Dead*, d. Sam Raimi, with Sharon Stone, Gene Hackman, and Russell Crowe. USA: Columbia, TriStar (DVD).
2003 *Pericles*, d. Yukio Ninagawa, with Masaaki Uchino, Masachika Ichmura, Kayoko Shiraishi, and Yuko Tanaka. London.
2005 *Pericles*, d. Kathryn Hunter, with Corin Redgrave, Patrice Naiambana, Hilary Tones, and Laura Rees. London.

Shakespeare as Medievalist: What It Means for Performing *Pericles*

R. F. Yeager

Writing circa 1998, Harold Bloom observes of *Pericles*:

it is the only play in Shakespeare I would rather attend again than reread, and not just because the text has been so marred by transmission. Perhaps because he declined to compose the first two acts, Shakespeare compensated by making the remaining three acts into his most radical theatrical experiment since the mature *Hamlet* of 1600–1601.[1]

Apart from placing *Pericles* and *Hamlet* in the same category (a judgment perhaps uniquely his, and one that — slyly — he leaves unexplained), Bloom's remarks capture in short space the reputational and scholarly histories of *Pericles* from its completion and first performance in 1607 or 1608 until the present day. Always better liked when seen than read, especially by those concerned to ascertain (and reserve their appreciation for) the "real" Shakespeare, the play's text has posed problems seemingly from the beginning.[2] John Hemminge and Henry Condell, for whatever reason, omitted *Pericles* from the First Folio, with the result that its Folio debut (in the Third in 1663 or 1664) and all subsequent editions derive from a single surviving source, a quarto defective especially in the opening two acts. From this omission, and from the sometimes line-by-line correspondence, especially in those "marred" first two acts, of the play with a novella by George Wilkins entitled *The Painfull Adventures of Pericles Prince of Tyre* and entered into the Stationers' Register in 1608, doubts developed early on about how fully *Pericles* reflects Shakespeare's hand.[3] That such doubts persist, Bloom offers witness.[4]

Why this history of textual transmission and attribution should matter when considering a "medievalist" Shakespeare in performance may be stated directly: what is not thought Shakespeare's is fairest game for cutting or transforming by directors always on the lookout for ways to put their own mark upon the Bard. Indeed, over the years those portions of the play most tampered with onstage have been the first two acts — the "Wilkins acts," as many, including Bloom, would have it — with consequent repercussions upon the shape of the "Shakespearean" (by agreement) latter three. And so, too, upon any view of Shakespeare's medievalism, which necessarily must devolve from his initial taking up and first conceiving of the raw material whence came *Pericles* — in this case, primarily the fourteenth-century English poet John Gower's *Confessio Amantis*.[5] And since "Gower," in full medieval rigging, was written in as the first player onstage, introducing act 1, early pruning of the script necessarily hampers any audience's recognition of *Pericles*'s medieval parameters. Thus, even as it well exceeds the present scope to resolve authorial issues so fraught for so long, yet they must be recognized, largely as hindrances, while looking past them to recuperate a medievalist Shakespeare.[6]

For Bloom is correct (and speaks for most scholars) in his ultimate assessment that *Pericles, Prince of Tyre* represents at least a "radical theatrical experiment," if not also marking something of a brash moment for Shakespeare. It was the first of four romances that he wrote just eight or nine years before the end of his life — years that together yielded but seven plays. Shakespeare was stepping back; Stratford was beckoning, and at such a juncture most, perhaps, might propitiate the reliable.[7] With *Pericles*, however, Shakespeare embarked into water that, if not altogether unsounded on the contemporary stage, was nonetheless original to him.[8] Apparently the daring leap was worth it: in the new (for him) genre, he seems to have found a secret sufficient to hold his interest and delight his audiences as well. *Pericles* was a great commercial success — the King's Men performed it often — and Shakespeare went on to write three more plays in like vein: *Cymbeline*, *A Winter's Tale* and *The Tempest*, of which the latter two are generally considered masterpieces.[9]

Viewed, then, from the vantage point of a new and original theatrical embarkation, one all the more striking by virtue of its occurrence late in a long-running, highly successful career, contemplating precisely how Shakespeare came to take up the writing of *Pericles* has significant pertinence. There are many theories. For present purposes, however, they may perhaps be elided into two: either (as the pervading wisdom has had it) Shakespeare came on board after *Pericles* was started by (an)other hand(s) (Wilkins is not alone as favored candidate), the writing having advanced as far as the first two acts; or he was involved from the beginning, either as sole author or as a *primus inter pares* who eventually absorbed the project whole, probably beginning no later than act 3.[10] Notably, in both cases the seminal question — what drew him to the material and held his interest? — remains the same.

The answer, I think, lies specifically in what Shakespeare recognized as "medieval" in *Pericles*'s primary source, the tale of "Apollonius of Tyre" as told by John Gower (d. 1408) in his polyvalent Middle English poem, the *Confessio Amantis* — and in what is revealed by all Shakespeare incorporated into his play to draw out the "medieval" from his source, pointedly foregrounding it for his audience. For this claim it matters not whether Shakespeare first found the play underway or sought out the *Confessio* himself; there is no doubt that he knew and used Gower's poem.

Indeed, although the narrative of Apollonius was available in several versions in seventeenth-century London,[11] Shakespeare apparently encountered Gower's poem early on, since he turned to it while writing *The Comedy of Errors*, dated usually around 1589 to 1593.[12] We can even be fairly sure about the form in which he saw it. During Shakespeare's lifetime the *Confessio Amantis* existed only in manuscript, in a black-letter edition of Caxton's of 1483, and in two quarto editions from Thomas Berthelette, "Printer to the Kingis grace," dated 1532 and 1554.[13] Berthelette's volumes were the most common, and for another reason (to be explained shortly) a copy of one of them was almost certainly what Shakespeare read.

This, it turns out, is no unimportant bit of knowledge. Berthelette's approach to printing the *Confessio Amantis* merits consideration, for it presents both Gower the poet in a biographical sketch filling several pages and his text in a manner "consistent with the early Renaissance conception of the Middle Ages."[14] Thus we learn from Berthelette in his prefatory matter that Gower was a friend of Chaucer with whom he shares honor as a father of English poetry and a model of proper English, that Gower was unexceptionably probative and moral, that he was deeply learned, and — because Berthelette records that still in 1532 masses were being sung for Gower at his tomb at St. Mary Overes in Southwark and describes a plaque hanging beside it "wherein appereth that who so euer praieth for the soule of John Gower, he shal so oft as he so dothe, haue a thousand and fyue hundred dayes of pardon" — that Gower was noteworthily medieval, that is, Roman Catholic.[15]

Berthelette's page layout also conjures the Middle Ages by mimicking, *mutatis mutandis*, the format of his manuscript copytext. While Gower composed the bulk of the *Confessio* in Middle English octosyllabic couplets, he added verses in Latin to designate sections and interpretive Latin prose paragraphs as well, which appear variously in the extant manuscripts either in the margins or within the columns of Middle English poetry, usually highlighted in red ink. The result of this mixture of English poetry and rubricized Latin prose and verse was a clearly intentional bilingual "conversation." In Gower's poem, the narrative fiction becomes the subject of what amounts to two running commentaries, each "speaking" in a distinct literary "voice."[16] Berthelette, who imbeds the Latin prose in the poetry, apparently worked from a manuscript of the latter kind, replicating his medieval model as far as he could by changing his typefaces: larger black letter for the Middle English verse, smaller black letter for the interpretive Latin prose, and roman for the Latin verses. The differing type maintains—even emphasizes—Gower's formalized "conversation," making especially the Latin prose seem to stand away from its placement in the column of English verse, as if (translating this into dramatic terms) speaking in an aside. (Indeed, the overall effect has even led one critic to suggest Berthelette's "medieval" page layout as Shakespeare's inspiration for the role of Gower in the play.)[17]

Arguably, then, when Shakespeare encountered Gower and his *Confessio Amantis* in Berthelette's edition, he was confronted, both overtly and subliminally, with an ancestral figure whose language(s), poetic expectations, and moral ethos were of the Middle Ages. Of course, Shakespeare would have shared this view of Gower and his poetry with a number, if not the majority, of his literate contemporaries, most of whom, like him, used Berthelette's editions, and in some cases— signally Robert Greene, Ben Jonson, and John Webster—cast Gower in similar light in compositions of their own.[18] Of these, Greene's treatment of Gower, in a work called *Greenes Vision*, is particularly interesting.[19] Unlike Jonson's masque *The Golden Age Restored* (1615) and Webster's pageant *Monuments of Honour*, written for the Merchant Taylors (1624), *Greenes Vision* was in print in 1592 and so could have influenced Shakespeare imagining *Pericles*.[20]

Gower has the major part in *Greenes Vision* (versus wordless cameos in Jonson's masque and Webster's pageant). The bulk of the text is a lengthy debate in prose between Chaucer and Gower, who appear to Greene on what he thinks will be his deathbed, about the true value of literature. Pointedly, the "aunticent"—that is, medieval—characteristics of both poets are stressed to some degree in their manner of speech and in the opinions each expresses, and in descriptions (in "Gowerian stanza": tetrameter couplets) of their clothing. Chaucer takes the position that, essentially, literature should be entertaining; Gower, on the other hand, upholds its primary value to be instructive. Each provides a tale to illustrate his claim. Chaucer's narrative recalls the plot and tone of the "Miller's Tale." Gower, condemning Chaucer for bawdry, offers an exemplum of a foolish husband who tests his wife's faithfulness, only to find her virtuous through and through. The testing provides "Gower" with the opportunity to moralize broadly about both life and art— and Greene, impressed by the poet's many "graue sentences" (and supported by Solomon, who arrives at the end to help pass judgment in favor not just of exemplary writing but also of theology as the only true study), falls in with "Gower's" position that literature should be morally and spiritually uplifting.

Greene's portrait of "Gower" in his *Vision*, then, reinforces a view both of the poet as moral authority and of the "medieval" as its essential field of discovery. It would be good to know whether Shakespeare read the *Vision* (how could he not?) and if it was in his mind when he sought out Berthelette to dramatize from the *Confessio*.[21]

Hence it is equally, if not *more*, important to point out that neither Shakespeare nor any in his audience had to find "moral Gower" the medieval poet in Berthelette alone. They might, for example, have turned him up as well at the conclusion of Chaucer's *Troilus and Criseyde*, where Chaucer gave his friend the sobriquet that has proven so unshakeable; Shakespeare surely did so when he converted Chaucer's poem into drama as *Troilus and Cressida* in 1601 to 1602.[22] And Shakespeare's world was, comparatively speaking, awash in volumes of Chaucer: alongside black letters of various individual works from the shops of William Caxton, Richard Pynson, Wynkyn de Worde, and Julian Notary, there was a collected *Works* edited by William Thynne in 1528 (revised, with additions, in 1542 and 1550), another (with much pseudo-Chaucerian material, falsely attributed) edited by John Stow in 1561, and in 1598, yet another *Works* compiled by Thomas Speght, who added a pair of (non–Chaucerian) poems and a "scholarly" apparatus.[23]

Or they could have gone to see "Gower" for themselves — as definitely many of them did, as often as once a week, at least in effigy. For Gower's tomb, described by Berthelette in his edition and topped by a near-life-size figure of the poet, his medieval clothing once painted in lifelike colors, his head supported by three labeled volumes of his works, then as now rested in the nave of what Shakespeare knew as St. Saviour's Church in Southwark (currently Southwark Cathedral).[24] St. Saviour's was the "theatrical parish": all the major Bankside theatres, including the Globe, resided within its bounds, and it served the religious needs of the dramatic community. Almost half the actors whose names appear in the First Folio are to be found listed in St. Saviour's registers, including Edward Alleyne, who, along with Philip Henslowe, owner of the Rose, was a vestryman. John Fletcher and Philip Massinger are both buried there. But doubtless more importantly for Shakespeare (and perhaps significantly for the writing of *Pericles*), William Shakespeare buried his brother Edmund at St. Saviour's in 1607, a year when it seems probable he was at work on the play.[25]

Even judging from these examples, it is clear that Shakespeare's encounters with John Gower were varied in kind and must have been numerous. Pointedly, their contexts all set the poet into full relief as a man of the Middle Ages. This was likely neither to have been overlooked by Shakespeare nor to have bothered him. On the contrary, many of Shakespeare's plays evince an ongoing excavation of the antique past in their choice of subjects: Rome, the Greek Mediterranean, early and late medieval Britain. Indeed, there is a cluster of them written in the years immediately before and after *Pericles*: *King Lear* (c. 1605–1606); *Macbeth* (c. 1606–1607); *Timon of Athens* (c. 1605–08); *Antony and Cleopatra* (1606–1607); *Coriolanus* (c. 1608); *Cymbeline* (c. 1608–1610). With the addition only of *The Winter's Tale* (c. 1609–1611) and *The Tempest* (c. 1611), these comprise the full output of Shakespeare's last years as an active playwright. It is difficult to argue from this list that Shakespeare was more antiquarian in his interests at the end of his life than at the beginning — the history plays are products of the 1590s, for example — but quite obviously he was no less so. Apparently he was looking for *something* in stories from the past: "something old" (as goes the wedding adage) to make something new. What *is* clear is that had Shakespeare turned his interests and search for materials elsewhere (back, say, to the urban Italy of the early comedies) and skipped the Middle Ages, *Pericles* might never have been written.

There are in fact several layers of debt to the Middle Ages discoverable in *Pericles*, any one or two of which might be independently explained away as accidental. Before turning exclusively to Gower and the *Confessio Amantis*, it is perhaps useful to consider some of them briefly. In concert and in context, these debts argue with some persuasion for Shakespeare's scrutiny of texts and sources in order purposefully to create effects that might translate medieval elements overt and covert to (and for) a Jacobean audience. And they make more easily visible what Shakespeare saw in Gower, both as a source and as a character in the cast.

One such debt is the dumb shows. The form is not, of course, strictly speaking medieval.[26] Indeed, unless Shakespeare were a far more scholarly student of the period's literature than likely he was and had somehow run across John Lydgate's mummings, he would have found nothing in the old books resembling a dumb show.[27] "Medieval drama" for Shakespeare undoubtedly meant the morality, miracle, and saints' plays he would have seen in his youth in Stratford and which continued to have some vogue in the countryside even later.[28] (These did have direct influence on *Pericles*, as will be seen below.) Nevertheless, Shakespeare clearly connected dumb shows with the past — and for good reason. The plays in which he would have encountered them were Elizabethan chestnuts: *Gorboduc*, Thomas Kyd's *Spanish Tragedy*, works of the "University Wits," such as *Locrine*.[29] When he wrote a dumb show for the mechanicals' "Pyramus and Thisbe" play in *A Midsummer Night's Dream*, he did so to send up a form at that point evidently so moribund in his view as to be laughable only.[30] And yet the idea of "old" has a way of transforming itself for

Shakespeare in the manner of so much else.[31] In *Hamlet* there are another group of players and another dumb show, but "The Murder of Gonzago," even as it once again demarcates an outmoded theatricality in contrast to Shakespeare's own, has yet another level of historicity, one closer to what is present in *Pericles*. *Hamlet* is, after all, the tale of a medieval Dane. *Macbeth*, too, is set in the Middle Ages. Its dumb show — the "Show of Kings" in act 4 — is closer in date of composition, if not precisely in function, to those in *Pericles*. Notably, however, the archaism of the "Show of Kings," unlike the mechanicals' play or "The Murder of Gonzago," is not the point of its presence in *Macbeth*. Rather, it is fully integrated into the action of the play — and in this it does resemble the later dumb shows, not only in *Pericles* but also in *Cymbeline* (the appearance of Jupiter), in *The Winter's Tale* (the oracle of Apollo), and Prospero's masque in *The Tempest* as well. Such a progression indicates a process in Shakespeare's thought to which the dumb show obviously contributed.

Certainly the form served his muse in several ways, variously to confer cohesion on otherwise disparate scenes, to facilitate the entry of the supernatural (especially at Blackfriars, where special effects were more easily achieved than at the Globe), and probably to capitalize on the rising stock of the masque in court circles under James I. In other words, Shakespeare's use of the dumb show continued to evolve as he turned its formal plasticity to hand in differing contexts and as (doubtless) he had available his own last version to reflect and build upon. Thus for our purposes it is especially important to recall that *Pericles* comes early in the sequence, with *Hamlet* and *Macbeth*—both "medieval" plays in subject if not in approach — as ancestors. And, of course, behind Shakespeare's own work stands *Gorboduc*, a drama in its way extremely medieval, far more so than Kyd's *Spanish Tragedy* or esoteric university work, not only in its particular treatment of the dumb show but also — and significantly — in its moralizing purpose. As a kind of activated *speculum principis*, *Gorboduc* itself hearkens backward to an earlier concept of dramatic necessity, one that has much in common with morality plays and Gower's *Confessio Amantis*. As an incubator for the dumb shows of *Pericles*, *Gorboduc* would have been ideal.

Indeed, arguing that "Obviously Shakespeare would not cultivate an archaic medievalism at this stage in his work without sophisticated ulterior motives," Howard Felperin some time ago successfully uncovered a deep substructure in *Pericles* traceable to miracle plays, saints' plays, and moralities that, while still performed for Shakespeare to observe, nonetheless had their formal and conceptual origins firmly in the Middle Ages and were recognized as archaic by Elizabethans generally.[32] For Felperin, the subject and goal of *Pericles* is "resurrection and restoration"— of Prince Pericles, assuredly, first as public man, then (across the last three acts) as private conscience but also through his experience, as a kind of Everyman, of humanity at large. It was thus to a backward-looking purpose that Shakespeare sought to put his play, however much of a wrenchingly different direction it represented in his work in 1607 and 1608. Pulling this off required, in Felperin's view, that a *Weltanschauung* both "Catholic" and "catholic" in its moral imperatives and scope be recuperated for an audience still "familiar with an exemplary or allegorical kind of drama"— one that could, to put it another way, be induced to revisualize the dramatic by exchanging a "mirror held up to nature" for a *speculum principis*, enough at least to ingest *Pericles*'s intended lesson.[33]

In many ways, this was Gower's purpose, too. Shakespeare's reversion to the *Confessio Amantis* to find a suitably medievalizing vehicle seems, against this background, hardly surprising. That he did not return again to rifle Edward Hall, Raphael Holinshed, or Geoffrey of Monmouth undoubtedly suggests the line in his mind between *history*— albeit of medieval figures who buckle on armor and kill each other with swords — and this new/old, magical/moralizing kind of drama he sought to encompass. (Indeed, it may indicate further a distinction of his between the Middle Ages as *prop*, as stage scenery — present in *Pericles* in the tournament of knights Shakespeare invented in 2.2, an addition puzzling to many — and the "medieval," a concept, even a moral category in his mind, embracing an anachronistic high seriousness bordering on the Roman Catholic.)[34] For if we turn now to Gower, it is clear how well his *Confessio Amantis* would compliment such other medievalizations as are present in *Pericles*. A poem at once didactic and narratively rich, conceived to induce rather than compel radical public and private reform, the *Confessio* works its way gently, much in the manner of *Pericles* itself. As Gower notes in his poem's Prologue, his lessons will emerge for his reader — *if* they emerge — as they do for Pericles, more or less organically, from amidst a lover's tale of woe.

Perhaps these dualities drew Shakespeare back to Gower; perhaps his interest was prompted by a serendipitous melding of James I's anticipated attendance at performances of Shakespeare's King's Men with the royal connections of the *Confessio Amantis*, as Shakespeare would have come to read it. Especially if Shakespeare's was a copy of the 1532 first edition, effusively dedicated by Berthelette to the "learned, good, just and gracious" Henry VIII, Gower's poem could have seemed a monarch's book indeed;[35] for, as the prefatory matter would have informed the reader, it was written at the express command of Richard II and later dedicated a second time to Henry IV.[36] Or perhaps, too, as seems quite likely, Shakespeare, along with Edmund Spenser and many Elizabethans, shared a broad sense that the medieval, with its greater apparent acceptance of the miraculous and magical, was somehow intrinsically apt soil for moral tillage, if done lightly, with sufficient adventure and amorous exercise thrown in.

In any case, Shakespeare evidently intended his audience to confront the action and import of his play through a recurrent, insistently "medieval" lens. It is a process apparently calculated to commence even as the character of Gower stepped onto the stage, prior to his uttering a single line — or so we must believe if, as seems most likely, the woodcut figure from the title page of Wilkins' exploitative *The Painfull Adventures of Pericles Prince of Tyre* ("Printed for T.P. by Nat: Butter, 1608") replicates how Gower appeared in performance.[37] Everything garbing "Gower," from the rounded "window-pane" shoes to the long coat and hose to the beard and earflapped cap, would have shouted "medieval" in the generically recognizable way of stage costume to a Jacobean viewer.[38]

Of course, Shakespeare himself may not have designed the outfit. He did, however, either create or complete the role — itself recalling the antique, since presenters (the technical term for what Gower the character does) would have been most familiar to contemporary audiences as being intrinsic to dumb shows and hence to "old plays" — mysteries, moralities — in general.[39] And certainly Shakespeare put appropriately outmoded words (whether all of them or not) into "ancient Gower's" mouth. It happens immediately. Consider Gower's first speech:

> To sing a song that old was sung,
> From ashes, ancient Gower is come,
> Assuming man's infirmities,
> To glad your ear and please your eyes.
> It hath been sung at festivals,
> On ember-eves and holy days,
> And lords and ladies in their lives
> Have read it for restoratives.
> The purchase is to make men glorious:
> *Et bonum quo antiquius eo melius.*
> If you, born in those latter times
> When wit's more ripe, accept my rhymes,
> And that to hear an old man sing
> May to your wishes pleasure bring,
> I life would wish, and that I might
> Waste it for you, like taper light [1.1.1–16].

The tetrameter couplets (Gower's measure in the *Confessio*), like the "medieval" formulations here — "sing a song that old was sung," "ember-eves and holy days," "lords and ladies" — strike a register impossible to mistake, immediately throwing long-departed time upon the audience.

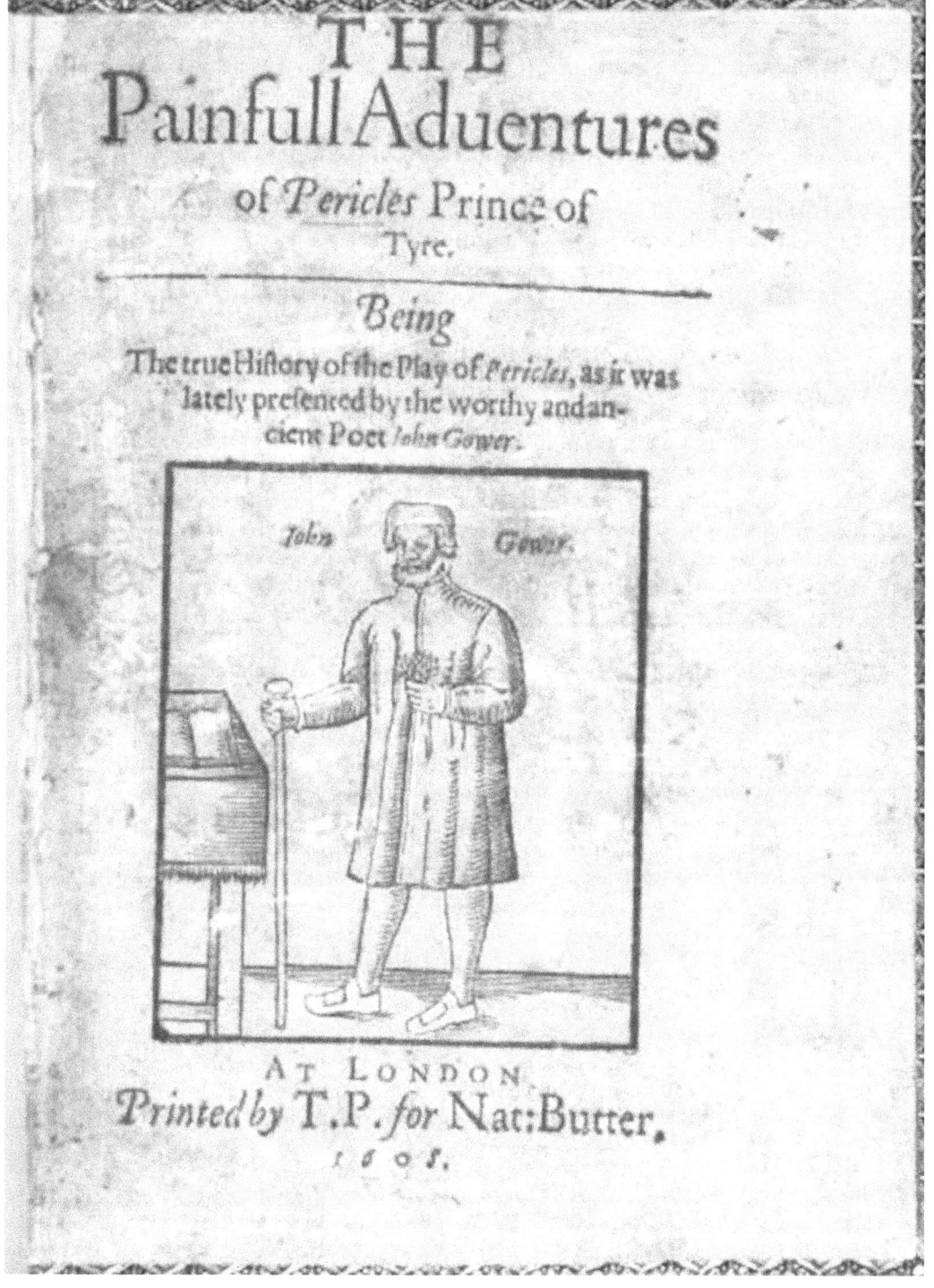

Title page, *The Painfull Adventures of Pericles Prince of Tyre*, represents how Gower appeared in performance. London, "Printed for T.P. by Nat: Butter, 1608." With permission from the British Library.

More and less strictly, such locutions are maintained in Gower's speeches and help define his character throughout *Pericles*.[40] Less readily noticeable, perhaps, is the level of study, especially of Berthelette's edition of the *Confessio*, that someone — Shakespeare — with a medievalist's eye surely had to engage in for these lines to have been written. The Latin tagline (*Et bonum quo antiquius eo melius*—"And the older a good thing is, the better") inserted into the English couplets, although a commonplace in itself, replicates precisely a reader's experience of Berthelette's page, where Gower's Latin commentaries appear sandwiched within the column amidst the English poem.

More subtle but doubtless a relic far more telling of the writer's "medievalist" research is Gower's self-description as "taper light" (1.1.16) — an echo, one might think, of a memorable comparison of Berthelette's from his preface: "this worthy olde wryter John Gower ... shall as a lanterne gyue hym lyghte to wryte counnyngly / and to garnyshhe his sentencis in our vulgar tonge."[41] Indeed, Berthelette's focus on Gower's language could have served as germ — or as permission — for what ultimately became the period-specific "counnyng" and "garnyshhe" of the "sentencis" of "ancient Gower" generally.

But there is more. If we delve beneath the thin antique patina of Gower's opening speech to parse the implications of his words for the unfolding play, again we confront the medieval. His "old song," Gower says, provides "restoratives" (1.1.8), usually glossed medicinally as "a means of healing or renewal."[42] But what sort of medicine is being offered here? Consider that in context, the following line itself designates a purpose for these "restoratives": "The purchase is to make men glorious." Consider also Gower's claim that he has come "from ashes ... / Assuming man's infirmities" (1.1.2–3), with its hints of Lazarus-like (or profounder) resurrection — associations perhaps rendered no less strong (if a trifle macabre) for those in Shakespeare's original audience familiar with the real Gower's five-foot effigy, recumbent upon his tomb in St. Saviour's nave, mere dozens of yards from the Globe.[43] "Restoration" and "the glorious" thus acquire a celestial weight and dimension hardly out of place were they found, say, in *Everyman* or *The Castle of Perseverance* and sufficient enough, surely, to qualify Gower's final admonition to the audience following his "anachronistic" summary of justice finally apportioned in the Epilogue: "New joy wait on you: here our play has ending" (Epilogue, 18).[44] A medieval viewer would have neither misunderstood what specific joy was meant, confusing it with merely random mirth, nor overlooked the apocalyptic warning implicit in the reference to the "ending" of "our play."

How important, then, is an understanding of Shakespeare's medievalism to presenting *Pericles* on stage? Probably the answer varies. "One of the greatest problems of theater history," as Stephen Orgel has remarked, "is to see with the eyes of the past."[45] If that is the intention — to animate an early modern playwright's goals for an audience — then clearly the medieval elements of *Pericles* are inviolable and requisite. In the "Letter of the Author's Expounding His Whole Intention" that the patent medievalizer Spenser attached to the supremely anachronistic *Faerie Queene*, he explains that:

> the generall end ... of all the booke is to fashion a gentleman or noble person in vertuous and gentle discipline: Which for that I conceived shoulde be most plausible and pleasing, being coloured with an historicall fiction, the which the most part of men delight to read, rather for variety of matter then for profit of the ensample: I chose the historye of king Arthure.[46]

Prince Pericles is, of course, not of the Round Table, but the impulse behind his creation out of what Spenser calls "historical fiction [i.e., in *Periclean* context, 'a song that old was sung'], the which the most part of men delight to read, rather for variety of matter than for profit of example," with emphasis on the final prepositional phrase, is precisely Shakespeare's and entirely medieval; and for that reason Spenser's self-consciously backward gaze, like his synthesized throwback English, serves as a contemporary and efficient gauge for Shakespeare's own inclusion of these things in the crafting of his first romance.

To say this is also to claim a level of high seriousness that, if it is sometimes invoked in discussions of *The Winter's Tale* or *The Tempest*, is not commonly afforded to *Pericles*: "Is it not, after all, just a *romance*?" Shakespeare's reaction to such a brush-off, apart from predictable surprise at an unfamiliar descriptor, can only be surmised. (Indeed, upon reflection, Shakespeare seems just as likely to have called *Pericles* "my Gower play"— with all the medieval ligatures that implies.)

"Romance" as a genre for the theater is a modern nomenclature — there are none so-called in the Folio — and represents a relatively recent attempt to classify and hence eliminate ambiguity from plays whose power is palpable but frustratingly elusive.[47] But while this method as applied to early modern texts has a long and star-studded trajectory, making sense by disposing things into boxes with other "like" things can be a Procrustean process and fraught with risks of the kind Orgel warns against. (Ben Jonson, after all, dismissed Spenser entirely on grounds that he "in affecting the ancients writ no language.")[48] Inevitably every director and audience is confronted with the "vision problem," that is, their own gaze, with direct effect upon performance and interpretation.

For *Pericles* onstage, this has meant a history, essentially, of revival. Having lost by mid-century what seems to have been great initial popularity (Jonson pronounced *Pericles* a "mouldy tale" in 1629),[49] as far as can be determined the play disappeared from the boards until 1854, when Samuel Phelps brought it to Sadler's Wells for a triumphant run of fifty-five performances.[50] Phelps's take on *Pericles* is as notable as it has proven prophetic over the years. What he saw in the play was action and wide-open opportunity for special effects, elements certainly not alien to Shakespeare's invention but perhaps not to the precise degree. Cutting Gower, the dumb shows, and all sexual references (no incest, no brothel — it was, after all, Victorian London!), Phelps, according to *The Times* reviewer, concentrated on exotic Mediterranean scenery and fantastic machinery:

> When Pericles is thrown upon the sands, it is with the very best of rolling seas ... when the storm afterwards rocks his vessel, it rocks in real earnest.... An admirably equipped Diana, with her car in the clouds orders his course to her sacred city, to which he is conducted by a moving panorama of excellently-painted coast scenery. The interior of the temple, where the colossal figure of the many-breasted goddess stands in all its glory amid gloriously attired votaries, is the last "bang" of the general magnificence.[51]

In many ways what the audience saw at Sadler's Wells in 1854 has remained the performance standard.[52] When the Royal Shakespeare Company (RSC) revived *Pericles* in 1947 under Nugent Monck's direction, Gower was again absent (though the brothel came back); the focus was on action, and the scenery was monumental.[53] Monck also excised and rearranged much of the script (he began with act 2 and omitted the dumb shows) — a zeal to curtail hardly uncommon among contemporary productions of Shakespeare generally.[54] In the RSC's next staging, a decade later at Stratford-upon-Avon, Tony Richardson restored much of the original text and brought Gower back, although (influenced perhaps by "moral Gower's" opening promise "To sing a song that old was sung") Chaucer's friend was transformed into a Trinidadian calypso singer. A partial exception to the Phelpsian trend was RSC's subsequent production in 1969 directed by Terry Hands, who, apparently, had gone back to Wilkins' *Painfull Adventures* woodcut for Gower's costume — an urge toward authenticity somewhat sadly undercut by offering up the poet (who, as far as is known, was born in Kent and seldom if ever left Southwark) as a Welsh bard.[55]

Certainly Phelpsianism was back in full display in the two most recent large equity productions in the United States: by the Shakespeare Theatre Company in 2004 and 2005 at Washington, D.C.'s Lansburgh Theatre (directed by Mary Zimmerman) and a reprise summer staging by the same company outdoors for three weeks in 2006 at the Carter Barron Amphitheatre in Washington, directed by David Muse, who followed Zimmerman's lead. For the Washington productions, the dumb shows were staged and only Gower was dropped, his lines being shared in various ingenious ways, sometimes as songs, sometimes spread around tag-team fashion, as well as spoken in full by single characters, none ever the same as another. Technical effects were in abundance and delightedly received.[56]

One conclusion to be drawn from these productions, even from so thumbnail-sized a review, might be that over the last hundred and fifty years the popularity of *Pericles* with audiences has increased as directors chose to diminish, either by transformation or excision, precisely those medieval elements that Shakespeare studied to put in. Indeed, because it is not inconceivable that Jacobean audiences similarly applauded what have become known as the play's "romance elements"—magic, multiple scene change, stage machinery, a plot rich with coincidence, and a happy, all-resolving ending—such a conclusion is probably neither anachronistic nor invalid for the larger history of the play's reception. But would such performances satisfy the medievalist in Shakespeare? Probably not. What goes missing in such productions is the moral cohesion that Shakespeare looked backward to find in medieval texts generally and specifically in Gower's.

It is an irony, perhaps, that Shakespeare selected as his source a poem whose history resembles that of his play: like *Pericles*, the *Confessio Amantis* has required revivals and over the years has been read rather more for its exotic stories individually than for its "restoratives"—the grand moral, social, and spiritual education Gower intended his poem cumulatively to provide his king and his readers in the simultaneously jaded and hope-filled manner characteristic certainly of late-medieval literature in England and also, I think, of *Pericles* and Shakespeare's romances generally. That Shakespeare was so obviously medievalist enough to recognize these elements in Gower's work and, valuing them, sought to construct a new kind of play upon them could be called sufficient reason to insist on the medieval presence when performing *Pericles*.

NOTES

1. Harold Bloom, *Shakespeare: The Invention of the Human* (New York: Riverhead Books, 1998), 604–605.
2. STC 22335. The search for the "real Shakespeare" in *Pericles* has taken a variety of forms. R. C. Churchill, *Shakespeare and His Betters: A History and a Criticism of the Attempts Which Have Been Made to Prove That Shakespeare's Works Were Written by Others* (Bloomington: Indiana University Press, 1958), opines that the "weakness" overall of *Pericles* assures its collaborative geniture and that its absence from the First Folio grew from Hemminge's and Condell's knowledge that "his part in it was so small—and the principal author still alive?" (140–41). Churchill's purism seems liberal, however, compared to that of fellow traveler T. W. Baldwin, *Shakspere's* [sic] *Five-Act Structure: Shakspere's Early Plays on the Background of Renaissance Theories of Five-Act Structure from 1470* (Urbana: University of Illinois Press, 1947; 1963), who manages to be certain only of a *single passage*: 3.1.10–14, which seems to him to be based upon Terence (546–47). Even those who credit Shakespeare's authorship have sometimes found odd ways of doing so: Henry Norman Hudson, in his introduction to the Aldus Shakespeare *Pericles, Prince of Tyre* (New York: Bigelow, Smith, for Funk & Wagnalls, 1909), attributes the play's uncharacteristic weaknesses to its being a work of Shakespeare's "boyhood"—"some exercise of the 'prentice hand'" before it became "the master's hand," that is, the "real" Shakespeare himself (xiv). Lest we imagine such concerns no longer occupy scholarly hours, consider the Oxford Shakespeare's edition by Roger Warren (Oxford: Oxford University Press, 2003), entitled *A Reconstructed Text of Pericles, Prince of Tyre by William Shakespeare and George Wilkins*. Here, very specifically, we learn of "Wilkins writing Scenes 1–9, Shakespeare Scenes 11–22" (4). Among Warren's reasons for asserting Wilkins's direct involvement are court records suggesting that Wilkins kept a bawdy house and physically abused his women (he may have been cited for kicking a pregnant woman in the abdomen)—facts that would make it "no surprise that Wilkins should relish a story which dramatizes the abuse of Antiochus' daughter, the attempted prostitution of Marina, and Pericles' striking Marina at the climax of the play" (6–7). All of this assumes, of course, one has the court record of the right Wilkins; on which, see Roger Prior, "The Life of George Wilkins," *Shakespeare Survey* 25 (1972): 137–52.
3. STC 25638.5. The relationship of Wilkins—author of a single known play, *The Miseries of Enforced Marriage* (1607)—to Shakespeare's *Pericles* remains (obviously!) a vexation to scholars. His *Painfull Adventures* claims in its introductory matter to be "the true History of the Play of Pericles," implying that it redacts from a play "Pericles" presumably to please an audience eager to have more of what they had enjoyed on stage. Such a play, of which no other record exists, would thus antedate Shakespeare's by at least two years; if Wilkins contributed to it—or wrote it—his work (so goes the argument) might have influenced Shakespeare, perhaps explaining (even to those holding the play to be primarily if not entirely Shakespeare's) the oft-remarked "unevenness" of the early sections as well as the decision to omit *Pericles* from the First Folio. The situation is further muddied by the existence of a prose history of Apollonius of Tyre by Laurence Twyne, *The Pattern of Painfull Adventures* (listed by the Stationer in 1576, although no edition is known before 1594–95 STC 709, 709.5, 710). Twyne's *Pattern* was reprinted in 1607, suggesting a revival of audience interest; Wilkins's *Painfull Adventures* also borrows passages from Twyne. Over the years the difficulties of reconciling these details, as David Bevington sums up, "have generally led to three hypotheses: that Shakespeare

worked with a collaborator such as Thomas Heywood or George Wilkins, that he revised an older play and left the first two acts pretty much as they were, or that he wrote the entire play, which was then 'pirated' by two unemployed actors whose portions differed markedly in accuracy"; see Bevington, ed., *The Complete Works of Shakespeare*, 5th ed. (New York: HarperCollins, 2003), 1398.

4. Not surprisingly, perhaps, these doubts took firm shape during the Enlightenment, when all four romances—*Pericles, Cymbeline, A Winter's Tale,* and *The Tempest*—were held in dim view. Apart from three performances in 1738 at Covent Garden of George Lillo's *Marina*—a rewrite of Acts 4 and 5, on the grounds that they alone were Shakespeare's—no other performance of *Pericles* is known during the century. See F. D. Hoeniger, "Introduction," in *Pericles*, by William Shakespeare, ed. F. D. Hoeniger, Arden Shakespeare (London: Methuen, 1963), lxix. Hoeniger comments further: "Most eighteenth-century editors, including Pope, Dr Johnson, and Capell, excluded the play from Shakespeare's canon" (lxx).

5. Many make the case for Shakespeare's dependencies on Gower's *Confessio*; but see esp. Gerard A. Barker, "Themes and Variations in Shakespeare's *Pericles*," *English Studies* 44 (1963): 401-14, and Richard Hillman, "Shakespeare's Gower and Gower's Shakespeare: The Larger Debt of *Pericles*," *Shakespeare Quarterly* 36 (1985): 427-37.

6. After a lengthy and contentious, albeit altogether informed, discussion of "Authorship," Doreen DelVecchio and Antony Hammond, editors of the New Cambridge Shakespeare *Pericles, Prince of Tyre* (Cambridge, UK: Cambridge University Press, 1998), conclude, "We as editors don't really care who wrote *Pericles* (though we do believe it to be the product of a single creative imagination): we really care that it is ... 'a masterpiece'" (15). For the most part, the present argument shares this opinion.

7. Or not: John Updike takes Shakespeare as his primary example to agree with Edward W. Said, in a *New Yorker* review (August 7 and 14, 2006) of the latter's *On Late Style: Music and Literature against the Grain* (New York: Pantheon, 2006) that characteristically genius in old age finds fresh voice in new forms (64-67). Said makes the argument for Beethoven.

8. Romances by various hands had been brought to the London stage before *Pericles*, among them Thomas Hughes (*The Misfortunes of Arthur*, c. 1588), Robert Greene (*The History of Orlando Furioso*, c. 1591), and John Day (*The Isle of Gulls*, 1606, based on Sidney's *Arcadia*—the latter an unlicensed satire, which sent its actors to jail); see John Dean, *Restless Wanderers: Shakespeare and the Pattern of Romance* (Salzburg: Institut für Anglistik und Amerikanistik, University of Salzburg, 1979), 116-66.

9. For evidence of *Pericles*'s popularity, Hoeniger quotes the title page of the surviving quarto: "it was 'diuers and sundry times acted by his Maiesties Seruants, at the Globe on the Banck-side,'" see Hoeniger, "Introduction," lxv.

10. Leading candidates, in addition to Wilkins, as likely collaborators have been William Rowley, first proposed by Sir Sidney Lee, *A Life of William Shakespeare* (London: Smith, Elder, 1898), 252; Thomas Heywood, argued especially by H. D. Gray, "Heywood's *Pericles*," *PMLA* 40 (1925): 507-29; and John Day, in Hoeniger, "Introduction," lxii-lxiii.

11. In addition to Gower's *Confessio*, Shakespeare evidently referred to Laurence Twyne's retelling of the Apollonius saga, *The Pattern of Painfull Adventures* (1576; 2nd ed. 1607), for certain details; there was also *Kyng Apollyn of Thyre*, a translation from the French by Robert Copland and printed by Wynkyn de Worde in 1510. Oxford, Bodleian Library MS Douce 216 preserves a fragmentary late-fifteenth-century recounting of the story in quatrains—evidence of a broader field of possibility. See Albert H. Smyth, *Shakespeare's Pericles and Apollonius of Tyre: A Study of Comparative Literature* (Philadelphia PA: MacCalla, 1898), 47-59 (Smyth prints a transcription of the fifteenth-century poem, 49-55); and further Elizabeth Archibald, *Apollonius of Tyre: Medieval and Renaissance Themes and Variations* (Cambridge, UK: D. S. Brewer, 1991), esp. 81-106, "Genre, Reception and Popularity," and Appendices I ("Latin and Vernacular Versions of HA [*Historia Apollonii*] to 1609") and II ("Medieval and Renaissance Allusions to the Story of Apollonius").

12. I am relying throughout for the chronology of Shakespeare's plays on the views of David Bevington. For the date of *Comedy of Errors*, see William Shakespeare, *The Complete Works of Shakespeare*, ed. David Bevington, 5th ed. (New York: HarperCollins, 2003), Appendix I.1. On Shakespeare's debt to Gower's *Confessio*, see the discussion in Marjorie Garber, *Shakespeare After All* (New York: Pantheon, 2004), 754-775.

13. STC 12142, 12143, 12144. On the early printing history, see N. F. Blake, "Early Printed Editions of *Confessio Amantis*," *Mediaevalia* 16 (1993 [for 1990]): 289-306; and Tim William Machan, "Thomas Berthelette and Gower's *Confessio*," *Studies in the Age of Chaucer* 18 (1996): 143-66. As Machan notes (144, n.3), an edition of 1544 was mentioned by Robert Watt, *Bibliotheca Britannica, or A General Index to British and Foreign Literature*, 4 vols. (Edinburgh: Archibald Constable, 1824), vol. 1, 430, as having been produced by Berthelette, but "Watt's identification is probably due to a misreading of the title page of a 1554 copy." See further Siân Echard, "Gower in Print," in *A Companion to Gower*, ed. Siân Echard (Cambridge, UK: D. S. Brewer, 2004), 115-135.

14. The phrase is Machan's, "Thomas Berthelette and Gower's *Confessio*," 163.

15. See Berthelette's edition of 1532, *Jo. Gower de Confessione Amantis*, sig. aaiii[v] (STC 12143). Berthelette's

preface to this edition and his letter to the reader are available in Alexander Chalmers, ed., *The Works of the English Poets: From Chaucer to Cowper*, 21 vols. (London: Whittingham, 1810), vol. 2, 1–5; and also in Blake, "Early Printed Editions," 296–301.

16. I discuss this relationship of Latin and English in detail in R. F. Yeager, "English, Latin and the Text as 'Other': The Page as Sign in the Work of John Gower," *Text* 3 (1987): 251–67. See further Joyce Coleman, "Lay Readers and Hard Latin: How Gower May Have Intended the *Confessio Amantis* to Be Read," *Studies in the Age of Chaucer* 24 (2002): 209–235; and two essays by Siân Echard, "Dialogues and Monologues: Manuscript Representations of the Conversation of the *Confessio Amantis*," in *Middle English Poetry: Texts and Traditions Essays in Honour of Derek Pearsall*, ed. A. J. Minnis (York, UK: University of York, 2001), 57–75; and Echard, "Last Words: Latin at the End of the *Confessio Amantis*," in *Interstices: Studies in Middle English and Anglo-Latin Texts in Honour of A.G. Rigg*, ed. Richard Firth Green and Linne Mooney (Toronto: University of Toronto Press, 2004).

17. See Stephen J. Lynch, "The Authority of Gower in Shakespeare's *Pericles*," *Mediaevalia* 16 (1993 [for 1990]): 361–378.

18. For a thorough overview of Gower's reputation in the sixteenth and seventeenth centuries with special reference to Shakespeare, see Neil Gilroy-Scott, "John Gower's Reputation: Literary Allusions from the Early Fifteenth Century to the Time of 'Pericles,'" *Yearbook of English Studies* 1 (1971): 30–47.

19. STC 12261. For the text of *Greenes Vision*, see Alexander B. Grosart, ed., *The Life and Complete Works in Prose and Verse of Robert Greene, M.A.*, 15 vols. (London, 1881–86; New York: Russell & Russell, 1964), vol. 12, 191–281.

20. On Greene's treatment of Gower in *Greenes Vision*, see esp. Helen Cooper, "'This Worthy Olde Writer': *Pericles* and Other Gowers, 1592–1640," in *Companion to Gower*, ed. Siân Echard, 99–113. For *Monuments of Honour*, see F. L. Lucas, ed., *The Complete Works of John Webster*, 4 vols. (London: Chatto & Windus, 1927), vol. 3, 317–327. For *The Golden Age Restor'd*, see *Ben Jonson*, ed. C. H. Herford and Percy and Evelyn Simpson, 11 vols. (1983; corrected ed. Oxford: Clarendon, 1954), vol. 7, 425. Jonson's greater interest in Gower is demonstrated in his work on language: see R. F. Yeager, "Ben Jonson's *English Grammar* and John Gower's Reception in the Seventeenth Century," in *The Endless Knot: Essays on Old and Middle English in Honor of Marie Borroff*, ed. M. Teresa Tavormina and R.F. Yeager (Cambridge, UK: D. S. Brewer, 1995), 227–239.

21. The probability of Shakespeare's having read *Greenes Vision* is quite high. Rival writers for the same stages, they frequented the same circles, viewed each other's work, and borrowed plots—Shakespeare most interestingly, perhaps, for present purposes, as in 1609, a year after writing *Pericles*, he turned to Greene's *Pandosto* for the plot of *The Winter's Tale*. Earlier, Greene himself seems to have served as Shakespeare's model for Falstaff's character. On Shakespeare's relations with Greene, see Stephen Greenblatt, *Will in the World: How Shakespeare Became Shakespeare* (New York: Norton, 2004), 203–211, 216–225; and, in the present volume, Louise Bishop, "A Touch of Chaucer in Shakespeare's *Winter's Tale*, 236–238, 242–243n25–31; and Martha Driver, "Reading *A Midsummer Night's Dream* through Middle English Romance," 142, 153, esp. n22.

22. STC 22331, 22332. For the date of *Troilus and Cressida*, see Bevington, *Complete Works of Shakespeare*, Appendix 1.7.

23. STC 5068, 5077, 5078, 5094. For the early printing history of Chaucer's works, see Paul G. Ruggiers, ed., *Editing Chaucer: The Great Tradition* (Norman, OK: Pilgrim Books, 1984).

24. See Kelly Jones, "'The Quick and the Dead': Performing the Poet Gower in Shakespeare's *Pericles*," in this volume, 203.

25. See Robert M. Garrett, "Gower in 'Pericles,'" *Shakespeare Jahrbuch* 48 (1912): 13–20, esp. 13; and also *Southwark Cathedral: The Authorized Guide* (London: Robert James Publications, for the Dean and the Chapter of Southwark Cathedral, 2002/2006), 19.

26. See further Driver, "Reading *A Midsummer Night's Dream*," in this volume, 147, 157n59–60.

27. For texts of the mummings, see Henry MacCracken, ed., *The Minor Poems of John Lydgate*, 2 vols., II, EETS o.s. 192 (1934 for 1933,1961), 668–701; for discussion, see Glynne Wickham, *Early English Stages 1300–1660*, 4 vols. (London: Routledge and Kegan Paul, 1959–2002), vol. 1 (2nd ed., Routledge, 1980), 191 ff.

28. Greenblatt traces Shakespeare's introduction to morality plays to 1569, when his father (then bailiff of Stratford) is on record as having arranged for payment to traveling companies of the Queen's Men and the Earl of Worcester's Men, whose repertoire was "for the most part 'morality plays,' or 'moral interludes,' secular sermons designed to show the terrible consequences of disobedience, idleness, or dissipation." See Greenblatt, *Will in the World*, 28–34, at 31.

29. STC 18684, 15086. On the place of the dumb show in early modern England, see Dieter Mehl, *The Elizabethan Dumb Show: The History of a Dramatic Convention* (Cambridge, MA: Harvard University Press, 1966).

30. STC 22302. See further Driver, "Reading *A Midsummer Night's Dream*," in this volume, 149–150, 158n71–72.

31. Indeed, Shakespeare seems to have incorporated the tableau-like scenic construction he had observed in Corpus Christi cycle drama into his own work; on which, see Clifford Davidson, "Positional Symbolism

and English Medieval Drama," in *Iconographic and Comparative Studies in Medieval Drama*, ed. Clifford Davidson and John H. Stroupe (Kalamazoo, MI: Medieval Institute Publications, 1991), 66–76; and, with specific reference to *Hamlet*, Cherrell Guilfoyle, "The Staging of the First Murder in the Mystery Plays in England," in *Iconographic and Comparative Studies in Medieval Drama*, 42–51.

32. Howard Felperin, *Shakespearean Romance* (Princeton, NJ: Princeton University Press, 1972), chap. 8, "This Great Miracle: *Pericles*," 143–176, at 146. In addition to *Everyman* (159), Felperin mentions as analogues the Digby *Mary Magdalene* (160), the moralities *The Castle of Perseverance* (170), *Mundus and Infans* (156), the Croxton *Play of the Sacrament* (153), and "miracle plays like that of St. Eustace" (165, n.12). See further Felperin, "Shakespeare's Miracle Play," *Shakespeare Quarterly* 18 (1967): 363–374.

33. Felperin, *Shakespearean Romance*, 171.

34. F. N. Hoeniger, "Gower and Shakespeare in *Pericles*," *Shakespeare Quarterly* 33 (1982): 461–479, finds an historical explanation for the tournament: "The vogue of tournaments was reaching its high point in popularity at the time. Knights parading past King James's or Queen Anne's pavilion before entering the lists, and presenting to them their elaborately adorned shields with emblematic devices and mottoes, were a frequent spectacle" (472). He records as well that in 1613 Shakespeare and the tragedian Richard Burbage, who acted Pericles for the King's Men, were paid forty-five shillings each by the Earl of Rutland to paint *imprese*—shieldlike emblems and mottoes. But the empty, even ludicrous performance that jousting had become by 1605 would hardly have been lost on Shakespeare, and being paid so outlandishly for daubing could only underscore it. More suggestive of the distinction between the "prop" Middle Ages and the "medieval" for Shakespeare is perhaps the record of a charge of sedition brought against a troupe of players in Yorkshire in 1610 for performing *King Lear* and *Pericles* on the grounds that the plays promoted Roman Catholic views, noted by Stephen Orgel in the introduction to his revised Pelican edition of *Pericles* (London: Penguin, 2001), xxxii. The players, who convinced the authorities they were merely staging what was already in print and hence officially licensed, got off; but Orgel's reading of the incident is relevant: "*Pericles* is [in a sense] not a romance ... but a tale about salvation through submission and abjection, through the patient endurance of suffering—a lesson, in the deepest sense, not for him but for us. This is no doubt what attracted the Roman Catholic actors in Yorkshire to it...: they would have viewed it as a saint's life; and its claims to transcendence are surely what ultimately earned it its place in the Shakespeare canon" (xl–xli). Shakespeare's own "complex relationship to Catholicism" (see Greenblatt, *Will in the World*, 101–109, 113–116, 318–321, 387–388, at 387) has obvious implications for such salvific elements as might have colored his sense of the "medieval." And see further Margaret Healy, "*Pericles* and the Pox," in *Shakespeare's Late Plays*, ed. Jennifer Richards and James Knowles (Edinburgh: Edinburgh University Press, 1999), 92–107, esp. 106, where she considers that perhaps the recusant company performed *Pericles* in Yorkshire "for counter-propaganda purposes."

35. Berthelette's dedication to Henry, filling two pages, is at once unmissable and potentially inspirational in its flattery, especially in its focus on elements important to James: the king's learning and (professed) interest in "morall doctrines."

36. As Berthelette noticed by comparing "writen copies" (i.e., manuscripts) with the "printed" (i.e., Caxton's blackletter), there were two dedications, to Richard II and to Henry IV, representing different stages (and historical moments) in the writing of the *Confessio*. With a politic care behooving Henry VIII's printer, Berthelette included both.

37. STC 25638.5. Variously replicated, including in George Wilkins, *George Wilkins: The Painfull Aduentures of Pericles Prince of Tyre*, ed. Kenneth Muir (Liverpool, UK: Liverpool University Press, 1967).

38. Or perhaps the cap might only have seemed antique. Compare the "scholar's cap" worn nearly universally in portraits of humanists and first-generation Protestant theologians painted before the death of Henry VIII: Martin Luther and Ulrich Zwingli, in Lucas Cranach's group portrait, with Friedrich of Saxony (Toledo [Ohio] Museum of Art); Erasmus, Thomas More, and Thomas Cranmer in portraits by Hans Holbein the Younger (Louvre; Frick Collection, New York, respectively); and the frontispiece image of Dr. Faustus from the so-called B-text quarto, *c*. 1616, of Christopher Marlowe's *The Tragicall History of the Life and Death of Doctor Faustus*—this last of particular pertinence since the appearance of such a cap on Faustus in a Jacobean publication offers clear indication of conscious antiquarianism. That said, it should be noted that the cap worn by Gower in the Wilkins edition woodcut more closely resembles that worn by the sower in the Limbourg Brothers' *Très Riches Heures du Duc de Berry*, "October" (*c*. 1413–16; Musée Condée, Chantilly), or even closer, in Gentile da Fabriano's "Adoration of the Magi" (*c*. 1423; Uffizi Gallery, Florence) by the fourth head from the top on the far right, next to (apparently) a lion.

39. See F.A. Foster, "Dumb Show in Elizabethan Drama before 1620," *Englische Studien* 44 (1912–1913): 8–17, esp. 11, on the origin of the role; and further Mehl, *Elizabethan Dumb Show*, 11–12. Shakespeare employs such chorus characters elsewhere, in *Henry IV, Part 2* (Rumor, "painted full of tongues," whose stage description reveals his origin in morality drama), *Henry V* (Chorus, a figure resembling Gower in function and importance but unlike Gower in that his is no authorial presence), and *The Winter's Tale* (where Time comes, again, directly out of the morality/allegory tradition). Authorial presenters, though hardly common, were

not unfamiliar on Elizabethan and Jacobean stages. Collectively "there is an inherent didactic value in the characterization of 'authorial presenters,' and the authority of their lessons is enhanced by a special feature of ... antiquity"; as a group they "inculcate in the audience ... the heroic values of an older generation or an earlier age." See Walter F. Eggers, Jr., "Shakespeare's Gower and the Role of the Authorial Presenter," *Philological Quarterly* 54 (1975): 434–443. Some measure of the morality-bred significance of the typical presenter is discerned even in *Henry V*'s most impersonal Chorus by J. Dover Wilson, who sees there "a priest leading his congregation in prayer or celebration"; see Wilson, "Introduction," in *Henry V*, by William Shakespeare, ed. J. Dover Wilson, New Cambridge edition (Cambridge, UK: Cambridge University Press, 1949), xv.

40. Gower's second and third choruses, preceding acts 2 and 3, are replete with antiquated grammar and vocabulary, e.g., "iwis, "benison, "speken can, "To killen" (act 2); "yslaked," eyne, "eche, "Y-ravished" (act 3). In subsequent choruses these forms are rare, and in choruses in acts 4 and 5 tetrameter couplets give way to blank verse, only to return in the second chorus in act 5 — though without "medieval" language. Nonetheless, Gower stays in medieval character as presenter, commenting, morality-fashion, on the meaning of the action, e.g., "See how belief may suffer by foul show!" (4.4.23). His entire final speech, which closes the play, is of this kind.

41. Berthelette, ed., *Jo. Gower de Confessione Amantis*, sig. aaii^v.

42. Shakespeare, *Pericles, The New Cambridge Shakespeare*, 85.

43. Doubtless some in Shakespeare's audience would have found "ember-eves," positioned four lines following "ashes" and two prior to "restoratives" in Gower's opening speech, a reinforcing hint toward resurrection, in that, by the 1500s, an euphonic "b" was commonplace between the "m" and "r" of what had been OE *ǽmerȝe*, "live coal," making "ember/er," identical in spelling and pronunciation with "ember," from OE *ymbryne*, "revolution of time" — the actual meaning of "ember-eves," i.e., quarterly periods of fasting and prayer established by the Catholic Church in 1095, and maintained by the Church of England after the dissolution. See *OED*, s.v. "ember^1" and "ember^2."

44. STC 10604.5, 10606, 10606.5. Felperin, who tends rather toward the term "archaistic," would find Gower's closing lines exemplary of characters who give *Pericles* its likeness to *Everyman* by making "a habit of stepping outside their roles and commenting on them from the moral perspective of the play as a whole"; see Felperin, *Shakespearean Romance*, 160–161.

45. Stephen Orgel, *Imagining Shakespeare: A History of Texts and Visions* (Houndmills, UK: Palgrave Macmillan, 2003), 163.

46. Edmund Spenser, *The Faerie Queene*, ed. Thomas P. Roche Jr. (Harmondsworth, UK: Penguin, 1978), 15.

47. Clearly, "romance" as a critical term applied to *poetry* was common medieval parlance: see, e.g., Derek Pearsall, "The Development of Middle English Romance," *Mediaeval Studies* 27 (1965): 91–116; Paul Strohm, "The Origin and Meaning of Middle English *Romaunce, Tragedie*: Generic Distinctions in the Middle English Troy Narratives," *Speculum* 46 (1971): 348–359; Dieter Mehl, *The Middle English Romances of the Thirteenth and Fourteenth Centuries* (New York: Barnes & Noble, 1969); and Carol Fewster, *Traditionality and Genre in Middle English Romance* (Woodbridge, UK: D. S. Brewer, 1987). Moreover, as Driver demonstrates in detail in her discussion, "Reading *A Midsummer Night's Dream*," in this volume, 140–160, Shakespeare both was sensitive to romance elements and made use of them himself in a variety of ways; and see further Cherell Guilfoyle, *Shakespeare's Play within Play: Medieval Imagery and Scenic Form in Hamlet, Othello, and King Lear* (Kalamazoo, MI: Medieval Institute Publications, 1990). Modern literary critical claims for "romance" as a descriptive category setting apart *Pericles, Cymbeline, A Winter's Tale,* and *The Tempest* from the rest of the Shakespearean canon are, however, a postmedieval (indeed, post–early modern) expansion of the term.

48. That Jonson included Chaucer and Gower among the "ancients" is clear from his concern that younger readers take their work in small doses, lest they fall "too much in love with Antiquity." See Jonson, *Ben Jonson*, vol. 8, 618.

49. Jonson, "Ode To Himselfe," in Jonson, *Ben Jonson*, ll. 21–22.

50. In 1660 the actor Thomas Betterton rose to fame in what seems to have been the final performance of *Pericles* before the long hiatus; in 1662 Charles II licensed the play for performance by Davenant, who apparently never exercised his option. See Stephen Orgel, "Introduction," in *Pericles* by William Shakespeare, ed. Stephen Orgel (London: Penguin, 2001), xliii. Orgel's edition has as its frontispiece, interestingly, the rescue of Thaisa from her coffer (3.2) as it appeared in Nicholas Rowe's 1709 Shakespeare. Orgel takes the "thoroughly classicized décor" to be the engraver's imaginary, rather than recollecting any actual stage practice. On Phelps's production, see also esp. William Shakespeare, *Pericles, Prince of Tyre*, ed. Doreen DelVecchio and Antony Hammond, New Cambridge Shakespeare (Cambridge, UK: Cambridge University Press, 1998), 18.

51. *The Times* London, October 16, 1854.

52. Of the only two performances of *Pericles* prior to Monck's, one — by John Coleman at Stratford in 1900 — was heavily edited in the manner of Phelps's; the other, at the Old Vic in 1921, used the full text uncut, but despite a good reception was not reprised.

53. DelVecchio and Hammond offer a look at Marina's tomb as conceived by Monck, in Shakespeare, *Pericles, Prince of Tyre*, 19. Some of Monck's cutting was apparently a response to postwar shortages in Britain: Micheline Steinberg reports the director's saying that his purpose was "to get the audience in and out and save on the electricity bills"; Steinberg, *Flashback: One Hundred Years of Stratford-upon-Avon and the Royal Shakespeare Company* (London: RSC Publications, 1985), 52.

54. Film versions, for example, retain on average about 40 percent of the full script. See Judith Buchanan, *Shakespeare on Film* (Harlow, UK: Pearson/Longman, 2005), 15, which quotes the figure.

55. For Gower's biography, see John H. Fisher, *John Gower, Moral Philosopher and Friend of Chaucer* (New York: New York University Press, 1964), 37–69. DelVecchio and Hammond, in Shakespeare, *Pericles, Prince of Tyre*, New Cambridge *Pericles*, 23, print a photo of Emrys James as Gower in the Hands production.

56. As I can attest from my own experience among the audience.

Works Cited

Archibald, Elizabeth. *Apollonius of Tyre: Medieval and Renaissance Themes and Variations.* Cambridge, UK: D. S. Brewer, 1991.
Baldwin, T. W. *Shakspere's [sic] Five-Act Structure: Shakspere's Early Plays on the Background of Renaissance Theories of Five-Act Structure from 1470.* Urbana: University of Illinois Press, 1947. Reprinted 1963.
Barker, Gerard A. "Themes and Variations in Shakespeare's *Pericles*." *English Studies* 44 (1963): 401–414.
Blake, N. F. "Early Printed Editions of *Confessio Amantis*." *Mediaevalia* 16 (1993 [for 1990]): 289–306.
Bloom, Harold. *Shakespeare: The Invention of the Human.* New York: Riverhead Books, 1998.
Buchanan, Judith. *Shakespeare on Film.* Harlow, UK: Pearson/Longman, 2005.
Chalmers, Alexander, ed. *The Works of the English Poets: From Chaucer to Cowper.* 21 vols. London: Whittingham, 1810.
Churchill, R. C. *Shakespeare and His Betters: A History and a Criticism of the Attempts Which Have Been Made to Prove That Shakespeare's Works Were Written by Others.* Bloomington: Indiana University Press, 1958.
Coleman, Joyce. "Lay Readers and Hard Latin: How Gower May Have Intended the *Confessio Amantis* to Be Read." *Studies in the Age of Chaucer* 24 (2002): 209–235.
Cooper, Helen. "'This Worthy Olde Writer': *Pericles* and Other Gowers, 1592–1640." In *A Companion to Gower*, edited by Siân Echard, 99–113. Cambridge, UK: D. S. Brewer, 2004.
Davidson, Clifford, and John H. Stroupe, eds. *Iconographic and Comparative Studies in Medieval Drama.* Kalamazoo, MI: Medieval Institute Publications, 1991.
———. "Positional Symbolism and English Medieval Drama." In *Iconographic and Comparative Studies in Medieval Drama*, 66–76. Kalamazoo, MI: Medieval Institute Publications, 1991.
Dean, John. *Restless Wanderers: Shakespeare and the Pattern of Romance.* Salzburg: Institut für Anglistik and Amerikanistik, University of Salzburg, 1979.
Echard, Siân, ed. *A Companion to Gower.* Cambridge, UK: D. S. Brewer, 2004.
———. "Gower in Print." In *A Companion to Gower*, 115–135. Cambridge, UK: D. S. Brewer, 2004.
———. "Dialogues and Monologues: Manuscript Representations of the Conversation of the *Confessio Amantis*." In *Middle English Poetry: Texts and Traditions Essays in Honour of Derek Pearsall*, edited by Alastair J. Minnis, 57–75. York, UK: University of York, 2001.
———. "Last Words: Latin at the End of the *Confessio Amantis*." In *Interstices: Studies in Middle English and Anglo-Latin Texts in Honour of A. G. Rigg*, edited by Richard Firth Green and Linne Mooney. Toronto: University of Toronto Press, 2004.
Eggers, Walter F., Jr. "Shakespeare's Gower and the Role of the Authorial Presenter." *Philological Quarterly* 54 (1975): 434–443.
Felperin, Howard. "Shakespeare's Miracle Play." *Shakespeare Quarterly* 18 (1967): 363–374.
———. *Shakespearean Romance.* Princeton, NJ: Princeton University Press, 1972.
Fewster, Carol. *Traditionality and Genre in Middle English Romance.* Woodbridge, UK: D. S. Brewer, 1987.
Fisher, John H. *John Gower, Moral Philosopher and Friend of Chaucer.* New York: New York University Press, 1964.
Foster, F. A. "Dumb Show in Elizabethan Drama before 1620." *Englische Studien* 44 (1912–1913): 8–17.
Garber, Marjorie. *Shakespeare After All.* New York: Pantheon, 2004.
Gilroy-Scott, Neil. "John Gower's Reputation: Literary Allusions from the Early Fifteenth Century to the Time of 'Pericles.'" *Yearbook of English Studies* 1 (1971): 30–47.
Gray, H. D. "Heywood's Pericles." *PMLA* 40 (1925): 507–529.

Greenblatt, Stephen. *Will in the World: How Shakespeare Became Shakespeare*. New York: Norton, 2004.
Grosart, Alexander B., ed. *The Life and Complete Works in Prose and Verse of Robert Greene, M.A.* 15 vols. London, 1881–1886. Reprinted New York: Russell & Russell, 1964.
Guilfoyle, Cherrell. "The Staging of the First Murder in the Mystery Plays in England." In *Iconographic and Comparative Studies*, edited by Clifford Davidson and John H. Stroupe, 42–51. Kalamazoo, MI: Medieval Institute Publications, 1991.
———. *Shakespeare's Play within Play: Medieval Imagery and Scenic Form in Hamlet, Othello, and King Lear.* Kalamazoo, MI: Medieval Institute Publications, 1990.
Healy, Margaret. "*Pericles* and the Pox." In *Shakespeare's Late Plays*, edited by Jennifer Richards and James Knowles, 92–107. Edinburgh: Edinburgh University Press, 1999.
Hillman, Richard. "Shakespeare's Gower and Gower's Shakespeare: The Larger Debt of *Pericles*." *Shakespeare Quarterly* 36 (1985): 427–437.
Hoeniger, F. N. "Gower and Shakespeare in *Pericles*." *Shakespeare Quarterly* 33 (1982): 461–479.
———. "Introduction." In *Pericles*, by William Shakespeare. Edited by F. D. Hoeniger. Arden Shakespeare. London: Methuen, 1963.
Jonson, Ben. *Ben Jonson*. Edited by C. H. Herford and Percy and Evelyn Simpson. 11 vols. Oxford: Clarendon, 1954; corrected ed. 1983.
Lee, Sir Sidney. *A Life of William Shakespeare*. London: Smith, Elder: 1898.
Lydgate, John. *The Minor Poems of John Lydgate*. Edited by Henry MacCracken. 2 vols. EETS e.s. 107 (1911), o.s. 192 (1934 for 1933, repr. 1961).
Lynch, Stephen J. "The Authority of Gower in Shakespeare's *Pericles*." *Mediaevalia* 16 (1993 for 1990): 361–378.
Machan, Tim William. "Thomas Berthelette and Gower's *Confessio*." *Studies in the Age of Chaucer* 18 (1996): 143–166.
Mehl, Dieter. *The Elizabethan Dumb Show: The History of a Dramatic Convention*. Cambridge, MA: Harvard University Press, 1966.
———. *The Middle English Romances of the Thirteenth and Fourteenth Centuries*. New York: Barnes & Noble, 1969.
Orgel, Stephen. *Imagining Shakespeare: A History of Texts and Visions*. Houndmills, UK: Palgrave Macmillan, 2003.
Pearsall, Derek. "The Development of Middle English Romance." *Mediaeval Studies* 27 (1965): 91–116.
Prior, Roger. "The Life of George Wilkins." *Shakespeare Survey* 25 (1972): 137–52.
Ruggiers, Paul G., ed. *Editing Chaucer: The Great Tradition*. Norman, OK: Pilgrim Books, 1984.
Shakespeare, William. *Pericles, Prince of Tyre*. Edited by Henry Norman Hudson. Aldus Shakespeare. New York: Bigelow, Smith & Co. for Funk & Wagnalls, 1909.
———. *Henry V*. Edited by J. Dover Wilson. New Cambridge Shakespeare. Cambridge, UK: Cambridge University Press, 1949.
———. *Pericles*. Edited by F. D. Hoeniger. Arden Shakespeare. London: Methuen, 1963.
———. *Pericles, Prince of Tyre*. Edited by Doreen DelVecchio and Antony Hammond. New Cambridge Shakespeare. Cambridge, UK: Cambridge University Press, 1998.
———. *Pericles*. Edited by Stephen Orgel. Pelican Shakespeare. London: Penguin, 2001.
———. *The Complete Works of Shakespeare*. Edited by David Bevington. 5th ed. New York: HarperCollins, 2003.
———. *A Reconstructed Text of Pericles, Prince of Tyre by William Shakespeare and George Wilkins*. Edited by Roger Warren. Oxford Shakespeare. Oxford: Oxford University Press, 2003.
Smyth, Albert H. *Shakespeare's Pericles and Apollonius of Tyre: A Study of Comparative Literature*. Philadelphia, PA: MacCalla, 1898.
Southwark Cathedral: The Authorized Guide. London: Robert James Publications, for the Dean and the Chapter of Southwark Cathedral, 2002/2006.
Spenser, Edmund. *The Faerie Queene*. Edited by Thomas P. Roche Jr. Harmondsworth, UK: Penguin, 1978.
Steinberg, Micheline. *Flashback: One Hundred Years of Stratford-upon-Avon and the Royal Shakespeare Company*. London: RSC Publications, 1985.
Strohm, Paul. "The Origin and Meaning of Middle English *Romaunce, Tragedie*: Generic Distinctions in the Middle English Troy Narratives." *Speculum* 46 (1971): 348–359.
Updike, John. Review of Edward W. Said, *On Late Style: Music and Literature against the Grain* (New York: Pantheon, 2006). *New Yorker*, August 7 and 14, 2006, 64–67.
Watt, Robert. *Bibliotheca Britannica, or A General Index to British and Foreign Literature*. 4 vols. Edinburgh: Archibald Constable, 1824.
Webster, John. *The Complete Works of John Webster*. Edited by F. L. Lucas. 4 vols. London: Chatto & Windus, 1927.
Wickham, Glynne. *Early English Stages 1300–1660*. 4 vols. London: Routledge and Kegan Paul, 1959–2002.

Wilkins, George. *George Wilkins: The Painfull Aduentures of Pericles Prince of Tyre*. Edited by Kenneth Muir. Liverpool, UK: Liverpool University Press, 1967.

Yeager, R. F. "English, Latin and the Text as 'Other': The Page as Sign in the Work of John Gower." *Text* 3 (1987): 251–267.

_____. "Ben Jonson's *English Grammar* and John Gower's Reception in the Seventeenth Century." In *The Endless Knot: Essays on Old and Middle English* in *Honor of Marie Borroff*, edited by M. Teresa Tavormina and R. F. Yeager. Cambridge, UK: D. S. Brewer, 1995.

Performances

1854 *Pericles*, d. Samuel Phelps. Sadler's Wells Theatre, London.
1900 *Pericles*, d. John Coleman. Stratford-upon-Avon.
1921 *Pericles*. Old Vic, London.
1947 *Pericles*, d. Nugent Monck, Royal Shakespeare Company, Stratford-upon-Avon.
1957 *Pericles*, d. Tony Richardson, Royal Shakespeare Company, Stratford-upon-Avon.
1969 *Pericles*, d. Terry Hands, Royal Shakespeare Company, Stratford-upon-Avon.
2004 *Pericles*, d. Mary Zimmerman, Shakespeare Theatre Company. Lansburgh Theatre. Washington, D.C.
2006 *Pericles*, d. David Muse. Shakespeare Theatre Company. Carter Barron Amphitheatre, Washington, D.C.

A Touch of Chaucer in *The Winter's Tale*

Louise M. Bishop

Rather than detailing modern productions' recognition of William Shakespeare's medieval roots, the following essay constructs a Shakespeare mindful of his medieval literary predecessors. It detects in Shakespeare's late play *The Winter's Tale* resonances of Geoffrey Chaucer's *Tale of Melibee* and the sixteenth-century deluxe folio editions in which it appears.[1] I argue that these resonances help Shakespeare place himself in England's literary history. In *The Winter's Tale*, Shakespeare augments his treatment of Robert Greene's *Pandosto*, the play's acknowledged source, with a model of successful female eloquence found in *The Tale of Melibee* to tweak Greene's literary reputation. Moreover, just as early modern readers reanimate medieval authors, the theater audience of *The Winter's Tale* sees Hermione's statue come to life: both she and Chaucer require their audiences' belief.

Taking Chaucer as his literary forebear, Shakespeare combines tales with romance in a drama that brings not only Hermione's statue but art — including literary art — to life. Even those productions of *The Winter's Tale* that avoid the trappings of costume drama, medieval sets, scenery, or clothing, for example, subtly demonstrate the play's concern for literary history that emphasizes the play's uncanny power of reanimation and reconciliation.

We know that Shakespeare knew the work of Chaucer. Carolyn Spurgeon, author of *Shakespeare's Imagery and What It Tells Us*, first published in 1935 but reprinted as late as 1999, completed her magisterial compendium of allusions to Chaucer, *Five Hundred Years of Chaucer Criticism and Allusion (1357–1900)*, in 1925.[2] This massive work cites Chaucer's influence on *Midsummer Night's Dream* and *Troilus and Cressida*. Her ginger manner characterizes twentieth-century approaches to this topic: "Although Shakespeare never refers to Chaucer by name, and only once to the title of one of his works (The House of Fame, in *Titus Andronicus*), yet there are many indications that he knew Chaucer and was indebted to him."[3]

More recent critics have made bolder assertions. Ann Thompson's *Shakespeare's Chaucer: A Study in Literary Origins* connects Chaucer and Shakespeare in proverbial sayings, names, images — albeit in very different contexts — and plots: "The sheer quantity of material involved implies that Shakespeare did not merely use Chaucer for a plot or two (as he did some authors) but knew him so well that he recalled his work (often unconsciously, one would imagine) in virtually every play."[4]

According to Thompson, *A Midsummer Night's Dream* owes a debt to Chaucer's "Knight's Tale," "Merchant's Tale," *The Legend of Good Women*, and *The Parlement of Foules*: "the borrowings are of every kind, from substantial parallels of plot to the briefest of one-line references."[5] E. Talbot Donaldson, in *The Swan at the Well: Shakespeare Reading Chaucer*, treats relationships between the Wife of Bath and Falstaff, and *Chaucerian Shakespeare*, the collection of essays he edited, widens the purview to parallel the Wife of Bath and *The Taming of the Shrew*, Pandarus and Iago, and "The Pardoner's Tale" and *Romeo and Juliet*.[6] Recent critics have used the terminology of intertextuality to articulate the relationship. In *Intertextuality and Romance in Renaissance Drama: The Staging of Nostalgia*, Richard Hillman characterizes intertextuality as "the possible intersection of parallel lines" because "texts extend beyond specific artifacts to literary codes of all sorts."[7] Helen Cooper, in her essay in Theresa Krier's collection *Refiguring Chaucer in the Renaissance*, characterizes Shakespeare's use of Chaucer as "a continuing and detailed dialogue with its original."[8]

But Shakespeare's connection to Chaucer as poet cannot surmount a critical difficulty: Shakespeare scholars have offered Shakespeare's seeming disregard for publishing his plays as proof of his disinterest in "literary" status. They consider *The Winter's Tale*'s revived statue in terms of theatrical action or visible tableau rather than in literary terms. For instance, in his seminal article on *The Winter's Tale*, Leonard Barkan situates Hermione's statue within a history of sculpture and characterizes Shakespeare's theater as "four-dimensional sculpture."[9] That supposition of Shakespeare's disinterest in literary status, however, has recently been challenged. Lukas Erne argues against Shakespeare's "little interest in his writings as personal property and even less interest in posterity" and, instead, for a self-consciously literary Shakespeare.[10] Using data from the Stationers' Register and noting relationships among stationers, printers, actors, and the playwright, Erne constructs a Shakespeare who, with his players, was involved in publication of quarto plays. Moreover, Erne notes that many plays exceed, in their printed form, the "two hours' traffic of our stage" and suggests that such printed plays can best be read as consciously *literary* productions.[11] Even without Shakespeare's literal "fingerprint" on quarto editions of his plays, Erne sees the playwright consciously organizing his plays' printing and arranging content in order to secure a literary reputation.

Perhaps Erne's most stirring argument for a literary Shakespeare is his contention that in the last decade of his career, Shakespeare and company withheld publication of individual plays to engage anticipation of a collected "works."[12] The death of Queen Elizabeth in 1603 followed by frequent theater closures brought on by plague had reduced immediate demand for individual quartos. Profit-oriented companies took to the idea of collections to replace the printing of individual plays, and posterity-oriented playwrights could also see the collection's potential value for establishing a permanent literary reputation. Ben Jonson's efforts to collect his works in a single edition are well documented.[13] After Shakespeare's death, John Heminge and Henry Condell produced the "First Folio," a deluxe edition of all Shakespeare's "Comedies, Histories, & Tragedies." Erne suggests that the idea of Shakespeare's plays in a folio edition was on the playwright's mind, most prominently in the last decade of his career.

One prompt for Shakespeare's interest in a folio edition of his works may have come from Ben Jonson, as Erne suggests. But deluxe editions of Chaucer may also have inspired appreciation for the role a "complete works" folio edition could and did play in establishing literary reputation and prominence. Folio editions of Chaucer's *Works*, such as John Stow's in 1561 and Thomas Speght's in 1598, had shaped Chaucer's reputation as the father of English poetry.[14] The sixteenth-century "folio canon" (Kathleen Forni's phrase for deluxe editions of Chaucer's *Works*) fully endorsed the creation of Chaucer as national poet.[15] Editions of Chaucer exemplify the perfect vehicle — the perfect book — through which to shape literary history and literary reputation.

If Shakespeare's interest in literary heritage drew him to Chaucer's *Works*, then the trace of Chaucer in Shakespeare's plays that critics since Spurgeon have noticed may be read as Shakespeare's conscious acknowledgment of his literary predecessor. The depth and breadth of Shakespeare's use of Chaucer suggest his interest in a literary history of a printed folio sort. While printing provides a wealth of metaphors throughout Shakespeare's canon, his last play, the very popular *Tempest*, reveals an abiding interest in literary history's physical instantiation: books.[16] *The Tempest* overtly concerns the meanings of books and dramatizes relationships among poet, book, heredity, and literary inheritance, wrapped in an aura of magic, as Peter Greenaway's 1991 film *Prospero's Books* demonstrates. This theme of magic books also appears in *Tempest*, John Schmor's 2004 adaptation of Shakespeare's play for the Lord Leebrick Theatre Company, Eugene, Oregon. Schmor describes the opening set: "A lost room — a last room — hundreds of books— thousands of esoteric codes, markings, map-lines, diagrams, formulae cover the floor" with "a 12′ diameter alchemical circle on the floor lined with the words 'Solvite Corpora' (dissolve the body)."[17] But the magic of books and the power of literary history have another sense appropriate to the stage and deeper even than Prospero's: readers revive (dead) authors.

I have written elsewhere about the way the sixteenth-century folio canon of Chaucer's *Works* constructs its Chaucer as a living father.[18] Paratexts in the folio canon — woodcut illustrations, charts, genealogies — picture Chaucer and his progeny, interwoven with fourteenth- and fifteenth-century nobility, in a fashion that suits the Tudor obsession with lineage.[19] With an image of Chaucer surmounting the tomb of his son Thomas and his wife, Maud (both shown in effigy), the folio canon also emphasizes Chaucer's living presence among his literary, as well as human, progeny. Even more obviously, *The Canterbury Tales*'s frame narrative gives us Chaucer as author and character. The pilgrim Chaucer tells two tales titled, in modern editions, "The Tale of Sir Thopas" and *The Tale of Melibee*. Lambasted for his turgid poetic "Tale of Sir Thopas," the pilgrim Chaucer gets a second chance and recounts in prose (one of only two prose performances in *The Canterbury Tales*) *The Tale of Melibee*, the story of the eponymous Melibee and his wife, Prudence. The folio canon includes both of these tales, but it titles them differently. Sixteenth-century readers would have read "The Rime," not the "Tale of Sir Thopas" and, even more significantly, they would have read *The Tale of Chaucer* rather than *The Tale of Melibee*. The folio canon invariably titles *The Tale of Melibee* as *The Tale of Chaucer*. It was possible to find Chaucer — his voice and person — in a folio edition of his *Works*, especially if the reader concentrated on the *Canterbury Tales*, and it was encouraged by the form, images, and words of Chaucer's *Works*.

The Tale of Chaucer with which the sixteenth-century folio canon identifies the father of English literature is a tale in prose that concerns, as does Shakespeare's *The Winter's Tale*, female eloquence successfully meeting patriarchal wrath.[20] *The Tale of Chaucer* stages a dialogue between King Melibee and his wife, Prudence, after "olde foes" have broken into Melibee's house, beating Prudence and wounding "in five sondry places" his daughter, Sophie.[21] The tale combines allegory with realpolitik as Prudence cautions Melibee against vengeance. Prudence is a clear and adept counselor, telling Melibee of his errors and giving him wisdom from Jesus Sirach, Seneca, and Cassiodorus, to name only a few of her many references to wisdom literature.[22] Indeed, early editions of the tale accentuated its sententious nature by literally "starring," with asterisks, the attributed and conventional aphorisms.

Despite its dramatic beginning fraught with mayhem — the old foes breaking into Melibee's house and attacking his wife and daughter — *The Tale of Chaucer* includes little action. But it does include characterization. Melibee needs repeated prompting to accede to Prudence's call to forgive his enemies: his thickheadedness requires Prudence's persistence and repetition before he gets the point. Besides Melibee's obtuseness and Prudence's determination, the tale has a "second act" climax: Prudence advises Melibee to review the advice doctors and surgeons had given him regarding vengeance (1264–1289). Essentially, physicians heal by contraries, although Melibee has initially misread the contraries. War is vanquished not with more war but with peace, she tells Melibee, and to certify her advice, Prudence invokes St. Paul: "Ne yeldeth nat harm for harm, ne wikked speche for wikked speche, but do wel to hym that dooth thee harm, and blesse hym that seith to thee harm" (1291).

This Pauline advice, coupled with physicians and surgeons serving as advisors, corresponds to the theme of healing urgency in *The Winter's Tale* but also, and more pointedly, to the play's character of Paulina, whose office to remonstrate with the lunatic king "becomes a woman best"[23] even as the play ends in forgiveness and reconciliation. In the play, Paulina eventually becomes Leontes' sole advisor and works her magic to chasten and heal. Unlike the failed and dead queen of *Pandosto* and the seemingly dead but surely absent (for sixteen years) queen, Hermione, in *The Winter's Tale*, Paulina, like Chaucer's Prudence, succeeds in meeting patriarchal wrath with female eloquence.

The Winter's Tale does include one specific reference to Chaucer: to "Dame Partlet" (2.3.74), the name of Chauntecleer's talking chicken wife in the "The Nun's Priest's Tale." But *The Winter's Tale* has a Chaucerian flavor in another fashion: it is the only one of Shakespeare's plays to use the word "tale" in its title. Subtle correspondences between *The Winter's Tale* and *The Tale of Chaucer* support their thematic connection. Although, unlike the peripatetic action of *The Winter's Tale*, the plot of *The Tale of Chaucer* stays in one locale, its queen, like both Queen Hermione and noble Paulina in Shakespeare's play, eloquently meets and defeats patriarchal wrath. Both *The Tale of Chaucer* and *The Winter's Tale* figure generational continuity through daughters, one injured, the other lost. In the case of *The Tale of Chaucer*, Prudence advises Melibee, "Youre doghter, with the grace of God, shal warisshe and escape" (982). The play's two women gear their efforts in service to a daughter, Perdita, as Hermione makes clear:

> I,
> Knowing by Paulina that the oracle
> Gave hope thou wast in being, have preserved
> Myself to see the issue [5.3.125–128].

A daughter's very specific injuries precipitate *The Tale of Melibee*; the rediscovery of a lost daughter closes *The Winter's Tale*. In Chaucer's tale, Prudence counsels Melibee to forgo violence on account of his minuscule family: "For al be it so that ye be mighty and riche, certes ye ne been but alone, / for certes ye ne han no child but a doghter, / ne ye ne han bretheren, ne cosyns germayns, ne noon oother neigh kynrede" (1365–1367). So, too, Leontes' family shrinks at Mamillius's death, its size a dramatic problem: "The King shall live without an heir, if that which is lost be not found" (3.2.134–136).

While an injured daughter begins the action of *The Tale of Chaucer*, a lost daughter links the two halves of *The Winter's Tale*. The play's lost daughter, like the tale's injured daughter, needs Time's passage, as well as her father's abjection, in order to be saved. Injury appears in both texts, but with fatal results only in *The Winter's Tale* and only for Mamillius and Antigonus. In Chaucer's tale, Prudence's debate with Melibee springs from an attack by Melibee's foes: "Thre of his olde foes ... betten his wyf [Prudence] and wound ... his doghter [Sophia]" (970–971).[24] His family's injuries prompt Melibee, husband and father, to call for revenge. In *The Winter's Tale*, conversely, the harm done Leontes—his conviction that his wife, Hermione, has been unchaste—exists only in his imagination. Even more tragically, death overtakes Leontes' son Mamillius, the result not of the acts of outside foes, as in Chaucer's tale, but of Leontes' own behavior. Leontes initially ignores female counsel with dreadful results but reconciles himself to it in the play's last act; he has been contrite for sixteen years. As Paulina has worked for sixteen years to keep Leontes in line, Prudence works overtime to temper Melibee's anger. After more than nine hundred lines of debate in which she answers Melibee's desire for vengeance with advice from classical authors like Cicero and Boethius and his antifeminist slanders with examples from the Bible and Cato, Prudence convinces Melibee to forgive those who have wronged his family and holdings. With his blessing, she negotiates with Melibee's enemies and brings all parties together for reconciliation. In his final, performative speech, Melibee speaks to his former enemies: "Wherefore I receyve yow to my grace / and foryeve yow outrely alle the offenses, injuries, and wronges that ye have doon agayn me and myne" (1882–1883). Prudence's eloquence and her eventual success in guiding her husband to forgiveness are parallel to Paulina's eventual success as Leontes' advisor, physician, and artist. *The Winter's Tale* expands the quality and consequences of patriarchal wrath found in *The Tale of Chaucer*, turning injury into death and allying reconciliation with reanimation in Hermione's living statue.

Post-partum Hermione (Miriam A. Laube) suffers the violent accusations of Leontes (William Langan) as the lord of Sicilia (Richard Baird) looks on in *The Winter's Tale*, Oregon Shakespeare Festival, 2006. Photograph by David Cooper.

At one point in her efforts to change Melibee's mind, Prudence uses a "semblaunt of wratthe" (1706) and *acts* for Melibee's profit. She chooses to chasten Melibee through an emotional outburst, then admits that her "semblaunt of wratthe" was a rhetorical ploy. In *The Winter's Tale*, Paulina's efforts to change Leontes also involve an emotional outburst and also involve a pretense: the death of Hermione. Like Prudence's outburst, Paulina's pretense of Hermione's death — "I say she's dead; I'll swear't" (3.2.203) — chastens her male interlocutor: "Go on, go on; / Thou canst not speak too much, I have deserv'd / All tongues to talk their bitt'rest" (3.2.214–216). The lie and the action of *The Winter's Tale* are more elaborate than Prudence's short-lived rhetorical guise, but both tale and play excuse the artifice of rhetorical deception when it cures patriarchal wrath. Prudence and Paulina use their rhetorical art to change the patriarch's vengeful wrath into remorse: fools need to be corrected, according to Prudence, and to prove their changed hearts through a changed face. By turning bodily injury — Sophia's — into the deaths of Hermione and Mamillius and laying the blame for their deaths at the feet of a father rather than outside foes, *The Winter's Tale* accentuates the horrors of patriarchal wrath met by the salvific power of the female voice recounted in the nondramatic family plot of Chaucer's prose tale. Both tale and play promote reconciliation through women's words of peace.

Of course, the main plot for *The Winter's Tale* derives not from Chaucer's tale but from *Pandosto*, a popular prose novel by Robert Greene (1558?–1592), the London literary wit and would-be Shakespeare competitor.[25] *Pandosto* provides characters, locations (Sicilia and Bohemia, although Shakespeare reverses their order), and plot for *The Winter's Tale*. There are, naturally enough, differences between Greene's prose and Shakespeare's drama. Greene's "Hermione" dies rather than faints at the news of her son's death. Greene's "Leontes" has no female advisor challenging and guiding him, and while he repents of his errors, he commits suicide at the end of the play. Shakespeare adds Paulina, the female advisor, to Greene's characters, revives Hermione's statue at the end of the play, and omits any hint of Leontes' suicide. Still, Greene's fingerprint remains on the play in ways visible only to readers concerned — as was Greene, apparently — with literary history. Yet Greene helps us to excavate the subterranean influence of literary history in Shakespeare's plays.

The Winter's Tale's audience may have noted Shakespeare's debt to Greene's *Pandosto* through often-exact parallels between novel and play. They may have laid at Greene's door the *Winter's Tale*'s confidence artist Autolycus because besides uplifting prose works like *The myrrour of modestie* (1584), Greene wrote cony-catching tales like *A notable discouery of coosenage* (1591). Ever the wit, Greene even wrote a satiric defense of confidence schemes, ostensibly penned by "Cuthbert Cunny-catcher, licentiate in Whittington Colledge" (1592). In another allusion to Greene, the name of Hermione's and Leontes' son, called "Garinter" in *Pandosto* but Mamillius in *The Winter's Tale*, echoes the title of Greene's 1583 play *Mamillia*. Those in the know may even have remembered Greene's veiled comment about Shakespeare, a "snarling reference," according to Sylvan Barnet to "an upstart crow, beautified with our feathers, that with his tiger's heart wrapped in a player's hide supposed he is as well able to bombast out a blank verse as the best of you, and being an absolute Johannes-factotum is in his own conceit the only Shake-scene in a country."[26] Evidently Greene's and Shakespeare's paths had crossed before, and although Greene died in 1592, his books and pamphlets continued in print well into the seventeenth century. One modern editor of *The Winter's Tale* finds that Shakespeare "seems for some reason to have been interested in Greene."[27]

One of Robert Greene's books, *Greene's Vision: Written at the Instant of His Death* (1592),[28] presents a colloquy on literary reputation, evidently a concern of Greene's. A dream vision in prose and poetry, *Greene's Vision* recounts Geoffrey Chaucer, John Gower, and Greene arguing about the morality of their several works as well as the meaning of literature more generally. Greene's own works hang in the balance. While scholarly opinion divides on whether Greene himself wrote the work, his dramatic ambiance pervades it. In *Greene's Vision*, after Greene states his case regarding the fitness of his own poetry and whether he wrote "The Cobler of Caunterburie"— a ribald pseudo-Chaucerian continuation of Chaucer's *Tales*— Chaucer tells Greene not to concern himself with the ascription of "The Cobler." Then "Chawcer sat downe and laught, and then rising vp and leaning his back against a Tree, he made this merry aunswer." In the event, "moral" Gower bests the tale-telling Chaucer with a story of wifely virtue one critic calls "little more than a framework for its abundance of *sententiae*."[29] When Greene accedes to Gower's injunction to leave off writing of love, "Chawcer shakt his head and fumed."[30] The last word belongs to Solomon, who, like a *deus ex machina*, enjoins Greene to "leave all other vaine studies, and applye thy selfe to feede upon that heauenly manna," to which the waking Greene accedes, concluding with "as you had the blossomes of my wanton fancies, so you shall haue the fruites of my better labours."[31]

While Gower's brand of sententious morality "wins," Chaucer's voice argues for tolerance. His tale, although lacking a moral issue like Gower's, teases authority through the comeuppance of a jealous husband. Helen Cooper reads *Greene's Vision* on the worth and morality of literature this way:

> Literature may indeed be wanton; but although its attractiveness may make it suspect, that does not in every case necessitate a denial of its worth, its power of persuading to virtue. The responsibility may, however, fall as much on the reader as on the writer.[32]

Greene's Vision explicitly concerns literary heritage and uses Chaucer and Gower to make its case. By this time, Gower had already earned the epithet "moral," while the phrase "a Canterbury Tale" had already become synonymous with scurrility and impropriety.[33] *Greene's Vision* dramatizes the Chaucer-Gower competition and, with the blessing of Solomon, trumps wit with author-

Leontes (William Langan), Perdita (Nell Geisslinger), Paulina (Greta Oglesby), and Florizel (Juan Rivera LeBron) gaze in wonder at the statue of Hermione in Paulina's garden in *The Winter's Tale*, Oregon Shakespeare Festival, 2006. Photograph by David Cooper.

ity, the ribald with the sententious, Chaucer with Gower. Thus *Greene's Vision*, through Chaucer and Gower, presents Greene's final word — as literally as it can — on literary reputation.

At about the same time as he was writing *The Winter's Tale*, Shakespeare — or perhaps his collaborator — put moral Gower on stage; in *Pericles*, Gower is the named chorus figure. Nowhere in Shakespeare's plays is there an equivalent role for Chaucer. Though he credits Chaucer as the source of his plot for *The Two Noble Kinsmen* ("The Knight's Tale"), Shakespeare never lets an embodied Chaucer strut the stage like *Pericles*'s Gower. Yet his interest in books in *The Tempest* along with his personification of Gower in *Pericles* suggests his concern with English literary history and the mechanisms of literary reputation. Perhaps *The Winter's Tale*, a late romance and, in the opinion of one director, Libby Appel, Shakespeare's greatest play, provided a place for subtle exposition on literary inheritance to complement, if not supersede, the Gower of *Pericles* and Prospero's books in *The Tempest*.[34] In *The Winter's Tale*, Shakespeare took various pages from Greene — both the plot of *Pandosto* and the characters and concerns of *Greene's Vision* — and added an inflection of Chaucer, both his tale and his *Works* as a whole, to honor female eloquence and, through allusion to the father of English poetry, make a case for "tales." Shakespeare's play, infused with Chaucer, stands up for tales and for female eloquence as answer to false, even deadly, masculine authority.

The character of Paulina best makes this case. There is no Paulina character in *Pandosto*, but her role is central to Shakespeare's play. Her good advice to Leontes, although ignored, is the best advice he could get, and she knows it: "These dangerous, unsafe lunes i' th' King, beshrew them! / He must be told on 't, and he shall; the office / Becomes a woman best" (2.2.29–31). As in *The Tale of Chaucer/Melibee*, women best speak truth to power: female eloquence meets patriarchal

With infant Perdita in her arms, Paulina (Greta Oglesby) prepares to confront the "unsafe lunes" of King Leontes in *The Winter's Tale*, Oregon Shakespeare Festival, 2006. Photograph by David Cooper.

wrath. Although Paulina does not prevent the deaths in Act 3, her success as the advisor of Leontes opens Act 5. The contrite king has had her advice for sixteen years, and she has reminded him continually of his disastrous wrath:

> Good Paulina,
> Who hast the memory of Hermione,
> I know, in honor: O, that ever I
> Had squared me to they counsel! Then, even now,
> I might have looked upon my queen's full eyes [5.1.49 53].

Leontes swears never to marry (5.1.71) except with Paulina's approval (5.1.83), much to the consternation of the courtiers Cleomenes and Dion, who express their country's desperate wish for an heir to the throne. Paulina's success, like Prudence's, is neither immediate nor easily won. Shakespeare adds a successful female rhetor to *Pandosto*, and the Pauline echoes of Chaucer's Prudence may contribute to Paulina's name. In this fashion Shakespeare interweaves the theme of female eloquence meeting patriarchal wrath with English literary history, inspired by *The Tale of Chaucer/Melibee* in Chaucer's reputation-making *Works*, titled in Speght's 1598 edition, "THE / Workes of our Anti- / ent and lerned English Poet / GEFFREY CHAVCER."

Nothing is more dramatic in *The Winter's Tale* than the revelation of a living Hermione in the play's last act. As Paulina avers, "It is required / You do awake your faith" (5.3.92–93). Besides the character of Paulina, Shakespeare's other addition to the plot he borrowed from Greene's *Pandosto* is the statue of the last act. A revived statue that stands for the reanimation of England's "father of English poetry"—a position for Chaucer that *Greene's Vision* allows even as it contests his worth—reveals Shakespeare's own hope for a literary legacy. It is a legacy that supersedes the

Paulina (Mimi Carr) awakens the faith of Perdita (Karin Johnson) and Leontes (Rex Rabold) as they circle the statue of Hermione (Liisa Ivary). *The Winter's Tale*, Oregon Shakespeare Festival, 1990. Photograph by Christopher Briscoe.

reputation and limitations of Robert Greene because it fits the *Works* of Geoffrey Chaucer not only within literary history but as English literature's voice for reconciliation. Through his attention to Greene's concern for literary reputation and his competition (real or imagined) with Greene for literary preeminence and the attentions of posterity, Shakespeare takes the subtle, mythic, literary, and dramatic to awaken his audience's faith in the power of the (printed) word and its alliance with timeless art to effect reconciliation. As in books, the once-dead speak; the lost are found. A living statue sustained by female hands, reputed to have been the creation of a man, Julio Romano, and saved for a daughter certifies the protean nature of a tale and *Tales*: of English literary history, of art's continuity, and of its powerful message of both faith and hope for reconciliation.

The dramaturge for the 2006 Oregon Shakespeare Festival production, Patricia Troxel, maintains that things medieval did not enter into director Libby Appel's preparation for the play.[35] Instead, the production emphasized the play's out-of-time character. But Appel had directed the play in 1990, and her papers, collected in the festival's archives, reveal a subtle strand of medieval considerations in her notes.[36] For instance, she mentions the Everyman quality of the play, a connection with medieval drama that also appears in her January 4, 2006, production presentation for festival members that calls *The Winter's Tale* a "cycle play." In the quotations Appel collected for the 1990 production, she includes one from *The Mists of Avalon*, the feminist retelling of the Arthur myths by Marion Zimmer Bradley. She also asks, in her suggestions for costume and set, for a sense of the Pre-Raphaelites as providing a myth and a kind of made-up religion. The Pre-Raphaelites were themselves reviving the Middle Ages, and this sense of literary revival subtly haunts her productions of the play. Appel's 1990 request for design that includes "Russian jeweled ikons" provides another trace of the medieval. In the 2006 production, a medieval offering appears in Troxel's description of the set's "art-gallery feel": according to dramaturge Troxel, it was meant to invoke St. Sebastian, the quintessential medieval erotic saint.[37]

Literary history, beginning with the folio canon, has created the Chaucer we recognize, but critical assessment of Chaucer's *Works*—or of Shakespeare's plays, for that matter—was far from secure in the early modern period. *The Winter's Tale* is not explicitly medieval; it fully incorporates its Chaucer. At the same time, *The Winter's Tale*'s interest in reconciliation sounds a note too often (and quite erroneously) thought absent from medieval literature, which is more customarily associated in the minds of modern readers with torture devices, warrior knights, and the Crusades. Instead, hard-won peace and reconciliation are the main themes of Chaucer's *Melibee*, themes echoed later by Shakespeare in *The Winter's Tale*. Shakespeare was a better and more subtle reader of Chaucer than we are.

Notes

1. The folio editions of Chaucer's *Works* are attributed to editors William Thynne (1532: STC 5068), John Stow (1561: STC 5075, 5076), and Thomas Speght (1598: STC 5077, 5078, 5079; 1602: STC 5080, 5081).
2. Carolyn Spurgeon, *Five Hundred Years of Chaucer Criticism and Allusion (1357–1900)*, 4 vols. (Cambridge, UK: University Press, 1925). Spurgeon's work has been only recently and only partially superseded by Jackson Campbell Boswell and Sylvia Holton, *Chaucer's Fame in England: STC Chauceriana, 1475–1640* (New York: Modern Language Association of America, 2004).
3. Spurgeon, *Five Hundred Years*, vol. 4, 45–46.
4. Ann Thompson, *Shakespeare's Chaucer: A Study in Literary Origins* (New York: Barnes & Noble Books, 1978), 59.
5. Ibid., 88.
6. E. Talbot Donaldson, *The Swan at the Well: Shakespeare Reading Chaucer* (New Haven, CT: Yale University Press, 1985); E. Talbot Donaldson and Judith J. Kollmann, eds., *Chaucerian Shakespeare: Adaptation and Transformation: A Collection of Essays* (Detroit, MI: Michigan Consortium for Medieval and Early Modern Studies, distributed by Fifteenth-Century Symposium, Marygrove College, 1983).
7. Richard Hillman, *Intertextuality and Romance in Renaissance Drama: The Staging of Nostalgia* (London: Macmillan, 1992), 4, 6.

8. Helen Cooper, "Jacobean Chaucer: *The Two Noble Kinsmen* and Other Chaucerian Plays," in *Refiguring Chaucer in the Renaissance*, ed. Theresa Krier (Gainesville, FL: University Press of Florida, 1998), 189–209, 189.

9. Leonard Barkan, "'Living Sculptures': Ovid, Michaelangelo, and *The Winter's Tale*," *English Literary History* 48, no. 4 (1981): 639–667, quotation on 664.

10. Lukas Erne, *Shakespeare as Literary Dramatist* (Cambridge, UK: Cambridge University Press, 2003), 4.

11. *Ibid.*, 131.

12. *Ibid.*, 108–110.

13. *Ibid.*, 31–33. There is even earlier precedence for publishing a collected works that bespeaks a poet's self-interest. John Skelton's *Garland of Laurel* offers an example of "a poet having deliberately written sixteen hundred lines in honour of himself"; see Martha W. Driver, "John Skelton, *The Garland of Laurel*," in *The Facts on File Companion to British Poetry before 1600*, ed. Michelle M. Sauer (New York: Facts on File, 2008), quoting Alexander Dyce (Skelton's earliest editor).

14. See Anne Hudson, "John Stow, 1525?–1605," and Derek Pearsall, "Thomas Speght, c. 1550–?" in *Editing Chaucer: The Great Tradition*, ed. Paul G. Ruggiers (Norman, OK: Pilgrim Books, 1984), 53–70 and 71–92; Alice Miskimin, "The 1598 Folio of Speght," in *The Renaissance Chaucer* (New Haven, CT: Yale University Press, 1975), 250–255; and Martha W. Driver, "Mapping Chaucer: John Speed and the Later Portraits," *Chaucer Review* 36, no. 3 (2002): 229–249.

15. Kathleen Forni, *The Chaucerian Apocrypha: A Counterfeit Canon* (Gainesville: University Press of Florida, 2001), coined the term for the deluxe folio editions of Chaucer published in the second half of the sixteenth century by John Stow and Thomas Speght. On Stow as editor, see the essays in Ian Anders Gadd and Alexandra Gillespie, eds., *John Stow (1525–1605) and the Making of the English Past: Studies in Early Modern Culture and the History of the Book* (London: British Library Publications, 2004). For more literary interpretation of the meaning of "Chaucer" for later periods, see Thomas Prendergast and Barbara Kline, eds., *Rewriting Chaucer: Culture, Authority, and the Idea of the Authentic Text, 1400–1602* (Columbus: Ohio State University Press, 1999); and Stephanie Trigg, *Congenial Souls: Reading Chaucer from Medieval to Postmodern* (Minneapolis: Minnesota University Press, 2002). On Shakespeare as national poet, see Patrick G. Cheney, *Shakespeare, National Poet-Playwright* (Cambridge, UK: Cambridge University Press, 2004).

16. For a recent analysis of printing as metaphor, see Douglas A. Brooks, *Printing and Parenting in Early Modern England* (Aldershot, UK: Ashgate, 2005).

17. From John Schmor's director's notes, used by permission. My thanks to my colleague at the University of Oregon for sharing his production notes with me.

18. See Louise M. Bishop, "Father Chaucer and the Vivification of Print," *Journal of English and Germanic Philology* 106, no. 3 (2007): 336–363.

19. See Sarah H. Kelen, "Climbing up the Family Tree: Chaucer's Tudor Progeny," *Journal of the Early Book Society* 6 (2003): 109–123; and also Driver, "Mapping Chaucer."

20. For a reading of *The Winter's Tale* that interprets the play on this basis, see Lynn Enterline, "'You Speak a Language I Understand Not': The Rhetoric of Animation in *The Winter's Tale*," *Shakespeare Quarterly* 48, no. 1 (Spring 1997): 17–44.

21. Geoffrey Chaucer, *The Riverside Chaucer*, 3rd ed., gen. ed. Larry D. Benson (Boston: Houghton Mifflin, 1987), 217–239, here ll. 970–971. All subsequent references to *The Tale of Melibee* (which I refer to as *The Tale of Chaucer* in this essay) are taken from this edition and cited by line rather than page numbers.

22. Martha Driver, "Romancing the *Rose*: The Readings of Chaucer and Christine," in *Writings on Love in the English Middle Ages*, ed. Helen Cooney, Studies in Arthurian and Courtly Cultures (London: Palgrave, 2006), 147–162, reads Chaucer's *Melibee* in conjunction with some poetry of his near-contemporary Christine de Pisan, including her *Livre de Prudence*, to note both authors' answers to the antifeminist stereotypes of the *Romance of the Rose* and to explain the "moral world view" of both poets (158).

23. William Shakespeare, *The Riverside Shakespeare*, ed. G. Blakemore Evans (Boston: Houghton Mifflin, 1973), 2.2.31. All further citations to the play are taken from this edition and cited by act, scene, and line numbers.

24. Daughter Sophia's injuries generally correspond to the five senses, lending support to an allegorical reading of the daughter's name; see the notes to the *Tale* in Chaucer, *Riverside Chaucer*, 3rd ed., 923–924.

25. For a compendious and enlightening analysis of the fortunes of Greene's play, see Lori Humphrey Newcomb, *Reading Popular Romance in Early Modern England* (New York: Columbia University Press, 2002).

26. Sylvan Barnet, "Shakespeare: Prefatory Remarks," in William Shakespeare, *The Winter's Tale*, ed. Frank Kermode, The Signet Classic Shakespeare (New York: New American Library, 1963), ix. STC 12278, 12279.4, 5656, 12269.

27. Frank Kermode, "The Source of *The Winter's Tale*," in Shakespeare, *The Winter's Tale*, ed. Frank Kermode, The Signet Classic Shakespeare (New York: New American Library, 1963), 155.

28. STC 12261. See Helen Cooper, "'This Worthy Olde Writer': *Pericles* and Other Gowers," in *A Com-

panion to Gower, ed. Siân Echard (Cambridge, UK: D. S. Brewer, 2004), 100–113, esp. 100–104. On *Greene's Vision* and "self-authorization," see Newcomb, *Reading Popular Romance*, 47, 52. Derek Brewer, *Geoffrey Chaucer, The Critical Heritage*, vol. 1, *1385–1837* (London: Routledge, 1978; repr. 1995), 130–135, prints a fair amount of *Greene's Vision*, as do Boswell and Holton, *Chaucer's Fame in England*, 136–138.

29. Cooper, "This Worthy Olde Writer," 104.
30. Accessed through the *Early English Books Online* (EEBO) database (Ann Arbor: University of Michigan, 1998–), http://eebo.chadwyck.com/home (February 13, 2005).
31. EEBO (February 13, 2005).
32. Cooper, "This Worthy Olde Writer," 104.
33. See the examples in Boswell and Holton, *Chaucer's Fame in England*, nos. 337 (calling Chaucer's tales "stale"), 375 (comparing "Caunterburie tales" to counterfeiting), and 497 (putting *Canterbury Tales* into a dung-cart).
34. From Libby Appel's presentation as director of the 2006 Oregon Shakespeare Festival production of *The Winter's Tale* in an introduction to the play, January 4, 2006. Provided through the courtesy of Kit Leary, archivist for the Oregon Shakespeare Festival, Ashland, Oregon.
35. Telephone interview, September 8, 2006.
36. My thanks to Oregon Shakespeare Festival archivist Kit Leary for providing me access to Libby Appel's notes for her 1990 production of *The Winter's Tale*.
37. St. Sebastian's medieval popularity is attested in scholarship; see Detlev, Baron von Hadeln, *Die wichtigsten Darstellungsformen des H. Sebastian in der italienischen Malerei bis zum Ausgang des Quatrocento* (Strassburg: J. H. E. Heitz, 1906), which details Italian depictions of the saint, primarily in paint but also in sculpture and mosaic, and the travels of these Italian artworks throughout Europe. The saint has also been a figure for modern adoration, especially for the gay community; see Derek Jarman's homoerotic film *Sebastiane*, the only film with exclusively Latin dialogue.

Works Cited

Barkan, Leonard. "'Living Sculptures': Ovid, Michaelangelo, and *The Winter's Tale*." *English Literary History* 48, no. 4 (1981): 639–667.
Barnet, Sylvan. "Shakespeare: Prefatory Remarks." In William Shakespeare, *The Winter's Tale*, edited by Frank Kermode, The Signet Classic Shakespeare. vii–xx. New York: New American Library, 1963.
Bishop, Louise M. "Father Chaucer and the Vivification of Print." *Journal of English and Germanic Philology* 106, no. 3 (2007): 336–363.
Boswell, Jackson Campbell, and Sylvia Wallace Holton. *Chaucer's Fame in England: STC Chauceriana, 1475–1640*. New York: Modern Language Association of America, 2004.
Brewer, Derek. *Geoffrey Chaucer, The Critical Heritage*. Vol. 1, 1385–1837. London: Routledge, 1978; repr. 1995.
Brooks, Douglas A. *Printing and Parenting in Early Modern England*. Aldershot, UK: Ashgate, 2005.
Cheney, Patrick Gerard. *Shakespeare, National Poet-Playwright*. Cambridge, UK: Cambridge University Press, 2004.
Cooper, Helen. "Jacobean Chaucer: *The Two Noble Kinsmen* and Other Chaucerian Plays." In *Refiguring Chaucer in the Renaissance*, edited by Theresa Krier, 189–209. Gainesville, FL: University Press of Florida, 1998.
———. "'This Worthy Olde Writer': and Other Gowers." In *A Companion to Gower*, edited by Siân Echard, 100–113. Cambridge, UK: D.S. Brewer, 2004.
Donaldson, E. Talbot. *The Swan at the Well: Shakespeare Reading Chaucer*. New Haven, CT: Yale University Press, 1985.
———, and Judith J. Kollmann, eds. *Chaucerian Shakespeare: Adaptation and Transformation: A Collection of Essays*. Detroit, MI: Michigan Consortium for Medieval and Early Modern Studies, distributed by Fifteenth-Century Symposium, Marygrove College, 1983.
Driver, Martha. "John Skelton, *The Garland of Laurel*." In *The Facts on File Companion to British Poetry before 1600*, edited by Michelle M. Sauer. New York: Facts on File, 2008.
———. "Mapping Chaucer: John Speed and the Later Portraits." *Chaucer Review* 36, no. 3 (2002): 228–249.
———. "Romancing the *Rose*: The Readings of Chaucer and Christine." In *Writings on Love in the English Middle Ages*, edited by Helen Cooney, 147–162. Studies in Arthurian and Courtly Cultures. London: Palgrave, 2006.
Enterline, Lynn. "'You Speak a Language I Understand Not': The Rhetoric of Animation in *The Winter's Tale*." *Shakespeare Quarterly* 48, no. 1 (1997): 17–44.
Erne, Lukas. *Shakespeare as Literary Dramatist*. Cambridge, UK: Cambridge University Press, 2003.

Forni, Kathleen. *The Chaucerian Apocrypha: A Counterfeit Canon*. Gainesville: University Press of Florida, 2001.
Gadd, Ian Anders, and Alexandra Gillespie, eds. *John Stow (1525–1605) and the Making of the English Past: Studies in Early Modern Culture and the History of the Book*. London: British Library Publications, 2004.
Greene, Robert. *Pandosto, or the Triumph of Time*. 1588. The Shakespeare Library, gen. ed. I. Gollancz. Toronto: Centre for Reformation and Renaissance Studies [n.d.].
———. *Greenes Vision, vvritten at the instant of his death. Conteyning a penitent passion for the folly of his pen*. STC 12261. London: Thomas Newman, 1588. Available at Early English Books Online. http://eebo.chadwyck.com/home.
Hadeln, Detlev, Baron von. *Die wichtigsten Darstellungsformen des H. Sebastian in der italienischen Malerei bis zum Ausgang des Quatrocento*. Strassburg: J. H. E. Heitz, 1906.
Hillman, Richard. *Intertextuality and Romance in Renaissance Drama: The Staging of Nostalgia*. London: Macmillan, 1992.
Hudson, Anne. "John Stow, 1525?-1605." In *Editing Chaucer: The Great Tradition*, edited by Paul G. Ruggiers, 53–70. Norman, OK: Pilgrim Books, 1984.
Kelen, Sarah H. "Climbing up the Family Tree: Chaucer's Tudor Progeny." *Journal of the Early Book Society* 6 (2003): 109–123.
Kermode, Frank. "The Source of *The Winter's Tale*." In William Shakespeare, *The Winter's Tale*, edited by Frank Kermode. The Signet Classic Shakespeare, 155–177. New York: New American Library, 1963.
Newcomb, Lori Humphrey. "'If That Which Is Lost Be Not Found': Monumental Bodies, Spectacular Bodies in *The Winter's Tale*." In *Ovid and the Renaissance Body*, edited by Goran V. Stanivukovic, 239–259. Toronto: University of Toronto Press, 2001.
———. *Reading Popular Romance in Early Modern England*. New York: Columbia University Press, 2002.
Pearsall, Derek. "Thomas Speght, c. 1550?" In *Editing Chaucer: The Great Tradition*, edited by Paul G. Ruggiers, 71–92. Norman, OK: Pilgrim Books, 1984.
Prendergast, Thomas A., and Barbara Kline, eds. *Rewriting Chaucer: Culture, Authority, and the Idea of the Authentic Text, 1400–1602*. Columbus: Ohio State University Press, 1999.
Shakespeare, William. *The Riverside Shakespeare*. Edited by G. Blakemore Evans. Boston: Houghton Mifflin, 1974.
Spurgeon, Caroline Frances Eleanor. *Five Hundred Years of Chaucer Criticism and Allusion 1357–1900*. Cambridge, UK: Cambridge University Press, 1925.
Thompson, Ann. *Shakespeare's Chaucer: A Study in Literary Origins*. New York: Barnes & Noble Books, 1978.
Trigg, Stephanie. *Congenial Souls: Reading Chaucer from Medieval to Postmodern*. Minneapolis: University of Minnesota Press, 2002.

FILMOGRAPHY AND PERFORMANCES

1991 *Prospero's Books*, d. Peter Greenaway, with Sir John Gielgud, Michael Clark, and Erland Josephson. European Union: Allarts, Cinéa, Caméra One, Penta Films S.L., Canal+, NHK, VPRO Television, Elsevier-Vendex Film Beheer, Channel 4 International, Pierson, Heldring & Pierson N.V., Stichting Produktiefonds voor Nederlandse Films, Eurimages, Palace Pictures.
1976 *Sebastiane*, d. Derek Jarman, with Barney James, Neil Kennedy, Leonardo Treviglio, and Richard Warwick. UK: Double Crown.
2004 *Tempest*, d. John Schmor, with Leon Johnson, Chris Hirsh, Kim Bates, Steve Wehmeier, Richard Lineweaver, and David Bull. Lord Leebrick Theatre Company, Eugene, Oregon.
1990 *The Winter's Tale*, d. Libby Appel, with Rex Rabold, Liisa Ivary, Mimi Carr, Patrick Page, James Edmondson, Karin Johnson, and Dennis Rees. Oregon Shakespeare Festival, Ashland, Oregon.
2006 *The Winter's Tale*, d. Libby Appel, with William Langan, Miriam A. Laube, Greta Oglesby, Christopher DuVal, Jeffrey King, Nell Geisslinger, and Juan Rivera LeBron. Oregon Shakespeare Festival, Ashland, Oregon.

Caliban's God: The Medieval and Renaissance Man in the Moon

Kim Zarins

What kind of man is Caliban? Or what kind of creature—fish-man, wodewose, demi-devil? His name, derived from the words *cannibal* and *Carib*, the name of a people of the Carribean, has led scholars to see Caliban as a Native American or African abused by Western colonialism.[1] Other scholars, prompted by the cast description of Caliban as a "salvage and deformed slave" and textual references to Caliban's misshapen form, fishlike smell, long nails, and demonic parentage, question his monstrosity.[2] While hardly offering a definitive statement on Caliban's almost protean identity, as a medievalist I hope to offer a new angle on him by exploring his belief in his god—not Setebos, but rather the Man in the Moon of medieval folklore. Postcolonial readings emphasize Setebos's importance to Caliban, but the reference to the Man in the Moon reveals a different if related aspect of Caliban's identity as a common laborer who longs for release from his hard master.

The passage I speak of follows on the heels of the comedy of errors in act 2, scene 2, in which Caliban, petrified at what mischief the spirits seem to be throwing his way, huddles under his gaberdine, only to be joined by Trinculo and, as the comedy builds, by Stephano. Just as Stephano mistakes the identity of the person (or people) under the gaberdine as a monster with four legs and two mouths, Caliban also misjudges Stephano. Starstruck, Caliban beholds Stephano's drunken exuberance, tastes his "celestial liquor" (2.2.112), and worships his new hero:

CALIBAN: Hast thou not dropped from heaven?
STEPHANO: Out o' th' moon, I do assure thee. I was the man i' th' moon when time was.
CALIBAN: I have seen thee in her and do adore thee. My mistress showed me thee, and thy dog, and thy bush.
STEPHANO: Come, swear to that: kiss the book. I will furnish it anon with new contents. Swear.

Caliban drinks

TRINCULO: By this good light, this is a very shallow monster. I afeard of him? A very weak monster! The man i' th' moon? A poor credulous monster! Well drawn, monster, in good sooth!
CALIBAN: I'll show thee every fertile inch o' th' island—and I will kiss thy foot. I prithee be my god [2.2.131–143].[3]

When Caliban asks if he has dropped from heaven, Stephano answers in jest, yet Caliban is not joking. He believes Stephano and adores his "brave god" (2.2.112). His instant falling for Stephano is comic yet questionable. Trinculo is astounded at Caliban's credulity. For the audience acquainted with Caliban's misery, this worship seems out of place, a necessary exaggeration on Shakespeare's part to play up the comic subplot—for why would one so embittered as Caliban fall for one so crude as Stephano?

The answer lies in the folkloric tale of the Man in the Moon, yet the medieval sources behind this scene have received little attention. Though folklorists have anthologized these lines in *The Tempest*, they do so without any discussion of the play's context. Perhaps in reaction to this seeming lack of relevancy, some films, such as Derek Jarman's 1979 *Tempest* and Fred McLeod Wilcox's 1956 sci-fi adaptation *Forbidden Planet*, omit the reference to the Man in the Moon — in Wilcox's case, probably because the setting on an alien planet renders the lunar reference irrelevant to characters light years away, but also because Caliban's loose counterpart, Robby the Robot, is a mechanical servant without desire for freedom or belief in folklore. The film recasts the drinking scene between Robby and the starship's cook (the Stephano figure), who is not adored by Robby but rather adores *him* for synthesizing 60 gallons of bourbon. In contrast to these films, Peter Greenaway's 1991 film adaptation, *Prospero's Books*, retains the reference to the Man in the Moon, but the words are visually drowned out by Caliban's graceful, tormented movements. His body, not these lines, represents his true voice. Indeed, the lines have an audibly backstage quality in that Greenaway's Prospero narrates them in penning his master-play of revenge. Because of this metatheatrical device and disembodied voice, Caliban's joyous lines seem severed from his tense physical movements. The lines do not belong to him, and the reference to the Man in the Moon and the passage as a whole remain untapped or at least inaccessible to a modern audience.

Shakespeare editors and scholars, likewise, have passed over the allusion to the Man in the Moon. The precedent seems to have been set by the 1892 Variorum *Tempest*, whose editor, Horace Howard Furness, dismisses the Man in the Moon's relevance to Caliban in a gloss: "The mass of folk-lore which has gathered around this 'man' is highly interesting, but is scarcely appropriate here."[4] Modern editions often concur by avoiding or obscuring references to the Man in the Moon.[5]

Without the Man in the Moon's story, though, the scene does little else besides contribute to Caliban's dramatic role as comic relief, a bumpkin of utter naïveté. Even Robby the Robot, upon swallowing the cook's last swig of Kansas City bourbon to analyze its molecular structure, belches with seeming appreciation. In Derek Jarman's production, one drink from Stephano's bottle leads Caliban to gasp, "Hast thou not dropped from heaven?" The Man in the Moon is eliminated because the dialogue on folklore and lunar observation detracts from the slapstick comedy for which the scene is famous. Caliban's is the ludicrous, misplaced reverence of the stereotypical native before the seemingly sophisticated European. If we read the scene exclusively in this way, however, it seems to me that there is an offensive suggestion that Caliban's provincial ignorance or even his Red Man's weakness for drink bring his misfortune and servitude upon him.[6] Unable to learn from previously betrayed trust, Caliban is again swayed by a European, and a flashy, crude, inebriated one at that.

In contrast to this view of Caliban, I read Stephano's association with the Man in the Moon as a claim that resonates deeply with Caliban. While mapping out the folkloric, medieval analogs to *The Tempest*'s themes of magic, monstrosity, and master-and-servant relationships, I am less interested in Stephano's posturing as the Man in the Moon and more interested in the Man in the Moon's similarities to Caliban. The two maligned creatures resemble one another remarkably, both in terms of social status and through the interplay of classical myth, folklore, and early modern science invoked throughout this brief scene. When Shakespeare — and Prospero, in turn — give Caliban a burden of logs to carry, they suggestively compare the two "dark" figures, thereby mythologizing Caliban in the role of the eternal outcast.

Rusticus in Luna: The Medieval Churl

The Man in the Moon has been a household name for centuries, yet modern people know little about him. Our main sources of information are from the nineteenth century: Jacob Grimm's *Teutonic Mythology*, Sabine Baring-Gould's *Curious Myths of the Middle Ages*, and Timothy Harley's

Caliban (Jack Birkett) in Derek Jarman's *The Tempest* (1979).

Moon Lore.[7] These books describe the Man in the Moon as a legend to explain the visible irregularity of the Moon's spots, which to European cultures usually resembled a man carrying a burden of thorns.

The English folkloric tradition is largely the story of a man sent to the Moon as punishment for stealing either thorns or brushwood, which he must now carry forever. The small-scale theft underscores the man's poverty. In a classic article, Robert J. Menner explains that village peasants mended manorial hedges with thorns.[8] To protect crops from cattle, peasants posted stakes around the perimeter of village crops or the lord's demesne. Then thorny plants were sown, and lastly dead thorns were piled around these saplings to protect the tender shoots from being eaten.[9] The brush-gathering Man in the Moon, then, is distinctly a common laborer. His earliest appearance in English literature is in the twelfth-century *De naturis rerum* of Alexander Neckham, who significantly calls the Man in the Moon not just a man but a "*Rusticus in luna*," underscoring his long-established role as a field hand.[10] A few centuries later, Robert Henryson in his *Testament of Creseide* calls him a "churle: "Beirand ane bunche of thornis on his bak, / Quhilk for his thift micht clim na nar the hevin" [Bearing a bundle of thorns on his back, / for his theft of which he might not climb nearer the heaven].[11] Henryson's matter-of-fact statement seems pitifully harsh: a desperate and petty theft results in perpetual suffering of mythic proportions, like that of Atlas shouldering the world, Sisyphus rolling a boulder perpetually uphill, or even (if parodic) Christ bearing the cross and crown of thorns.

As an iconic sufferer, the Man in the Moon is an object lesson to the laborer: steal, and this is what happens to you. A personal seal belonging to Walter de Grendon from about 1335 says as much with its image of the Man in the Moon with his bundle of thorns and his dog. The seal is encircled with a Latin inscription: *Te Waltere dicebo cur spinas phebo gero* [I will tell you, Walter, why I carry thorns on the Moon].[12] The inscription has a pat, proverbial quality, as though the Man in the Moon were a common exemplum to admonish the pilferer. The homoeoteleuton draws attention to the seven-syllable lines' potential (or pretense) as a couplet with internal (*dicebo / phebo*) and end-line rhyme. Such singsong verse is characteristic of Man in the Moon literature, from Neckham's prosy rhymes (*Rusticus in Luna, / Quem sarcina deprimit una / Monstrat per opinas / Nulli prodesse rapinas*) to twentieth-century nursery rhymes.[13] The pronounced rhyme in Latin and English underscores the reductive moral outlook of this tradition.

Reading the Man in the Moon as a warning against bad behavior probably owes something to two biblical associations not recorded in English literature but found in oral tradition and Continental sources. The first is a story "as told by nurses" and based on Numbers 15:32–36, which tells the story about a man who gathered wood on the Sabbath.[14] In the scriptural account the man is stoned to death, but his punishment in fable is to carry his wood eternally on the Moon. Just as poems about the Man in the Moon often depend upon heavy rhymes, this narrative moralizes through emphasized wordplay: mistreat Sun-day, the tale warns, and you may lose the sun and live in perpetual Moon-day. The other association, based on Scripture and most famously recounted by Dante, is the story of Cain, who offered to God an unworthy sacrifice of thorns and in his wanderings comes to the Moon with his thorny burden (*Inferno* 20.126; *Paradiso* 2.50).[15] These biblical traditions authenticate the most rigid world imaginable:

The 1335 Seal of Walter de Grendon, Public Records Office.

one slip, and the punishment is dire and eternal. The harsh punishment, brought on through a sweeping act of divine intervention and judgment for so mundane an offense as theft, creates a striking imbalance in the story. The only way to resolve the vastly uneven crime and punishment is to give the Man in the Moon Cain-like proportions, to make him a symbol of evil rather than a sympathetic body of flesh and blood.

One notable variation on this tradition seems more attuned to this gross imbalance in power. In "Man in the Moon," a forty-line alliterative poem from the thirteenth-century Harley Lyrics, we get a fuller history of the Man in the Moon's past before he took up a lunar residence. The poem, grounded in manorial peasant life, tells the anguished story of a peasant who steals thorns to make hedges but is caught in the act:

> Whider trowe þis mon ha þe wey take?
> ...
> Wher he were o þe feld pycchynde stake
> For hope of ys þornes to dutten is doren,
> He mot myd is twybyl oþer trous make,
> Oþer al is dayes werk þer were yloren.
>
> Þis ilke mon vpon heh when er he were,
> Wher he were y þe mone boren ant yfed,
> He leneth on is forke ase a grey frere;
> þis crokede caynard sore he is adred!
> Hit is mony day go þat he was here,
> Ichot of his ernde he naþ nout ysped;
> He haþ hewe sumwher a burþen of brere,
> þarefore sum hayward haþ taken ys wed.[16]

[Translation by Thomas Duncan: Where does this man think he is going? ... Wherever he might be planting cuttings in the field, hoping with his thorns to stop up his gaps, he must with his two-edged axe make another bundle (of thorns), or else all his day's work there would be lost. This same man up there, whatever his origin, whether he was the Man in the Moon born and nurtured, he leans on his fork like a grey friar, this hunched idler, he is sore afraid. It is many a day gone since he was here. I reckon that in his errand he has not succeeded. He has cut somewhere a bundle of thorns. For this some hedge-keeper has taken his pledge.][17]

"Man in the Moon" is a dramatic monologue whose sly, chatty narrator offers his view of the Man in the Moon as a pathetic, contemptible creature fearing the legal consequences of his theft.[18] However, the narrator also seems to admit that the theft was practically unavoidable. After planting new thorns, the peasant must find some old thorns to finish the job, or else "al is dayes werk þer were yloren." If anything, the man is pathetic for being caught rather than for stealing. The second and third stanzas abound with the more technical aspects of manorial law, a force of justice that effectively replaces the God of the Book of Numbers. Caught red-handed by the hayward, who oversees the lord's lands, the peasant hands over a "wed," an object relinquished as a pledge to appear in the manorial court for sentencing. The peasant, however, is afraid to go: "þis crokede caynard sore he is adred!" This fear drives him to run away, and thus when the narrator talks about the Man in the Moon, he speaks of him as a fugitive who fled his village: "Hit is mony day go þat he was here."[19]

Hence, in this version, the Moon is a place of voluntary refuge, not of punishment. The Moon may be a cold land, but so are the fields in the frost; there may be fearful lunar heights to fall from, but they are less fearful than manorial law. Indeed, when the narrator mocks the Man in the Moon's circumstances, it is often not clear whether he is mocking the man's lunar residence or his bleak life as a laborer, and that may be part of the author's point if this poem is charged with issues of social justice, as some other Harley Lyrics are.[20] The Moon, then, though not utopia, is a refuge set apart from society. Significantly, at the end of the poem the narrator tries to convince the Man in the Moon to return to the village, but the man chooses not to come down.

Besides the Harley Lyrics' nuanced portrayal of the Man in the Moon, there is another tradition discussed in Raymond A. Urban's brief 1976 article, "Why Caliban Worships the Man in the Moon," on medieval and early modern drinking games.[21] Medieval clerics playfully engaged in a burlesque religion with the Man in the Moon as their Bacchic god, presumably because he rises at night with a flushed face as though from too much drink. With the bottle as their sacred book, taverns as their churches, and drinking songs as their hymns, they sang songs such as "The Man in the Moon Drinks Clarret":

> Our man in the moon drinks clarret,
> With powder-beef, turnep, and carret;
> If he doth so, why should not you
> Drink until the sky looks blew?[22]

Three taverns were called the Man in the Moon in Shakespeare's London, which lends strength to Urban's argument that Shakespeare knew and used this medieval tradition in his play. To my knowledge, Urban's essay from 1976 has received only passing references, including one comment in 1991 that the allusions to drinking games are "scarcely probable" sources for Shakespeare, nor have I seen anyone otherwise address the Man in the Moon's role in *The Tempest*.[23] Urban still offers the best statement on Stephano as a comic Bacchic figure initiating his new worshipper. Invited to compare himself to a heavenly figure, Stephano associates himself with the god closest to his heart. His tavern joys recall the woodcuts of "The Man in the Moon Drinks Clarret" found in the *Bagford Ballads* and *Roxburghe Ballads*.

And yet, however well Urban explains Stephano's perspective and what the Man in the Moon would mean to *him*, it is overly reductive to say *Caliban* worships the Man in the Moon because he worships drink. Even if this ludic tradition thrived in Shakespeare's London so that audiences compared Stephano to a drunk Man in the Moon, Caliban would not recognize him as such. Miranda, who taught Caliban the legend, mentioned the Man in the Moon's bush and dog, not his bottle. Thus Stephano and Caliban draw upon two different medieval versions, tavern man and folkloric churl. Stephano's lighthearted references to the Man in the Moon and Caliban as a "Mooncalf" reflect his flippant humor and ridicule; the metaphor is only a game (2.2.102, 129). For Caliban, the role is serious, and his joy is the thrill of rebellion and deliverance in his grasp. Caliban seems to get roaring drunk in record time, to Trinculo's disgust — "a

The Man in the Moon with his glass in hand. From the Bagford Collection ii.119. With permission from the British Library.

drunken monster!"—but the instant signs of inebriation seem an emotional high more than physical drunkenness (2.2.174). The Man in the Moon and drink mean different things to Stephano and Caliban.

The juxtaposition of incompatible medieval or early modern traditions with the Moon as their focal point recalls the counterpart scene in *A Midsummer Night's Dream*, in which the rude mechanicals perform "A tedious brief scene" of Pyramus and Thisbe.[24] In deciding how to stage the Moon, they worry about issues of timing and consult an almanac to ensure the Moon would actually shine on the night of the performance. Their solemn efforts result in ridiculous anachronism, with Starveling chosen to play the folkloric Man in the Moon identified with "a bush of thorns and a lantern" (3.1.46). The Athenian court seems knowledgeable of medieval folklore, but their derision has a contemporary feel, as though the medieval man were a dated timepiece. Two eras and two social strata clash as a medieval, folkloric figure acts before a cast dressed royally, perhaps in Renaissance garb. For the Athenians, part of the fun is that the Man in the Moon does not belong in a classical love story nor before any urbane audience.

In both plays, naïve literalism is something mocked. Caliban receives Stephano's words as literal truth, causing him, as Trinculo says, "to make a wonder of a poor drunkard" (2.2.159–160). The Athenian court, in turn, mocks the mechanicals' efforts to lend realism to the performance that instead distract the audience with a talking wall and Moon. Caliban's Man in the Moon, however, is not just a personified backdrop but the center of his drama. He reads into the performance more than Stephano put there, employing a literalism that stems from his awareness of an active spiritual world all around him (he was hiding from spirits at the time of Trinculo's and Stephano's appearance). Because Caliban grew up in a world of screaming trees and shape-shifting sprites, the Man in the Moon is not such a tall order for his credibility.

Besides underscoring the importance of the Moon, the scene with Stephano and his "Mooncalf" offers a comic version of the master-and-servant relationship between Prospero and Caliban. Both masters seem greater than ordinary men because of their books, which Caliban either fears (Caliban warns Stephano, "Remember / First to possess his books; for without them / He's but a sot, as I am"; 3.2.89–91) or kisses upon Stephano's orders, "kiss the book." In different ways, both masters mistreat their books and their servants, and by linking Caliban with the Moon and monstrosity, they reenact the old folktale of abused peasantry. Prospero especially evokes the Man in the Moon's toiling image by his exorbitant display of magic, geared to bully Caliban into carrying wood. Caliban's opening lines are a protest that he has brought Prospero "wood enough" (1.2.314). Prospero contends that he has "other business" for Caliban, yet at his next appearance in act 2, scene 2, the stage directions indicate that Caliban enters with yet another "burden of wood" (1.2.315). Being a powerful magician with the sprite Ariel at his command, Prospero could have as much sprite-delivered wood as he requires. Instead, he directs Ariel and others to pinch Caliban black and blue, pen up his breath with cramps, slither around him with serpentine shapes that "hiss [him] into madness" (2.2.14), and otherwise mistreat him with an overdose of magical bullying—all for the trivial cause of bringing in "wood enough," or whatever menial chore needs doing. "For every trifle are they set upon me," Caliban laments (2.2.8). This strange and fascinating overkill comments on Prospero's pettiness in micromanaging Caliban for lack of anything nobler to do with his considerable supernatural powers.

Prospero also plays master to Caliban's Man in the Moon by calling Caliban a thief and generally berating him. For example, he scornfully calls Caliban a tortoise, just as the Harley narrator calls the Man in the Moon "þe slowest mon þat euer was yboren!" (12). This is not to say that Prospero consciously invokes the Man in the Moon myth with this tortoise reference, but it is part of a pattern of scorn and power imbalances that reenacts the myth, casting Prospero as God or the manor lord. This very slowness as the *sine qua non* of the Man in the Moon turns up in Antonio's lines in act 2, scene 1—the scene immediately preceding Stephano's visit in act 2, scene 2—when he tries to persuade Sebastian that were Ferdinand drowned and Claribel heir to the throne, the distance between Algiers and Naples would effectively deprive her of her inheritance, for "The man i' th' moon's too slow" to bring her the news (2.1.247). Antonio's dismissal of the Man in the Moon and Prospero's scorn for wood-burdened Caliban yoke the two brothers. This proximity of Man in the Moon allusions makes it appealing to retain both references in act 2, scene 1 and scene 2, though Jarman's and Greenaway's film adaptations omit the Man in the Moon reference in act 2, scene 2 and act 2, scene 1, respectively.

Antonio's and Prospero's mockery of the slow servant shows a social gap as wide as that between Theseus and Starveling. In *A Midsummer Night's Dream*, the comical play within a play echoes the melodramatic actions of the noble lovers, though the royal audience is blind to this fact. Likewise, *The Tempest*'s Man in the Moon offers a subversive reflection of high culture with an unflattering link between Prospero and Antonio. Both brothers have elaborate stratagems to achieve power, and the Man in the Moon is a pawn in the game. Antonio's Man in the Moon is hopelessly remote, like Algiers, "Ten leagues beyond man's life" (2.1.245). Shut out from the Western world by her marriage to an African, Claribel is effectively the Man in the Moon's consort. It is this pairing of Man in the Moon and a secluded woman that gives Prospero reason to fear for his own daughter's shared space with Caliban, who must be demonized before Miranda is cut off from a more politically suitable match.

Caliban, then, like the rustic of the Harley Lyrics, is a figure both of folklore and of the agricultural field—and in both cases an outcast. Miranda calls Caliban a "villain"; it is a term that reveals her distaste for and anxiety toward him, yet it is precisely his status as a *villein* that makes him necessary (1.2.308).[25] Prospero answers Miranda's complaint with an elaboration of the villein's duties to his manor lord: "He does make our fire, / Fetch in our wood, and serves in offices / That profit us" (311–313). Even if Miranda originally taught Caliban the Man in the Moon myth with no overt agenda, the myth's applicability to her higher social position in relation to Caliban's informs her instruction. They are not peers under Prospero's tutelage, and the divide between them increases until those early language lessons are remembered in a way slanted against Caliban.

Hauling wood and looking skyward at his mirror image engaged in the same toil, Caliban would see his likeness to the Man in the Moon. To Caliban, the Man in the Moon has been a fairy tale, so it must be a shock for him when he meets the *real* Man in the Moon — mistreated of old by God and man and living to tell the tale — or perhaps the man described in the Harley Lyrics who escaped from servitude. If such things can happen, anything can happen, even Caliban's freedom, with the help of this man who toiled in his former village yet managed to get away. The Man in the Moon is not a traditional god, but traditional gods have disappointed Caliban. Early in the play he explains his rejection of Setebos, since Prospero's "art is of such power, / It would control my dam's god Setebos / And make a vassal of him" (1.2.371–373).

Caliban does not want to worship his master's vassal. He wants someone entirely set apart from Prospero and finds that figure in a villein and outcast like himself. "I prithee, be my god," Caliban gasps, and Trinculo mocks his drunkenness, but Caliban is drunk on the possibility of deliverance as well as belonging. The role assigned to him and designed to put him down may be his salvation.

Diana Maculosa: Caliban's Darkness, Miranda's Light

The folkloric tradition discussed in the previous section is better understood in the context of relevant classical and scientific lore. The Moon is a crowded repository of classical myth, English folktales, and, especially in 1610 and beyond, scientific observation, and these stories blend together — though by no means do Moon gazers treat these traditions equally. The interplay of these lunar traditions within early modern literary and social milieus, particularly the Man in the

Moon's proximity to the classical goddess Cynthia, suggests hierarchies of value that delineate *The Tempest*'s master-servant relationships.

Learning European language and lore is a treacherous gift that Caliban initially welcomes. When Prospero first came to the island, he would, says Caliban:

> teach how
> To name the bigger light and how the less,
> That burn by day and night; and then I loved thee,
> And showed thee all the qualities o'th'isle,
> The fresh springs, brine pits, barren place and fertile —
> Cursed be that I did so! All the charms
> Of Sycorax, toads, beetles, bats light on you!
> For I am all the subjects that you have,
> Which first was mine own king, and here you sty me
> In this hard rock, whiles you do keep from me
> The rest o'th'island [1.2.334–344].

The two men differ in their pedagogy: Caliban shows natural wonders, Prospero names them, and this naming shapes Caliban's perceptions of the world that he has shared and lost.[26] Foremost in Prospero's instruction is naming the Sun and Moon, what Caliban calls "the bigger light and ... the less." Later in Caliban's education, stories are attached to the names. When Stephano identifies himself as the Man in the Moon, Caliban replies that he has already seen the figure: "I have seen thee in her [the Moon].... My mistress showed me thee, and thy dog, and thy bush." In teaching this lore, though, Miranda takes more than she gives. As Kim Hall notes, Miranda's language lessons "rather than fostering communication, reveal an epistemic 'difference' that serves only to heighten her sense of racial difference and her estrangement from Caliban."[27] Whatever attitudes Prospero and Miranda have when they begin Caliban's instruction, by the end of it, their education is designed to make his world not larger but smaller — literally and figuratively. Thus Caliban, formerly king of a sensuous island, becomes Prospero's subject, perpetually carrying wood and imprisoned: "you sty me / In this hard rock, whiles you do keep from me / The rest o'th'island." Fixed on a hard rock with his burden of wood, Caliban looks very much like the Man in the Moon of old.

Prospero later invokes Caliban's connection to the Moon when he informs Alonso and his court of Caliban's evil nature. He defines Caliban through his mother, "one so strong / That could control the Moon, make flows and ebbs, / And deal in her command without her power." Prospero performs for Alonso at Caliban's expense — Stephano, Trinculo, and Antonio have all remarked on Caliban's freakish, "marketable" body (5.1.266), but Prospero markets Caliban's supernatural pedigree, turning Caliban into a demonic offspring rather than the "dead Indian" Trinculo wishes to profit by (2.2.32). However, it is an odd strategy for a magician to accuse a witch of sorcery. Moreover, rather than speaking of Sycorax's cruelty to Ariel, for example, or raising corpses or committing sensational acts of witchery, he anticlimactically emphasizes her influence over the Moon to horrify a king and his court. This suggests how much Prospero values the Moon as a benchmark of power. Although he next tries to link mother's and son's evil natures by describing Caliban's foiled crimes, there is a more suggestive connection between the sorcerers. Prospero, not Caliban, inherits Sycorax's power over the Moon. Caliban, by contrast, is a whelp "freckled" with lunar spots (1.2.283).

The connection between the Moon and woman — both Hecate and Cynthia — is as old as myth, and the play complicates this theme with plots of rape and a Man in the Moon. Prospero's fear of sexual union between Caliban and Miranda — Caliban, he claims "didst seek to violate / The honour of my child" (1.2.347–348[U1]) — suggestively juxtaposes the Man in the Moon and the Moon herself. In one variation of the tradition, Moon gazers saw two bodies in the Moon: fair Cynthia and the folkloric man, as shown in Robert Henryson's *Testament of Creseide*:

> Hir [Cynthia's] gyse was gray and full of spottis blak,
> And on hir breist ane churle paintit full evin
> Beirand ane bunche of thornis on his bak,
> Quhilk for his thift micht clim na nar the hevin [260–264].

It is jarring if comic to see the Man in the Moon's cameo in Henryson's very classical tale of Troy. Henryson's Cynthia is a lesser goddess because of her dim light but rendered lowlier because the Man in the Moon and his thorns sully her bosom like so much graffiti. The pairing feels wrong: she is a goddess, he a churl.

This scorn for the churl paired with those above him is replayed in *A Midsummer Night's Dream*. While Starveling plays Moonshine, the royal party interrupts him at every opportunity: "He is no crescent"; "I am aweary of this moon. Would he would change!"; "the man should be put into the lantern. How is it else the man i' th'moon?" (5.1.230; 238; 234–235). The criticism centers on Starveling's inadequate body, too thin to be a growing or crescent Moon. Notwithstanding the scene's humor, the royal party seems anxious to deny Starveling his role and the drama's application to them, because to attend to his performance is to look into the mirror and see a rustic on one's breast; it is a self-knowledge and syncretism that they revile.

Syncretism, the combination of different and even conflicting beliefs and traditions, typifies lunar descriptions, though the contrast between the Man in the Moon and classical mythology was not always antagonistic. Some Renaissance texts classicized the Man in the Moon with conventions of love poetry, along the lines of the earthly man and heavenly lady in Sidney's *Astrophil and Stella*. For example, in John Lyly's 1591 play, *Endymion, or The Man in the Moone*, the Man in the Moon is no churl but handsome and wise Endymion.[28] Lyly's Prologue circuitously declares, "we must tell you a tale of the Man in the Moon, which, if it seem ridiculous for the method ... we can make but one excuse: it is a tale of the Man in the Moon." Lyly's opening sets up Endymion's equally vague confession that he loves someone not above or below the Moon. His friend Eumenides jokes that "I hope you be not sotted upon the Man in the Moon." Endymion, still speaking in riddles, replies that he is in love with the Moon itself and seems madly lovesick for either a rustic man or a bright ball in the sky. Quickly, though, Lyly moves beyond these comic, literal readings of mythology and folklore and instead establishes the text as an elevated, classical retelling of Endymion as Man in the Moon, the only man privileged with chaste Cynthia's favor.

Classical syncretism in the seventeenth century resembles Henryson's bosom-besmirched Moon but often blends classical mythology with the new science born of Galileo's 1610 *Sidereus Nuncius* (*The Starry Message* or *The Starry Messenger*), a text revolutionary for proving a lack of perfection hitherto assumed in heavenly bodies. The Moon, not smooth and featureless as long thought, was a richly textured world, "rough and uneven," writes Galileo, "covered everywhere, just like the earth's surface, with huge prominences, deep valleys, and chasms."[29] The lunar spots noted since Pliny were not optical illusions but signs of rugged terrain.[30] One illustration from the 1714 *Novum Atlas* of John Baptist Homann reconfigures classical myth with early modern science by showing Diana with a face covered in spots. The inscription reads, "Sit maculosa licet tamen est formosa Diana" [Although she is spotted, Diana is nonetheless beautiful].[31] Though the illustration shows scientific interest in natural phenomena, spots are an odd thing for a goddess to have. Similarly, the Man in the Moon's figure—the shape of those spots—looks odd on Henryson's Cynthia. In both cases, whether folklore or science is invoked, an otherwise perfect celestial body is personified as a goddess whose beauty is compromised.

Something of this goddess-with-spots syncretism is at play in Caliban and Miranda's relationship. Though living in close proximity, Caliban and Miranda, like the Man in the Moon and Cynthia, are worlds apart in terms of race and economic status. That the Man in the Moon, Caliban, and later Ferdinand all occupy themselves in gathering wood is curious, as though Prospero is staging his own version of Lyly's drama, rewriting the Man in the Moon myth with Ferdinand

The Diana maculosa detail, upper right, from John Baptist Homann's "Tabula Selenographica," first printed in the *Atlas Novum* (1714), reprinted for Frederik V (1723-1766). With permission from the Royal Library of Denmark, Department of Maps, Prints and Photographs, Frederik den Femtes Atlas, vol. 1, side 24.

as Endymion. By "bearing a log," as the stage directions indicate in act 3, scene 1 (immediately following a scene with Caliban bearing *his* logs), Ferdinand performs Caliban's labor and is supposedly rewarded with Miranda's hand, when in fact Prospero has chosen Ferdinand as a son-in-law from the beginning because he is a prince.

Miranda, as her gerundive name from *mirari* suggests (Latin *miror*, to wonder), is set out by Prospero as an object to be desired — but not by Caliban. Their union would make her a *Diana maculosa*, ruined in her father's eyes and her own. If Ferdinand is Endymion, worthy of Cynthia's (Miranda's) love, Caliban is the medieval churl, "A thing most brutish" on her brilliant surface (1.2.356). Just as Miranda, in teaching Caliban language, taught him of his ignorance and savagery in contrast to her culture, so with folklore: teaching him how to see the Man in the Moon has given him a classical and folkloric model with which to understand her beauty and his ugliness. Like Caliban, the Man in the Moon is a dark character set against a glitteringly white, feminine, and classical backdrop. Both the Man in the Moon and Caliban are characters represented as earthy, besmirching darkness in the presence of light.

If Henryson, Lyly, and others recognize the degrading, even sullying, presence of the Man in the Moon, Caliban takes the Man in the Moon's side: "I have seen thee in her and I do adore thee." *Thee*, not *her*. The brief words indicate Caliban's awareness of the interplay between folkloric man and Cynthia, but he chooses the dark figure in rejection of the classical education he has received. Instead of adoring the goddess, he chooses a god who represents a projection of his fantasies of freedom and perhaps the sexual pleasure of being, in Henryson's words, a churl with thorns "on hir breist": "O ho, O ho! Would't had been done! Thou didst prevent me — I had peopled else / This isle with Calibans" (1.1.348–350). Whether guilty of intended rape or not, Caliban may be insisting here that he does not feel like a blight next to Miranda, in spite of Prospero's instruction to the contrary.

Novello Endimion: Colonizing the Moon and Clothing Caliban

When Prospero confines Caliban to "this hard rock" and takes the island, there is another layer of early modern syncretism suggestively at work: the Moon as a New World ripe for exploration, even colonization. In 1638 John Wilkins writes that Kepler believes his nation would be the first to colonize the Moon, but Wilkins has a different idea: "as soone as the art of flying is found out, some of [our British] nation will make one of the first Colonies, that shall transplant into that other world."[32] Around 1600 William Gilbert drafted the earliest map of the Moon, containing descriptive Latin nomenclature such as "Insula longa" for a long island, except for one island named simply Brittania, a Roman name recently invoked with new political import during England's efforts to annex Scotland.[33] Michael Florent Van Langren's 1645 map, in turn, names craters with Catholic Europe's royalty, saints, and scholars.[34]

This drive to map and remake new worlds began mostly with Galileo, who was lauded as an explorer of mythic proportions. Contemporary poets called him Columbus; Giambattista Marino in his 1623 *L'Adone* also hails him as the "novello Endimion."[35] The speaker in Thomas Gray's 1737 Latin poem "*Luna habitabilis*" takes on this scientific and mythic mantle, rising to lunar heights not with wings but with the telescope ("*Non pennis*," 19, but "*tubulo*," 26). By so doing he becomes "novus Endimion" (23), whose remarkably sharpened *acies* or vision (27) foreshadows the new Columbus (86) whose *acies* or battlelines (88) of English colonists conquer the Moon and make it English territory.[36] Despite this rhetoric of myth and colonialism, Galileo's monumental achievement is also an armchair affair. "Me thinkes," writes Sir William Lower, a pupil of Thomas Harriot (famous for his own drawing of the Moon), "my diligent Galileus hath done more in his threefold discoverie than Magellane in openinge the streights to the South Sea ... with more ease and safetie to him selfe & more pleasure to mee."[37] Lower wryly suggests that this is something folks can try at home. Thus the seventeenth century was an age of "Galilaeusses," according to Francis Godwin's protagonist in *The Man in the Moone, or A Discourse of a Voyage Thither by Domingo Gonsales the Speedy Messenger* (1638), for many could follow the path outlined in Galileo's *Starry Messenger*, including Gray's protagonist as well as Godwin's character, the "speedy" instead of "starry" messenger.[38]

Just as Lower notes that Galileo voyages farther than Magellan yet "with more ease and safetie to him selfe," so supine Endymion travels to Cynthia's embrace. It is not a traditional, physical voyage so much as a rapture, and this intellectual ascent to the heavens frames Galileo's science with myth. Intimate with Cynthia, Galileo becomes her beloved Endymion. He hints that we too may become so, when he addresses his reader as the "*candidus Lector*," *candidus* signifying the shining white of the Moon.[39] Vicariously *candidus* from basking in Cynthia's beauty, the new Endymion possesses her celestial body through text and telescope.

Caliban has often been noted for his poetic awe at the natural and supernatural beauty around him, attuned to "Sounds, and sweet airs" and tactile delights (3.2.134).[40] His sensuous appreciation has its analogue in Galileo's possessive descriptions of the Moon. For example, Galileo invokes the myth of Danae and the golden shower, referring to the Sun "who penetrates the Moon's vast mass with his rays" ("qui radiis suis profundam Lunae solidatem permet").[41] However, Caliban, though sensitive to natural wonder, is not permitted to be seen as a new Endymion. Rather, Prospero is the scholarly colonist, conquering new worlds with his books and nomenclature, and Ferdinand plays Endymion to Miranda's Cynthia. To Prospero, Caliban remains the Man in the Moon, an unenlightened churl. Though Caliban predates Godwin's picaresque protagonist of *The Man in the Moone*, both physically are outcasts: Caliban is misshapen in some way, and Gonsales is dwarfish. For both, the identification with the Man in the Moon is something they make the most of, but it is a pejorative, categorizing label.

It may seem to be reading too much into the text to insert the Man in the Moon into Prospero's mythological fantasies, yet Prospero suggestively clothes Caliban as such and casts him as the Man in the Moon near the end of the play. Against the threat on his life posed by Caliban, Stephano, and Trinculo, he hatches a curious plot and commands Ariel, "The trumpery in my house, go bring it hither, / For stale to catch these thieves.... Come, hang them on this line" (4.1.187–188, 193). [U2]The ploy seems irrelevant to the legendary Man in the Moon until we remember that he is a stereotypical thief. This explains why Prospero categorizes these men as thieves, not murderers—"These three have robbed me," he tells Alonso (5.1.269)—even though Prospero stages the theft while they engage in a murder plot. Theft is also Antonio's crime, and the scene is perhaps staged as Prospero's rebuke of his brother, who is invited to see himself as a thieving, murderous monster like Caliban. However, the theft of trumpery is more like the petty theft of the Man in the Moon, who suffers much for stealing little.

Also unusual is Prospero's choice of bait, clothes hung about on the trees: "hang them on this line." Stephen Orgel's footnote indicates that there were no clotheslines in Renaissance England, so "line" referred to a linden or lime tree—the branches would not be too tall, or else no one could reach the clothes (the stage directions tell us that Trinculo "*takes a robe from the tree and puts it on*"; 4.1.224[U3]). Elsewhere in the play, trees are a source of Prospero's power to confine and contain; he threatens to peg Ariel in an oak, and Alonso and his followers are "prisoners," says Ariel, "In the line-grove which weather-fends your cell" (5.1.10). Here he ensnares Caliban and his followers with trees baited with gaudy clothing. The low branches seem reminiscent of the hedges of the Man in the Moon tradition, especially when we consider the opening stanza from the Harley "Man in the Moon":

> Mon in þe mone stond and strit,
> On is bot-forke his burþen he bereþ;
> Hit is much wonder þat he n'adoun slyt,
> For doute leste he valle, he shoddreþ and shereþ.
> When the forst freseþ muche chele he byd,
> Þe þornes beþ kene, is hattren totereþ.
> Nis no wyþt in þe world þat wot wen he syt,
> Ne—bote hit bue þe hegge—whet wedes he wereþ [1–8].

[Duncan: The Man in the Moon stands and strides out. On his hay fork he carries his bundle. It is a great wonder that he does not fall down. For fear lest he fall, he trembles and swerves. When the frost freezes, great chill he endures. The thorns are sharp which tear his clothes to pieces. There is nobody in the world who knows when he sits down, nor, unless it be the hedge, what garments he wears.]

The stanza rings of ridicule framed in riddles, including the last lines: "Nis no wyþt in þe world þat wot wen he syt, / Ne—bote hit bue þe hegge—whet wedes he wereþ." However, the riddle is easily solved by considering the man's poverty and toil. He never seems to sit because he is always on the job, nor are his ragged clothes discernable in the distance. However, the personified hedges know the answer to both questions, for the sharp thorns tear the man's clothing every time he sits or leans in too closely, and the hedges gather motley scraps of cloth.

The Harley riddle and its derogatory answer suggestively inform Prospero's trap for Caliban. Prospero's behavior is not what we would expect from a man trying to catch a murderer, but it is in line with Prospero's treatment of Caliban as the Man in the Moon, to the point of dressing him like an English churl to make the boundaries between master and servant plain. Caliban wears a coarse gaberdine—distinctly English attire, unlike the exotic pelts and feathers Caliban has historically worn on stage, or no clothes at all, as in Peter Greenaway's *Prospero's Books* (a decision that underscores the nobility of Caliban's form yet removes him from the English peasantry suggested at times by Shakespeare's lines). Having outfitted his slave as an English laborer, Prospero then plots to ensnare him with a stash of glitzy clothes strewn upon the trees. Prospero's otherwise inexplicable ploy suggests that there is a connection between the hedges of rags from the Harley

Lyrics and Prospero's hedges of trumpery. It is as though, knowing the thieving Man in the Moon is in need of clothes, Prospero provides some where the man would most likely go looking.

Caliban does not fall for Prospero's script, but Stephano does. Significantly, this is the scene in which Caliban finally loses faith in Stephano as the Man in the Moon. If Stephano had lived up to his Harley reputation as a fugitive, Caliban would have served him as a "foot-licker" not unlike the Man in the Moon's dog (4.1.218). Caliban's companions, however, ultimately disappoint him, and when a chastised Caliban reappears on stage in act 5, scene 1, he swears upon the name of his dam's god, "O Setebos," not out of any belief in Setebos's supremacy but to signify the end of his rebellious devotion to Stephano (5.1.261–262). Repentant, as though confronted with the Seal of Walter de Grendon and its moralizations on the thieving Man in the Moon, he exclaims, "What a thrice-double ass / Was I to take this drunkard for a god, / And worship this dull fool!" (5.1.295–297). Ashamed of his former god, Caliban promises to be "wise hereafter, / And seek for grace" (5.1.294–295). The Christian tenor of his words is new, but the religious element is not: all along, Caliban has been a creature eager to believe in divine companionship and deliverance.

Caliban's story is the tale not just of a faraway islander but of a man close to home. His plight as a common laborer was a topic readily understood by Shakespeare's audience but not readily resolved. Where can such a man turn? Caliban's native god Setebos fails him, but his stubborn belief in divine power and need for companionship opens him up to a new faith in the Man in the Moon. It is not the contents of Stephano's bottle that primarily move him; it is the joy of finding a fellow laborer and god of the marginalized. It is a rebellious choice of companionship, for this man was visible to all as a dark stain on the Moon, a sign of theft properly punished, but in other contexts he signified freedom from human oppression and access to a higher realm.

Caliban's eager worship of Stephano, then, is not just the slapstick comedy that it seems to be in film adaptations, from Jarman's drunk Caliban to Wilcox's burping robot. Greenaway's staging of the scene, which at least retains the lines, though they are spoken by Prospero, proves the most complex in its blend of Stephano's frivolity and Caliban's intensity, making this version more difficult to pigeonhole as comic foolery. However, in contrast to these performances which elide the Man in the Moon's connection to Caliban, the text's folkloric reference provides Caliban with a focal point of hope. It explains his misplaced trust as well as underscoring the tension between master and servant that drives Caliban to look beyond the world for help. As master, Prospero loosely uses this folkloric association to make Caliban seem a thing of darkness in his and his daughter's presence. However, just as the Man in the Moon upstages Cynthia literally, but also insofar as early modern astronomers study the spots rather than the goddess, it could be said that Caliban eclipses Prospero and Miranda in the play's recent reception. As Harold Bloom puts it, "We are now in the Age of Caliban rather than the Time of Ariel or the Era of Prospero."[42] No one today wonders how Miranda and Ferdinand fare as married people, nor how much longer Prospero lives, or even what Ariel does next, but many audiences do long for more stories about Caliban that fill the gaps and narrate what becomes of him. Many of us see the good in him and want his prayers answered.

Acknowledgments

I especially thank Mimi Yiu of Georgetown University for her valuable criticism throughout the writing process, as well as Andrew Galloway and Winthrop Wetherbee, both of Cornell University.

Notes

1. Alden T. Vaughan and Virginia Mason Vaughan, *Shakespeare's Caliban: A Cultural History* (New York: Cambridge University Press, 1991), 26–36, 37–38; Kim Hall, *Things of Darkness: Economies of Race and Gen-*

der in Early Modern England (Ithaca, NY: Cornell University Press, 1996), 141–153; Bernard W. Sheehan, Savagism and Civility: Indians and Englishmen in Colonial Virginia (New York: Cambridge University Press, 1980); Paul Brown, "'This Thing of Darkness I Acknowledge Mine': *The Tempest* and the Discourse of Colonialism," in *Political Shakespeare*, ed. Jonathan Dollimore and Alan Sinfield (Ithaca, NY: Cornell University Press, 1985), 48–71; and Jyotsna G. Singh, "Caliban versus Miranda: Race and Gender Conflicts in Postcolonial Rewritings of *The Tempest*," in *Feminist Readings of Early Modern Culture*, ed. Valerie Traub, M. Lindsay Kaplan, and Dympna Callaghan (New York: Cambridge University Press, 1996), 191–209.

  2. See John W. Draper, "Monster Caliban," in *Caliban*, ed. Harold Bloom (New York: Chelsea House Publishers, 1992), 89–94; Jacqueline E. M. Latham, "*The Tempest* and King James' *Daemonologie*," in *Caliban*, ed. Bloom, 151–158; and Virginia Mason Vaughan, "Caliban's Theatrical Metamorphoses," in *Caliban*, ed. Bloom, 192–206.

  3. William Shakespeare, *The Tempest*, ed. Stephen Orgel (New York: Oxford University Press, 1998).

  4. William Shakespeare, *The Tempest, A New Variorum Edition*, vol. 9, ed. Horace Howard Furness (Philadelphia: Lippincott, 1892).

  5. The 1997 Norton edition makes no comment on this exchange between Caliban and Stephano; the 2004 edition glosses line 135 only to remark that "The Man in the Moon has with him a dog and a thornbush"; the Arden says, "Stephano claims to be the man whose face appears in a full Moon," which glosses over the story of the Man in the Moon as well as misleading the reader into thinking that the Man in the Moon is only a face with two eyes and a mouth on the Moon's surface rather than the full-body outline of a man carrying a bundle of brushwood—for if it were only a face, where would the dog and bush fit? By contrast, Stephen Orgel, editor of the Oxford *Tempest*, defines the basic myth of a man banished for stealing brushwood or for gathering it on the Sabbath, offers the line references to *Midsummer Night's Dream* 3.1.55–57 for comparison, and points out that the myth was widespread enough in the fifteenth century to figure in the Lollard Reginald Pecock's writings as an example of a harmless superstition. See Shakespeare, *The Tempest*, ed. Orgel, 149; Pecock, *The Repressor of Over Much Blaming the Clergy*, edited by C. Babington (London, 1860), i.155. For editions, see William Shakespeare, *The Norton Shakespeare*, ed. Stephen Greenblatt, Walter Cohen, Jean E. Howard, and Katharine Eisaman Maus (New York: W. W. Norton, 1997); Shakespeare, *The Tempest*, ed. Peter Hume and William H. Sherman (New York: W. W. Norton, 2004); Shakespeare, *The Arden Shakespeare*, ed. Virginia Mason Vaughan and Alden T. Vaughan, 3rd ser. (London: Thomson Learning, 1999).

  6. G. Wilson Knight, "Caliban as a Red Man," in *Caliban*, ed. Bloom, 182.

  7. Jacob Grimm, *Teutonic Mythology*, trans. James Steven Stallybrass (New York: Dover, 1966), ii, 716–720; Sabine Baring-Gould, *Curious Myths of the Middle Ages* (London: Rivington's, 1875); Timothy Harley, *Moon Lore* (Rutland, VT: Charles E. Tuttle, 1970 [1885]).

  8. Robert J. Menner, "The Man in the Moon and Hedging," *Journal of English and Germanic Philology* 48 (1949): 1–14.

  9. These medieval practices continued in sixteenth-century England, attested in part by John Fitzherbert's 1523 *Book of Husbandry*; Menner, "The Man in the Moon and Hedging," 7.

  10. Alexander Neckham, *De naturis rerum*, ed. Thomas Wright. Rolls Series (London: Longman, Green, Longman, Roberts, and Green, 1863), xviii, 54–54.

  11. Robert Henryson, *The Poems of Robert Henryson*, TEAMS Middle English Texts Series (Kalamazoo, MI: Medieval Institute Publications, 1997), 164, ll. 260–264.

  12. My translation differs from those of P. D. A. Harvey and Andrew McGuinness as well as Jonathan Alexander and Paul Binski, who provide a literal rendering of *phebo*, masculine dative of Phoebus, not his sister Phoebe: "from the Sun," not "on the Moon." Phoebus, however, seems a nonsensical reading, since the legendary theft of wood was from Earth, and, besides, the Sun would incinerate the Man in the Moon's burden of wood. Perhaps the error can be attributed to the medieval writer's difficulty with Greek nouns, and perhaps also the internal rhyme of *dicebo* and *phebo* was desired. The Seal of Walter de Grendon, ca. 1335, has been reproduced in Harley, Baring-Gould, Turville-Petre, and others. See Harvey and McGuinness, *A Guide to British Medieval Seals* (London: British Library and the Public Record Office, 1996), 90 and 114; Roger H. Ellis, *Catalogue of Seals in the Public Record Office: Personal Seals* (London: Her Majesty's Stationery Office, 1978–1981), 348; Alexander and Binski, *Age of Chivalry* (London: Royal Academy of Arts, 1987), 116–167.

  13. "The Man in the Moon was caught in a trap / For stealing the thorns from another man's gap. / If he had gone by, and let the thorns lie, / He'd never been a Man in the Moon so high." Angelina Parker, "Oxfordshire Village Folklore," in *Folk-Lore*, 24 (1913): 77; and Alta Jablow and Carl Withers, *The Man in the Moon: Sky Tales from Many Lands* (New York: Holt, Rinehart and Winston, 1969), xi.

  14. Baring-Gould, *Curious Myths*, 191–192. Harley, *Moon Lore*, 21–22.

  15. Oliver F. Emerson, "Legends of Cain, Especially in Old and Middle English," *PMLA* 21, no. 4. (1906), 840–845.

16. "The Man in the Moon" in Thorlac Turville-Petre, ed., *Alliterative Poetry of the Later Middle Ages* (Washington, D.C.: Catholic University of America Press, 1989), 32–33, ll. 9, 13–24.

17. Thomas Duncan, *Medieval English Lyrics 1200–1400* (New York: Penguin Books, 1995), 158.

18. Carter Revard, "The Lecher, the Legal Eagle, and the Papelard Priest: Middle English Confessional Satires in Ms. Harley 2253 and Elsewhere," in *His Firm Estate: Essays in Honor of Franklin James Eikenberry*, ed. Donald E. Hayden (Tulsa, OK: University of Tulsa, 1967), 54–71.

19. Richard Firth Green, *A Crisis of Truth: Literature and Law in Ricardian England* (Philadelphia: University of Pennsylvania Press, 1999), 53, 270; V. J. Scattergood, *Politics and Poetry in the Fifteenth Century* (London: Blandford Press, 1971), chap. 10 and esp. 351–353.

20. For example, "The Song of the Husbandman" offers the perspective of oppressed laborers. The hayward is specifically criticized: "þe hayawrd heteþ vs harm to habben of his" (15); Scattergood, *Politics and Poetry*, 351–352.

21. Raymond Urban, "Why Caliban Worships the Man in the Moon," *Shakespeare Quarterly*, 17, no. 2 (Spring 1976): 203–205.

22. *The Roxburghe Ballads*, vols. 1–3 ed. W. Chappell and vols. 4–8 ed. J. Woodfall Ebsworth (1890–1891; repr. New York: AMC Press, 1966), 258, ll. 49–52.

23. Vaughan and Vaughan, *Shakespeare's Caliban*, 60–61; Cosmo Corfield, "Why Does Prospero Abjure His 'Rough Magic'?" *Shakespeare Quarterly* 36, no. 1 (Spring 1985): 36.

24. William Shakespeare, *A Midsummer Night's Dream*, ed. R. A. Foakes (Cambridge, UK: Cambridge University Press, 1990), 5.1.56.

25. Francis and Joseph Gies, *Life in a Medieval Village* (New York: HarperPerennial, 1990), 74–77.

26. Hall, *Things of Darkness*, 143–147.

27. *Ibid.*, 143.

28. John Lyly, *Endymion*, ed. David Bevington (New York: Manchester University Press, 1996). Michael Drayton comically connected the two figures in his "Man in the Moone," a revision of his earlier *Endimion and Phoebe* (1595): "Thus yonder man that in the moone you see / Rap'd vp from Latmus, thus she doth prefer / And goes about continually with her," to enjoy her presence but also to peep on every unsuspecting "base churle" below. Drayton, *Poems*, Early English Books Online (London: R. Bradock for N. Lind and I. Flasket, 1606), Harvard University Library, STC 923:09, 63.

29. Galileo Galilei, *Discoveries and Opinions of Galileo*, trans. Stillman Drake (New York: Anchor Books, 1957), 28.

30. Scott L. Montgomery, *The Moon and the Western Imagination* (Tuscon: Arizona University Press, 1999), 42.

31. Marjorie Hope Nicolson, *A World in the Moon* (Northampton, MA: Smith College, 1936), 19–20.

32. *Ibid.*, 49; for the "Luna habitabilis," ibid., 36ff.; Montgomery, *Moon and the Western Imagination*, 149; Mary Baine Campbell, *Wonder and Science: Imagining Worlds in Early Modern Europe* (Ithaca, NY: Cornell University Press, 1999), 146.

33. Montgomery, *Moon and the Western Imagination*, 98–103.

34. *Ibid.*, 159, 167, 210.

35. Marjorie Hope Nicolson, "The Telescope and the Imagination," *Modern Philology* 32, no. 3 (February 1935): 249–251. The phrase from *l'Adone* is from Canto X, ottava 43.

36. Nicolson, *World in the Moon*, 52. Gray's Latin poem with a translation is available online at www.thomasgray.org.

37. Montgomery, *Moon and the Western Imagination*, 112.

38. *Ibid.*, 144. For samples of seventeenth- to nineteenth-century lunar voyage literature, see Faith K. Pizor and T. Allan Comp, eds., *The Man in the Moone* (New York: Praeger, 1971).

39. Campbell, *Wonder and Science*, 127. For *candidus*, see *Aeneid* 7. When Aeneas sets sail, "nec candida cursus / luna negat, splendet tremulo sub lumine pontus" [a bright Moon / Favored their voyage, its radiance dancing on the water]. Virgil, *Aeneid VII–XII*, ed. R. Deryck Williams (London: Bristol, 1998), 7.8–9. Virgil, *Aeneid*, trans. C. Day Lewis (Oxford: Oxford University Press, 1986).

40. Shakespeare, *The Tempest*, ed. Orgel, 23.

41. Campbell, *Wonder and Science*, 125.

42. Bloom, *Caliban*, 1.

Works Cited

Alexander, Jonathan, and Binski, Paul. *Age of Chivalry: Art in Plantagenet England, 1200–1400*. London: Royal Academy of Arts, 1987.

Baring-Gould, Sabine. *Curious Myths of the Middle Ages*. London: Rivington's, 1875.

Bloom, Harold, ed. *Caliban*. New York: Chelsea House Publishers, 1992.
Brown, Paul. "'This Thing of Darkness I Acknowledge Mine': *The Tempest* and the Discourse of Colonialism." In *Political Shakespeare*, edited by Jonathan Dollimore and Alan Sinfield, 48–71. Ithaca, NY: Cornell University Press, 1985.
Campbell, Mary Baine. *Wonder and Science: Imagining Worlds in Early Modern Europe*. Ithaca, NY: Cornell University Press, 1999.
Corfield, Cosmo. "Why Does Prospero Abjure His 'Rough Magic'?" *Shakespeare Quarterly* 36, no. 1 (Spring 1985): 36.
Draper, John W. "Monster Caliban." In *Caliban*, edited by Harold Bloom, 89–94. New York: Chelsea House Publishers, 1992.
Drayton, Michael. *Poems*. Early English Books Online (London: R. Bradock for N. Lind and I Flasket, 1606), Harvard University Library, STC. 923:09, 63[0].
Duncan, Thomas. *Medieval English Lyrics 1200–1400*. New York: Penguin Books 1995.
Ellis, Roger H. *Catalogue of Seals in the Public Record Office: Personal Seals*. London: Her Majesty's Stationery Office, 1978–1981.
Emerson, Oliver F. "Legends of Cain, Especially in Old and Middle English." *PMLA* 21, no. 4. (1906): 831–929.
Galilei, Galileo. *Discoveries and Opinions of Galileo*. Translated by Stillman Drake. New York: Anchor Books, 1957.
Gies, Francis, and Joseph Gies. *Life in a Medieval Village*. New York: HarperPerennial, 1990.
Green, Richard Firth. *A Crisis of Truth: Literature and Law in Ricardian England*. Philadelphia: University of Pennsylvania Press, 1999.
Grimm, Jacob. *Teutonic Mythology*. Translated by James Steven Stallybrass, ii, 716–720. New York: Dover, 1966.
Hall, Kim. *Things of Darkness: Economies of Race and Gender in Early Modern England*. Ithaca, NY: Cornell University Press, 1996.
Harley, Timothy. *Moon Lore*. Rutland, VT: Charles E. Tuttle, 1970 [1885].
Harvey, P. D. A., and McGuinness, Andrew. *A Guide to British Medieval Seals*. London: British Library and the Public Record Office, 1996.
Henryson, Robert. *The Poems of Robert Henryson*. TEAMS Middle English Texts Series. Kalamazoo, MI: Medieval Institute Publications, 1997.
Jablow, Alta, and Withers, Carl. *The Man in the Moon: Sky Tales from Many Lands*. New York: Holt, Rinehart and Winston, 1969.
Knight, G. Wilson. "Caliban as a Red Man." In *Caliban*, edited by Harold Bloom, 179–191. New York: Chelsea House Publishers, 1992.
Latham, Jacqueline E. M. "*The Tempest* and King James' *Daemonologie*." In *Caliban*, edited by Harold Bloom, 151–158. New York: Chelsea House Publishers, 1992.
Lyly, John. *Endymion*. Edited by David Bevington. New York: Manchester University Press, 1996.
Menner, Robert J. "The Man in the Moon and Hedging." *Journal of English and Germanic Philology* 48 (1949): 1–14.
Montgomery, Scott L. *The Moon and the Western Imagination*. Tuscon: Arizona University Press, 1999.
Neckham, Alexander. *De naturis rerum*. Edited by Thomas Wright, xviii, 54–54. Rolls Series. London: Longman, Green, Longman, Roberts, and Green, 1863.
Nicolson, Marjorie Hope. *A World in the Moon*. Northampton, MA: Smith College, 1936.
_____. "The Telescope and the Imagination." *Modern Philology* 32, no. 3 (February 1935): 233–260.
Parker, Angelina. "Oxtordshire Village Folklore." in *Folk-Lore* 24 (1913): 77.
Pecock, Reginald. *The Repressor of Over Much Blaming the Clergy*. Edited by C. Babington. London, 1860.
Pizor, Faith K., and T. Allan Comp. *The Man in the Moone*. New York: Praeger, 1971.
Revard, Carter. "The Lecher, The Legal Eagle, and the Papelard Priest: Middle English Confessional Satires in Ms. Harley 2253 and Elsewhere." In *His Firm Estate: Essays in Honor of Franklin James Eikenberry*, edited by Donald E. Hayden, 54–71. Tulsa, OK: University of Tulsa, 1967.
The Roxburghe Ballads. 8 vols. Vols. 1–3 edited by W. Chappell and 4–8 by J. Woodfall Ebsworth. Reprint New York: AMC Press 1966.
Scattergood, V. J. *Politics and Poetry in the Fifteenth Century*. London: Blandford Press, 1971.
_____. "Authority and Resistance: The Political Verse." In *Studies in the Harley Manuscript*, edited by Susanna Fein, 163–201. Kalamazoo, MI: Medieval Institute Press, 2000.
Shakespeare, William. *The Tempest, A New Variorum Edition*, vol. 9. Edited by Horace Howard Furness. Philadelphia: Lippincott, 1892.
_____. *A Midsummer Night's Dream*. Edited by R. A. Foakes. Cambridge, UK: Cambridge University Press, 1990.
_____. *The Norton Shakespeare*. Edited by Stephen Greenblatt, Walter Cohen, Jean E. Howard, and Katharine Eisaman Maus. New York: W. W. Norton, 1997.

_____. *The Tempest*. Edited by Stephen Orgel. New York: Oxford University Press, 1998.
_____. *The Arden Shakespeare*. Edited by Virginia Mason Vaughan and Alden T. Vaughan. 3rd series. London: Thomson Learning, 1999.
_____. *The Tempest*. Edited by Peter Hume and William H. Sherman. New York: W. W. Norton, 2004.
Sheehan, Bernard W. *Savagism and Civility: Indians and Englishmen in Colonial Virginia*. New York: Cambridge University Press, 1980.
Singh, Jyotsna G. "Caliban versus Miranda: Race and Gender Conflicts in Postcolonial Rewritings of *The Tempest*." In *Feminist Readings of Early Modern Culture*, edited by Valerie Traub, M. Lindsey Kaplan, and Dympna Callaghan, 191–209. New York: Cambridge University Press, 1996.
Skura, Meredith Anne. "The Case of Colonialism in *The Tempest*." In *Caliban*, edited by Harold Bloom, 221–248. New York: Chelsea House Publishers, 1992.
Smith, James. "Caliban." In *Caliban*, edited by Harold Bloom, 124–150. New York: Chelsea House Publishers, 1992.
Turville-Petre, Thorlac, ed. *Alliterative Poetry of the Later Middle Ages*. Washington, D.C.: Catholic University of America Press, 1989.
Urban, Raymond. "Why Caliban Worships the Man in the Moon." *Shakespeare Quarterly* 17, no. 2 (Spring 1976): 203–205.
Vaughan, Alden T., and Vaughan, Virginia Mason. *Shakespeare's Caliban: A Cultural History*. New York: Cambridge University Press, 1991.
Vaughan, Virginia Mason. "Caliban's Theatrical Metamorphoses." In *Caliban*, edited by Harold Bloom, 192–206. New York: Chelsea House Publishers, 1992.
Virgil, *Aeneid*. Translated by C. Day Lewis. Oxford: Oxford University Press, 1998.
_____. *Aeneid VII–XII*. Edited by R. Deryck Williams. London: Bristol, 1998.

Filmography

1956 *Forbidden Planet*, d. Fred McLeod Wilcox. USA: MGM/CBS Home Video.
1979 *The Tempest*, d. Derek Jarman. UK: London Films.
1991 *Prospero's Books*, d. Peter Greenaway, with John Gielgud. USA: Media Films.

About the Contributors

Michael Almereyda's film adaptation of *Hamlet* is set in pre-millennial New York and features Ethan Hawke in the title role. The film was released by Miramax in 2000. Almereyda's other movies include *Nadja* (1995), *The Rocking Horse Winner* (1997), *This So-Called Disaster* (2002), *William Eggleston in the Real World* (2005), and *Paradise* (2008). Almereyda is the editor of *Night Wraps the Sky: Writings by and about Mayakovsky*, published by Farrar, Straus, and Giroux. His writing has appeared in *The New York Times*, *The Believer*, *Film Comment*, and *ArtForum*.

Louise M. Bishop is an associate professor of literature at the Robert D. Clark Honors College, University of Oregon. Bishop earned her Ph.D. in English from Fordham University and held the position of associate dean of Fordham's Graduate School of Business before relocating to Eugene, Oregon. An award-winning teacher, she publishes on Middle English and early modern literature. Her book *Words, Stones, and Herbs: The Healing Word in Medieval and Early Modern England* was published by Syracuse University Press in 2007.

Julia Ruth Briggs (1943–2007), professor of literature and women's studies at De Montfort University in Leicester, was awarded the OBE for her services to English literature and education in 2006. A writer and critic of extraordinary breadth, she published *Night Visitors*, on the English ghost story, in 1977; *This Stage Play World: Texts and Contexts, 1580–1625*, in 1983 (revised in 1997); *A Woman of Passion*, a life of E. Nesbit, the children's writer and Fabian socialist, in 1987; and *Children and Their Books: A Celebration of the Work of Iona and Peter Opie*, coedited with Gillian Avery in 1989. She published extensively on Middleton and Marlowe, on Shakespeare's late plays, on modernism, on women writing in early modern England, and on late nineteenth- and early twentieth-century literature, and was especially well known for her important work on Virginia Woolf. *Virginia Woolf: An Inner Life*, published in 2005, was described in the *London Times* as "quietly wonderful" and by the *New York Times* as "intelligent and well-researched." She helped to form the British Shakespeare Association and was a friend of the Virginia Woolf Society of Great Britain. In Briggs's obituary in *The Guardian* (August 30, 2007), Alison Light described her as "a nurturer of others, while insisting upon the highest standards of research" (with thanks to Marilyn Deegan).

Jim Casey is an assistant professor at High Point University in North Carolina. He received his Ph.D. from the Hudson Strode Program in Renaissance Studies at the University of Alabama. Although primarily a Shakespearean, he has also published articles or chapters on textual theory, performance theory, gender theory, Chaucer, Alan Moore, chivalry, old age, comics, *Battlestar Galactica*, and the work of artist David Mack.

Patrick J. Cook received his Ph.D. in comparative literature from the University of California, Berkeley. An associate professor of English at George Washington University, he teaches classical humanities, literary theory, and film, as well as Renaissance, medieval, and classical literatures.

He serves as director of the university's undergraduate interdisciplinary humanities program. The author of *Milton, Spenser, and the Epic Tradition* and numerous articles and reviews, he has recently completed a book manuscript on adaptions of *Hamlet* to film.

Martha W. Driver is distinguished professor of English and women's and gender studies at Pace University in New York City. A cofounder of the Early Book Society for the study of manuscripts and printing history, she writes about illustration from manuscript to print, book production, and the early history of publishing. In addition to publishing some forty-five articles in these areas, she has edited fourteen journals over eleven years, including *Film & History: Medieval Period in Film* and the *Journal of the Early Book Society*. Her books about pictures (from woodcuts to film) include *The Image in Print: Book Illustration in Late Medieval England* (British Library Publications and University of Toronto, 2004), *An Index of Images in English MSS*, fascicle four, with Michael Orr (Brepols, 2007), and *The Medieval Hero on Screen: Representations from Beowulf to Buffy*, edited with Sid Ray (McFarland, 2004).

Carl James Grindley is an assistant professor of English at Eugenio María de Hostos Community College of the City University of New York. Grindley studied paleography and codicology and earned his Ph.D. at the University of Glasgow in Scotland. His academic work focuses mostly on the intersection of medieval textual scholarship and film studies. His first three novels have just been published by San Francisco's No Record Press under the title *ICON: Three Works of Fiction*.

Kelly Jones is a senior lecturer in drama at the University of Lincoln. Kelly's primary research areas lie in Shakespeare in performance (from the Renaissance to the present day), English theater history and historiography from the medieval period to the nineteenth century, theater and popular culture, representations of authorship in performance, and theatrical realizations of the supernatural.

Catherine Loomis is an associate professor of English and women's studies at the University of New Orleans. She is the compiler of *William Shakespeare: A Documentary Volume* for the *Dictionary of Literary Biography* (Gale, 2002). Her research interests include Shakespeare, early modern drama, original staging practices, and early modern women writers.

Dakin Matthews is an associate artist of the Old Globe Theatre, a founding member of John Houseman's Acting Company, artistic director of Andak Stage Company, former artistic director of California Actors Theatre, Berkeley Shakespeare Festival, and the Antaeus Company, and an emeritus professor of English at California State, East Bay. He played Warwick and Glendower in his own adaptation of Shakespeare's *Henry IV* at Lincoln Center Theatre (multiple Tony Awards), receiving a Drama Desk Award for the adaptation and a Bayfield Award for his performance. He has dramaturged Shakespeare for directors Jack O'Brien, John Rando, Darko Tresnjak, and Daniel Sullivan, including the Denzel Washington *Julius Caesar* on Broadway. His handbook on verse-speaking *Shakespeare Spoken Here* has been used in universities and training programs throughout California; he has given masterclasses in Shakespearean acting across the country and has taught and directed in professional training programs at The Juilliard School, American Conservatory Theatre, Cal Arts, and USD/Old Globe.

Sid Ray is a professor of English and women's and gender studies at Pace University, New York City. She has published essays in *Shakespeare Quarterly*, *Film & History*, and *Conradiana* and in several collections on gender in the early modern period. She is the coeditor, with Martha W. Driver, of *The Medieval Hero on Screen: Representations from Beowulf to Buffy* (McFarland, 2004) and the author of *Holy Estates: Marriage and Monarchy in Shakespeare and His Contemporaries*

(Apple-Zimmerman Series in Early Modern Culture, Susquehanna University Press, 2004). She is working on a book on maternity and monarchy in early modern England.

Linda K. Schubert is a musicologist who studies scores for historical films. She is particularly interested in how music affects viewers' perceptions and interpretations of film scenes and, by extension, viewers' understanding of history itself. She holds a Ph.D. from the University of Michigan and has presented lectures in the United States, Germany, and Canada. She has also reviewed classical music websites for the online magazine *BRIEFME.COM*. The former book reviews editor for the *Journal of Film Music*, she has also worked as assistant editor for the online *Polish Music Journal*. Dr. Schubert teaches at the University of Wisconsin, Stevens Point.

Gary Waller is a professor of literature, cultural studies, and drama at Purchase College, State University New York, and the author or editor of more than a dozen books and many articles on medieval and Renaissance literature, including editions of Mary Wroth and Mary Sidney, Countess of Pembroke, and books on *The Sidney Family Romance: Gender Construction in Early Modern England*; *English Poetry of the Sixteenth Century*, *Edmund Spenser: A Literary Life*, *Mary Sidney, Countess of Pembroke*; and *All's Well That Ends Well: New Critical Essays*. He is currently finishing a study of the Virgin Mary and the Shrine of Our Lady of Walsingham in the late Middle Ages and Reformation and is editing (with Dominic Janes) a collection of essays on Walsingham from the Middle Ages to the present. His next project is a study, with Michael R. Carroll, of English popular religion and literature in the fifteenth century.

R. F. Yeager is a professor and chair of the Department of English and Foreign Languages at the University of West Florida. He has published widely on topics from *Beowulf* to Ben Jonson. Recent books include *Who Murdered Chaucer? A Medieval Mystery*, with Terry Jones, Terry Dolan, Alan Fletcher, and Juliette Dor (2003); *John Gower: The Minor Latin Poems* (2005); and, as editor, *On John Gower: Essays at the Millennium* (2007). His current project is a facing-page translation of Gower's two Anglo-French *balade* sequences.

Kim Zarins is a Ph.D. candidate in the Department of English at Cornell University, where she has taught Shakespeare to first-year students. She will be an assistant professor of English at California State University, Sacramento, in fall 2009. She has published on Matthew Arnold and Victorian medievalism (in *Beyond Arthurian Romances: The Reach of Victorian Medievalism*, edited by Jennifer Palmgren and Lorretta Holloway, 2006), as well as on the subject of her dissertation, the poetics and wordplay of fourteenth-century poet John Gower (in *On John Gower: Essays at the Millennium*, edited by R. F. Yeager).

Index

*Page numbers in **bold italics** refer to illustrations.*

Abbots Bromley horn dance 155n39
Act of Supremacy (England, 1534) 10, 12, 179
Adams, John Quincy 53
L'Adone (Marino) 256
The Adventures of Robin Hood (film) 65
Aeneas 167
Aethiopica. Tragicomedy (Heliodorus) 195
"Agincourt Carol" 13, 64, 67, 69
Alexander, Bill 32, 33
Alexander, Geraldine 34
Alexander, Jonathan 259n12
Alexander Nevsky (film) 13, 62, 65, 67, 68, 69
Alexander the Great 154n31
allegory 2–3
Alleyne, Edward 218
All's Well, That Ends Well (Shakespeare) 10–11, 14, 54, 178–91, 183, ***184***, ***185***
Almereyda, Michael 1–6, ***5***, 7, 9, 81, 84–86, ***86***, 112
Alonso, Maria Conchita 40
Althaus-Reid, Marcella 180
Ambrose (saint) 63
American Company 49
American Revolution 51–52
American Shakespeare Center 60n45
anachronism 9, 50, 206, 208, 210, 219, 251
Anderegg, Michael 120
Anders, H. R. D. 142, 153n25
Anderson, Scott M. 40–41
Andrew of Wyntoun 128n5
Anglicanism *see* Protestantism
Anglo-Saxons 106–7
Annales (Stow) 12
Annis, Francesca ***122***, 122–23, ***123***
Antony and Cleopatra (Shakespeare) 218
"L'Antouèno" (folksong) 67
Appel, Libby 238, 241
Apsion, Annabelle 34, 35
Aquinas, Thomas 3
Arbeau, Thoinot 65
Archibald, Elizabeth 154n31
aristocrats: Hackett's claims of links to 53; in Shakespeare plays 50, 63, 89–92, 101, 138, 162; *see also* class; masques

Aristotle 3
Arthur (mythical king of England) 11, 57, 154n32, 169, 222; *see also Morte Darthur*
Morte Darthur (Malory)
As You Like It (Shakespeare) 54, 135–38, ***136***, ***137***
Ashmore, Lawrence 69
Astrophil and Stella (Sidney) 254
Atlas Novum (Homann) 254, ***255***
Augustine (saint) 63, 179, 183
Australia 117

Bacon, Roger 195
Bagford Ballads 250
"Bailèro" (folksong) 67
Balanchine, George 144
Baldwin, T. W. 224n2
Bale, Christian ***71***
Ballmann, Otto 141
Banks, Elizabeth 126
Baring-Gould, Sabine 246
Barkan, Leonard 233
Barlet, Keith 36–37
Barnet, Sylvan 237
Barr, Roseanne 58
Bartels, Emily 40
Barton, John 9, 32, 37, 164, 167, 183
Baskervill, C. R. 147
Bassuk, David 183, 184, 185, 186
Battersby, Christine 187
Battersea Arts Center 86
Baugh, A. C. 152n16, 156n57
Bayeux tapestry 13, ***110***, 111–12
Bazin, André 120
BBC 37
BBC Time-Life 208, 209
BBC TV 167, 168, 183, 185
Beale, Simon Russell 34–35, 39
Beatles (band) 157n63
Beaumont, Francis 163, 169, 170, 195
Beaumont and Fletcher Folio 163
Beckerman, Bernard 32–33
Beckwith, Sarah 13
Bedford, James Gavin 41
Beerbohm Tree, Herbert 144
The Beggar's Opera (Gay) 137
Bellenden, John 117, 119, 130n34
Belushi, John 58
Benoît de Sainte-Maure 165
Bentley, Greg W. 174n30
Beowulf 207
bergomasks 147–49, ***149***

Berkeley Shakespeare Festival 170
Berlioz, Hector 166
Bernard (saint) 180
Berthelette, Thomas 216, 217, 218, 220, 221–22
Bertram, Paul 162
Bethurum, Dorothy 141, 150
Betterton, Rosemary 187
Betterton, Thomas 228n50
Bevington, David 143, 173nn17, 24, 174n43, 175n44, 224n3
Bible 36, 235, 248–49; *see also* mystery plays
Billington, Michael 36
Binski, Paul 259n12
Birkett, Jack ***247***
Bishop, Louise M. 14, 197, 232–44
Blackfriars Theatre 170, 196, 219
Blackness Castle (Scotland) 110
Blits, Jan 105
Bloom, Claire ***30***, 31
Bloom, Harold 215, 258
Bloomfield, Morton W. 50
Bly, Mary 187
Boccaccio, Giovanni 15, 165, 178
Boece, Hector 12, 117, 119, 128, 130n34
Boethius 161, 235
Bogdanov, Michael 37
The Boke of Duke Huon of Burdeux *see Huon of Burdeux*
Bolingbroke, Henry 49–50; *see also* Henry IV (king of England)
A Bomb-itty of Errors 137
Bonelli, Elena 179
The Book of Common Prayer 63, 64, 210n1
Book of Durrow 112
Book of Hours 109
Book of Husbandry (Fitzherbert) 259n9
"Book of the Duchess" (Chaucer) 140
books (in Shakespeare's plays) 233–34, 238, 241, 251, 256
Booth, John Wilkes 51, 108
Booth's Theatre (New York City) 53
Bostridge, Ian 155n45
Boswell, Jackson Campbell 241n2
Boudicca 196
Bourchier, John 142
Boyd, Michael 36, 37, 167

Boys, Rowland de 135
The Boys from Syracuse (Rodgers and Hart) 137
Bradbrook, Muriel 170
Bradford, Jesse 126
Bradley, A. C. 129n20
Bradley, Marion Zimmer 241
Branagh, Kenneth 63, 136, 137, *138*; *Henry V* film of 7, 55, *56*, 62, 64, 65, 67–72, *70, 71*
Braunmuller, A. R. 124
Braveheart (film) 40
Brecht, Bertolt 38, 208
Brewer, Anthony 106
Bridcut, John 155n45
Briggs, Julia Ruth 11, 13–14, 138, 161–77
Briggs, Katharine Mary 154n33, 156n46
British Ministry of Information 62
Britten, Benjamin 166; *Midsummer Night's Dream* opera by 13, 138, 144, 145, 147, 148–49, 150, 155n42
Brode, Douglas 37, 39, 40
Brome, Richard 203–4
Brook, Peter 147, 148, 149, 150, 151n1, 154nn34, 35, 155n43
Brooke, Michael 42n12
Brooklyn Academy of Music 86
Brother Sun, Sister Moon (film) 110
Brown, Georgina 36, 37
Brown, Joe E. *149, 150*
Brown, Keith 106
Brueghel, Pieter 56
Bruster, Douglas 204, 205, 206, 210n9
Bryden, Ronald 151n1
Buccola, Regina 178
Buchanan, George 117, 119
Buchanan, Judith 41
Bullough, Geoffrey 113n1, 174n42
Burbage, Richard 14, 98, 227n34
Burden, Suzanne *168*
Burkholder, J. Peter 73n18
Burnett, Kenyan *185*
Burnett, Mindi *184*

Cagney, James *149, 150*
Cahiers du Cinéma 55–56
Cain (biblical figure) 248–49
Cambridge Shakespeare Festival 187
Campbell, Cheryl 129n8
Canteloube, Joseph 67
Canterbury Tales (Chaucer) 2, 11, 13, 195, 234, 237; *see also specific tales in*
Carlin, Nancy 170
carnivalesque 49
Carr, Mimi *240*
Carradine, David 40
Cartelli, Thomas 85
Carter Barron Amphitheatre (Washington, D.C.) 223
Casey, Jim 13, 27–48
Cassavetes, John 197
Castiglione, Baldassare 105
The Castle of Perseverance (morality play) 204, 222, 227n32
Catholicism: in Denmark 106, 107; Gower's 216; in *Hamlet* 2, 3, 105, 107; music associated with 63–64;
in *Pericles* 219, 227n34; and the Pregnant Virgin 179–83, 186, 187; and romance genre 196; Shakespeare's 9, 179, 219; and Soviet Union 65; in *Troilus and Cressida* performances 167–68; *see also* convents; medievalism; morality plays; mystery plays
Cato, Marcus Porcius 235
Caviness, Madeline 181
Caxton, William 161, 167, 216, 217
Cerasano, S. P. 33, 34
Ceremony of Carols (Britten) 155n42
Chanson de Roland 135–37
Chants d'Auverne (Canteloube) 67
Chapel Street Theater (New York City) 49
Chapman, George 167
Charles II (king of England) 170, 228n50
Charles VIII (emperor of France) 162
Chaucer, Geoffrey: as actual father 234; contemporaries of 13, 209, 216; in *Greenes Vision* 217, 237–38; humor associated with 135, 137, 170–71; as influence on Shakespeare 2, 7, 12, 13–14, 84, 161, 197, 232–36, 238, 241; as medieval writer 15, 168; patron of 10; as proto-Protestant 9; *Works* of 233, 239, 241; *see also specific works by and editors of*
Chaucer to Spenser (Pearsall) 8–9
Chaucerian Shakespeare (Donaldson) 232
Chettle, Henry 161
Chicago Shakespeare Theater Company 60n43
Chicago World's Fair (1934) 54
Chichester Festival Theatre 86
The Children's Midsummer Night's Dream (film) 156n49
Chimes at Midnight (film) *22*, 51, 55–56, *57*
chorus figures *see* prologue presenters
Christine de Pisan 242n22
Chronicles of England (Stow) 12
Chronicles of England, Scotlande, and Ireland (Holinshed) 12, 55, 105, 106
Churchill, R. C. 224n2
Cibber, Colley 13, 27, 29, 32, 42
Cicero 235
class (social hierarchy): dances enjoyed by 149; Falstaff's violations of 50, 51; in *Midsummer Night's Dream* 100, 138, 141, 142, 145–51, 162, 170–71, 218, 251, 252, 254; Renaissance conflicts between 162; in *Romeo and Juliet* 87, 89–104; in Shakespeare comedies 138; in *The Tempest* 245–62; in *Two Noble Kinsmen* 169, 170–71; and warfare perspectives 63; *see also* aristocrats; merchant class; peasants
Clifford, Hubert 67
clogging (dance) 149
Cloisters (New York City) 4, 7
Clopper, Lawrence M. 210n3
Close, Glenn 125, *125*, 126, 130n38
Cnut (Danish ruler) 106
Cohen, Ralph Alan 60n45
Coleman, John 229n52
collective action 89–104
Colley, Scott 42n3
colonialism: in Renaissance period 162; in *The Tempest* 197, 245, 246, 256; and *Troilus and Cressida* performances 167–68
Coltrane, Robbie *56*
Columbus, Christopher 256
comedy: in *All's Well, That Ends Well* 186; American 58; and the Middle Ages 135; moral functions of 52; in morality plays 50; Restoration 51; in *Richard III* 35, 38; in *The Tempest* 246; *see also* tragicomedies
Comedy of Errors (Shakespeare) 54, 137, 216
communalism 111–12; *see also* women: solidarity among
Condell, Henry 195, 209, 215, 233
Confessio amantis (Gower) 197, 203, 206, 215–22, 224
Confessions of an Actor (Olivier) 67
Connor, Edric 208
Continental Congress 51
convents 10–11
Cook, Patrick J. 13, 87, 105–15
Cooke, Dominic 198
Cooper, Helen 196, 233, 237
Copland, Robert 225n11
Corineus (first duke of Cornwall) 135
Coriolanus (Shakespeare) 101, 218
Corman, Roger 37
costumes: for Falstaff 53, 54; in *Hamlet* 108, 109; in *Macbeth* 9, 107, *120*, 121, 122; in *A Midsummer Night's Dream* 144; in *Pericles* 206, 209, 220, 223; in *The Tempest* 196, *197*, 257; in *Troilus and Cressida* 167, 168; in *Two Noble Kinsmen* 170, 175n55; in *A Winter's Tale* 241
Council of Constantinople 180
Council of Trent 182
Coursen, H. R. 31, 38, 40
Courtyard Theatre (Stratford-upon-Avon) 37
Covent Garden (London) 107, 225n4
Cowan, Edward J. 130n25
Craik, T. W. 64
Cranach, Lucas 168, 227n38
Cranmer, Thomas 63, 227n38
Crimean War 168
Crist, Judith 175n44
Crowl, Samuel 37, 38, 39, 55
Cumberland, Richard 170
Cuningham, Henry 153n25
Curious Myths of the Middle Ages (Baring-Gould) 246
Cusack, Sinead 129n8, 130n28
Cutlack (play) 106
Cymbeline (Shakespeare) 186, 216, 218; medieval aspects of 11, 195, 196, 219; performance history of 197–98, 225n4

Cynthia (classical goddess) 253–54, 255, 256, 258

Dalí, Salvador 11
Danae (classical goddess) 256
Danes, Claire 9, 94
Dangerous Liaisons (film) 130n38
Daniels, Ron 209
Dante 3, 90, 248
Davenant, William 107, 170, 228n50
Davies, Anthony 83
Davies, Howard 165, 168
Davis, Mary (Moll) 170
Dawson, Anthony 84, 164, 173nn17, 24–25, 174nn39, 40
Day, John 225n10
Dekker, Thomas 161
Delany, Paul 93
DelVecchio, Doreen 225n6, 229nn53, 55
De naturis rerum (Neckham) 248
Dench, Judi 56, 96, 183
Denmark 105, 106–7
Devine, George 156n51
de Worde, Wynken 217, 225n11
Diana (classical goddess) 254, 255, 255
DiCaprio, Leonardo 9, 94, 95
Diet of Worms 105
Digby Day, Richard 170
Dillane, Stephen 5
"diptych structure" *see* doubling
Disney, Walt 29
Docetic heresy 180
Dr. Faustus (Marlowe) 54, 227n38
Donaldson, E. Talbot 151nn6, 13, 156n54, 232–33
Donaldson, Peter 38
Donmar Warehouse 86
Doran, Greg 183
Dorn, Dieter 198
doubling ("diptych structure") 141, 143–44, 150
Douglass, David 49, 51
Dover Castle (England) 110
Doyle, Patrick 13, 62, 67, 68–72
Drabble, Margaret 156n49
Draper, John W. 153n24
Drayton, Michael 260n28
Dreyfuss, Richard 37
drinking games 250
Driver, Martha 4, 15n4, 138n3, 210, 242n22; introduction to essays 21–26, 81–88; on medieval Shakespeare 7–17; on *A Midsummer Night's Dream* 138, 140–60, 228n47
Droeshout, Martin 197
Dromgoole, Dominic 168
Drury Lane Theatre (London) 27, 107
Dryden, John 166
dumb shows (pantomimes) 147, 149–50, 207, 218–19, 223
Duncan (king of Scotland) 118, 119
Duncan, Thomas 249, 257
Dunnottar Castle (Scotland) 110
Dürer, Albrecht 168

Earl Godwin and His Three Sons (play) 107
early modern period (Renaissance): characteristics of 1, 10, 12, 105, 136; in *Hamlet* 13, 105, 106, 111; themes in 2; warfare in 162; *see also* Protestantism; *specific playwrights in*
Eder, Bruce 42n12
Edge, Simon 212n41
Edinburgh Festival 156n49
Edmund Ironside (play) 106
Edward (of Westminster) 31
Edwards, Philip 161
Edwards, Richard 161
Edzard, Christine 156n49
Eggers, Walter F., Jr. 228n39
Ehle, Jennifer 35
Eisenstein, Sergei 13, 65, 67
Elizabeth I (Tudor queen of England) 13, 161, 169, 233; in *Shakespeare in Love* 96, 99, 100, 101
Ellis, Peter 129n13
Elsinor (Helsingor) 106, 109, 110
embodiment (of Richard III by different actors) 27–48
Endymion, or The Man in the Moone (Lyly) 254
England: Act of Supremacy in 10, 12, 179; break between medieval and early modern periods in 10; Catholicism in 179; identification of, with Trojans 167; nostalgia for medieval times in 56–57, 135–36; *Richard III* performed in 27–37; royal succession in 1–2, 9, 10, 14–15; unification of 10; *see also* early modern period; medievalism; *specific people and places in*
English country dancing 149
The English Dancing Master (Playford) 149
English language *see* language
Erasmus, Desiderius 162, 227n38
Erne, Lukas 233
Essay on the Dramatic Character of Falstaff (Morgann) 52
Evans, Edith 117, 124, 173n17
Eve (biblical figure) 36
Everett, Barbara 203, 209
Everett, Rupert 143
Everyman (morality play) 2, 222, 227n32, 241
Eyre, Richard 37

Faerie Queene (Spenser) 142, 222
Faire Em, the Miller's Daughter (play) 106
fairies 152n9; in Chaucer's works 146; in *Midsummer Night's Dream* 141, 142–45, 150
fairy tales 195, 197–98; *see also* folklore
The Faithful Shepherdess (Beaumont and Fletcher) 195
Falkland Islands War 62, 68, 72
Falstaff (character) *see* Henry IV; Henry V
Falstaff (Welles's film) *see Chimes at Midnight*
Fatal Attraction (film) 130n38
Fechter, Charles 108
Feldman, Charles 121
Felix Brutus 167

Felperin, Howard 219, 228n44
feminism 14, 127–28, 138, 186–87, 196, 234–39; *see also* women
Fenwick, Henry 172n6, 175n45
Feretti, Dante 110
Fewster, Carol 141–42
fiction vs. history 12, 117
Fiennes, Joseph 94
Fiennes, Ralph 163
"The Fight between Carnival and Lent" (Brueghel) 56
Fight Club (Palahniuk) 89, 102
film noir 84–85
film versions: of *All's Well, That Ends Well* 183, 185; of *Hamlet* 1–7, 9, 13, 24, 81, 83, 84–86, 109–12, 110, 112; of *Henry V* 7, 13, 24, 30, 55, 56, 62–77, 66, 109; of *King Lear* 81–82, 83–84, 84; of *Macbeth* 15, 81, 82, 116–17, 120, 120–28, 121, 122, 123, 125, 126, 130n34; of *Midsummer Night's Dream* 143, 143–44, 144, 145, 147, 149, 150, 156n49; of *Othello* 84; of *Pericles* 208, 209; of *Richard III* 11, 14, 24, 28, 29–31, 30, 33, 34, 37–42, 38; of *Romeo and Juliet* 9, 9, 13, 89–104, 110; of *Taming of the Shrew* 110, 137; of *The Tempest* 196, 197, 198, 198, 233–34, 246, 247, 247, 252, 257, 258; of *Troilus and Cressida* 167, 168, 168
Il Filostrato (Boccaccio) 165
Finch, Jon 122, 122
Finlayson, John 141
Fire over England (film) 65
The First Book of Ayres (Morley) 137
Firth, Colin 96
Fitzherbert, John 259n9
The Fitzwilliam Virginal Book 67
Five Hundred Years of Chaucer Criticism and Allusion (Spurgeon) 232
Five Kings (Welles) 55
Fletcher, John 13, 162, 163, 169, 171, 195, 218
Folger Shakespeare Library 52
Folios (of Shakespeare's works) 163, 196, 203, 207, 209, 215, 218, 223, 224n3, 233
folklore 13, 15, 138, 141, 143, 147–49, 151n1, 155n39, 156n46; and *All's Well, That Ends Wel* 178; and *The Tempest* 197, 245–62; *see also* bergomasks; fairy tales; morris dancing
Forbes-Robertson, Jean 175n52
Forbes-Robertson, Johnston 109
Forbidden Planet (film) 197, 246
Forni, Kathleen 233
Forrest, John 157n67
Fortune Theater 54
Fox, Amy 124, 125, 128
Francis of Assisi (saint) 110
François de Belleforest 105
"The Franklin's Tale" (Chaucer) 170–71
Frederick V (Elector Palatine) 169
Freedman, Barbara 38–39
French, Philip 37
Freud, Sigmund 35
Friedhofer, Hugo 73n18, 74n43

Frye, Roland Mushat 113n3
Funny Stories 52
Furness, Howard 246

Gable, Clark 39
Galileo Galilei 254, 256
gangster film genre 38, 94
Garber, Marjorie 129n13
Garland of Laurel (Skelton) 242n13
Garrick, David 27
Gay, John 137
Geisslinger, Nell **238**
genitalia 182, 187; *see also* sexuality
Gennep, Arnold van 210n9
Gentile da Fabriano 227n38
Geoffrey of Monmouth 135, 167, 219
Gesta Henrici Quinti 63
Geva, Tamara 144
Ghibelline family 90, 94
Gibson, Gail 179
Gibson, Mel 40, 111
Gielgud, John 196, **197, 198**
Gielgud Theatre (London) 86
Gilbert, William 256
Glen, Georgie **96**
Globe Theatre 170, 196, 208, 209, 218, 219, 222; in Olivier's *Henry V* film 65, 66–67, 109; in World's Fairs 54
Glyndebourne Festival Opera 145, 155n44
goddess cults 181; *see also specific classical goddesses*
Godfrey of Viterbo 207
Godsalve, William H. L. 155n42, 156n47
Godwin, Francis 256
Gogmagog 135
The Golden Age Restored (Jonson) 217
The Goodbye Girl (film) 37
Goold, Rupert 5
Gorboduc 218, 219
Gower, John 2, 7; as character in *Pericles* 11, 13, 14, 195, 197, 201–14, 238; in *Greenes Vision* 217, 237–38; as icon of medieval literature 206–7, 209, 215, 216–22, **221**, 224; as influence on Shakespeare 14, 203, 215–18; tomb of 203, 206, 209, 216, 218, 222
"The Gower Project" 212n43
"Grand Mechanism" idea 32
Granville Barker, Harley 144, 147
Gray, Thomas 256
Greece (ancient) 164, 167; *see also Troilus and Cressida*
Green Man myth 58, 155n43
Greenaway, Peter 196, 197, 198, 233–34, 246, 252, 257, 258
Greenblatt, Stephen 210n9, 226n28
Greene, Robert 142, 206, 209, 217, 226n21, 232, 236–39, 241
Greenes Vision (Greene) 206, 217, 237, 238, 239
"Greensleeves" (song) 148
Grieve family 107
Griffin, Alice 29
Grimm, Jacob 246
Grindley, Carl James 11, 13, 87, 89–104

Gruoch (queen) 13, 116–32
Guarini, Giambattista 195
Guelph family 90, 94
Guggenheim Museum (New York City) 4
Guilfoyle, Cherrell 105–6
Guinizelli, Guido 90
Guneratne, Anthony R. 155n40
Guntner, J. Lawrence 121

Hackett, James Henry 51, 52–54, 57
Hales, John W. 140
Hall, Edward 12, 13, 42n3, 63, 219
Hall, Kim 253
Hall, Peter: *All's Well, That Ends Well* of 183, 186; *Cymbeline* of 197; *Midsummer Night's Dream* of 145, 147, 149, 150, 155n44, 156n49; *Richard III* of 32, 37; *The Tempest* of 196–97; *Troilus and Cressida* of 173
Hallam, Lewis 49, 51
Hamlet (Shakespeare) 215, 219; film versions of 1–7, 9, 13, **24**, 81, **83**, 84–86, 109–12, **110, 112**; medieval aspects of 2, 3–4, 7, 10, 105–15; and national identity 87, 105–15; performances of **5**, 54, 68, 81, **86**, 107, 108; social hierarchy in 101; *Troilus and Cressida* compared to 164–65
The Hamlet of Edwin Booth (Shattuck) 109
Hammond, Anthony 225n6, 229nn53, 55
Hammond, Eleanor 16n14
Hand, Terry 208
Hands, Terry 41, 223
Hankey, Julie 33
Harada, Mieko **84**
Hardicanewtes (play) 107
Haridcute (play) 106
Harlan, Otis **149**
Harley, Timothy 246
Harley Lyrics 249–50, 251, 252, 257–58
Harold (king of England) 111
Harriot, Thomas 256
Harris, Jed 29
Hart, Lorenz 137
Harvey, P. D. A. 259n12
Hassall, Christopher 166
Hassel, Chris 31, 32
Hattaway, Michael 196
Hawke, Ethan 2, 4, 7, **86**
Healy, Margaret 227n34
Heavey, Lorna 86
Hefner, Hugh 9, 122, 123–24
Heights (film) 116, 117, 124, **125**, 125–28, **126**
Heliodorus 195
Heminge, John 195, 209, 215, 233
Henderson, Diana E. 140
Henry IV (king of England) 49–50, 220
Henry IV (Shakespeare) 10; Falstaff's character in 49–58, 226n21; Lincoln Center production of 1, 2–3, 60n45; *Merry Wives of Windsor* combined with 50, 54, 55; performances of 51, 53, 54; prologue

presenters in 205, 227n39; social hierarchy in 101
Henry V (king of England) 63
Henry V (Shakespeare) 10, 50, 108, 204, 227n39; film versions of 7, 13, **24**, 30, 55, **56**, 62, 64–72, **66, 70, 71**, 109; music for films of 13, 62–77; propaganda uses of 62, 65–66, 67; social hierarchy in 101
Henry V (Vaughan Williams) 67
Henry VI (king of England) 10, 31
Henry VI (Shakespeare) 50
Henry VI, Part 3 (*This England* series) 36
Henry VII (king of England) 2, 10, 147, 149
Henry VIII (king of England) 63, 147, 149, 179, 220
Henry VIII (Shakespeare) 10, 54, 108, 149, 163
Henryson, Robert 2, 161, 165, 168, 248, 253–54, 255
Henslowe, Philip 98, 106–7, 142, 161, 218
Herald, Heinz 144
Herbert, Hugh **149**
"heritage film" genre 38
Heywood, Thomas 225n3
Hibbard, Laura A. 157n58
Hill, Nicholas 15n4
Hill, Victoria 124–25
Hillman, Richard 233
Hirschorn, Clive 33
Historia Apollonii Regis Tyrii (Velserius) 207
history: alternative versions of 5, 37–38; vs. fiction in early modern period 12, 117; Lady Macbeth in 116–32; medievalists vs. early modernists on 8–9; and memory 85–86; in mystery plays 1–2; Shakespeare's inaccuracies about 9, 10, 12, 14, 24, 27, 105, 116–28; Shakespeare's questioning of official versions of 49, 63; Shakespeare's views of 10, 32, 36, 57, 161–62; vs. theology 12; *see also* medievalism; political emphases; *specific countries, rulers, and Shakespearean history plays*
Hobson, Harold 32
Hocktide (folk tradition) 106
Hoeniger, F. D. 207, 225nn4, 9–10, 227n34
Hoffman, Michael 143, 147
Holbein, Hans 109, 227n38
Holden, Stephen 38
Holderness, Graham 68
Holinshed, Raphael 119, 128, 130n34, 219; as Shakespeare source 12, 42n3, 55, 57, 63, 64, 105, 117; on Denmark 106
Holland, Peter 35, 36, 37
Hollywood 40, 41, 74n43, 145
Hollywood Bowl 145
Holm, Ian 32–33, 34, 35, **71**, 145
Holton, Sylvia 241n2
Homann, John Baptist 254, 255
Homer 167, 195
Homily on Idolatry 181

homosexuality *see* sexuality
Howard, Alan 154n34
Howard, Bryce Dallas *136*, *137*
Howard, Jean 51
Howell, Jane 37
"Howe's Thespians" 51–52
Hoyt, Diana *184*, *185*
Hudson, Anne 15n4, 16n9
Hudson, Henry Norman 224n2
Huneycutt, Lois L. 119
Hunter, Kathryn 208
Hunter, R. G. 179
Huntington Library Quarterly 11–12
Huon of Burdeux 140, 142–43, 145, 150

Iceland 106
Iliad (Homer) 167
illiteracy: in *Romeo and Juliet* 91, 95; in Shakespeare's time 210
"In exitu Israel" (psalm) 64
Instruction of a Christen Woman (Vives) 195–96
intertextuality 164, 165, 233
Intertextuality and Romance in Renaissance Drama (Hillman) 233
Iraq War 168
Irving, Henry 109, 117
Isherwood, Lisa 180
Ivary, Liisa *240*

Jackson, Kevin 37
Jackson, Nagle 175n56
Jackson, Russell 37, 157n66
Jacobi, Derek 129n8
James, Emrys 229n55
James, Heather 164, 165, 168
James I (king of England) 4–5, 10, 118, 179, 219, 220; *see also* James VI (king of Scotland)
James IV (Greene) 142
James VI (king of Scotland) 106; *see also* James I (king of England)
Jankowski, Theodora 187
Japan 81–84, 171, 208
Jarman, Derek 246, 247, 252, 258
Jefferson, Thomas 51
Jesus 180, 182
The Jew of Malta (Marlowe) 205
John (king of England) 10
John of Fordun 128n5
Johns, Eric 32
Johnson, Karin *240*
Johnson, Samuel 118, 225n4
Jones, David 208
Jones, Emrys 32, 40, 208
Jones, Griffith 209
Jones, Kelly 14, 201–14
Jonson, Ben 142, 169, 195, 196, 203, 217, 223, 233
Jorgens, Jack 109
Jory, Victor 144, *144*
A Jovial Crew (Brome) 203–4
Jowett, John 32, 33, 39
Judaism 179
Judge, Ian 165, 167
Julius Caesar 142, 154n31
Julius Caesar (Shakespeare) 54, 166
Jung, Carl 33
Jutland 106

Kaleidoscope (radio program) 35
Kammerspiele (Munich) 198
Kane, John 154n34
Karloff, Boris 37
Kassel, Maria 181
Kaut-Kowson, Helena 186
Kean, Charles 107, 108, 109, 111
Kean, Edmund 14
Keith, Elspeth 167
Kemble, Charles 54
Kendall, Paul 27
Kent, Gill 172n1
Kepler, Johannes 256
Kermode, Frank 129n17
Kestelman, Sara *148*, 154n34
Kewes, Paulina 11–12
Kimball, Frederic 39–40
King, Ros 198
King John (Shakespeare) 10, 54, 108
King Lear (Shakespeare) 10, 15, 54, 105, 218, 227n34; Kurosawa's versions of 81, 82, 83–84, *84*
King's Men (Shakespeare's company) 169, 203, 216, 220, 227n34
Kiss Me, Kate (Porter) 137
Kline, Kevin 2, 60n45
Knewtus (play) 107
Knights, L. C. 129n20, 173n26
"The Knight's Tale" (Chaucer) 135; as *Midsummer Night's Dream* source 13, 138, 140, 141, 232; as *Two Noble Kinsmen* source 2, 147, 161, 169, 170, 172n9, 238
Knights Templar 179
Korngold, Erich Wolfgang 65, 74n43
Kott, Jan 4, 32, 164, 168
Kozikowski, Stanislaus 106
Kozintsev, Grigori 41, 109
Krier, Theresa 233
Kronborg Castle (Denmark) 106
Kurosawa, Akira 41, 81–84, *84*, *85*
Kyd, Thomas 42n3, 165, 218, 219
Kyle, Barry 171, 183, 187
Kyng Apollyn of Thyre 225n11

Lamb, Mary Ellen 156nn46, 50
Langan, William *236*, *238*
language: Chaucer's 12; filmmakers' abandoning of Shakespeare's 41; Gower's 216–17, 220–22; Latin 201, 216–17, 221–22, 248, 256; modern English 10, 12, 56; Shakespeare's 1, 40; in *The Tempest* 253, 255, 256
Lanier, Douglas M. 84–85
Lansburgh Theatre (Washington, D.C.) 223
Larrington, Carolyne 154n31
The Last King of Scotland (film) 39
Lateran Council 180
Latin language: in church services 201; in Gower's *Confessio* 216–17, 221–22; Gray's moon poem in 256; on Walter de Grendon's seal 248, *248*
Laube, Miriam A. *236*
LeBron, Juan Rivera *238*
Lee, Rowland 37
Lee, Sidney 225n10
Lee, Sung Hi 40

Legend of Good Women (Chaucer) 13, 138, 140, 232
Leigh, Vivien 117
leprosy 165–66
Lesser, Anton 34, 36, *168*
Lessons in Elocution (Scott) 52
Lester, Adrian *138*
"Letter of the Author's Expounding His Whole Intention" (Spenser) 222
Lewis, C. S. 165
The Life and Death of Falstaff 54, 55
Light on the Piazza 183
Lillard, Matthew *138*
Lillo, George 207–8, 225n4
Limbourg brothers 7, 227n38
Lincoln Center (New York City) 1, 2–3, 60n45
Lives (Plutarch) 12
Loch Levin 119
Locke, Philip 154n34
Locrine 218
Lodge, Thomas 135
Loehlin, James 33, 34, 35, 38
Loncraine, Richard 37–39
London: Man in the Moon taverns in 250; theatrical companies from, in America 51; *see also specific theaters, companies, and places in*
London Times 223
Loney, Glenn 156n49
Looking for Richard (film) 7, *8*, 39–40
Loomis, Catherine 11, 13, 49–61
López-Morillas, Julian 170, 175n55
Lord Leebrick Theater (Oregon) 234
Lorenz, Sarah L. 94
Los Angeles (California) 40, 41, 94; *see also* Hollywood
Love and Madness (Waldron) 170
The Love-Sick King (Brewer) 106
Love's Labour's Lost (Shakespeare) 137, *138*
Low, Lisa 129n17
Lower, William 256
Luhrmann, Baz 156n49; *Romeo + Juliet* film by 9, *9*, 13, 89, 94–100, *95*, 102
Lulach (Lady Macbeth's son) 118, 119
Lull, Janis 27, 32
"Luna habitabilis" (Gray) 256
Luther, Martin 105, 227n38
Lydgate, John 7, 15, 147, 149, 167, 218
Lyly, John 42n3, 254, 255

MacArthur, John R. 153n23
Macauley, G. C. 208
Macbeth (Australian film) 116, 117, 124–25
Macbeth (Shakespeare): and historical context of women in 105, 116–32, 218; historical inaccuracies in 9, 12, 13, 116–28; Kurosawa's versions of 81–82, *85*; medieval aspects of 2, 3, 5, 10, 219; performances of 15, 51, 54, 81, *82*, 86, 108, 116–28, *120*, 129n8; settings for 107; violence in 4–5, 86, 122, 124–25
Macbeth, Scotland, PA (film) 15

"The Macbeth Murder Mystery" (Thurber) 81, 87
Machan, Tim William 225n13
Machiavelli, Niccolò 205
Macklin, Charles 107
MacNeil, Robert 86
Macowen, Michael 164
Macready, William 107
Madden, John 13, 89, 94, 95, 96, 98, 100–101
Madonna del Parto tradition 14, 178–91
Magellan, Ferdinand 256
The Magnetic Lady (Jonson) 142
Malcolm II (king of Scotland) 118
Malcolm III (king of Scotland) 118, 119
Malory, Thomas 15, 75n48, 143, 195, 196
Mamillia (Greene) 237
Man in the Moon 14, 197, 245–62, **248**, **250**
"The Man in the Moon Drinks Claret" 250
"Man in the Moone" (Drayton) 260n28
The Man in the Moone (Godwin) 256
"The Man of Law's Tale" (Chaucer) 15
Mankind (morality play) 204, 205
Margaret (of Scotland) 119, 130n31
Marina (Lillo) 207–8, 225n4
Marino, Giambattista 256
Marlowe, Christopher (Kit) 42n3, 50, 54, 98, 142, 205, 227n38
Marlowe, Sam 86
Marowitz, Charles 37, 39
marriage: in *All's Well, That Ends Well* 183; as compulsory 138; convents as alternatives to 10–11; as ideal vocation for women 181, 184, 187, 195
Marsden, James 126
Mary (Queen of Scots) 106, 196
Mary (virgin) 179–83, 186, 187
Mary Magdalene 179
Mary Magdalene (morality play) 227n32
Mary Stuart *see* Mary (Queen of Scots)
masques 169, 170, 217, 219
Massinger, Philip 218
master-servant relationships *see* class
Matthews, Dakin 1–6, 170
Matthews, David 8, 155n45
McArdle, Aidan 36–37
McConnell, Bridget **96**
McDonald, Russ 12
McGuckin, Aislin 36–37
McGuinness, Andrew 259n12
McHugh, Frank **149**
McKellen, Ian 14, 37–39, **38**, 40, 41
McMullan, Gordon 8
Measure for Measure (Shakespeare) 13
"Medieval Shakespeare" seminar 8
medievalism: characteristics of 1–5, 50, 162; *see also* Catholicism; folklore; history; language; morality plays; mystery plays; peasants; romance genre; *specific medieval writers*
Medievalism in America (Rosenthal and Szarmach) 49
Megahey, Leslie 56–57
Mehl, Dieter 146, 147, 152n16, 158n72
Melibee (Chaucer) 14
melodrama 32, 34, 51
Mendelssohn, Felix 65
Mendes, Sam 34, 163
Menner, Robert J. 247
merchant class 89, 98, 101, 138; *see also* class
The Merchant of Venice (Shakespeare) 51, 92, 108, 138
Merchant Taylors 217
"The Merchant's Tale" (Chaucer) 140, 141, 232
meritocracy 101
Merry Wives of Windsor (Shakespeare) 50, 53, 54, 55
Metamorphoses (Ovid) 12
Middle Ages *see* medievalism
A Midsummer Night's Dream (Shakespeare) 259n5; medieval sources for 10–11, 13, 15, 138, 140–60, 232; musical scores for 65; performances of 54, 108, **143**, 143–44; social hierarchy in 100, 138, 141, 142, 145–51, 162, 170, 218, 251, 252, 254; *Two Noble Kinsmen* as sequel to 162, 170
Miller, Jonathan 167, 168, 172n6
"The Miller's Tale" (Chaucer) 135, 170, 217
Milton, Ernest 175n52
A Mirror for Magistrates 12
mirror imagery 3–4, 6, 12
The Miseries of Enforced Marriage (Wilkins) 224n3
The Mists of Avalon (Bradley) 241
Moisan, Thomas 92
Monck, Nugent 223, 229n52
Monette, Richard 183
Monterchi (Italy) 179
Monuments of Honour (Webster) 217
Moon Lore (Harley) 247
moon spots 247, 254, 258; *see also* Man in the Moon
morality plays: description of 2–3, 204, 220; elements of medieval consciousness in 106; Shakespeare's knowledge of 218, 219, 222; Shakespeare's plays read as 52; Vice figure in 2, 14, 49, 50, 204; Virtue figure in 204, 205; *see also Everyman*; mystery plays
More, Thomas 42n3, 227n38
Moreau, Jeanne 55
Morgann, Maurice 52, 53
Morley, Thomas 65, 137
morris dancing 147, 149, 162, 169, 170, 171
Morrison, Susan 181
Morrissette, Billy 15
Morte Darthur (Malory) 15, 75n48, 143
Mosinsky, Elijah 183
The Most Lamentable Comedy of Sir John Falstaff (Cohen) 60n45

Moulton, Ian 39
Much Ado about Nothing (Shakespeare) 54, 92, 100
Muir, Kenneth 141
Mullaney, Steven 204, 206–7
multiculturalism 168, 208
Mumming at Windsor (Lydgate) 147
Mundus and Infans (morality play) 227n32
Murphy, Eddie 58
Muse, David 223
music: in *As You Like It* 137; for *Henry V* films 13, 62–77; and *Midsummer Night's Dream* 13, 138, 144, 145, 147, 148–49, 150, 155n42; in other Shakespeare plays 139n5
musical theater 137
My Own Private Idaho 58, **58**
The Myrrour of modestie (Greene) 237
mystery plays: abridged plays likened to 54–55; description of 2, 50, 201, 220; Protestant suppression of 106; Shakespeare's familiarity with 1; *see also* morality plays

Naiambana, Patrice 208
Nanagawa, Yukio 208
narrative closure 7
Nashe, Thomas 196
nationalism 87, 105–15, 162
National Portrait Gallery 31
National Theatre 37, 164, 168, 208
Nativity plays 186
Neckham, Alexander 248
Neill, Michael 63
Neilson-Terry, Dennis 144
Nelson, Janet 119, 130n22
Neues Theatre am Schiffbauerdamm (Berlin) 144
New Shakespeare Company (York) 170
New World 256
New York: corporate culture in 4, 85, 112; as setting for Shakespeare plays 4, 7; Shakespeare performances in 1, 2–3, 49, 53, 184, 197, 198
Newcomb, L. H. 153n22
Newman, Barbara 181
Nicene Creed 210n1
Niles, John D. 207
Nivola, Alessandro **138**
Noble, Adrian 34, 43n31, 129n8, 130n28; *Midsummer Night's Dream* film of 143–44, 145, 147, 149
Noble, Richmond 64
Noh theater 81, 82
Nolan, Jeannette **121**, 121–22, 130n28
"Non nobis" (song) 13, 63–64, 69–72, 75n45
Nora, Pierre 85
Norman, Marc 94
Norman Conquest 111
Normans 106–11
The Norton Shakespeare 259n5
Norway 106
Nosworthy, J. M. 199n2
A notable discouery of coosenage (Greene) 237

Notary, Julian 217
Notes and Comments upon Certain Plays and Actors of Shakespeare (Hackett) 53
Noye's Fludde (Britten) 155n42
nudity 9, 121, 123
Nunn, Trevor 168, 183
"The Nun's Priest's Tale" (Chaucer) 235

O (film) 41
"Obal, dinlou Limouzi" (folksong) 67
Oberon (Jonson) 169
O'Brian, Jack 2, 3
Odo (bishop of Bayeux) 111
The Odyssey (Homer) 195
Oglesby, Greta **238**, **239**
Oldcastle, John 49
Old Globe Theater (San Diego) 54
Old Vic (London) 168, 170, 196, 229n52
Olivier, Laurence: Cibber's influence on 27, 29; *Hamlet* film of 13, **24**, 81, **83**, 84; *Henry V* film of 7, 13, 30, 55, 62, 64–67, **66**, 68, 69, 72, 109; in *Macbeth* 117; as Richard III **11**, 14, **24**, 29–31, **30**, 33, 34, 37, 38, 39, 41
Olson, Glending 210n3
On Acting (Olivier) 29
Open Air Theatre (Regent's Park) 170
orality *see* storytelling
orchestrators 69
Oregon Shakespeare Festival (Ashland) 171, 241
Orgel, Stephen 222, 223, 227n34, 229n50, 257, 259n5
Osherow, Michele 186–87
Othello (Shakespeare) 2, 10, 84, 107
Ovid 12, 84
Oxford Stage Company 168
Oyelowo, David **136**

Pacific National Exhibition *see* World's Fairs
Pacino, Al 7, **8**, 14, 39–40
paganism 181
The Painfull Adventures of Pericles Prince of Tyre (Wilkins) 203, 206, 215, 220, **221**, 223, 224n3
Painter, William 178
Palahniuk, Chuck 89
Palamon and Arcite (Cumberland) 170
Palestrina, Giovanni Pierluigi da 65
Palmer, Christopher 65–66, 67
Paltrow, Gwyneth 94
Pandosto (Greene) 226n21, 232, 235, 236–39
Panofsky, Erwin 155n39
Pantheon (Godfrey of Viterbo) 207
pantomimes *see* dumb shows
"The Pardoner's Tale" (Chaucer) 233
"Parliament of Fowles" (Chaucer) 140, 170, 232
Il Pastor Fido (Guarini) 195
The Patterne of Painefull Adventures (Twyne) 210n6, 224n3, 225n11

Payne, Ben Iden 54
Pears, Peter 145
Pearsall, Derek 8, 15n4, 145
peasants: in *A Midsummer Night's Dream* 100, 141, 142, 145–51, 162, 170, 218, 251, 252, 254; in *Romeo and Juliet* films 13, 87–104; in *The Tempest* 197, 245–62; *see also* class
Pecock, Reginald 259n5
Pepys, Samuel 107
Perceval (romance) 142
Pericles (Shakespeare) **202**; as collaborative writing effort 163, 203, 207–8, 209–10, 215, 216; dumb show in 149; Gower as character in 11, 13, 14, 195, 197, 201–14, 238; medieval aspects of 2, 11, 13, 195, 208–10, 215–31; performance history of 203–4, 207–8, 215, 216, 223–24, 225n4, 229n52; in Shakespearean canon 203–4, 207; sources for 203, 210n6, 215
Peter Grimes (Britten) 155n45, 166
Petherbridge, Edward 209
Petrarca, Francesco 90
Pfeiffer, Michelle **143**
Phaedra 86
Phelps, Samuel 208, 223, 229n52
Philaster (Beaumont and Fletcher) 195
Phillips, James 30, 31
Phoenix, River **58**
Pidgeon, Walter 197
Piero della Francesca 179, 182
Pilkington, Ace G. 73n23
Pimlott, Stephen 35
The Pit (theater) 208
The Place of the Stage (Mullaney) 204, 206–7
plague 233
The Plantagenets (Noble production) 34, 36, 43n31
Plato 3
Playboy magazine 122, 123–24; *see also* Hefner, Hugh
Playford, John 149
Play of the Sacrament (morality play) 227n32
Pliny, Gaius 254
Plummer, Christopher 32
Plutarch 12, 42n3, 84
Poel, William 164, 167
Polanski, Roman 9, 116, 117, 122–24, 125, 128, 130n34
political emphases: in *Hamlet* performances 4, 85; of *Henry IV* performances 49–61; of modern readings of Shakespeare's plays 81; of motives in *Macbeth* 116–32; of *Richard III* adaptations 32; in *Romeo and Juliet* 89–104; of Shakespeare's plays 10, 13, 14; *see also* warfare
Pope, Alexander 225n4
Porter, Andrew 156n49
Porter, Cole 137
Potter, Lois 170, 173n13, 175n55
Prah-Perechon, Anne 112
Pre-Raphaelites 241
presenters *see* prologue presenters
Preston, Travis 5

Price, Jonathan 129n8, 130n28
Price, Vincent 37, 39
Pride and Prejudice (film) 30
primogeniture 14
The Prince and the Pauper 65
Prince Henry's Barriers (Jonson) 169
Princess's Theatre (London) 107, 108, 111
The Private Life of Henry VIII (film) 65
Prokofiev, Sergei 13, 65
prologue presenters 204–5, 206, 208, 220, 227n39, 228n40, 238
Prologues to Shakespeare's Theatre (Bruster and Weimann) 204
Prospero's Books (film) 196, **197**, 198, **198**, 233–34, 246, 252, 257
Protestantism: Chaucer as precursor of 9; under Elizabeth I 169, 179; in *Hamlet* 105, 107; on marriage 181, 184, 187, 195; music associated with 63–64; rise of 10; and the Virgin 181–82; *see also* Puritanism
Protevangelium 180
Public Theater (New York) 197
Purchas, Samuel 106
Purchase Repertory Theatre 183, 185
Purgatorio (Dante) 90
Puritanism 58, 98–99
Pynson, Richard 217

The Quick and the Dead (film) 210n1

Rabey, David 212n42
Rabold, Rex **240**
race 168, 208
Rackin, Phyllis 12, 51
Raden, Bill 172n1
Rafferty, Terence 39
Raimi, Sam 210n1
Ran (film) 81–82, 83–84, **84**
rape 165, 171, 253, 255
Ratcliffe, Michael 33
Rathbone, Basil 37
Ravenscroft, Christopher **70**
Ray, Sid 157n63; introduction to essays 135–39, 195–200; on *Macbeth* 11, 13, 87, 116–32; on medieval Shakespeare 7–17
Reading the Medieval in Early Modern England (McMullan and Matthews) 8
Rebhorn, Wayne 93
Recuyell of the Historyes of Troye (Caxton) 161, 167
Reduced Shakespeare Company 147
"The Reeve's Tale" (Chaucer) 170
Refiguring Chaucer in the Renaissance (Krier) 233
Reinhardt, Max 144, 145, 147, 148, 149, 150, 157n66
religious emphases (of Shakespeare's plays) 14, 258; *see also* Catholicism; paganism; Protestantism; Puritanism
Renaissance *see* early modern period
Renaissance Films 68
Renaissance Theatre Company 68

Republic (Plato) 3
The Resistible Rise of Arturo Ui (Brecht's adaptation of) 38
"Reveillez-vous Piccars" (song) 67
rhyme and rhythm 141, 146, 164, 206, 209, 220, 248
Richard I (the Lionheart, king of England) 10, 136, 137
Richard II (king of England) 2, 10, 32, 220
Richard II (Shakespeare) 12, 50, 55, 108, 111
Richard III (king of England) 10
Richard III (Shakespeare) 10, 13, 14, **24**, 27–48, **28**, 50, 51, 205, 206
Richard Plantagenet (3rd Duke of York) 36
Richardson, Tony 208, 223
Richert, William **58**
Richmond (earl of; later, Henry VII) 2, 10
Richmond, Hugh 29, 31, 33–34, 170
"The Rime" (Chaucer) *see* "Tale of Sir Thopas" (Chaucer)
The Rivals (Davenant) 170
Robert of Cisyle 157n58
Robin Goodfellow 143, 145
Robin Good-Fellow, His Mad Prankes, and Merry Jests 145
Robin Hood 65, 136
Robinson, Dewey **149**
Rodgers, Richard 137
Le Roman de la Rose (*Romance of the Rose*) 182, 242n22
Roman de Troie (Benoît de Sainte-Maure) 165
romance genre (medieval) 13, 14; characteristics of 141–42, 195, 224; as influence on *As You Like It* 135–38, 178; as influence on *Midsummer Night's Dream* 140–60; and later Shakespeare's plays 195–96, 216, 222–23
Romanesque style 108
Romans 11
Romeo + Juliet (Luhrmann) 9, **9**, 13, 89, 94–100, **95**, 102
Romeo and Juliet (Shakespeare) 233; adaptations of 9, **9**, 13, 54, 89–104, 110; medieval aspects of 10, 15, 89–104; musical scores for 65
Romeo and Juliet (Zeffirelli) 13, 89, 94–97, 99, 100, 102, 110
Rooney, Mickey 145
Rorik (Viking king) 105
Rosalynde (Lodge) 135
"Rosa Solis" (song) 67
Rose, Mary Beth 172n5
Rose theatre (London) 98, 218
Rosenberg, Marvin 129n20
Rosenthal, Bernard 49
Rosenthal, Daniel 38, 42n12
Ross, A. Elizabeth 50
Rowe, Katherine 85
Rowe, Nicholas 228n50
Rowley, William 225n10
Roxburghe Ballads 250
Royal Ballet (London) 170
Royal National Theatre *see* National Theatre
Royal Shakespeare Company (RSC):

All's Well, That Ends Well at 183, 186; *Henry IV* at 60n43; *Henry V* at 68; *Midsummer Night's Dream* at 154n35; *Pericles* at 209, 223; *Richard III* at 29–37; *Tempest* at 86; *Troilus and Cressida* at 164, 167; *Two Noble Kinsmen* at 171
Royal Shakespeare Theatre (Stratford) 208
Royal Supremacy Act *see* Act of Supremacy (1534)
RSC *see* Royal Shakespeare Company
Rutherford, Margaret 55
Ryder, Winona 40

Saccio, Peter 27
Sadler's Wells 223
Said, Edward W. 225n7
St. Andrew's Church 128
St. Saviour's Church *see* Southwark Cathedral
San Diego (California) *see* World's Fairs
Sanders, Wilbur 186
Sargent, John Singer 122
Satan 5
Saxo Grammaticus 7, 105, 108
scenery (theatrical): for *All's Well, That Ends Well* 184; for *Hamlet* 107–10; for *Henry IV* 54; for *Pericles* 223
Schein, Harry 31
Schmor, John 234
Schoch, Richard 107–8
Schubert, Linda K. 13, 62–77
Scotland: annexation of 10, 245; gradations of kingship in 130n25; medieval clothing in 9, 123; royal succession in 9, 14–15, 118; women's position in 14, 116–32; *see also Macbeth* (Shakespeare)
Scotorum historia (Boece) 12, 117
Scott, William 52
Scott Thomas, Kristin **38**, 39
Seaton, Ethel 153n24
Sebastian (saint) 241
Seda, Jon 41
Segal, George 127
Selbourne, David 147
Seneca 42n3
Serban, Andrei 197
Setebos 245, 252, 258
Settlement of 1559 179
sexuality: in *All's Well, That Ends Well* 179–91; Britten's 145n55; Jesus's 182; in *Midsummer Night's Dream* productions 145, 156n51; morris dancing and 162; in *Pericles* 208, 223; of Piero's *Madonna del Parto* 179, 182–83; in *Richard III* 29–30, 32, 33, 35, 37, 39–40; *see also* genitalia
Shakespeare, Edmund 218
Shakespeare, William: abridgments of works by 54–55, 147; appearance of 197, 209; first American edition of works by 52; folios of plays by 163, 196, 203, 207, 209, 215, 218, 223, 224n3, 233; historical inaccuracies in works by 9, 10,

12, 14, 24, 27, 105, 116–28; historical views of 10, 32, 36, 57, 161–62; as influence on how nonmedievalists view the Middle Ages 14; interest of, in his literary legacy 233, 238, 239, 241; as literary genius 4, 209; as living during the transition between medieval and early modern era 89; medieval "footprints" in works by 1; social status of 101; sources used by 1, 2, 7–8, 10–15, 42n3, 55, 63, 64, 84, 87, 119, 128, 135–38, 147, 161, 164–67, 169–71, 178, 195–97, 203, 206n6, 215–18, 226n21, 232, 238, 241; universal appeal of 84, 162; *see also* political emphases; religious emphases; *specific plays by*
Shakespeare Association of America 8
Shakespeare in Love (film) 13, 89, 94–96, **96**, **97**, 98–99, 100–101, 102
Shakespeare Memorial Theatre (Stratford-upon-Avon) 156n51, 208
Shakespeare, Our Contemporary (Kott) 4
Shakespeare Theatre Company 223
Shakespeare's Chaucer (Thompson) 232
Shakespeare's Imagery and What It Tells Us (Spurgeon) 232
Shakespeare's Victorian Stage (Schoch) 107–8
Shapiro, James 135
Sharp, Cecil 148, 149
Shattuck, Charles 51
Shaw, Glen Byam 129n12
Shelby, Nicholas **123**
Shepard, Sam **5**
Sher, Antony 32–34, 39
Sher, Bartlett 198
She's the Man (film) 41
Shrapnel, John 168
Sidereus Nuncius (Galileo) *see Starry Messenger*
Sidney, Philip 157n58, 254
Simon, Neil 37
Simpson, James 12
Sir Clyomon and Sir Clamydes (play) 106, 157n58
Sir Lanval (romance) 142, 146
Sir Orfeo (romance) 146
"Sir Thopas" (Chaucer) *see* "Tale of Sir Thopas" (Chaucer)
Skelton, John 242n13
slasher film genre 38
Slinger, Jonathan 37
Smallwood, Robert 34–35, 36
social hierarchy *see* class
Southern, Richard 107
Southwark Cathedral (St. Saviour's Church) 203, 206, 216, 218, 222
Southwark Theatre (Philadelphia) 51
Spain 106
Spanish Tragedy (Kyd) 165, 218, 219
Speaight, Robert 32
Speght, Thomas 12, 161, 218, 233, 239, 241n1
Spencer, Charles 36

Spenser, Edmund 42n3, 142, 220, 222, 223
spider imagery 31, 33–34, 39
Spotswood, Jerald 89, 93
Spurgeon, Carolyn 232, 233
Staffordshire pottery 53
stage versions: of *All's Well, That Ends Well* 183, **184**, **185**, 186, 187; of *Macbeth* 117, 129n8, 130n28; of *Midsummer Night's Dream* 143–44, 145, 147, 154n34, 155nn43, 44, 156n49; of *Pericles* 203–4, 208, 223; of *Richard III* 14, 29–37; of *Taming of the Shrew* 54; of *The Tempest* 234; of *Troilus and Cressida* **163**, 164, 165, 167–68; of *Two Noble Kinsmen* 170–71; of *A Winter's Tale* **236**, 238, **238**, **239**, **240**, 241
Stalin, Joseph 65
Star of David 179
The Starry Messenger (Galileo) 254, 256
Stein, Peter 168
Steinberg, Leo 182
Steinberg, Micheline 229n53
Steiner, Max 74n43
Stevens, John 74n44
Stevens, Thomas Wood 54
Stevenson, Juliet 165
Stewart, Patrick 5, 86
Stoicism 105, 161
Stock, Brian 207
Stockholder, Kay 129n17
Stoppard, Tom 94, 95, 98, 99, 100, 101
storytelling (orality) 207–10
Stothart, Herbert 65
Stow, John 12, 156n56, 161, 218, 233, 241n1
Stratford (Ontario) 183
The Street King (film) 41
Strong, Roy 169, 175n47
Suetonius 42n3
"Sumer is icumen in" (folksong) 65
Summarie of Englyshe Chronicles (Stow) 12
A Survey of London (Stow) 12
Suzman, Richard 32
The Swan at the Well (Donaldson) 232
Swan Theatre (Stratford) 171, 198
syphilis 162, 166
Szarmach, Paul 49

Tacitus 42n3
The Tale of Chaucer see *Tale of Melibee* (Chaucer)
"The Tale of Gamelyn" 135
Tale of Melibee (Chaucer) 197, 232, 234–35, 238–39, 241
"The Tale of Sir Thopas" (Chaucer) 13, 138, 140, 141, 145–46, 149, 234
Taming of the Shrew (Shakespeare) 54, 92, 110, 137, 232
tanistry (in royal succession) 9, 14–15, 118
Tate, Sharon 130n32
Tatham, John 203–4
Taylor, Gary 203
Tchaikovsky, Pyotr Ilich 65

"Te Deum" (medieval Latin plainchant) 63, 64, 67, 75n45
"Teaching the Middle Ages on Film" (Driver) 210, 212n45
The Tempest (film) 197, 246
The Tempest (Shakespeare) 216, 218, 222; adaptations of 54; books in 233–34, 238, 251; medieval aspects of 11, 14, 195, 197, 219, 245–62; pantomime in 149–50; performances of 86, 225n4, 246, 247, **247**, 252, 258; regarded as Shakespeare's final play 163
10 Things I Hate About You (film) 41
Terrio, Chris 117, 127–28
Terry, Ellen 117, 122
Teruyo, Nogami 82
The Testament of Cresseid (Henryson) 161, 165, 248, 253–54
Teutonic Mythology (Grimm) 246
Thacker, David 208
Theater for a New Audience (New York) 184, 198
This England series 36, 37
Thompson, Ann 140–41, 173n30, 232
Thompson, Sophie 186
thorns (in Man in the Moon imagery) 247–49, 254, 257
Three Little Pigs (Disney) 29
Throne of Blood (film) 81–82, **85**
Thurber, James 81, 87
Thynne, William 12, 161, 217, 241n1
Timon of Athens (Shakespeare) 218
Titian 109
Titus Andronicus (Shakespeare) 86, 232
Tommasini, Anthony 155n45
tournaments 169, 219, 227n34
Tower of London 108
Tower of London (film) 37
tragicomedies 196
Treacher, Arthur **149**
Trejo, Danny 40
Tresnjak, Darko 184
Très Riches Heures du Duc de Berry (Limbourg brothers) 7, 67, 227n38
The Tretise of Miraclis Pleyinge 201, 203
Trewin, J. C. 33
Troilus and Cressida (Dryden) 166
Troilus and Cressida (Shakespeare) 206, 211n26; Chaucer's influence on 161, 171, 217, 232; medieval aspects of 2, 10, 13–14, 138, 164–68, 171–72; performance history of **163**, 164, 165, 167, 169; syphilis in 162
Troilus and Cressida (Walton) 166
Troilus and Crisedye (Chaucer) 15, 161, 217
The Trojans (Berlioz) 166
Troughton, David 35–36, 39
Troxel, Patricia 241
Troy Book (Lydgate) 15, 147, 167
Tudors: lineage interests of 234; as marking medieval vs. early modern break 10; Richard III propaganda of 27; see also Elizabeth I; Henry VI; Henry VIII

Turner, Victor 210n9
The Turn of the Screw (Britten) 155n45
Tutin, Dorothy 173n17
Twelfth Night (Shakespeare) 54, 68, 138, 165–66
Two Gentlemen of Verona (Shakespeare) 54
The Two Noble Kinsmen (Shakespeare and Fletcher): medieval aspects of 2, 10, 13–14, 138, 169–72; performance history of 169–70; in Shakespearean canon 162–63, 170; as Shakespeare's final play 162; sources for 2, 147, 161, 169, 170, 172n9, 238; warfare in 162
Twyne, Laurence 210n6, 224n3, 225n11
Tylee, Claire 164
Tynan, Kenneth 122
Tyndale, William 156n46
Tyrwhitt, Thomas 141

Understanding Macbeth (Nostbakken) 118
Unicorn Tapestries 7
The Union of the Two Noble and Illustre Families of Lancaster and York (Hall) 12
United States: and American Revolution 51–52; Civil War in 168; Falstaff's portrayal in 13, 49–61
University of Wittenberg 105
Updike, John 225n7
Urban, Raymond A. 250

Valbuena, Olga 117, 118, 128
Valois, Ninette de 170
Van Langren, Michael Florent 256
Vaughan Williams, Ralph 67
Velserius, Marcus 207
Vergil, Polydore 167
Vestris, Lucia Elizabeth 144
Vice figure (in morality plays) 2, 14, 49, 50, 204
violence: in *Macbeth* performances 4–5, 86, 122, 124–25; transfer of British throne through 36; transfer of Scottish throne through 118; see also rape; warfare
Virgil, Polydore 42n3, 167
virgins 138, 178–91
Virtue figure (in morality plays) 204, 205
Visconti, Luchino 109–10
Vives, Juan Luis 195–96

Wagner, Richard 69, 166
Waldron, Francis Godolphin 170
Wales 10, 195
Walker, Roy 31
Walker, Rudolph 208
Die Walküre (Wagner) 166
Wall, Wendy 152n9, 156nn46, 52
Wallace, David 15n3
Wallace, William 40
Waller, David **148**
Waller, Gary 14, 138, 178–91
Walsingham (England) 181
Walter de Grendon's seal 248, **248**, 258

Walton, William: *Henry V* music of 13, 62, 65–67, 68, 69, 72; *Troilus and Cressida* opera of 166
War of the Roses 55
The War of the Roses (Barton and Hall production) 32
The War of the Roses (Bogdanov production) 37
Wardle, Irving 187
warfare 14; in *Henry V* adaptations 62–77; Shakespeare on 138, 162, 171–72
Warren, Roger 224n2
Washington, George 51
"Watkin's Ale" (song) 67
Watt, Robert 225n13
Webb, Danny *71*
Webster, John 217
Weil, Simone 174n38
Weimann, Robert 40, 204, 206, 210n9; *locus* vs. *platea* distinctions by 29, 211n15
Weinberger, Jerry 90, 92–94
Welles, Orson: *Chimes at Midnight* film of *22*, 51, 55–56, *57*; *Five Kings* of 55; *Macbeth* of 81, *82*, 86, 116–17, *120*, 120–22, *121*, 124, 126, 128; *Othello* of 84
Wells, Stanley 34
Werfel, Franz 155n39
western film genre 38
Westminster Abbey (London) 110
Wheel of Fortune motif 15

Whitaker, Forest 39
Whitrow, Benjamin 168
"Why Caliban Worships the Man in the Moon" (Urban) 250
Wickham, Glynne 162, 169, 170
"The Wife of Bath's Tale" (Chaucer) 152n9
Wilcox, Fred McLeod 246
Wilkins, George 203, 206, 215, 216, 220, 223, 224nn2, 3
Wilkins, John 256, 258
William the Conqueror 106, 111
Williams, Gary Jay 155n45, 156n49, 157n63
Williamsburg (Virginia) 51
Wilmington, Michael 83–84
Wilson, J. Dover 228n39
The Winter's Tale (Shakespeare) 216, 218, 222, 227n39; *All's Well, That Ends Well's* similarities to 186; medieval aspects of 11, 14, 195, 196, 219, 226n21, 232–44; performances of 108, 225n4, *236*, *238*, *239*, *240*
women: as battlefield robbers 72; connection between moon and 253–54; medieval vs. early modern representations of 14, 178–91; men dressed as, in *Troilus and Cressida* 167; playing male fairies on stage 144, *145*; romances forbidden to 195–96; Scottish 14, 87, 116–32; solidarity among, in *All's*

Well, That Ends Well 180, 185, 187; as war victims 165, 167, 171, 172; in Welles' versions of Falstaff 55; in Zeffirelli's *Hamlet* 111–12; *see also* feminism; sexuality; *specific plays*
Woolf, Virginia 128
World War II: nostalgia for medievalism during 56–57; and Olivier's *Henry V* film 62, 65–66, 67, 68, 72; post–, as setting for *All's Well, That Ends Well* 184; as setting for Richard III adaptation 38
World's Fairs 51, 54–55, 57
Worthen, William 207
wrestling 135
Wright, Geoffrey 117, 124, 128
Wryesdale dance 148
Wuthering Heights (film) 30

Yale Repertory Theater 183–84
Yeager, R. F. 2, 11, 14, 215–31
Year of the King (Sher) 33
York Theatre Royal 170
Yvain (romance) 142

Zarins, Kim 14, 197, 245–62
Zeffirelli, Franco: *Hamlet* adaptation by 13, 109–12, *110*, *112*; *Romeo and Juliet* adaptation by 13, 89, 94–97, 99, 100, 102
Zimmerman, Mary 223
Zwingli, Ulrich 227n38

www.ingramcontent.com/pod-product-compliance
Lightning Source LLC
Chambersburg PA
CBHW081545300426
44116CB00015B/2757